The Great Skiing & Snowboarding Guide 2007

Cadogan Guides
2nd Floor 233 High Holborn London WC1V 7DN
info@cadoganguides.co.uk
www.cadoganguides.com

The Globe Pequot Press
246 Goose Lane, PO Box 480, Guilford,
Connecticut 06437–0480

Cover photograph: Tom Stillo for Skishoot
Other photographs: p.1 Avoriaz AgenceNuts, Skishoot, Scott Markewitz; p.8 Stowe; p.9 Jackson Hole/Gilman; p.11 Eric Schramm, Skishoot; p.17 TVB Ischgl, OT Mègeve; p.22 Skishoot; p.28 Scott Markewitz; p.23 OT Méribel; p.35 TVB Ischgl; p.35 Skishoot; p.72 Skishoot; p.94 Skishoot; p.94 Scott Markewitz; p.110 Perisher Blue; p.116 Matt Peterson/Skishoot; p.118 OT Val Thorens; p.127 Skishoot; p.132 Skishoot; p.132 Avoriaz/Pascal Lebeau; p.141,147 OT Méribel; p.152 Mègeve Nuts.fr; p.181 OT Val Thorens; p.203 Skishoot; p.237, 238 OT Méribel; p.247 Will Wissman, OT Méribel; p.261 Skishoot; p.273 Skishoot; p.285 OT Méribel, OT Val Thorens; p.292 Avoriaz AgenceNuts, OT Méribel; p.297 Avoriaz/Christophe Vaury, Pascal Lebeau; p.298 OT Val Thorens; p.299 Christophe Vaury; p.329 Skishoot; p.345 Rob Bossi/The Canyons, Stowe, Scott Markewitz; p.347 Stowe; p.354 Marc Meunch/The Canyons; p.360 Larry Pierce; p.362 Marc Meunch; p.412 Stowe; p.416 Ken Redding/The Canyons, Scott Markewitz; p.470 OT Méribel; p.486 Stowe

Art Director: Sarah Gardner
Managing Editor: Natalie Pomier
Editor: Alison Copland
Assistant Editor: Nicola Jessop
Editorial Assistant/Advertising: C S Randall
Proofreading: Elspeth Anderson

Printed in the Italy by Legoprint

A catalogue record for this book is available from the British Library

ISBN 13: 978-1-86011-348-2
ISBN 10: 1-86011-348-6

The publishers would like to thank the resorts for the kind provision of maps for this guide.

The author and publishers have made every effort to ensure the accuracy of the information in this book at the time of going to press. However, they cannot accept any responsibility for any loss, injury or inconvenience resulting from the use of information contained in this guide.

Please help us to keep this guide up to date. We have done our best to ensure that the information in this guide is correct at the time of going to press. But places and facilities are constantly changing, and standards and prices in hotels and restaurants fluctuate. We would be delighted to receive any comments concerning existing entries or omissions. Authors of the best letters will receive a copy of the Cadogan Guide of their choice.

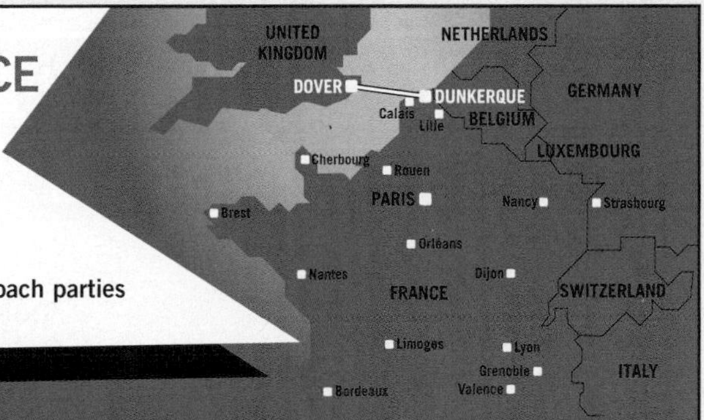

UNITED KINGDOM
NETHERLANDS
DOVER
DUNKERQUE
GERMANY
Calais
Lille
BELGIUM
LUXEMBOURG
Cherbourg
Rouen
PARIS
Nancy
Strasbourg
Brest
Orléans
Nantes
Dijon
FRANCE
SWITZERLAND
Limoges
Lyon
Grenoble
ITALY
Bordeaux
Valence

About the authors

Peter and Felice Hardy are both full-time travel writers and acknowledged worldwide as the two most authoritative experts on ski resorts and the ski industry. They have spent many years skiing in some 500 resorts around the globe. In an average 18-week winter, Peter alone commutes from Britain to some 45 resorts on both sides of the Atlantic. When not up to their knees in fresh powder somewhere in the Alps, the Rockies or the Andes, you can find them at their rural home in Hampshire with their three children and two dogs, all of whom are expert skiers and accomplished snowboarders (not the dogs).

Peter and Felice are the joint authors of some 20 travel books and Peter is the ski correspondent of the *Daily Telegraph* and the *Daily Mail*. Felice is travel editor of *With Kids* magazine and writes regularly in the *Guardian* and the London *Evening Standard*. Their work also appears in an enormous number of lifestyle and travel magazines, including *Condé Nast Traveller* and *Tatler*.

Contents

Scandinavia

Spain

Switzerland

USA

Introduction

Last year, the first edition of *The Great Skiing & Snowboarding Guide* proved to be such a success that we had to reprint halfway through the season. Our aim was to provide informed and detailed assistance on choosing where to spend your ski holiday and how to get there. We hope that the 2007 edition, revised and in full colour throughout, will prove an even more invaluable aid in organizing your holiday this winter.

We have spent half a lifetime collecting, collating and constantly updating information on resorts around the world. Here we examine in detail what we consider to be the cream of these. Unlike other guide books, *The Great Skiing & Snowboarding Guide* is heavily opinionated, a fact that does not always endear us to resorts that we criticize. We make no apologies for the fact that creature comforts are high on our list of priorities. Unusual hotels, as well as great places to eat both on and off the mountain, are apportioned equal space to the actual skiing. You may not always second our opinions, but they do provide a yardstick from which to make your own personal judgement.

Madness in the Mountains

Don't be fooled. Winter 2005–6 has been hailed as one of the vintage seasons for snow-cover out of the past 50, thereby chucking ice-studded snowballs at the heads of the global warming lobby. But when the spring melt at altitude began at the beginning of May 2006 – at least three weeks later than usual – by no means everything on the mountainside was as deep and crisp and even as it might have appeared from news reports.

Vintage indeed was the snow-cover in many European resorts – with Austria once again leading the way. But wallowing in knee-deep powder in Val d'Isère or Les Arcs in late April sunshine, we found it all too convenient to forget that the most popular French resorts suffered a pretty miserable start to the season. After the driest November and December on record, the first proper falls in the Tarentaise didn't arrive until New Year's Eve. January was poor, and the 'vintage' snow didn't come until February. Until a month before the Olympic Games, Sestriere and sister resorts in the Milky Way looked to be in serious trouble. Destinations in Norway and Sweden recorded less than half their normal snowpack and never really got off the ground.

Of course this doesn't seriously detract from the fantastic skiing found across most of Europe and North America for much of last season. But it is worth noting that increased amounts of precipitation in winter, along with the high winds that have now become commonplace at altitude in the French Alps, are the hallmarks of global warming. Fortunately, unusually low temperatures caused by an Arctic airstream, meant that all that moisture – this year – fell as snow.

The inescapable fact remains that mean temperatures in the Alps and the Rockies are rising at an alarming rate – double the figures that were predicted only five years ago. A new report suggests that Colorado – which had a superb winter in 2005–6 – could lose half its spring snowpack by 2050, making winter sports no longer economically viable in many resorts.

The long-term future of year-round skiing in Europe is already in doubt. In 2006, Sölden, Les Diablerets and Alpe d'Huez joined the growing number of resorts that have either suspended or curtailed summer skiing. The list includes Alagna, St Moritz, Verbier and Val Thorens, and amounts to around one-third of the 30 glaciers that have been developed for snow sports.

Avalanches

A tragic by-product of such irregular weather patterns was the record number of avalanche deaths in Europe - nearly 60 in France alone and 100 in total. In an average year 'only' 30 die in such accidents in France. The figures are the highest since records began 35 years ago.

The reason for the instability of the main European snowpack last winter is complex: a combination of substantial falls that failed to adhere to the established layers because of fluctuating temperatures and abnormally high winds at altitude. The reasons for the deaths in too many cases is much simpler: crass stupidity and what often amounted to criminal irresponsibility.

The user-friendly shape of the latest generation of skis and snowboards mean that almost anyone who has tried sliding on snow for a week or two can manage to turn in deep snow and enjoy the unbeatable sensation of powder. Away they go without any knowledge of snowcraft or the natural dangers that should be apparent as soon leaving the roped runs of a resort.

Avalanches remain one of the most awesome forces of nature. That white fluffy stuff is transformed into debris with a mass greater than concrete. The best way to survive an avalanche is not to get caught in one. If you are, your chances of survival depend on your wearing a transceiver that will enable rescuers to pinpoint your location. Your chance of being dug out alive plummets dramatically after 15 minutes.

Yet a mountain survey by police in Verbier this winter showed that only a minimal number of off-piste skiers were properly equipped with bleepers, probes and shovels. American expert Henry Schniewind who gives regular lectures in snowcraft in Val d'Isère to tour operator staff and to the public says: 'Telling skiers and riders about danger is a little like trying to teach safe sex to adolescents – they will try it anyway.' Too many fatal and near-fatal avalanches this winter were caused by inexperienced skiers or snowboarders ignoring all warning signs, cutting a loaded slope, and bringing tons of snow down onto parties of skiers below.

The French Minister for Sports, Jean-François Lamour, has called these deaths 'unacceptable' and, as a result, French police are no longer treating them with the time-honoured Gallic shrug of the past. At the time of writing, a number of skiers and snowboarders – including Britons – face potential charges of causing death by irresponsible behaviour. No one wants to see rules or regulations on the open mountainside, but if this level of death toll continues these will become inevitable. It's preferable that such limitations are imposed by skiers and riders than by suits in cities. In the past we have firmly stated our opposition to the kind of curbs on freedom that exist in most North American resorts. Here you are not allowed to leave marked trails without the permission of the snow patrol – and then only to certain areas. However, we note that, despite even bigger snowfalls this winter than in Europe, the number of avalanche deaths in North America – already nominal by comparison – has been no higher than usual.

A no-tolerance policy on blatant offenders may have some effect, but the biggest problem is the one that Henry Schniewind has been trying address for the past 17 years: how to educate skiers and snowboarders in mountain safety.

The Great Skiing & Snowboarding 2007 Awards

The Great Skiing & Snowboarding Awards are judged by a panel of experts including the authors of the guide and take into account nominations supplied by readers. These prestigious awards go to the resorts, hotels and restaurants that demonstrate particular merit. Two winners have been selected for each category: one in Europe and the other in North America.

Readers are invited to submit their nominations for The Great Skiing & Snowboarding 2008 Awards. Please send them by email to info@skishoot.co.uk

BEST SKI RESORT

Europe: Verbier, Switzerland
North America: Telluride, Colorado

BEST SMALL RESORT

Europe:Baqueira Beret, Spain
North America: Kicking Horse, BC

BEST FAMILY RESORT

Europe: Les Gets, France
North America: Beaver Creek, Colorado

MOST CHILLED RESORT

Europe: Kitzbühel, Austria
North America: Taos, New Mexico

BEST LUXURY SKI HOTEL

Europe: La Pleta, Baqueira Beret, Spain
North America: The Peaks Resort & Golden Door Spa, Telluride, Colorado

BEST SMALL SKI HOTEL

Europe: La Bouitte, St-Marcel, near St-Martin-de-Belleville, France
North America: Hotel Lenado, Aspen, Colorado

BEST MOUNTAIN RESTAURANT

Europe: Bélliou La Fumée, Les Arcs, France
North America: The Lookout Cabin, The Canyons, Utah

BEST RESORT RESTAURANT

Europe: La Bouitte, St-Marcel, near St-Martin-de-Belleville, France
North America: Elements Urban Tapas Parlour, Whistler, BC

The Best

These are the resorts or ski areas we consider to be the best in a variety of categories. The 10 entries in each are listed alphabetically rather than in order of merit.

First-timers

Bansko
Beaver Creek
Big White
Flaine
Livigno
Mayrhofen
Saas-Fee
Pal-Arinsal/Vallnord
Poiana Brasov
Westendorf

Intermediates

Banff-Lake Louise
Courchevel
Park City
La Plagne
Sauze d'Oulx
Serre Chevalier
Soldeu/Grandvalira
Söll/SkiWelt
Vail
Wengen

Challenge-hunters

Aspen
Chamonix
Jackson Hole
St Anton
Snowbird and Alta
Taos
Telluride
Val d'Isère
Verbier
Zermatt

Mixed groups

Les Arcs/Paradiski
Aspen
Banff-Lake Louise
Courchevel
Flaine
Lech and Zürs
Morzine
Park City
Vail
Whistler

Snowboarders

Avoriaz
Axamer Lizum
Breckenridge
Chamonix
Davos
Mammoth
St Anton
Serre Chevalier
Verbier
Whistler

Steep and deep

Alagna
Chamonix
La Grave
Jackson Hole
Kicking Horse
Snowbird and Alta
Val d'Isère
Verbier
Whistler
Zermatt

Mogul-hoppers

Avoriaz
Breckenridge
Killington
Klosters
Mürren
Red Resort
St Anton
Taos
Telluride
Verbier

Ski to lunch

The Canyons
Cervinia
Cortina d'Ampezzo
Courchevel
Courmayeur
Kicking Horse
Klosters
Megève
St Anton
Zermatt

Luxury

Aspen
Beaver Creek
Courchevel 1850
Deer Valley
Gstaad
Jackson Hole
Lech and Zürs
Méribel
St Moritz
Zermatt

Après-ski gourmets

Aspen
Cortina d'Ampezzo
Courchevel
Courmayeur
Kitzbühel
Megève
Park City
St Anton
Telluride
Zermatt

Party-goers

Banff
Baqueira-Beret
Chamonix
Ischgl
Kitzbühel
Pas de la Casa/
Grandvalira
St Anton
Sauze d'Oulx
Verbier
Zermatt

Ski and shop

Arinsal/Andorra La Vella
Aspen
Breckenridge
Cortina d'Ampezzo
Jackson Hole
Livigno
Mammoth
Megève
Park City
Whistler

Ski and spa

Aspen
Bad Gastein
Banff
Beaver Creek
Kitzbühel
Megève
St Moritz
Snowbird
Telluride
Whistler

Cosmopolitan sophistication

Aspen
Courchevel 1850
Davos
Grindelwald
Kitzbühel
St Moritz
Sun Valley
Telluride
Whistler
Zermatt

Families with young children

Åre
Beaver Creek
Deer Valley
Geilo
Lake Louise
Mayrhofen
Obergurgl
La Tania
Valmorel
Villars

Families with older children

Fernie
Flims
Les Gets
Saalbach
Schladming
Soldeu/Vallnord
Tignes
Vail
Vaujany
Whistler

Non-skiers

Åre
Aspen
Banff
Cortina d'Ampezzo
Kitzbühel
Megève
St Moritz
Seefeld
Telluride
Zermatt

Value

Arinsal/Vallnord
Bansko
Barèges
Fernie
Levi
Livigno
Niederau
Poiana Brasov
Red Resort
Serre Chevalier

Snow-sure

Cervinia
Kaprun
Neustift/Stubai
Obergurgl-Hochgurgl
Obertauern
Passo Tonale
Saas-Fee
Tignes/Val d'Isère
Val Thorens
Zermatt

Romantic

Alpbach
Courmayeur
Jackson Hole
Kitzbühel
Megève
Mürren
Saas-Fee
Telluride
Zell am See
Zermatt

Off the beaten track

Alagna
Bohinj
Crested Butte
Filzmoos
La Grave
Kicking Horse

Red Resort
Sainte-Foy
St-Martin-de-Belleville
Taos

Resorts in exotic locations

Chamonix
Cortina d'Ampezzo
Grindelwald
Heavenly
Las Leñas
Mammoth
Portillo
Ruapehu
Thredbo
Zermatt

Purpose-built convenience

Les Arcs
Big White
Courchevel
Flaine
Kicking Horse
Obertauern
La Plagne
Snowbird
Tignes
Valmorel

State-of-the art lifts

Bansko
The Canyons
Copper Mountain
Keystone
Kicking Horse
Kronplatz
Saalbach-Hinterglemm
Tremblant
Trois Vallées
Yellowstone Club

Village backdoors to large ski areas

Champagny/Montchavin (Paradiski)
Champéry (Portes du Soleil)
Corvara (Sella Ronda)
Dorfgastein (Gasteinertal)
Ellmau (SkiWelt)
Flachau/Wagrain (Salzburger Sportwelt)
St-Martin-de-Belleville (Trois Vallées)
Samoëns (Flaine)
Stuben (St Anton)
Vaujany (Alpe d'Huez)

Close to an interesting city/airport convenience

Baqueira-Beret (Toulouse)
Chamonix (Geneva)
Cortina d'Ampezzo (Venice)
Sauze d'Oulx (Turin)
Seefeld (Innsbruck)
Mont-Sainte-Anne (Québec City)
Park City (Salt Lake City)
Valle Nevado (Santiago)
Whistler (Vancouver)
Winter Park (Denver)

Heli- or cat-skiing

Fernie
Grand Targhee
Grindelwald
Humber Valley
Kicking Horse
Panorama
La Thuile
Verbier
Whistler
Zermatt

Family Skiing

The number of families taking a childcare-inclusive ski holiday in recent years has increased to the point where demand is beginning to outstrip supply. The crucial factor for many people each winter is no longer 'where' but 'when' to take your school-age children to the snow. Indeed, if you are hoping to go to the Alps over New Year or at February half-term, a call to any of the 20-something specialist family tour operators couldn't be soon enough.

One way of travelling is by organizing your own holiday: contacting your chosen hotel to get an individual quote, booking low-cost flights, car hire or transfers online and organizing childcare through the local tourist board. This may result in a saving, but it is worth noting that your investment will not necessarily be secure in the event of an unforeseen problem such as overbooking – nor will you have the services of the tour operator's staff in the resort.

Childcare

We would personally recommend going with a tour operator who offers dedicated childcare. More than 30 operators have a crèche or nanny service. Most provide baby care, as well as indoor and outdoor play for children up to six years old. This takes place from around 9am to 4.30pm, which gives parents enough time to go skiing.

Non-skiing children under the age of four require full-day care with lunch provided. Skiing children under eight may be happy to go to ski school in the morning, but few will have the energy for a whole day on the slopes. Ideally, you find an operator with a 'nanny escort service' that picks up your child at lunch time and then either returns them to ski school in the afternoon or entertains them with activities such as skating or tobogganing until you return.

The tour operator's crèche – and indeed the resort kindergarten – provides cots for little ones to have a rest during the day. Potties, highchairs and bottle warmers are usually provided, as well as toys, books, games, colouring equipment and videos. Bring your own nappies and milk formula. Trying to buy your usual size of nappies or favourite brand of baby milk in a ski resort can be difficult – and the French don't use baby wipes.

When do we start?

Doting parents have been known to start their children skiing when they are still in nappies – more for their own benefit than for their child's. If you have to, **Bobo's Miniclub**, **t** +43 (0)4285 8241, *www.skiarena.at*, in Nassfeld, Austria, offers lessons to bandy-legged two-year-olds. However, you run the risk of putting your child off the sport for years to come. The ideal age to start it is between five and eight years old.

Where to stay?

Getting a couple of children dressed, breakfasted, booted and off to ski school each morning complete with lift pass and equipment, as well as not one but two mittens

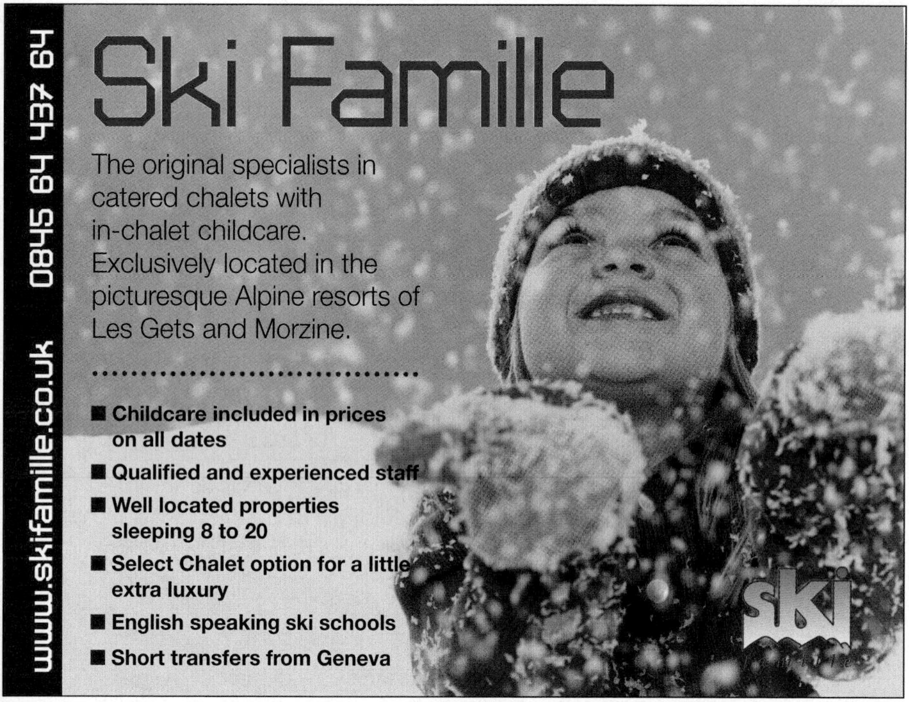
www.skifamille.co.uk 0845 64 437 64
Ski Famille
The original specialists in catered chalets with in-chalet childcare. Exclusively located in the picturesque Alpine resorts of Les Gets and Morzine.
Childcare included in prices on all dates
Qualified and experienced staff
Well located properties sleeping 8 to 20
Select Chalet option for a little extra luxury
English speaking ski schools
Short transfers from Geneva
ski

family ski company
The ski company designed with the family in mind
Choose from among the world's best skiing and boarding resorts:
Three Valleys / Portes du Soleil
Les Arcs / La Plagne
Stay in hand-picked catered chalets with ski-in ski-out access in family friendly villages. Add unrivalled childcare and fun clubs from 3 months up to teenage skiers and boarders, including ski school helpers for young beginners. Choose when you ski as a family and when you take time out.
Call us for more information
01684 540 333
www.familyski.co.uk
enquiries@familyski.co.uk

ESPRIT
Ski
No.1 FOR FAMILY SKIING
17 TOP RESORTS
Switzerland ★ France ★ Austria ★ Italy ★
Huge range of guaranteed child care in every resort.
★ Exclusive Esprit Nurseries
★ Exclusive Esprit Ski Classes
★ Afternoon Activity Clubs
★ Free evening Cocoa Clubs
★ Free babysitting
No.1 FOR FAMILY SKIING
For a free brochure
visit www.esprit-holidays.co.uk
or call 0871 310 1000

is hard. Getting all four of you there – on time and into separate classes – is a task of Herculean proportions. The overall success of your holiday is dependent on choosing the right resort. Proximity to the nursery slopes, the lifts and ski school rendezvous point is a great energy-saver for families with children of all ages.

The best hotels have a relaxed atmosphere and plenty of like-minded families around you. If you are taking a baby or toddler they can pre-book extras such as cots and highchairs. Check whether evening babysitting is available so that you can escape when you need to. An in-house crèche, larger-than-normal 'family bedrooms' or two linked rooms are big bonuses.

Apartments provide flexible accommodation best suited to families with older children, allowing the option of eating in or out each evening. Cooking for your family saves money and it is fun – as well as educational – to shop in foreign supermarkets.

Chalets are the home-from-home option and you won't have to worry about your noisy children running around and disturbing other guests. The living areas usually have satellite television, DVD and CD players, some even have games rooms and other useful extras. An early children's supper is provided, and the chalet staff will often babysit for an extra fee.

Which country?

France is the most popular country for British families with some of the best-equipped crèches in Europe, but the 'you are here to learn' attitude of some ski schools can be off-putting. Try: Morzine, Les Gets, La Tania, Tignes, Valmorel and Vaujany.

Switzerland can be more expensive but it offers efficiency, excellent skiing, and traditional villages full of atmosphere. Try: Villars and Flims (near Laax).

Avoid **Italy** if you're taking small children, as many resorts (Ortisei is an exception) do not have childcare due to the Italian penchant for bringing granny in tow on the family holiday.

Austria is the traditional place to learn. It is pretty and jolly, with comfortable and friendly family-run hotels and some great hotel spas for parents to relax in after skiing. Try: Mayrhofen, Obergurgl, Saalbach and Schladming.

Andorra has a marginal price advantage, and several resorts have linked to form impressive intermediate ski areas. Try: Soldeu in the Grandvalira area.

Eastern Europe offers much lower prices, with Bansko in Bulgaria now competing in terms of ski infrastructure with comparable-sized alpine resorts.

North America provides a less frenetic alternative at any time of the winter. Nowhere in Europe can beat the enthusiastic welcome your child will receive wherever you go, and the advantage of tuition in your native language outweighs almost everything else. For younger kids try: Beaver Creek, Deer Valley, Lake Louise. For older ones try: Fernie, Vail and Whistler.

Many people in **Norway** and **Sweden** are fluent English-speakers (this matters enormously to you if you are four years old and have been left for the week in a strange environment). Safety is paramount, with free helmets offered wherever you go. Try: Åre, Hemsedal and Geilo.

How to dodge the crowds

There are several ways to minimize the inconvenience of the half-term and New Year crowds. The first is to choose a resort with a really modern lift system (*see* 'The Best: State-of-the-art Lifts', page 17) that can cope with large numbers swiftly and efficiently. The second is to opt for a lesser-known resort (*see* 'The Best: Village Backdoors', page 17), which is part of a bigger ski area. The third is to go for a resort off the beaten track (*see* 'The Best: Off the Beaten Track', pages 16–17).

Teen scene

It is important for them to be seen in all the right places – so check 'The Best' lists and the resort descriptions if you're unsure. If you don't want to waste their expensive lift passes, parents should insist that adolescents vacate their beds and hit the slopes by 10am. Do not stay in a hotel (the extras of drinks and telephone calls may necessitate a second mortgage), but go for an apartment or chalet instead.

Ski Weekends

Panda marks around the eyes and a permanent grin on a grey Monday morning in the office are the greatest giveaway during the winter months. A couple of quality days on snow can feel like a full week away, and an increasing number of skiers are opting this season for two or more weekends in the Alps rather than the tradition full-length holiday. The advantage over the annual week-long outing to the snow is the chance to ski more than once a season. You don't have to wait for a whole year before clicking into your bindings once again. Unfortunately the idea of the spontaneous short break – deciding on Wednesday that you fancy skiing this Saturday and Sunday – rarely works. The secret of the successful ski weekend lies in forward planning.

What you want is maximum time on skis and minimum time away from the office, at a reasonable price. Much depends on your definition of a weekend. If you want to catch the last flight out on Friday evening without any loss of working hours and be back at your desk at 8am on Monday then you need to book your airline tickets months in advance. If you can be more flexible – flying out on Thursday evening and

WEEKEND RECOMMENDATIONS:

Chamonix: 1hr by car, taxi, bus or train from Geneva
Courmayeur: 1½hrs by car from Geneva
Cortina d'Ampezzo: 2hrs by car from Venice
Engelberg: 1hr by car or train from Zurich
Flaine: 1½hrs by car from Geneva
La Clusaz: 1hr by car from Geneva
Obertauern: 1hr 20mins by car from Salzburg
Verbier: 2hrs by car from Geneva
Villars: 1½hrs by car or train from Geneva

returning on Monday morning – the price will be lower and you don't need to make arrangements so far ahead.

The so-called low-cost airlines do not always live up to their name. As the departure day approaches, the price of the flight can more than triple according to demand. Regular ski-smitten commuters block book their Friday and Sunday evening flights for the season as they come on sale. Prices are at their most reasonable in January, March and April. Geneva airport is by far the most popular hub for weekends, but it is by no means the only option. Consider also Lyon, Zurich, Venice, Trieste, Turin and Treviso, as well as Salzburg and Innsbruck.

You then have to choose a resort and, almost more importantly, find the right accommodation. Few hotels will consider letting rooms for less than a week, especially during high season. Pick a destination that is preferably within two hours of your chosen airport. A rental car is usually the best form of weekend transport. But remember that with the one-hour time difference the 18.45 Friday flight to Geneva doesn't land until 21.20 and therefore you are not going to reach your hotel before midnight. Always insist in advance that the car is equipped with snow tyres – by no means standard practice for even the major rental companies – and that snow chains are provided. Before you leave the airport, check that the chains match the tyre size. At 1am on a mountain pass in a blizzard you don't want to find out that they don't.

If your destination is in Switzerland, consider the convenience of travelling by train directly from the airport to your resort. The Swiss Card (*www.myswissalps.com*) allows a return trip to any resort.

Luggage, equipment rental and lift pass are all the enemies of the weekender. Veteran Friday night travellers pack boots and ski clothes in hand luggage to avoid baggage hall delays. If time is truly precious you should consider going with one of the specialist weekend tour operators. They will greet you on arrival and whisk you straight to your resort. You will also save valuable ski hours by having your ski rental, lift pass, and a mountain guide or instructor – if required – arranged in advance. A bonus is that they can arrange short-stay hotel bookings.

For two or three days' skiing you don't necessarily have to choose one of the largest resorts. If travelling late in the season, you are strongly advised to choose a high-altitude village where snow quality will be guaranteed. However, one major advantage of booking accommodation shortly before departure is that you can check current snow conditions and choose your resort accordingly.

REP IN RESORT

The Ski Club of Great Britain icon, which appears in the Top Resort chapters of this guide, highlights resorts where you will find a representative of the Ski Club of Great Britain. See page 4 for details of the Ski Club of Great Britain 2007 offer.

01

The Top Resorts: Andorra

Pal-Arinsal and Ordino-Arcalis

***BEST FOR**

First-timers, families, duty-free shopping, nightlife

ESSENTIALS

Altitude: Pal-Arinsal: 1940m (6,363ft)–2624m (8,609ft) Ordino-Arcalis: 1950m (5,084ft) –2573m (8,442ft)
Further information: Pal-Arinsal, t +376 737 000, Ordino-Arcalis, t +376 739 900, *www.vallnord.com* for both
Lifts in area: 38 (3 cableways, 17 chairs, 18 drags) serving 89km of piste
Lift pass: Vallnord adult €125–149, child 6–11yrs €97.50–101.50, both for six days. All Andorra adults and children €152 for five consecutive weekdays
Access: Toulouse airport 3½hrs, Barcelona airport 3hrs

Profile

Friendly area with good nightlife, ideally suited to beginners, intermediates and families with small children. Atmosphere in Arcalis is more intimate and alpine than in other Andorran resorts

Resorts

The village of Arinsal and the linked ski area of Pal have now joined forces with the valley town of La Massana and the quite separate ski area of Ordino-Arcalis in this corner of Andorra. Together they form the single lift pass region of Vallnord.

It's all part of the dramatic €160 million regeneration of Andorra in recent years as a serious ski destination. It has binned its bargain basement image and the once humble resort of Arinsal, still renowned for its low-cost nightlife, has even managed to twin itself with glitzy Gstaad in Switzerland.

Most skiers and riders choose to stay in Arinsal, an attractive little resort with easy gondola access to some easy beginner and low intermediate pistes.

A sleek 12-person gondola now connects La Massana into the Pal-Arinsal circuit, transforming it into an alternative and convenient place in which to stay. It is also a useful base for the more demanding and much underrated ski area of Ordino-Arcalis, situated a 20-minute drive away up a remote valley.

When the snow is good and the sun is shining, the easy, undulating pistes can match those of any resort. But no amount of investment can give the mountains here the thrilling high-altitude terrain of the Alps.

One of the major reasons to choose the Vallnord region is its proximity to the capital, Andorra La Vella. Here you can shop your heart out on the Avenida Carlemany. Boutiques sell designer names like Versace, Armani, Donna Karan, Ralph Lauren and Dolce & Gabbana at discount prices.

Mountain

Arinsal's skiing begins with a gondola ride from the middle of the village up to the mid-mountain station at 1950m. You can also take a venerable double-chair from the end of the village – or drive up the mountain road.

Lifts from here bring you up towards the 2569m Pic Negre and allow for some smooth novice and easy runs back down to 1950m. In good snow conditions the descent through the trees to the valley is hugely enjoyable.

From the top of Arinsal, a cable-car spans the valley to the Coll de la Botella and the start of the Pal ski area. Runs here

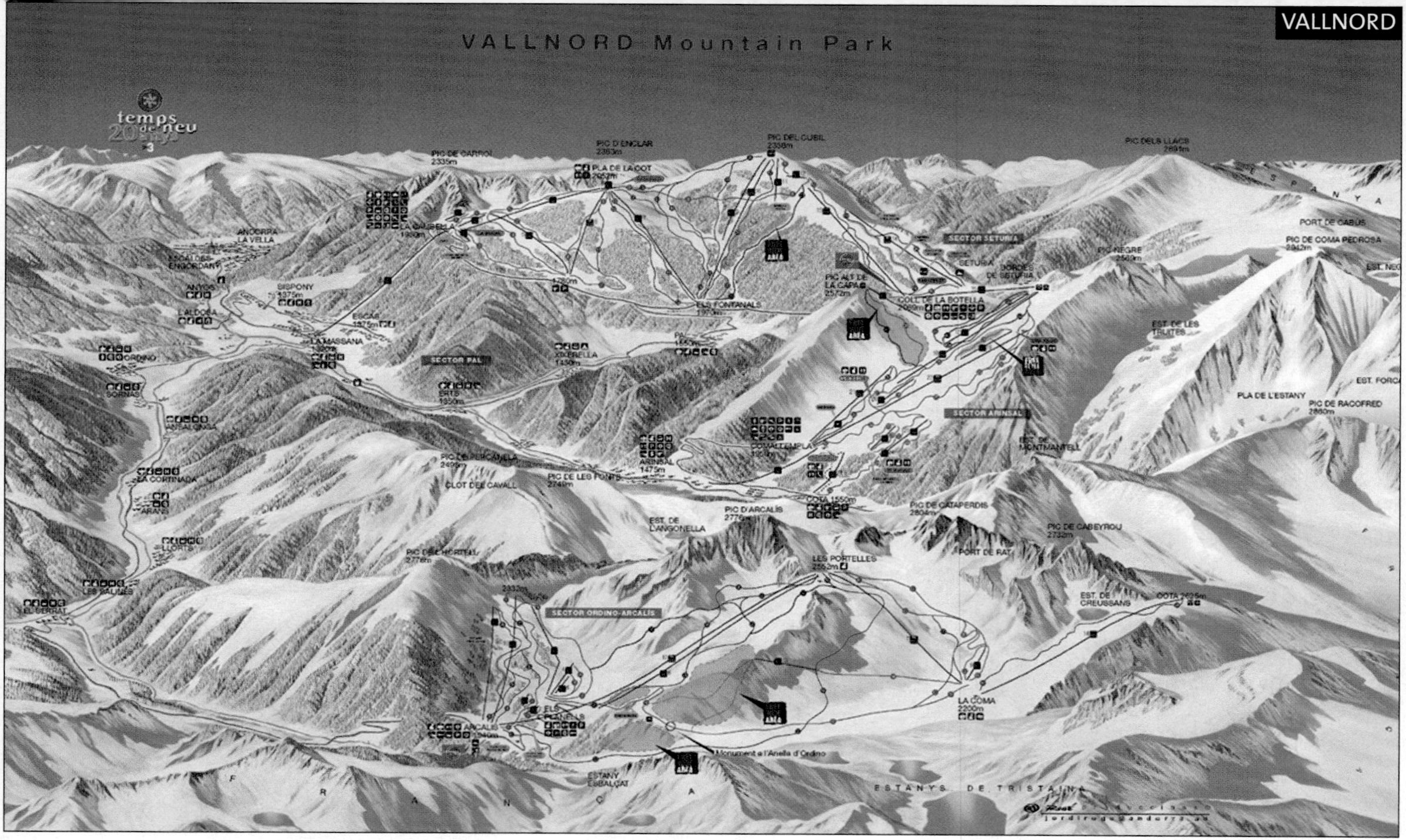
VALLNORD Mountain Park
temps de neu
PIC DE CARROI
2335m
PIC D'ENCLAR
2383m
PLA DE LA COT
PIC DEL CUBIL
2358m
PIC DELS LLACS
2691m
E S P A N Y A
PORT DE CABUS
PIC DE COMA PEDROSA
2942m
PIC NEGRE
SECTOR SETURIA
SETURIA
BORDES DE SETURIA
ANDORRA LA VELLA
ESCALDES-ENGORDANY
LA CAUBELLA
ANYÓS
SISPONY
L'ALDOSA
ESCÀS
LA MASSANA
ELS FONTANALS
PIC ALT DE LA CAPA
2572m
COLL DE LA BOTELLA
ORDINO
SECTOR PAL
XIXERELLA
1450m
PAL
ERTS
1650m
SORNÀS
ANSALONGA
EST. DE LES TRUITES
EST. FORCAT
PLA DE L'ESTANY
PIC DE RACOFRED
2860m
SECTOR ARINSAL
ARINSAL
1475m
COMA TEMPLA
LA CORTINADA
CLOT DEL CAVALL
PIC DE LES FONTS
2748m
EST. DE MONTMANTELL
ARANS
COTA 1550m
PIC DE CATAPERDIS
2804m
PIC D'ARCALÍS
2776m
EST. DE L'ANGONELLA
PIC DE CABEYROU
2732m
LLORTS
PIC DE L'HORTELL
PORT DE RAT
LES PORTELLES
2553m
LES SALINES
EL SERRAT
SECTOR ORDINO-ARCALIS
EST. DE CREUSSANS
COTA 2625m
LA COMA
2200m
ELS PLANELLS
ARCALÍS
Monument a l'Anella d'Ordino
ESTANY ESBALÇAT
ESTANYS DE TRISTAINA
F R A N Ç A

come to Andorra
come to Vallnord
Come to VALLNORD, your family-friendly resort in Andorra.
Arinsal, Pal and Arcalis... an unforgettable holiday experience in the heart of the Pyrenees
ANDORRA
VALLNORD
PAL ARINSAL ORDINO ARCALÍS
www.vallnord.com

are slightly more demanding, but the whole area is best suited to beginners and low intermediates.

Ordino-Arcalis is of considerably more interest for advanced skiers. Its remote position and limited base facilities deter most foreign tourists except the Spanish from across the border. This is where you will find Andorrans skiing at weekends.

A couple of black runs on the front face of the 2552m mountain provide a serious challenge, as well as several long reds served by modern quad-chairs.

Vallnord has a high percentage of riders among its clientele. The FreeStyle Area at Arinsal contains a half-pipe, jumps and other obstacles.

Learn

Arinsal, **t** +376 737 029, and **Pal**, **t** +376 737 008, ski schools have lots of experience in teaching foreign skiers. **Arcalis**, **t** +376 739 600, is the third school.

Children

Babyclub cares for children from 12 months at Comallempla above Arinsal and Els Planells at Pal. **Snowpark** ski kindergarten is from four years at Pal, all **t** +376 737 014. Ordino-Arcalis has a **Jardin d'Enfants**, **t** +376 739 600.

Lunch

At Arinsal, the midday meal is multi-cultural. Eat Chinese at **Xina Igloo** and Tex-mex at **MexicObelix**, British burgers at **Panoramix**, and pork 'n' beans in the **Far West**, or pasta at **Bella Italia**, **t** +376 737 020 for all. **La Borda**, **t** +376 737 020, at Pal serves chicken tikka, Thai red curry, and authentic Catalan cuisine of sausages and peppery salads. At Ordino-Arcalis, **La Coma**, **t** +376 850 201, specializes in barbecued meat.

Dine

The incomparable **El Rusc**, **t** +376 838 200, in La Massana is one of the finest restaurants in Andorra. Starters include oyster soup with a hint of saffron, a main course of steamed cod with rosemary, tomato, olives and port wine jus. **La Borda** mountain restaurant in Pal, **t** +376 737 020, is also open in the evenings.

Party

Arinsal's nightlife involves sustained drinking in bars such as **El Cau** and **Quo Vadis**. **Surf** and the **Derby** are also popular. In La Massana the action is at **El Cocktail de l'Avi** and **El Xtu en el Complejo Tabola**.

Escaldes-Engordany, on the outskirts of Andorra La Vella, is home to **Caldea**, **t** +376 800 999, *www.caldea.ad*, a futuristic spa inspired by Gaudí and made entirely from glass and metal. Inside is a miniature mosque housing Turkish, Roman, Aztec and Icelandic baths, as well as a thermal lagoon.

Sleep

Arinsal:

******Hotel Princesa Park** and **Princesa Diana**, **t** +376 736 400 for both, *www.hotelprincesapark.com* for both, attracts 93 per cent of its visitors from the UK. The establishment is a melange of eccentric styles, with a bar called The Bog and a room full of kitsch classical statues.

*****Poblado Apartments**, **t** +376 835 122, are recommended.

****Residencia Janet**, **t** +376 835 088, is a small, family-run apartment building at Erts between Arinsal and La Massana.

La Massana:

******Hotel Rutllan**, **t** +376 835 000, *www.hotelrutllan.ad*, is the best hotel in town and is ideally situated close to the gondola.

Pas de la Casa

*BEST FOR
20–30-somethings, beginners and intermediates, spirited nightlife, value

ESSENTIALS
Altitude: 2095m (6,872ft)–2580m (8,465ft)
Further information: Grandvalira, **t** +376 808 900, *www.grandvalira.com*
Lifts in area: 58 (4 cableways, 30 chairs, 24 drags) serving 193km of piste
Lift pass: Grandvalira adult €175–180, child 6–11yrs €131–138, both for six days. All Andorra pass adults and children €152 for five consecutive weekdays
Access: Toulouse airport 3hrs, Barcelona airport 3hrs

Profile

Frontier town with cheap and unsophisticated nightlife at the foot of Andorra's largest ski area. Suits 20-somethings looking for Ibiza-style partying with piste-bashing

Resort

Over the past four years, Andorra has dramatically reinvented itself as a world-class destination. Pas de la Casa on the French frontier now shares the Grandvalira lift pass with neighbouring El Tarter. The single ski area also extends to Canillo, and outlying Encamp in the middle of the country. Last season saw its expansion into France with the construction of a six-pack lift on Mt Pedrus on the far side of the River Ariège, which marks the frontier. It is the first of three lifts that will give access to 12 slopes in the new Porte des Neiges sector.

New lifts and hotels abound, but Pas remains largely unchanged, a concrete dormitory with duty-free booze and some of the best skiing in the principality. It is ideal for 20-somethings who want to sandwich some slope time with otherwise uninterrupted inebriation. Other resorts in Andorra are better suited to families and older skiers and riders.

Mountain

Main mountain access from the town is by a choice of chair-lifts that take you up to the ridge overlooking the hamlet of Grau Roig. From here you can either explore the lift-served terrain on either side of the ridge, or take the Cubil quad-chair and work your way across to the wooded slopes above Soldeu. The terrain park is on the Tubs piste at Pas. The new ski area on the French side of the frontier is a great improvement.

Learn

Pas de la Casa Ski, t +376 871 920, and **Grau Roig, t** +376 872 920, schools both have considerable experience in teaching foreigners to ski and snowboard.

Children

Pas de la Casa, t +376 871 920, and **Grau Roig, t** +376 872 920, crèches care for children from 12 months to three years. Grau Roig also offers an introduction to skiing from three years.

Lunch

Llac de Pessons, t +376 759 015, near Grau Roig, is the best mountain

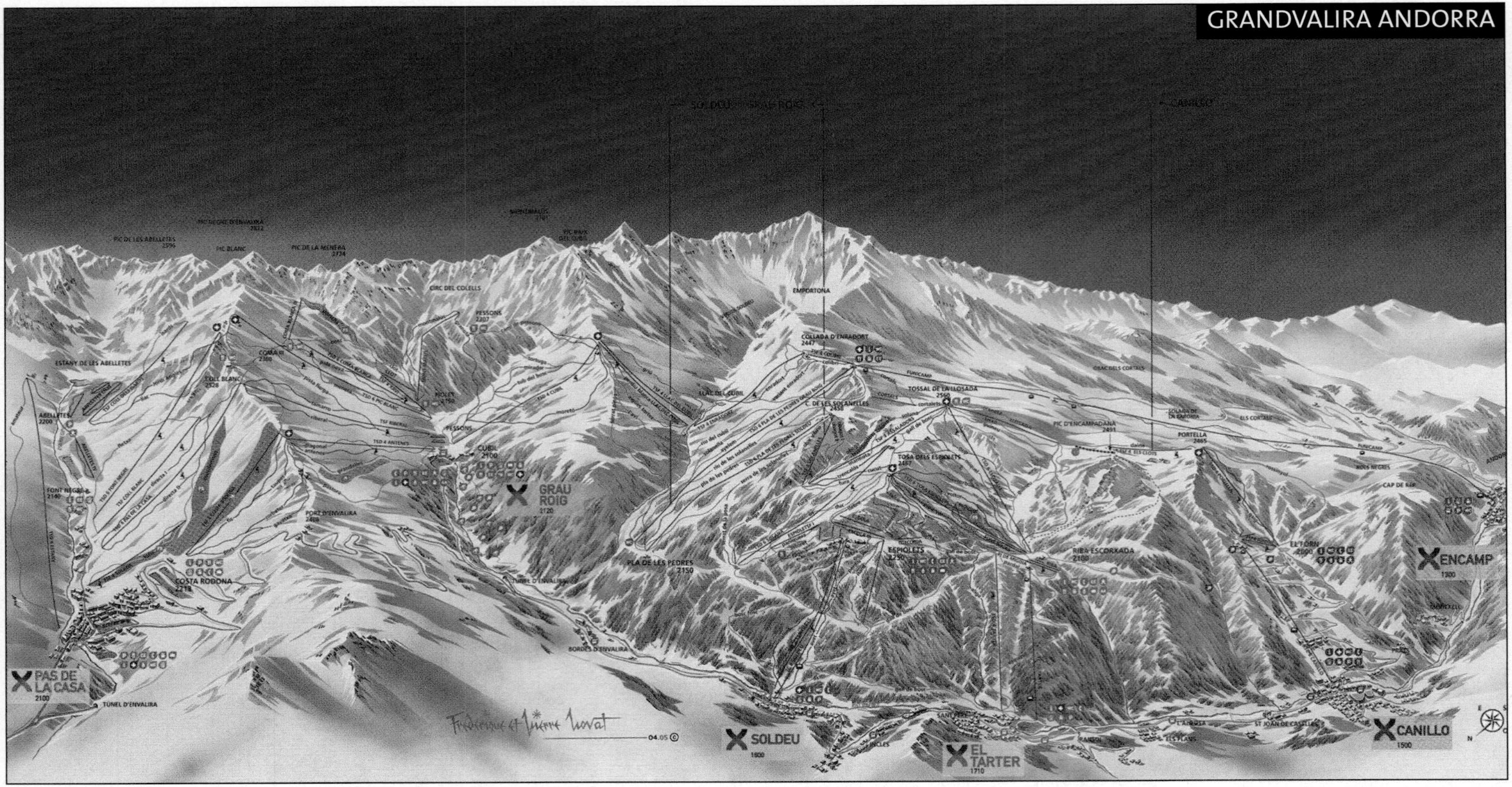
GRANDVALIRA ANDORRA
PAS DE LA CASA
2100
TUNEL D'ENVALIRA
ESTANY DE LES ABELLETES
ABELLETES
2200
FONT NEGRE
2140
COSTA RODONA
2218
PORT D'ENVALIRA
2408
PIC DE LES ABELLETES
PIC BLANC
PIC DE LA MENERA
2724
CIRC DEL COLELLS
PESSONS
2307
CUBIL
2100
GRAU
ROIG
2120
BORDES D'ENVALIRA
EMPORTONA
COLLADA D'ENRADORT
2447
PLA DE LES PEDRES
2150
TOSSAL DE LA LLOSADA
2560
TOSA DELS ESPIOLETS
ESPIOLETS
PIC D'ENCAMPADANA
2491
PORTELLA
2465
RIBA ESCORXADA
2180
EL FORN
FUNICAMP
CAP DE RIU
SOLDEU
1800
EL TARTER
1710
CANILLO
1500
ENCAMP
1300
ST JOAN DE CASELLES
04.05 ©

searching for
SNOW
& SUN
?

restaurant in Andorra. It serves fine grilled meat and has dramatic views across the lake.

Dine

Chez Paulo, t +376 855 596, offers pizzas and French cuisine. **El Carli, t** +376 855 211, is renowned for its mussels and trout with almonds. **Refugo Calones, t** +376 856 040, has fondues and raclette. **La Tagliatelle, t** +376 750 656, serves pizza and pasta dishes.

Party

'I've never been anywhere with so many free drinks', said one reporter. **Milwaukee** is the largest and most crowded bar, while the **Underground**, **Mulligans Irish Pub**, **KYU Disco-pub**, **Havana**, **The Pirate** and **Kamikaze Surf** all provide serious competition. **The Outdoor Centre** offers paintballing in the snow.

Sleep

- ★★★★**Hotel Himalaia Pas, t** +376 735 515, *www.hotansa.com*, has a pool, sauna and a gym.
- ★★★★**Aparthotel Alaska, t** +376 756 056, was new in 2005. It is situated in the upper part of town and houses La Tagliatelle restaurant.
- ★★★★**Hotel Font d'Argent, t** +376 739 739, *www.fontdargent.com*, is an attractive boutique hotel.
- ★★★**Hotel Cristina, t** +376 736 800, is a friendly hotel at the top of town.

Soldeu-El Tarter

Profile

This is the skiing capital of the new Andorra, a village with considerable charm that provides much the most agreeable base in the principality. It suits families and others in search of creature comforts and good, easy skiing. Nightlife is hectic but less brash than in neighbouring Pas de la Casa

Resort

Soldeu is a smart little resort just over the pass from Pas de la Casa, but a world away in style. The ribbon of stone-and-wood buildings stretching along the main road to adjoining El Tarter has undergone a physical and social transformation.

New lifts and hotels abound, and last winter the resort saw the opening of a five-star with a four-storey spa centre of the kind of proportions you might only otherwise encounter in Ancient Rome.

Like other Andorran resorts, Soldeu is still popular with budget skiers, but you have to ask yourself for how much longer. The new Andorra, recipient of lavish €160 million funding in recent years, is in danger of losing sight of why it was ever popular in the first place – low prices.

Soldeu is part of the Grandvalira, a single ski pass area that includes Pas de la Casa, El Tarter and the ancient community of Canillo further along the valley. The skiing can also be accessed by a long gondola from the town of Encamp in the middle of the country. In recent years the snow record across Andorra has been excellent.

✱ BEST FOR

Beginners and intermediates, families, night-owls, value

ESSENTIALS

Altitude: 1710m (5,610ft)–2580m (8,465ft)
Further information: Grandvalira, t +376 808 900, *www.grandvalira.com*
Lifts in area: 58 (4 cableways, 30 chairs, 24 drags) serving 193km of piste
Lift pass: Grandvalira adult €175–180, child 6–11yrs €131–138, both for six days. All Andorra pass adults and children €152 for five consecutive weekdays
Access: Toulouse airport 3hrs, Barcelona airport 3hrs

Mountain

The skiing area is reached by a gondola or chair-lift from Soldeu and by the same choice from El Tarter. From the mid-mountain station of Espiolets, lifts fan out in both directions towards Pas and further down the valley to Canillo.

The undulating terrain above and below the treeline is best suited to beginners and intermediates. However, the substantial size of the Grandvalira should keep more advanced skiers fully occupied. Off-piste opportunities down through the trees are particularly good and new snow does not get tracked out within hours.

Recent lift improvements include the c5.3 million 10-person gondola, which takes skiers up the mountain from El Tarter. Bosc Fosc (it means Dark Forest) is a new blue piste leading down to Soldeu.

Learn

Soldeu's ski school, **t** +376 890 591, deservedly has the reputation of being the best in Andorra and one of the top half-dozen learning academies in Europe.

Much of this is due to the enthusiasm of its veteran teaching director, Yorkshireman Gordon Standeven. Some 100 of the 240 instructors are native English speakers. **Canillo**, **t** +376 890 691, and **El Tarter**, **t** +376 890 641, also have good reputations. All of them become very crowded over February half-term.

Children

Mickey Snow Club in Soldeu, **t** +376 890 591, **Canillo**, **t** +376 890 691, and **El Tarter**, **t** +376 890 641, cares for non-skiing children aged two to three years and the **Jardin de Neige** ski kindergarten from three years.

Lunch

Roc de les Bruixes, **t** +376 890 696, above Canillo is warmly recommended along with refurbished **Solanelles**, **t** +376 759 008, in the Encamp sector. **Gall de Bosc**, **t** +376 890 607, above Soldeu has mountain Catalan cuisine and spectacular views. Try *faves* (warm bean, pea and ham salad) or *trinxat* (bubble-and-squeak topped with slithers of black pudding).

Dine

Soldeu's **Cort de Popaire**, **t** +376 851 211, is renowned for its grilled lamb and steaks. **La Fontanella**, **t** +376 871 787, in the Hotel Piolets, serves pasta and pizza. **La Llar del Artesa**, **t** +376 851 078, just out of town at Bordes d'Envalira, has good-value Catalan mountain dishes. **Borda de l'Horto**, **t** +376 851 622, outside El Tarter, serves grilled meat and fish and is popular with the locals.

Party

Caldea spa, **t** +376 800 999, in Escaldes-Engordany on the outskirts of the capital Andorra La Vella, has a giant 68°C thermal pool and is one of the largest spas in the whole of Europe.

Soldeu's main street is lined with shops, bars and restaurants. Nightlife is frenetic all season but, unlike brasher Pas, revellers here are not confined to the 16–25 age bracket. Venues include the **Avalanche**, **Roc Bar**, **Aspen**, **Ice Berg**, **Pussy Cat** and the popular **Villager** bar. Most atmospheric is **Fat Albert's**, a cavernous barn with videos and live music.

Sleep

All accommodation can be booked through a central reservations office, **t** +376 890 501.

Soldeu:

★★★★★**Sport Hermitage**, **t** +376 870 500, *www.andorramania.com/ hotelsportvillage*, under the same ownership as the Sport Hotel Village, is the resort's first five-star. It is linked internally to a colossal four-storey spa with 14 treatment rooms and a giant basement pool.

★★★★**Sport Hotel Village**, **t** +376 870 500, *www.andorramania.com/ hotelsportvillage*, has a vast lobby with hacienda-style atrium. The wood-panelled bedrooms are large and comfortable. The main mountain access gondola is actually in the hotel.

★★★★**Hotel Piolets Park**, **t** +376 872 787, *www.ahotels.ad*, has comfortable rooms and contains a steakhouse, swimming pool and gym ('very comfortable and excellent food').

★★★★**Hotel Himalaia Soldeu**, **t** +376 878 515, *www.hotansa.ad*, has been refurbished and has a recommended buffet-style restaurant.

★★★**Hotel Soldeu Maistre**, **t** +376 801 963, is rated 'very clean and comfortable, with an excellent choice of food'.

Canillo:

★★★★★**Hotel Ski Plaza**, **t** +376 739 444, *www.hotelskiplazaandorra.com*, is a charming hotel located at the heart of Canillo and has an indoor swimming pool, gym, kids' club, family suites, games room and nightclub.

★★★★**Hotel Font d'Argent**, **t** +376 753 753, *www.fontdargent.com*, in the old town centre, was new last season.

★★★**Hotel Bonavida**, **t** +376 851 300, is a cosy place with a swimming pool.

El Tarter:

★★★★**Hotel Llop Gris**, **t** +376 751 515, *www.llopgris.com*, is convenient for the slopes, with squash courts and a swimming pool.

★★★★**Hotel Nordic**, **t** +376 739 500, *www.grupnordic.ad*, has a wood-and-stone decor and an entrance hall dominated by a Rolls-Royce.

★★★★**Hotel Euro Ski**, **t** +376 736 666, *www.hotansa.com*, is highly recommended by one reporter.

★★★**Hotel del Tarter**, **t** +376 802 080, *www.hotel-eltarter.com*, has a well-regarded restaurant.

★★★**Hotel del Clos**, **t** +376 851 500, *www.grupnordic.ad*, is ski-in/ski-out and modern.

Encamp:

★★★★**Hotel Guillem**, **t** +376 832 133, 500m from the Funicamp lift, has a heated pool, sauna and hot tub.

02

The Top Resorts: Austria

Pinguin-Design © anaplus
www.austria.inf

Alpbach

* BEST FOR

Authentic Tyrolean ambience, intermediates, families, romantics

Profile

Typically Tyrolean village with loads of alpine charm. Family-friendly with good intermediate skiing and some surprisingly varied off-piste possibilities

ESSENTIALS

Altitude: 1000m (3,281ft)–2100m (6,890ft)
Further information: t +43 (0)5336 5233, *www.alpbach.at*
Lifts in area: 20 (3 cableways, 5 chairs, 12 drags) serving 40km of piste
Lift pass: adult €127.50–144, child 6–15yrs €61.50–71, both 6 days
Access: Innsbruck airport 30mins

Resort

Alpbach is officially the prettiest village in Austria, a small friendly resort with enduring charm that has maintained close ties with British skiers for the past 50 years. The overriding key to its success is that in the early 1970s the wise village fathers took an ice axe to future development plans in their determination to avoid the commercial path taken by some of its Tyrolean rivals. As a result, it remains a largely unspoilt, traditional village where farming continues outside the ski season.

Daily life still revolves around the church, which is backed by two buttressed village inns where, between services, drink has been taken and gossip exchanged for 1,100 years.

Mountain

With the exception of one nursery slope in the middle of the village, the skiing takes place a five-minute free bus ride away on the Wiedersbergerhorn. Some reporters say that this is an annoying inconvenience, while one maintains 'you have to walk less here in ski boots than in any other resort I have visited'.

Main mountain access is by a two-stage gondola that brings you up to Hornsboden at 1850m. A small network of lifts rise a further 150m on the Wiedersbergerhorn, and runs overall are more challenging than in the better-known nearby resorts of similar size.

Alpbach still has plenty of novice terrain, but the skiing is best suited to intermediates. Experts will find enticing off-piste opportunities adjacent to the marked runs.

The new eight-person Pöglbahn gondola which opened last season has replaced the two 17-year-old Pögl fixed double-chairs. It takes you from the hamlet of Inneralpbach to the top station on the Wiedersbergerhorn in less than eight minutes.

The local piste map understates the potential of the region, which includes lifts in neighbouring Reith. Our favourite piste is the former FIS downhill course, which tracks the fall line of the main mountain access gondola to the Wiedersbergerhorn.

A new lake created last summer between Reith and Alpbach has provided a much-needed reservoir for the resort's snow cannon network. Alpbach has a half-pipe. Plans remain on the drawing board to link the Alpbach Valley with the adjoining Wildschönau.

Learn

Alpbach-Inneralpbach Ski School, t +43 (0)5336 5515, has a fine reputation and **Alpbach Aktiv Ski School, t** +43 (0)5336 5351, is the alternative.

Children

Both ski schools operate all-day ski kindergartens for children from four years, with free helmets provided.

Lunch

The choices include **Berggasthaus Hornboden**, t +43 (0)5336 5366, near the top of the access gondola, **Gasthof Almhof** by the Wiedersbergerhorn mid-station, t +43 (0)5336 5379, and **Schihütte Böglalm**, t +43 (0)664 9161743, at Inneralpbach.

Dine

Try **Gasthof Wiedersbergerhorn**, t +43 (0)5336 5612, at Inneralpbach, or **Jo Margreiter's Hotel Post**, t +43 (0)5336 5203. **Gasthaus Rossmoos**, t +43 (0)5336 5305, and **Gasthof Jakober**, t +43 (0)5336 5171, both have fine food.

Party

The liveliest bars are the **Messnerwirt**, the **Postalm** and the **Waschkuchl**, but Alpbach can be quiet mid-week.

Sleep

★★★★**Romantikhotel Böglerhof**, t +43 (0)5336 52270, *www.boeglerhof.com*, is ski-in/ski-out, with a swimming pool and spa.
★★★★**Hotel Galtenberg**, t +43 (0)5336 5610, *www.galtenberg.com*, has a new restaurant, a children's play area and a swimming pool.
★★★★**Hotel Alphof**, t +43 (0)5336 5371, *www.hotel-alphof.at*, is in a peaceful location.
★★★**Hotel Post**, t +43 (0)5336 5203, *www.tiscover.at/post.alpbach*, is in the heart of the village, with a popular bar and restaurant.

★★★**Gästehaus Larch**, t +43 (0)5336 5875, *www.gaestehaus-larch.at*, offers B&B or self-catering.

The Gasteinertal

Profile

The skiing is suited to all standards, especially for those wanting to cover a high mileage. The resort is also ideal for non-skiers who like walking, spas and eating

Resort

The ancient watering-hole of Bad Gastein is the original and still the most important of the four resorts dotted along this scenic valley which sits on a giant reservoir of bath-temperature thermal water, a 90-minute drive from Salzburg. The Romans, the Habsburgs and later the Nazis, viewed it as the ideal holiday hideaway. An impressive

> ✳ BEST FOR
> Long-distance cruisers, waterbabes, ski gourmets, non-skiers

ESSENTIALS

Altitude: 840m (2,756ft)–2686m (8,810ft)
Further information: t +43 (0)6432 33930, *www.gastein.com*
Lifts in area: 44 (1 funicular, 10 cableways, 18 chairs, 15 drags) serving 201km of piste. Skiverbund Amadé

region 276 (30 cableways, 74 chairs, 172 drags) serving 860km of piste
Lift pass: Skiverbund Amadé adult €164–176, child 6–15yrs €85–91.50, both for 6 days
Access: Salzburg airport 1½hrs, railway station in Bad Gastein

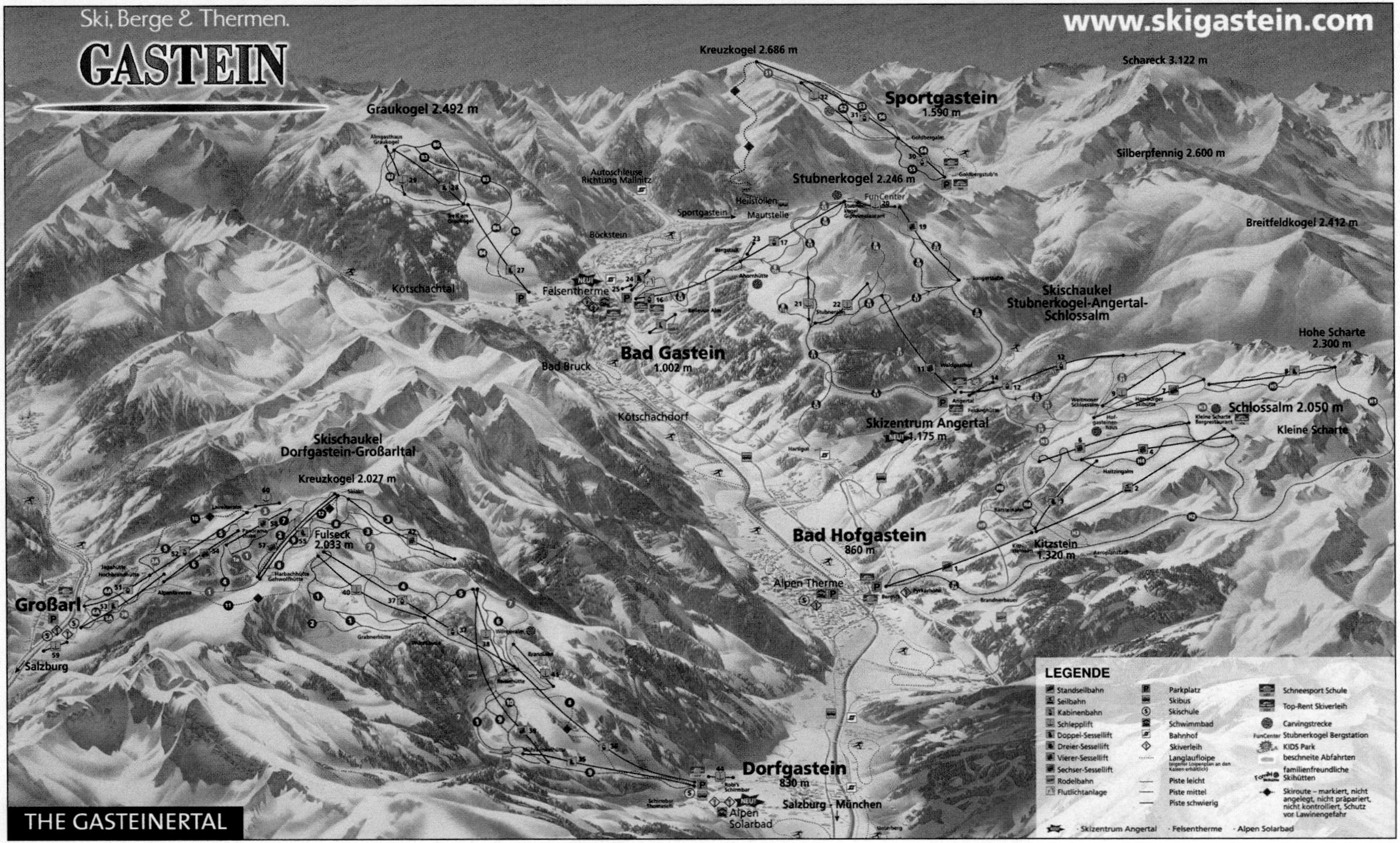
Ski, Berge & Thermen.
GASTEIN
www.skigastein.com
Kreuzkogel 2.686 m
Schareck 3.122 m
Graukogel 2.492 m
Sportgastein
1.590 m
Silberpfennig 2.600 m
Autoschleuse Richtung Mallnitz
Stubnerkogel 2.246 m
FunCenter
Heilstollen
Sportgastein
Mautstelle
Breitfeldkogel 2.412 m
Böckstein
Kötschachtal
Felsentherme
Skischaukel
Stubnerkogel-Angertal-
Schlossalm
Hohe Scharte
2.300 m
Bad Gastein
1.002 m
Bad Bruck
Schlossalm 2.050 m
Kleine Scharte
Kötschachdorf
Skizentrum Angertal
1.175 m
Skischaukel
Dorfgastein-Großarltal
Kreuzkogel 2.027 m
Fulseck
2.033 m
Bad Hofgastein
860 m
Kitzstein
1.320 m
Alpen Therme
Großarl
Salzburg
Dorfgastein
830 m
Salzburg - München
Alpen
Solarbad
THE GASTEINERTAL
LEGENDE
Standseilbahn
Seilbahn
Kabinenbahn
Schlepplift
Doppel-Sessellift
Dreier-Sessellift
Vierer-Sessellift
Sechser-Sessellift
Rodelbahn
Flutlichtanlage
Parkplatz
Skibus
Skischule
Schwimmbad
Bahnhof
Skiverleih
Langlaufloipe
Piste leicht
Piste mittel
Piste schwierig
Schneesport Schule
Top-Rent Skiverleih
Carvingstrecke
FunCenter Stubnerkogel Bergstation
KIDS Park
beschneite Abfahrten
familienfreundliche Skihütten
Skiroute – markiert, nicht angelegt, nicht präpariert, nicht kontrolliert, Schutz vor Lawinengefahr
Skizentrum Angertal · Felsentherme · Alpen Solarbad

23 million litres of this curative water bubble up each day from 17 springs. This is piped to the leading hotels and to public indoor and outdoor baths. You can enjoy the surreal experience of soaking at the foot of the pistes while snow falls around you.

Johann Strauss and Franz Schubert were both inspired to compose here. Hotel Mozart is named not after the supreme maestro, but after his mother, who was a regular guest. Visitors should be aware that the hotels, an interesting mix of revamped imperial and gleaming modern, are set on extraordinarily steep gradients. If you don't like walking in ski boots, choose your base with care. However, it is possible to leave equipment overnight close to the lifts. The town centre is flanked by smart boutiques and expensive jewellery shops that rely largely for their living on the high number of wealthy non-skiing customers who visit Bad Gastein throughout the year.

Bad Hofgastein, further along the valley, is a modern and spacious resort built at a less challenging angle. It shares the main alpine ski area but is more suited to families and those who enjoy cross-country skiing, snowshoeing and walking. It also has good ice rinks, a sophisticated sports centre and its own assortment of thermal pools and accompanying health treatments.

Dorfgastein is contrastingly different – a sleepy farming settlement by the entrance to the valley. It has considerable rural charm as well as some of the best skiing in the area, which stretches across the shoulder of the 2027m Kreuzkogel to link with the village of Grossarl.

Sportgastein, at the head of the valley, is a high-altitude ski area rather than a resort, a lift station built on the site of a medieval gold mine that was briefly reopened by Hermann Goering in the Second World War in the hope of finding fresh natural resources to fund the war machine of the Third Reich. Health-conscious visitors should pay a visit to the nearby Healing Galleries, a naturally heated underground chamber reached by a 2km train journey into the mountain. The Gastein resorts are included in the regional Amadé lift pass.

Mountain

The valley is best suited to high-mileage intermediates looking for a large ski area with plenty of challenges. Advanced skiers and riders should head to Sportgastein and Graukogel, which both have fine off-piste runs in the right conditions. Each resort has its own beginner slopes as well as a good nursery area in the Angertal. However, a general lack of ski convenience does not commend it as an area for absolute novices.

More than €30 million has been spent in recent years on improving the lift system and other mountain facilities including snowmaking in the valley. A much-needed new home piste back to Bad Gastein should be completed in time for this ski season.

Bad Gastein and Bad Hofgastein share the main Stubnerkogel/Schlossalm ski area, reached respectively by gondola and funicular. This complex of constantly updated lifts on both sides of the Angertal is a pleasant intermediate playground with lots of varied blue and red runs both above and below the treeline – and no overtly demanding surprises. When the slopes get crowded on high season weekends wise skiers head across Bad Gastein to the steeper and more peaceful Graukogel ski area, reached by a two-stage chair-lift.

Dorfgastein has the pick of the skiing in the Gasteinertal, although this is not apparent at village level. A modern gondola from just above the village takes you up to the 2000m ridge. From here you can either enjoy the choice of easy blue or more challenging sweeping red runs back towards Dorfgastein, or you can head over to Grossarl in the neighbouring valley.

Sportgastein is considerably higher – the base is at 1590m and the top at 2686m – and usually provides good skiing when cover is thin elsewhere. However, it is a bleak place when the weather suddenly closes in. Ski-buses link all the areas. Taxis are plentiful, but expensive.

Learn

Bad Gastein, t +43 (0)6434 2260, **Bad Hofgastein, t** +43 (0)6432 6339, and **Dorfgastein, t** +43 (0)6433 7538, are the three main ski and board schools. Small and friendly **Schlossalm, t** +43 (0)6432 3298, operates from Bad Hofgastein and **Dorf Aktiv, t** +43 (0)6433 20048, has a strong following in Dorfgastein.

Guiding is available through the ski schools or from **L. Kravanja, t** +43 (0)6434 2941, **F. Sendlhofer, t** +43 (0)6434 2879, and **Hans Zlöbl, t** +43 (0)6434 5355.

Children

The geography of the valley with its separate ski areas does not make the Gasteinertal a good choice for a family holiday with small children. The three main ski schools operate ski- and non-ski kindergartens for children from three years with lessons from four years. **Hotel Grüner Baum, t** +43 (0)6434 2516, has a crèche for guests. The **Fun Centre** at the Stubnerkogel lift has a kids' cinema, table tennis, a climbing wall and a ball pond. **Restaurant Angertal 1180, t** +43 (0)6432 7475, in the futuristic Angertal Ski Centre, offers supervised meals for children aged three to 12 years.

Lunch

The Gasteinertal is dotted with welcoming huts serving typical mountain fare. **Aeroplanstadl, t** +43 (0)6432 8603, on the home run to Bad Hofgastein has to be visited not just for its *Apfelstrudl* but for its extraordinarily original *Damen* and *Herren*. We also recommend **The Jungerstube, t** +43 (0)6433 7370, and the **Wengeralm, t** +43 (0)6433 7257, as well as the cosy **Waldgasthof Angertal, t** +43 (0)6432 8418, for its home-made *Gulaschsuppe*.

Dine

Restaurant Thom, t +43 (0)6434 5101, at the Villa Solitude is a favourite of ours, along with the **Fischerstüberl, t** +43 (0)6434 4505, **Orania Stüberl, t** +43 (0)6434 2717, and the **Mediterran, t** +43 (0)6434 30004, by the waterfall. **Gisela & Co, t** +43 (0)6434 225350, and the **Bahnhofrestaurant, t** +43 (0)6434 2166, are also recommended. **Bellevue Alm, t** +43 (0)6434 3881, and the **Hofkeller, t** +43 (0)6434 2037245, both specialize in fondue. The restaurant in **Hotel Grüner Baum, t** +43 (0)6434 2516 has won awards as one of the outstanding restaurants in the region.

Party

The bars at and near the Felsentherme outdoor baths are the focal point as skiers return from the slopes. The action moves on to a huge assortment of bars and clubs in town. **Haeggbloms**, **Oslags**, **Silver Bullet**, **Eden's Pub** and the **Gatz Music Club** are among the most popular. **Ritz** in the Salzburgerhof has regular live music, while the British-owned **Tannenburg Hotel** near the top of town claims to have the cheapest beer. Bad Hofgastein has five discos and a dozen bars.

Sleep

Bad Gastein has an unusually wide range of hotels, pensions and student hostels as befits a resort that caters for wealthy middle-aged bankers, euro-skint British snowboarders, and everybody in between. Some arduous uphill walking is unavoidable although the ski bus operates between 8am and 6pm daily.

Bad Gastein:

★★★★**Arcotel-Elizabethpark**, t +43 (0)6434 2551, *www.arcotel.at*, is modern, central and has an indoor pool and wellness centre.

★★★★**Hotel Wildbad**, t +43 (0)6434 3761, *www.hotel-wildbad.com*, is much nearer the lifts and recommended for its half-board cuisine that includes tea as well as dinner.

★★★★**Hotel Grüner Baum**, t +43 (0)6434 2516, *www.grunerbaum.com*, is a 19th-century imperial hunting lodge in its own rural hamlet, just outside the resort. The stylish hotel has a spa and a children's club, and attracts a celebrity crowd.

★★★★**Villa Solitude**, t +43 (0)6434 5101, is a magnificently restored 19th-century town house near the casino and the waterfall.

★★★**Hotel Mozart**, t +43 (0)6434 2686, *www.hotelmozart.at*, is conveniently located and reasonably priced.

Bad Hofgastein:

★★★★★**Grand Park Hotel**, t +43 (0)6432 6356, *www.grandparkhotel.at*, is the smartest address as well as being piste-side.

★★★★**Österreichischer Hof**, t +43 (0)6432 62160, *www.oehof.at*, is warmly recommended.

★★★★**Hotel Alte Post**, t +43 (0)6432 62600, *www.bergwelthotels.at*, is a traditional hotel in the town centre.

Dorfgastein:

★★★★**Hotel Römerhof**, t +43 (0)6433 7777, *www.roemerhof.com*, has a pool and spa.

★★★★**Dorfhotel Kirchenwirt**, t +43 (0)6433 7251, *www.kirchenwirt-gastein.at*, is friendly and family run.

★★★**Gasthof Steindlwirt**, t +43 (0)6433 7219, *www.steindlwirt.com*, has a cheerful children's playroom and provides everything from baby baths to bottle warmers.

★★★**Landgasthof Gasteiner Einkehr**, t +43 (0)6433 7248, *www.einkehr.com*, is situated close to the main lift.

★★★**Gasthof Mühlbachstüberl**, t +43 (0)6433 7367, *www.muehlbachstueberl.com*, has a reputation for fine food.

Ischgl

Profile

A resort surrounded by beautiful scenery and a large intermediate ski area. It boasts the biggest terrain park in Europe as well as some of the liveliest après-ski. This is not a place for those on a budget

✳ BEST FOR

Table-dancers, intermediates, off-piste, ski gourmets

ESSENTIALS

Altitude: 1400m (4,592ft)–2864m (9,394ft)
Further information: t +43 (0)5444 5266, *www.ischgl.com*
Lifts in area: 42 (2 funiculars, 3 cableways, 21 chairs, 16 drags) serving 205km in Ischgl-Samnaun

Lift pass: Silvretta Regional (covers Galtür, Ischgl, Kappl, Samnaun, See) adult €184–214, child 7–15yrs €122, both for 6 days
Access: Innsbruck airport 1½hrs, Zurich airport 2½hrs, Landeck station 30km, frequent buses from station

Silvretta Arena
ISCHGL
SAMNAUN
MUTTLER 3294 m
STAMMERSPITZE 3254 m
VAL MAISAS
VAL CHAMINS
SAMNAUN DORF 1840 m
PIZ OT 2758 m
SAMNAUN RAVAISCH
SAMNAUN PLAN
SAMNAUN LARET
SAMNAUN COMPATSCH
STRASSE NACH SPISS/PFUNDS & VINADI
PIZ MUNSCHUNS 2656 m
ALP TRIDA SATTEL 2488 m
ALP TRIDA ECK
OBSTACLE PARK
GRIVALEA 2700 m
Projekt Laret Muller
OBERALP 2380 m
ALP BELLA
ALP TRIDA 2263 m
VISNITZKOPF 2744 m
MULLER
2640 m
NEU
WESTL. VISNITZJOCH
BÜRKELSPITZEN 2933 m
VESULSPITZE 3089 m
BÜRKELKOPF 3033 m
FLIMSPITZ 2928 m
VIDERJOCH 2732 m
IDJOCH 2760 m
Rennstrecke
Funpark
VELILLSCHARTE 2556 m
PARDATSCHGRAT 2624 m
VELILLSPITZE 2704 m
VELILLTAL
SALAAS
GREITSPITZ 2872 m
ZEBLASJOCH 2539 m
ZEBLASWIESEN
INNERES VIDERJOCH 2704 m
PALINKOPF 2864 m
HÖLLENSPITZE
HÖLLENKAR
IDALP 2320 m
Skischule
PIZ TASNA
PIZ VAL GRONDA 2811 m
Projekt
HEIDELBERGER HÜTTE 2264 m
ZAHNJOCH
FLUCHTHORN 3398 m
FIMBAALP 2123 m
VESIL
FIMBATAL
GAMPENALP 1975 m
PAZNAUNER THAYA 2000 m
DREIKÖPFL 2970 m
BODENALP 1840 m
TSCHAMATSCHKOPF
MITTELSTATION
PARDATSCHALP
UNTERE VELILLALP
GALTÜR 1584 m
MATHON 1454 m
PAZNAUNTAL
KAPPL 8 km
SEE 15 km
LANDECK/ARLBERG
FERNPASS
ISCHGL.com
1400 m
STUDIO VELKINZ

Resort

Ischgl is considered by the Germans to be Austria's second most important resort behind St Anton. The two ski centres, which are only 45km apart, developed along parallel lines during the early 20th century. But St Anton found international fame while Ischgl remained largely the private haunt of ski-tourers.

Today it has a sophisticated lift system, and the old farming village houses a collection of sophisticated hotels and cavernous bars. An airport-style pedestrian walkway, cut through the rock around which the town was built, provides easy access to pistes, shops and restaurants – regardless of where you choose to stay.

If St Anton is the skiing capital of Europe, then Ischgl – against strong opposition from its rival – wears the après-ski crown and waves the sceptre of a never-empty *Stein* of beer. The resort is linked on piste across the Swiss frontier to the duty-free village of Samnaun. It is also connected to the small resort of Galtür by a free shuttle bus during the day.

Mountain

The ski area has been hugely improved in recent years with lifts being upgraded and pistes widened on an annual basis. Main mountain access is by three swift gondolas from different parts of town that take you up to Idalp, the mid-mountain station at 2320m that forms the hub of the lift system. Lifts extend up to and over the ridge which forms the territorial frontier with Switzerland. Some of the best skiing is at Palinkopf, which at 2864m is the highest point, reached by two chair-lifts from Idalp. Long red and black runs sweep down into the beautiful Fimbatal on the edge of the ski area. Some of the most rewarding off-piste runs here can be found off the Gampenbahn chair.

However, whenever the day dawns bright and sunny it seems that almost everyone in the resort heads over to Samnaun to indulge in a Swiss mountain lunch and fill their rucksacks with duty-free cigarettes, drink, perfume and electrical goods at supposedly bargain prices.

The return journey begins with a ride on what was the world's first double-decker cable-car. Multiple chair-lifts – Ischgl had the first eight-seater – help to ferry skiers homeward. However, one shortfall of the resort are the final runs down to the village. These are narrow and steep – too difficult for many of Ischgl's habitual clients, but that does not stop them trying and falling in the path of others.

This is a serious snowboarding resort. Boarders Paradise at Idjoch has a half-pipe and over 30 obstacles and is one of the largest in the Alps.

Learn

Ischgl Ski School, **t** +43 (0)5444 5257, has plenty of good English speakers, but don't expect to pick up any cutting-edge technique from most of the locally born instructors.

Children

The **Ski Kindergarten**, **t** +43 (0)5444 5257, at Idalp is run by the ski school and provides all-day care with lunch for children aged from three years. Ski lessons start at four years.

Lunch

A new restaurant opened last season in the giant glass-and-steel Pardatschgrat complex at the top of the gondola. **Panorama-Restaurant Alp Trida Sattel**, **t** +41 (0)81 868 5117, has the recommended Gourmet-Stüberl'n on the first floor. **La Marmotte** in the Bergrestaurant Alp Trida,

t +41 (0)81 868 5221, and **Bodenalp, t** +43 (0)5444 5285, in the Fimbertal are also suitable escapes from the ubiquitous self-services.

Across the frontier, the **Samnaunerhof, t** +41 (0)81 861 8181, is good for *Rösti* and **Hotel Chasa Montana, t** +41 (0)81 861 9000, has great pizzas.

Dine

Paznauner Stube, t +43 (0)5444 600, in the Trofana Royal, has a Michelin star. Martin Sieberer, former Austrian Chef of the Year, specializes in gourmet local cuisine. **Feuer & Eis, t** +43 (0)5444 591956, and **Salz & Pfeffer, t** +43 (0)5444 591956, both have good pizzas. **Gasthaus Alt-Paznaun, t** +43 (0)5444 5380, has a comprehensive menu of regional and international dishes.

Hotel Madlein, t +43 (0)5444 5226, serves light Austrian food inspired by the Far East. **The Goldener Adler, t** +43 (0)5444 5217, is known for its baked fresh trout. The rustic **Heidelberger Hütte, t** +43 (0)5444 5418, **Bodenalp, t** +43 (0)5444 5285, and **Vider Alp, t** +43 (0)5444 5385, are all mountain huts offering fondue evenings.

Party

By 4pm Germans and Austrians are in full swing, dancing on table-tops to jaded euro anthems and New Wave Oompah while downing litres of beer and shots of schnapps. Go-go girls clad in minimalist parodies of Austrian national dress are an intrinsic part of Ischgl's tea-time scene.

The **Schatzi Bar** in the **Hotel Elisabeth, Kitzloch, Kuhstall** at the **Sporthotel Silvretta, Trofana Alm, the Eisbar** and **Niki's Stadl** form the hard core of this sozzled spectacle. Those still sober enough (and others, too) then tackle the famous toboggan run on Mondays and Thursdays. The track from the top of the Silvrettabahn is a gruelling 7km with a vertical drop of nearly 1000m.

Remaining energy is expended on the late-night dance floors of **Pacha** in the **Hotel Madlein, Feuer & Eis, Hölle** and **Trofana Arena** in the **Trofana Royal**.

Every winter the resort holds open-air pop concerts featuring big-name stars. Previous performers include Peter Gabriel, The Corrs, Enrique Iglesias, Elton John, Sugababes and Sting.

Sleep

*****Trofana Royal, t** +43 (0)5444 600, *www.trofana.at*, has an extensive wellness centre – anti-ageing is the speciality.

****Hotel Madlein, t** +43 (0)5444 5226, *www.madlein.com*, is a minimalist hotel with Oriental overtones.

****Hotel Elisabeth, t** +43 (0)5444 5411, *www.ischglelisabeth.com*, is a popular resort meeting-place.

****The Goldener Adler, t** +43 (0)5444 5217, *www.goldener-adler.at*, is in a 350-year-old building with an ultra-modern interior and a wellness centre.

****Hotel Jägerhof, t** +43 (0)5444 513650 is conveniently placed for the underground walkway and has a friendly atmosphere.

****Hotel Seiblishof, t** +43 (0)5444 5425, *www.seiblishof.com*, has a separate children's restaurant.

Kitzbühel

MOST CHILLED RESORT 2007

***BEST FOR**

Authentic Tyrolean ambience, all levels of skier and rider, party-goers, non-skiers

ESSENTIALS

Altitude: 760m (2,493ft)–2,000m (6,562ft)
Further information: t +43 (0)5356 777, *www.kitzbuehel.com*
Lifts in area: 54 (9 cableways, 30 chairs, 15 drags) serving 148km of piste in linked area
Lift pass: Area pass covers Jochberg, Kitzbühel, Kirchberg, Pass Thurn. Adult €152–175, child 6–15yrs €87.50, both for 6 days
Access: Salzburg airport 1½hrs, Innsbruck airport 2hrs, Munich airport 2½hrs, railway station in Kitzbühel

Profile

Architecturally the most beautiful ski resort in Austria, with lots of alpine charm, scenic intermediate skiing and lively après-ski

Resort

Watching the Hahnenkamm on TV, the toughest of all the downhills on the World Cup circuit, it's easy to see why Kitzbühel holds a special place in the hearts of racers. Austrian Olympic hero Franz Klammer, who in the 1970s made the course his own, once famously said that every one of them who got to the bottom was a winner. The Blue Riband event on the racing calendar signals a bacchanalian frenzy among supporters who party a whole January weekend away in the picturesque medieval town with its heavily buttressed walls and delicate frescoes.

This annual television portrayal gives the erroneous impression that Kitz is a resort reserved strictly for experts who can jump 75 metres over the jaws of the Mausefalle and then tackle the reverse camber of the Steilhang at 80mph.

In fact, nothing could be further from the case. When not prepared for competition, the notorious Streif race course reverts to its more sedate role as a *Familienabfahrt* – a family run. Without the wickedly iced surface and with the jumps cordoned off, almost anyone who can ski parallel will enjoy themselves here on the Hahnenkamm as well as on the Kitzbüheler Horn, the town's second classic ski area. Kitzbühel also has excellent beginner slopes as well as a few serious piste challenges for experts.

This attractive medieval silver-mining town, set against the dramatic backdrop of the Wilderkaiser mountains, has been a ski centre ever since local hero Franz Reisch managed to acquire a pair of long wooden skis from Norway in 1893. His antics on the Horn incited a combination of curiosity and amusement that quickly spread across the Tyrol. These days, wealthy couples in designer ski suits and fur coats browse expensive boutiques in the pedestrianized centre and dine in Kitzbühel's sumptuous restaurants.

Mountain

Kitzbühel's critics argue that the town rested on its laurels for much of the second half of the 20th century and showed a marked reluctance to re-invest in the mountains that provide its livelihood. For those who come here to actually ski rather than revel in its scenic surroundings, Kitzbühel is seriously lacking in modern lifts. Unacceptable queues of 15 minutes or more are the norm to ride fixed chairs that should have

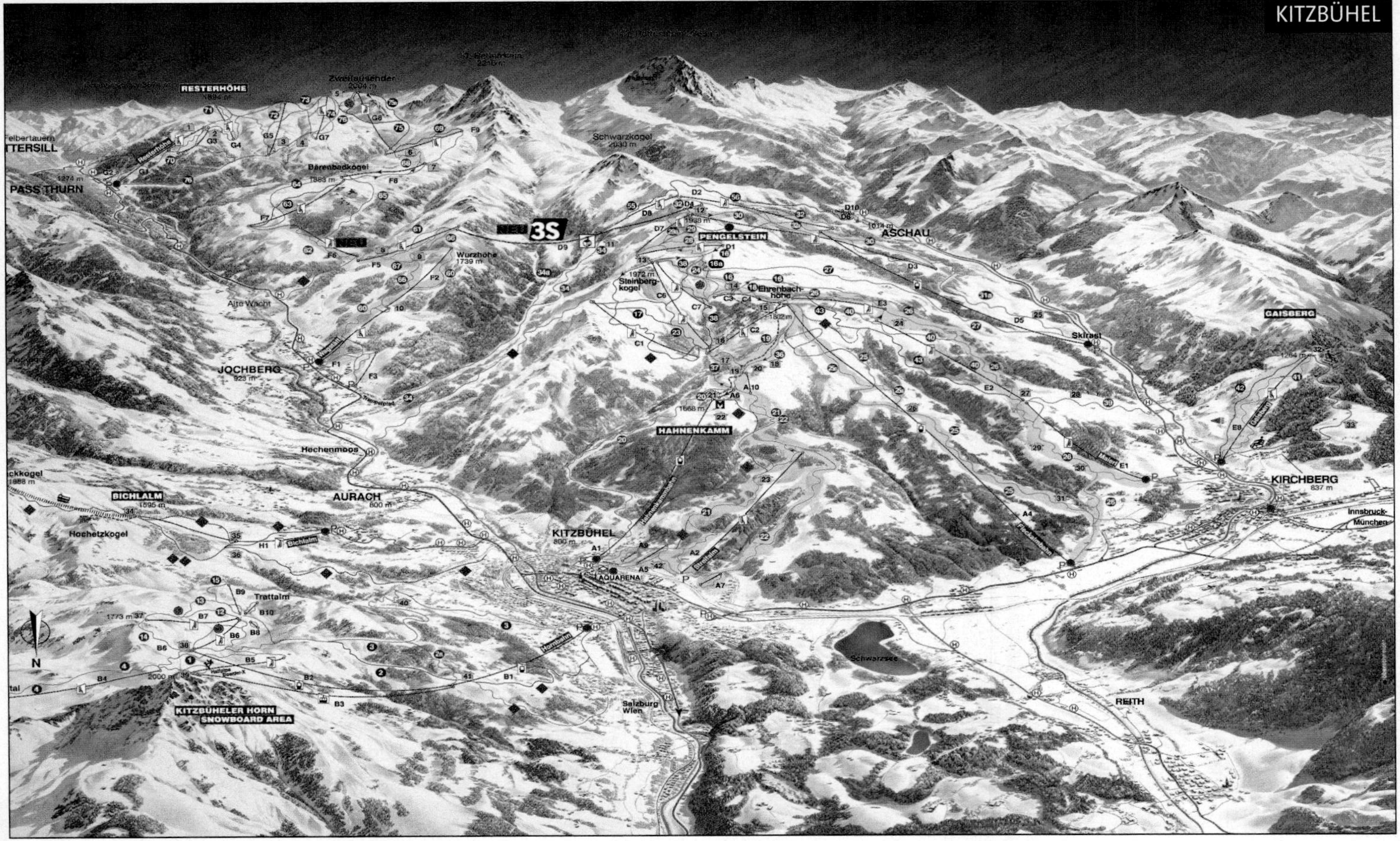
RESTERHÖHE
Zweitausender
2004 m
Schwarzkogel
2030 m
PASS THURN
1274 m
Bärenbadkogel
1883 m
NEU
3S
Wurzhöhe
1739 m
PENGELSTEIN
ASCHAU
1014 m
Steinberg-
kogel
1972 m
Ehrenbach-
höhe
1802 m
Alte Wacht
JOCHBERG
923 m
HAHNENKAMM
1668 m
Hechenmoos
AURACH
800 m
BICHLALM
1595 m
Hochetzkogel
KITZBÜHEL
800 m
AQUARENA
Trattalm
1773 m
2000 m
KITZBÜHELER HORN
SNOWBOARD AREA
Salzburg
Wien
Schwarzsee
REITH
GAISBERG
Skirast
KIRCHBERG
837 m
Innsbruck-
München
N

been replaced a generation ago. However, some of that seems about to change.

Two new six-packs open this season and a gondola now spans the deep valley between Pengelstein and Jochberg, allowing Kitzbühel-based skiers to complete the ski safari to Jochberg and Pass Thurn in both directions.

Last season another new gondola connected the ski manufacturing town of Mittersill with Pass Thurn and Kitzbühel. A third, the Ki-West, also links Kirchberg with Westendorf and the other resorts of the Wilder Kaiser Brixental SkiWelt.

This doesn't create 'the third largest ski area in Europe' as SkiWelt claimed with indecent haste. But when fully integrated SkiWelt's 150 lifts will make it a sizable intermediate region in an increasingly competitive market at a time when Big is considered essential to being Beautiful.

For the present, the area is by no means fully linked. You still have to rely on a bus link between Kirchberg and the base of the new lift, while Westendorf is also only connected to the rest of SkiWelt by bus across the Brixen Valley. None of these innovations compensate for Kitzbühel's ancient chairs, which need upgrading.

The 2000m Hahnenkamm is the main ski area and it is best reached by a six-person gondola from the centre of town. However, at busy times it can make sense to employ one of a number of alternative routes. The Fleckalmbahn gondola near the neighbouring town of Kirchberg takes you directly to the top of the mountain. The Wagstäst chair at Jochberg now provides a back door into the system, as does the Pengelstein gondola that rises from a car park beyond Kirchberg on the main road to Aschau.

The Kitzbüheler Horn, the town's second mountain, is on the far side of the valley and reached from the centre by regular ski bus. A gondola followed by a cable-car brings you to the summit. But the views from the top are better than the skiing. Apart from a token black run, the area consists of banal blue and red trails that meander through summer pastures.

However, the presence of a half-pipe, boardercross course and a terrain park makes the Horn of major interest to riders and twin-tippers.

Learn

Kitzbühel's assorted ski schools have now all amalgamated under the banner of **Rote Teufel/The Red Devils**, **t** +43 (0)5356 62500, with 350 instructors. The resort's schools have come in for some criticism in recent years for overcrowding and a consequent fall-off in service at peak times. Hopefully, under centralized management this will now be resolved – although absence of competition is usually not conducive to a high standard of tuition. However, we already have a couple of favourable reports from last season.

Children

The ski school has a kindergarten and runs group lessons. **Anita Halder**, **t** +43 (0)5356 75063, provides private childcare.

Lunch

Sohnbühel, **t** +43 (0)5356 62776, on the Hahnenkamm has a good sun terrace and great food. **Hochkitzbühel**, **t** +43 (0)5356 6957230, at the top of the Hahnenkamm gondola, serves typical Austrian dishes and also has a popular sun terrace.

Staudachstub'n, **t** +43 (0)5357 2084, on the main run down to the Fleckalm gondola is recommended; **Streifalm**, **t** +43 (0)5356 64690, is famous for its home-made ravioli. **Seidlalm**, **t** +43 (0)5356 63135, on the Hahnenkamm is renowned for its cheese dishes and has great views of the resort.

Dine

Rosengarten, t +43 (0)5357 2527, in the Hotel Taxacherhof at Kirchberg, is one of the finest restaurants in the Tyrol. Acclaimed chef Simon Taxacher has created his own outstanding style of Austrian nouvelle cuisine. **Golf-Hotel Rasmushof, t** +43 (0)5356 6525249, at the bottom of the Streif, has 'great food and a traditional atmosphere, as well as a wonderfully intimate conference room'. **Hotel zur Tenne, t** +43 (0)5356 64444, in Kitzbühel's Vorderstadt, is known for its fresh trout and is a personal favourite of ours. **Huberbräu-Stüberl, t** +43 (0)5356 65677, serves simple dishes at reasonable prices. **La Fonda, t** +43 (0)5356 73673, in the Hinterstadt, serves Mexican food. **Lois Stern, t** +43 (0)5356 74882, has Asian fusion cuisine.

Party

Kitzbühel's long-established British pub, **The Londoner**, takes central stage as the après-ski venue as soon as the lifts close for the day. However, it now has a serious British rival in **Brass Monkeys**. Others include the tiny **Waschkuchl**, **Stamperl**, **S'Lichtl**, **Jimmy's**, **Funferl**, **Bergsinn** and **Barrique**. The coolest nightclub is **Club Take Five. Olympia**, **Royal** and the new **Club Phyton** are the alternatives. The **Casino** has been entirely revamped and now offers a sophisticated evening out in contemporary surroundings. **Aquarena** leisure complex, **t** +43 (0)5356 64385, has a 25m pool and offers a full range of spa treatments.

Sleep

★★★★★**Grand SPA Resort A-ROSA, t** +43 (0)5356 656600, *www.a-rosa.de*, is a brand new building on the golf course just outside the town ('lots of teething problems, but impressive potential').

★★★★★**Romantikhotel Tennerhof, t** +43 (0)5356 63181, *www.tennerhof.com*, was originally an elegant Tyrolean country house.

★★★★★**Hotel Weisses Rössl, t** +43 (0)5356 625410, *www.weisses-roessl.com*, is the other sophisticated hotel. Its facilities include the two-storey Cheval Blanc spa with an indoor pool and pool bar.

★★★★**Golf-Hotel Rasmushof, t** +43 (0)5356 6525249, *www.austria-tourist.net*, is 'off the beaten tourist track, a smart, welcoming establishment that is a favourite with the Hahnenkamm racers'.

★★★★**Sport-und Beautyhotel Schweizerhof, t** +43 (0)5356 62735, *www.hotel-schweizerhof.at*, is 'comfortable, handy for the town centre and the food is excellent'.

★★★★**Hotel Goldener Greif, t** +43 (0)5356 64311, *www.hotel-goldener-greif.at*, is warmly traditional.

★★★★**Hotel Jägerwirt, t** +43 (0)5356 64067, *www.hotel-jaegerwirt.at*, has its own Irish pub, Sigi's Sport Bar.

★★★★**Schloss Lebenberg, t** +43 (0)5356 6901, *www.tiscover.com/schloss-lebenberg*, is a converted hunting lodge with a medieval-style interior complete with four-poster beds, and a health centre.

★★★★**Hotel Zur Tenne, t** +43 (0)5356 64444, *www.hotelzurtenne.com*, in the town centre, is a comfortable designer hotel. Many bedrooms have open fireplaces, and some suites have whirlpools and steam baths.

★★★★**Villa Mellon, t** +43 (0)5356 66821, *www.villa-mellon.at*, is à private house formerly owned by the banking family. Decorated like a hunting lodge, it offers haute cuisine and beautiful views.

★★★★**Golfhotel Bruggerhof, t** +43 (0)5356 62806, outside town, is recommended for the quality of its food.

Lech and Zürs

Profile

Two adjoining resorts for comfort-seekers who prefer a flattering piste to a tricky challenge. Not for anyone on a tight budget

Resort

Lech is an attractive traditional village tucked away in a narrow valley on the banks of a river, with a large collection of sumptuous four- and five-star hotels.

Zürs is perched 5km away at a snow-sure high altitude on the Flexen Pass, in a region that looks more towards Switzerland than to the rest of Austria and is best reached by car or train from Zurich. It shares its ski area with larger Lech and is included with St Anton in the regional Arlberg Ski Pass.

This is one of the birthplaces of modern skiing. Victor Sohm, a founding father of the original technique, gave the first lessons in Zürs on the open slopes of the Trittkopf and Hexenboden over 100 years ago. His international clients were mainly wealthy British, Swiss and Germans wanting to learn the new sport and relax in beautiful surroundings. In this respect, not much has changed.

Today, the two villages are the most exclusive resorts in Austria with six five-star hotels between them ('we even spotted a Moet et Chandon delivery truck'). Both attract a higher age group of visitors than nearby St Anton.

For many years, Princess Caroline of Monaco has been the unofficial patron of Zürs, while Princess Diana was her counterpart in Lech. The Dutch and Jordanian royal families, as well as former tennis champion Boris Becker and Russian president Vladimir Putin, are numbered among the fans of the region.

The terrain here is markedly easier than in St Anton, with plenty of benign cruising runs best suited to intermediates. As a result, large numbers of skiers and riders based in St Anton come here for the day. However, overcrowding is not an issue.

Zürs is no more than a huddle of smart hotels and precious little else. Hotels, restaurants and the slopes are set on either side of the little river that meanders through the centre, past a magnificent onion-domed church.

Oberlech, on the higher summer pastures, provides a traffic-free environment. Winter access is only by cable-car and luggage is cunningly transported to your hotel through a network of tunnels beneath the piste.

Zug, a tiny hamlet reached along a narrow lane through the woods from Lech, offers an alternative tranquil base that is linked into the lift system.

The galleried road across the Flexen Pass is prone to the occasional closure due to avalanche danger. Skiers wanting to explore further afield can join the St Anton ski area by taking a 20-minute bus ride to Alpe Rauz. It is possible for experts

* BEST FOR

Older intermediates, comfort-seekers, free spenders, families

ESSENTIALS

Altitude: Lech 1450m (4,756ft), Zürs 1720m (5,642ft)–2450m (8,036ft)
Further information: t +43 (0)5583 2161229, *www.lech-zuers.at*
Lifts in area: 33 (4 cableways, 18 chairs, 11 drags), serving 110km in Lech/Zürs and 82 lifts serving 286km and 86 lifts in Arlberg Ski Pass area
Lift pass: Arlberg Ski Pass (covers Lech and Zürs, Klösterle, Pettneu, St Anton, St Christoph, Stuben) adult €136–194, child 7–14yrs €82–116, both for 6 days. 6yrs and under €10 for whole season
Access: Innsbruck airport 2hrs, Zurich airport 2½hrs, Langen station 17km by postbus

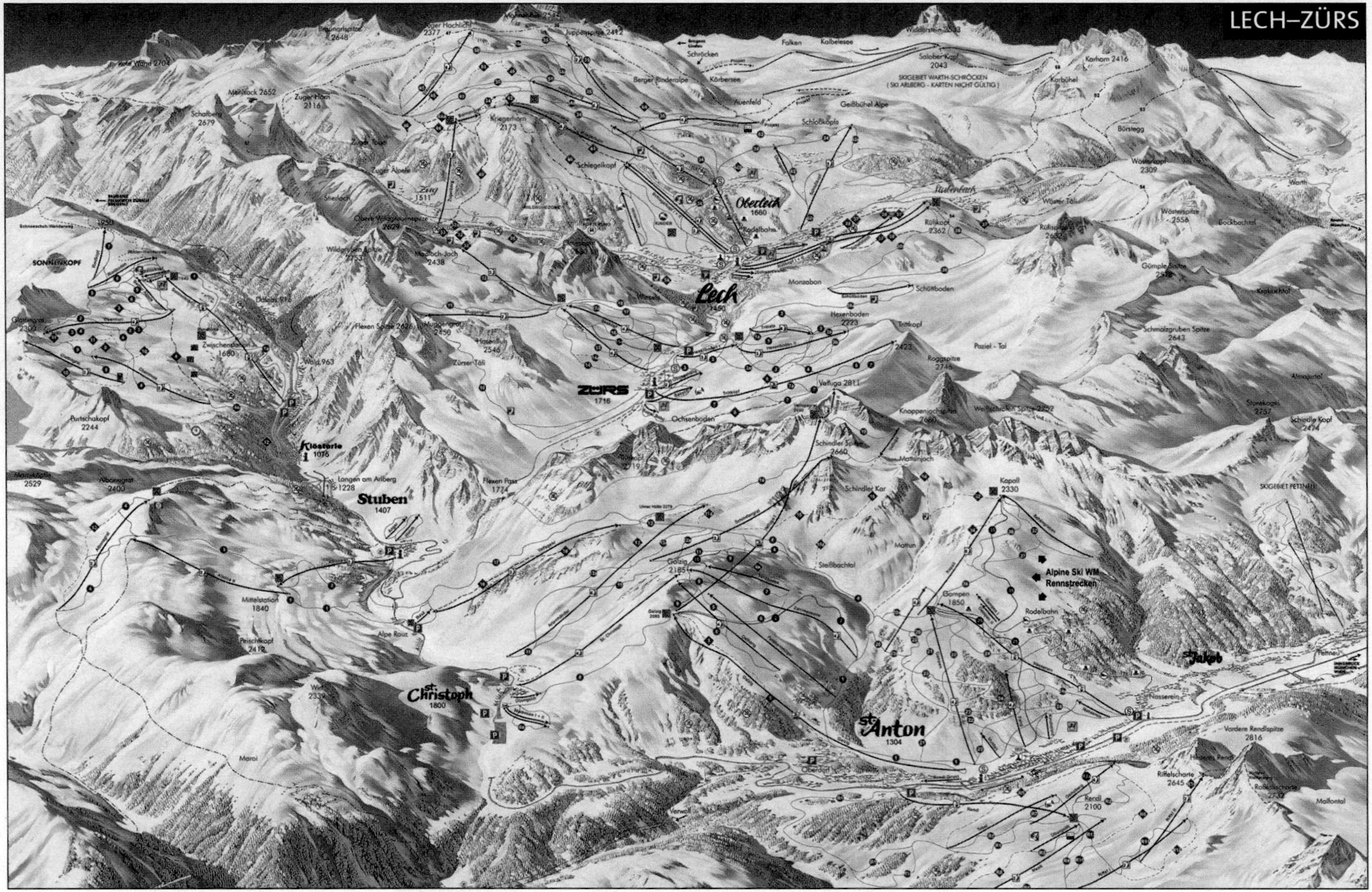
Rote Wand 2704
Braunarlspitze 2648
Zuger Hochlicht 2377
Juppenspitze 2412
Schröcken
Falken
Kalbelesee
Widderstein 2533
Saloberkopf 2043
Karhorn 2416
SKIGEBIET WARTH-SCHRÖCKEN
(SKI ARLBERG - KARTEN NICHT GÜLTIG)
Berger Binderalpe
Körbersee
Auenfeld
Geißbühel Alpe
Schloßkopfe
Karbühel
Bürstegg
Mohnenfluh 2652
Zuger Horn 2116
Schafberg 2679
Kriegerhorn 2173
Schlegelkopf
Zuger Alpele
Zug 1511
Stierloch
Oberleck 1660
Rodelbahn
Stubenbach
Wartherkopf 2309
Warth
Wöster Tal
Rüfikopf 2362
Rüfispitze 2632
Wösterspitze 2558
Bockbachtal
SONNENKOPF
Obere Wildgrubenspitze 2629
Wildgrubenspitze 2753
Madlochjoch 2438
Monzabon
Schüttboden
Lech 1450
Gümple Spitze 2538
Krabachtal
Glattingrat 2300
Zwischenalp 1680
Wald 963
Flexen Spitze 2626
Muggengrat 2450
Hasenfluh 2546
Hexenboden 2223
Trittkopf
Schmalzgruben Spitze 2643
Paziel - Tal
Zürser Täli
Zürs 1716
Ochsenboden
Valluga 2811
Roggspitze 2746
Almajurtal
Putschakopf 2244
Klösterle 1076
Knoppenjochspitze 2660
Weißschrofen Spitze 2752
Stanskogel 2757
Schindler Kopf 2474
Schindler Spitze 2660
Mattunjoch
Albonaköpfle 2529
Albonagrat 2400
Langen am Arlberg 1228
Stuben 1407
Flexen Pass 1773
Schindler Kar
Kapall 2330
SKIGEBIET PETTNEU
Mattun
Steißbachtal
Galzig 2185
Alpine Ski WM Rennstrecken
Gampen 1850
Mittelstation 1840
Rodelbahn
Alpe Rauz
Peischlkopf 2412
St. Jakob
Pettneu
St. Christoph 1800
Nasserein
St. Anton 1304
Vordere Rendlspitze 2816
Maroi
Oberdorf
Verwall
Rendl 2100
Riffelscharte 2645
Malfontal

to ski home off-piste – with a guide – from the top station of the 2811m Valluga.

Mountain

Zürs and Lech provide a pleasant playground of three mountains that can be skied in a clockwise direction only. The more challenging slopes are at the Zürs end of the circuit and on the Kriegerhorn and Zuger Hochlicht. The easiest runs are to be found on the sunny meadows surrounding Oberlech.

From Lech, the circuit begins with a ride up the twin Rüfikopf cable-cars. A combination of easy pistes takes you over the Schüttboden and Hexenboden and down into Zürs.

From Zürs, you take either the Seekopf or Zürsersee chairs followed by the Madloch chair for the long itinerary run down to Zug and on towards Lech.

It's worth noting that unpatrolled ski itineraries are marked by orange triangles and either orange or black broken lines. Most of these runs are so well skied that they are effectively pisted, but you should check the small print of your insurance policy to ensure that you are covered.

In good snow conditions, the area has sufficient challenge for accomplished skiers. Zürs has the steep black Sonnenberg, but otherwise the most challenging routes are all marked as itineraries.

Off-piste skiing through the woods is forbidden for environmental reasons and anyone caught doing so is liable to forfeit their lift pass.

Beginners have good nursery slopes at Oberlech as well as a dedicated area behind the church in Lech. The Boarderland terrain park on the Schlegelkopf in Lech has a half-pipe, a quarter-pipe and lots of obstacles.

Learn

For a resort that has produced a clutch of ski champions, the ski schools at **Lech**, **t** +43 (0)5583 2355, **Oberlech**, **t** +43 (0)5583 200, and **Zürs**, **t** +43 (0)5583 2611, are disappointing. If you come away with the impression that jobs are passed from father to son, you may not be far wrong.

It is a reflection of their financial status that some 80 per cent of visitors to Zürs and 50 per cent to Lech choose to take private rather than group lessons. What they get for their money is year-to-year continuity, but this is by no means the home of the kind of cutting-edge technique that wins medals for Austria. Guiding can be arranged through the ski schools and heli-skiing with **Wucher Heli-skiing**, **t** +43 (0)5583 2950.

Children

Children six years and under ski for €10 for the whole season. **Kinderland Oberlech**, **t** +43 (0)5583 2007, takes children aged from four-and-a-half years. **Miniclub Lech**, **t** +43 (0)5583 3530, provides a programme of play and skiing for children from three years. **Little Zürs Kindergarten**, **t** +43 (0)5583 224515, also takes children from three years.

Lunch

The pick of the lunch spots are attached to hotels. **Alter Goldener Berg**, **t** +43 (0)5583 2205, at Oberlech is recommended, along with the nearby **Bergkristall**, **t** +43 (0)5583 2678, **Montana**, **t** +43 (0)5583 2460, and the **Sonnenburg**, **t** +43 (0)5583 2147. In Zürs, **Gasthof Seekopf**, **t** +43 (0)5583 2143, and the **Trittalm**, **t** +43 (0)5583 2831, are also rated.

Dine

Most of the best restaurants are in the hotels. These include the **Post**, **t** +43 (0)5583 2206, **Arlberg**, **t** +43 (0)5583 2134, and **Brunnenhof**, **t** +43 (0)5583 2349 in Lech, as well as the **Rote Wand**, **t** +43 (0)5583 3435, in Zug, the **Albona Nova**, **t** +43 (0)5583 2341, and **Chesa** in Hotel Edelweiss, **t** +43 (0)5583 2662, in Zürs.

Other restaurants in Lech include tiny **Hüs Nr. 8**, **t** +43 (0)5583 33220, opposite the Post, serving grilled meat and light regional cooking with a superb wine list. **Fux**, **t** +43 (0)5583 2992, offers Asian fusion dishes. **Don Enzo Due**, **t** +43 (0)5583 2225, has great pizzas.

Party

In Lech, the evening gets under way with drinking at the ice bar outside the **Tannbergerhof** and 5pm tea-dancing inside the hotel. The **Schneggarei** bar by the Schlegelkopf lift catches the crowd as they come off the slopes. Later on, the action switches to **Klausur** in the **Schneider-Almhof**, **Fux** and **Pfefferköndl**. **Archiv** stays open until 2am. You can dance at the **Tannbergerhof**, **Hotel Krone** and Egon Zimmerman's **Scotch Club**.

In Zürs, **Vernissage** in **Skiclub Alpenrose**, the bar in the **Hotel Hirlanda** and **Kaminstüble** in the **Schweizerhaus** are all popular.

Disco Zürsserl in **Sporthotel Edelweiss** is the late-night venue.

A collective taxi service called 'James' runs until 4am and will take you home to your hotel for a flat fee.

Sleep

*****__Schneider-Almhof__, **t** +43 (0)5583 3500, *www.almhof.at*, has rooms decorated with natural materials, wooden furniture and stone-made accessories.

*****__Hotel Gasthof Post__, **t** +43 (0)5583 22060, *www.postlech.com*, is small but sumptuous and attracts an older clientele.

*****__Hotel Arlberg__, **t** +43 (0)5583 2134, *www.arlberghotel.at*, is on the edge of the piste and has comfortable suites and a gourmet restaurant.

****__Sporthotel Kristiania__, **t** +43 (0)5583 2561, *www.kristiania.at*, is a boutique hotel founded by 1952 Olympic champion Othmar Schneider.

****__Hotel Pension Haldenhof__, **t** +43 (0)5583 24440, *www.haldenhof.at*, is friendly and family-run.

****__Romantik-Hotel Krone__, **t** +43 (0)5583 2551, *www.romantikhotelkronelech.at*, is on the river bank opposite the church and has a Moroccan-influenced spa.

****__Hotel Tannbergerhof__, **t** +43 (0)5583 3313, *www.tannbergerhof.com*, is a principal resort rendezvous.

***__Hotel-Café Stülzis__, **t** +43 (0)5583 2471, *www.stuelzis.com*, has 'large, clean and comfortable rooms, a new wellness suite, and excellent half-board food and wine'.

Oberlech:

****__Hotel Sonnenburg__, **t** +43 (0)5583 2147, *www.sonnenburg.at*, is the best hotel in the hamlet. Facilities include an indoor swimming pool and two saunas with 'fog grottos'.

Zug:

****__Hotel Rote Wand__, **t** +43 (0)5583 3435, *www.rotewand.com*, has a swimming pool, indoor golf, wellness centre and a minimalist apartment wing.

Zürs:

*****__Thurnhers Alpenhof__, **t** +43 (0)5583 21910,*www.thurnhersalpenhof.com*, is a favourite and a member of *Leading Hotels of the World*.

*****__Hotel Lorünser__, **t** +43 (0)5583 22540, *www.loruenser.at*, is worthy of its rating.

*****__Hotel Zürserhof__, **t** +43 (0)5583 25130, *www.zuerserhof.at*, continues to have a popular following.

★★★★**Arlberghaus**, t +43 (0)5583 2258, *www.arlberghaus.com*, has a roof-top curling rink.

★★★★**Sporthotel Edelweiss**, t +43 (0)5583 2662, is convenient for the nightlife.

Mayrhofen

Profile

Large intermediate ski area with a well-regarded ski school make it a good place to learn and to take children, but nightlife is noisy. This is not a resort for advanced skiers and riders or for people looking for skiing convenience

Resort

The once quaint village of Mayrhofen was one of the original migration points for British skiers back in the 1970s and early 1980s. In those days, Austria in general and the Tyrol in particular attracted more British skiers than anywhere else in the world.

The mass market has long since deserted rival resorts in the region in favour of the more demanding slopes of France, but curiously the allure of Mayrhofen has never faded. An unfettered nightlife, reasonable accommodation, as well as good tuition and childcare gloss over the fact that this is one of the worst resorts for skiing convenience in the Alps – with heavy high-season queues to go up and down the main access lift ('20–45 minutes on a sunny day and 10 minutes when overcast').

Its big plus point is that outlying hamlets have been incorporated into the ski area branded as Zillertal 3000, making it the largest complex in the valley and, regardless of the vagaries of nature, you can ski on the glacier at Hintertux, at the end of the valley, throughout the year. However, overcrowding on the glacier can be a serious problem when Mayrhofen and other resorts in the region are short on snow.

The Zillertal Superskipass covers all 11 different villages in the valley. Buses are frequent and a free train goes down the valley to Zell am Ziller and to the mainline station at Jenbach.

*BEST FOR

beginners and intermediates, big drinkers, families

ESSENTIALS

Altitude: 630m (2,066ft)–2500m (8,202ft)
Further information: t +43 (0)5285 6760, *www.mayrhofen.at*
Lifts in area: 52 in Zillertal 3000 (8 cableways, 17 chairs, 27 drags) serving 175km of piste, 590km in the whole Zillertal area
Lift pass: Zillertal Superskipass adult €172, child 6–15yrs €86, both for 6 days
Access: Innsbruck airport 1hr, Munich and Salzburg airports 2½hrs, railway station in resort

Mountain

Mayrhofen's own ski area is split between two mountains. Beginners must make their way to the edge of town to the Ahorn, a 2000m peak now served by a new cableway this season, replacing the slow 25-year-old cable-car. The top is given over to snow-sure nursery runs. The 5.5km black Ebenwald piste from the top also gives more accomplished skiers and riders a reason to explore Ahorn.

The main skiing takes place on higher slopes on the other side of the valley, reached by the modern Penkenbahn gondola from the centre of town. Unfortunately the topography dictates that there is no home run and skiers and riders must return by lift at the end of the day – and cope with further high-season queues. Alternative access is provided by gondolas from Finkenberg and

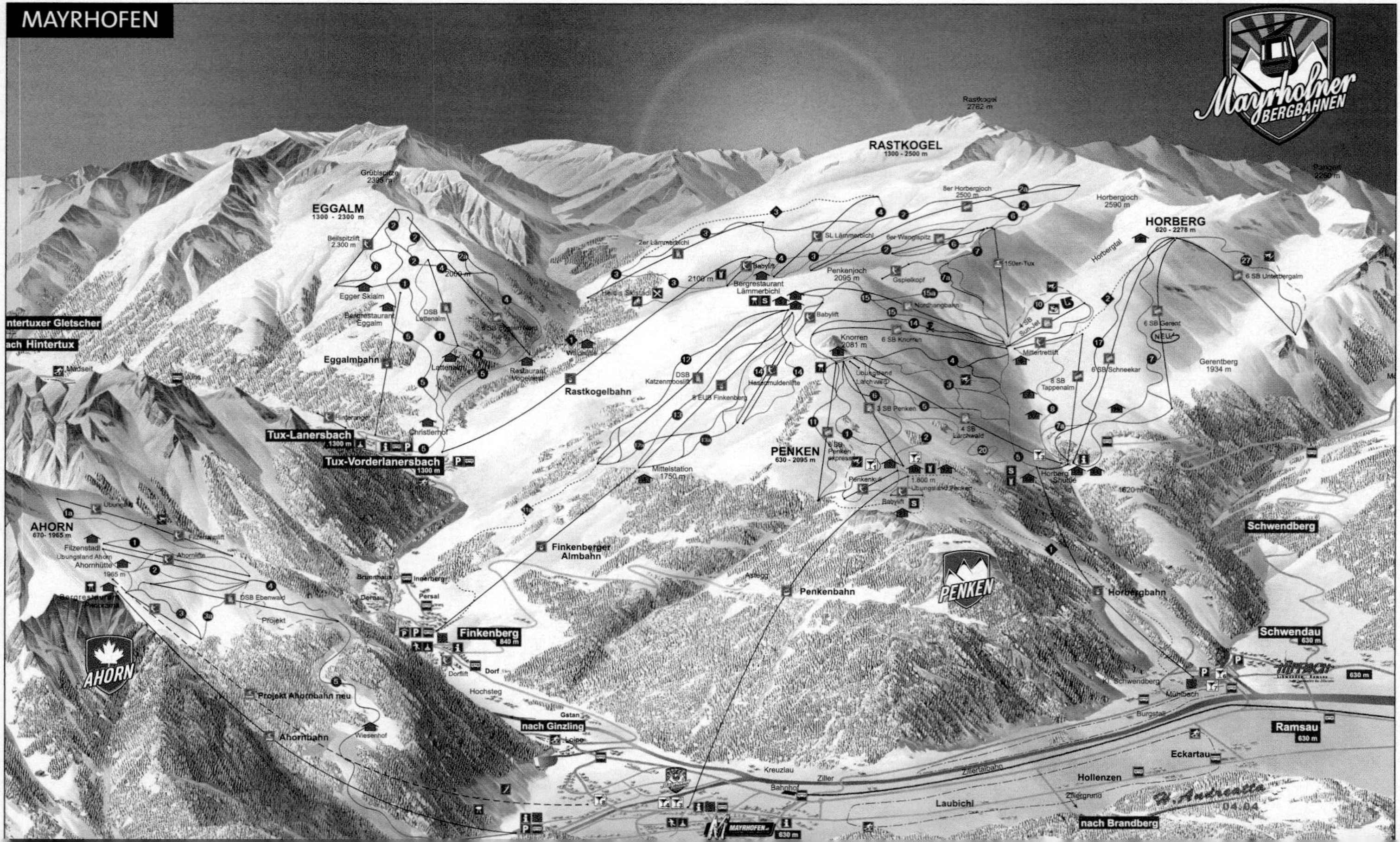
Mayrhofner Bergbahnen
RASTKOGEL
1300 - 2500 m
Rastkogel
2762 m
EGGALM
1300 - 2300 m
Grüblspitze
2395 m
HORBERG
620 - 2278 m
Horbergjoch
2590 m
Gerentberg
1934 m
PENKEN
630 - 2095 m
Penkenjoch
2095 m
Knorren
2081 m
AHORN
670 - 1965 m
Bergrestaurant
Lämmerbichl
Mittelstation
1750 m
Rastkogelbahn
Eggalmbahn
Finkenberger
Almbahn
Penkenbahn
Horbergbahn
Ahornbahn
Projekt Ahornbahn neu
Tux-Lanersbach
1300 m
Tux-Vorderlanersbach
1300 m
Finkenberg
840 m
Schwendberg
Schwendau
630 m
Ramsau
630 m
nach Ginzling
nach Brandberg
Hintertuxer Gletscher
nach Hintertux
Hollenzen
Eckartau
Laubichl
Ziller
Zillertalbahn
Hochsteg
Gstan
Kreuzlau
Bahnhof
Astegg
Dornau
Persal
Innerberg
Brunnhaus
Dorf
Dorflift
Wiesenhof
Mühlbach
Burgstall
Hippach
Egger Skialm
Bergrestaurant
Eggalm
DSB
Lattenalm
Lattenalm
Restaurant
Vogelnest
Christlerhof
Heidi's Skistadl
2er Lämmerbichl
SL Lämmerbichl
8er Horbergjoch
2500 m
6er Wanglspitz
150er-Tux
Gspielkopf
Nordhangbahn
6 SB Knorren
DSB
Katzenmooslift
8 EUB Finkenberg
Hasenmuldenlifte
Mittertrettlift
8 SB
Tappenalm
6 SB Schneekar
6 SB Gerent
NEU
6 SB Unterbergalm
4 SB
Lärchwald
3 SB Penken
8 SB
Penken
express
Penkenkuh
1.800 m
Übungsland Penken
Babylift
Horberg
Shuttle
1620 m
Ahornlifte
Filzenalmlift
Filzenstadl
Übungsland Ahorn
Ahornhütte
1965 m
DSB Ebenwald
Projekt
PENKEN
AHORN
MAYRHOFEN
630 m
04.04

Vorderlanersbach further up the valley, and from Schwendau further down the Zillertal. You can – snow conditions permitting – ski back down to these bases but must then take a usually overcrowded peak hour bus back to Mayrhofen. The resort therefore gets a minus point for skiing convenience.

The terrain park, with a 150m half-pipe and served by a dedicated four-person chair, has been voted the best in the German-speaking Alps.

If you can't leave your work behind on holiday or need to commune with iTunes, it is worth noting that one of the first wireless hotspots in a ski area is situated on Penken.

Learn

Four schools with over 100 instructors between them cope with the annual influx of predominantly beginner and lower intermediate clients as well as a few experts who are drawn to the recommended **Mount Everest** ski school, **t** +43 (0)5285 62829. Its charismatic owner, Peter Habeler, climbed Everest without oxygen in 1978. His school teaches all standards and he personally guides off-piste tours with overnight stops in a mountain hut. The other schools are: **Roten Profis**, **t** +43 (0)5285 63800, Max Rahm's **Mayrhofen Total**, **t** +43 (0)5285 63939, and **Mayrhofen 3000**, **t** +43 (0)5285 64015.

Children

Back in the 1970s, Mayrhofen pioneered the first ski kindergarten in the Alps. The resort maintains its long tradition of childcare, which remain as good as any in the Alps. **Wuppy's Kinderland**, **t** +43 (0)5285 63612, takes children from three months to seven years. **Roten Profis**, **t** +43 (0)5285 63800, looks after children from 12 months, and **Mayrhofen Total**, **t** +43 (0)5285 63939, accepts children from two years.

Lunch

Some 28 huts are dotted on the mountainside. **Ahornhütte** on the Ahorn is owned by ex-World Cup racer Uli Spiess. **Josef's Biohütte**, **t** +43 (0)5285 62309, has organic fare. **Schneekarhütte**, **t** +43 (0)5285 64940, is renowned for its fresh prawns and salmon steaks. On Penken, the **Penkentenne**, **t** +43 (0)5285 62115, and **Hilde's Skitenne**, **t** +43 (0)664 3857574, are recommended. **Grillholfalm**, **t** +43 (0)664 3126426, by the terrain park, has good pizzas. **Christa's Skialm**, **t** +43 (0)5285 63033, and **Schiestl's Sunnalm**, **t** +43 (0)5282 4182, are both popular.

Dine

Most visitors to Mayrhofen eat at their hotels. **Ciao**, **t** +43 (0)5285 63299, is a friendly Italian. **Café Dengg**, **t** +43 (0)5285 64866, has fine pizzas. The modern **Sport Bar Grill**, **t** +43 (0)5285 6705, in Fun & Spa Hotel Strass serves international food until 2am. **Bruggerstube**, **t** +43 (0)5285 63793, and the **Eckartauerhof**, **t** +43 (0)5285 62435, are atmospheric.

Party

Après-ski starts up the mountain at Penken before spreading to the **Ice Bar** at the foot of Penken gondola and the new **Speak Easy** in the **Fun & Spa Hotel Strass**, **Happy End**, **Niki's Schirmbar**, **Mo's** and the **Piccadilly Pub**. **Schlüsselalm** and **Sport's Arena** are the discos.

The **Erlebnis Mayrhofen** swimming-pool complex is one of the leading waterparks in this corner of Austria.

Sleep

★★★★★**Elisabethhotel**, t +43 (0)5285 6767, *www.elisabethhotel.com*, at the entrance to the village, sets the pace. This is a charming, traditional Tyrolean hotel with a fine pool and spa.

★★★★**Fun & Spa Hotel Strass**, t +43 (0)5285 6705, *www.hotelstrass.com*, is next to the Penken lift.

★★★★**The Waldheim**, t +43 (0)5285 62211, *www.waldheim.at*, is recommended.

★★★★**Hotel Berghof**, t +43 (0)5285 62254, *www.berghof.cc*, has three indoor tennis courts.

★★★★**Alpenhotel Kramerwirt**, t +43 (0)5285 6700, *www.kramerwirt.at*, was established by the Kröll family in 1624 and is stylishly traditional.

★★★**Hotel-Gasthof Perauer**, t +43 (0)5285 62566, *www.perauer.at*, is a converted Tyrolean hotel. It offers regional, international and vegetarian cuisine.

★★★**Gasthof Brücke**, t +43 (0)5285 62232, *www.gasthof-bruecke.com*, has 'a brilliant atmosphere, friendly and helpful staff, but fairly ordinary food'.

Neustift and the Stubaital

Profile

Large attractive village located close to Innsbruck, with its own simple ski area and the snow-sure Stubai Glacier. Neustift is the first Disney-franchised resort in Europe

*BEST FOR

Families, beginners and intermediates, guaranteed snow-cover (Stubai Glacier)

ESSENTIALS

Altitude: Fulpmes 937m (3,074ft) –2200m (7,218ft), Neustift 1000m (3,281ft)–3200m (10,499ft)
Further information: Fulpmes, t +43 (0)5225 62235, *www.stubai.at*, Neustift, t +43 (0)5226 2228, *www.neustift.com*
Lifts in area: 59 (9 cableways, 16 chairs, 34 drags) serving 149km
Lift pass: Superskipass Stubai adult €167–185, child 10–14yrs €120, both for 6 days
Access: Innsbruck airport 20mins, Munich airport 1½hrs

Resort

Neustift is the most important community in the broad valley between Innsbruck and the Brenner Pass to Italy. The large, attractive village is gateway to the Stubai Glacier, a training centre for national ski teams. Schönberg, Fulpmes, Mieders and Telfes villages are dotted along the valley and act as further bed-bases.

Mountain

Apart from the glacier, a 20-minute drive away, Neustift has its own little ski area that stretches over undulating pastures. Schlick 2000 at Fulpmes is in a sheltered bowl on the 2230m Sennjoch. Both areas are ideal for families with young children. The Stubai Glacier is served by twin gondolas that form part of a network of 21 lifts serving 110km of piste. It is a good out-of-season training area for racers that closes from the middle of June until the last week in September.

Learn

Neustift has two ski schools: **Neustift Stubaier Gletscher**, t +43 (0)5226 8108, and **Neustift Olympia**, t +43 (0)5226 3682. Fulpmes has the **Stubai ski school**, t +43 (0)664 3332222.

Children

The **Micky Mouse Ski Club**, **t** +43 (0)5226 8108, based up on the glacier, teaches kids from four years to learn to ski while having fun. The children's magic carpet lift is inside a tunnel and the nursery slope has ski-through Disney characters. Non-skiers from three years are cared for in the slope-side **Micky Mouse Clubhouse**.

Lunch

Fulpmes has 10 self-service restaurants on the mountain at Schlick 2000. There are five eateries on the **Stubai Glacier**, **t** +43 (0)5226 8141.

Dine

In Neustift, **Grillstube**, **t** +43 (0)5226 3147, has great steaks and **Café Anni Platzl**, **t** +43 (0)5226 3613, has good pizzas, but the **Hotel Jagdhof**'s restaurant, **t** +43 (0)5226 2666, serves the best food in town. Restaurants in Fulpmes include the hip **Kla4vier**, **t** +43 (0)5225 63744, which serves Tex-Mex.

Party

Bierfassl and **Harry's Pub** in Neustift are popular meeting places. The **Mutterberg**, **Hully Gully** and **Rumpl** discos are the late-night spots. In Fulpmes, **Café Corso**, **Platzwirt**, **Jump-In** and the **Dorfalm** provide the action.

Sleep

★★★★★**Hotel Jagdhof & Spa**, **t** +43 (0)5226 2666, *www.hotel-jagdhof.at*, in Neustift village centre, has excellent food. It houses the comprehensive Vitality World spa with 30 different types of sauna and steam room.

★★★★**Alpenhotel Tirolerhof**, **t** +43 (0)5226 3278, *www.alpenhoteltirolerhof.com*, is family-run, with a wellness centre and a traditional Tyrolean interior.

★★★★**Sporthotel Neustift**, **t** +43 (0)5226 2510, *www.sporthotelneustift.at*, has a wellness suite and an entire floor for non-smokers.

★★★★**Alpenhotel Mutterberg**, **t** +43 (0)5226 8116, *www.stubaital.at/mutterberg*, is a comfortable hotel for keen skiers who prefer to stay at the base of the Stubai lifts.

★★★★**Alpenhotel Tirolerhof**, **t** +43 (0)5225 62422, *www.tirolerhoffulpmes.at*, in Fulpmes, has been recently refurbished.

★★★★**Sporthotel Cristall**, **t** +43 (0)5225 634240, *www.sporthotelcristall.at*, is also recommended.

Niederau

Profile

The traditional village attracts a large influx of British and is suited to beginners and lower intermediates. Neighbouring Auffach and Oberau provide further skiing on the shared lift pass

Resort

Niederau is a modest traditional village in the Wildschönau region, which includes the surrounding Tyrolean communities of Thierbach, Oberau, and Auffach. Together they have acted as a winter playground for overseas visitors for 70 years. Much of the appeal has been based on lower-than-average prices and benign but beautiful slopes. Plans have been approved in principle to connect the Wildschönau to the neighbouring and perceivedly smarter Alpbach valley, a move that should be beneficial to both.

***BEST FOR**

Traditional Tyrolean ambience, beginners and low intermediates, families

ESSENTIALS

Altitude: 830m (2,722ft)–1903m (6,243ft)
Further information: t +43 (0)5339 8255, *www.wildschoenau.com*
Lifts in area: 25 (2 cableways, 3 chairs, 20 drags) serving 70km of piste
Lift pass: Area adult €128.40–142.60, child from 6yrs €77–85.60, both for 6 days
Access: Innsbruck airport 45mins, Wörgl station 10mins

Mountain

All the villages are linked by free ski-bus. Main mountain access from Niederau is by a modern eight-person gondola. From the summit of the Markbachjoch you have a choice of three pisted and one unpisted run back to the valley. The old single-chair is scheduled to be replaced by a double in time for the 2006–7 season.

Auffach has the pick of the skiing. A gondola takes you through the woods to a network of five drag-lifts and a chair. Oberau has eight short drags, while skiing in Thierbach is confined to just two drag-lifts. Riders congregate in Auffach, which has a terrain park with a half-pipe.

Learn

Niederau has two ski and board schools: **Aktiv**, **t** +43 (0)5339 2701, and **Wildschönau**, **t** +43 (0)5339 2200. English is widely spoken in both.

Children

Niederau crèche takes children from two years. The Wildschönau ski school runs **Bobo's Kinderclub** for two- to six-year-olds.

Lunch

In Niederau, **Anton-Graf-Hütte**, **t** +43 (0)5339 2547, and **Markbachjochalm**, **t** +43 (0)5339 8202, offer wholesome fare. In Oberau, try **Achentalalm**, **t** +43 (0)5339 8578, or **Zauberwinkel**, **t** +43 (0)5339 8126.

Dine

Hotel Wastlhof, **t** +43 (0)5339 8247, has the best cuisine. **Hotel Austria**, **t** +43 (0)5339 8188, houses the most popular restaurant in Niederau. There are two Italian eateries, **Ferrari**, **t** +43 (0)5339 2733, in Niederau, and **Italia 90**, **t** +43 (0)5339 8109, in Oberau.

Party

Bobo's Heustadl at the gondola base in Niederau and the **Gruttn-Bar** in Auffach draw skiers off the slopes long before the lifts stop. **Sno Blau** in **Hotel Tirolerhof** and the **Starchentstüberl** are the hotspots in Oberau. The **Cave Bar**, **Alm Pub** and **Dorfstub'n** are nightspots in Niederau.

Sleep

Niederau:

★★★★**Hotel Sonnschein**, **t** +43 (0)5339 8353, *www.harmony-hotels.com*, has an indoor swimming pool and a playroom.

★★★★**Hotel Wastlhof**, **t** +43 (0)5339 8247, *www.tiscover.at/wastlhof*, is less conveniently located on the cross-country skiing track. It has a new spa.

★★★**Hotel Alpenland**, **t** +43 (0)5339 8258, *www.alp1.at*, is well situated but 'food a bit plain and slightly unimaginative'.

Oberau:

★★★★**Hotel Silberberger**, **t** +43 (0)5339 8407, *www.silberberger.at*, is charming.

★★★**Hotel Tirolerhof**, **t** +43 (0)5339 81180, *www.hoteltirolerhof.at*, is ski-in/ski-out and the main resort meeting place.

★★★**Gasthof Kellerwirt**, **t** +43 (0)5339 8116, *www.kellerwirt.alpinerose.net*, is a former monastery.

Auffach:

★★★**Auffacher Hof**, **t** +43 (0)5339 8837, *www.auffacherhof.at*, is in the centre.

Obergurgl-Hochgurgl

✻BEST FOR

Reliable snow-cover, families with young children, ski-touring

ESSENTIALS

Altitude: 1930m (6,330ft)–3080m (10,104ft)
Further information: t +43 (0)5256 6466, *www.obergurgl.com*
Lifts in area: 23 (4 cableways, 12 chairs, 7 drags) serving 110km of piste
Lift pass: adult €175–195, child 9–16yrs €110, both for 6 days
Access: Innsbruck airport 1½hrs, Ötztal station 54km, with regular buses

Profile

Charming high-altitude family resort with magnificent glacial scenery, a long ski season that stretches to Easter and beyond, cheerful après-ski and good ski-touring

Resort

Obergurgl is a traditional village set around its church at 1930m in the high 67km Ötz Valley close to the frontier with Italy, an easy drive from Innsbruck. Back in 1931, Swiss aviation pioneer Auguste Piccard first put Obergurgl on the ski map when he landed his hot-air balloon on the Gurgler-Ferner glacier after achieving a world altitude record of 16000m. In a triumphant rescue operation, local guide Hans Falkner led the explorers across to crevasses to safety and glory. More recently, Oetzi, the 5,300-year-old hunter whose perfectly preserved body was found on one of the 23 glaciers above the resort, has brought renewed fame to the valley.

Higher Hochgurgl is a collection of ski-in/ski-out hotels perched on the mountainside and linked by gondola to Obergurgl. Much of the appeal of the joint resort lies in secure snow conditions that last from November to the end of April. Obergurgl has a few shops and an open-air ice rink.

Mountain

This is an easy family ski area with few challenges on piste but plenty of opportunities for guided excursions into magnificent terrain leading up to the Italian frontier.

The skiing takes place in three topographically separate, but lift-linked areas spread across the northwestern side of the Ötztal. Obergurgl's main Festkogl sector is reached either by a gondola at the beginning of the village or by a two-stage chair-lift from the centre. From the top you can reach two further lifts and together these give access to a pleasant choice of blue and red cruising runs as well as a couple of steeper blacks.

From mid-mountain, the 3.6km Top Express gondola spans two valleys to reach Hochgurgl. The glacial terrain here is much more extensive with plenty of long, mainly blue, descents. The two-stage Hochgurglbahn gondola allows swift access from the valley to the modest collection of drag-lifts and chairs – including a new six-seater – and a continuous vertical drop of 1500m.

The third smaller area of Gaisberg lies to the south of Obergurgl and is reached by chair-lift from the village centre. Gaisberg offers delightful blue runs as well as well as three more challenging reds between the trees, served by the swift six-person Steinmannbahn chair. A glorious off-piste route begins from the Hohe Mut and ends up near the Schönwieshütte.

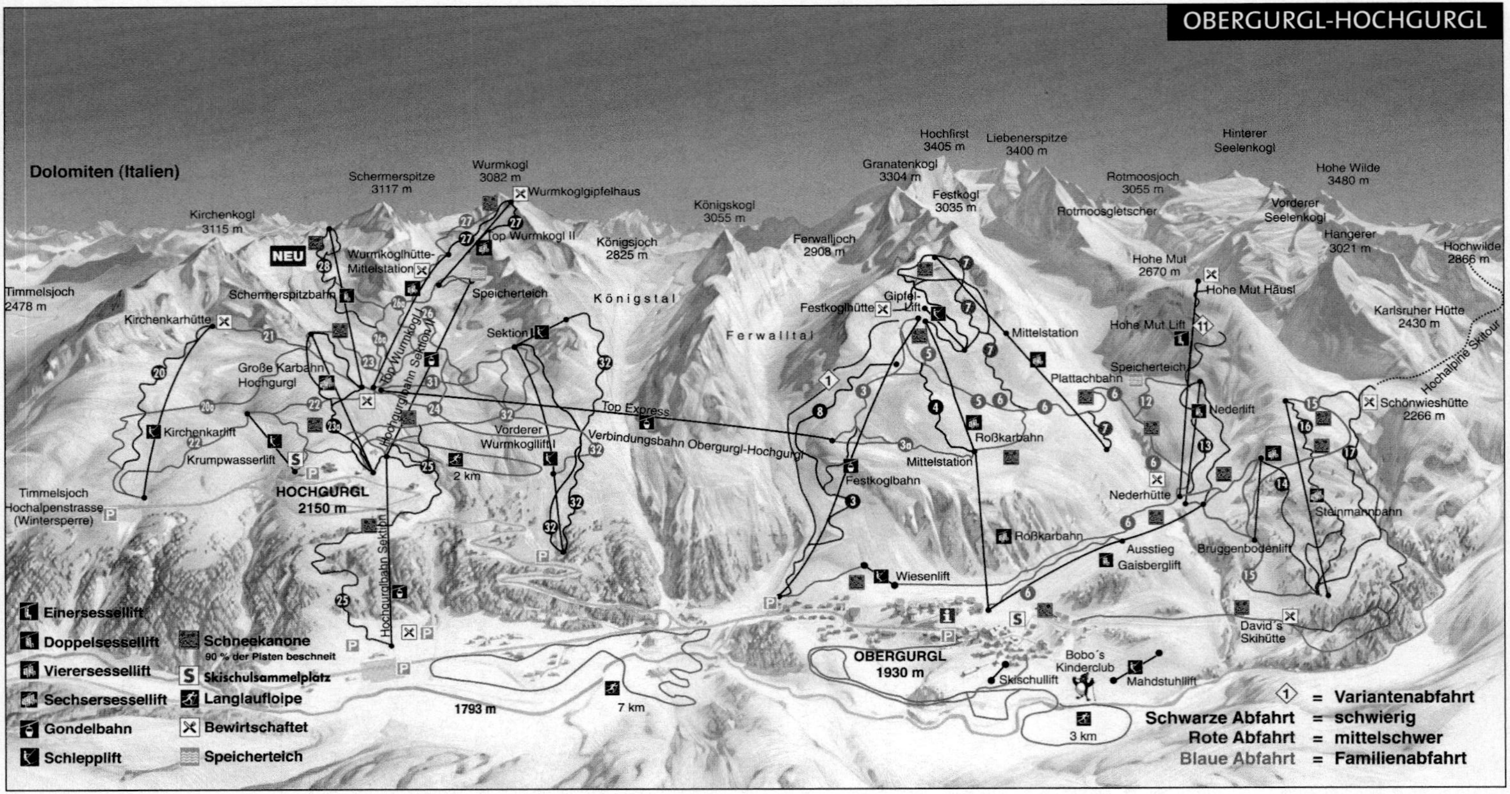
OBERGURGL-HOCHGURGL
Dolomiten (Italien)
Timmelsjoch
2478 m
Kirchenkogl
3115 m
Schermerspitze
3117 m
Wurmkogl
3082 m
Wurmkoglgipfelhaus
Königskogl
3055 m
Königsjoch
2825 m
Ferwalljoch
2908 m
Granatenkogl
3304 m
Hochfirst
3405 m
Festkogl
3035 m
Liebenerspitze
3400 m
Rotmoosjoch
3055 m
Rotmoosgletscher
Hinterer
Seelenkogl
Vorderer
Seelenkogl
Hohe Wilde
3480 m
Hangerer
3021 m
Hochwilde
2866 m
Hohe Mut
2670 m
Hohe Mut Häusl
Karlsruher Hütte
2430 m
Hochalpine Skitour
NEU
Wurmkoglhütte-
Mittelstation
Top Wurmkogl II
Speicherteich
Schermerspitzbahn
Kirchenkarhütte
Königstal
Ferwalltal
Sektion I
Top Wurmkogl
Hochgurglbahn Sektion II
Große Karbahn
Hochgurgl
Kirchenkarlift
Krumpwasserlift
Top Express
Verbindungsbahn Obergurgl-Hochgurgl
Vorderer
Wurmkogllift I
2 km
Timmelsjoch
Hochalpenstrasse
(Wintersperre)
HOCHGURGL
2150 m
Hochgurglbahn Sektion I
Festkoglhütte
Gipfel-
lift
Mittelstation
Plattachbahn
Hohe Mut Lift
Speicherteich
Nederlift
Schönwieshütte
2266 m
Roßkarbahn
Mittelstation
Festkoglbahn
Nederhütte
Steinmannbahn
Roßkarbahn
Ausstieg
Gaisberglift
Bruggenbodenlift
Wiesenlift
David´s
Skihütte
OBERGURGL
1930 m
Bobo´s
Kinderclub
Skischullift
Mahdstuhllift
1793 m
7 km
3 km
Einersessellift
Doppelsessellift
Vierersessellift
Sechsersessellift
Gondelbahn
Schlepplift
Schneekanone
90 % der Pisten beschneit
Skischulsammelplatz
Langlaufloipe
Bewirtschaftet
Speicherteich
= Variantenabfahrt
Schwarze Abfahrt = schwierig
Rote Abfahrt = mittelschwer
Blaue Abfahrt = Familienabfahrt

Learn

Obergurgl, t +43 (0)5256 6305, and **Hochgurgl, t** +43 (0)5256 6265, schools have been successfully teaching the basics to international visitors for generations, but don't expect to learn cutting-edge technique here.

Children

Bobo's Kinderclub, t +43 (0)5256 6305, provides care for non-skiing children from three years. The ski school accepts children as young as three years. The resort allows children aged nine and under to ski for free – a higher age limit than in many other resorts. A number of hotels operate their own crèches. These are usually free of charge for older children, but you need to check ages carefully before booking. They include **Alpina, Austria, Bellevue, Bergwelt, Crystal** and **Hochfirst** as well as **Hotel Edelweiss & Gurgl** and **Top Hotel Hochgurgl**.

Lunch

Hohe Mut Häusl, t +43 (0)699 1141 4045, is a popular lunch venue with magnificent views at the top of the Gaisberg sector. It is reached by chair-lift but the only route from here is a unclassified itinerary. Less accomplished skiers are advised to take the lift back down. The **Schönwieshütte, t** +43 (0)664 4428113, is a touring refuge renowned for its *Gulaschsuppe* and *Kaiserschmarren* (plum pancakes).

David's Skihütte, t +43 (0)5256 6332, at the bottom of the Steinmann lift, is a popular lunch venue with good food and lively après-ski. **Festkoglalm, t** +43 (0)5256 6370, and **Nederhütte, t** +43 (0)5256 6425, are also recommended.

In Hochgurgl, the **Wurmkoglhütte, t** +43 (0)5675 6100, offers traditional mountain fare.

Dine

With only a handful of exceptions, restaurants in both Obergurgl and Hochgurgl are located within the hotels. **Dorf-Alm, t** +43 (0)5256 6570, offers regional dishes and cheese fondue. **Pizzeria Romantika** in the Hotel Madeleine, **t** +43 (0)5256 63550, and **Pizzeria Belmonte, t** +43 (0)5256 6533, both have good pizzas.

Party

Nightlife is generally muted and one reader described it as 'not a resort for party animals'. The **Nederhütte** and other mountain restaurants start the ball rolling with music and dedicated drinking in the late afternoon. Later on, the **Josl-Keller** has the best atmosphere. **Krump'n'Stadl** is crowded and noisy. **Austria-Keller** in Obergurgl and **African Bar** in Hochgurgl have dancing and stay open into the early hours.

Sleep

Obergurgl:
★★★★**Hotel Deutschmann, t** +43 (0)5256 6594, *www.hotel-deutschmann.com*, at the entrance to the village, is warmly recommended. It is named after the family that own it.
★★★★**Hotel Austria, t** +43 (0)5256 6282, *www.austria-bellevue.com*, dates back to 1561.
★★★★**Hotel Crystal, t** +43 (0)5256 6454, *www.hotel-crystal.com*, is a monster of a building, but extremely comfortable.
★★★★**Hotel Bergwelt, t** +43 (0)5256 6274, *www.hotelbergwelt.com*, is a traditional

hotel with great ambience and a good swimming pool.

★★★★**Hotel Edelweiss & Gurgl**, **t** +43 (0)5256 6223, *www.edelweiss-gurgl.com*, in the centre, is one of the resort's original hotels ('food was fab and the staff are brill. Can't rate it highly enough').

★★★★**Hotel Jenewein**, **t** +43 (0)5256 6203, *www.hotel-jenewein.com*, offers exceptional half-board cuisine.

★★★★**Hotel Madeleine**, **t** +43 (0)5256 63550, *www.hotel-madeleine.com*, has 'pristine accommodation, excellent food, and very pleasant staff'.

★★★**Haus Schönblick**, **t** +43 (0)5256 6251, *www.tiscover.at/schoenblick.obergurgl*, has large rooms and serves up excellent breakfasts.

Hochgurgl:

★★★★★**Top Hotel Hochgurgl**, **t** +43 (0)5256 6265, *www.tophotelhochgurgl.com*, leads the field in Hochgurgl and has a crèche and health club.

★★★★**Hotel Riml**, **t** +43 (0)5256 6261, *www.hotel-riml.com*, is on the piste. Owner Gerold Riml has turned the hotel into a well-balanced energy zone, with a colour scheme designed for relaxation, as well as some strategically placed 'energy pyramids'.

★★★**Alpenhotel Laurin**, **t** +43 (0)5256 6227, *www.laurin.at*, serves first-rate food.

Obertauern

Profile

Purpose-built resort with convenient snow-sure skiing. Not suitable for non-skiers or committed party-goers

*BEST FOR

Reliable snow-cover, purpose-built convenience, beginners and intermediates

ESSENTIALS

Altitude: 1740m (5,708ft)–2313m (7,587ft)
Further information: **t** +43 (0)6456 7252, *www.obertauern.com*
Lifts in area: 26 (1 cableway, 18 chairs, 7 drags) serving 95km of piste
Lift pass: adult €147.50–162.50, children up to 15yrs €81.50, both for 6 days
Access: Salzburg airport 90km, Radstadt station 20km

Resort

When snow-cover is light elsewhere in Austria, this high-altitude ski area has virtually guaranteed conditions. Its position on a mountain pass in the Niedere Tauern mountain range, 90km south of Salzburg, attracts a favourable microclimate.

Until local ski enthusiasts 'colonized' the pass in the early 1930s the only building was Hotel Tauernpasshöhe. During the intervening decades a straggle of hotels and bars has sprung up along the roadside to give Obertauern more of an American ski resort atmosphere.

Mountain

The peaks on both sides of the road rise to over 2200m and the lifts complete a circuit that can be skied in either direction. There is plenty of novice terrain close to the village centre as well as a couple of testing blacks. The area provides plenty of variety as well as some sensational off-piste. Reporters heavily criticize the piste map ('dreadful layout, completely unintelligible').

Learn

Competition among teaching academies is healthily high. Of the five main schools

Krallinger, **t** +43 (0)6456 7258, is most favoured by tour operators. **CSA Willi Grillitsch**, **t** +43 (0)6456 7462, **Frau Holle**, **t** +43 (0)6456 766384, **Koch**, **t** +43 (0)6456 72285, and **Top**, **t** +43 (0)6456 7678, are worthy contenders. **Blue Tomato**, **t** +43 (0)6456 20036, is for boarders. **Vertical**, **t** +43 (0)6456 7594, is the guiding company.

Children

Petzi-Bär crèche, **t** +43 (0)6456 7252, cares for children from three. **CSA Willi Grillitsch** has a non-skiing kindergarten, **t** +43 (0)6456 7462. All the ski schools run ski kindergartens.

Lunch

The resort has over 20 enticing restaurants. **Lürzer Alm**, **t** +43 (0)6456 7289, and **Hochalm**, **t** +43 (0)6456 7318522, have good food. **Almrausch**, **t** +43 (0)6456 7407, is also open in the evening. Also try **Flubachalm**, **t** +43 (0)6456 7217, and **Edelweiss Hütte**, **t** +43 (0)6456 7653.

Dine

Bacchuskeller, **t** +43 (0)6456 7561, and **Restaurant Sailer**, **t** +43 (0)6456 7328, are both recommended. **Edelweiss-Stüberl**, **t** +43 (0)6456 7245, and **Wagner Stub'n**, **t** +43 (0)6456 7256, have reasonable prices.

Party

The **Edelweisshütte** and the **Achenrainhütte** are lively in the late afternoon. **Der Turm** and **Römerbar** are popular. The **Lürzer Alm** is central to the evening action, which progresses to **Monkey's Heaven** in Hotel Rigele Royal.

Sleep

★★★★**Sporthotel Edelweiss**, **t** +43 (0)6456 7245, *www.luerzer.at*, is situated beside the village nursery slope.

★★★★**Sporthotel Cinderella Spa & Resort**, **t** +43 (0)6456 7589, *www.cinderella.at*, is decorated true to its fairy-tale name. The dining room has low turreted walls painted with pastel frescoes.

★★★★**Alpenhotel Römerhof**, **t** +43 (0)6456 72380, *www.roemerhof.at*, has a traditional interior and a piste-side terrace.

★★★★**Sportinghotel Marietta**, **t** +43 (0)6456 7262, *www.marietta.at*, is a lavish place at the foot of the slopes.

★★★★**Hotel Kohlmayr**, **t** +43 (0)6456 7272, *hotel-kohlmayr.at*, is 'a great hotel. Food is exceptional and it's convenient for slope access'.

Saalbach-Hinterglemm

Profile

These adjoining villages share an extensive ski circuit with confidence-building slopes, reliable snow-cover and a modern lift system. Great for ski-to-lunchers and night-owls, but not for anyone who is early-to-bed

Resort

The villages of Saalbach and Hinterglemm, which lie in the Glemm Valley a short drive from Zell am See, are attractive bases for some of the best skiing in Austria outside the Arlberg. This fact has not been lost on generations of mainly Dutch and British visitors who

*** BEST FOR**

All levels of skier and rider, dedicated lunchers, night-owls

ESSENTIALS

Altitude: 1,000m (3,280ft)–2096m (6,877ft)
Further information: t +43 (0)6541 680068, *www.saalbach.com*
Lifts in area: 54 (15 cableways, 16 chairs, 23 drags) serving 200km of piste
Lift pass: Area (Saalbach-Hinterglemm and Leogang) adult €163–181, child 7–15yrs €81.50–90.50, both for 6 days
Access: Salzburg airport 1½hrs, Zell am See station 19km

return here each year in numbers proportionate to their respective economies. Euro-free British skiers and riders are currently in ascendance. Last winter Saalbach introduced a four-times-a-day shuttle service from Salzburg airport for €65 return.

The 10 peaks that rise on both sides of the valley are lined with an impressive array of modern lifts that can be skied equally well in both directions.

In terms of ski convenience, choice of base is relatively unimportant. Saalbach has a wider variety of hotels, shops, restaurants and nightlife. Hinterglemm is much more tranquil and consequently popular with families, although it still has plenty of après-ski.

The village of Leogang in the adjoining valley is linked into the ski area by a modern gondola and three high-capacity chairs. It provides a more rural alternative base.

Mountain

The skiing here is ideal for adventurous intermediates who want to feel that they are travelling somewhere each day rather than skiing the same stretch of mountainside over and over again. The main circuit is made up of easy blue and undemanding red runs that can be tackled by anyone who can ski parallel. Unlike a lot of other circuits, such as the Sella Ronda in Italy, you don't have to complete it – just descend to the valley floor and hop home on a free ski-bus.

Whether you start from Saalbach or Hinterglemm you move seamlessly into the 200km circuit – few areas in Austria can match the modern lift system, which is being continuously upgraded. Last season saw the opening of a new eight-person gondola on Hochalm, as well as a couple of chair-lifts being upgraded to six-packs. This winter the new Westgipfelbahn gondola replaces two old chairs. A new six-pack replaces the old Kar and Weissbach lifts on the 1910m Wildenkarkogel.

The clockwise circuit from Saalbach starts with a two-stage gondola ride to Schattberg Ost. From Hinterglemm the new Westgipfelbahn gondola also provides greatly improved access. On the other side of the valley the Bernkogel triple-chair, followed by one of the few remaining drag-lifts, brings you up to the 1740m summit of Bernkogel and the start of the anticlockwise circuit.

This is a big resort for snowboarding, with a terrain park situated just above Hinterglemm and another served by the six-person Asitzmuldenbahn between Vorderglemm and Leogang. The nearby quad Polten lift gives access to a boardercross course, while the half-pipe is beneath the Bernkogel chair. The valley offers considerable opportunities for cross-country and the resort has three dedicated toboggan runs. The north side of the valley offers some outstanding powder runs.

Learn

Saalbach has no fewer than seven competing ski schools while Hinterglemm has two and the hamlet of Vorderglemm has one. The continued survival of all of

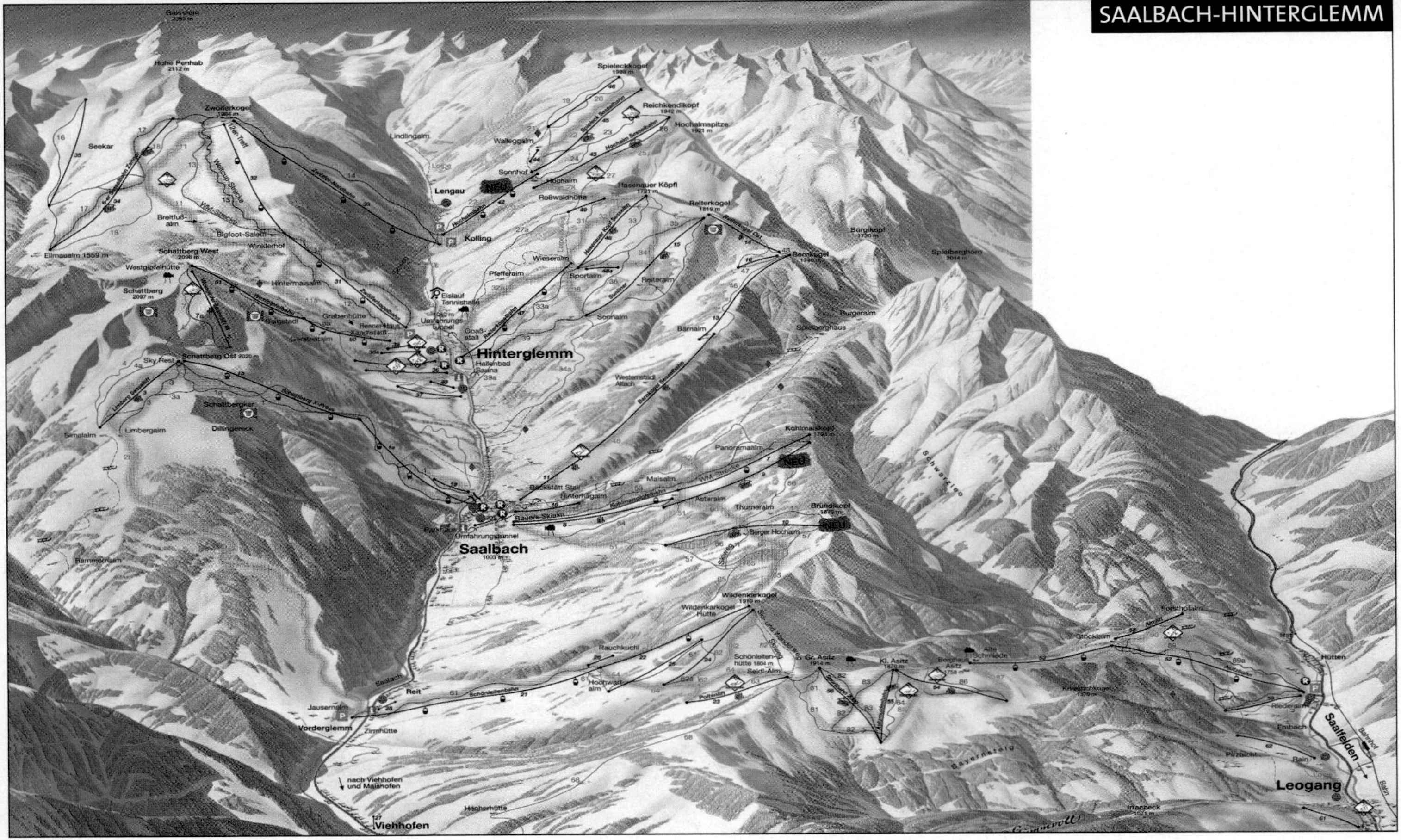
Gaisstein
2363 m
Hohe Penhab
2112 m
Zwölferkogel
1984 m
Seekar
Ellmaualm 1559 m
Breitfuß-
alm
Bigfoot-Saloon
Winklerhof
Schattberg West
2096 m
Westgipfelhütte
Schattberg
2097 m
Hintermaisalm
Grabenhütte
Renner-Haus
Xandlstadl
Berg-stadl
Gerstreitalm
Sky Rest
Schattberg Ost 2020 m
Schattberger
Limbergalm
Dillingereck
Samalm
Rammeralm
Lindlingalm
Lengau
Kolling
Spieleckkogel
1998 m
Reichkendlkopf
1942 m
Hochalmspitze
1921 m
Walleggalm
Sonnhof
Hochalm
Hasenauer Köpfl
1781 m
Roßwaldhütte
Reiterkogel
1819 m
Bernkogel
1740 m
Bürglkopf
1730 m
Spielberghorn
2044 m
Wieseralm
Sportalm
Pfefferalm
Reiteralm
Sonnalm
Bärnalm
Burgeralm
Spielberghaus
Eislauf
Tennishalle
Umfahrungs-
tunnel
Goaß-
stall
Hinterglemm
Hallenbad
Sauna
Westernstadt
Altach
Kohlmaiskopf
1794 m
Panoramaalm
NEU
Malsalm
Backstätt Stall
Hinterhagalm
Asteralm
Thurneralm
Bründlkopf
1879 m
NEU
Berger Hochalm
Bauers Skialm
Umfahrungstunnel
Saalbach
1003 m
Schwarzleo
Wildenkarkogel
1910 m
Wildenkarkogel
Hütte
Rauchkuchl
Hochwart
alm
Schönleiten-
hütte 1804 m
Seidl-Alm
Gr. Asitz
1914 m
Kl. Asitz
1878 m
Alte
Schmiede
Berghaus
Asitz
Stöcklalm
Forsthofalm
Hütten
Riederalm
Krallerkogel
Saalach
Reit
Schönleitenbahn
Jausernalm
Vorderglemm
Zirmhütte
nach Viehhofen
und Maishofen
Viehhofen
Hecherhütte
Bayernsteig
Saalfelden
Bahnhof
Bahn
Leogang
Bain
Embach
Irrachbeck
1071 m

them gives an indication of the popularity of the Glemmtal during the main holiday period. In Saalbach we recommend **Aamadall Snow Academy, t** +43 (0)6541 668256, **Green Discount, t** +43 (0)664 4998465, **Zink, t** +43 (0)664 1623655, and **Fürstauer, t** +43 (0)6541 8444. In Hinterglemm, **Thomas Wolf & Bartl Gensbichler, t** +43 (0)6541 63460, has an enduring reputation. Off-piste guiding is available through **Sepp Mitterer, t** +43 (0)6541 7008.

Children

Thomas Wolf & Bartl Gensbichler, operates a ski kindergarten for children from three years. In Hinterglemm, **Hotel Lengauerhof, t** +43 (0)6541 7255, and **Hotel Glemmtalerhof, t** +43 (0)6541 71350, both have crèches. **Annaliese Kröll, t** +43 (0)6541 7183, and **Manuela Griesler, t** +43 (0)664 3762553, provide babysitting.

Lunch

The ski circuit is dotted with huts that vary from proper restaurants to the simplest of snack bars. **Pfefferalm, t** +43 (0)6541 6325, an ancient farmhouse above Hinterglemm, is a favourite of ours. Try *Speckknödel* (bacon dumplings) and *Kasnock'n* (shank of pork).

Rosswaldhütte, t +43 (0)6541 6959, situated beside the Rosswald lift, has good food and staff in traditional dress. **Sportalm, t** +43 (0)6541 7972, **Thurner Alm, t** +43 (0)6541 8418, **Gerstreit Alm, t** +43 (0)6541 6565, and **Maisalm, t** +43 (0)6541 7409, are all recommended.

Dine

In Saalbach, **La Trattoria Italiana** and **Vitrine Asia Wok** are both in the Alpenhotel, **t** +43 (0)6541 6666, and make a change from traditional Austrian mountain fare. **Bäckstättstall, t** +43 (0)6541 7652, is the best smart eatery.

In Hinterglemm we recommend the **Fuhrmannstube** in Hotel Dorfschmiede, **t** +43 (0)6541 740862. **Restaurant Kendler, t** +43 (0)6541 6225, has a rustic atmosphere. Signature dishes include roast venison and sole.

Party

Late afternoon comes to alcoholic life in **Hinterhagalm** above Saalbach and at **Bauer's Schialm** by the church. It's equally noisy at the rustic **GoassStall** and **Hexenhäusl** in Hinterglemm. The snow bar outside **Hotel Dorfschmiede** is always busy as the lift closes.

Later on, attention in Saalbach focuses on **King's Disco** and the **Kuhstall**. The **Crazy Bear** and **Zum Turn** (a converted jail) are lively. In Hinterglemm the **Glemmerkeller**, **Road King** and **Tanzhimmel** attract the late-night crowd.

The Nightliner bus service operates along the valley road between the two villages until late evening on weeknights and until 2.30am on Saturday nights.

Sleep

Saalbach:

★★★★**Kunst-Hotel Kristiana, t** +43 (0)6541 6253, *www.kunsthotel.at*, in Saalbach, has a typically Tyrolean interior transformed by a modern art collection.

★★★★**Gartenhotel Theresia, t** +43 (0)6541 74140, *www.hotel-theresia.co.at*, is a stylish hotel filled with contemporary art. It has won awards for 'the use of natural and organic produce' in its kitchen and offers especially good family facilities.

★★★★**Saalbacherhof, t** +43 (0)6541 7111, *www.saalbacherhof.at*, has a swimming pool surrounded by rocks and is described as 'very comfortable, with superb cuisine'.

****Alpenhotel, t +43 (0)6541 6666, *www.alpenhotel.at*, is a multiple nightlife centre.

Hinterglemm:

****Sport & Vitalhotel Ellmau, t +43 (0)6541 7226, *www.sporthotel-ellmau.at*, has an impressive spa, and a kitchen specializing in healthy cuisine including Ayurvedic food. The hotel has a children's funpark with tubing, snowmobiling, a children's gym and sauna.

****Hotel Glemmtalerhof, t +43 (0)6541 7135, *www.alpinparadies.at*, is long established and conveniently situated in the village centre.

****Blumenhotel Tirolerhof, t +43 (0)6541 64970, *www.blumenhotels.at*, has a wellness centre and a heated outdoor pool.

****Hotel Zur Dorfschmiede, t +43 (0)6541 74080, *www.wolf-hotels.at*, also in Hinterglemm village centre, has outstanding half-board cuisine and comfortable rooms.

St Anton

Profile

A lively town with some of the most challenging skiing and nightlife in Europe. This is not a place recommended for beginners, wobbly intermediates or anyone of a nervous disposition

Resort

The Arlberg is the major European home of skiing. While the Swiss caught on to the idea of what were called 'Norwegian snow shoes' at the start of the 1890s, they had little idea what to do with them. It was ski instructors in St Anton who perfected the original technique that allowed you not only to go downhill, but also to turn (almost) at will. The first races were held in the neighbouring hamlet of St Christoph in 1903. But it wasn't until 1921 that the great Hannes Schneider opened his Arlberg Ski School on the slopes below Galzig, and St Anton began to shape the history of modern skiing.

Back in the 1950s, St Anton earned itself a place among the top five ski resorts in the world. It is remarkable, given the enormous development of the sport in both hemispheres over the past half century, that it easily holds on to its position. In the hall of fame, St Anton rubs shoulders with Chamonix, Val d'Isère/Tignes, Verbier, Zermatt, Jackson Hole and Whistler as one of the world's Truly Greats.

Anyone going for the first time should be aware that the terrain here varies from quite steep to the near sheer. It is not a place for novices and certainly not a place for wobbly second-weekers looking for a little confidence-building. St Anton is popular with experienced snowboarders, but if you can't manage steep moguls then stay away.

*BEST FOR

Sophisto-cats, strong intermediates and experts, off-piste, party-goers

ESSENTIALS

Altitude: 1304m (4,278ft)–2811m (9,222ft)
Further information: +43 (0)5446 22690, *www.stantonamarlberg.com*
Lifts in area: 82 on Arlberg Ski Pass (10 cableways, 38 chairs, 35 drags) serving 260km of piste
Lift pass: Arlberg Ski Pass (covers Klösterle, Lech and Zürs, Pettneu, St Anton, St Christoph, Stuben) adult €136–194, child 7–14yrs €82–116, both for 6 days. 6yrs and under €10 for whole season
Access: Innsbruck airport 1hr, Friedrichshafen airport 1½hrs, Zurich airport 2–3hrs, Munich airport 3–4hrs, railway station in resort

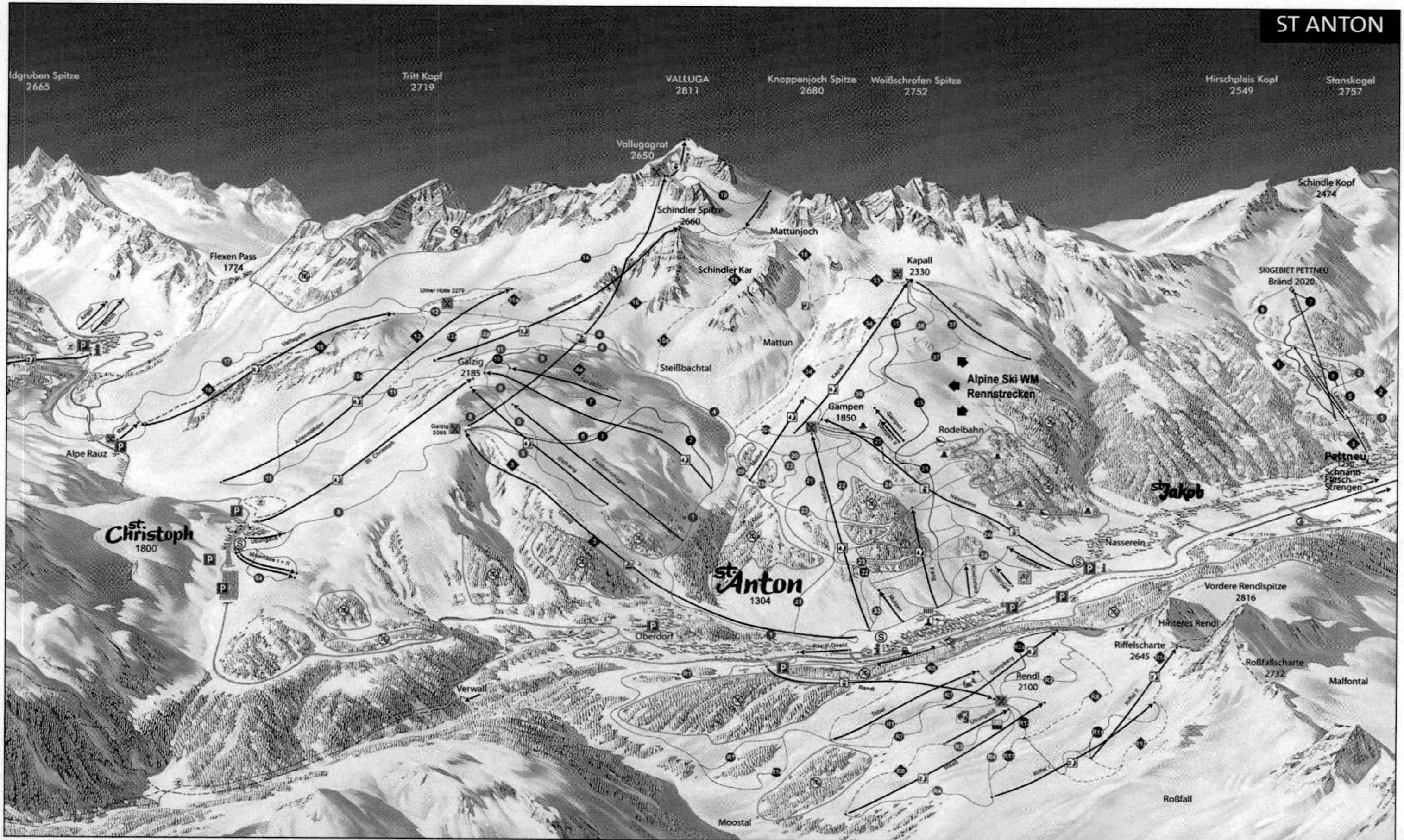

ldgruben Spitze 2665
Tritt Kopf 2719
VALLUGA 2811
Knoppenjoch Spitze 2680
Weißschrofen Spitze 2752
Hirschpleis Kopf 2549
Stanskogel 2757
Vallugagrat 2650
Schindler Spitze 2660
Mattunjoch
Schindle Kopf 2474
Flexen Pass 1774
Schindler Kar
Kapall 2330
SKIGEBIET PETTNEU Bränd 2020
Ulmer Hütte 2279
Mattun
Galzig 2185
Steißbachtal
Alpine Ski WM Rennstrecken
Gampen 1850
Rodelbahn
Galzig 2085
Alpe Rauz
Pettneu 1250
Schnann
Flirsch
Strengen
St. Jakob
St. Christoph 1800
Nasserein
St. Anton 1304
Vordere Rendlspitze 2816
Hinteres Rendl
Oberdorf
Riffelscharte 2645
Roßfallscharte 2732
Rendl 2100
Malfontal
Verwall
Roßfall
Moostal

The village itself is a blend of old and new, much improved by the relocation of the railway line that used to bisect it. The attractive centre is pedestrianized during day time with a modest selection of sports shops and boutiques, as well as some fine old hostelries and modern bars.

The village stretches in both directions, to the outlying and popular alternative bed-base of Nasserein as well as in the west towards Mooserkreuz. A ski-bus runs throughout the day and a night bus until 2am, but some walking is inevitable. However, it's possible to leave skis and boots overnight in storage near the bottom of the Galzig cable-car.

Mountain

Much has been done to update St Anton's once antiquated lift system. Most of this effort was concentrated into the build-up of the 2001 Alpine World Championships. The Nasserein gondola was a major improvement as was the scrapping of the venerable Gampen funicular. The venerable Galzigbahn cable-car built in 1937 is being replaced this season by a revolutionary 24-person jumbo gondola, which should transform mountain access and dispose of the high-season lift queues that have plagued the resort in the past.

The ski area is in two sections, one on either side of the St Anton Valley. Rendl, the smaller and easier of these, is a pleasant suntrap with a choice of red and blue runs reached by a gondola which rises inconveniently a short bus ride or awkward walk in boots from outside the village. Rendl has a terrain park and is popular with riders.

However, most skiers head each morning for the opposite side of the valley. A quad-chair followed by a six-pack take you up Gampen and Kapall for the easiest intermediate skiing in the main area. That said, the long black descent from the top follows the course used for the downhill races in the World Championships.

This sector connects – by piste and chair from Gampen, or by cable-car from St Anton – with 2185m Galzig, the true hub of the ski area. From here you can ski down to the charming hamlet of St Christoph. Alternatively you can take the cable-car up to the 2811m Valluga, the highest point in the ski area. From the top station it is possible to ski off the back down to Zürs, but you have to be accompanied by a guide.

It is fair to describe almost all St Anton's skiing as difficult and the standard of skier and rider is high. The main runs become bumped up within hours of a major snowfall. The powder skiing is sensational, with unlimited possibilities. This is high alpine skiing, avalanche danger is ever present, and a guide is essential when straying beyond the ropes.

Learn

The two ski schools retain their separate identities but are under the same ownership. The original **Arlberg Ski School**, **t** +43 (0)5446 3411, founded by Hannes Schneider, has 250 instructors. **Franz Klimmer's St Anton**, **t** +43 (0)5446 3563, has 60 teachers. Both offer an outstanding level of tuition, although standards can fall during peak weeks. British-run **Piste to Powder Mountain Guided Adventures**, **t** +43 (0)6641 7462 820, or **t** +44 (0)1661 824 318, teaches off-piste and offers guiding to small groups. We rate it highly.

Children

Kinderwelt, **t** +43 (0)5446 2526, run by the Arlberg school, has a kindergarten at the ski school meeting place, on the Gampen, in Nasserein, and at St Christoph.

Small skiers are accepted once they are out of nappies. **Kiki Club, t** +43 (0)5446 3563, operated by the St Anton school, runs ski classes for older children.

Lunch

Best mountain meal in the Arlberg is at Galzig in the **Verwall Stube, t** +43 (0)5446 2352501, for modern Austrian cuisine with an emphasis on fresh fish and seafood. Also recommended are **Kaminstube, t** +43 (0)5446 2681, and **Rodelhütte, t** +43 (0)5446 22690, as well as **Albona-Grat, t** +43 (0)5582 761, and **Ulmerhütte, t** +43 (0)5446 30200, on the descent from the Schindler Spitze. **Sennhütte, t** +43 (0)5446 2048, has live music.

Our favourite lunchspot is the sunny terrace of the **Arlberg-Hospiz-Alm, t** +43 (0)5446 2611, in St Christoph, where waiters wear Austrian national dress and descent to the loo is by a helter-skelter slide. The **Maiensee Stube, t** +43 (0)5446 2804, also in St Christoph, and the **Hotel Post, t** +43 (0)5582 761, in Stuben have a warm atmosphere and good food.

Dine

By night the Werner family's **Arlberg-Hospiz-Alm, t** +43 (0)5446 2611, in St Christoph puts on the tablecloths and becomes a serious gourmet restaurant with an astonishing wine cellar.

In St Anton, warehouse-style **Benvenuto, t** +43 (0)5446 30203, serves mainly Oriental dishes. Family-run **Floriani, t** +43 (0)5446 2330, is recommended, as is **Hazienda, t** +43 (0)5446 2968, which serves excellent steaks and seafood. The **Museum, t** +43 (0)5446 2475, is like eating in someone's large private home. **Sportcafé Schneider, t** +43 (0)5446 2548, is in the pedestrian zone. **Café Aquila, t** +43 (0)5446 2217, is decorated 1960s style. The **Funky Chicken, t** +43 (0)664 4043360, is popular with snowboarders and has some of the best-value food in town. Nasserein's **San Antonio, t** +43 (0)5446 3474, is a popular pizzeria.

Party

The afternoon warms up with a *Glühwein* at the **Sennhütte** before the descent into degenerate behaviour at the infamous **Krazy Kanguruh** and/or the **Mooserwirt** on the meadow above the resort. The party gets truly under way with raucous music and much drinking and dancing as the light fades. Most make it back down the nursery slope in one piece, ready for a full evening of entertainment ahead. Hotspots include the **Piccadilly**, **Funky Chicken**, **Scotty's Bar**, **Bar Cuba**, **Hazienda**, **Train** and **Vino**. **Scotty's Bar** in the Hotel Rosanna is also a popular meeting place. The **Kandahar** comes to life in the early hours as other establishments close.

Sleep

★★★★★**Hotel Arlberg-Hospiz, t** +43 (0)5446 2611, *www.hospiz.com*, in St Christoph, counts President Putin of Russia among its patrons.

★★★★★**Hotel St Antoner Hof, t** +43 (0)5446 2910, *www.st.antonerhof.at*, is comfortable and modern.

★★★★**Hotel Post, t** +43 (0)5446 2213, *www.hotel-post.co.at*, is convenient for the lifts.

★★★★**Hotel Alte Post, t** +43 (0)5446 2553, *www.hotel-alte-post.at*, is the original coaching inn. It's well located and has a good spa.

★★★★**Hotel Karl Schranz, t** +43 (0)5446 25550, *www.arlberg.com/hotel.karl. schranz*, owned by the former world champion, has pleasant rooms and good food but is slightly out of town.

★★★★**Hotel Arlberg, t** +43 (0)5446 22100, *www.arlberg.com*, has a relaxed atmosphere and is furnished in traditional Tyrolean style.

★★★★**Hotel Tyrol**, **t** +43 (0)5446 2340, *www.tyrolhotel.com*, near the church, is a pleasant place to stay ('very friendly and helpful staff').

★★★★**Hotel Bergschlössl**, **t** +43 (0)5446 2220, *www.bergschloessl.at*, is well located next to the Galzig cable-car and is owned by Johanna Moosbrugger, whose brother owns Gasthof Post in Lech. Bedrooms are spacious and individually decorated.

★★★★**Hotel Schwarzer Adler**, **t** +43 (0)5446 22440, *www.schwarzeradler.com*, is 'good, central, friendly, and comfortable, with a great pool'.

A large number of visitors to the resort choose to stay in catered chalets.

St Johann in Tirol

Profile

Unpretentious Tyrolean village of frescoed houses surrounded by less attractive suburbs. A modern lift system and benign slopes suit both beginners and families

Resort

St Johann in Tirol found popularity with foreign visitors in the 1970s and 1980s before fading from the frame. But now, thanks to new lifts and a reaffirmed sense of identity, it is enjoying a fresh lease of winter life.

The pretty Tyrolean village with its ornately frescoed inns and old coaching inns is marred by heavy traffic and industrial estates on the outskirts, but the centre retains considerable charm.

*BEST FOR

Beginners and low intermediates, families

ESSENTIALS

Altitude: 670m (2,198ft)–1,700m (5,576ft)
Further information: **t** +43 (0)5352 633350, *www.st.johanntirol.at*
Lifts in area: 17 lifts (3 cableways, 4 chairs, 10 drags) serving 60km of piste. 60 lifts and 170km of piste in linked Schneewinkel area
Lift pass: Schneewinkel adult €138–162, child €69–81, both for 6 days
Access: Innsbruck airport 1hr, railway station in resort

Mountain

This is a particularly good area for beginners, with a series of dedicated nursery slopes on the gentle meadows behind the station and in the hamlet of Eichenhof.

Main mountain access is by a two-stage gondola, which brings you up to the 1700m summit of Harschbichl. Reporters complain of 'horrendous' queues at around 10am each morning during high season. It is advisable to take the alternative, and usually near-deserted, eight-seater gondola that rises from Penzing on the edge of Oberndorf.

The resort has a terrain park beneath the Penzing chair and a half-pipe at Eichenhof. Cross-country skiing is extensive with 275km of prepared trails just outside the village.

Learn

St Johann has five ski schools: **St Johann**, **t** +43 (0)5352 64777, **Eichenhof**, **t** +43 (0)5352 65930, **Wilder Kaiser**, **t** +43 (0)5352 64888, **Ski-Akademie St Johann in Tirol**, **t** +43 (0)5352 624888, and **White Eagle**, **t** +43 (0)664 7620481.

Children

St Johann ski school, t +43 (0)5352 64777, runs **Bobo's** ski kindergarten, which accepts children from four years. Eichenhof school's **Kinderland**, t +43 (0)5352 65930, also cares for children from four years. Babysitters can be booked through the tourist office, t +43 (0)5352 63335.

Lunch

The **Harschbichlhütte**, t +43 (0)5352 64671, has great *Gulaschsuppe*. **Koasaburg**, t +43 (0)65063 94001, has home-cooked food and a sunny terrace. **Grander Schupf**, t +43 (0)5352 63925, and **Bassgeigeralm**, t +43 (0)5352 62117, are recommended.

Dine

Lange Mauer, t +43 (0)5352 62174, serves Chinese cuisine. **La Rustica-Antonio**, t +43 (0)5352 62843, and **Rialto**, t +43 (0)5352 64168, are pizzerias. **Edelweiss**, t +43 (0)5352 63580, serves unpretentious mountain dishes.

Party

Popular bars include **Bunny's**, **Humungus**, **Max Pub** and **Rogi's Stad**. **Club Humungus** and the **Scala-Bar Club** provide the late-night entertainment.

Sleep

★★★★**Sporthotel Austria**, t +43 (0)5352 62507, *www.sporthotelaustria.at*, is traditional and in a central yet quiet location. Facilities include an indoor pool and family apartments with two adjoining bedrooms.
★★★★**Hotel Gasthof Park**, t +43 (0)5352 62226, *www.park.at*, is near the gondola.

★★★**Hotel Post**, t +43 (0)5352 62230, *www.hotel-post.tv*, dates from 1225 and is beautifully frescoed on the outside, with each room individually decorated.
★★★**Hotel Fischer**, t +43 (0)5352 62332, *www.hotel-fischer.com*, is located in the pedestrian area and has comfortable rooms.

Schladming

Profile

Large intermediate playground that is included in the 276-lift Skiverbund Amadé lift pass, which covers five main areas in this corner of Austria. Glacier skiing and extensive cross-country trails are nearby, but the terrain is not suited to advanced skiers

Resort

Schladming is a fine medieval town with an industrial and cultural life of its own rather than a village that has expanded into a ski resort. It has two beautiful Romanesque and Gothic churches and a magnificent 18th-century town square. In earlier times the whole town was enclosed by heavily buttressed walls. But, apart from one gateway, these were removed during bitter social unrest in 1525, which culminated in a peasants' revolt.

The town makes a charming base from which to explore not just the rather banal skiing immediately around the town, but also the other areas such as Flachau/Wagrain and the Gasteinertal. All are included in the regional lift pass and are situated just a short drive away.

*** BEST FOR**

Unadventurous intermediates, mountain huts, families, cross-country

ESSENTIALS

Altitude: 745m (2,224ft)–2,015m (6,609ft)
Further information: t +43 (0)3687 22777, *www.schladming-rohrmoos.com*
Lifts in area: 78 (8 cableways, 23 chairs, 47 drags) serving 115km of piste
Skiverbund Amadé region: 276 (30 cableways, 74 chairs, 172 drags) serving 860km of piste
Lift pass: Skiverbund Amadé adult €164–176, child €85–91.50, both for 6 days
Access: Salzburg airport 1hr, Munich airport 2½hrs, railway station in resort

Be warned: this is a resort much loved by the Austrians, and the slopes can be very crowded during the national school holidays in February.

Mountain

The central Planai ski area is reached by a gondola that rises from the edge of town. Alternatively, you can drive up an all-weather road to a car park just below the mid-station. A network of modern mainly high-capacity chairs serve easy blue and red runs that wind down between the trees.

Pistes and chair-lift provide links to the peaks of Hauser Kaibling on one side and Hochwurzen and Reiteralm on the other. Fageralm, a few kilometres further along the valley towards Radstadt and Salzburg, is another small but enjoyable ski area.

In the other direction towards Linz and Graz lies the pretty village of Haus-im-Ennstal, flanked by two gondolas that rise to the top of Hauser Kaibling. Beyond Haus, the 1986m Galsterbergalm above Pruggern provides slightly more demanding terrain. Schladming is not a place for off-piste skiers. In the main ski area above the resort, leaving the marked piste is positively discouraged. Planai and the Dachstein Glacier both have good half-pipes.

The Ramsau plateau, situated just a few minutes' drive from Schladming, is one of Austria's most scenic cross-country areas, and is a former venue for the World Championships. It has 145km of snow-sure marked trails between 1100m and 1300m.

High-altitude skiing is possible on the adjoining Dachstein Glacier, reached by cable-car from Turlwand.

Learn

Hopl, **t** +43 (0)3687 23582, and **Tritscher**, **t** +43 (0)3687 22137, provide the full range of ski and snowboard lessons. **Blue Tomato**, **t** +43 (0)3687 24223, is the specialist board school. Off-piste guiding is available from **Helli Team Bedarfsflug**, **t** +43 (0)3687 81323.

Children

Meine Kleine Schule, **t** +43 (0)3687 24407, and **Frau Ladreiter**, **t** +43 (0)3687 61313, are the resort's two non-ski kindergartens.

Trischer ski school operates a highly acclaimed ski kindergarten.

Lunch

Schladming has an abundance of friendly huts scattered across the mountainside and should win a prize for being one of the only resorts in the world to list its mountain restaurants with telephone numbers on the piste map.

Seiterhütte, **t** +43 (0)3687 61615, below the summit of Hochwurzen, has a welcoming sun terrace. **Märchenwiesenhütte**, **t** +43 (0)3687 61251, near the lift of the same name, has reliable home cooking. **Onkel Willy's Hütte**, **t** +43 (0)3687 23105, has live music and a sunny terrace. The **Eiskarhütte**, **t** +43 (0)6454 7234, at Reiteralm, is recommended.

Schladming-Dachstein Tauern
mit der 4-Berge-Skischaukel
NATURPARK SÖLKTÄLER
GALSTERBERGALM 1986 m
HAUSER KAIBLING 2015 m
PLANAI 1894 m
HOCHWURZEN 1850 m
REITERALM 1860 m
FAGERALM 1885 m
PRUGGERN 680 m
MARTIN AM GRIMMING
AICH 750 m
GRÖBMING 776 m
STODERZINKEN 2045 m
HAUS/ENNSTAL 752 m
ROHRMOOS 1050 m
PICHL 800 m
GLEIMING 810m
FORSTAU 930 m
MANDLING 820 m
SCHLADMING 745 m
Rittisberg 1600 m
RAMSAU AM DACHSTEIN 1100 m - 1300 m
DACHSTEINGLETSCHER 2700 m

Dine

L'Osteria da Giorgio, t +43 (0)3687 23173, and **Va Bene**, t +43 (0)3687 23226, provide an Italian alternative to Austrian mountain fare along with **Giovanni's Pizza & Pasta**, t +43 (0)3687 24638. **Planaistub'n Charly Kahr**, t +43 (0)3687 23544, is a favourite of Californian governor Arnold Schwarzenegger when he returns to these parts. **Arnoldstub'n Charly Kahr**, t +43 (0)3687 23544, is under the same ownership. The **Rôtisserie Royer Grill**, t +43 (0)3687 2000, in Sporthotel Royer, is recommended. **Kirchenwirt**, t +43 (0)3687 22435, has good-quality food, a warm atmosphere and excellent service. **China Restaurant Peking**, t +43 (0)3687 22688, rings the changes.

Party

Onkel Willy's Hütte on Planai and the **Schirmbar** draw a large crowd long before the lifts close. Later on the action moves to **Charly's Treff** which is a resort meeting point, along with **La Porta**, **Das Beisl**, **Mariah's Mexican**, the **Hanglbar**, **Ferry's**, **Twister Bar**, **Siglu** and the **Sonderbar** disco. The 8km toboggan run from the top of Hochwurzen is open in the evenings. Schladming has a good swimming pool 'made of stainless steel with superb water quality'.

Sleep

★★★★**Sporthotel Royer**, t +43 (0)3687 2000, *www.royer.at*, has a swimming pool, indoor tennis and squash, bowling alley and a wellness centre. It is crowded with Russians in January.

★★★★**Hotel-Restaurant Alte Post**, t +43 (0)3687 22571, *www.alte-post.at*, is an old coaching inn in the main square, with a fine restaurant and wellness centre.

★★★★**Hotel zum Stadttor**, t +43 (0)3687 24525, *www.hotelzumstadttor.at*, is a family-run hotel next to the church.

★★★**Appartement-Hotel Ferienalm**, t +43 (0)3687 23517, *www.ferienalm.com*, has a panoramic view of Schladming and the Planai ski area and is five minutes by ski bus from the Planai gondola.

★★★**Gasthof zum Kaiserweg**, t +43 (0)3687 22038, *www.members.a1.net/kaiserweg*, is in a quiet position five minutes from the centre. It has simple rooms, and a good restaurant with all fresh ingredients and everything home-made.

Seefeld

Profile

Attractive old town with elegant hotels and a sophisticated nightlife. This is the cross-country ski capital of the Austrian Alps, with the downhill variety best suited to beginners and low intermediates

Resort

Seefeld is a mini-Kitzbühel with 280km of cross-country tracks and a much more modest amount of downhill

*** BEST FOR**

Beginners, low intermediates, families, value, night-owls, cross-country

ESSENTIALS

Altitude: 1200m (3,937ft)–2100m (6,890ft)
Further information: t +43 (0)5212 2313, *www.seefeld.at*
Lifts in area: 31 (1 mountain railway, 2 cableways, 7 chairs, 21 drags) serving 35km of piste
Lift pass: adult €147–159.50, child 7–15yrs €88–96, both for 6 days
Access: Innsbruck airport 20mins, railway station in resort

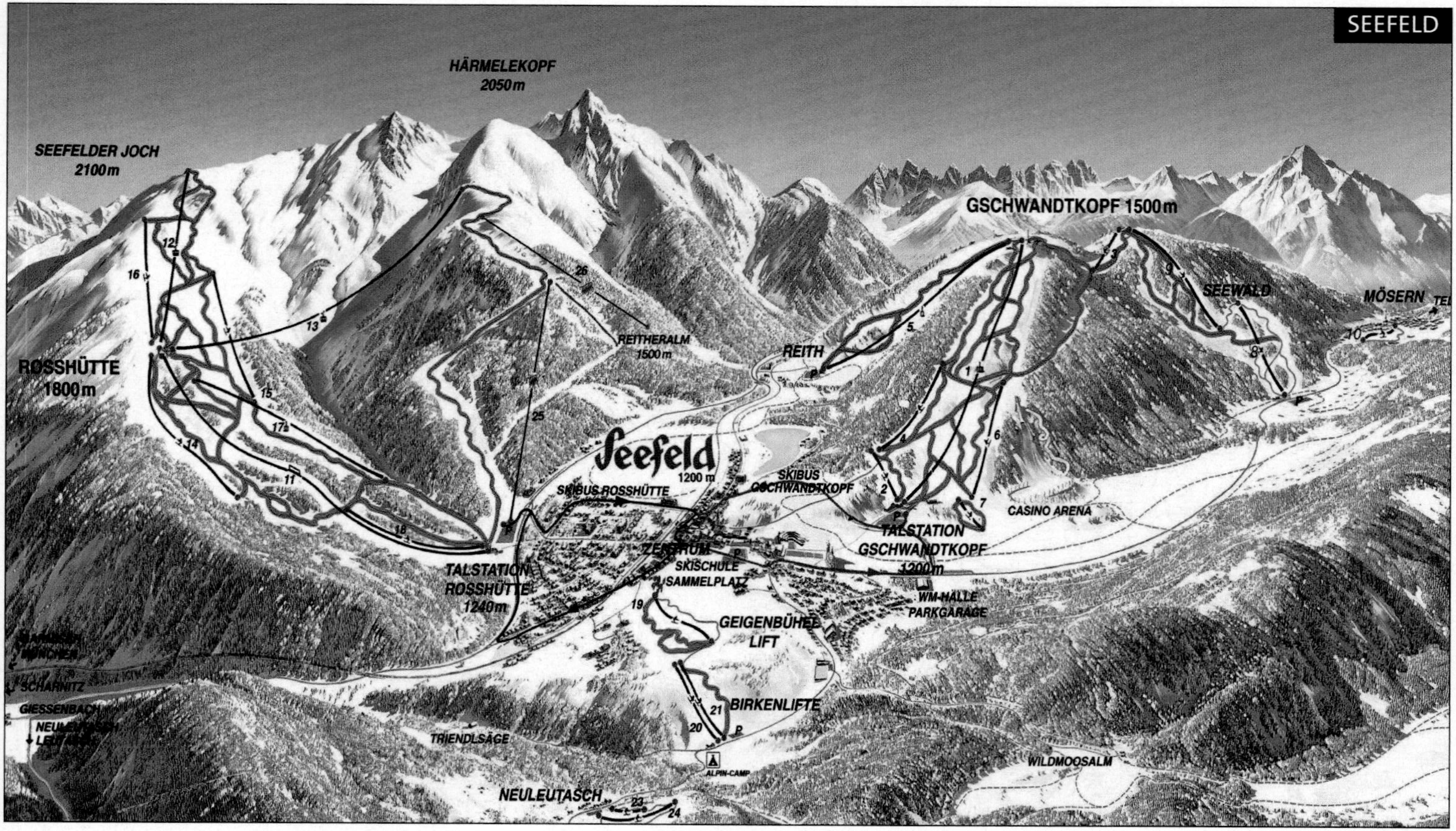
SEEFELDER JOCH
2100m
HÄRMELEKOPF
2050m
GSCHWANDTKOPF 1500m
SEEWALD
MÖSERN
REITH
REITHERALM
1500m
ROSSHÜTTE
1800m
Seefeld
1200 m
SKIBUS ROSSHÜTTE
SKIBUS
GSCHWANDTKOPF
CASINO ARENA
TALSTATION
GSCHWANDTKOPF
1200m
ZENTRUM
SKISCHULE
SAMMELPLATZ
WM-HALLE
PARKGARAGE
TALSTATION
ROSSHÜTTE
1240m
GEIGENBÜHEL
LIFT
BIRKENLIFTE
SCHARNITZ
GIESSENBACH
TRIENDLSÄGE
ALPIN-CAMP
WILDMOOSALM
NEULEUTASCH

skiing, set around a large village with frescoed medieval architecture above the Inn Valley.

Visitors come here not just for the skiing, but for an all-round winter holiday complete with sleigh rides, skating, tobogganing, exotic spa treatments, a casino and a clutch of superlative hotels and restaurants.

Mountain

The serious skiers here are langläufers who want to explore the 280km of marked tracks in the area. The 2km floodlit loipe opens four evenings a week.

Downhill skiers have three small areas. Novices congregate at Geigenbühel. Gschwandtkopf is a hill next to the cross-country track used mainly by the ski school. Rosshütte is the more extensive area with some more challenging runs, a long off-piste trail, night-skiing and a snowboard park.

Learn

Ski School Seefeld, **t** +43 (0)5212 2412, is the largest school and has a good reputation ('among the best private lessons we have ever had'). **Sport Aktiv**, **t** +43 (0)699 1461 0000, in Reith is based in the Gschwandtkopf area. **Mösern**, **t** +43 (0)5212 4736, has a beginner slope in the hamlet of the same name and also teaches on the Gschwandtkopf.

Children

The resort kindergarten, **t** +43 (0)5212 3220, is in the Olympia Sport and Congress Centre. **Ski School Seefeld**, **t** +43 (0)5212 2412, offers childcare as well as a games zone and designated pistes.

Lunch

Sonnenalm, **t** +43 (0)5212 2490 is an enticing mountain restaurant on the Gschwandtkopf. **Rosshütte**, **t** +43 (0)5212 24160, has been completely refurbished.

Dine

Gourmets can try the **Alte Stube** in the Casinohotel Karwendelhof, **t** +43 (0)5212 2655. **Café Nanni**, **t** +43 (0)5212 2229622, and **Café Moccamühle** in the Hotel Elite, **t** +43 (0)5212 2901, are popular for après-ski. The gourmet restaurant in the **Klosterbräu**, **t** +43 (0)5212 26210, has a 500-year-old cellar housing 9,000 bottles.

Party

Batzenhäusl, hotels **Royal**, **Kaltschmid** and **Karwendelhof** all have live music. The **Tenne** has tea-dancing, **Siglu** is always crowded, and late-night entertainment is focused on the **Jeep** and **Buffalo** discos. The sports centre has an Olympic-sized swimming pool, as well as skating and curling.

Sleep

*******Dorint Vital Royal & Spa**, **t** +43 (0)5212 44310, *www.sofitel.com*, has a large pool and a spa specializing in Chinese treatments.

*******Hotel Klosterbräu**, **t** +43 (0)5212 26210, *www.seefeld.klosterbraeu.com*, is a former 16th-century monastery with sumptuous bedrooms.

******Hotel A-Vita Viktoria**, **t** +43 (0)5212 4441, *www.viktoria.at*, has suites with apt names such as Laura Ashley, La Dolce Vita and St Paul de Vence.

******Casinohotel Karwendelhof**, **t** +43 (0)5212 2655, *www.karwendelhof.com*, is in the pedestrian precinct.

★★★★**Hotel Kaltschmid, t** +43 (0)5212 2191, *www.kaltschmid.info.* Free kindergarten.

★★★★**Gartenhotel Tümmlerhof, t** +43 (0)5212 2571, *www.tuemmlerhof.at*, offers daycare.

★★★★**Wellnesshotel Schönruh, t** +43 (0)5212 2447, *www.kaltschmid.info*, is 'slightly starchy and formal, but the staff there made our stay special'.

Sölden

*BEST FOR

Snow-sure slopes, long season, vibrant après-ski

ESSENTIALS

Altitude: 1377m (4,517ft)–3250m (10,663ft)

Further information: t +43 (0)5254 508, *www.soelden.com*

Lifts in area: 34 (7 cableways, 19 chairs, 8 drags) serving 150km of piste

Lift pass: adult €179–199.50, child 7–13yrs €108, both for 6 days

Access: Innsbruck airport 1hr.,Ötztal station 45mins

Profile

High-altitude destination for all standards and for those who want jolly après-ski. Two glaciers offering snow-sure skiing and boarding throughout a long season

Resort

High-altitude Sölden is renowned for reliable snow-cover and unfettered nightlife, two products that endear it to substantial numbers of fun-loving visitors who ski hard and party even harder. This is not a place to experience the tranquil ambience of a rural Austrian village.

Hochsölden is a car-free satellite set on summer pastures above the village with a handful of ski-in/ski-out hotels and panoramic views of the Ötztal.

Mountain

Sölden's reputation for snow-sure skiing hinges on the presence of the adjoining Tiefenback and Rettenbach glaciers. These were incorporated seven years ago into the resort's mainstream terrain by the addition of a gondola that spans the Rettenbach Valley.

However, the resort's own skiing goes up to 3058m, allowing for an impressive vertical drop of 1680m. Sölden's skiing is suited to all standards, with plenty of intermediate terrain and a few testing black runs.

Main mountain access is by two gondolas, one at either end of the village. Giggijoch terrain park, reached by the Hainbachkar chair, has a half-pipe and a boardercross course. Another terrain park is built each autumn on the Rettenbach glacier.

Learn

Sölden has five schools: **Sölden-Hochsölden, t** +43 (0)5254 2364, **Yellow Power, t** +43 (0)664 4424866, **Skiaktiv, t** +43 (0)5253 6313, **Vacancia Total, t** +43 (0)5254 3100, and **Freeride Center Tirol, t** +43 (0)650 2665292. All have established reputations.

Children

Sölden-Hochsölden, t +43 (0)5254 2364, has a non-ski kindergarten for children from six months. It also runs **Bobo's Ski Kindergarten** for children from three years. **Yellow Power, t** +43 (0)664 4424866, operates **Fiddel Bambini Club** ski kindergarten on Giggijoch for little ones from three years.

Lunch

Mountain huts are in abundance. **Gampe Thaya**, **t** +43 (0)5254 5010 has plenty of atmosphere. **Heide Alm**, **t** +43 (0)5254 508875, offers beautiful views.

Dine

Mangia Bene, **t** +43 (0)5254 5010, is a new eatery serving pasta and fish. **La Tavola**, **t** +43 (0)5254 2674, has pizzas and Austrian specialities. **Pizzeria Gusto**, **t** +43 (0)5254 2272, and **Gasthof Waldcafé**, **t** +43 (0)5254 2319 are recommended, along with the **Schnalser Stube** in the **Hotel Liebe Sonne**, **t** +43 (0)5254 2203.

Party

Après-ski begins at **Top Ok**, **Felsenstüberl**, **Grüner's Almstube**, **Kuhstall** and at **Philipp** at Innerwald. Later on, some 12 nightclubs, including the new **Bierhimml**, keep visitors on their feet until the early hours. In Hochsölden the action centres around **Eugens Obstlerhütte**.

Sleep

★★★★★**Central Sölden**, **t** +43 (0)5254 22600, *www.central-soelden.at*, has a vast spa.

★★★★**Hotel Regina**, **t** +43 (0)5254 2301, *www.hotel-regina.com*, has a swimming pool and is convenient for the Gaislachkoglbahn.

★★★★**Hotel Stefan**, **t** +43 (0)5254 2237, *www.hotel-stefan.at*, is close to the Giggijoch lift station and has good food.

★★**Gasthof Sonnenheim**, **t** +43 (0)5254 2276, *www.kraxner.com/sonnenheim*, is a recommended budget option.

Söll and the SkiWelt

Profile

Large linked ski area that is good value for money. Best for beginners, families and skiers on a budget. This is not the place to come if you're looking for other activities besides skiing and nightlife

Resort

By virtue of being the largest bed-base in the region, Söll is the uncrowned capital of what is still Austria's largest interconnected ski area. The network of lifts spans the mainly gentle mountainsides surrounding seven resorts near Kitzbühel. Two further resorts, Westendorf (now, in turn, linked to Kirchberg and Kitzbühel) and Kelchsau, are linked into the system only by bus but consider themselves part of the network and are included in the lift pass. Reporters complain that the regional piste map is of little assistance: 'We kept getting lost, but it didn't really matter as we kept finding new runs.' This winter, in a bid to attract more families, the region is dramatically

*BEST FOR

Beginners, low intermediates, families, value, night-owls

ESSENTIALS

Altitude: 703m (2,306ft)–1829m (6,001ft)
Further information: **t** +43 (0)5358 505, *www.skiwelt.at*, *www.wilderkaiser.info*
Lifts in area: 93 (1 funicular, 10 cableways, 38 chairs, 44 drags) serving 250km of piste in the SkiWelt.
Lift pass: SkiWelt adult €143–168, child 6–16yrs €71.50, both for 6 days
Access: Innsbruck airport 45mins, Wörgl station 10mins

SÖLL AND THE SKIWELT

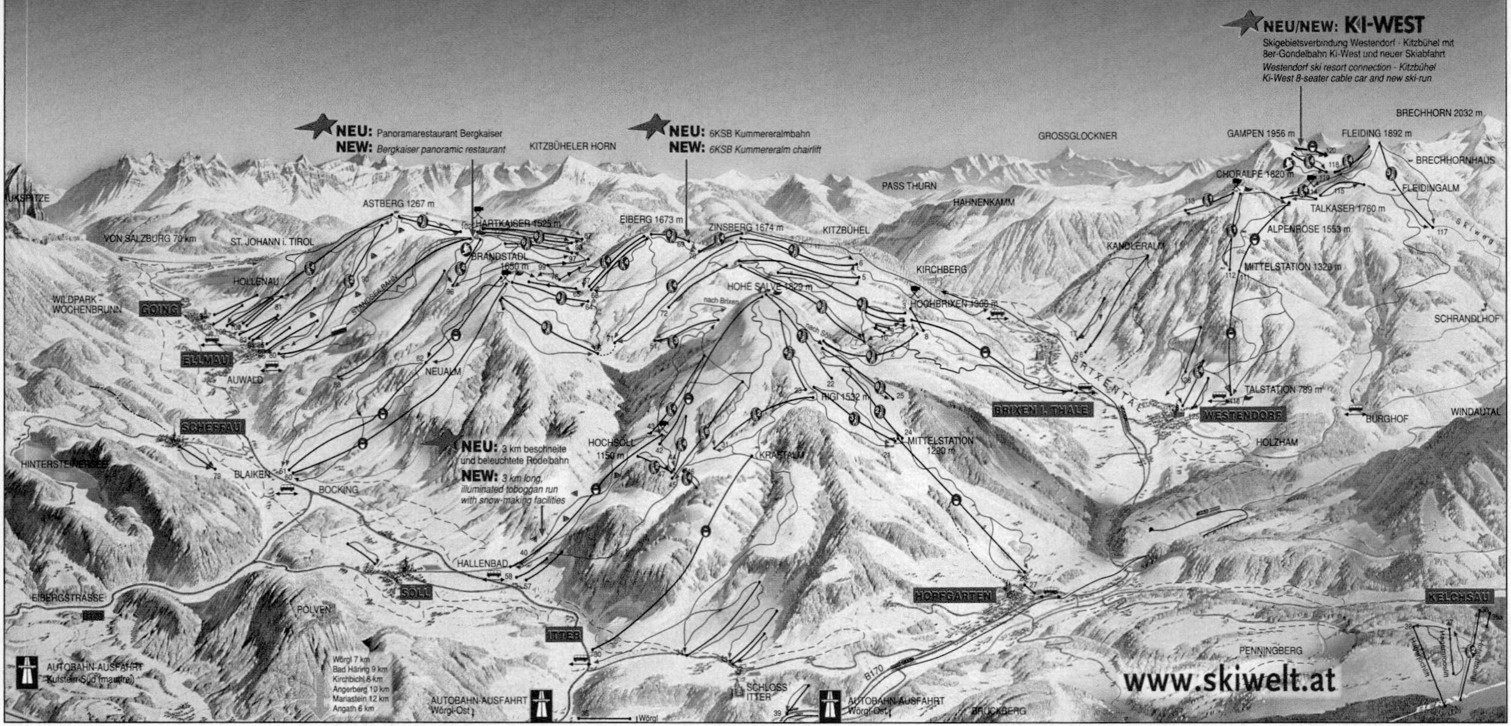

reducing the cost of a six-day child's lift pass by as much as €20 in high season.

This is prime cruising country over undulating summer pastureland, best suited to skiers who have progressed from the nursery slopes and are in need of daily confidence-building mileage.

Söll is a large, friendly village set around an onion-domed church in the middle of a wide valley. The ski area is 1km away and best reached by ski-bus ('this can be a very crowded and unpleasant experience in the rush hour – think Tube journey with skis and poles prodding into you').

Back in the 1980s the resort was an annual mustering point for British and Dutch youth who did more drinking than skiing. However, it has long since shrugged off its overtly laddish image and is now popular with families and couples of all ages.

Après-ski still plays an important role, although the resort along with its clientele has matured to the point of respectability but not sophistication.

Mountain

Mountain access is by a two-stage gondola, which brings you swiftly up to Hohe Salve, the high point of the linked area. The other linked villages of Going, Ellmau, Scheffau, Itter, Hopfgarten and Brixen-im-Thale all line the valley around the dome-shaped massif. Each of these resorts provides alternative access into the system, either by gondola or by funicular from Ellmau, or by quad-chair from Going.

The resorts are linked on the main road by postbus, but not by free ski-bus, so in the afternoon it is advisable to keep an eye on your watch.

All of them, except south-facing Hopfgarten and Brixen, have dedicated nursery slopes at the bottom of the mountain. Scheffau, our favourite here, is set back on the other side of the valley and has its novice area on a sloping meadow beneath the church.

The home run back to Söll is marked red on the piste map. It is covered by snow-cannon, but lack of natural cover can lead to difficult icy conditions. Regular blue-run skiers are advised to return to the valley by gondola.

This is not a place for advanced skiers who, despite the beauty of the scenery, will soon tire of the lack of challenge. Lärchenhang, on the north side of Hohe Salve, is a short and testing pitch. Other steep terrain as well as some rewarding off-piste can be found with the help of a guide. The terrain park and half-pipe at Söll are situated above Salvenmoos.

If you don't want to ski alone the SkiWelt has introduced a find-a-ski-mate scheme. The area has seven fixed meeting points and you are given an appropriate sticker for your jacket. Further information at *www.skiwelt.at*.

Learn

The various ski schools here have now amalgamated into the **Söll-Hochsöll**, **t** +43 (0)5333 5454, which over the past 40 years has acquired considerable experience in teaching foreigners to ski. As a place to get to grips with the basics, we warmly recommend it. However, like a lot of Austrian ski schools in major beginner and intermediate resorts, there seems to be little emphasis on adapting teaching methods to encompass the latest generation of skis.

Children

Bobo's Kinderclub, **t** +43 (0)5333 5454, is run by the school and cares for children from five years. Small guests at the Alphotel can join the **Smiley Tiny Tots Ski School**, **t** +43 (0)5517 5449, from two years.

Lunch

The mountainside is dotted with welcoming huts and larger self-service restaurants. **Gründalm**, **t** +43 (0)5333 5060, and **Gipfelrestaurant Hohe Salve**, **t** +43 (0)5335 2216, are both recommended. **Schernthannstuberl**, **t** +43 (0) 5333 5273, is a welcome spot on a cold day. **Stöcklalm**, **t** +43 (0)5333 5127, and **Kraftalm**, **t** +43 (0)5332 75152, are both extremely busy from 11.30am onwards.

Dine

Most restaurants are in the hotels. **Giovanni**, **t** +43 (0)5333 57050, **Venezia**, **t** +43 (0)5333 6191, and **Hexenalm**, **t** +43 (0)5333 5544, are all good pizzerias. **Schindlhaus**, **t** +43 (0)5333 516136, offers more gourmet fare. **Panoramabad Café**, **t** +43 (0)5333 544212, is out of the way but worth the walk for coffee and cakes.

Party

Whisky Mühle is the original and still the best bar/disco here, a resort institution that receives rave reviews from visitors, with live music most nights including UK bands. Après-ski begins much earlier at **Hexenalm** by the gondola station, and at **Hexenkessel** and **Salvenstadl**. The **Moonlight Bar** is a noisy pub and the **Sports Bar** shows Premier League football and has Guinness on tap. Early-to-bedders complain of noisy drunks in the street at 3am.

Sleep

****Hotel Postwirt**, **t** +43 (0)5333 5081, *www.hotel-postwirt-soell.at*, in the village centre, has an outdoor swimming pool heated to 33°C ('brilliant – lovely food and plenty of it, as well as a friendly bar').

****Hotel AlpenSchlössl**, **t** +43 (0)5333 6400, *www.hotel-alpenschloessl.com*, is more luxurious, with an indoor pool complex and frescoed Sleeping Beauty Tower Rooms.

****Alphotel**, **t** +43 (0)5517 5449, *www.alphotel.at*, is a member of Kinderhotels, which offer indoor 'splash pools', children's menus and organized activities, a children's ski school and soft drinks round the clock.

***Hotel Feldwebel**, **t** +43 (0)5333 5224, is a newly converted traditional building in the village centre, recommended for its rooms and half-board food.

Hotel Gänsleit, **t** +43 (0)5333 5471, is a five-minute walk from the village centre and welcomes children.

Wagrain and the Salzburger Sportwelt

Profile

Large intermediate ski area covering a dozen villages within easy reach of Salzburg. The main resorts are linked by lift, while regular buses serve the outlying corners of the ski area. Towns and villages vary considerably in character, so choose your base with care

Resort

This easily accessible ski area is extremely popular with Austrians from

*** BEST FOR**

Austrian village ambience, high-mileage cruisers

ESSENTIALS

Altitude: 650m (2,132ft)–2188m (7,177ft)
Further information: **t** +43 (0)6457 2929, *www.salzburgersportwelt.at*
Lifts in area: 89 (12 cableways, 34 chairs, 43 drags) serving 350km of piste. Skiverbund Amadé region 276 (30 cableways, 74 chairs, 172 drags) serving 865km
Lift pass: Skiverbund Amadé adult €164–176, child €85–91.50, both for 6 days
Access: Salzburg airport 45mins

Salzburg and elsewhere, but much underrated by overseas visitors. St Johann im Pongau is the regional capital of this corner of the country and is a ski resort in its own right. However, the cathedral city was burnt to the ground in 1852 and lacks the medieval charm of Salzburg or Innsbruck. It has its own small ski area and from the pistes above the town you get a panoramic view of the cathedral.

Of far more interest to the skier are the outlying villages of Alpendorf, Wagrain, Kleinarl, Flachau and Zauchensee, which are linked from valley to valley by a complex network of modern lifts. Other resorts including Radstadt/Altenmarkt and Filzmoos add extra variety and are alternative places in which to stay. All are included in the regional Skiverbund Amadé lift pass.

Wagrain and Flachau are the most centrally placed and convenient resorts. Altenmarkt and Radstadt, linked by piste and lift across the 1677m Kemahdhöhe, are pleasant little market towns. Their main ski area of Zauchensee is a few minutes' bus ride away. Filzmoos, hot-air balloon capital of the Austrian Alps and a winter bolt hole for Viennese aristocracy in the first years of the 20th century, shares its ski area with neighbouring Neuberg, just off the edge of the circuit.

Mountain

The whole Wagrain region comprises a dozen resorts served by 89 lifts covering undulating pastures and woodland as well as a handful of rounded 2000m summits. Runs here are of limited challenge to true experts, although that did nothing to arrest the development of Austrian downhill hero Hermann Maier who was raised and still lives in Flachau. However, the area should prove enormously enjoyable for the vast majority of skiers. Lifts are mainly fast and modern, allowing you to travel a considerable distance from scenic valley to valley in a single day. The postbus service is efficient, but it makes sense to keep track of time when venturing far from home.

Learn

Each of the resorts has at least one ski school. Wagrain has **Skischule Wagrain**, **t** +43 (0)6413 7100. Flachau has six including **Hermann Maier**, **t** +43 (0)6457 2812. St Johann has four including **Alpendorf**, **t** +43 (0)6412 8455, and its board school, **Vitamin B**.

Schools In Altenmarkt include **Der Erste S**, **t** +43 (0)6452 60700. In Zauchensee the choice is between **Happy Maier**, **t** +43 (0)6452 4315, and **Radstadt Pichler**, **t** +43 (0)6452 7382.

Children

Wagrain **ski kindergarten**, **t** +43 (0)6413 7100, cares for children from three years. In Flachau the ski schools accept children from four years. **Miniclub Flachau**, **t** +43 (0)6457 3134, is the non-ski kindergarten. Altenmarkt's **Balla** kindergarten, **t** +43 (0)6452 4737, cares for children from three years. In Alpendorf **Wellness & Sporthotel Alpina**, **t** +43 (0)6412 8282, runs a supervised activity programme for its small guests.

Lunch

The mountainside is dotted with welcoming huts. In the Flachau area try **Hoflalm**, **t** +43 (0)6457 2332, **Hubertusalm**, **t** +43 (0)6457 2756, and the **Griessenkar Hütte**, **t** +43 (0)6457 2575. In the Wagrain area **Almstadl**, **t** +43 (0)6413 7444, is recommended. In Zauchensee both **Arlhofhütte**, **t** +43 (0)6452 54856, and **Hochnössleralm**, **t** +43 (0)6452 6242, have plenty of atmosphere.

Dine

In Wagrain, **Gasthof Kalkhofen**, **t** +43 (0)6413 8206, dates back to the 16th century and serves traditional Salzburgerland dishes. **Haar-Trog Alm**, **t** +43 (0)6413 7286, has pasta and Asian fusion cuisine.

Mennerhäusl, **t** +43 (0)6413 8965, is recommended. **H.C. Andersen**, **t** +43 (0)6413 8170, specializes in fresh fish.

In Flachau, **Alter Jagdhof**, **t** +43 (0)6457 2228, is a family restaurant serving mainly Italian cuisine. **Rustic Hoagascht–Das Restaurant**, **t** +43 (0)6457 32490, has Asian, Italian and Austrian dishes. **Hotel Schartner**, **t** +43 (0)6452 5469, in Altenmarkt, is famed for its modern Austrian cuisine.

Party

Wagrain's returning skiers head for the outdoor **Schirmbar** at the end of the day. The **Haar-Trog Alm** and the **Kuhstall** are both extremely lively, while the **Point** has live music and karaoke. You can dance on the floor or on the tables at the **Tenne**.

In Flachau, **Franzl's Schirmbar**, **Dampfkessel**, **Bergwerk**, **Ema's Pub** and **Double Dutch** are the hotspots. Late-nighters dance at **Burg** and **Yeti's Partyhaus**. Altenmarkt's après spots include **Napa Valley**, **S'Kessei** and **Webers Bar**.

Sleep

Wagrain:

******Wagrainerhof**, **t** +43 (0)6413 8204, *www.wagrainerhof.com*, has good half-board food and welcomes children.

******Hotel Alpenhof Edelweiss**, **t** +43 (0)6413 8447, *www.alpenhof.edelweiss*, has a relaxed atmosphere and the restaurant uses local organic produce.

******Hotel Alpina**, **t** +43 (0)6413 8337, *www.hotelalpina.at*, has a large swimming pool and spa.

*****Hotel Sonne**, **t** +43 (0)6413 8242, *www.wagrain.at/hotel/sonne*, is a pleasant establishment with a sauna, gym and a sun terrace.

Flachau:

******Vierjahreszeiten**, **t** +43 (0)6457 2981, *www.vierjahreszeiten.co.at*, has a central but quiet location.

******Hotel Tauernhof**, **t** +43 (0)6457 2311, *www.tauernhof.at*, calls itself 'a four-star base camp for sporty guests'.

******Flachauerhof**, **t** +43 (0)6457 2225, *www.flachauerhof.at*, is a comfortable traditional establishment in the village centre.

*****Hotel Wieseneck**, **t** +43 (0)6457 2276, is in a peaceful, ski-in/ski-out position.

Altenmarkt:

******Hotel Alpenrose**, **t** +43 (0)6452 4027, *www.hotel-alpenrose.at*, has a wellness and fitness centre, and serves 'creative cuisine'.

Alpendorf:

******Wellness & Sporthotel Alpina**, **t** +43 (0)6412 8282, *www.sporthotel-alpina.com*, contains apartments, a playroom, and an impressive indoor swimming pool.

Westendorf

Profile

Appealing village with lots of Tyrolean atmosphere. Has its own modest beginner and intermediate skiing, and is linked by bus into the giant SkiWelt circuit and to Kirchberg and Kitzbühel

*BEST FOR

Beginners, intermediates, families, party-goers in high season

ESSENTIALS

Altitude: 789m (2,589ft)–1892m (6,207ft)
Further information: t +43 (0)5334 6230, *www.westendorf.com*
Lifts in area: 94 (11 cableways, 38 chairs, 44 drags) serving 250km of piste in the whole SkiWelt
Lift pass: SkiWelt adult €143–168, child 6–16yrs €71.50, both for 6 days
Access: Innsbruck airport 45mins. Wörgl station 15mins

Resort

Westendorf has the best and highest skiing in the SkiWelt, a network of lifts covering nine villages. Last season saw it linked with Kirchberg by a new piste and the Ki-West gondola that in turn connects by a 1km bus ride to the Kitzbühel/Pass Thurn ski area.

However, its allegiance is still to the nine-resort Skiwelt despite being one of the two villages (the other is Kelchsau) that are linked by bus into the system. The attractive village has plenty of atmosphere and has been popular with foreign skiers since the 1960s. Many families congregate here during school holidays, but be warned that noisy après-ski can last well into the night.

Mountain

Lazy skiers avoid the 1km walk or bus ride to the gondola, the only means of mountain access, by riding the Schneebergbahn quad up the nursery slope and traversing to the main lift station. The two-stage gondola takes you up to a small network of high-capacity chairs that bring you to the peak of Fleiding, the highest point in the SkiWelt.

The new gondola tranforms Westendorf from a small Tyrolean village into a link between two giant ski areas. Whether this will change the intimate character of the resort remains to be seen.

Learn

Westendorf has three ski schools: **Ideal**, **t** +43 (0)5334 2919, **Top**, **t** +43 (0)5334 6737, and **Westendorf**, **t** +43 (0)5334 6181.

Children

All the ski schools accept children. **Kindergruppe Simba**, **t** +43 (0)5334 20603, cares for non-skiing children from 18 months to four years.

Lunch

Alpenrosenhütte, **t** +43 (0)5334 6488, and **Bergrestaurant Choralpe**, **t** +43 (0)5334 61290, have plenty of atmosphere. **Jausenstation Alte Mittel**, **t** +43 (0)5334 2324, beneath the gondola, is also recommended.

Dine

Most of the restaurants are in hotels, with the **Vital-Landhotel Schermer**, **t** +43 (0)5334 6268, providing gourmet cuisine. **Liftstüberl**, **t** +43 (0)5334 30014, serves Italian food. **Marcel's**, **t** +43 (0)5334 30111, is recommended along with **Gasthof Maierhof**, **t** +43 (0)5334 6412, and **Gery's Inn**, **t** +43 (0)5334 6334.

Party

The après-ski atmosphere is extremely lively. The hotel bars and the **Village Pub** are the main meeting points, while **Bruchstall** is a new après-ski bar next to the nursery slope. The **Wunderbar** disco stays open until 6am.

Sleep

- ****Hotel Jakobwirt, t +43 (0)5334 6245,** *www.jakobwirt.at*, is on the edge of the piste and is warmly recommended for its food and facilities.
- ****Vital-Landhotel Schermer, t** +43 (0)5334 6268, *www.vitalhotelschermer.at*, is on the edge of the village with a major wellness centre offering thalasso treatments ('cannot speak too highly of the hotel and of the spa').
- ***Vital Hotel Sportalm, t** +43 (0)5334 6495, *www.sportalm-schwaigeralm.at*, next to the Alpenrose piste, has a spa.
- ***Hotel Post, t** +43 (0)5334 6202, *www.hotelpost.co.at*, built in 1593, has 40 rooms, including some that sleep six ('recommended for location and food').

Zell am See and Kaprun

Profile

A pretty resort (Zell) on the shore of Austria's most scenic lake. It offers substantial intermediate skiing backed up by snow-sure glacial skiing on the Kitzsteinhorn at nearby Kaprun. Also summer skiing, good nightlife and plenty of alpine atmosphere

* BEST FOR

Beginners and intemediates, beautiful scenery, certain snow-cover (Kaprun Glacier)

ESSENTIALS

Altitude: 758m (2,487ft)–3029m (9,938ft)
Further information: t +43 (0)6542 770, *www.europasport region.info*
Lifts in area: 57 in Zell am See/Kaprun (12 cableways, 15 chairs, 30 drags) serving 77km of piste in Zell am See, 58km in Kaprun
Lift pass: Europa Sport Region (covers Abtenau, Kaprun, Leogang, Saalbach-Hinterglemm, Zell am See) adult €161–179, child 6–15yrs €80.50–89.50, both for 6 days. Free for under 6yrs if accompanied by parent
Access: Salzburg airport 1hr, railway station in Zell am See

Resort

Zell is one of those rare places where in summer you can ski in the morning and sunbathe, swim and sail in the afternoon. The lakeside town acts as the tourist gateway to the Grossglockner, Austria's highest mountain, and attracts a year-round clientele that is as sedate in summer as it is lively in winter.

Above it rises the dome of the 2000m Schmittenhöhe, a charming and mainly wooded ski area best suited to intermediates but with dedicated learning areas at base and mid-mountain.

Zell was first established by a monastic order in the eighth century and had considerable commercial importance in medieval times. The legacy of fine old buildings has been transformed over the years into a See-side Kitzbühel. It has smart hotels and boutiques as well as villas dotted along the shore that are the holiday homes of wealthy Salzburgers.

Less cosmopolitan Kaprun, 8km up the road, is much more of a traditional ski village, with its own little mountain. However, focus here is up the valley on the 3000m Kitzsteinhorn Glacier where skiing continues throughout the year, except for a fortnight in June.

ZELL AM SEE AND KAPRUN

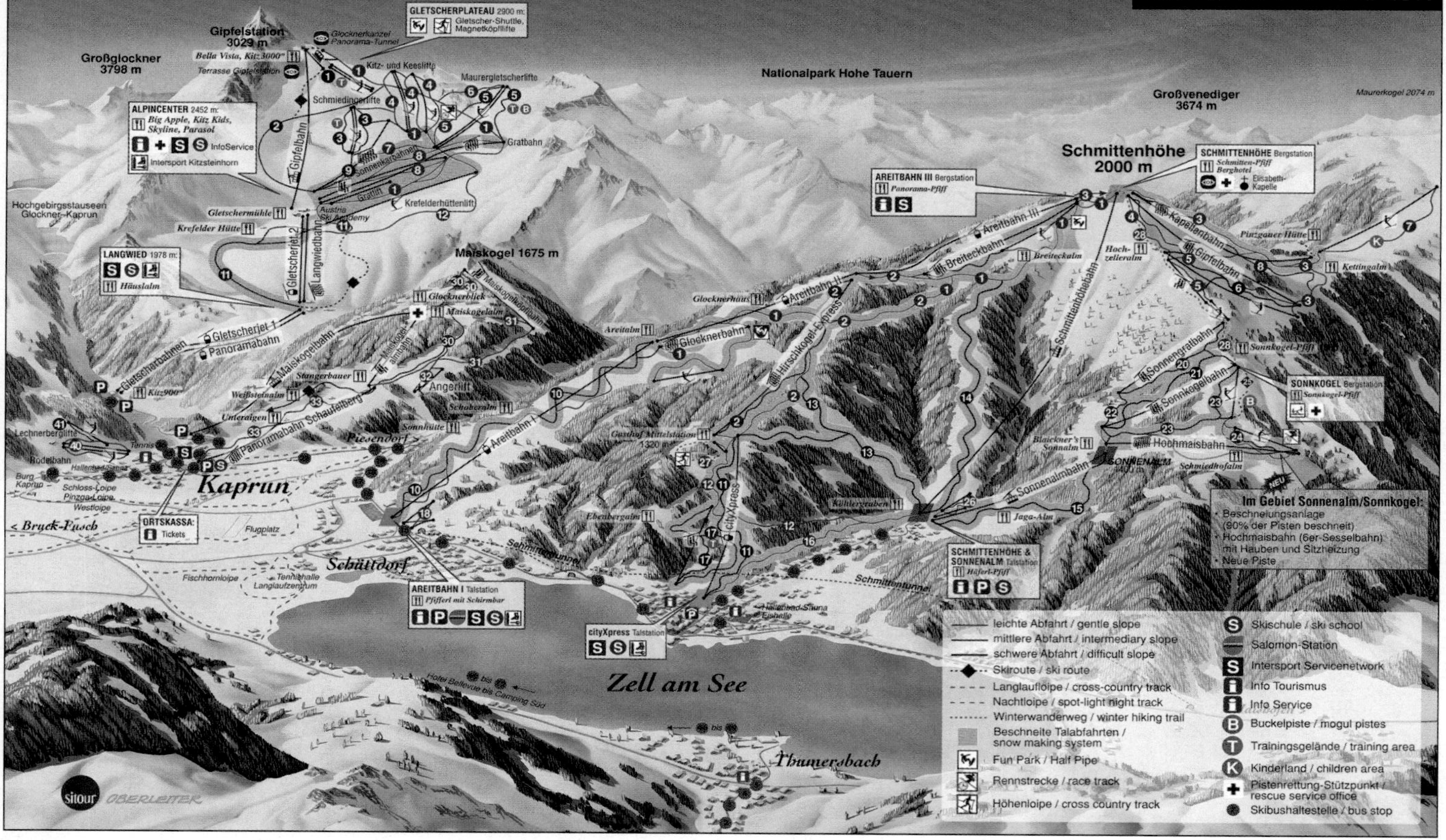

Mountain

A modern gondola rises from Zell, but the quickest way to the top of the mountain is by ski-bus to Schüttdorf and a three-stage gondola. Alternatively, you can catch a bus and join the cable-car from Schittental, the base of the main ski area, but this is prone to overcrowding at peak times.

A glance at the piste map gives the erroneous impression that the skiing here is testing. While the western shoulder of the mountain is given over to easy blue and red runs, the front face features seven blacks. In fact, in many other resorts most of these would be graded as moderate reds.

The severe classification is only barely justified in icy conditions when cover is thin. The whole area is ideally suited to intermediates.

Kaprun has its own winter area on Maiskogel, reached by a new six-pack with pull-down covers this season. The glacier is served by twin cableways that take you up to the Alpincenter mid-mountain hub at 2452m. A network of lifts fan out between here and the 3029m top station. In winter conditions you can ski all the way down to the cable-car station at Langwied. Terrain parks are located on the Kitzsteinhorn and at Jumping City on the Schmittenhöhe, where there is also a half-pipe.

Learn

Of the 10 schools in both resorts, **Sport-Alpin** Zell am See, **t** +43 (0)664 4531419, receives the most praise along with **Kitzsteinhorn, t** +43 (0)6547 8621363, in Kaprun. **Ski Safari, t** +43 (0)664 3361487, teaches off-piste and has a strong reputation. **Oberschneider, t** +43 (0)6547 82320, is strongly recommended. **Snowboard Academy, t** +43 (0)664 2530381, is the dedicated riding school.

Children

The **Sport-Alpin, t** +43 (0)664 4531419, and **Zell-am-See, t** +43 (0)6542 56020, schools in Zell, and five schools in Kaprun offer lessons to children from three years. **Play & Fun, t** +43 (0)6542 56020, is the non-ski kindergarten. **Babyboom, t** +43 (0)664 3762553, provides babysitting.

Lunch

On Schmittenhöhe try **Ebenbergalm, t** +43 (0)664 3512307, **Jaga Alm, t** +43 (0)6542 72969, for local game dishes, **Schmiedhofalm, t** +43 (0)6542 72868, for Pinzgauer specialities and panoramic views, and **Hochzeller Alm, t** +43 (0)6542 72113, for home cooking.

On Maiskogel, **Weisssteinalm, t** +43 (0)6547 7439, has plenty of atmosphere. On Kitzsteinhorn, **Gletschermühle, t** +43 (0)6547 8621371, is popular.

Dine

Nearly all the restaurants here are in hotels. In Zell, the **Steinerwirt, t** +43 (0)6542 72502, is recommended along with the **Kupferkessel, t** +43 (0)6542 72768. **Hotel St Georg, t** +43 (0)6542 768, **Zur Einkehr, t** +43 (0)6542 72363, **Landhotel Erlhof, t** +43 (0)6542 566370, and the **Salzburgerhof, t** +43 (0)6542 765, are all worth a visit.

In Kaprun, **Hotel Orgler, t** +43 (0)6547 8205, has some of the best food in the village. **Zucchini, t** +43 (0)6547 20010, makes a change from the ubiquitous *Wienerschnitzel*.

Party

In Zell, **Villa CrazyDaisy** and **Diele** are the hotspots. **Sunrise** disco and the **Rock-Bar** are also important hang-outs. In Kaprun nightlife is more muted. **Kitsch & Bitter** has regular live bands.

The **Optimum** sports centre contains an indoor pool, sauna and fitness centre, as well as a giant outdoor water-slide.

Sleep

Zell:

★★★★★**Hotel Salzburgerhof**, t +43 (0)6542 765, *www.salzburgerhof.at*, is the most comfortable base and has a good spa.

★★★★**Romantikhotel Zum Metzgerwirt**, t +43 (0)6542 72520, *www.romantik-hotel.at*, has pastel-decorated bedrooms, with a fireplace and water bed in one of the suites.

★★★★**Alpin Sporthotel**, t +43 (0)6542 769, *www.alpinhotel.at*, has modern rooms.

★★★★**Hotel Alpenblick**, t +43 (0)6542 5433, *www.alpenblick.at*, has wood-panelled rooms and studios.

★★★★**Hotel Schwebebahn**, t +43 (0)6542 72461, *www.schwebebahn.at*, is at the bottom of two cable-cars and convenient for the skiing.

★★★★**Hotel St Georg**, t +43 (0)6542 768, *www.grossglockner.co.at/stgeorg*, has traditional rooms and views of the lake.

★★★★**Hotel Berner**, t +43 (0)6542 779, *www.bernerhotel.com*, is in a quiet position and has a heated outdoor pool.

★★★★**Kinderhotel Hagleitner**, t +43 (0)6542 571870, *www.kinderhotel-hagleitner.at*, at Schüttdorf, is good for young families.

★★★★**Hotel Fischerwirt**, t +43 (0)6542 781, *www.fischerwirt.com*, has 'lovely rooms, full English breakfast, and a four-course dinner. We would all return without hesitation.'

★★★★**Hotel zum Hirschen**, t +43 (0)6542 72152, *www.zum-hirschen.at*, is 'fantastic, with superb food and a great staff'. It has a wellness centre containing a jetstream splash pool, massage rooms, sauna and steam bath.

★★★**Hotel Bellevue**, t +43 (0)6542 73104, *www.zellamsee.at/bellevue*, is located on the lakeside.

★★★**Gasthof Der Wildbachhof**, t +43 (0)6547 72244, is 'a 20- to 30-minute walk from town, but very convenient for the skiing'.

Kaprun:

★★★★**Active by Leitner's**, t +43 (0)6547 8782, *www.active-kaprun.at*, is a 1960s-style hotel run like an action-packed club. As well as skiing and snowboarding, the owners will arrange tobogganing and snowball-throwing parties.

★★★★**Alpen-Wellness Hotel Barbarahof**, t +43 (0)6547 7248, *www.hotel-barbarahof.at*, has a good spa and is next to the ski school meeting place ('excellent service and food').

★★★★**Hotel Orgler**, t +43 (0)6547 8205, *www.hotel-orgler.at*, is the original village inn with comfortable rooms.

★★★★**Hotel Sonnblick**, t +43 (0)6547 8301, *www.hotel-sonnblick.at*, is decorated in modern Tyrolean style.

★★★★**Hotel Tauernhof**, t +43 (0)6547 8235, *www.tauernhof-kaprun.at*, is at the base of the nursery slopes ('excellent food and ideal for first-time skiers').

★★★**Haus Annelies**, t +43 (0)6547 8689, *www.sbg.at/haus-annelies*, is 'a very nice B&B, budget rather than three-star'.

03

The Top Resorts: Canada

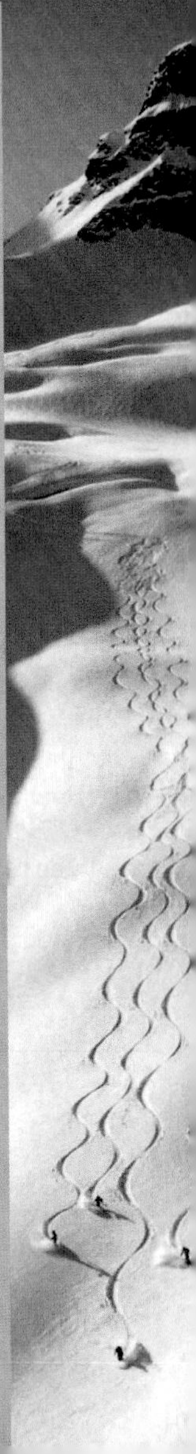

Banff-Lake Louise, Alberta

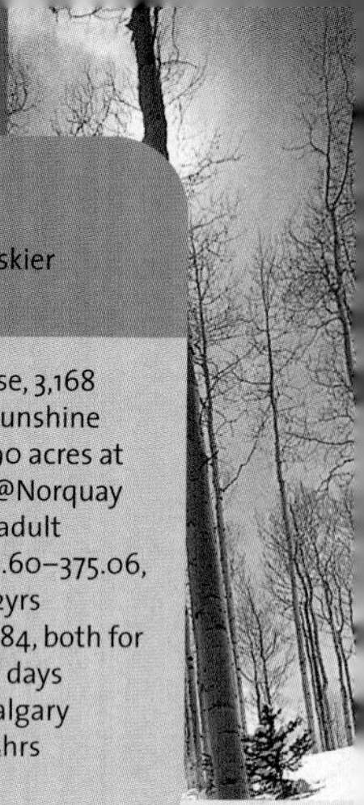

*** BEST FOR**

Beautiful scenery, all levels of skier and rider, value, nightlife (Banff)

ESSENTIALS

Altitude: 5,350ft (1631m)–8,650ft (2637m)
Further information: **t** +1 403 762 4421, *www.skibig3.com*
Lifts in area: 23 (2 cableways, 19 chairs, 2 drags) serving 7,558 acres of terrain in area: 4,200 acres at Lake Louise, 3,168 acres at Sunshine Village, 190 acres at Ski Banff@Norquay
Lift pass: adult CDN$309.60–375.06, child 6–12yrs CDN$195.84, both for 6 out of 8 days
Access: Calgary airport 1½hrs

Profile

Lake Louise is a peaceful village surrounded by stunningly beautiful scenery, while the historic town of Banff has a lively nightlife. The snow-sure slopes offer great skiing variety and few queues. This is a resort for skiers and riders on a budget, but not for those who dislike low temperatures

Resort

It is a triumph of successful Canadian marketing that two such totally different resorts in Alberta so far apart from each other should be bracketed together, not to mention similarly separate Sunshine Village which sits on a mountain top between them.

'Banff is an ordinary little tourist resort,' wrote the First World War poet Rupert Brooke in the year before his death, 'but Lake Louise – Lake Louise is of another world.' Ninety winters later, his description is still apt. Banff is a busy but bland little town just inside the gates of the Banff National Park. This is a traditional summer destination for thousands of North Americans, but not until relatively recently one that excited much interest in wintertime. It has its own little ski area of Mount Norquay nearby which it has unsuccessfully tried to brand as SkiBanff@Norquay.

Since hoteliers discovered that overseas skiers would pay to fill their empty beds in the closed season, Banff has become an important destination for temporary migrants from the slopes of Andorra and Austria in search of fresh low-cost ski fields and an equally frenetic nightlife.

Lake Louise lies 56km away across the park down the Trans-Canadian highway, which is dotted with little bridges so that elk and other animals can cross in safety. It is so small that 'village' is an exaggeration; a handful of hotels and a couple of shops that originally owed their *raison d'être* to the Canadian Pacific railway line. It built the splendid Victorian hotel, the Château Lake Louise, here so that passengers could rest in comfort while drinking in one of most dramatic glacial vistas of the Rockies. Lake Louise has its own substantial ski area situated an inconvenient five-minute bus ride away from the 'village' and hotels.

Sunshine Village is again not a 'village', but the name of the third ski area sandwiched between the two, 16km from Banff and 24km from Lake Louise. Its skiing rivals that of Lake Louise, but the only place to stay is in a hotel at the mid-mountain base, reached by gondola and far from any serious hope of evening entertainment beyond a glass of wine with dinner.

We recommend visitors stay in Banff and commute to the ski areas. All three

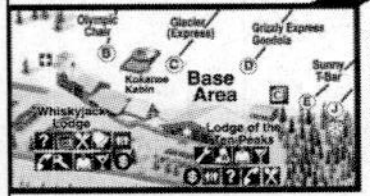

LIFTS	LENGTH	VERT.	CAP./HR.
(A) Summit Platter	3,670 ft/1,119m	1,345 ft/410 m	930
(B) Olympic Chair	7,000 ft/2,134m	2,100 ft/640 m	800
(C) Glacier Express Quad	5,975 ft/1,822m	1,450 ft/442 m	2,640
(D) Grizzly Express Gondola	9,571 ft/2,918m	2,414 ft/736 m	1,730
(E) Sunny T-Bar	1,185 ft/ 361m	145 ft/ 44 m	1,200
(F) Paradise Triple Chair	3,608 ft/1,100m	1,292 ft/394 m	1,800
(G) Ptarmigan Quad Chair	3,350 ft/1,021m	1,350 ft/412 m	2,200
(H) Larch Express Quad	4,800 ft/1,463m	1,230 ft/375 m	2,640
(I) Top of the World 6 Person Chair	4,407 ft/1,344m	1,350 ft/411 m	2,640
(J) Play Station Kid's Tow	200 ft/ 61m	60 ft/ 18 m	300

Wiwaxy
Boulevard
Bald Eagle
Easy Street
Pinecone Way
Men's Downhill
Double Trouble
Ladies' Downhill
Grizzly Bowl
Juniper
Juniper Jungle
Wrong Turn
Sunnyside
Outer Limits
Sunset
Skyline
Sunset Terrace
Gully
Upshoot Trail
Eagle Flight
Wapta
Deer Run
Eagle Meadows
Upper Meadowlark
The Ski Out
Saddleback
Flight Chutes
Home Run
Meadowlark
Meadowlark Crossover
Headwall
Good Intentions
Eagle Trees
STM
Tickety Chutes
Kernshan's
Mirkwood
Eagle Poma
Cameron Way
Tight Turn
Sunset Gully
Whitehorn Cat Track
Steep & Flat
Lower Flight
Eagle's Beak
Meadow Race Pitch
Lower Meadowlark

Guest Services

Restaurants
Phones
Customer Service
Rental Equipment
Ski Accessory Shop
Parking
Bar
Ski Tuning/Repair
Washrooms
Ski School
Day Care/Nursery
Lift Tickets
Cash Machine
Kids Learning Centre/Magic Carpets
Super Pipe
Terrain Park
Slow Skiing/ Snowboarding Zone

Trail Markings

Easiest
More Difficult
Patrol Boundary
Most Difficult
Extreme
Ski Patrol

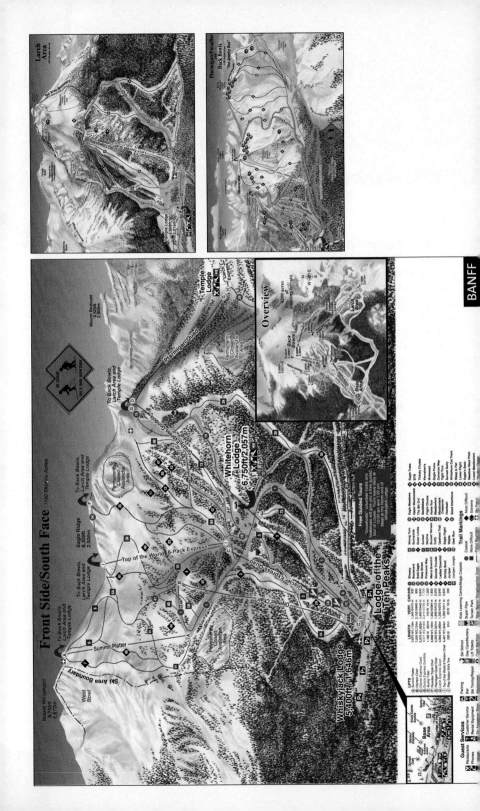

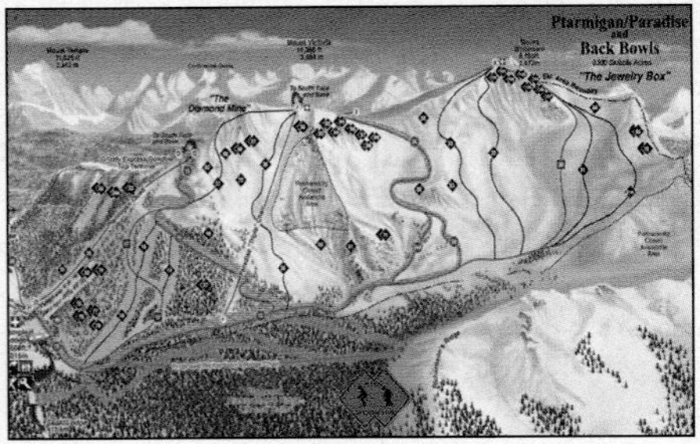

share a regional lift pass and are connected by a regular bus service. However, renting a car adds considerable convenience and avoids any hanging around in what can be mind-numbingly low temperatures in mid-winter. We have persistent and alarming reports of poor ski and board hire in Banff, with iniquitous 'excess' damage charges on top of local insurance. We advise you to take your own equipment.

Mountain

Mount Norquay is much more than a local hill, but you didn't cross the Atlantic to spend a week or 10 days riding three quad-chairs. Nevertheless we spent an enjoyable morning here repeatedly cruising beautifully groomed but short trails cut through the trees. The pitch dictates whether each is classified as easy or intermediate. Four of them correctly get a double-black-diamond rating.

Lake Louise is far more exciting. A multi-mountain area with every type of terrain from gentle tree-lined trails to steep chutes and awesome open bowls. It's all challenging stuff, but less confident skiers should not be scared away. An easy run descends from every lift. The Larch Express Quad gives access to a couple of easy motorways as well as four hugely enjoyable blue trails.

For strong intermediates as well as advanced skiers and riders, the pick of the action is off the backside. A host of demanding or downright impossible chutes are reached along the heavily corniced ridge from the top of the Summit Platter lift and the Top of the World Express. On a big powder day the locals just ski lap after lap here. The new Grizzly Express gondola accesses some steep double-diamond-graded tree-skiing that is served on the backside by the Ptarmigan quad.

The whole area is popular with snowboarders and we rate the terrain park as one of the best we have ever experienced.

Sunshine Village has three separate mountains. Mount Standish is a rounded, exposed peak with a mixture of terrain for all standards. Look Out Mountain suits strong intermediates and more advanced skiers, while Goat's Eye Mountain is the domain of the hardcore.

Delirium Dive is a classic steep here. While not in the same league as Corbet's in Jackson Hole, it is spoken off in reverentially hushed tones by the cognoscenti. The ski patrol adds to the hype by insisting that you wear a transceiver and have shovel and probe in your backpack. In fact, the idea is to confine this pitch to dedicated off-piste enthusiasts who are already sufficiently experienced to have bought their own gear – you can't rent a transceiver anywhere nearby. After a usually tricky entrance it opens into a steep bowl with a choice of exits: the more direct involves a walk-out, while a lengthy traverse to the skier's right offers more powder and a speedier return to a lift.

Wild West is a similar adrenalin-fuelled experience that opened last season – three rock-walled couloirs and a series of 30m cliffs accessed from the western end of Goat's Eye.

Learn

The **Lake Louise**, **t** +1 403 522 1333, **Banff@Norquay**, **t** +1 403 760 7717, and **Sunshine Village**, **t** +1 403 762 6560, ski and snowboard schools all offer group and private lessons. **Club Ski/Snowboard**, **t** +1 403 760 7731, runs three-day courses for groups of similar ability, with guided tours of all three resorts.

Children

At Lake Louise, **Telus Play Station**, **t** +1 403 522 1333, takes babies from three weeks old. **Club Ski Junior programme**, **t** +1 403 760 7731, offers a cool mix of guiding and instruction. **Tiny Tigers Daycare**, **t** +1 403 762 6560, at Sunshine Village and **SkiBanff@Norquay Day Care**, **t** +1 403 762 4421, offer daycare from 19 months.

Lunch

At Mount Norquay, Cascade Lodge houses the **Lone Pine** restaurant, **t** +1 403 762 4421, serving hearty mountain fare.

At Lake Louise, **Sawyers Nook** upstairs at the Temple Lodge, **t** +1 403 522 3555, has waiter-service food and an intimate atmosphere. **Kokanee Kabin**, **t** +1 403 522 3555, at the base has barbecues and beer. **Lodge of the Ten Peaks**, **t** +1 403 522 3555, and the **Whisky Jack Lodge**, **t** +1 403 522 3555, house a cafeteria. **The Great Bear Room**, **t** +1 403 522 3555 has self-service dining with soups, pasta and roast beef.

At Sunshine, all the restaurants are at the mid-mountain base area, **t** +1 403 762 4421 for all. **Lookout Bistro** on the top floor of the Day Lodge has a full menu and a warm fireplace. We recommend **The Eagle's Nest** in Sunshine Inn for a long, relaxed lunch. **Mad Trapper's Saloon** in Old Sunshine Lodge is a Western-style saloon on two floors with the ubiquitous burger.

Dine

Banff has a wonderfully wide choice of restaurants that reflect its multi-cultural clientele. **Maple Leaf Grill**e, **t** +1 403 760 7680, is essentially Canadian with an emphasis on elk, bison, duck and lobster. **Melissa's**, **t** +1 403 762 5511, is a rustic log cabin with great steaks and BBQ ribs. **Le Beaujolais**, **t** +1 403 762 2712, is French, romantic and regularly wins Canadian culinary awards. **Giorgio's Trattoria**, **t** +1 403 762 5114, is Italian. Try the osso buco with polenta. **El Toro**, **t** +1 403 762 2520, is Greek. **The Silver Dragon**, **t** +1 403 762 3939, serves Cantonese and Peking cuisine. **Pad Thai**, **t** +1 403 762 4911, is Thai, and **Miki**, **t** +1 403 286 2860, is Japanese.

In Lake Louise Village, the **Post Hotel**, **t** +1 403 522 3989, and **Deer Lodge**, **t** +1 403 522 3747, are the pick of a limited choice. **Timber Wolf Pizza** at the **Lake Louise Inn**, **t** +1 403 522 3791 is recommended. **The Fairmont Chateau Lake Louise**, **t** +1 403 522 3511, has four restaurants including the **Walliser Stube Wine Bar**, **t** +1 403 522 1817. **Mountain Restaurant**, **t** +1 403 522 3573 serves Asian fusion cuisine and pasta.

Party

Après-ski in Banff largely revolves around the enormous number of bars scattered along Banff Avenue. These include **Tommy's Neighbourhood Pub**, **Magpie & Stump**, **Rose & Crown**, and **St James's Gate** – an Irish pub originally built in Dublin and shipped over in pieces to Canada. **Wild Bill's** has Country and Western bands, and the **Barbary Coast** has live rock bands. **Hoodoo Lounge** and **Aurora** are both popular nightclubs. The nightlife at Lake Louise is considerably quieter and restricted to a few hotel bars.

Sleep

Luxury:

Banff:

Fairmont Banff Springs, **t** +1 403 762 2211, *www.fairmont.com/banffsprings*, Château Lake Louise's majestic 'sister' hotel is designed to look like a Scottish castle with one of the best spas in Canada.

Rimrock Resort Hotel, **t** +1 403 762 3356, *www.rimrockresort.com*, is elegant and modern, located on Sulphur Mountain, a short walk from Banff's natural hot springs.

Lake Louise:

Fairmont Château Lake Louise, **t** +1 403 522 3511, *www.fairmont.com/lakelouise*, is in a quiet wilderness setting with spectacular views over the frozen lake.

The Post Hotel, **t** +1 403 522 3989, *www.posthotel.com*, is a luxuriously elegant recreation in Edwardian style.

Moderate/Budget:

Banff:

Buffalo Mountain Lodge, **t** +1 403 410 7417, *www.crmr.com/lodgebuffalo.php*, is ruggedly luxurious, with open fires and beams.

The Mount Royal, **t** +1 403 762 3331, *www.mountroyalhotel.com*, is ideally placed for the nightlife of Banff.

Banff Caribou Lodge, **t** +1 403 762 5887, *www.bestofbanff.com*, is a 15-minute walk from downtown and is in rustic Western style.

The Banff King Edward, **t** +1 403 762 2202, is the town's second oldest hotel.

Siding 29 Lodge, **t** +1 403 762 5575, *www.bestwesternsiding29.com*, is a no-frills hotel with an indoor pool.

The Rundle Manor Hotel, **t** +1 403 762 5544, is a good-value apartment-style hotel.

Juniper Inn, **t** +1 403 762 2281, *www.decorehotels.com/juniper*, has newly renovated chalets and suites.

Lake Louise:

Deer Lodge, **t** +1 403 522 3747, *www.crmr.com/lodgedeer.php*, is two minutes' walk from the lake shore, and ideal for those wanting a quiet retreat. It has a roof-top hot tub.

Sunshine Village:

Sunshine Village Inn, **t** +1 403 762 6564, *www.skibanff.com/accommodation/inn.html*, is reached by a 15-minute gondola ride from Sunshine base and is the area's only on-mountain accommodation.

Big White, BC

Profile

Attractive village with doorstep skiing for intermediates and powder skiers. More suited to families than party-goers, with a lack of mountain restaurants and après-ski venues

Resort

Big White is a big hitter among the more recently developed clutch of Canadian resorts that have successfully sought international acclaim on the coat-tails of Whistler. It is hidden away in BC in the beautiful Okanagan Valley, the country's equally successful wine-growing region.

Big White takes its name from the sometimes all-enveloping moisture-filled cloud cover, which creates a phantom forest of snow-ghosts – trees frozen into eerie monster-like shapes. It is under the same Australian ownership as nearby Silver Star.

*BEST FOR

Beginners and intermediates, off-piste, families

ESSENTIALS

Altitude: 4,950ft (1508m)–7,606ft (2319m)

Further information: **t** +1 250 765 3101, *www.bigwhite.com*

Lifts in area: 13 (1 cableway, 9 chairs, 3 drags) serving 85km of trails

Lift pass: adult CD$349, child 6–12yrs CD$157, both for 6 days

Access: Kelowna airport 35 miles (56km), Vancouver airport 4½hrs

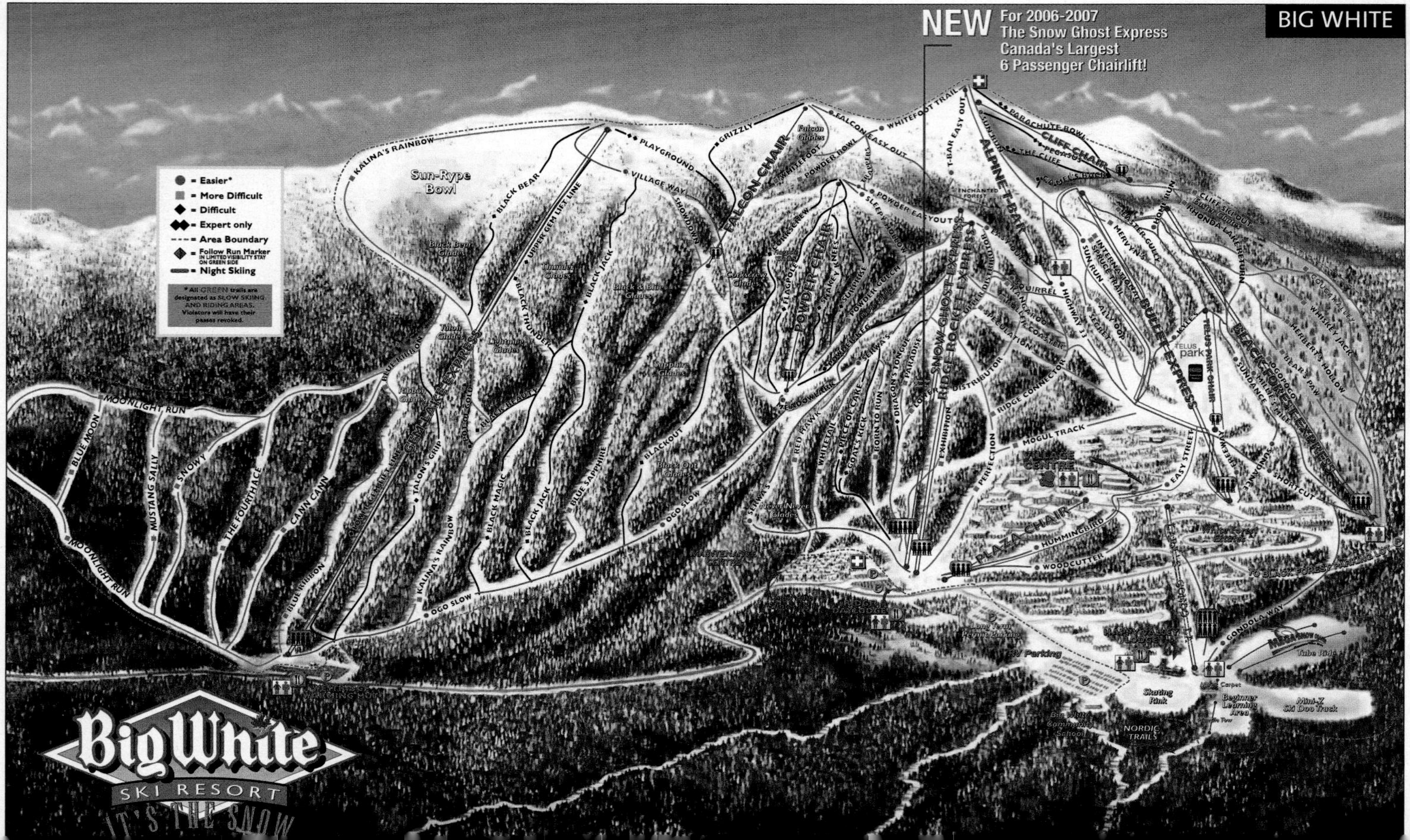
NEW
For 2006-2007
The Snow Ghost Express
Canada's Largest
6 Passenger Chairlift!
● = Easier*
■ = More Difficult
◆ = Difficult
◆◆ = Expert only
= Area Boundary
= Follow Run Marker IN LIMITED VISIBILITY STAY ON GREEN SIDE
= Night Skiing
* All GREEN trails are designated as SLOW SKIING AND RIDING AREAS. Violators will have their passes revoked.
Sun-Rype Bowl
KALINA'S RAINBOW
BLACK BEAR
UPPER GEM LIFT LINE
PLAYGROUND
VILLAGE WAY
SHOWDOWN
GRIZZLY
FALCON CHAIR
WHITEFOOT
POWDER BOWL
FALCON EASY OUT
WHITEFOOT TRAIL
T-BAR EASY OUT
ALPINE T-BAR
PARACHUTE BOWL
CLIFF CHAIR
PEGASUS
THE CLIFF
POWDER CHAIR
POWDER EASY OUT
SLEEPY HOLLOW
SNOW GHOST EXPRESS
RIDGE ROCKET EXPRESS
BULLET EXPRESS
BLACK FOREST EXPRESS
TELUS PARK CHAIR
TELUS park
PLAZA CHAIR
GEM LAKE EXPRESS
HOME RUN
MERVYN'S
CLIFF SKI OUT
RHONDA LAKE RETURN
COUGAR ALLEY
WHISKEY JACK
HERBERT'S HOLLOW
BEAR'S PAW
SUNDANCE
SHORTCUT
SUN RUN
SPRUCE TRAIL
HIGHWAY 33
SQUIRREL
KANGAROO
SPECULATION
RIDGE CONNECTOR
DISTRIBUTOR
EXHIBITION
PERFECTION
MOGUL TRACK
PARADISE
DRAGON'S TONGUE
BORN TO RUN
GOAT'S KICK
PIECE OF CAKE
WHITETAIL
RED HAWK
SERWA'S
BLACKOUT
BLUE SAPPHIRE
BLACK JACK
BLACK MAGIC
BLACK THUNDER
KALINA'S RAINBOW
TALON'S GRIP
BLUE RIBBON
POT OF GOLD
OGO SLOW
CANN CANN
THE FOURTHACE
SNOWY
MUSTANG SALLY
BLUE MOON
MOONLIGHT RUN
VILLAGE CENTRE
HUMMINGBIRD
WOODCUTTER
EASY STREET
GONDOLA WAY
Skating Rink
Beginner Learning Area
Mini-Z Ski Doo Track
Tube Park
NORDIC TRAILS
Big White Community School
RV Parking
Long Term Permit Parking
HAPPY VALLEY LODGE
Big White SKI RESORT
IT'S THE SNOW

Mountain

This is much more than the local hill for Kelowna, a small but testing intermediate area with magical charm. Beginners congregate around the Humming Bird quad below the village, while others head directly for the Ridge Rocket Express and the new Snow Ghost Express six-pack, which give smooth access to the main network of runs. Best off-piste is between the snow-ghosts in Sun Ripe Bowl. Big White has a long history of snowboarding with the first riders congregating here back in 1983. The terrain park has an Olympic-sized superpipe, a snowcross course and a rail.

Learn

Big White's Ski and Snowboard School, **t** +1 250 491 6113, incorporates **Telus Heavy Metal Flight School**, which teaches terrain park technique.

Children

Tot Town Day Care, **t** +1 250 491 2711, takes non-skiing children from 18 months. **The Kids' Centre**, **t** +1 250 418 6118, cares for kids all day from four years. Both are warmly recommended.

Lunch

The West Ridge Warming Hut, **Day Lodge** and **Happy Valley Lodge**, **t** +1 250 765 3101 for all, provide limited alcohol-free options. Wise skiers return to the resort. Try **Frank's Chinese Laundry**, **t** +1 250 765 7866.

Dine

Snowshoe Sam's, **t** +1 250 765 1416, has been newly renovated. It has good steaks and burgers. **Kettle Valley**, **t** +1 250 491 0130, has the best gourmet fare.
The Swiss Bear, **t** +1 250 491 7750, has authentic fondues.

Party

Snowshoe Sam's is the main rendezvous, with pool tables and dance floor.

Sleep

All the accommodation adjoins the piste and includes a range of condos. For further details, **t** +1 250 765 8888, or visit *www.bigwhite.com*.

Luxury:

Chateau Big White is the resort's best address at the top of the village. It has a small spa.

Big White Condos throughout the resort include 14 new mountain rental homes.

Moderate/Budget:

Inn at Big White is the only hotel here, with a pool.

White Crystal Inn is in a good location with large family rooms.

Fernie, BC

Profile

Good-value, but remote ski-in/ski-out resort with uncrowded slopes, extensive piste grooming, a friendly atmosphere and a good snow record. Well suited to families, very limited nightlife

Resort

Fernie has been likened to Argentière without glaciers, a wonderfully challenging ski area in a remote corner of BC that has the topographical potential to

***BEST FOR**

All levels of skier and rider, families, ski convenience

ESSENTIALS

Altitude: 3,500ft (1068m)–6,316ft (1925m)
Further information: t +1 250 423 4655, *www.skifernie.com*
Lifts in area: 10 (6 chairs, 4 drags) serving 2,504 acres of terrain
Lift pass: adult CDN$384, youth 13–17yrs CDN$270, child 6–12yrs CDN$120, all for 6 days
Access: Calgary airport 3½hrs

become the new Whistler. International powderhounds tend to rate Fernie in their top five destinations in North America. Few destinations can offer such premium pistes and powder within the infrastructure of a modern ski village that is backed by all the charm and historical association of an attractive Victorian railway town.

Over the past 10 years this small and once unfashionable resort has achieved pipe-dream fame as luxurious apartment blocks and mountain homes sprouted around the ski village.

Real estate developers have now started on a CDN$1.5 billion development between the ski area and the old town that is the setting for a Greg Norman championship golf course due to open in 2007. To their surprise and delight, 30 of the first 50 homes attracted British buyers. Nearby Cranbrook airport has got the go-ahead to increase its runway to take large airliners, and the whole region looks set for its biggest boom since the 19th-century gold rush.

But where are the new lifts? Fernie's ski area has somehow managed its metamorphosis from ugly duckling to swan with six chairs – none of them covered and only two of them quads. Fernie now belongs to Resorts of the Canadian Rockies, which also owns Banff-Lake Louise, Kimberley, Stoneham and Mont-Sainte-Anne. An initial CDN$6 million investment over two years has resulted in new base facilities but so far no fresh uphill transport.

Despite all the comfortable living accommodation, it is foolish to suppose that international skiers will continue to support Fernie unless it dramatically overhauls its antiquated lift system. Go-ahead Kicking Horse is waiting in the wings to grab Whistler's crown, while two major new resorts are under construction in BC.

Visitors have the choice of staying in ski-convenient hotel rooms and condos at the base area or in the old town of Fernie, three miles below the resort. By slumbering with minimal change throughout the 20th century it has managed to retain its considerable Victorian charm. A regular bus service operates between the mountain village and the town.

Mountain

This is one of these rare resorts that truly suits all levels, and its compact size lends itself particularly well to families. It has a good beginner area at the base, and plenty of tree-skiing for all standards. However the real action is found in the series of five deep powder bowls that stand side by side beneath the 2000m peaks of Elephant Head, Polar Peak and Grizzly Peak. These provide an astonishing variety of challenging terrain that will keep a strong intermediate or advanced skier happy for a whole season.

Main mountain access is by two successive quads from the base area that take you up into Lizard Bowl, setting for the notorious Face Lift. Originally this was a meat-hook tow, which would be more at home on a Kiwi club field, but it has now been fitted with platters for greater ease of use. The slow and cold Timber Bowl Express quad from the base area brings you to the steep terrain of Siberia Bowl at the other end of the ski area. Fernie is popular with riders. It has a terrain park

Mammoth Head
6807 ft, 2074 m
Elephant Head
6789 ft, 2045 m
Polar Peak
7000 ft, 2134 m
Grizzly Peak
6900 ft, 2103 m
SIBERIA BOWL
TIMBER BOWL
CURRIE BOWL
LIZARD BOWL
CEDAR BOWL
(See inset map)
FISH BOWL
FACE LIFT
HAUL BACK
BOOMERANG TRIPLE CHAIR
GREAT BEAR EXPRESS QUAD
TIMBER BOWL EXPRESS QUAD
WHITE PASS QUAD
DEER CHAIR
ELK QUAD
MIGHTY MOOSE
Legend
Easiest
More Difficult
Most Difficult
Extreme
Extreme Hazard
Permanent Closure
Daycare
Public Payphones
Restrooms
Tickets
Rentals
Retail Shop
Lodging Check-In
NASTAR Race Centre
Ski Patrol & First Aid
World Cup Freestyle Venue
Snowshoe Trails
Ski School
Restaurants & Snack Bars
Bars
Repairs & Equipment Check
Groceries & Liquor
Information
Snowboard Terrain Park*
Snowboard Half Pipe*
*Snow conditions permitting
Slow Zone
Cross CountrySki Trails

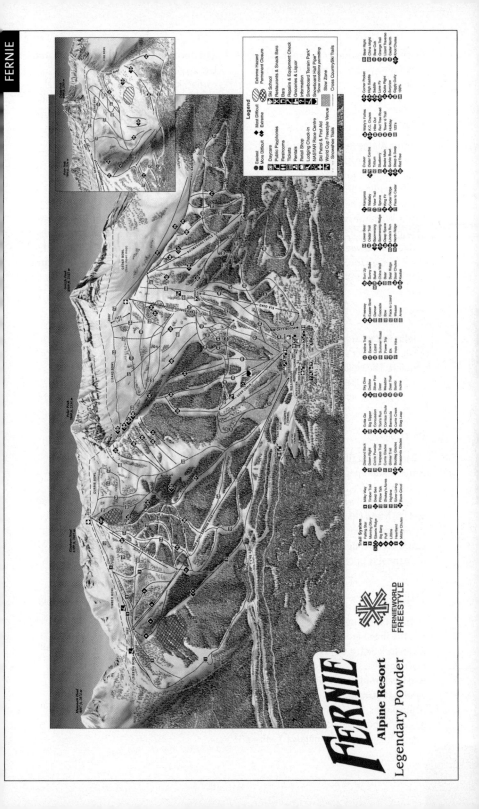

FERNIE
Alpine Resort
Legendary Powder
FERNIEWORLD
FREESTYLE
Trail System
Falling Star
Morning Glory
Siberia Ridge
Big Bang
Puff
Liftline
Heartland
Mitchy Chutes
Milky Way
Timber Trail
Deep Sea
Pillow Talk
Shakey's Acres
Highline
Silver Lining
Black Cloud
Diamond Back
Down Right
Currie Powder
Trespass Trail
Currie Glades
Gilmar Trail
Bootleg Glades
Anaconda Glades
Gotta Go
Big Dipper
Concussion
Tom's Run
Cornice Chute
Barracuda
Currie Creek
Stag Leap
Sky Dive
Decline
Silver Fox
Deer
Meadow
Deer Trail
Bambi
Incline
Incline Trail
Downhill
Lizard
Summer Road
Power Trip
Elk
Holo Hike
Freeway
Easter Bowl
Dancer
Cascade
Bow
Face to Lizard
Weasel
Arrow
Sun Up
Sunny Side
Ballet
China Wall
Bear
Bear Ridge
Bear Chutes
Kodiak
Lower Bear
Cedar Trail
Boomerang
Boomerang Ridge
Deep Space
Linda's Run
North Ridge
Kangaroo
Wallaby
View Trail
Spruce
King Fir
Cedar Ridge
Face to Cedar
Cruiser
Cedar Centre
Trillium
Blueberry
Snake Main
Gorbie Bowl
Steep & Deep
Red Tree
Wally's Follies
K.C. Chutes
Hike Out
Red Tree Road
Tower 6 Trail
Holiday
123's
Corner Pocket
High Saddle
Saddle
Lone Fir
Quite Right
Surprize
Giggly Gully
100%
Bear Right
China Might
Bear Cub
Orange Trail
Lizard Traverse
Cedar North
Knot Chutes

reached by the Timber chair-lift, and a half-pipe on Bambi trail, close to the base area.

Learn

Fernie Alpine Resort Winter Sports School, **t** +1 250 423 4655, is warmly recommended for lessons in alpine skiing, snowboarding and telemark. Backcountry excursions can be arranged through **Fernie Wilderness Adventures Snowcat Skiing**, **t** +1 250 423 6704, **Island Lake Lodge** and **Powder Cowboy Cat Skiing**, **t** +1 250 423 3700, and **RK Heli-ski** in nearby Panorama, **t** +1 250 342 3889.

Children

Telus Resort Kids Daycare, **t** +1 250 423 4655, looks after small babies and toddlers. The children's ski programme is extensive. The Freeriders Programme is aimed at experienced teenagers.

Lunch

The Wood on the Hill, **t** +1 250 423 4597, is the best proper lunch option. **Kelsey's**, **t** +1 250 423 6855, in the Cornerstone Lodge in the village centre, has English-style fish and chips and Mexican dishes, as well as ubiquitous chili and burgers. **Lizard Creek Lodge**, **t** +1 250 423 2057, has a reasonably priced bar menu.

Dine

Lizard Creek Lodge, **t** +1 250 423 2057, has the finest food in the ski village. **River Rock Bistro**, **t** +1 250 423 6871, in Park Place Lodge is recommended for steaks and local trout. **Gabriella's**, **t** +1 250 423 7388, is Italian and serves good-value pasta dishes. The **Alpine Lodge**, **t** +1 250 423 4237, above the base area, is Asian fusion. In old Fernie, **Yamagoya**, **t** +1 250 430 0090, serves sushi. **The Old Elevator**, **t** +1 250 423 7115, features Ahi tuna carpaccio and pan-seared venison rack. **Rip 'n' Richard's Eatery**, **t** +1 250 423 3002, has more basic Canadian fare. The historic **Royal Hotel**, **t** +1 250 423 7743, features modern Australian cuisine.

Party

The **Griz Bar** is where the après-ski starts, but dog-sledding and *skijoring* take precedence over Alpine Oompah here. Have a go at ice-skating or curling in the old town. **Eldorado Lounge**, **Grand Central Hotel & Bar** and the **Royal Hotel** are popular meeting places with regular live music.

Sleep

Luxury:

Lizard Creek Lodge, **t** +1 250 423 2057, *www.lizardcreek.com*, is the best address on the mountain, with spacious condos, a gym, swimming-pool and hot tub. The bar serves snacks while you sit in squashy sofas around the open fire.

Moderate/Budget:

Fernie Alpine Lodge, **t** +1 250 423 4237, *www.alpinelodge.com*, is a ski-in/ski-out B&B with a warm atmosphere.

Cornerstone Lodge, **t** +1 250 423 6855, *www.cornerstonelodge.ca*, is at the foot of Deer chair and houses Kelsey's Restaurant.

Park Place Lodge, **t** +1 250 423 6871, *www.parkplacelodge.com*, is in the old town and has modern rooms.

The Old Nurses Residence, **t** +1 250 423 3091, *www.oldnurse.com*, is a B&B built in 1908, with large and attractively restored rooms.

Royal Hotel, **t** +1 250 423 7743, *www.fernieroyalhotel.com*, is Victorian and has great atmosphere.

Humber Valley, Newfoundland

*** BEST FOR**

Comfortable accommodation, families, cat-skiing

ESSENTIALS

Altitude: 33ft (10m)–1,791ft (546m)
Further information: **t** +1 709 637 7601, *www.humbervalley.com*, *www.skimarble.com*
Lifts in area: 4 (3 chairs, 1 drag) serving 175 acres of terrain
Lift pass: adult CDN$42, child 5–12yrs CDN$10, both per day
Access: Deer Lake airport 20mins, Stephenville airport 1hr

Profile

Small pisted ski area at Marble Mountain, rough and ready cat-skiing in the Blomidon Mountains, and high-quality accommodation

Resort

Newfoundland, previously more famous for its cod than its pistes, has the closest North American skiing to the UK, with a 5-hour flight and a 3½-hour time difference. The area is part of the foothills of the Appalachians above the Humber River, which cuts a winding path through the valley to the Bay of Islands. The scenery is beautiful, but temperatures can be low. The resort of Humber Valley is an alternative to the over-commercialized and over-priced mainstream resorts on both sides of the Atlantic. You can buy luxury chalets here at incredibly low prices.

Mountain

Marble Mountain, 10 minutes' drive from Humber Valley, is a small area with 35 trails, a terrain park and half-pipe. However, the area does receive a large annual snowfall of 16ft (5m).

The main attraction is cat skiing, **t** +1 709 783 2712 – a rugged off-piste experience like no other. Located in the Bay of Islands, 30 minutes from Humber Valley Resort, a heated snowcat transports skiers and boarders 2,200 vertical feet (670m) to the top of the spectacular Blomidon Mountains. Here the mountains reach down to the sea where whales, dolphins and porpoises swim among the icebergs off the coast.

Learn

Marble Mountain Snow School, **t** +1 709 637 7601, offers group and private tuition in skiing and snowboarding.

Children

Marble Children's Center has a supervised play area filled with toys and activities to keep kids entertained for hours. In the evening, a fleet of babysitters is available. **Marble Mountain Snow School** accepts children from three years, with Kids Kamp for ages three to six years, and Marble Krunchers and Marble Riders from seven years.

Lunch

There is a basic self-service in the lodge at the base of Marble Mountain.

Dine

The restaurants at Corner Brook, Pasadena and Deer Lake provide a range of dining. **Gitanos'**, **t** +1 709 634 4389,

Marble
MOUNTAIN
A
B
C
D
P

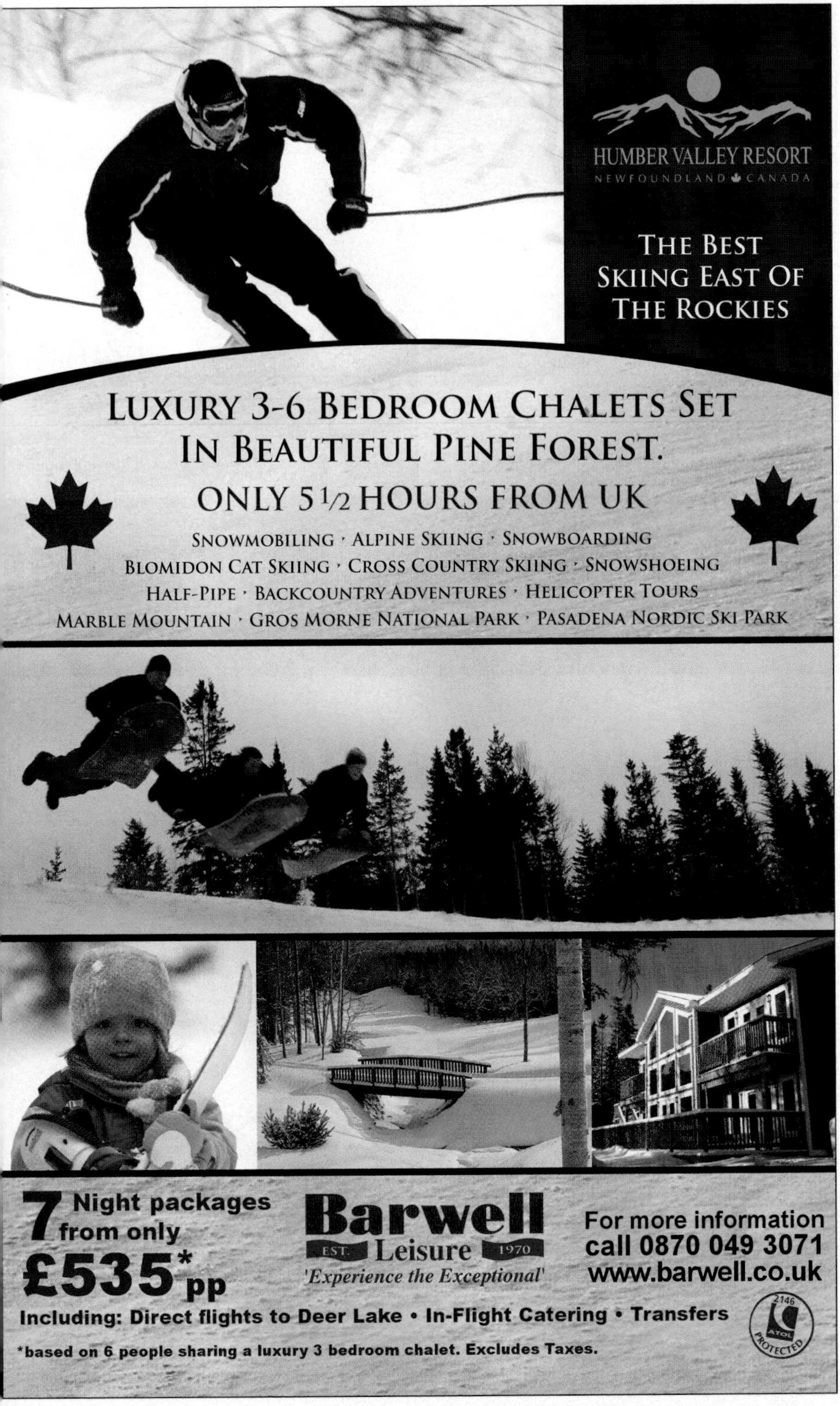

HUMBER VALLEY RESORT
NEWFOUNDLAND CANADA
THE BEST SKIING EAST OF THE ROCKIES
LUXURY 3-6 BEDROOM CHALETS SET IN BEAUTIFUL PINE FOREST.
ONLY 5 1/2 HOURS FROM UK
SNOWMOBILING · ALPINE SKIING · SNOWBOARDING
BLOMIDON CAT SKIING · CROSS COUNTRY SKIING · SNOWSHOEING
HALF-PIPE · BACKCOUNTRY ADVENTURES · HELICOPTER TOURS
MARBLE MOUNTAIN · GROS MORNE NATIONAL PARK · PASADENA NORDIC SKI PARK
7 Night packages from only
£535* pp
Barwell
EST. Leisure 1970
'Experience the Exceptional'
For more information
call 0870 049 3071
www.barwell.co.uk
Including: Direct flights to Deer Lake • In-Flight Catering • Transfers
2146 ATOL PROTECTED
*based on 6 people sharing a luxury 3 bedroom chalet. Excludes Taxes.

serves European cuisine. **Thirteen West**, **t** +1 709 634 1300, has traditional hearty Newfoundland tucker such as seafood chowder. **The Fine Dining Restaurant** is at Humber Valley Resort and serves the best lobster, while **Strawberry Hill Dining**, **t** +1 877 434 0066, at nearby Little Rapids offers seven-course 'tasting menus'. A shopping service is available for the chalets, and takeaway pizzas and burgers can be delivered.

Party

Rural Newfoundland is not party-land. Nightlife is restricted to a few bars including **Waylands Gate**, which is Irish, and **Union Station** – both are at Corner Brook. Snowshoeing is a popular evening activity, with two-night survival courses organized where you learn how to light a fire and follow tracks. Snowmobiling is another resort pastime, with 745 miles (1200km) of groomed trails and guided evenings with drinks around a bonfire as the focus. The tubing park is open on Fridays, Saturdays and Sundays. You can also go ice-skating on Deer Lake.

Sleep

Marble Villa, **t** +1 709 637 7601, at the base of Marble Mountain, is the resort's only ski-in/ski-out accommodation.

Humber Valley Resort Chalets, **t** +1 709 686 8100, have a minimum of three bedrooms and three bathrooms. All are light and spacious with modern kitchens, satellite TV, log fireplaces, and laundry rooms. Many have saunas and outdoor hot tubs as well. Most visitors stay in these excellent chalets.

Kicking Horse, BC

BEST SMALL RESORT 2007

Profile

Rugged terrain best suited to good skiers and riders wanting serious challenges without having to ignore creature comforts. KH has one of the best mountain restaurants in North America and new, comfortable accommodation at its base. Not suited to easy cruisers

Resort

When it opened six years ago, Kicking Horse was billed as the first new resort in the world to be built in a generation. This was not strictly true, but after a tricky start in a bad-snow winter the ski area in a remote corner of BC has far exceeded all expectations and become one of our favourite resorts on both continents. It now has world-class ranking with tough terrain comparable to Whistler and Jackson Hole.

The secret of its international appeal lies in an agreeable blend of Canadian

*BEST FOR

Strong intermediates and experts, ski gourmets, comfort-seekers

ESSENTIALS

Altitude: 3,902ft (1190m)–8,037ft (2450m)
Further information: **t** +1 250 439 5424, *www.kickinghorseresort.com*
Lifts in area: 4 (1 cableway, 3 chairs) serving 2,750 acres
Lift pass: adult CDN$321, youth 13–18yrs CDN$266, child 7–12yrs CDN$143, all for 6 days
Access: Calgary airport 3hrs

KICKING HORSE

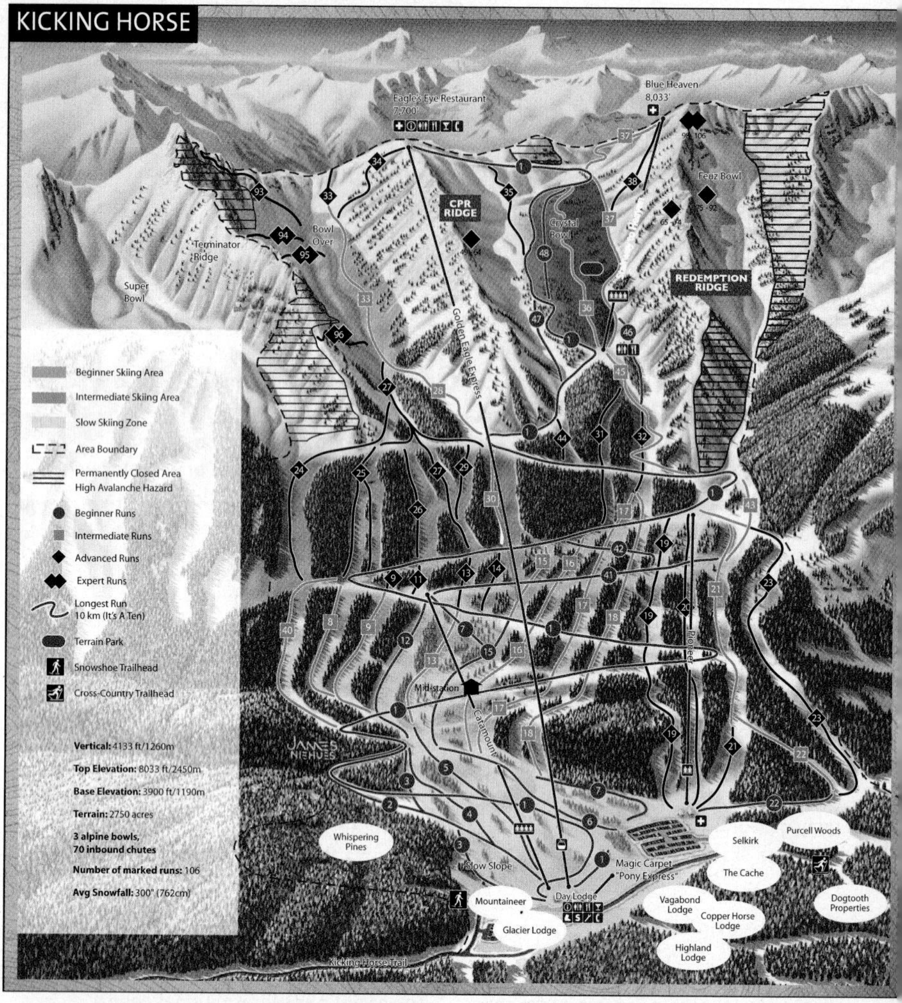
Eagle's Eye Restaurant
7,700'
Blue Heaven
8,033'
Feuz Bowl
CPR RIDGE
Crystal Bowl
REDEMPTION RIDGE
Bowl Over
Terminator Ridge
Super Bowl
Golden Eagle Express
Pioneer
Midstation
Catamount
Whispering Pines
Slow Slope
Magic Carpet
"Pony Express"
Day Lodge
Mountaineer
Glacier Lodge
Selkirk
Purcell Woods
The Cache
Vagabond Lodge
Copper Horse Lodge
Highland Lodge
Dogtooth Properties
Kicking Horse Trail
JAMES NIEHUES
Beginner Skiing Area
Intermediate Skiing Area
Slow Skiing Zone
Area Boundary
Permanently Closed Area
High Avalanche Hazard
Beginner Runs
Intermediate Runs
Advanced Runs
Expert Runs
Longest Run
10 km (It's A Ten)
Terrain Park
Snowshoe Trailhead
Cross-Country Trailhead
Vertical: 4133 ft/1260m
Top Elevation: 8033 ft/2450m
Base Elevation: 3900 ft/1190m
Terrain: 2750 acres
3 alpine bowls,
70 inbound chutes
Number of marked runs: 106
Avg Snowfall: 300" (762cm)

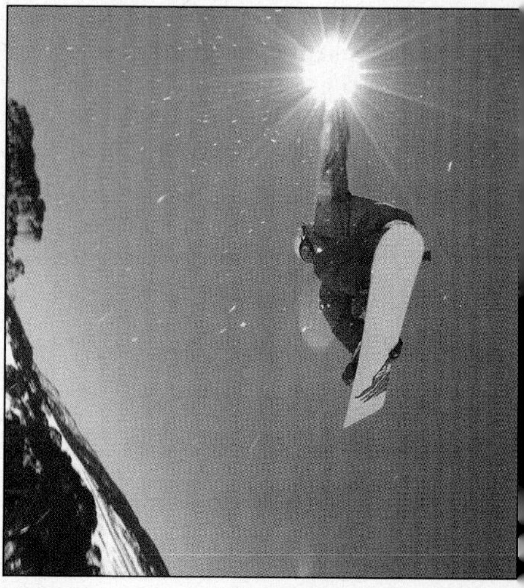

know-how and European sophistication, coupled with substantial Dutch finance. Backbone of KH is a high-speed gondola, which gives a respectable 1260m vertical drop on a ski mountain of near perfect shape. The bottom third of the mountain used to be the old community ski hill of White Tooth above the valley town of Golden. Certainly it needed vision to choose this remote spot.

This is no quaint Victorian mining town awaiting a little gentrification, but a busy blue-collar railway junction awkwardly sprawled across both sides of the tracks and lacking even an ounce of charm.

But, having completed the gondola, the stroke of European-inspired genius was to build, at the top of it, one of the best mountain restaurants in North America.

However, no one would willingly choose to spend a week or a fortnight in a Golden roadside motel. Therefore commensurate accommodation had to be constructed. So far this has taken the form of delightful mountain homes and new guest lodges that ring the base area.

Mountain

Either through lack of finance or foresight, the developers failed to build a halfway station for the Golden Eagle Express gondola. The number of cabins has now been doubled, but queues inevitably develop at peak times. A nearby quad-chair serves the beginner area and an old fixed-grip double gives access to some easy and advanced runs on the lower half of the mountain. But Eagle's Eye on the summit is why you make the effort to travel all this way. Unlike Jackson Hole's now-defunct aerial tram, the gondola does offer an easy route down for those who have either eaten and drunk too much in the restaurant – or lost their nerve when they began to discover the nature of the terrain.

The choice of *entrées* starts right outside the door of the Eagle's Eye restaurant. Wicked black-diamonds fall away from both sides of the ridge to produce some sensational tree- and bowl-skiing. Some of this is steep by any standards, and for anyone lacking in confidence it pays to study the topography before immediately committing yourself to runs that may test your ability to its limits.

Stairway to Heaven, a detachable-quad on the far side of the ski area, takes you up to Blue Heaven, highest point on the mountain. More steep runs follow down through the trees on one side of Redemption Ridge. The other leads down into Feuz Bowl, a glorious powder cache after a fresh fall. Kicking Horse's 2,600-acre ski area is now larger than Breckenridge.

Learn

Kicking Horse Snow School, **t** +1 866 754 5425, has established a reputation as a worthy powder academy. Heli-skiing can be arranged through **Purcell Heli Skiing**, **t** +1 250 344 5410.

Children

No kindergarten facilities. The ski school teaches children from three years.

Lunch

Corks, **t** +1 250 344 7644, in the Copper Horse Lodge serves pasta and pizza. **Glacier Lodge**, **t** +1 250 439 1160, has a sushi bar and café. A mid-mountain yurt – called **Heaven's Door** – serves sushi. The base lodge has a self-service restaurant but the **Eagle's Eye**, **t** +1 250 439 5400, at the gondola summit, has a roaring log fire, floor-to-ceiling windows, and wooden rafters which all add to the atmosphere. Local game is the culinary speciality.

Dine

The Eagle's Eye, **t** +1 250 439 5400, is open on weekend evenings. **Corks**, **t** +1 250 344 7644 and **Sushi Bar & Café** in Glacier Lodge, **t** +1 250 439 1160, are both open for dinner. Golden boasts a number of coffee shops, bars and cafés, such as the smoky **Mad Trapper Pub**, **t** +1 250 344 2330, and the **Dogtooth Café**, **t** +1 250 344 3660. **Cedar House**, **t** +1 250 344 4679, on the edge of town, is strongly recommended. **The Kicking Horse Grill**, **t** +1 250 344 2330, which has a Dutch chef/owner, is highly recommended for its atmospheric log-cabin setting and adventurous cuisine.

Party

The **Mad Trapper Pub** in Golden has been the only establishment to rise to the evening needs of skiers and snowboarders. However, the new **Vagabond Lodge**, near the ski area base, has a bar and games room.

Sleep

Luxury:

The Eagle's Eye restaurant, **t** +1 250 439 5400, *www.kickinghorseresort.com/eagles_eye* has two suites where you can stay after dinner and make 'first tracks' down in the morning.

The ski-in/ski-out chalets, **t** +1 250 439 5424, at the area base are beautifully equipped with large rooms and modern kitchens, outdoor hot tubs and garages.

Copper Horse Lodge, **t** +1 250 344 7644, *ww.copperhorselodge.com*, is a 10-room boutique hotel housing Corks restaurant.

Glacier Lodge, **t** +1 250 439 1160, is just 100ft from the Eagles Express gondola and comprises a health club, sushi bar and ski shop.

Vagabond Lodge, **t** +1 250 344 2622, *www.vagabondlodge.ca*, opened last season with 10 suites and a lounge with fireplace.

Emerald Lake Lodge, **t** +1 403 410 7417, *www.crmr.com/lodgeemerald.php*, about 45km away on the other side of Kicking Horse Pass, is a lakeside mountain retreat built of hand-hewn timber and featuring massive stone fireplaces. Accommodation is in 24 cabin-style buildings.

Budget:

Golden, a 10-minute drive away, has half-a-dozen B&Bs, and a handful of motels and lodges.

Ramada Golden, **t** +1 250 439 1888, *www.ramadagolden.com*, has an indoor swimming pool.

Prestige Inn, **t** +1 250 344 7990, *www.prestigeinn.com*, has simple rooms.

Panorama, BC

Profile

Purpose-built village close to some of Canada's best heli-skiing. The piste skiing best suits intermediates and families

Resort

Panorama is an attractive village built by resort developer Intrawest, with comfortable accommodation and good skiing for all standards. It lies a two-hour drive to the south-west of Banff and is on the edge of the Bugaboos.

Mountain

The mainly easy and intermediate terrain here received a major boost a

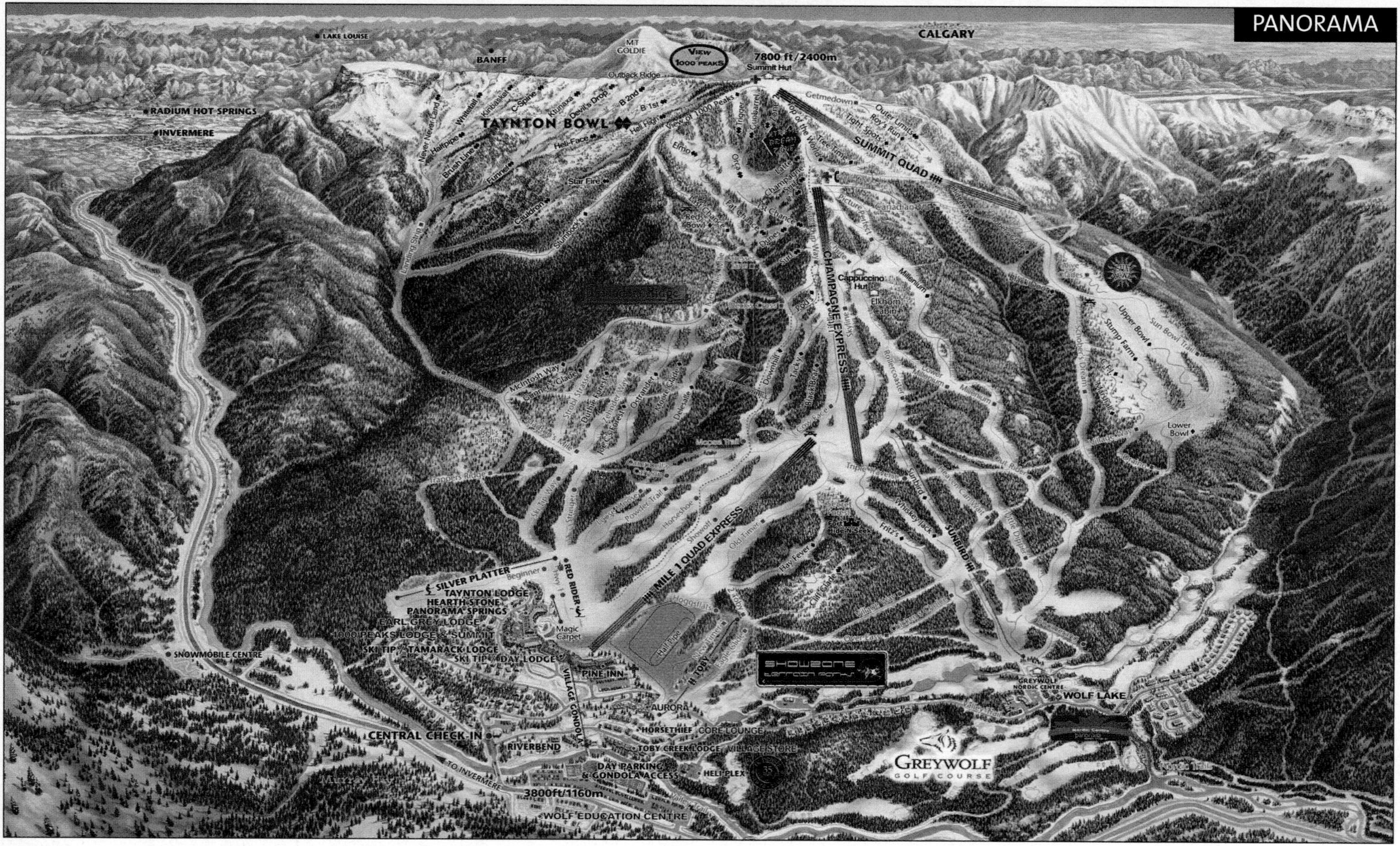
LAKE LOUISE
BANFF
MT GOLDIE
VIEW of 1000 PEAKS
7800 ft/2400m
Summit Hut
CALGARY
Outback Ridge
RADIUM HOT SPRINGS
INVERMERE
TAYNTON BOWL
Never Never Land
Halfpipe
Whitetail
C-Spine
Kinbasket
Kurnoxa
Devil's Drop
B 2nd
B 1st
Hell High
Hell-Face
View of 1000 Peaks
Trigger
Gunbarrel
Brush Line
Funnel
Star Fire
Cauldron
Elmo
Orca
Getmedown
Outer Limits
Roy's Run
Tight Spots
Top of the World
SUMMIT QUAD
Landing Strip
Champagne
Last Chance
Reds Bowl
Picture Perfect
Canadian
Dunes
CHAMPAGNE EXPRESS
Cappuccino Hut
Elkhorn Cabin
Millenium
Skyline
Upper Bowl
Stump Farm
Sun Bowl Trail
Schober's Dream
Lower Bowl
McIntosh Way
Strobl Stress
Dalhie Forest
Ostrander
Kokanee Glade
Daleslie
Downhill
Tacky
Black Bear
Rollercoaster
Bell's Landing
Jacks Forest
Triple Trees
Sunbird
Whiskey Jack
Fritz's
Little Dipper
SUNBIRD
Stringer
Powder Trail
Horseshoe
Showoff
Old Timer
Hay Fever
Cliff Glade
MILE 1 QUAD EXPRESS
SILVER PLATTER
Beginner
RED RIDER
Magic Carpet
TAYNTON LODGE
HEARTHSTONE
PANORAMA SPRINGS
EARL GREY LODGE
1000 PEAKS LODGE & SUMMIT
SKI TIP
TAMARACK LODGE
SKI TIP
DAY LODGE
Half Pipe
TOBY
SNOWMOBILE CENTRE
PINE INN
VILLAGE GONDOLA
AURORA
HORSETHIEF
CORE LOUNGE
TOBY CREEK LODGE
VILLAGE STORE
CENTRAL CHECK-IN
RIVERBEND
DAY PARKING & GONDOLA ACCESS
HELIPLEX
TO INVERMERE
3800ft/1160m
WOLF EDUCATION CENTRE
GREYWOLF NORDIC CENTRE
WOLF LAKE
GREYWOLF GOLF COURSE

***BEST FOR**
Intermediates, families, heli-skiing

ESSENTIALS
Altitude: 3,800ft (1158m)–7,800ft (2360m)
Further information: t +1 250 342 6941, *www.panoramaresort.com*
Lifts in area: 8 (1 cableway, 5 chairs, 2 drags) serving 2,847 acres of terrain
Lift pass: adult CDN$299, teen 13–18yrs CDN$239, child 7–12yrs CDN$139, all for 6 days
Access: Calgary airport 4hrs

few years ago when the old T-bars on the front face were replaced by three quad-chairs. The enjoyable trails cut through the trees offer few challenges but are ideal for anyone wanting the Canadian ski experience in a thoroughly agreeable environment. Taynton Bowl, off the backside with 1,000 acres of chutes, gullies and difficult tree-skiing, is a worthy off-piste playground for more advanced skiers.

The resort is included in the Canadian Rockies Super Pass covering eight other resorts, including Banff-Lake Louise, Fernie, Nakiska and Kimberley.

Learn

The School of Skiing and Snowboarding, **t** +1 250 342 6941, organizes group and private lessons.

Children

Wee Wascals, **t** +1 250 341 3041, provides daycare for children from 18 months. **Snowbirds ski kindergarten**, **t** +1 250 342 6941, accepts children from three years.

Lunch

The Summit Hut, **t** +1 250 342 0217, has a limited menu but great views. **Scott Nordic Centre**, **t** +1 250 342 6941 x3840, has a restaurant and is at the base of Sunbird chair.

Dine

Wildfire Grill, **t** +1 250 342 6941, is relaxed and reasonably priced, serving burgers, salads and ribs. **Ferrari's on Toby Creek**, **t** +1 250 341 3056, has affordable family dining. **Earl Grey Lodge**, **t** +1 250 341 3641, specializes in French and Italian dishes. You can also eat at the **Heli-Plex restaurant**, **t** +1 250 342 6941, where the local heli-skiing is based.

Party

This is not a great resort for partying. The **Crazy Horse Saloon** and **Jackpine Pub** are the main rendezvous points. The **Glacier Nightclub** is for music and dancing. You can relax at the **Panorama Springs** outdoor waterpark, or take the shuttle bus to the valley town of Invermere to bathe in the radium hot springs.

Sleep

Luxury:

For all accommodation contact Resort Reservations, **t** +1 250 342 6941.

Riverbend Townhomes on Toby Creek have easy access to the Village gondola.

Wolf Lake Townhomes are in a ski-in/ski-out position by the Sunbird chair-lift.

Gold Premium Lodging is in condos in the Upper Village.

Earl Grey Lodge, **t** +1 250 341 3641, *www.earlgreylodge.com*, is a privately-owned boutique hotel situated 200m from the main mountain access lift.

Moderate/budget:

Silver Lodging is at Creekside.

Bronze Lodging is at the Pine Inn at the base of the Mile 1 chair.

Red Resort, BC

***BEST FOR**
Advanced skiers and riders, retro-chic

ESSENTIALS
Altitude: 3,888ft (11296m)–6,800ft (2266m)
Further information: t +1 800 663 0105, *www.redresort.com*
Lifts in area: 5 (4 chairs, 1 drag) serving 1,585 acres of terrain
Lift pass: adult CDN$308, child 7–12yrs CDN$154, both for 6 out of 7 days
Access: Castlegar airport 30mins, Spokane airport in Washington State 2½hrs

Profile

Rough and tough skiing for accomplished intermediates to advanced skiers and boarders. Accommodation choice lies between small ski base area and historic valley town

Resort

Red is under potentially dynamic new ownership and it has dropped the 'Mountain' from its name. For a while back in 2005 it looked as if this cult resort in BC, with a rugged reputation for some of the steepest terrain in Canada, was going to go out of business. However, to the delight of the people of the nearby distressed Victorian mining town of Rossland, Red was saved in the nick of time by a businessman from San Diego in California.

What he is going to do with it still remains to be seen, but he has begun with a major property development around the base area. Retro-chic is what Red has traded upon for a generation – a last frontier of Canadian machismo where slow lifts, mighty moguls and big drop-offs were the name of the game. But commercial reality is that retro-chic makes money for no one.

Mountain

Red and adjoining Granite Mountains can be skied 360 degrees on all faces, although they are served by only six lifts. Together they offer 83 trails of which a high 45 per cent are graded at least black-diamond. The vertical drop is only 887m but the longest run – Long Squaw – is a respectable 7km. The off-piste opportunities down through the trees are endless and the overall quality of the skiing is nothing short of phenomenal. Red's terrain park on the T-bar slope has 15 rails, funboxes and table-tops.

Learn

Red Snowsports School, **t** +1 800 663 0105, offers lessons and guiding.

Children

Club Red Kindercare, **t** +1 800 663 0105, accepts children from 18 months, and combines skiing with childcare for three- to six-year-olds.

Lunch

Paradise Lodge has been revamped and provides simple but good food. **Rafters Lounge** at the base lodge is recommended. For information contact, **t** +1 800 663 0105.

Dine

Mountain Gypsy Café, **t** +1 250 362 3342, in Rossland has good fusion cuisine.

Party

The laid-back town of Rossland has little more than bars with pool and air-hockey tables. The **Powder Keg Pub** in the Prestige Mountain Resort is the town's hotspot.

Sleep

Moderate/Budget:

Prestige Mountain Resort-Rossland (formerly the Uplander), **t** +1 250 362 7375, has simple rooms.

Black Bear B&B, t +1 250 362 3398, *www.blackbearinn.ca*, is five minutes' drive from Red, was built in 1898 and has an outdoor hot tub.

The Ram's Head Inn, t +1 250 362 9577, *www.ramshead.bc.ca*, a pleasant B&B, is almost ski-in/ski-out, with communal breakfast/dining and a hot tub.

Silver Star, BC

Profile

Intriguing neo-Victorian village with convenient skiing for intermediates as well as advanced skiers and riders. Recommended ski school

Resort

Silver Star is one of a trio of resorts in the heart of the the scenic wine-growing country of BC that has come to prominence over the past few years. It's not big, but combined with Big White, its Australian-owned stable mate, this area makes for a great holiday.

At first sight, the nine-lift resort near Vernon suggests that it is a restored *fin de siècle* mining town. In fact the 'old' vividly painted town houses and streets lit with soft sodium lamps are a complete sham. For a purpose-built resort it has considerable panache, but it is not a place for non-skiers.

Mountain

The ski area, our favourite in the Okanagan Valley, is underrated. The front face comprises the usual North American menu of gladed easy and intermediate runs. However, the backside is much more demanding. Double-diamond runs such as vertiginous Freefall and the infamous Cowabunga are of sufficiently steep pitch to make even the most jaded powderhound think edge control. The terrain park is one of the most highly rated in BC.

The new Silver Woods area, served by a high-speed detachable quad, opens up 360 acres of mainly intermediate terrain with 10 runs and five areas of tree-skiing. A new quad-chair built in summer 2006 will improve service to the steep terrain to the skier's right of the Summit Chair.

The terrain park is one of the most highly rated in BC and it features a rail

* BEST FOR

Backwater village ambience, intermediate and advanced skiing, terrain park

ESSENTIALS

Altitude: 3,780ft (1155m)–6,280ft (1915m)
Further information: **t** +1 250 542 0224, *www.skisilverstar.com*
Lifts in area: 9 (5 chairs, 4 drags) serving 2,725 acres of terrain
Lift pass: adult CDN$349, youth 13–18yrs CDN$295, child 6–12yrs CDN$157, all for 6 out of 7 days
Access: Kelowna airport 55mins

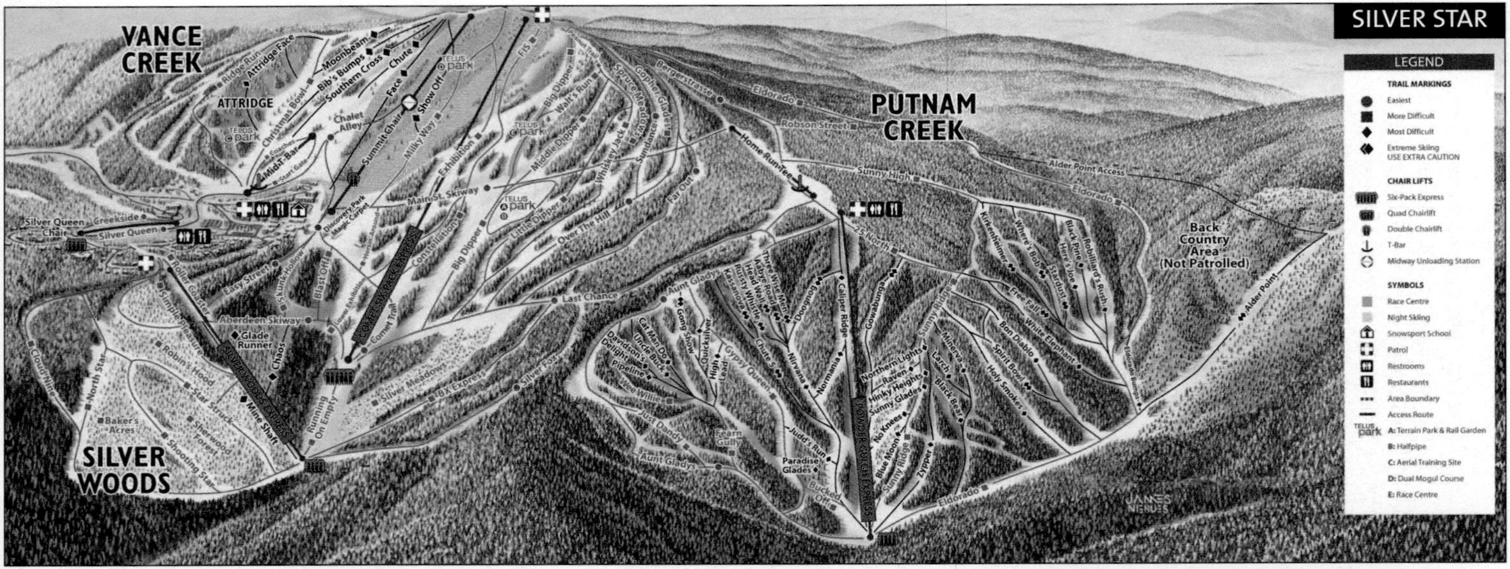
SILVER STAR
LEGEND
TRAIL MARKINGS
Easiest
More Difficult
Most Difficult
Extreme Skiing USE EXTRA CAUTION
CHAIR LIFTS
Six-Pack Express
Quad Chairlift
Double Chairlift
T-Bar
Midway Unloading Station
SYMBOLS
Race Centre
Night Skiing
Snowsport School
Patrol
Restrooms
Restaurants
Area Boundary
Access Route
TELUS park A: Terrain Park & Rail Garden
B: Halfpipe
C: Aerial Training Site
D: Dual Mogul Course
E: Race Centre
VANCE CREEK
PUTNAM CREEK
SILVER WOODS
ATTRIDGE
Back Country Area (Not Patrolled)
Ridge Run
Attridge Face
Moonbeam
Bib's Bumps
Southern Cross
Chute
Face
Show Off
Christmas Bowl
Chalet Alley
Summit Chair
Milky Way
Mid T-Bar
Silver Queen Chair
Greekside
Silver Queen
Roller Coaster
Easy Street
Skunk Hollow
Blast Off
Discovery Park Magic Carpet
Main St. Skiway
Exhibition
FIS
Big Dipper
Walt's Run
Middle Dipper
Little Dipper
Spruce Meadows
Gopher Glades
Whiskey Jack
Sundance
Over The Hill
Far Out
Bergerstrasse
Eldorado
Robson Street
Home Run
Sunny High
Alder Point Access
Constellation
Comet Trail
Last Chance
Aberdeen Skiway
Glade Runner
Chaos
Simple Pleasure
Robin's Hood
Star Struck
Sherwood Forest
Shooting Star
Mine Shaft
Running On Empty
Silver Meadows
BX Express
Silver Fox
North Star
Cloud Nine
Baker's Acres
Aunt Gladys
Gong Show
Cat Man Doo
Uncle Buck
Davidson's Delight
Pipeline
Wee Willie
Just Dandy
Quicksilver
High Lead
Gypsy Queen
Fearn Gully
Three Wise Men
Aabye Road
Head Wall
Russty Whistle
Kassanova
Chute 5
Nirvana
Doognog
Normania
Caliper Ridge
Judd's Run
Paradise Glades
Bucked Off
Powder Gulch Express
Gowabunga
Northern Lights
Raven
Hinky Heights
Sunny Glades
No Knees
Blue Moon
Sunny Ridge
Zypper
Black Bear
Larch
Minerva
Holy Smokes
Spirit Bowl
Bon Diablo
White Elephant
Free Fall
Kirkenheimer
Where's Bob
Stardust
Here's Joe
Black Pine
Robilliard's Rush
Eldorado Bumps
Alder Point
Comet Six-Pack Express
Silver Woods Express

BURTON

garden, a half-pipe, an aerial training site, a race centre and a dual mogul race course.

Learn

Silver Star Snowsport School, **t** +1 250 558 6065, has a strong reputation for teaching cutting-edge ski and snowboard technique.

Children

Star Kids Center, **t** +1 250 558 6065, accepts little ones from newborn to six years old, and skiers and riders from four years.

Lunch

Paradise Camp, **t** +1 250 558 6087, near the top of the Powder Gulch Express, offers the only on-mountain lunch. **Longjohn's Pub**, **t** +1 250 549 2992, is back in the village.

Dine

The Italian Garden Restaurant, **t** +1 250 558 1448, has pizzas and pasta, **Clementine's**, **t** +1 250 545 3208, has live piano at weekends, and the **Silver Lode Restaurant**, **t** +1 250 549 5105, serves international cuisine. The Craigellachie Room at **Putnam Station Inn**, **t** +1 250 542 2459, is warmly recommended.

Party

Après-ski here is what you make it. **Beyond Wrapture Mind and Body Care Day Spa** is one place in which to relax, while the tubing park is another. The action then shifts rather slowly to a pre-dinner drink in the **Wine Cellar** below Putnam Station followed by the pool table in the **Saloon**.

Sleep

Luxury:

Victorian Vacation Homes range from simple studios to five-bedroom town houses with private hot tubs, **t** +1 250 542 0224.

Moderate:

Bookings for all, **t** +1 250 558 6083.

Silver Star Club Resort is a complex of three buildings in a ski-in/ski-out position.

Creekside Condos are beside the tubing park and suitable for families.

Putnam Station is a colourful wooden building with rustic charm.

Silver Lode Inn is a European-style property with simple rooms in a good location.

Sun Peaks, BC

Profile

An up-market resort for all standards with comfortable accommodation, good restaurants and nightlife, and doorstep skiing for all standards. Not the place for non-skiers

Resort

Sun Peaks has come a long way in the 14 years since a Japanese company bought Mount Tod outside the BC mining town of Kamloops. Lying nearly four hours by road from Vancouver, it seemed an unlikely location for an international resort.

But Nancy Greene, the *grande dame* of Canadian skiing who won Olympic gold in Grenoble, was summoned to give her

***BEST FOR**

Comfort-seekers, all levels of skier and rider, cat-skiing

ESSENTIALS

Altitude: 3,933ft (1199m)–6,824ft (2080m)
Further information: t +1 250 578 7222, *www.sunpeaksresort.com*
Lifts in area: 10 (6 chairs, 4 drags) serving 3,678 acres of terrain
Lift pass: adult CDN$342, child 6–12yrs CDN$180, both for 6 days
Access Kamloops airport 20mins

opinion on the terrain. 'It took me rather less than 30 minutes to say "yes",' she said. Nancy set about promoting newly named Sun Peaks while owners Nippon Cable Company stomped up CDN$225 million. The result is a delightful three-mountain ski area set around a well-designed purpose-built village with world-class accommodation. This season sees a further CDN$4 million spent on a new lift and new terrain.

Mountain

The skiing is suited to strong intermediates who will enjoy the mainly short but searching runs on Sundance and on Mount Tod, which has a new quad-chair this season. Advanced skiers will find plenty of challenging pistes to keep them busy. But the real excitement is the well-organized cat-skiing on the upper reaches of Mount Tod.

Novices and wobbly second-weekers will find their ski legs on Mount Morrisey, where the gentlest of scenic trails have been cut through the trees. Sun Peaks has a terrain park, which is being expanded for this season, and a 100m half-pipe.

Learn

Sun Peaks Snowsports School, t +1 250 578 5505, is for group and private lessons.

Children

Sundance Playschool, t +1 250 578 5433, cares for babies from 18 months. **Sun Tots** gives private ski lessons from three years, and **Sun Kids Adventure Club**, both **t** +1 250 578 5505, accepts children from six years for skiing and eight years for snowboarding. The **Kids Ranch**, an animated theme park, opens this season at the top of the Village Platter.

Lunch

Mountain eating is limited to the grim **Sunburst Self-service, t** +1 250 578 7222, at the top of the Sunburst Express.

Dine

Sun Peaks Village has an Asian restaurant called **Toro, t** +1 250 578 7870. **The Val, t** +1 250 578 8111, in Sun Peaks Lodge and **Macker's Bistro & Bar, t** +1 250 578 7454, in Nancy Green's Cahilty Lodge, are both recommended. **Powderhounds Restaurant, t** +1 250 578 8588, in the Fireside Lodge, offers a European/ Canadian menu.

Party

Macdaddy's, in the Delta Sun Peak Resort, is the liveliest nightspot.

Sleep

Luxury:

Delta Sun Peaks Resort, t +1 250 578 6000, *www.deltasunpeaks.bcresorts.com*, is one of the country's finest ski hotels.

Moderate:

Nancy Greene's **Cahilty Lodge, t** +1 250 578 7454, *www.cahiltylodge.com*, is ski-in ski-out.

Fireside Lodge, t +1 270 578 8588, *www.woodlandsatsunpeaks.com/Lodges*

Fireside.html, condos have fully equipped kitchens.

Hearthstone Lodge, **t** +1 250 578 8588, *www.hearthstonelodgeatsunpeaks.com*, is a charming boutique hotel.

The Ice Palace Hotel, **t** +1 604 328 2663, *www.icepalacehotel.com*, featuring themed ice rooms, ice bar, ice chapel and ice sculptures, is new for this season.

Tremblant, Québec

Profile

State-of-the-art lift system, beautifully groomed slopes, extensive snowmaking, attractive purpose-built village, and *cuisine québecoise*. Bitterly cold mid-winter temperatures unfortunately might deter some people

Resort

Tremblant has achieved phenomenal success. A decade has slipped by since developer Intrawest began pumping in tens of millions of dollars in one of its first lucrative explorations of the relationships between real estate, ski areas and golf courses. Work started in summer 2006 on the latest stage – a whole new village on the Versant Soleil side of the mountain.

What's surprising is that the company behind Whistler in BC and Arc 1950 in France chose such a modest mountain in chilly Québec rather than the Rockies. What's even more surprising is that Tremblant now ranks close to Whistler as the most popular destination in Canada for European skiers. However, an 18-day strike last season over Christmas and New Year by 1,500 Intrawest employees no doubt damaged its position in the league table.

Tremblant lies in the Laurentian Mountains, 150km northwest of Montréal. Intrawest retained the original village of Vieux-Tremblant while creating a new one of steeply terraced streets with painted wooden buildings modelled on the old quarter of Québec City. A visit here is a chance to appreciate *québecois* culture and cuisine in contrived but charming surroundings. The ambience is warm, but the same cannot be said about the air temperature in mid-winter. European February half-term is the most popular time to visit, but for families with young children the temperature can be too low for enjoyable skiing.

*BEST FOR

Ski convenience, groomed slopes, comfort-seekers

ESSENTIALS

Altitude: 870ft (265m)–3,001ft (915m)
Further information: **t** +1 819 681 2000, *www.tremblant.ca*
Lifts in area: 9 (1 cableway, 8 chairs) serving 628 acres of terrain
Lift pass: adult CDN$287, youth CDN$237, children 6–12yrs CDN$178, all for 6 days
Access: Montréal airport 1½hrs

Mountain

The nine-lift ski area stretches in four sectors across both faces of the mountain. The main Equilibre beginner area lies just above the village, and most of the easy intermediate terrain is also on the South Side. The heated gondola ride up from the village to the Grand Manitou temporarily shelters you from the reality of skiing in a cold climate. But low temperatures do not necessarily equate with high snowfall. To compensate for nature's not infrequent failure, Tremblant has Canada's largest artificial snowmaking system.

VERSANT NORD
NORTH SIDE
GRAND MANITOU
VERSANT EDGE / THE EDGE
BOOMERANG
BON VIVANT
PARC À NEIGE
SNOWPARK
SHORTCUT
EDGE
LOWELL THOMAS
BUZZ
DUNCAN EXPRESS
EXPO EXPRESS
TREMBLANT

VERSANT SUD
SOUTH SIDE
GRAND MANITOU
VERSANT EDGE / THE EDGE
VERSANT SOLEIL / SOLEIL SIDE
BON VIVANT
VERTIGE
STANDARD
BELVÉDÈRE
PARC À NEIGE
SNOWPARK
DERNIER CRI
PROMENADE
ROY SCOTT
CASCADES
LE SOLEIL
PLACE
ST-BERNARD
PORTE DU SOLEIL
ÉQUILIBRE

The North Side receives little sunshine in winter – a fact you may well feel, or rather not feel, in your fingers – and consequently retains good cover throughout the winter. It offers considerably more scope for strong intermediates and advanced skiers and riders. A couple of trails have short sharp pitches of 42 degrees and these call for a high level of technique in the often icy conditions.

The Edge, served by its own quad-chair, is an area set aside for accomplished skiers and riders. Haute-Tension, an expert run that follows the fall line beneath the lift, is guaranteed to raise blood pressure.

The main terrain park, Nintendo Park, on the North Side, has a superpipe, quarter-pipe and a variety of obstacles. Two further parks on the South Side are for experts and beginners. The nearby intermediate runs of Réaction and Sensation wind down through the frozen spruces and provide a dramatic introduction to tree-skiing.

Learn

The Tremblant Snow School, **t** +1 819 681 5666, has a first-rate reputation but new visitors to this part of Canada may be surprised to discover that not all instructors are necessarily fluent English speakers.

Children

Kidz Club, **t** +1 819 681 5666, at the base of the slopes, provides daycare for non-skiing children from 12 months, and runs ski programmes from three years of age.

Lunch

Mountain eating includes a wide range of cafeteria-style places, including **Le Grand Manitou**, **t** +1 819 681 3000, at the summit. **Le Refuge du Trappeur**, **t** +1 450 533 1091, on the Versant Soleil is a log cabin that serves soups and drinks by the fireplace.

Dine

The cost of eating out in Tremblant is high at the eclectic choice of restaurants from pizzas and *cuisine québecoise* to sushi. **Aux Truffes**, **t** +1 819 681 4544, is for truffles, foie gras and game, and **La Forge** has steaks and grills. **La Grappe à Vin**, **t** +1 819 681 4727, is an intimate eatery serving creative French cuisine with an extensive wine list. **Coco-Pazzo**, **t** +1 819 681 4774, offers Italian and vegetarian food, and **Crêperie Catherine**, **t** +1 819 681 4888, specializes in Breton crêpes. **Restaurant U**, **t** +1 819 681 4141, combines sushi with international creations. **Mexicali Rosa's**, **t** +1 819 681 2439, is Californian-Mexican. **Loup-Garou** in the Fairmont Tremblant, **t** +1 819 681 7685, offers 'daring Québec cuisine'.

Party

Bar Café d'Époque is a main resort meeting place, open from mid-afternoon until 3am with a DJ and dancing. **Octobar** has rock, and **Le P'tit Caribou** in Vieux-Tremblant offers a more intimate atmosphere.

Microbrasserie La Diable brews its own beer and is a popular bar before dinner. The pool at **La Source Aquaclub** provides good family entertainment. **Spa Le Scandinave** is a relaxing wellness centre a few kilometres out of town. **Hammam Vaporium** and **Slope-Side Spa** are more convenient. Other activities nearby include dog-sledding, sleigh rides, ice-climbing, tubing, snowmobiling and moonlit snowshoe hikes.

Sleep

All accommodation, unless otherwise stated, can be booked through central reservations, **t** +1 819 681 2000.

Luxury/moderate:

Fairmont Château Mont Tremblant, **t** +1 819 681 7000, on the edge of the piste, with a large spa and outdoor pool, is still the premier hotel address.

Le Westin Resort & Spa, **t** +1 819 681 8000, is a comfortable hotel with a choice of restaurants.

Hilton Homewood Suites are in the Town Square, just a short walk from the lifts.

Le Lodge de la Montagne is a ski-in/ski-out condo hotel next to La Source Aquaclub.

Le Tour des Voyageurs, at the entrance to the village, has both hotel rooms and condos. A people-mover lift links it to the ski area.

Outside Tremblant Village:

Club Tremblant, **t** +1 819 425 8781, is 10 minutes' drive away on the shore of Lake Tremblant, with fine views over the lake and to the ski slopes.

Le Grand Lodge, **t** +1 819 425 2734, also 10 minutes away, is a smart log-cabin-style hotel close to the Gray Rocks ski area.

Whistler, BC

🏆 BEST RESORT RESTAURANT 2007: Elements

Profile

Still the top resort in North America. Twin mountains with an enormous vertical act as showcases for every conceivable type of terrain from glacier to glade and from steep to deep. Its Pacific Rim position makes it a melting pot of different nationalities. Vibrant atmosphere, excellent accommodation and restaurants as well as a buzzing nightlife

*BEST FOR

Sophisto-cats, all levels of skier and rider, off-piste, foodies

ESSENTIALS

Altitude: 2,140ft (652m)–7,494ft (2284m)

Further information: **t** +1 604 664 5625, *www.whistlerblackcomb.com*, *www.tourismwhistler.com*

Lifts in area: 34 (3 cableways, 19 chairs, 12 drags) serving 8,071 acres of terrain

Lift pass: adult CDN$426, youth 13–18yrs CDN$360, child 7–12yrs CDN$216, all for 6 days

Access: Vancouver airport 2hrs

Resort

After the worst season for snow in its history (2004–5), Whistler struck back last winter with one of its best. Low-pressure systems, backing up one behind the other like buses in the rush hour, crept in from the Pacific throughout the season to produce record amounts of snow.

The weather in Whistler is always the prime subject of conversation. Normally the village, which lies at an altitude of only 652m – but on the same latitude as Labrador – attracts abundant winter precipitation. Much of this falls as rain in the resort and as powder on the top half of the mountain. The number of blue-sky days is significantly lower than in Colorado, but the snow quality is usually excellent. Mid-winter temperatures can be chilly, although not as low as in Banff–Lake Louise and the central Rockies. Whistler suits all standards of skier and rider. Glacier skiing continues on Blackcomb through most of the summer.

Whistler is the setting for the 2010 Winter Olympics and it is right that what is still indisputably Number One in North

WHISTLER MOUNTAIN
LITTLE WHISTLER PEAK
BLACKCOMB PEAK
PERMANENTLY CLOSED AREA
FLUTE BOWL
GLACIER BOWL
WHISTLER BOWL
WEST BOWL
BAGEL BOWL
LAKESIDE BOWL
JERSEY CREAM BOWL
GARIBALDI PROVINCIAL PARK
BLACKCOMB GLACIER PROVINCIAL PARK
OVERLORD GLACIER
PICCOLO
GARIBALDI
DECKER
SPEARHEAD
KIDS
TERRAIN PARKS
EASIEST
BASE II
VILLAGE
BLACKCOMB
CREEKSIDE

SKI INDEPENDENCE
THE UK'S NO.1 SKI SPECIALIST
USA · CANADA · FRANCE · SWITZERLAND
EXCLUSIVE EARLY BOOKING OFFERS
· FREE NIGHTS ·
· FREE SKIING & KIDS SKI FREE ·
IN SELECTED RESORTS
0845 310 3030 www.ski-i.com
AITO
ABTA V3690

Chalet-hotel Alta Vista

Alta Vista lounge

America has been given the honour of hosting the Games. Whistler and Blackcomb mountains have the longest vertical drop on the continent, awesome terrain, and a cosmopolitan atmosphere. You can stay and eat here better than in almost any other resort in either Canada or the USA.

Mountain

Whistler and Blackcomb provide equally enjoyable intermediate and advanced skiing on their gladed lower slopes, but the top halves of both offer contrastingly different experiences. While Whistler is given over to a succession of glorious powder bowls, Blackcomb has steep couloirs and long glacial descents. Both offer thrilling top-to-bottom skiing on long cruising trails, and part of the enjoyment of a stay here is deciding which to choose each morning. Both are reached from adjoining lifts in Whistler Village. Plans to provide a mid-mountain gondola link are on the drawing board but show no signs off progressing to the pylon stage.

Whistler Village gondola provides the main two-stage access to mid-mountain Roundhouse Lodge. At peak times wise skiers take the much underused Fitzsimmons Express quad-chair beside it. This links to a second quad that provides a trouble-free backdoor into the system.

Creekside, down Highway 99 from Whistler, is an alternative accommodation base with car parks designed to attract the large numbers of day visitors from Vancouver and deter them from clogging up Whistler itself. Access from here to the Roundhouse and top lifts is by the Creekside gondola, followed by the Big Red Express quad. Peak to Creek, a 7km intermediate run with a vertical drop of 1650m on the west side of Whistler Mountain, opened last season.

Blackcomb Mountain is accessed by the Excalibur gondola from Whistler Village or by the Wizard Express chair from Upper Village, formerly called Blackcomb Village. You can ski from Blackcomb mountain to Whistler Village but not vice versa. Whistler is spending CDN$22 million on mountain improvements this winter. Innovations include a new detachable-quad from the bottom of Flute Bowl to the top of Piccolo, which will provide access to a further 1,000 acres of intermediate and expert terrain.

Blackcomb has nursery slopes served by a chair-lift just above the village. Whistler has dedicated higher beginner terrain reached by the first stage of the Village gondola.

Whistler is considered to be among the top snowboarding resorts in North America, with sophisticated terrain parks on both mountains, and a Nintendo superpipe and snowcross track on Blackcomb. The Chipmunk Park on Whistler is for expert riders and skiers. Entry requires a separate pass and a helmet is compulsory.

Numerous heli-ski companies operate in and around Whistler, including **Blackcomb Helicopters**, **t** +1 604 938 1700, **Coast Range Heliskiing**, **t** +1 604 894 1144, **Helico Presto**, **t** +1 604 938 2927, **Spearhead Mountain Guides**, **t** +1 604 932 8802, **TLH Heliskiing**, **t** +1 250 558 5379, **Whistler Alpine Guides Bureau**, **t** +1 604 932 4040, and **Whistler Heli-skiing**, **t** +1 604 932 4105.

Learn

Whistler Blackcomb Ski and Snowboard School, **t** +1 604 932 3434, is an established academy for cutting-edge ski and riding instruction. Make use of the free daily tours of the piste hosted by volunteers who include some of Canada's greatest skiers. **Extremely Canadian**, **t** +1 604 932 4105, provides guiding and powder instruction, while **Lauralee Bowie Ski**

Adventures, **t** +1 604 689 7444, offers tuition with video.

Children

Whistler Kids, **t** +1 604 932 3434, looks after children from three months with all-day care and lessons for appropriate ages. It also runs special classes for teenagers. Evening babysitting in your hotel or condo can be arranged through **The Nanny Network**, **t** +1 604 938 2823.

Lunch

A lack of good mountain restaurants is Whistler's only true failing.

On Whistler Mountain the **Roundhouse Lodge**, **t** +1 604 932 3434, offers hamburgers, Asian stir-fry, and pasta in cavernous and compellingly unpleasant self-service surroundings. **Steeps**, **t** +1 604 932 3434, in the same building, has waiter-service West Coast cuisine. **Garibaldi Lift Company**, **t** +1 604 905 2220, has good hamburgers and a warm atmosphere. **Ravens Nest**, **t** +1 604 905 2176, at the top of Creekside gondola, offers soups and stews. **Dusty's**, **t** +1 604 905 2171, at Creekside base, has barbecued burgers and plenty of ambience.

On Blackcomb, **Christine's Restaurant**, **t** +1 604 938 7437, in Rendezvous Lodge, is the resort's best shot at a waiter-service mountain restaurant with international cuisine – but standards of cuisine and service seem to yo-yo. **The River Rock Grill**, **t** +1 604 938 7417, upstairs at the Glacier Creek Lodge, is a good self-service. **Monks Grill**, **t** +1 604 932 9677, in the Upper Village, is highly recommended.

Dine

In Whistler Village, **Bearfoot Bistro**, **t** +1 604 932 3433, specializes in French and other European cuisine. **Il Caminetto di Umberto**, **t** +1 604 932 4442, and **Trattoria di Umberto**, **t** +1 604 932 5858, are Italian. **Araxi**, **t** +1 604 932 4540, and **Apres**, **t** +1 604 935 0200, have seafood and Pacific Rim cuisine. **Zueski's Taverna**, **t** +1 604 932 6009, is good-value Greek. **Teppan Village**, **t** +1 604 932 2223, is a Japanese steakhouse. **Elements Urban Tapas Parlour** in Summit Lodge, **t** +1 604 932 2778, serves 'refreshingly innovative cuisine in contemporary surroundings'.

In Upper Village, try **La Rua**, **t** +1 604 932 5011, for West Coast cuisine or **Thai One On**, **t** +1 604 932 4822, for Thai. In Village North **Sushi-Ya**, **t** +1 604 905 0155, has great sushi. **Ciao-Thyme Bistro**, **t** +1 604 932 9795, is warmly praised by reporters: 'Looks like a bikers' café but is anything but.'

In Whistler Creek, **The Rim Rock Cafe**, **t** +1 604 932 5565, has seafood and fine European dishes. **Zen Whistler**, **t** +1 604 932 3667, is Japanese.

Party

Après-ski begins noisily at the **Dubh Linn Gate** Irish pub, and **Longhorn**, at the base of the Excalibur and Whistler Village gondolas. **Garibaldi Lift Co** in Whistler and **Merlin's** at Blackcomb base have live bands. The shopping – which continues until 10pm – is a core part of the evening entertainment. Zip-wiring is an alternative sport in Whistler and an exhilarating way to spend the afternoon.

Later on, the action switches to **Garfinkel's**, the **Savage Beagle**, **Tommy Africa's** and **Maxx Fish**. **Moe Joe's** is smaller and more intimate. **Buffalo Bill's** attracts the over-30s. **Citta's Bar** in the Village Square is a friendly hang-out for a quiet drink. The **Mallard Bar** in the Château Whistler is more sophisticated and expensive.

Sleep

Luxury:

Fairmont Château Whistler, **t** +1 604 938 8000, *www.fairmont.com/whistler*, is one of the world's great ski hotels, right on the piste at Blackcomb base, with a good restaurant, heated outdoor pools and the outstanding Vida spa.

The Four Seasons Resort, **t** +1 604 935 3400, *www.fourseasons.com/whistler*, is slightly less well positioned, but a true contender for Whistler's most luxurious hotel.

The Westin Resort & Spa, **t** +1 604 905 5000, *www.westinwhistler.com*, at Whistler Mountain base, has a shopping mall and is conveniently located.

Adara Hotel, **t** +1 604 905 4009, *www.adarahotel.com*, is a new boutique hotel with contemporary design.

Whistler Chalets, **t** +1 604 905 5287, *www.whistlerchalets.com*, offers a portfolio of luxury self-catering homes.

Moderate:

Delta Whistler Village Suites, **t** +1 604 905 3987, *www.deltahotels.com*, has a rustic mountain atmosphere.

Pan Pacific Mountainside, **t** +1 604 905 2999, *www.panpacificwhistler.com*, and **Pan Pacific Village Centre**, **t** +1 604 966 5500, both offer apartments with fireplaces and floor-to-ceiling windows.

Timberline Lodge, **t** +1 604 932 5211, *www.whistler-timberline.com*, is comfortable and well situated.

Crystal Lodge, **t** +1 604 932 2221, *www.crystal-lodge.com*, is conveniently located.

Listel Hotel Whistler, **t** +1 604 932 1133, *www.listelhotel.com*, has a heated outdoor pool and is a short walk from the shops.

Summit Lodge, **t** +1 604 932 2778, *www.summitlodge.com*, in the heart of Whistler Village North, has a spa and free in-room yoga.

Budget:

Alpine Springs B&B, **t** +1 604 905 2747, *www.bc-bed-and-breakfast.com*, is in a peaceful setting.

Blue Spruce Lodge B&B, **t** +1 604 932 3508, *www.bluesprucelodgewhistler.com*, sleeps 8–10 people and is good value.

04

The Top Resorts: Eastern Europe

Bansko, Bulgaria

***BEST FOR**

Modern lift system, beginners and intermediates, value

ESSENTIALS

Altitude: 936m (3,079ft)–2560m (8,399ft)
Further information: t +359 (0)7443 8060, *www.banskoski.com*
Lifts in area: 11 (1 cableway, 7 chairs, 3 drags) serving 65km of piste
Lift pass: adult €144, child up to 12yrs €79, both for 6 days
Access: Sofia airport 160km

Profile

Best-developed ski resort in Eastern Europe, an attractive old town with a modern lift system and hotels of international standard

Resort

Bansko, previously better known for its school of Orthodox icon painting than for its pistes, is now Boomtown Bulgaria, much the most successful and challenging resort in Eastern Europe – and, thanks to an investment of €130 million by a Sofia-based consortium, the only one to have a modern lift system.

What began in the 1980s as a one-lift ski resort in the Pirin Mountains has been transformed in recent years into the ski capital of the Wild East. Every second completed building appears to house an estate agent cashing in on the property boom – and the biggest customers are the British.

A modest €100,000 secures a luxurious two-bedroom apartment by the base of the lifts, provided of course that you can locate your plot among the cranes and burgeoning concrete shells that blot the landscape.

For €20,000 you can still buy a run-down stone-and-wood farmhouse in the outlying villages such as Dobrinishte, although it will probably cost you at least twice that to do it up. What investors get for their money is a ticket to what potentially could become one of the great ski areas of Europe. For, unlike Borovets, the mountains here are perfectly shaped for snowsports with the kind of awe-inspiring terrain that befits a future Verbier, or at least a Les Arcs. The resort has a long season that usually runs from mid-December until mid-May, and it had excellent snow-cover last season.

Investment has been sufficient to encourage the building of a British-designed golf course and the five-star Grand Arena Hotel, which is managed by the German Kempinski group. Plenty of other less exalted, but clean and cheerful, accommodation can be found in the old town with its cobbled streets. Walking along those streets is like entering a scene from *The Third Man*. Ancient houses – most of them ripe for renovation – give the place a time-warped character. It's icy underfoot and you have to watch out for potholes and the odd gaping drain.

In the days of the Ottoman Empire, Bansko was an important staging post on the caravan route from Constantinople to Thessaloniki. The downside to any visit here, especially for those new property owners, is the tedious two-and-a-half-hour journey southwards on bone-jarring potholed roads from Sofia. Bansko lies close to the Macedonian and Greek frontiers and on a clear day you can see the Aegean Sea.

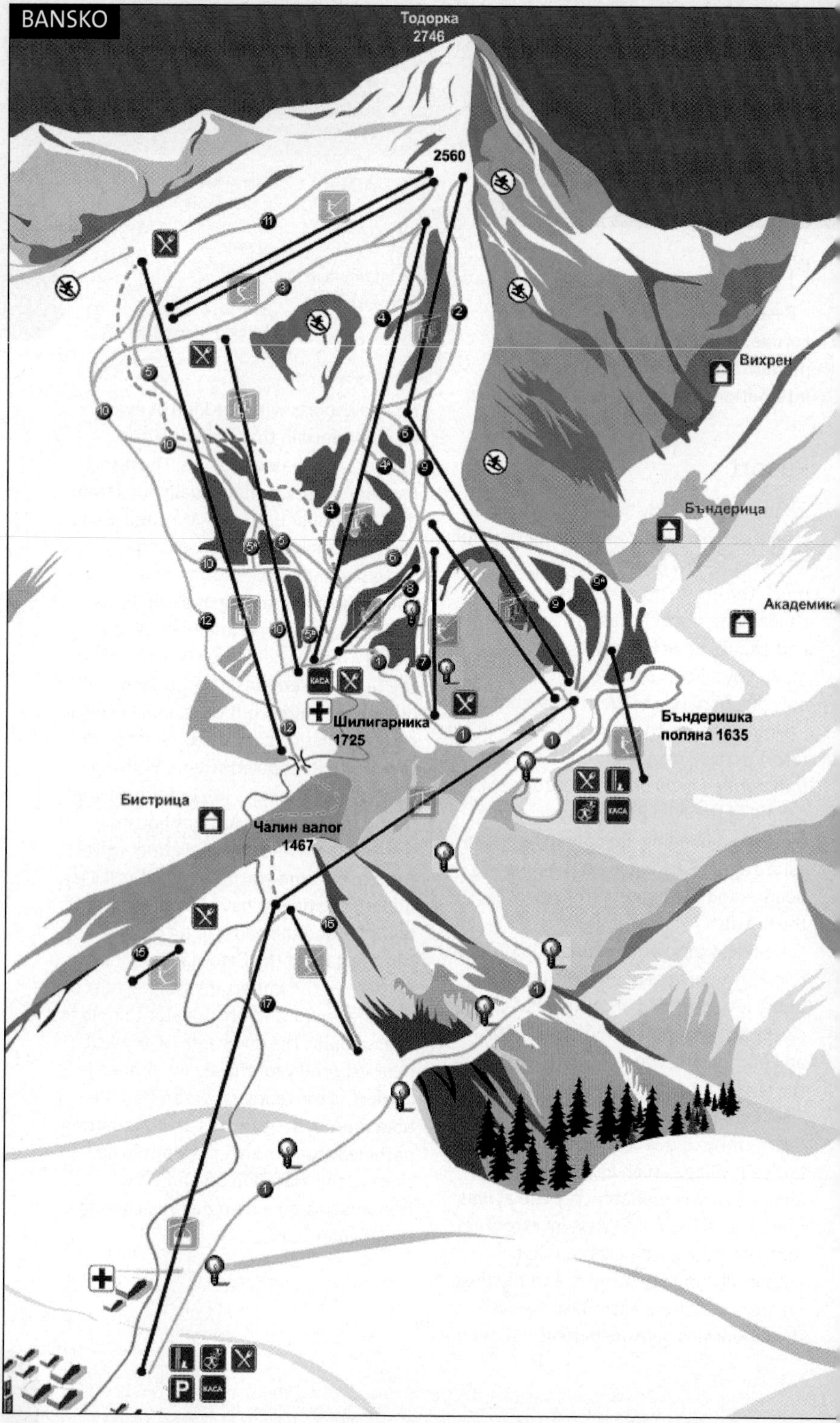

BANSKO
Тодорка
2746
2560
Вихрен
Бъндерица
Академика
Шилигарника
1725
Бъндеришка
поляна 1635
Бистрица
Чалин валог
1467
КАСА

Mountain

To put it in a Western perspective, the ski area is of a similar size to Alpbach and larger than Niederau in Austria. A new 'village' of modern hotels is being built just above the town around the Doppelmayr gondola that forms the backbone of the lift system. The gondola takes you up to the mid-mountain area at 1725m, where a small network of lifts takes you on to the highest point at 2560m. At present Bansko has a vertical drop of 1100m – or 1600m if you include the long, gentle coast-and-pole back to town. The final 7km is floodlit and covered by snow-cannon. Bansko has an electronic hands-free lift pass.

The present piste map represents a creative view of future development rather than a current record of available mountain transport. So far Ulen, the Sofia-based company developing the ski area, has built seven fast lifts including the gondola, and more are planned including a second gondola.

Learn

The **Ulen school**, **t** +359 (0)7443 8060, is recommended, with most instructors speaking good English.

Children

The **Ulen school** runs its own ski kindergarten and has a dedicated beginner area with a magic carpet.

Lunch

Mountain restaurants, **t** +359 (0)7443 8049 for all, serving simple local dishes at reasonable prices, are located at the foot of the gondola and at mid-mountain. **Bla-Bla** and the **Bachvite** waiter-service restaurant in the **Banderishka Polyana** building are both recommended. A two-course lunch for two costs around €15 including a bottle of local wine.

Dine

Reporters repeatedly warned that half-board food in the hotels was to be avoided, but eating out was so cheap that this was no financial hardship. Eating out is centred upon 100 traditional taverns called Mehanas. Competition is keen and 'greeters' dressed in national costume loiter outside the larger ones, beckoning tourists to enter. Once inside, the ambience is invariably warm with an open fire, checked tablecloths, and a good selection of Bulgarian wines. Hearty meals of barbecued lamb and assorted offal are not for the faint-hearted or vegetarians. **Beli Noshti**, **t** +359 (0)7443 5088, and **Kamenitsa**, **t** +359 (0)7443 4635, are recommended, along with **Georgeo's Pizzeria**, **t** + 359 (0)7443 2948, **Steak House**, **t** + 359 (0)7443 2416, and **Come Prima** in the Kempinski, **t** +359 (0)7443 8933, which has gourmet Italian cuisine.

Party

Happy End and **The Lions Pub**, at the gondola end of town, are Bansko's best shots at international après-ski. More traditional Bulgarian entertainment is to be found in the Mehanas, which offer live folk music. The best include **Dedo Pene**, **Motikata**, **Kassapinova Kashta**, **Kadiyata**, **Molerite**, **Bai Koce** and **Baryakova Mehana**. The **Torino** cabaret bar attracts smart Sofian weekenders. **Amnesia** and **No Name** are the most popular late-night clubs.

Sleep

*******Kempinski Grand Arena**, **t** +359 (0)7443 8933, *www.kempinski.com*, is a smart new establishment opposite the gondola station. It has an indoor pool, two restaurants and a spa.

****Hotel Bansko, t +359 (0)7443 8054, *www.hotelbansko.bansko.bg*, is popular with the locals and has huge rooms with intricate wood-carved ceilings.

****Hotel Glazne, t + 359 (0)7443 8021, *www.glazne.bansko.bg*, has a sports centre and separate villas for families.

****Hotel Pirin, t +359 (0)7443 8051, is in the town centre, a 10-minute walk from the gondola. It has a swimming pool and a Mehana restaurant.

****Hotel Strazhite, t +359 (0)7443 8117, *www.banskoski.com*, has a swimming pool and a bowling alley.

****Hotel Tanne, t + 359 (0)7443 8100, *www.hotel-tanne.com*, is decorated in authentic Bulgarian style. Its Tavern restaurant has live music.

**Hotel Zornitza, t +359 (0)7443 8200, is in the old town and is 'clean, cheerful, and friendly'.

Bohinj, Slovenia

Profile

Beginner and limited intermediate skiing in a retro-Austrian atmosphere with beautiful scenery, low prices, excellent tuition and a high standard of food and hotels

Resort

Bohinj is pronounced 'Bocking' and lies just 27km beyond the beautiful lakeside town of Bled, which is dominated by a fairy-tale castle and an enchanting island church. This is the most entertaining of Slovenia's 26 ski areas (Bled itself is not really a ski resort). Slovenia is reminiscent of neighbouring Austria as it was a couple of decades ago. Imagine, for a moment, a ski holiday in quaint traditional alpine surroundings where a lift pass costs €20 a day, a three-course meal with wine €15, and a pint of beer €1.85.

Mountain

Bohinj's three separate ski areas are 10 minutes' drive apart in the rugged mountains above Lake Bohinj. Vogel is reached by a cable-car, which rises over cliffs from the far end of Lake Bohinj. The 18km area is much larger than its statistics suggest, and you can ski around the shoulder of the mountain back down to the cable-car station.

Kobla, the second area and the country's original ski resort, is our favourite. Its three antiquated double chair-lifts add to, rather than detract from, its charm as you rise slowly over farmland from the village to the mountain top.

The steep and long run down the front face has the pedigree of the FIS downhill course it once was. The third little area of Soriska Planina has three drag-lifts and 3km of nursery slopes.

*BEST FOR

Beginners, value for money

ESSENTIALS

Altitude: 512m (1,680ft)–1800m (5,905ft)
Further information: **Vogel**, t +386 (0)4572 4236, **Kobla**, t +386 (0)4574 7100, *www.bohinj.si*
Lifts in area: 18 (1 cableway, 7 chairs, 10 drags) serving 65km of piste
Lift pass: adult €147.30, child €103, both for 6 days
Access: Ljubljana airport 1hr

Learn

Vogel, **t** +386 (0)4572 1451, **Kobla**, **t** +386 (0)4574 7100, and **Soriska Planina**, **t** +386 (0)4511 7835, schools all offer friendly tuition at a low price.

Children

No special facilities.

Lunch

Mountain huts in Vogel and Kobla provide a good range of hot dishes. **Vogel Bar**, **t** +386 (0)5063 7921, at Vogel, is recommended for pizzas and grilled meat.

Dine

Rupa, **t** +386 (0)4572 3401, at Sednja Vas, has good home-cooked food. **Erlah**, **t** +386 (0)4572 3309, at the Vogel end of the lake, is renowned for its fresh trout and *strukljі* (cheese- or nut-filled buckwheat dumplings).

Party

Bohinj has a few bars that liven up at weekends. Nearby Bled has a disco and a famous casino.

Sleep

Bohinj:

★★★★**Hotel Bohinj**, **t** +386 (0)4572 6000, *www.alpinum.net*, is modern and highly recommended.

★★★★**Hotel Jezero**, **t** +386 (0)4572 9100, *www.bohinj.si*, overlooks the lake and is convenient for both main ski areas.

★★★**Hotel Zlatorog**, **t** +386 (0)4572 3381, is in a beautiful setting just back from the lake.

Bled:

★★★★★**Grand Hotel Toplice**, **t** +386 (0)4579 1000, *www.hotel-toplice.com*, is a traditional hotel.

★★★★**Vila Bled**, **t** +386 (0)4579 1500 has an intimate atmosphere.

Borovets, Bulgaria

Profile

Old lift system and unimaginative food are offset by an appealing forest setting, low prices, a lively nightlife and good beginner instruction

Resort

Borovets is the oldest resort in Bulgaria. Skiing started here as long ago as 1896 and cynics would argue that the lift system has scarcely improved since. Borovets failed in its combined bid with Bansko to host the 2014 Winter Olympics, but will rebid for 2018. Plans are afoot to create a new lift network linked to a series of purpose-built satellite villages over the next seven years, effectively doubling the size of Borovets. The first stage should be the construction of a gondola to a new

***BEST FOR**

First-timers, forest setting, low prices

ESSENTIALS

Altitude: 1323m (4,339ft)–2540m (8,333ft)

Further information: **t** +359 (0)2987 9778 or **t** +359 (0)7226 6171, *www.bulgariaski.com*

Lifts in area: 8 (1 cableway, 1 chair, 6 drags) serving 40km of piste

Lift pass: adults €129, child €82

Access: Sofia airport 1hr

Super Borovets above the existing village. The village, in a pine forest at the foot of Mount Moussala, 73km from Sofia, was originally the site of a hunting lodge for the Bulgarian royal family.

It developed into a popular ski resort in the 1970s and, after the fall of Communism in Eastern Europe, Borovets looked set to attract overseas investment. But it never happened and now Bansko has stolen its title of top ski destination in Bulgaria. Despite its mountain shortcomings, Borovets has a lively atmosphere and continues to attract a large number of overseas skiers, from Britain in particular. Many of these are people who proclaim that they would not ski anywhere else. A visit here cannot fail to be an interesting experience – as one reporter aptly put it: 'don't go with any expectations and you won't be disappointed'.

Mountain

The antiquated lift system is headed by an ageing gondola and an assortment of fixed-grip chair-lifts and drag-lifts. Inevitably, high-season lift queues are irritatingly long. The skiing is divided into two sectors, linked by a long walk on an ice-rutted road. The Markoudjik sector, reached by a 1970s gondola, offers the best of the resort's skiing, which is mainly above the treeline with a highest ski point of 2540m. All the nursery slopes are situated at the base of the separate Martinovi Baraki area. In good conditions there are plenty of off-piste opportunities, including low-cost heli-skiing.

Learn

Borovets ski and snowboard school, **t** +359 (0)7128 2441, has a strong reputation for teaching the basics in a friendly and efficient manner. Ski classes do not have priority on the lifts.

Children

The **ski school's kindergarten, t** +359 (0)7128 2441, in the Rila Hotel accepts non-skiers from 12 months to four years old and skiers from four to eight years.

Lunch

A couple of snack bars are located on the mountain, but it is best to return to the resort.

Dine

Reporters repeatedly comment that half-board hotel food should be avoided. Small restaurants abound serving burgers, pasta and pizzas as well as Bulgarian fare. Chips are big here in Bulgaria's biggest potato-growing region. Try **The Hungry Horse**, **Mamacita's**, **The White Horse**, **Franco's**, **Blue Café** and **White Magic** (telephone numbers not available).

Party

The Buzz Bar is the main resort rendezvous. **The Samakov** and the **Rila** hotels both have nightclubs.

Sleep

******Ice Angels Hotel**, *www.bulgariaski.com*, is the newest and smartest hotel in Borovets, situated in the centre.

******Samokov Hotel, t** +359 (0)7128 2306, *www.samokov.com*, has 'cramped' rooms and a swimming pool, bowling alley and nightclub ('hotel is very dated and in desperate need of a facelift').

******Hotel Rila, t** +359 (0)7128 2441, *www.bulgariaski.com*, is convenient for the skiing, but the rooms are small ('basic, but fine').

Poiana Brasov, Romania

*BEST FOR

Beginners, value, hectic nightlife (Brasov)

ESSENTIALS

Altitude: 1021m (3,350ft)–1775m (5,823ft)
Further information: t +40 (0)268 417 866, *www.poiana-brasov.com*
Lifts in area: 10 (3 cableways, 7 drags) serving 14km of piste
Lift pass: adult €59, child €37, both for 6 days
Access: Bucharest airport 186km

Profile

Budget beginner skiing with competent, friendly tuition, blighted by a primitive lift system. High standard of hotels and unlimited nightlife in nearby Brasov

Resort

Poiana Brasov opened as a ski resort in 1906 and has slowly grown into a small town at the foot of 1799m Mount Postavaru in the Carpathian mountains. It lies a 13km drive up a mountain road from the attractive medieval town of Brasov with its famous Black Church, Romania's most important cathedral.

Beautiful surroundings and a high standard of accommodation and cuisine, together with the friendliness of the people, make this one of our favourite destinations in Eastern Europe. However, snowfall is variable. In 2005–6 it was one of the only resorts in Europe to have poor-to-adequate cover throughout.

Mountain

This a pleasant beginner and lower intermediate area for anyone who wants to get to grips with the basics without breaking the bank.

Mount Postavaru is accessed by a gondola and two ancient cable-cars. Nursery slopes are located by the Sport and Bradul hotels.

Learn

The six ski schools teach modern technique and are all of a similar high standard. **Ana Hotels, t** +40 (0)268 407330, **Club Montana Schi, t** +40 (0)722 269411, **Euro Inter Ski, t** +40 (0)268 151735, **Impera International, t** +40 (0)744 321065, **Poiana SA, t** +40 (0)268 262310, and **Valona Tour, t** +40 (0)722 269411.

Children

All schools take children from four years. Non-skiing activities include tobogganing, paintballing in the woods and excursions to **Dracula's Castle** and to **Peles Castle** at Sinaia.

Lunch

Two mountain restaurants, **Cristianu Mare** and **Postavaru**, serve pizzas, burgers, soup and sandwiches at wonderfully low prices.

Dine

In Poiana Brasov, **Sura Dacilor, t** +40 (0)268 262327, has Romanian cuisine and folk music. **Coliba Haiducilor, t** +40 (0)268 2621370, also known as **The Outlaws' Hut**, has barbecued bear and traditional dancing. **Vanatorul, t** +40 (0)268 2623540, serves venison, pheasant and wild boar.

In Brasov, **Le Stradivari, t** +40 (0)268 476945 is Italian and specializes in seafood. **Pepper Jack, t** +40 (0)268 417349 has Mexican and Transylvanian cuisine.

Party

In Poiana the **Ciucas**, **Alpin**, **Bradul** and **Poiana** hotel bars are the liveliest. In Brasov, try **Festival 39**, **Cabana** and **Blue Night**. **Blitz** is the hippest late-night hotspot. Other discos are **Pro-Club**, **Hacienda** and **No Problem**.

Sleep

★★★**Hotel Miruna, t** +40 (0)268 262120, *www.mirunahotel.ro*, built four years ago, is recommended.

★★★**Piatra Mare, t** +40 (0)268 262029, *www.piatramare.ro,* has a good restaurant.

★★★**Sport Hotel, t** +40 (0)268 407330, *www.anahotels.ro*, is convenient for the nursery slopes.

★★★**Tirol Hotel, t** +40 (0)268 262460, has a good restaurant.

★★★**Alpin Hotel, t** +40 (0)268 262111, has a swimming pool and a gym ('excellent service and good food').

★★**Hotel Bradul, t** +40 (0)268 407330, *www.anahotels.ro*, adjoins the Sport and is well located ('food plain, but plentiful').

05

The Top Resorts: France

Alpe d'Huez

***BEST FOR**

Intermediates, big ski area, eating out

ESSENTIALS

Altitude: 1120m (3,674ft)–3330m (10,922ft)
Further information: t +33 (0)4 76 11 44 44, *www.alpedhuez.com*
Lifts in area: 82 (16 cableways, 24 chairs, 42 drags) serving 240km of piste
Lift pass: Area (covers linked resorts, 2 days in Les Deux Alpes, 1 day in La Grave, The Milky Way, Puy-St-Vincent and Serre Chevalier) adult €192, child 5–15yrs €137, both for 6 days
Access: Grenoble airport 1½hrs, Lyon airport 2hrs

Profile

A large and architecturally unattractive resort with plenty of high-altitude, snow-sure skiing from before Christmas until after Easter. The lift system extends down to Vaujany and other smaller and more pleasing resorts in neighbouring valleys

Resort

Alpe d'Huez is one of France's oldest resorts and is the hub for the fifth largest ski circuit in the country. Back in 1934, a young engineer called Pomagalski invented the drag-lift here just days ahead of a rival in Davos. It was also a venue for the 1968 Winter Olympics. However, Alpe d'Huez is better known to millions of cycle fans each July when the approach road becomes one of the most energy-sapping climbs of the Tour de France.

Over the years the resort has grown without design along a sunny balcony above the beautiful Oisans Valley, reached by 22 hairpin bends. Lifts link the various sectors of the village, which provides a utilitarian base for some excellent skiing for all standards.

Mountain

Alpe d'Huez is one of the few resorts that a few years ago started quietly responding to the threat of global warming – and it has paid huge dividends. The lift company took the decision to develop the summer ski area on the glacier above the resort. The plan was to ensure that, even in the worst winters, skiers and riders would have plenty of snow-sure terrain at high altitude. However, such is the onward march of global warming that the resort no longer runs the glacier lifts in summer.

Two quad-chairs now serve long runs on the glacier, which can be reached by a new extension of the Marmottes gondola at one end of the resort and by the Pic Blanc cable-car at the other.

Skiers and riders must return to mid-mountain by lift unless they are capable of descending the notoriously difficult and often icy Tunnel run down the front face or the 16km Sarenne that leads into the Sarenne Gorge below the resort.

Alpe d'Huez-based skiers tend to congregate on the easy and intermediate runs directly above the resort, which are served by gondolas from either end. In fact the best skiing is to be found off both sides leading down to the neighbouring villages of Oz, Vaujany and Auris-en-Oisans, as well as the lower satellites of Villard-Reculas, and Huez.

The 3330m Pic Blanc is the starting point for a number of off-piste itineraries. These include the Grand Sablat, the Combe du Loup and a long, tricky descent via the Couloir de Fare. A 20-minute climb from the cable-car station takes you to the top of La Pyramide. From here you can ski more than 2000m of vertical down to

ALPE D'HUEZ
MASSIF DU MONT BLANC
L'ETENDARD 3470
PIC BAYLE
PIC DE LA PYRAMIDE
PIC BLANC 3330
GLACIER DE SARENNE
AIGUILLES D'ARVES
LA MEUE
GLACIER DE BARBARATE
GLACIER DES ROUSSES
CLOCHER DE MACLE 2800
DÔME DES PETITES ROUSSES 2800
COL DU COUARD
2700
LAC BLANC
BARRAGE DU CHAMBON
LE FRENEY
PLAT DES MARMOTTES
MINE DE L'HERPIE
GORGES DE SARENNE
2300
L'ALPETTE 2050
SIGNAL DE L'HOMME 2176
2100
MONTFRAIS 1650
SIGNAL 2115
LA VILLETTE
OZ EN OISANS STATION 1350
ALPE D'HUEZ 1860
AURIS EN OISANS 1600
Connexion Auris
VAUJANY 1250
LE BESSEY
LE ROSAY
L'ENVERSIN D'OZ
LA GARDE
LE CHATELARD
MARONNE
VILLARD RECULAS 1480
HUEZ 1500
OZ EN OISANS VILLAGE
SARDONNE
LAC DU VERNEY
ALLEMONT
BOURG D'OISANS GRENOBLE AURIS VILLAGES
BOURG D'OISANS GRENOBLE
mod.2003

Vaujany. Alpe d'Huez has a half-pipe on the Signal piste as well as a terrain park at Plat des Marmottes.

Learn

The **ESF**, **t** +33 (0)4 76 80 94 23, has a number of English-speaking instructors. The **ESI**, **t** +33 (0)4 76 80 42 77, offers smaller classes and tuition in English, while **British Masterclass**, **t** +33 (0)4 76 80 93 83, is strongly recommended. Guiding is available through the **Bureau des Guides**, **t** +33 (0)4 76 80 42 55, while **SAF Isère Heliskiing**, **t** +33 (0)4 76 80 65 49, will pick you up at the end of day ski tours into neighbouring valleys.

Children

The **ESF**, **t** +33 (0)4 76 80 94 23, accepts children from four years and guarantees 10 or fewer pupils per class, although we have seen up to 16 during high season. The **ESI**, **t** +33 (0)4 76 80 42 77, teaches children from three-and-a-half, and **Les Eterlous**, **t** +33 (0)4 76 80 67 85, alternates skiing and games for little ones from two-and-a-half years. **Les Crapouilloux**, **t** +33 (0)4 76 11 39 23, is a crèche for children from two-and-a-half years. **Les Intrépides**, **t** +33 (0)4 76 11 21 61, is the alternative for non-skiers aged six months to three years.

Lunch

La Cabane du Poutat, **t** +33 (0)4 76 80 42 88, beneath the Marmottes gondola, has a serious gourmet menu. **La Bergerie**, **t** +33 (0)4 76 80 36 83, on the way down to Villard-Reculas, is an alpine museum with simple dishes. **Auberge de l'Alpette**, **t** +33 (0)4 76 80 70 00, above Oz, has the best omelettes and salads on the mountain. The **Chalet du Lac Besson**, **t** +33 (0)4 76 80 65 37, on the cross-country trail, has an open fireplace and a large sun terrace. **L'Altibar**, **t** +33 (0)4 76 80 41 15, beside the altiport runway, is a local favourite. **Le Signal**, **t** +33 (0)4 76 80 39 54, offers panoramic views. **Bonsoir Clara**, **t** +33 (0)4 76 80 37 20, at Villard-Reculas, is recommended.

Dine

Alpe d'Huez has a fine choice of restaurants. **Au P'tit Creux**, **t** +33 (0)4 76 80 62 83, is one of the best restaurants but expensive, while **Passe Montagne**, **t** +33 (0)4 76 11 31 53, is good value. **Les Caves**, **t** +33 (0)4 76 80 92 44, has fine food and wine. **Le Génépi**, **t** +33 (0)4 76 80 36 22, was praised by reporters. **Lily Muldoon's**, **t** +33 (0) 476 80 35 39, is an Irish restaurant with a popular following.

Party

Alpe d'Huez has a vibrant atmosphere and après-ski lasts well into the early hours at **The Underground** and **Le Sporting**. Others recommended include **Crowded House**, **Sphere Bar**, **Les Caves**, **Zoo Music Bar**, **Freeride Café** and **L'Etalon**. **Magoos**, **The O Bar**, **The Last Bar** and **O'Sharkeys** are all popular venues.

Sleep

★★★★**Royal Ours Blanc**, **t** +33 (0)4 76 80 35 50, *www.eurogroup-vacances.com,* has an indoor swimming pool.

★★★★**Au Chamois d'Or**, **t** +33 (0)4 76 80 31 32, *www.chamoisdor-alpedhuez.com,* is at the top of the village, with some delightful wood-panelled suites.

★★★★**Pierre et Vacances Les Bergers**, **t** +33 (0)4 76 80 85 00, *www.pierreetvacances.com,* are the best apartments in the resort.

★★★**Le Christina**, **t** +33 (0)4 76 80 33 32, *www.lechristina-alpedhuez.com,* is a chalet-style building with a restaurant serving local cuisine.

★★★**Hôtel Le Pic Blanc**, **t** +33 (0)4 76 11 42 42, *www.hmc-hotels.com*, is a very welcoming place.

★★★**Le Printemps de Juliette**, **t** +33 (0)4 76 11 44 38, *www.leprintempsdejuliette.com*, is a delightful hotel with just four rooms and four suites.

Les Arcs

🏆 BEST MOUNTAIN RESTAURANT 2007: Bélliou La Fumée

*BEST FOR

Ski convenience, big ski area, reliable snow-cover

ESSENTIALS

Altitude: 1200m (2,788ft)–3226m (10,581ft)
Further information: **t** +33 (0)4 79 07 12 57, *www.lesarcs.com*
Lifts in area: 141 in Paradiski (1 mountain railway, 16 cableways, 66 chairs, 58 drags) serving 425km of piste
Lift pass: Paradiski adult €229 (covers linked Les Arcs/La Plagne area and one day in each of Val d'Isère/Tignes, Pralognan-La Vanoise, Les Saisies), child 6–13yrs €172, both for 6 days
Access: Chambéry airport 2hrs, Lyon airport 2½hrs, Geneva airport 2½hrs, Bourg-St-Maurice station (for Eurostar) 15km, with buses and funicular to Arc 1600

Profile

Part of the giant Paradiski area linking the resort with La Plagne and providing snow-sure, high-altitude skiing in purpose-built villages. Good terrain for all standards and abundant off-piste opportunities

Resort

Les Arcs was one of France's great new areas developed during the boom years of the 1960s. This was a time when every Parisian and quite a few others flocked to the Alps for at least one week each winter in search of snow, sunshine and a shoebox-sized apartment they could call their own.

Local skier Robert Blanc conceived the idea of building a series of villages at different altitudes on the mountain above his home town of Bourg-St-Maurice. Ex-Olympic champion Emile Allais lent his name to the project and the first village of Arc 1600 opened in 1968. Les Arcs has come a long way since then.

Villages at 1800 and 2000 were followed much more recently by the development of another at 1950. Intrawest, the giant North American resort developer, chose Les Arcs for the first of what are planned as a number of property-led commercial forays in the Alps.

Arc 1950 is now the focal point of the whole resort – with a true village ambience. The last apartment building will be completed in 2008. It provides sympathetic architecture and reasonably priced apartments finished to a level not previously found in the French Alps.

The timing of initial construction coincided with the creation of Paradiski, the name given to the combined ski area of Les Arcs and adjoining La Plagne. Both resort lift companies are under the same ownership of the Compagnie des Alpes, who decided to link two of France's largest ski areas together to provide a rival to the Trois Vallées.

After years of discussion and oiling of the cogs of French bureaucracy, the 200-passenger double-decker Vanoise Express cable-car was built at a cost of €16 million across the deep Ponturin gorge that separates the two resorts. From the beginning, the lift company admitted that the number of visitors in either centre who would use the lift in any one week

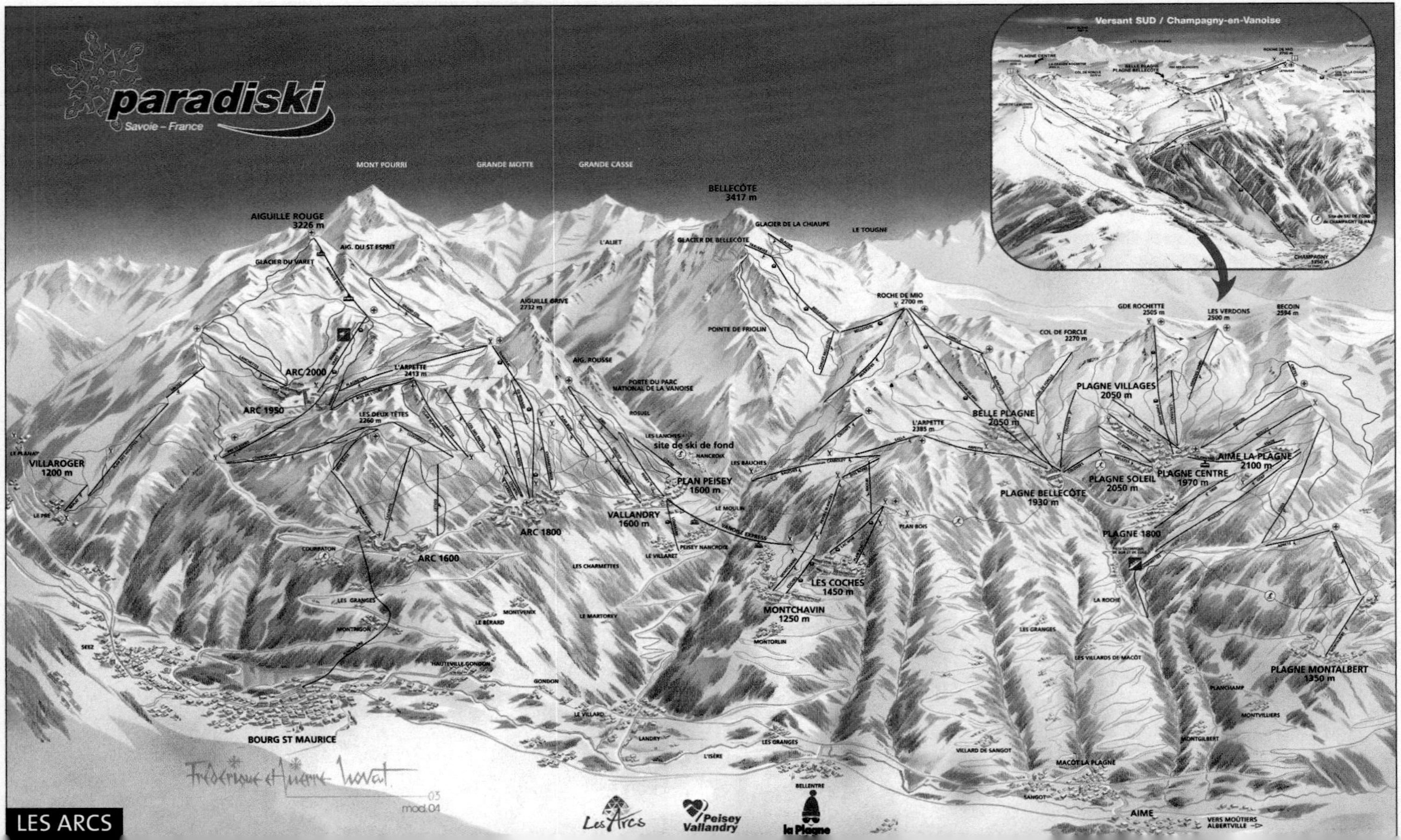
paradiski
Savoie - France
MONT POURRI
GRANDE MOTTE
GRANDE CASSE
BELLECÔTE
3417 m
AIGUILLE ROUGE
3226 m
AIG. DU ST ESPRIT
GLACIER DU VARET
GLACIER DE LA CHIAUPE
GLACIER DE BELLECÔTE
L'ALIET
LE TOUGNE
AIGUILLE GRIVE
2732 m
ROCHE DE MIO
2700 m
POINTE DE FRIOLIN
ARC 2000
L'ARPETTE
2413 m
ARC 1950
LES DEUX TÊTES
2260 m
AIG. ROUSSE
PORTE DU PARC
NATIONAL DE LA VANOISE
ROSUEL
LES LANCHES
site de ski de fond
NANCROIX
LES BAUCHES
L'ARPETTE
2385 m
BELLE PLAGNE
2050 m
COL DE FORCLE
2270 m
GDE ROCHETTE
2505 m
LES VERDONS
2500 m
BECOIN
2594 m
PLAGNE VILLAGES
2050 m
AIME LA PLAGNE
2100 m
PLAGNE CENTRE
1970 m
PLAGNE SOLEIL
2050 m
PLAGNE BELLECÔTE
1930 m
LE PLANAY
VILLAROGER
1200 m
LE PRÉ
PLAN PEISEY
1600 m
VALLANDRY
1600 m
LE MOULIN
VANOISE EXPRESS
PEISEY NANCROIX
LE VILLARET
ARC 1800
ARC 1600
COURBATON
PLAN BOIS
PLAGNE 1800
LES COCHES
1450 m
MONTCHAVIN
1250 m
LES CHARMETTES
LES GRANGES
MONTRIGON
LE BÉRARD
MONTVENIX
LE MARTOREY
MONTORLIN
LA ROCHE
LES GRANGES
LES VILLARDS DE MACÔT
SEEZ
HAUTEVILLE GONDON
GONDON
LE VILLARD
LANDRY
L'ISÈRE
LES GRANGES
BELLENTRE
VILLARD DE SANGOT
MACÔT LA PLAGNE
SANGOT
PLANCHAMP
MONTVILLIERS
MONTGILBERT
PLAGNE MONTALBERT
1350 m
AIME
VERS MOÛTIERS
ALBERTVILLE
BOURG ST MAURICE
Versant SUD / Champagny-en-Vanoise
PLAGNE CENTRE
BELLE PLAGNE
PLAGNE BELLECÔTE
ROCHE DE MIO
CHAMPAGNY
Frédérique et Pierre Novat
03
mod.04
Les Arcs
Peisey Vallandry
la Plagne

would not exceed 30 per cent. In reality the figure is much lower.

Nevertheless, skiers in both Les Arcs and La Plagne now have the daily choice of a quite stupendous amount of terrain. The hamlets of Vallandry, Peisey Nancroix and higher Plan-Peisey beside the new lift have also developed as resorts in their own right.

The original village Arc 1600 remains the most compact and child-friendly. Arc 1800 is the largest and liveliest, soulless 2000 has guaranteed snow-cover but precious little else to commend it. Arc 1950 is the brave new heart of the resort. Les Arcs founder Robert Blanc would be proud of it had he lived to see it. Sadly he died in an avalanche in 1980.

Mountain

The 425km of skiing in Paradiski covers every conceivable type of terrain, but most of it is given over to enjoyable red and blue motorway pistes that are ideal intermediate terrain. Long runs start above the treeline and descend through the woods to outlying hamlets, and in good mid-winter conditions you can ski all the way down to Bourg-St-Maurice at 850m.

The easy pistes above Arc 1800, served by the Transarc gondola and a whole series of chairs spread across the mountainside attract the crowds – but more enterprising skiers and riders will explore further afield.

A gondola and a cable-car from Arc 2000 take you up to the 3226m Aiguille Rouge, the highest point in the ski area and starting point for some classic steep runs including a 7km descent down to Le Planay or Le Pré. The area is so large that even accomplished skiers must work at travelling by lift and piste in a single day from Le Pré at one end of Paradiski to Champagny-en-Vanoise at the other – and back again. Each of the Arc villages has its own dedicated nursery slopes, but the best are found at 1800.

Les Arcs is famous for its speed-skiing track above Arc 2000, the setting over the years for a number of world records. For a modest fee anyone is allowed to have a go from a lower starting point that keeps your speed down to a sensible level. Les Arcs was a pioneer of snowboarding in Europe. The terrain park is situated between Arc 1800 and Arc 1600 with a half-pipe and snowcross course.

Learn

The **ESF**, **t** +33 (0)4 79 07 40 31, has a branch in each village. We recommend **Arc Aventures**, **t** +33 (0)4 79 07 41 28, in Arc 1800 and **Spirit 1950**, **t** +33 (0)4 79 04 25 72, in Arc 1950. **Initial Snow**, **t** +33 (0)6 12 45 72 91, is a small school based in Bourg-St-Maurice with meeting points in Les Arcs. **Privilege**, **t** +33 (0)4 79 07 23 38, is another small school in Arc 1800. **Darentasia**, **t** +33 (0)4 79 04 16 81, specializes in off-piste. Guiding can also be arranged through the **Bureau des Guides**, **t** +33 (0)4 79 07 71 19.

Children

In Arc 1600, **Hôtel La Cachette**, **t** +33 (0)4 79 07 70 50, cares for children from four months to two years and has a mini-club for under-12s.

In Arc 1800, **Les Pommes des Pins**, **t** +33 (0)4 79 04 24 31, looks after children from 12 months to six years.

In Arc 200, **Les Marmottons**, **t** +33 (0)4 79 07 64 25, provides a mix of daycare and lessons, but not lunch.

Lunch

Bélliou La Fumée, **t** +33 (0)4 79 07 29 130, is a 500-year-old hunting lodge in Pré-St-Esprit below Arc 2000 ('an ancient family-run hut with a wonderful atmosphere and truly outstanding home-cooked haute cuisine'). The **Aiguille Grive**, **t** +33 (0)4 79 07 43 97, has good food in a panoramic setting. **Chalet de Luigi**, **t** +33 (0)6 08 57 23 36, at 1950 is renowned for its ham-based gourmet cuisine. **Les Chalets de l'Arc 2000**, **t** +33 (0)4 79 04 15 400, has a warm atmosphere and serves traditional *savoyarde* cuisine.

Dine

In Arc 1600, **La Rive** in the Hotel La Cachette, **t** +33 (0)4 79 07 70 50, is recommended, along with **Pizza 1600**, **t** + 33 (0)4 79 04 27 73.

In Arc 1800, try **Casa Mia**, **t** +33 (0)4 79 07 05 75, **La Marmite**, **t** +33 (0)4 79 07 44 28, **L'Equipe**, **t** +33 (0)4 79 07 49 34 and **Le Chalet Bouvier**, **t** +33 (0)4 79 04 14 68.

In Arc 1950, **Chalet de Luigi**, **t** +33 (0)6 08 57 23 36, is the focal point for fine dining. **East**, **t** +33 (0)4 79 11 19 57, is a new oriental fusion restaurant.

In Arc 2000, **El Latino Loco**, **t** +33 (0)4 79 07 79 49, has some of the best food in the village.

In Bourg-St-Maurice, **L'Hostellerie du Petit Saint Bernard**, **t** +33 (0)4 79 07 04 32, is the kind of old-fashioned *bourgeois* French restaurant that serves snails, frogs' legs and wonderful steaks.

Party

This is definitely not a place for lively après-ski. At the end of the day the French seem to disappear into their self-catering apartments and do not reappear until morning. Apart from a few busy bars, the main action – what there is of it – is found in **Apokalypse** and **L'Igloo** at Arc 1800. **Chalet de Luigi** at 1950 has a new nightclub, which is building a reputation as the best in the resort.

Sleep

Most accommodation is in self-catering apartments. Arc 1950 has the newest and the best, **t** +44 (0)870 750 6820, *www.ernalow.co.uk*.

Arc 2000:

★★★★Les Chalets des Neiges, **t** +44 (0)20 7244 8764, is a complex containing chalet-apartments sharing an indoor pool and bar. They include **Chalet Turia** and **Chalet Charvet**, which sleep 10 people each.

Arc 1950:

★★★★Radisson SAS, **t** +44 (0)870 750 6820, was completed for last season and is the most comfortable *résidence* with a pool and underground parking ('best ski apartment I have ever stayed in').

Arc 1800:

★★★★Les Alpages du Chantel apartments, **t** +33 (0)1 58 21 58 21, *www.residences mgm.com*, are piste-side and have a swimming pool, sauna and massage.

★★★Hôtel du Golf Maeva, **t** +33 (0)4 79 41 43 43, *www.maeva.com*, is the village's original hotel with sloping walkways rather than staircases.

★★★Hôtel Mercure Coralia, **t** +33 (0)4 79 07 65 00, *www.mercure.com*, makes up in efficiency for what it lacks in character.

Arc 1600:

★★★Hôtel La Cachette, **t** +33 (0)4 79 07 70 50, *www.lesarcs.com*, has a deserved reputation as one of the best hotels in the Alps for families with small children.

★★Hôtel Béguin, **t** +33 (0)4 79 07 72 61, *www.lesarcs.com*, is small and simple.

★★Hôtel Explorers, **t** +33 (0)4 79 04 16 00, *www.lesarcs.com*, provides cheerful accommodation.

Bourg-St-Maurice:

★★Hostellerie du Petit-St-Bernard, **t** +33 (0)4 79 07 04 32, has a celebrated restaurant.

Hôtel La Petite Auberge, **t** +33 (0)4 79 07 05 86, on the edge of town, has clean rooms and good restaurant.

Avoriaz

Profile

Part of the vast Portes du Soleil ski area, this car-free resort is in a dramatic clifftop setting offering skiing and snowboarding for all standards

Resort

The Portes du Soleil, a trans-frontier alliance of a dozen ski villages in France and Switzerland, largely came into being as a consequence of the 1960 Olympics which were held 8000km away in Squaw Valley in California.

Jean Vuarnet won gold in the downhill for France and on his return was asked to oversee the creation of a high-altitude *station de ski* above his native Morzine. At the same time it was suggested he might try linking his new ski area to Champéry in Switzerland.

He called the new resort Avoriaz and the Portes du Soleil now includes 206 lifts, which serve a mighty 650km of piste covering a large area of mountainside above Lac Léman.

Ironically Vuarnet is better-known today for his sunglasses than for his speed on snow, but it is a tribute to him that his vision all those years ago remains as futuristic-looking today as it did then.

Avoriaz clings to the cliff face at the top of the cable-car that brings you up from Les Prodains in the Morzine Valley. The French government has already correctly listed it as a Landmark of the Twentieth Century.

Most of the original 'shoebox' *résidence* buildings have been completely gutted to provide a smaller number of decent-sized apartments. Other new ones in the Falaise and Festival *quartiers* fulfil the much more luxurious expectations of present-day skiers who can't remember cable bindings and leather ski boots – and have spent summer holidays in much more spacious surroundings in Florida. But the concept remains unchanged: a series of apartment buildings on different levels that are linked by exterior boulevard pistes and interior stairs, lifts and walkways.

You can also drive up to Avoriaz, but the covered parking is expensive and in a pedestrianized resort you have no need of your own transport. Baggage is conveyed to your apartment or hotel by horse-drawn sleigh or snow tractor.

Avoriaz is the best place to base yourself in the Portes du Soleil, which falls short of being one of the world's outstanding ski circuits only because of uncertainty of snow-cover. The top of the ski area, in this the highest resort in the region, only goes up to 2466m which is simply not high enough in these variable winters. When cover is poor or non-existent elsewhere, the overcrowding here can become unacceptable. That said, snow conditions throughout 2005–6 were some of the best in France.

The resort has been a champion of snowboarding since the boards arrived here in the 1970s, and in 1993 it was the first resort in France to build a dedicated terrain park and half-pipe. The resort now

* BEST FOR

Big ski area, intermediates and advanced, ski convenience

ESSENTIALS

Altitude: 1000m (3,280ft)–2466m (8,090ft)
Further information: **t** +33 (0)4 50 74 02 11, *www.avoriaz.com*
Lifts in area: 206 in Portes du Soleil area (14 cableways, 82 chairs, 110 drags) serving 650km of piste
Lift pass: Portes du Soleil (covers 13 resorts) adult €152–179, child 5–16yrs €102–120, both for 6 days
Access: Geneva airport 2hrs

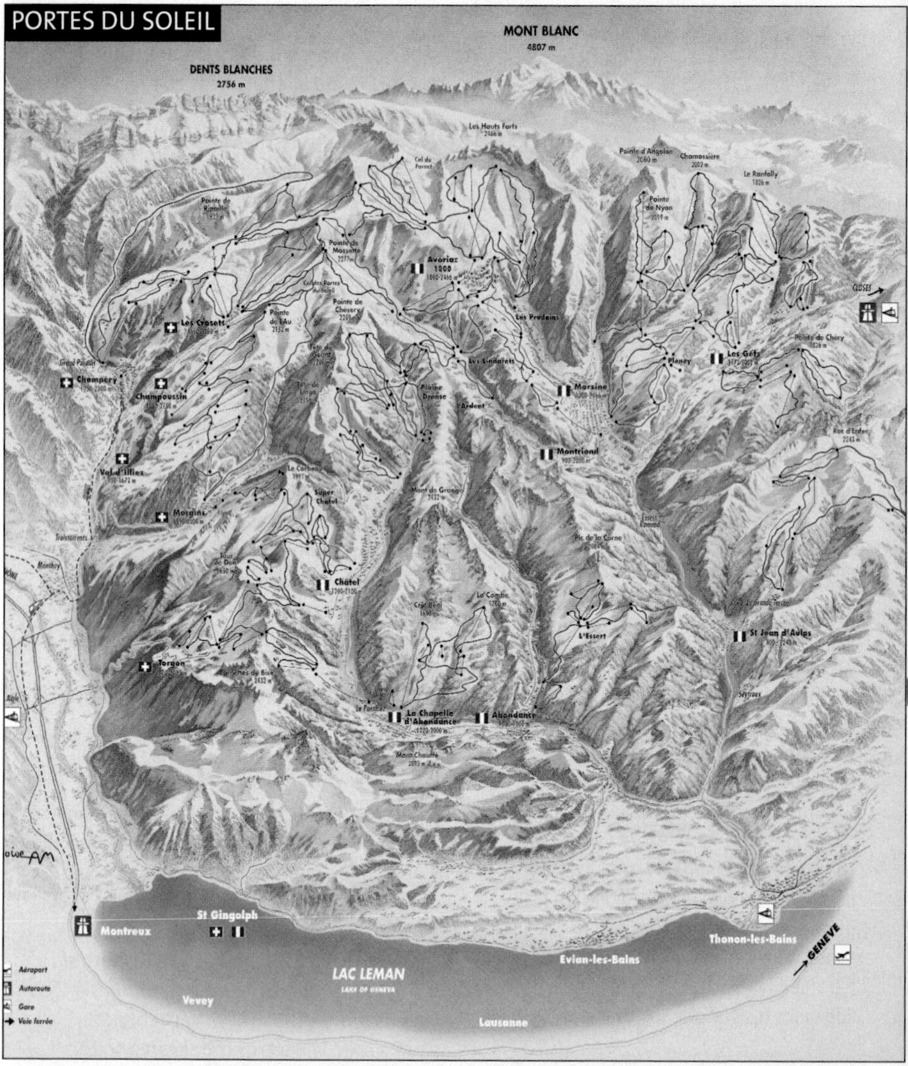
PORTES DU SOLEIL
MONT BLANC
4807 m
DENTS BLANCHES
2756 m
Les Hauts Forts
Pointe d'Angolon
Chamossière
Le Ranfolly
Pointe de Nyon
Pointe de Ripaille
Pointe de Mossette
Avoriaz 1800
Les Crosets
Pointe de l'Au
Pointe de Chesery
Les Prodains
Les Lindarets
Planey
Les Gets
Pointe de Chéry
Cluses
Champéry
Champoussin
Plaine Dranse
Ardent
Morzine
Montriond
Roc d'Enfer
Val-d'Illiez
Le Corbeau
Super Chatel
Mont de Grange
Morgins
Troistorrents
Monthey
Pic de la Corne
Châtel
Crêt Béni
La Combe
L'Essert
St Jean d'Aulps
Torgon
La Chapelle d'Abondance
Abondance
Seytroux
Mont Chauffé
Aigle
Montreux
St Gingolph
Thonon-les-Bains
Genève
Evian-les-Bains
LAC LEMAN
LAKE OF GENEVA
Vevey
Lausanne
Aéroport
Autoroute
Gare
Voie ferrée

has three terrain parks, including La Chapelle park, which is designed for beginners. The Tête aux Bœufs, which is 120m long and 4.5m high, plays host to a number of international snowboard competitions. A constantly updated lift system allows you to explore the main villages of the Portes du Soleil and return to base by evening. A few, such as St-Jean-d'Aulps and Abondance, remain entirely independent and require a separate excursion.

As with Sella Ronda in Italy, completing the actual tour of the principal French and Swiss resorts in a single day restricts the amount of time spent going downhill, with most of your day taken up riding lifts. It makes more sense to explore one sector of the area at a time.

Decide on where you want to go and the quickest way of getting there. Comprehensible lift maps covering such a large and diverse area have always been a problem. Every few years the Portes du Soleil radically changes them, but with no discernible improvement. The current generation of maps provide only a rough indication of where you are and where you want to go. Fortunately the piste signage is good.

Border controls are unusual, but not unheard of. We strongly advise you to carry your passport as well as euros and Swiss francs. If you, or one of your party, has an accident along the way, you could be stranded in another country.

Border guards on skis are increasingly a rarity and few goods are so much cheaper in one country than the other that it pays to lug them them home in a rucksack. However, Switzerland is not part of the EU and restrictions apply as to what you may take from one country to the other without paying duty.

Both currencies are widely accepted, but you will find the exchange rate more favourable if you tender the appropriate one for lunch or goods purchased.

Mountain

Avoriaz is suited to all levels of skier and rider, but in particular to intermediates who will enjoy the feeling of 'going somewhere' each day rather than being forced to repeatedly ski the same slopes over and over again for the whole week. Part of the charm of the resort is that the village streets are pistes – making this the definitive destination for doorstep skiing. The main nursery slopes are above the village and a number of different lifts serve a series of pleasant green runs that connect to lifts coming up from the valley town of Morzine.

Most of Avoriaz's own intermediate terrain lies on the lift-served slopes leading up to the ridge that marks the Swiss border as well as in the adjoining Les Hauts Forts sector, accessed by a chair-lift near the lower 'gate' of Avoriaz. Skiers here can explore some outstanding blue and red runs above and below the treeline with lots of off-piste variations that are superb after a fresh snowfall. A long and testing black run descends from Le Plan Brazy following the basic steep line of the FIS downhill course and brings you down eventually – by bus or green run in good snow conditions over the last bit – to Les Prodains where you can take the cable-car directly back to Avoriaz.

Aventurous skiers or riders will soon want to explore further afield either by taking the Chaux Fleurie chair to the Col de Bassachaux and Châtel beyond, or by tackling the notorious Wall and heading into Switzerland for a cheesy lunch.

The Wall – its correct name is La Chavanette – has achieved considerable notoriety over the years as one of the most difficult descents marked as a black run on any piste map. In reality its bark is usually much worse than its bite, although the toxicity of the latter is dependent on the quality of the snow.

A piste sign at the top warns that the run should be attempted only by experts. At the start, the angle of descent does not allow you to see what lies ahead. But once you have completed the first half dozen turns it eases into a relatively straightforward but heavily mogulled run.

Alternative routes, including a moderately steep and narrow gully on skier's left, may well be preferable in high season traffic conditions when the moguls on The Wall tend to be poorly cut. If conditions are hard-packed and you don't like what you see – or rather don't see – at the top of The Wall, then you should ride the chair down. More lifts take you up to a point above Les Crosets, Champéry and the rest of the Portes du Soleil.

The hamlet of Les Crosets is little more than a few holiday homes and a hotel that doubles as a lift station. It is surrounded by wide north-facing pistes served by lifts leading back up in the direction of Avoriaz. It's worth spending some time exploring this sector.

A chair-lift to the Pointe de l'Au takes you deeper into the Portes du Soleil in the direction of little Champoussin and Morgins beyond. Morgins has an enjoyable north-facing run that takes you down through the woods to the village. On the far side, a lift takes you up to Super-Châtel over the Pas de Morgins and back into France. Alternatively you can ski down into Switzerland again to the remote purpose-built village of Torgon.

At Châtel you have to cross the village by bus to take the gondola up to Linga and the series of lifts and piste beyond that complete the circuit to Avoriaz. Plan your day carefully and allow plenty of time. If you don't manage to finish your tour before the lifts close, you must decide between an expensive taxi ride, an even more expensive phone call to **Mont Blanc Helicopters**, t +33 (0)4 50 74 22 44, or an unscheduled overnight stay.

The best powder runs are found on both sides of the Swiss border. The area is prone to considerable avalanche danger, and the services of a qualified guide are essential.

Learn

Avoriaz has the **ESI Ecole de Glisse, t** +33 (0)4 50 74 02 18, which received favourable comments from reporters, and the **ESF, t** +33 (0)4 50 74 05 65. Both schools also teach snowboarding, in healthy competition with **Emery Snowboard School, t** +33 (0)4 50 74 12 64, and **Free Ride, t** +33 (0)4 50 74 00 36. **The British Alpine Ski and Snowboarding School, t** +44 (0)1237 451 099, is warmly recommended.

Children

Le Village des Enfants/Le Village Snowboard, t +33 (0)4 50 74 04 46, cares for children from three years in a dedicated area in the centre of the resort, using methods developed by the celebrated French ski champion, Annie Famose. **Les P'tits Loups, t** +33 (0)4 50 74 00 38, cares for non-skiing children.

Lunch

The main self-service restaurants are prone to overcrowding during high season or when snow-cover is poor elsewhere. It pays to seek out one of the authentic mountain huts. **Coquoz, t** +41 (0)24 479 1255, at Planachaux has a circular open fireplace and good food. The goat-farming hamlet of Les Lindarets has a number of enticing eateries including **La Crémaillère, t** +33 (0)4 50 74 11 68. **L'Abricotine, t** +33 (0)4 50 74 17 43, at Les Brochaux and **Les Crêtes de Zorre, t** +33 (0)4 50 79 24 73, are also recommended.

Dine

Avoriaz has a wide choice of restaurants. **La Table du Marché** and **Restaurant Gastronomique**, both **t** +33 (0)4 50 74 08 11, are in Hôtel Dromonts. **Le Bistro**, **t** +33 (0)4 50 74 14 08, opposite Le Village des Enfants, is good but expensive. **La Réserve**, **t** +33 (0)4 50 74 02 01, has wonderful lamb dishes. **Chez Flo**, **t** +33 (0)4 50 74 19 24, and **Le Petit Dru**, **t** +33 (0)4 50 74 02 24, are also recommended.

Party

The Place, **Le Shooter's** and **Le Globe Trotters Café** are all popular international pubs with live music. **Le Tavaillon-Pub** attracts predominantly young British customers. **Le Fest** and **Pub Le Choucas** are the late-night venues.

Sleep

Most visitors to Avoriaz stay in apartments. Bookings can be made through **Pierre et Vacances**, **t** +33 (0)8 25 82 08 20, **Agence Immobilière des Dromonts**, **t** +33 (0)4 50 74 00 03, **Agence Immobilière des Hauts Forts**, **t** +33 (0)4 50 74 16 08, and **Selectis**, **t** +33 (0)4 50 74 13 33. As all the skiing is from your door, it makes little difference where you stay.

*****Hôtel Dromonts**, **t** +33 (0)4 50 74 08 11, *www.christophe-leroy.com/dromont.htm*, has a Thalgo spa and a handy children's playroom.

*****Hôtel Neige & Roc**, **t** +33 (0)4 50 79 03 21, *www.neige-roc.com*, is down at Les Prodains.

Chamonix and Argentière

Profile

Strikingly beautiful glacial scenery and rugged off-piste beneath the soaring peaks of the Mont Blanc massif. This is a high alpine area best suited to strong intermediate and expert skiers and riders looking for new challenges. Beginners and nervous skiers should steer clear. Vibrant après-ski scene, a cosmopolitan ambience, and easy airport access

Resort

Chamonix first ventured into tourism in 1741 when two heavily armed English explorers, William Windham and Richard Pococke, took three days rather than the

* BEST FOR

Steep 'n' deep, rugged scenery, airport access, nightlife

ESSENTIALS

Altitude: 1035m (3,396ft)–3842m (12,605ft)
Further information: **t** +33 (0)4 50 53 00 24, *www.chamonix.com*
Lifts in area: 46 (1 funicular, 12 cableways, 17 chairs, 16 drags) serving 155km of piste; 729km in Mont Blanc ski area
Lift pass: Cham'Ski (covers Chamonix valley except Les Houches) €186, child 4–15yrs €130–158. Ski Pass Mont Blanc (covers all local resorts including Chamonix, Courmayeur, Les Houches) adult €252, child 5–15yrs €203, all for 6 days
Access: Geneva airport 1hr, railway station in resort

CHAMONIX

Mont-Blanc 4810m
Grandes Jorasses 4208 m
Dent du Géant 4013 m
Helbronner 3466 m
Blanc du Tacul 4248 m
Dome du Gouter 4304 m
Aiguille du Gouter 3817 m
Aiguille du Midi 3842 m
St-Gervais
Tramway du Mont-Blanc
Le Brévent 2525 m
Glacier des Bossons
Glacier du Géant
Vallée Blanche
Les Houches
Chamonix 1035 m
Planpraz 2000 m
Col Cornu 2414 m
L'Index 2385 m
Plan de l'Aiguille 2317 m
Le Savoy
La Salle à Manger
Aiguille Verte 4121 m
Aiguille du Dru 3754 m
Les Planards
Montenvers 1913 m
Mer de Glace
Les Praz 1060 m
La Flégère 1877 m
La Trappe
Les Grands Montets 3275 m
Bochard 2765 m
Glacier d'Argentière
La Herse 2595 m
Chosalets
Lognan 1972 m
Argentière 1252 m
Le Tour 1462 m
La Vormaine
Aiguillette des Posettes 2201 m
Chalets de Balme
Glacier du Tour
Charamillon 1856 m
Vallorcine 1264 m
Tête de Balme 2270 m
Domaine de Balme 2270 m
Col de Balme 2186 m

present one hour to reach the valley from Geneva. Pococke, for reasons best known to himself, was dressed as an Arab.

They gazed up at the ice fields of Mont Blanc, but it was another 45 years before the highest peak in Western Europe was successfully conquered by local crystal collector Jacques Balmat. Since then it has become the climbing – and more recently skiing – capital of the world.

The little town with its *fin de siècle* villas and grand hotels acts as a magnet for powderhounds. They are attracted by the extraordinarily steep and awe-inspiring terrain that takes no prisoners.

After a fresh overnight snowfall you must rise with the sun to cut first tracks. By mid-morning not a bowl or a single gully will be left unsullied by the passage of ski and board.

There are plenty of groomed pistes, but they are much steeper than in most other resorts. This is not the place for those who demand doorstep skiing and enjoy miles of conveniently linked motorways, nor is it a good resort for families or groups of mixed ability.

Mountain

Chamonix is dominated by the 3842m Aiguille du Midi, reached by cable-car from the southern side of town. This is the starting point for the famous Vallée Blanche, a glorious 22km descent past yawning crevasses and house-sized *séracs* (ice boulders) all the way back to Chamonix. Anyone who can ski parallel and who is not afraid of heights can tackle the easiest of the four main routes, but you must take a guide.

At the start you have to negotiate the ice steps cut into the spine of the ridge leading down from the cable-car station. They are not difficult, but the 2000m sheer drop to your left can have an unsettling psychological effect. The return to Chamonix is by rack-and-pinion railway from Montenvers or via a short climb and a long descent down a narrow path and piste to a cowbell factory on the outskirts of Chamonix.

But the town's main skiing is on the other side of the valley, reached either from the outskirts of the resort or from a lift station at Les Praz higher up the valley. Linked Le Brévent and La Flégère provide plenty of scope for intermediate and strong skiers.

However, for powderhounds the main course starts at the little village of Argentière, where an 80-person cable-car and a quad-chair give access to Lognan. From this mid-mountain station a cable-car (not included in the lift pass) rises to the 3275m Grands Montets, one of the world's greatest ski mountains. The descents from here through the glacier are as staggeringly beautiful as they are demanding. Pas de Chèvre, a run from the top of Bochard via one of several extreme couloirs down to the Mer de Glace is a Chamonix classic.

At the head of the valley, Le Tour offers some good novice terrain as well as rewarding runs on the Col de Balme and a long descent to Vallorcine. The Grands Montets and Le Tour both have terrain parks but the majority of snowboarders here are usually busy elsewhere, climbing up or riding down a vertiginous couloir.

Learn

The **ESF**, **t** +33 (0)4 50 53 22 57, offers traditional tuition. **Sensation Ski Ecole Internationale**, **t** +33 (0)4 50 53 56 46, takes a more offbeat approach. **Evolution 2**, **t** +33 (0)4 50 55 90 22, is strongly praised by reporters. The ESF also has a branch in **Argentière**, **t** +33 (0)4 50 54 00 12, and **Summit Ski Montagne**, **t** +33 (0)4 50 54 05 11, is the specialist board school. Other schools include **Kailish Adventure**, **t** +33 (0)4 50 53 18 99, and **Stages Bernard Muller**, **t** +33 (0)4 50 53 18 99.

Guiding is available through **Association Internationale des Guides du Mont-Blanc**, **t** +33 (0)4 50 53 27 05, **Compagnie des Guides de Chamonix**, **t** +33 (0)4 50 53 00 88, **Mont Blanc Ski Tours**, **t** +33 (0)4 50 53 82 16, **Roland Stieger**, **t** +33 (0)4 50 55 84 77, **Sensation Ski Ecole Internationale**, **t** +33 (0)4 50 55 94 26, **Stages Vallençant**, **t** +33 (0)4 50 54 05 11, and **Yak & Yeti**, **t** +33 (0)4 50 53 53 67.

Children

Two ski areas, Les Planards and Le Savoy, are reserved for children. The **ESF Piou Piou Club**, **t** +33 (0)4 50 53 22 57, cares for children from three years. The **ESF** runs its **Panda Club** ski kindergarten in **Chamonix**, **t** +33 (0)4 50 55 86 12, and in **Argentière**, **t** +33 (0)4 50 54 04 76. Both provide daycare and tuition from three years. **Evolution 2** gives lessons from three years at **Chamonix**, **t** +33 (0)4 50 55 93 03, and at **Argentière**, **t** +33 (0)4 50 54 21 36.

Lunch

At Lognan, **La Crèmerie du Glacier**, **t** +33 (0)4 50 55 90 10, in the woods above the base station of the Lognan cable-car, is one of the only restaurants not owned by the lift company. It is renowned for its *croûte fromage*. **Plan Joran**, **t** +33 (0)4 50 53 05 42, has good food and a sunny terrace.

We recommend **La Bergerie de Planpraz**, **t** +33 (0)4 50 53 93 40, at Brévent and **La Chavanne** at Flégère, **t** +33 (0)4 50 53 06 13.

In Chamonix, **Le Robinson**, **t** +33 (0)4 50 53 45 87, on the cross-country track, has a great atmosphere and serves mountain cuisine.

Dine

La Maison Carrier, **t** +33 (0)4 50 53 05 09, has outstanding Savoyard cuisine. **L'Auberge du Bois Prin**, **t** +33 (0)4 50 53 33 51, is also warmly recommended along with **Hôtel Eden in Les Praz**, **t** +33 (0)4 50 53 18 43. **Atmosphere**, **t** +33 (0)4 50 55 97 97, serves gourmet food. **La Calèche**, **t** +33 (0)4 50 55 94 68, specializes in traditional Savoyard dishes. **Le Satsuki**, **t** +33 (0)4 50 53 21 99, has sushi. **The Rusticana**, **t** +33 (0)4 50 55 88 28, in Argentière offers fish and chips and Irish stew.

Party

Chamonix has better and more lively après-ski than almost any other French resort. Start the evening with cocktails at **Chambre Neuf**, **Le Choucas**, **Le Privilege**, **Jekyll** or **Expedition** – rue du Docteur Paccard is paved with welcoming bars. **La Terrasse** on the main square occasionally has live music on its balcony. Other bars include **Elevation**, **Cybar**, **Bard'Up**, **Bar Moulin** and **Queen Vic**. The **MBC** bar and restaurant on the road towards Les Praz is a favourite with the locals. Real late-nighters end up at the **BPM**, or **The Garage** in Chamonix Sud.

In Argentière, **The Office** is a resort institution where you can drink, eat, listen to live music – or even stay.

Sleep

Chamonix offers the full spectrum, from youth hostels to four-star hotels, plus a wide choice of chalets and apartments. All bookings can be made through **Chamonix Reservations Centre**, **t** +33 (0)4 50 53 23 33.

****Le Hameau Albert 1er**, **t** +33 (0)4 50 53 05 09, *www.hameaualbert.fr*, is a stylish and atmospheric hotel owned by the Carrier brothers.

****L'Auberge du Bois Prin**, **t** +33 (0)4 50 53 33 51, *www.boisprin.com*, has considerable charm as well as a fine restaurant.

****Les Balcons du Savoy**, **t** +33 (0)4 50 55 32 32, *www.lesbalconsdusavoy.com*, are the resort's prime apartments.

★★★★**Grand Hôtel des Alpes, t** +33 (0)4 50 55 37 80, *www.grandhoteldesalpes.com*, is new and extremely comfortable.

★★★★**The Clubhouse, t** +33 (0)4 50 90 96 56, *www.thebigfriendlyhouse.com*, is a contemporary boutique hotel inside an Art Deco mansion built in 1927. Accommodation is in custom-built bunkhouses. Each has a plasma screen, Xbox, and 'rainforest' shower.

★★★**Hôtel Gustavia, t** +33 (0)4 50 53 00 31, *www.hotel-gustavia.com*, is lively and central ('food is fantastic and it has a lively après-ski bar separated from the hotel by a huge sound-proof door').

★★★**Park Hôtel Suisse, t** +33 (0)4 50 53 07 58, *www.chamonix-park-hotel.com*, is friendly and rated 'superb' by reporters.

★★**Hôtel Richemond, t** +33 (0)4 50 53 08 85, *www.richemond.fr*, is an old favourite in the town centre.

Argentière:

Hôtel Le Dahu, t +33 (0)4 50 54 01 55, *www.hotel-le-dahu.com*, is warmly recommended.

Le Lavancher:

★★★★**Hôtel Jeu de Paume, t** +33 (0)4 50 54 03 76, *www.jeudepaumechamonix.com*, is a romantic boutique hotel with an outstanding gourmet restaurant.

★★★**Les Chalets de Philippe, t** +33 (0)4 50 54 56 35, are tiny but stylishly converted wood-and-stone *mazots* (ancient barns).

La Clusaz

Profile

One of the closest resorts to Geneva airport with lots of low-level intermediate skiing, good mountain restaurants and modest hotels

✻ BEST FOR

Easy intermediate skiing, families, airport access

ESSENTIALS

Altitude: 1100m (3,608ft)–2600m (8,528ft)
Further information: t +33 (0)4 50 32 65 00, *www.laclusaz.com*
Lifts in area: 88 in Aravis (8 cableways, 27 chairs, 53 drags) serving 220km of piste
Lift pass: Aravis (covers La Clusaz, Le Grand-Bornand, Manigod and St-Jean-de-Sixt) adult €155, child 5–15yrs €114; La Clusaz adult €121.50–143.50, child 5–15yrs €103
Access: Geneva airport 1hr, railway station at Annecy 30mins

Resort

La Clusaz has been a resort since 1908 when local lad Pierre-Noël Vittoz experimented wth skis and an invention called *Le Paret*, the first-ever snowbike. The attractive village is built around an early 19th-century church and a mountain stream.

Mountain

The skiing is divided into five sectors. Access to Beauregard and L'Aiguille is by lifts from the resort centre. The other areas (Balme, L'Etale and Croix-Fry/Merdassier) are reached by ski-bus. Most of the skiing is ideal for intermediates. The terrain park on L'Aiguille receives much praise from reporters.

Learn

ESF, t +33 (0)4 50 02 40 83, is rated excellent, while the **ESI Sno-Académie, t** +33 (0)4 50 32 66 05, and **Aravis Challenge, t** +33 (0)4 50 02 81 29, are recommended. The others are **Evolution 2, t** +33 (0)4 50 23 52 77, **Alter Ego, t** +33 (0)6 07 39 72 53, and **Dimension Freeride, t** +33 (0)4 50 03 54 39.

Children

The **ESF** and **ESI** provide lessons. **Club des Mouflets**, **t** +33 (0)4 50 02 48 91, is the non-ski kindergarten, the ESF **Piou-Piou Club** offers daycare with optional ski lessons, and – unusually – there is a **cross-country ski kindergarten** for children from four years, **t** +33 (0)4 50 02 40 83 for all.

Lunch

Try **Altitude 1647**, **t** +33 (0)4 50 02 44 00, in the Beauregard area, and **Chalet des Praz**, **t** +33 (0)4 50 02 59 84, an atmospheric Savoyard chalet built in 1792 on the Crêt du Merle pistes. **Le Bercail**, **t** +33 (0)4 50 02 43 75, on the Massif de L'Aiguille, is a fine lunching experience.

Dine

Au Cochon des Neiges, **t** +33 (0)4 50 02 62 62, serves Savoyard cuisine. **La Calèche**, **t** +33 (0)4 50 02 42 60, is renowned for its fresh fish and home-made foie gras. **L'Arbé**, **t** +33 (0)4 50 02 60 54, has a chalet ambience. **Le Symphonie** in Hotel Beauregard, **t** +33 (0)4 50 32 68 00, is gastronomic.

Party

Après-bars include **La Grolle**, **Les Caves du Paccaly** and **La Braise**. **Le Pressoir** is a snowboarders' haunt and **Le Grenier** attracts the locals. **L'Ecluse** nightclub has a glass dance floor over the river, and at **Club 18** you can dance away until the early hours.

Sleep

★★★**Hôtel Beauregard**, t +33 (0)4 50 32 68 00, *www.hotel-beauregard.fr*, has an attractive interior and a swimming pool.

★★★**Hôtel L'Alpage de Tante Pauline**, **t** +33 (0)4 50 02 63 28, *www.chaletalpage.com*, has 10 rooms.

★★★**Hôtel Vieux Chalet**, **t** +33 (0)4 50 02 41 53, *www.levieuxchalet.fr*, is even smaller, with eight rooms.

★★★**Hôtel Alpen Roc**, **t** +33 (0)4 50 02 58 96, *www.hotel-alpenroc.fr*, a stable mate of the Beauregard, is 'very friendly and way above its star rating'.

★★**Hôtel Les Sapins**, **t** +33 (0)4 50 63 33 33, *www.clusaz.com*, is in a good position.

Courchevel

Profile

At its highest level, Courchevel is the most chic and the most expensive resort in France, and it also happens to have outstanding skiing. But that is just the top bit. Courchevel is made up of four quite separate villages at different altitudes and has something to suit everybody. You just need to know your geography

*BEST FOR

Cosmopolitan sophistication (1850), all levels of skiing, families, luxury accommodation

ESSENTIALS

Altitude: 1300m (4,265ft)–2738m (8,983ft)
Further information: **t** +33 (0)4 79 08 00 29, *www.courchevel.com*
Lifts in area: 167 in Trois Vallées (40 cableways, 69 chairs, 58 drags) serving 600km of piste
Lift pass: Trois Vallées adult €145.50–215, child 5–13yrs €109.50–161, both for 6 days
Access: Chambéry airport 1½hrs, Lyon airport 2½hrs, Geneva airport 3hrs, Eurostar at Moûtiers, 25km

les 3 vallées
savoie france
AIGUILLE DU FRUIT
3051 m
ROC MERLET
2734 m
MONT DU VALLON
2952 m
MONT DU BORGNE
3153
GLACIER
DU BORGNE
AIGUILLE DE PECLET
3562 m
POINTE DE THORENS
3266 m
MONT BREQUIN
3130 m
LA MAURIENNE
ORELLE
900
POINTE DE LA MASSE
2804 m
LES ENCOMBRES
LES AVALS
LA VIZELLE
2659 m
SAULIRE
COL DE LA LOZE
MONT DE PECLET
MONT DE LA CHAMBRE
3 MARCHES
MONT DE LA CHALLE
TOUGNETE
CHERFERIE
ROC DE FER
BRECHE DE ROSAËL
CIME DE CARON
VAL THORENS
2300
LES MENUIRES
1800
Le Bettex
Praranger
Saint Marcel
Le Châtelard
SAINT MARTIN DE BELLEVILLE
1400
COURCHEVEL
1850
COURCHEVEL
1650
COURCHEVEL
1550
COURCHEVEL 1300
LE PRAZ
LA TANIA
1350
MERIBEL MOTTARET
1750
MERIBEL
1450
MERIBEL VILLAGE
1400
Le Raffort
Les Allues
Saint Bon
Bozel
La Perrière
BRIDES LES BAINS
600
Téléski - Surface lift
Télésiège - Chairlift
Télésiège débrayable
High speed slow boarding chairlift
Télésiège débrayable à bulle
High speed slow boarding bubble chairlift
Télécabine - Gondola
Funitel
Téléphérique - Cable car
Point de passage entre les vallées
Links between the valleys
Gare intermédiaire
Intermediate station
Poste de secours
First aid

Resort

Courchevel has been reigning supreme since 1946 as the resort closest to the heart of Parisians. Ever since the Mugnier family first cashed in their cow pastures and agreed to the construction of the first lift, Courch', as the locals call it, has caught the eye of capital café society. In present-day terms what we are talking about is Courchevel 1850, the highest of these villages with direct links to Méribel and the other resorts of the Trois Vallées.

Courchevel 1850 is the only centre here with Le Jet Set appeal, a purpose-built portfolio of extraordinarily hedonistic hotels and private chalets perched on the mountainside above the still unspoilt valley town of Bozel. It has few alpine rivals for comfort and cuisine – and none for cost. It caters for an international clientele that includes Russians, and now Chinese and Bollywood, who frankly don't give a damn what it costs to stay, ski and eat here as long as they enjoy themselves. That's 1850.

Some 200 vertical metres down the mountain in both altitude and social standing comes Courchevel 1650, a more authentic French mountain village with reasonable restaurant prices and affordable chalet accommodation. It also has the best skiing.

Courchevel 1550, which is geographically directly below 1850 and now served by a new six-person chair, is becoming a serious satellite of its sophisticated sister, while 1650 retains a less affluent and earthy character entirely of it own.

At the bottom of the mountain lies the original farming village of Le Praz or Courchevel 1300. This is a delightful place to stay with good accommodation, one of the best restaurants in the area, and easy access by gondola to the other Courchevels. However, it is likely that resort-level snow-cover will be limited for a large proportion of the season.

Mountain

The number of lifts and the sheer scale of the skiing in the Trois Vallées is simply staggering. Mere statistics mean nothing, you have to see it for yourself. It is worth noting that the resort lift map takes considerable licence with the compass. Courchevel appears to be the most westerly resort in the region, when in fact it is the most easterly, a fact to be borne in mind when searching for sunshine or north-facing slopes.

From the hub of La Croisette at 1850 a network of gondolas and a cable-car take you up to 2738m Saulire. You can either ski down the far side to Méribel and further into the Trois Vallées, or return towards Courchevel. The main arterial run back down to 1850 can become horrendously overcrowded and it pays to spend time around the adjoining 2659m peak where most slopes are slightly more challenging and therefore less popular.

For accomplished skiers and riders, the black Les Suisses is particularly enjoyable. In the right snow conditions it is possible to ski from Saulire all the way down to Bozel below Courchevel – a vertical drop of over 2000m.

Courchevel is famed for its Couloirs, three ribbons of snow between the rocks that unfurl from the ridge on the right-hand side of the top station of the cable-car. Grand Couloir, Sous le Téléphérique and Emile Allais can be extremely demanding when icy. However, in good mid-winter snow conditions they should present no great problem to an experienced skier or rider. Catch them as soon as they are declared open after a major dump. They quickly become bumped up with some awkward VW-sized moguls in the high reaches. If you fall here, it is a long way down, but there are no obstacles and the likelihood of serious injury is small. However, you should treat the often icy approach route from the cable-car with considerable caution.

The Altiport sector of Courchevel just to the east of 1850 is good beginner terrain with green and easy blue runs that are ideal for building confidence before heading further afield. Topographically, the Trois Vallées is the perfect ski area. The links between different sectors are natural rather than contrived. This allows for more real ski time rather than hours wasted on paths. From almost everywhere there is an easy way down and anyone who can vaguely ski parallel can explore far afield.

During peak high season the cognoscenti head for Courchevel 1650 – unless they are already staying here. Its own extensive ski area beneath a trio of peaks is off the Trois Vallées beaten track. The runs on Col de Chanrossa, Signal and Bel Air above the village are suited to all standards and are some of the most enjoyable in the whole region. From Roc Merlet you can ski off-piste on the higher slopes of the Vallée des Avals on a glorious itinerary that brings you back down to 1650.

Snowboarders will find a good supply of natural hits throughout Courchevel. The terrain park at Plantrey has a half-pipe. Riders also congregate at Les Verdons and Biolley and there is a snowcross course near La Loze.

Learn

Ski lesson are big businees in Courchevel and there is intensive rivalry between the various schools. Large numbers of 'blacks' – unqualified ski bums – also tout for business and should be avoided. The **ESF**, **t** +33 (0)4 79 08 07 72, has branches in all the villages and, with over 700 teachers working during peak February, the quality of instruction is a lottery. We recommend **New Generation**, **t** +33 (0)4 79 01 03 18, owned and operated by **British BASI instructors. Supreme**, **t** +33 (0)4 79 08 27 87, is another long-established British school. **Ski Academy**, **t** +33 (0)4 79 08 11 99, has a strong reputation. **Absolute Ski**, **t** +33 (0)6 68 51 74 94, is a small school with local instructors. **Magic in Motion**, **t** +33 (0)4 79 01 01 81, is a favourite with tour operators. Guiding can be arranged through the ski schools or the **Bureau des Guides**, **t** +33 (0)4 79 01 03 66.

Children

Courchevel has the French government's *P'tits Montagnards* award for childcare. The **ESF** runs non-ski and ski kindergartens that come in for criticism during peak holiday times when they are stretched to capacity.

1850: **Village des Enfants**, **t** +33 (0)4 79 08 08 47, provides all-day care and an introduction to skiing from three years. **Magic in Motion**, **t** +33 (0)4 79 01 01 81, runs English-only classes for four- to six-year-olds. **Ski Academy**, **t** +33 (0)4 79 08 11 99, has morning classes for children from four years as well as dedicated classes for children aged 10 to 13 years and 14 to 16 years. **Supreme**, **t** +33 (0)4 79 08 27 87, has classes for children aged six to 12 years during school holidays.

1650: **Les Pitchounets**, **t** + 33 (0)4 79 08 33 69, is a dedicated play area for small children. **Le Club des Oursons**, **t** +33 (0)4 79 08 26 08, teaches children from three years. The **Garderie**, **t** +33 (0)6 20 66 37 23, cares for children under 18 months.

1550: **Le Club des Piou-Piou**, **t** +33 (0)4 79 08 21 07, takes children from three to five years for a mix of lessons and snow fun.

Lunch

Courchevel has lots of overpriced self-services and a portfolio of elegant piste-side eateries that cater for a clientele that sees a gourmet lunch and a €60 bottle of wine as a basic component of the skiing day. Booking is essential. Best value is **Bel-Air**, **t** +33 (0)4 79 08 00 93, at the top of the Courchevel 1650 gondola. It serves traditional Savoyard cuisine in a beautiful setting, with friendly and attentive staff.

Le Cap Horn, **t** +33 (0)4 79 08 33 10, by the Altiport, offers seafood and Asian dishes served by liveried waiters. **Chalet de Pierres**, **t** +33 (0)4 79 08 18 61, on the descent from Saulire, is a comfortable but costly resort institution with a sunny terrace, more liveried waiters, and an enticing display of desserts. In 1650, **Le Petit Savoyard**, **t** +33 (0)4 79 08 27 44, and **L'Eterlou**, **t** +33 (0)4 79 08 25 45, both serve pizzas.

Dine

In 1850, double Michelin-starred **Le Bateau Ivre**, **t** +33 (0)4 79 08 36 88, in Hotel Pomme de Pin, has inspirational cooking that stands head and shoulders above its many rivals. **Hôtel Le Chabichou**, **t** +33 (0)4 79 08 00 55, has a similar Red Guide accolade. **La Saulire** (known as **Jacques' Bar**), **t** +33 (0)4 79 08 07 52, is our favourite here; it has an impressive menu and wine list, intimate surroundings and impeccable, friendly service.

In 1650, prices are considerably lower. We recommended **L'Eterlou**, **t** +33 (0)4 79 08 25 45, and **La Montagne**, **t** +33 (0)4 79 08 09 85. In 1550, **L'Œil de Bœuf**, **t** +33 (0)4 79 08 22 10, is in an old mountain barn. In Le Praz, **La Table de mon Grand-Père** in Hotel Les Peupliers, **t** +33 (0)4 79 08 41 47, offers traditional cooking using fresh ingredients and is one of the finest restaurants in the region. **L'Ecurie**, **t** +33 (0)4 79 00 28 14, is in a 300-year-old converted stable in St Bon and is full of atmosphere.

Party

At **Prends Ta Luge et Tire-toi** in Courchevel 1850 you can check your emails, have a drink or buy a snowboard. The iniquitously expensive **Le Pyggys Pub** is popular, and **The Purple** is a new 'fashion bar' with a DJ. **Les Caves** is the shockingly expensive, late-night venue. In 1650, the British celebrate and check their emails in **Le Bubble**. **Le Plouc** is an intimate late-night bar. In 1550, après-ski centres around the friendly **Taverne**, the **Glacier Bar**, **Le Barouf** and **Chanrossa**. Family-oriented **Le Praz** (Courchevel 1300) falls asleep early, but you can enjoy a drink in L'Escorch'vel.

Sleep

Courchevel 1850:

- ★★★★*deluxe* **Hôtel Les Airelles**, **t** +33 (0)4 79 09 38 38, *www.airelles.fr*, is tastefully discreet.
- ★★★★*deluxe* **Hôtel Byblos Courchevel**, **t** +33 (0)4 79 00 98 00 attracts celebrities and has a sister hotel in St Tropez.
- ★★★★*deluxe* **Hôtel Kilimandjaro**, **t** +33 (0)4 79 01 46 46, *www.hotelkilimandjaro.com*, is a collection of chalets grouped around a central building with a restaurant and La Prairie spa.
- ★★★★*deluxe* **Hôtel Lana**, **t** +33 (0)4 79 08 01 10, has a spa with swimming pool.
- ★★★★*deluxe* **Le Mélézin**, **t** +33 (0)4 79 08 01 33, *www.amanresorts.com*, is the stylish alpine headquarters of Aman-resorts, with a gym and swimming pool.
- ★★★★*deluxe* **Hôtel Le Saint-Joseph**, **t** +33 (0)4 79 08 16 16, in the heart of the village, offers understated luxury combined with a retro style in its 11 rooms and three apartments.
- ★★★★**Chalet Aurea**, **t** +44 (0)20 8682 5050, *www.scottdunn.com*, is a short walk from the village centre and the main lift station. It has a sublime little swimming pool, hot tub and steam room.

★★★★**Hôtel Chabichou, t** +33 (0)4 79 08 00 55, *www.chabichou-courchevel.com*, is in a large chalet-style building, and offers weekly cookery courses.

★★★★**Hôtel des Neiges, t** +33 (0)4 79 03 03 77, has a gastronomic restaurant and Banyan Spa.

★★★★**La Sivolière, t** +33 (0)4 79 08 08 33, has recently been upgraded to four-star status.

★★★★**Hôtel Trois Vallées, t** +33 (0)4 79 08 00 12, has panoramic views.

★★★**Ducs de Savoie, t** +33 (0)4 79 08 03 00, has a swimming pool and is in the Jardin Alpin residential area.

★★★**La Loze, t** +33 (0)4 79 08 28 25, *www.la-loze.com*, has a library that doubles as a bar.

Courchevel 1650:

★★★**Hôtel du Golf, t** +33 (0)4 79 00 92 92, *www.hoteldugolf-courchevel.fr*, is ski-in/ski-out.

★★★**Le Seizena, t**+33 (0)4 79 01 46 46, *www.hotelseizena.com*, is a new B&B for this winter with 20 attractive and minimalist rooms.

★★★**Chalet Rikiki** is right on the edge of the piste, and **Chalet Les Sorbiers** has great views, both **t** +44 (0)870 754 4444, *www.leski.com*.

Le Praz:

★★★**Hôtel Les Peupliers, t** +33 (0)4 79 08 41 47, *www.lespeupliers.com*, is a delightful place to stay.

Les Deux Alpes

Profile

Large ski area with snow-sure glacial slopes served by a modern lift system. Suited to novices, intermediate cruisers, families and off-piste skiers in search of fresh challenges. The nightlife is some of the most frenetic in France

* BEST FOR

Certain snow-cover, wild après-ski, intermediates, snowboarding

ESSENTIALS

Altitude: 1650m (5,412ft)–3600m (11,808ft)
Further information: t +33 (0)4 76 79 22 00, *www.les2alpes.com*
Lifts in area: 49 (1 funicular, 6 cable-ways, 23 chairs, 19 drags) serving 220km of piste
Lift pass: Area (includes 1 free day in Alpe d'Huez, La Grave, The Milky Way, Puy-St-Vincent, Serre Chevalier) adult €168, child 6–13yrs €126, both for 6 days
Access: Grenoble airport 1½hrs, Lyon airport 2hrs

Resort

Les Deux Alpes lies between Grenoble and Briançon in a remote corner of the Dauphiné. Its biggest asset is its high altitude, which allows skiing to continue throughout much of the year and makes it a popular venue for out-of-season ski and snowboard camps. It has been a ski resort since 1939 when a primitive rope-tow was installed. Unfortunately this fell down 15 minutes after the opening ceremony. Hostilities with Germany then got in the way of any further development plans until the late 1950s when a gondola paved the way for Les Deux Alpes to become an important French resort.

The purpose-built village was conceived as a *station de ski* on the sunny balcony above the ancient community of Venosc to which it is connected by gondola but not by piste. Venosc, with its cobbled lanes, craft shops and enticing restaurants provides a welcome contrast and a tranquil alternative bed-base to the functional ski factory above it.

L2A sprawls along a narrow ledge below what were once the high summer pastures of sheep and goat farmers. The village lacks aesthetic appeal but is by no means an architectural eyesore on the scale of Tignes, Les Menuires and other French resorts that developed during the the 1960s.

L2A is suited to all levels of skier and rider. However, lower intermediates should note that on the main mountain the gradient is 'reversed'. Some of the easiest skiing is higher up on and around the glacier. The benefit of this is that complete beginners can learn against the panoramic backdrop of the high Alps rather than on a shaded slope tucked away on the outskirts of a village. The downside is that newcomers and other inexperienced skiers will find the much steeper final descent to L2A beyond their capabilities. The alternative is to follow a narrow and often icy green path. This is not made easier by the number of better skiers whizzing by. Until you have gained sufficient confidence it makes sense to download by gondola.

Advanced skiers will want to explore the glacial terrain of La Meije, reached by a 20-minute hike from the top of the ski area to the 3568m Dôme de la Lauze. From here you can ski all the way down to the ancient climbing village of La Grave.

Here and elsewhere in the L2A area it is important always to be aware that you are in high mountains where the weather can change within minutes. It is the kind of territory where anyone who goes off-piste without a qualified local mountain guide is risking their life. Even then, it is up to the individual to take overall responsibility for his or her own safety. Mountain guides, like everyone else, are fallible.

Mountain

A choice of gondolas and cable-cars provides main mountain access. The most important of these, the Jandri Express jumbo gondola, takes you to an underground funicular station at 3200m for the final ride to the top of the glacier. The whole journey from the village takes around 45 minutes, a practical indication of the enormous vertical drop here. The bulk of the skiing revolves around the hubs of Les Crêtes at 2100m and Toura at 2600m. The terrain flattens out on the lower reaches of the glacier to provide easy pistes where the snow quality is always excellent.

La Fée sector, off the shoulder below Toura, is usually uncrowded and offers some of the best blue and black runs on the mountain. On the other side of the resort, the Pied Moutet sector provides gentle sunny blue runs served by three lifts. From here, snow conditions permitting, you can also ski down to the village of Bons at 1300m.

L2A is an important resort for riders and each October hosts the World Snowboard Meeting. The terrain park has a 120m half-pipe and is one of the most sophisticated in Europe.

Learn

The **ESF**, **t** +33 (0)4 76 79 21 21, and **ESI St Christophe**, **t** +33 (0)4 76 79 04 21, are the main teaching establishments. The British-run **European Ski School**, **t** +33 (0)4 76 79 74 55, offers tuition in English for classes of up to four pupils. **Ski Privilège**, **t** +33 (0)4 76 79 23 44, and new British-run **Easiski**, **t** +33 (0)6 82 79 57 34, are alternatives. **Primitive**, **t** +33 (0)6 07 90 71 35, and **Burton Connexion**, **t** +33 (0)6 15 07 94 42, are the dedicated snowboard academies. Race-training is with **Stages Pierre Alain Carrel**, **t** +33 (0)4 76 80 51 99, and **Stages Damien Albert**, **t** +33 (0)4 76 79 50 38. Guiding is through **Bureau des Guides ESF**, **t** +33 (0)4 76 79 50 12.

Children

L2A has the coveted *Les P'tits Montagnards* award from the French

La Meije
3982
Les Ecrins
4102
Le Rateau
3809
Aiguille du Plat de la Selle
3596
Pic de la Grave
3669
Massif du Soreiller
Tête de Lauranoure
3323
Glacier de la Meije
Glacier du Râteau
Dôme de la Lauze
3568
Dôme de Puy Salié
3421
Grotte de Glace
Table d'orientation
Le Jandri
3288
La Toura
2914
Col des Ruillans
3211
Glacier de la Girose
Glacier de Mantel
GLACIER 3200m
Lac Noir
Snowpark
Tête du Diable
2868
Tête Moute
2813
TOURA 2600m
DIABLE 2400m
Clot de Chalance
Refuge Chancel
Itinéraire La Grave - La Meije
Conditions particulières d'accès aux remontées mécaniques
Renseignements :
Caisse centrale - Le Meijotel
Lac du Plan
LES 2 ALPES 1650m
CRÊTES 2100m
LA FÉE 2100m
Signal
2800
Roche Mantel
Funiculaire
Lauze
Trifides
Girose
Puy-Salié I & II
Jandri Express II
Glaciers I
Glaciers II
Grand Nord
Bellecombes
Super Diable
Vallons
Petite Aiguille
Village
Vallée Blanche
Belle Etoile
Jandri Express
Jandri I
Jandri II
Pied Moutet
Super Venosc
Mont-de-Lans
1300m
Mont de Lans
Bons
Cuculet
Lac du Chambon
1040
www.2alpe

government for excellence in childcare. **Crèche Les 2 Alpes 1800**, **t** +33 (0)4 76 79 02 62, cares for children aged six months to two years. **Garderie Le Bonhomme de Neige**, **t** +33 (0)4 76 79 06 77, looks after children aged two to six years. **Espace Luge** is a children's play area at the base of the mountain with animal characters, a trampoline, slalom course, snow-biking, tobogganing, tubing and an inflatable bob-run.

The **ESF**, **t** +33 (0)4 76 79 21 21, runs ski kindergartens in the village, at Champamé, and at Les Crêtes with lessons for little ones from three years combined with fun in the snow and indoor play and videos. **ESI St Christophe**, **t** +33 (0)4 76 79 04 21, is for children up to eight years. **The European**, **t** +33 (0)4 76 79 74 55, also runs classes for children.

Lunch

La Molière, **t** +33 (0)4 76 80 18 99, is at the foot of the pistes, and **Le Diable au Cœur**, **t** +33 (0)4 76 79 99 50, at 2400m, has an open fireplace and well-prepared regional cuisine. Both are recommended. **Les Glaciers**, **t** +33 (0)4 76 79 21 36, at 3200m, is a new self-service that also has separate gastronomic restaurants with 40 covers. **Le Panoramic**, **t** +33 (0)4 76 79 06 75, at 2600m, is a mountain hut with a great atmosphere and some of the best mountain fare in the resort.

Dine

The gourmet choices are the **Bel Auberge**, **t** +33 (0)4 76 79 57 90, which is 'Austrian style' with inventive cuisine, and **Le P'tit Polyte**, **t** +33 (0)4 76 80 56 90 , which has an excellent wine list. **L'Abri**, **t** +33 (0)4 76 79 21 41, has an alpine ambience. **La Spaghetteria**, **t** +33 (0)4 76 79 05 77, is recommended for pasta, and **Tribeca Caffé**, **t** +33 (0)4 76 80 58 53, for pizzas. **Blue Salmon**, **t** +33 (0)4 76 79 29 56, serves simple fish dishes, and **Il Caminetto**, **t** +33 (0)4 76 79 51 54, is a typical Italian restaurant. **Smokey Joe's**, **t** +33 (0)4 76 79 21 70, offers good-value Tex-Mex. **La Patate**, **t** +33 (0)4 76 79 23 55, serves raclette and fondue in an alpine atmosphere. **Hôtel-Chalet Mounier**'s restaurant, **t** +33 (0)4 76 80 56 90, has reasonable prices and romantic surroundings.

Party

'The nightlife is amazing', says one reporter. Popular watering holes include **The Irish Bar**, **Pub Le Windsor**, **Smokey Joe's**, **The Secret**, **Smithy's** and **Le Pressoir**. **L'Opéra** is the recommended disco. **L'Avalanche** and **La Casa** also have a strong following.

Sleep

Most of the accommodation is in apartments.

★★★★**Alpina Lodge**, **t** +33 (0)4 76 79 75 17, *www.les2alpes.com*, contains some very comfortable apartments for two to 10 people.

★★★★**Les Balconnes de Sarenne**, **t** +33 (0)4 76 79 57 97, *www.lesbalconnesdesarenne.com*, are luxury apartments.

★★★★**Hôtel La Bérangère**, **t** +33 (0)4 76 79 24 11, *http://berangerehotel.free.fr*, is ski-in/ski-out, with indoor and outdoor heated pools, games room and gym.

★★★★**Hôtel La Farandole**, **t** +33 (0)4 76 80 50 45, *www.utaf.com/lafarandole*, is a traditional chalet with gastronomic restaurant and a piano bar.

★★★**Hôtel Le Souleil'Or**, **t** +33 (0)4 76 79 24 69, *www.le-souleil-or.fr*, is a modern hotel with friendly owners and lots of alpine character.

★★★**Hôtel-Chalet Mounier**, **t** +33 (0)4 76 80 56 90, *www.chalet-mounier.com*, was a mountain refuge and alpine farm back in 1879. Today it is attractively decorated, and has a swimming pool and spa.

★★★**Hôtel Muzelle Sylvana, t** +33 (0)4 76 80 50 93, *www.skisystem.net*, is 50m from the Diable cable-car and has a good wine cellar.

Flaine

Profile

Large ski area with an excellent snow record near the Mont Blanc massif. Suitable for all standards of skier and rider looking for a no-frills holiday in delightful alpine surroundings. A short airport transfer and piste-side accommodation makes it popular with families

Resort

Flying down the red Lucifer run or blue Belzebuth above Flaine, it is easy to imagine you have somehow become in entangled in a devilish time warp. While other famous resorts in the French Alps over the past 38 years have expanded out of all recognition, this temple of Modernism, once worshipped by the British in general and by the Scots in particular, has so far remained largely undeveloped since the 1960s – but not for much longer.

The harsh diamond-shaped blocks of apartments conceived by architect Marcel Breuer still sit in a natural bowl on the edge of the Mont Blanc massif, little more than a one-hour drive from Geneva. Depending on your cultural viewpoint they are either an eyesore or a shining example of the Bauhaus School. True, the raw concrete edifices have mellowed in colour, but to us they still look as alien now to their majestic mountain setting as they did when the Beatles ruled the charts.

Indeed the only 'new' addition is the so-called Scandinavian Village, and that was built 20 years ago. This contrastingly pretty, but isolated collection of pastel-painted cabins on the outskirts now looks, like the rest of the village, run-down and in serious need of a makeover.

Weather-beaten sculptures by Picasso and Dubuffet still adorn the ski school meeting place. They serve as reminders that Flaine was originally planned by geophysicist and wealthy banker Eric Boissanas not only as a ski resort, but also as a cultural centre on snow.

Flaine's history as a major ski resort has been marked by more troughs and crests than anywhere else but, after a decade in the doldrums, it is suddenly about to become the hottest property in the Alps.

Resort developer Intrawest, the force behind the creation of the successful Arc 1950 village at Les Arcs, has picked Flaine for its next major investment in the Alps. The area around the main gondola base station is to be completely redeveloped and a new 'village' will be constructed below the Scandinavian village.

*BEST FOR

All levels of skier and rider, big ski area, ski convenience, reliable snow-cover

ESSENTIALS

Altitude: 1600m (5,248ft)–2480m (8,134ft)
Further information: t +33 (0)4 50 90 80 01, *www.flaine.com*
Lifts in area: 73 in Le Grand Massif (7 cableways, 28 chairs, 38 drags) serving 265km of piste
Lift pass: Grand Massif (covers Les Carroz, Flaine, Morillon, Samoëns, Sixt) adult €176, child 5–15yrs €130, both for 6 days
Access: Geneva airport 90mins, railway station at Cluses 25km, frequent bus service to resort

AIGUILLE VERTE
LE DRU
AIGUILLE DU MIDI
DOMES DE MIAGE
LE GRAND MASSIF
AIGUILLE DE WARENS 2544m
TETE DU COLONNEY 2692m
TETE DES LINDARS 2561m
LES GRANDES PLATIÈRES 2480m
TETE PELOUSE 2474m
LA CROIX DE FER 2337m
SALLANCHES
TETE DE VERET 2214m
LES GRANDS VANS 2204m
GERS 1718m
SIXT FER À CHEVAL
SALVAGNY
SIXT
FLAINE 1600m
flaine 1600-2500
ARBARON 1916m
TETE DES SAIX 2120m
VERNANT
LE LAC
LES MOLLIETS
1900 m
1800 m
VALLON
SAMOËNS VILLAGE
SAMOËNS 1600
Samoëns
LA VIELLE 1500m
Les Carroz 1200m
MORILLON été/hiver

The first of 550 apartments – increasing the number of beds in Flaine by 30 per cent – are scheduled for completion by 2008 and all should be completed by 2012. Each building will have a different cultural theme – contemporary is the watchword – in keeping with the resort's original avant-garde image. Canny skiers who did not buy in Les Arcs will be reaching for their chequebooks, for Flaine has just as much to offer.

Despite its modest altitude, Flaine has a more reliable snow record than any resort of comparable altitude in France, thanks to the microclimate created by nearby Mont Blanc. Snow-cover is virtually guaranteed from early December until late April. Equally important is the high quality of the ski terrain, which extends to the traditional villages of Samoëns, Morillon, Les Carroz and Sixt.

Mountain

Main mountain access is by gondola, which takes you up to the Grandes Platières at 2480m. This is the starting point for a whole series of runs graded blue, red and black leading down into the main bowl of Flaine. The natural amphitheatre is rimmed by a series of lifts all going up to around 2500m. Good nursery slopes are located in and outside the village, making it an ideal spot for families with young children.

For more adventurous skiers and riders, Flaine is a base for exploring further afield into the Grand Massif. The Intrawest development plan has spurred the Compagnie des Alpes – owners of the lift system – to promise a series of upgrades including a link to the main part of the new village, situated just below the Scandinavian complex.

The main link out of the bowl is a fast eight-person chair. From the 2204m summit of the Tête des Saix, north-facing runs drop down steep mogul slopes towards Samoëns. Alternatively you can choose easier cruising pistes that bring you all the way down to Morillon or to Les Carroz. The ancient village of Sixt has its own small ski area and is directly linked into the Grand Massif via a piste, but ski-buses provide the only means of return.

Anyone who can ski parallel can enjoy day-long excursions to the far corners of the Grand Massif. However, the lift system is prone to high-season bottlenecks in the afternoon when everyone is heading for home.

Flaine was one of the first resorts in France to embrace snowboarding. The 1500m Jam-Park has a half-pipe and snowcross course. Fantasurf has a half-pipe for children.

Learn

The **ESF**, **t** +33 (0)4 50 90 81 00, has a large presence. Anglo-Saxon visitors tend to favour the **ESI**, **t** +33 (0)4 50 90 84 41, which has small classes of six to seven pupils. We have good reports of **Moniteurs Independants**, **t** +33 (0)6 07 19 56 09, a co-operative of individual teachers run by veteran instructor Guy Pezet. They offer group and private instruction for adults and children. **Stages François Simond**, **t** +33 (0)4 50 90 80 97, and **Stages Flaine Super Ski**, **t** +33 (0)6 81 06 19 06, both offer race training. Guiding is available through the ski schools.

Children

All the ski schools offer lessons, with the **ESI La Souris Verte**, **t** +33 (0)4 50 90 84 41, putting children into small groups. The **ESF Rabbit Club**, **t** +33 (0)4 50 90 81 00, is more Gallic. Both offer a collection and drop-off service. **MMV** in Hotel Aujon and **Le Flaine**, **t** +33 (0)4 92 12 62 12, have mini-clubs for four to 11 years and a youth club for 12 to 14 years. **Club Med**, **t** +33 (0)4 50

90 81 66, has childcare for its small residents. Crystal's Hotel Totem **Whizz Kids**, t +44 (0)870 160 6040, was rated 'first class' by reporters. **Les P'tits Loups**, t +33 (0)4 50 90 87 82, accepts children from six months to three years.

Lunch

Blanchot, t +33 (0)4 50 90 82 44, is renowned for its onion soup. **Epicéa**, t +33 (0)4 50 90 83 79, between Flaine Forêt and Forum, has good pasta. **L'Eloge**, t +33 (0)4 50 90 85 91, by the Flaine gondola, provides simple food and service with a smile. **L'Igloo**, t +33 (0)4 50 90 14 31, at the top of the Morillon chair, has reasonable food at good prices. The **Oréade**, t +33 (0)4 50 90 03 61, at the top of the Kédeuse gondola, has local mountain dishes. **Le Bissac**, t +33 (0)4 50 90 81 32, is a busy self-service with a good range of lunch-time dishes.

Dine

In Flaine Forum, try friendly **Chez La Jeanne**, t +33 (0)4 50 90 81 87, for excellent pizzas. **L'Auroch**, t +33 (0)4 50 90 12 83, and **Le Grain de Sel**, t +33 (0)4 50 90 80 49, serve traditional French cuisine. **Chez Daniel**, t +33 (0)4 50 90 81 87 has a warm alpine ambience. **La Pizzeria Chez Pierrot**, t +33 (0)4 50 90 84 56, has the best pizzas in town. **Les Chalets du Michet**, t +33 (0)4 50 90 80 08, has plenty of atmosphere. In Flaine Forêt, the British-run **La Perdrix Noire**, t +33 (0)4 50 90 81 81, specializes in Savoyard cuisine and has a fine reputation.

Party

'Ideal family resort – too quiet for a boys' holiday' said one reporter. Certainly other destinations have livelier après-ski. The **Flying Dutchman** has karaoke and **Le Diamant Noir** is busy at weekends and in high season. You can also try your hand at driving a saloon car on ice. **The Motoring School**, t +33 (0)4 50 90 44 07, is one of the most famous in France.

Sleep

All the original hotels are now run by French or British tour operators; accommodation can also be booked through **Flaine Reservations**, t +33 (0)4 50 90 89 09, *www.flainereservations.com*.

- ★★★**Le Hameau de Flaine**, t +33 (0)4 50 90 40 40, on the mountain at 1800m, has Scandinavian-inspired chalets.
- ★★**Cap'Vacances Les Lindars**, t +33 (0)4 71 50 80 88, *www.capvacances.com*, is in the centre, with a sun terrace and a theatre.
- ★★**The Totem**, t +44 (0)870 160 6040, is run by Crystal Holidays and has good-sized rooms. 'The food was 10 out of 10' said reporters.
- ★★**Hôtel-Club Le Flaine MMV**, t +33 (0)4 50 90 47 36, *www.mmv.fr*, has spacious rooms and good food.
- ★★**Hôtel-Club Aujon MMV**, t +33 (0)4 50 90 80 10, *www.mmv.fr*, has comfortable, clean rooms.
- ★★**Résidence de la Forêt**, t +33 (0)4 50 90 86 99, situated at the top of the resort, has old-style Pierre et Vacances apartments.

La Grave

Profile

For experts only. Rugged off-piste skiing on the glacial slopes of the mighty 4000m La Meije. The ski area is tenuously linked to Les Deux Alpes

*BEST FOR
Steep 'n' deep, off the beaten track

ESSENTIALS
Altitude: 1450m (4,757ft)–3550m (11,647ft)
Further information: **t** +33 (0)4 76 79 90 05, *www.lagrave-lameije.com*
Lifts in resort: 4 (2 cableways, 2 drags) serving 5km of piste
Lift pass: adult €158, child under 16yrs €138, both for 6 days
Access: Grenoble airport 2hrs

Resort

La Meije, which rises above the rugged little village of La Grave between Grenoble and Briançon, was the last great peak of the Alpes to be conquered. Local guide Pierre Gaspard finally reached the 3982m summit in 1877. This corner of L'Oisans is one of the poorest, least populated, and most wildly beautiful areas of France, a place of jagged peaks and rushing waterfalls.

La Grave has some of the most demanding high-altitude skiing and snowboarding in Europe, with an extraordinary vertical drop of 2200m through dramatic glacial scenery.

The top of the ski area can be reached by a long gondola and drag-lift from La Grave or by a 20-minute hike from the top of the ski area at Les Deux Alpes.

Mountain

The old but efficient gondola takes half an hour to climb from the village of La Grave to the top station. You must then find your own way down between the giant *séracs* and yawning crevasses. The main routes are clearly indicated but stray from the well-beaten path and you may encounter some spectacular couloirs. Runs at le Pan de Rideau start with a traverse along the edge of cliffs that requires a certain degree of concentration even for the most experienced powderhound.

From the top of the ski area you can either descend to the valley or ski off the backside with a guide to the remote village of of St-Christophe-en-Oisans. You can take a taxi back to Venosc below Les Deux Alpes, climb through the lift system to the glacier, and return to La Grave down the front face of La Meije.

Learn

This is not teaching terrain. You can hire a guide from the **Bureau des Guides**, **t** +33 (0)4 76 79 90 21, but the only tuition is with the **ESF**, **t** +33 (0)4 76 79 92 86, 5km away at **Le Chazelet**.

Children

The **ESF** in Le Chazelet accepts children from four years. Babysitting can be arranged through the tourist office.

Lunch

The area has three mountain refuges, but most people have lunch in the village.

Dine

La Meije, **t** +33 (0)4 76 79 21 27, is a new pizzeria close to the tourist office. The other restaurants are in the hotels.

Party

La Grave itself has little to offer anyone who does not climb or ski off-piste.

Sleep

★★★**Hôtel les Chalets de la Meije**, **t** +33 (0)4 76 79 97 97, has double, triple and quadruple rooms, and a restaurant.

★★**Hôtel Edelweiss**, **t** +33 (0)4 76 79 90 93, *www.hotel-edelweiss.com*, has a bar and restaurant.

La Roche Méane, **t** +33 (0)4 76 79 91 43, *www.rochemeane.com*, is a charming and good-value B&B that was once an old stone barn. It has five bedrooms.

Les Houches

Profile

Family-friendly resort in the Chamonix Valley with good tree-skiing for all levels and a revered World Cup downhill course. Ski area linked by lift only to St-Gervais

Resort

Les Houches is a pleasant family resort with the best tree-skiing in the Mont Blanc region. It has an FIS World Cup downhill course considered by racers to be second only in technical difficulty to the Streif on the Hahnenkamm in Kitzbühel.

Mountain

Main mountain access is by an old cable-car from the village, or by a brand-new eight-person gondola which will open in time for the start of the season. Don't be surprised to see a railway carriage slowly crossing the pistes near the cable-car top station. The rack-and-pinion Mont Blanc Tramway, which comes up from St-Gervais, opened in 1904 and is still going strong.

The pistes offer a wide variety of skiing for all levels with some excellent trails winding through the woods. The slopes are used by the **British Ski Academy**, **t** +44 (0)20 8399 1181, a skiing school (with academic as well as ski lessons) for young British hopefuls, based in Les Houches.

Learn

ESF, **t** +33 (0)4 50 54 48 79, and **Evolution 2**, **t** +33 (0)4 50 54 31 44, are the two schools. The **Compagnie des Guides de Chamonix**, **t** +33 (0)4 50 47 21 68, has a branch in Les Houches.

Children

The **ESF Jardin des Neiges**, **t** +33 (0)4 50 54 48 79, is for skiers from three years. **La Garderie des Chavants**, **t** +33 (0)4 50 54 48 19, looks after little ones from three months.

Lunch

Try **Les Vieilles Luges**, **t** +33 (0)6 84 42 37 00, at Maisonneuve, **Le Prarion**, **t** +33 (0)4 50 54 40 07, at Prarion and **Le Courant d'Air**, **t** +33 (0)4 50 55 99 65, on the Col de Voza.

* BEST FOR

All levels of skier and rider, families, boy/girl racers

ESSENTIALS

Altitude: 1000m (3,281ft)–1860m (6,102ft)
Further information: t +33 (0)4 50 55 50 62, *www.leshouches.com*
Lifts in area: 19 (1 mountain railway, 2 cableways, 4 chairs, 12 drags) in Les Houches serving 55km of piste; 729km in Mont Blanc ski area
Lift pass: Chamonix-Mont Blanc adult €216, child 5–11yrs €173
Access: Geneva airport 1hr, railway station in resort

Dine

La Sabaudia, t +33 (0)4 50 54 47 72, **Le Kandahar**, t +33 (0)4 50 54 26 34, and **La Ferme des Agapes**, t +33 (0)4 50 54 50 69, offer regional specialities.

Party

Nightlife is restricted to a couple of quiet bars. If you require after-dinner entertainment, it's best to head into Chamonix.

Sleep

- ★★★**Hôtel Beau-Site**, t +33 (0)4 50 55 51 16, *www.hotel-beausite.com*, is in the heart of the village with a restaurant and a swimming pool.
- ★★★**Hôtel Chris-Tal**, t +33 (0)4 50 54 50 55, *www.chris-tal.fr*, has a games room and a swimming pool.
- ★★★**Hôtel du Bois**, t +33 (0)4 50 54 50 35, *www.hotel-du-bois.com*, is decorated in traditional chalet style, and houses Le Caprice restaurant.
- **La Ferme d'en Haut**, t +33 (0)4 50 54 74 87, *www.lafermedenhaute.fr*, is an early 19th-century farmhouse with four bedrooms.

Megève

Profile

A smart ski town near Chamonix that is much loved by Parisians. It has alpine ambience, superlative designer hotels, Michelin-rated restaurants and sophisticated nightlife. It's best suited to families, intermediates and non-skiers

Resort

Megève vies with Courchevel 1850 for the title of France's smartest resort. It was founded in 1914 by Baroness de Rothschild who, during the years following the First World War, turned it into her own winter salon for European aristocracy. The rich and famous built houses here and, at one point, the resort liked to boast that it was the winter home to more kings and queens – both crowned and uncrowned – than any other resort in Europe.

Its heyday was in the 1950s and 1960s when artist and author Jean Cocteau, as well as celebrities such as Charles Aznavour, Sacha Distel, Johnny Halliday and Brigitte Bardot, made it the focus of Parisian café society.

Patronage has continued from other influential families such as Citroën, Taittinger and Benetton. However, the only royals left these days are the House of Saudi who have a lavish chalet just above the town.

Megève's position, just an hour's drive from Geneva airport, makes it popular with weekenders and families wanting to avoid long transfers. Its only downside is that low altitude can restrict snow-

* BEST FOR

Sophisto-cats, ski gourmets, intermediate cruisers, window-shoppers

ESSENTIALS

Altitude: 1113m (3,651ft)–2350m (7,708ft)

Further information: t +33 (0)4 50 21 27 28, *www.megeve.com*

Lifts in area: 111 in Evasion Mont Blanc (13 cableways, 38 chairs, 60 drags) serving 450km of piste; 729km in Mont Blanc ski area

Lift pass: Ski Pass Mont Blanc (covers all local resorts including Chamonix, Courmayeur, Les Houches) adult €252, child 5–15yrs €203, both for 6 days

Access: Geneva airport 1hr, TGV railway station at Sallanches 10km, regular bus service to resort

AIG. DE ROSELETTE 2384
MONT JOLY 2525
AIG. CROCHE 2487
CRÊT DU MIDI 1890
2353
CÔTE 2000
L'EPAULE 2112
LES CONTAMINES
MT JOUX 1958
LE PLANAY
ALTIPORT
ROCHEBRUNE 1764
LE TORRAZ 1930
FLUMET
PRAZ S/ ARLY
LE CHRISTOMET 1853
CHARMOTS
CASSIOZ
FREDDY 1833
MT D'ARBOIS 1840
LE PLANELLET
LE VILLARD
ST NICOLAS DE VEROCE
LES CHATTRIX
LES COMMUNAILLES
LE JAILLET 1580
LA MOTTAZ
LES PLANS
LES PETTOREAUX
MEGÈVE
LES PRAZ
LE BETTEX
MONT D'ARBOIS
PONT D'ARBON
LE VERNAY
MONTS ROSSET
VAUVRAY
LA PRINCESSE
DEMI-QUARTIER
LE CHATELET
CUPELIN
LE FREYNET
ORMARET
ST GERVAIS MONT-BLANC
COMBLOUX
GARE TGV
LE FAYET
Frédérique et Pierre Novat
© 04

cover in the village, although it had a stupendous season in 2005–6.

The focal point of Megève is a central square surrounded by mellow 18th-century buildings, a fine medieval church, and the Aallard department store where the world's first ski trousers were tailored.

Brightly painted sleighs driven by local farmers ply for hire to reach the lift stations and hotels. They are more fun but more expensive that the free ski-buses and regular services to Chamonix and other resorts in the region covered by the extensive Evasion Mont Blanc lift pass.

Mountain

This enormous ski area extends from the spa town of St-Gervais and the village of Saint-Nicolas-de-Véroce through Megève and on to the little resort of La Giettaz where wooded slopes lead down to Praz-sur-Arly in the Val d'Arly. The next step will be for Megève to join the new 73-lift Espace Diamant circuit here that includes Flumet, Notre-Dame-de-Bellecombe, Les Saisies and Crest-Voland.

For the present, Megève's skiing is divided into three sectors with two of them, Mont d'Arbois and Rochebrune, joined by cableways.

A gondola from the town centre or a cable-car from the outskirts takes you up to Rochebrune. The area offers the most attractive runs in the resort and is usually less crowded than Mont d'Arbois. From the top of the gondola, a sequence of further lifts and pistes lead up to Côte 2000, which has some of the most challenging runs in the region.

The main beginner and intermediate area of Mont d'Arbois is reached by cable-car and gondola from Rochebrune or by a choice of two gondolas from the other side of town. A network of green and blue pistes provide easy skiing back towards Megève, or you can venture almost endlessly further afield. From 1958m Mont Joux you cruise wood-fringed pastures to Le Bettex and St-Gervais, or you can tackle higher and more demanding exposed terrain at 2350m on Mont Joly.

Le Jaillet, Megève's third and least-known area, is reached by gondola from the edge of town. The front face, leading back to the resort, has a good variety of mainly red runs and usually remains uncrowded even in high season. A new six-seater chair takes you up to the 1853m summit of Christomet where you can ski down to La Giettaz. Some outstanding off-piste can be found on the wooded slopes beneath the Tête de Bonjournal, as well as runs from La Torraz into the Val d'Arly.

Megève is a popular destination for cross-country skiers with four circuits totalling 70km, including a long, scenic track from the Mont d'Arbois cable-car to Le Bettex and Saint-Nicolas-de-Véroce.

The resort's only terrain park is at Mont Joux, and there is a snowcross course at Rochebrune.

Learn

Both the **ESF**, **t** +33 (0)4 50 21 00 97, and the **ESI**, **t** +33 (0)4 50 58 78 88, are warmly recommended ('excellent, friendly tuition. The best lesson I have had in many years'). **Ecole Freeride**, **t** +33 (0)4 50 93 03 52, and **Summits**, **t** +33 (0)4 50 93 03 52, are the alternatives. Guiding can be arranged through the long-established **Bureau des Guides de Megève**, **t** +33 (0)4 50 21 55 11.

Children

Megève has a justified reputation for providing good childcare. The non-ski kindergarten, **Meg Accueil**, **t** +33 (0)4 50 58 77 84, situated next to the Palais des Sports, cares for children from 12 months. **Club Piou-Piou**, **t** +33 (0)4 50 58 97 65, accepts skiers from three to five years.

La Princesse, **t** +33 (0)4 50 93 00 86, looks after skiers from two-and-a-half years. All the ski schools offer children's classes. **Ecole Freeride**, **t** +33 (0)4 50 93 03 52, limits the class size to six.

Lunch

You can eat better on the mountain in Megève than in any other resort in France, but you will pay for the privilege. At Rochebrune, **L'Alpette**, **t** +33 (0)4 50 21 03 69, has been a lunch-time institution since 1935. **Côte 2000**, **t** +33 (0)4 50 21 31 84, is also praised. At Mont d'Arbois, **Les Mandarines**, **t** +33 (0)4 50 21 31 27, and **L'Igloo**, **t** +33 (0)4 50 93 05 84, both have good food. At Le Jaillet, **Auberge du Christomet**, **t** +33 (0)4 50 21 11 34, is warmly recommended. **Chez Ernestine**, **t** +33 (0)4 50 93 13 08, on the route from Mont d'Arbois to St Gervais via Mont Joly, is warmly praised ('an amazing steak with superb views of Mont Blanc').

Dine

Chef Marc Veyrat's **La Ferme de Mon Père**, **t** +33 (0)4 50 21 01 01, has three Michelin stars and is one of the top restaurants in France. **Le Cintra**, **t** +33 (0)4 50 21 02 60, is famed for its seafood. **Flocons de Sel**, **t** +33 (0)4 50 21 49 99, has a Michelin star. **L'Alpage**, **t** +33 (0)4 50 21 30 39, has a good ambience and serves Savoyard specialities. Delightfully named **Le Sapin Chaud**, **t** +33 (0)4 50 91 08 88, is in an old wooden chalet. **Le Prieuré**, **t** +33 (0)4 50 21 01 79, and **Mirtillo**, **t** +33 (0)4 50 21 69 33, are both recommended.

Party

Après-ski is taken just as seriously as the skiing, with window-shopping for jewellery, antiques and designer clothing a major part of the early evening entertainment. **Club de Jazz Les Cinq Rues**, off the church square, is both an apéritif and late-night focal point. Its cosy surroundings draw some of the biggest names in jazz from both sides of the Atlantic. **Bar Tabac St-Paul** attracts the locals. The **Palo Alto** houses two popular discos. The **Casino**, originally a 1930s bus station, also has a restaurant. **Le Pallas** is popular with the young crowd. **Bar des Alpes**, opposite the Post Office, is an Internet café. **Wake Up** is a cocktail and tapas bar.

The **Palais des Sports** has an outdoor Olympic-size skating rink and a swimming pool. Electric-powered ice bumper cars are an unusual sport on the skating rink.

Sleep

The standard of Megève's four-stars is outstanding.

******Chalet Hôtel du Mont d'Arbois**, **t** +33 (0)4 50 21 25 03, *www.chalet-montarbois.com*, used to be the Rothschild family home and is located close to the Mont d'Arbois cable-car. The hotel also has a separate chalet, **Le Réfuge du Planay**, which has four double rooms.

******Le Fer à Cheval**, **t** +33 (0)4 50 21 30 39, *www.feracheval-megeve.com*, is attractively decorated and serves a good English breakfast.

******Les Fermes de Marie**, **t** +33 (0)4 50 93 03 10, *www.c-h-m.com*, 10 minutes' walk from the centre, is an exquisite place to stay, based around an ancient cowshed and other farm buildings. A swimming pool is set into rocks and the spa is one of the finest in Europe.

******Le Hameau de Mavarin**, **t** +33 (0)4 50 91 48 70, *www.skicollection.co.uk*, is a collection of five de luxe chalets and four apartments offering hotel service.

★★★★**Lodge Park**, **t** +33 (0)4 50 93 05 03, *www.c-h-m.com*, looks like a private club decorated in hunting-shooting-fishing style.

★★★★**Le Manège**, **t** +33 (0)4 50 21 41 09, *www.hotel-le-manege.com*, is small and chalet-style with 30 rooms.

★★★★**Mont Blanc**, **t** +33 (0)4 50 21 20 02, *www.c-h-m.com*, is perfectly placed in the centre of the pedestrian district and is one of the best small hotels in the Alps.

★★★★**Chalet Saint Georges**, **t** +33 (0)4 50 93 07 15, *www.hotel-chaletstgeorges.com*, provides excellent accommodation.

★★★★**Le Chalet Saint Philippe et Son Hameau**, **t** +33 (0)4 50 91 19 30, *www.chalet-saint-philippe.com*, are four luxury chalets with hotel service.

★★★★ **La Ferme du Châtel and La Ferme d'Hauteluce**, **t** +33 (0)4 50 93 03 10, *www.c-h-m.com*, are two beautiful chalets, the latter with an indoor swimming pool.

★★★**Hôtel Coin du Feu**, **t** +33 (0)4 50 21 04 94, *www.coindufeu.com*, is a delightful small hotel.

★★★**La Grange d'Arly**, **t** +33 (0)4 50 58 77 88, *www.grange-darly.com*, is a comfortable place to stay.

★★★**Au Vieux Moulin**, **t** +33 (0)4 50 21 22 29, *www.vieuxmoulin.com*, is tastefully decorated, with excellent food.

★★**La Chauminé**, **t** +33 (0)4 50 21 37 05 is a B&B with 11 rooms.

Les Menuires

Profile

Large sunny purpose-built resort in the giant Trois Vallées area favoured by the budget-conscious who want to ski Méribel and Courchevel without the high cost of staying there. Suits all standards of skier and rider

Resort

The ugly duckling of French ski resorts from the 1960s has grown positively handsome in middle age. A swan it is not, but Les Menuires has long since matured from the low-cost concrete dormitory that it once was into a comfortable and convenient ski base that lies 450 vertical metres short of Val Thorens up the winding road from Moûtiers.

The original eyesore of La Croisette had a makeover for the Albertville Olympics (the slalom events took place here) and then a couple of years ago the worst *résidence* was bulldozed to make way for

*BEST FOR

All levels of skier and rider, value, ski convenience

ESSENTIALS

Altitude: 1850m (6,068ft)–3300m (10,827ft)

Further information: Les Menuires, **t** +33 (0)4 79 00 73 00, *www.lesmenuires.com*

Lifts in area: 167 in Trois Vallées (40 cableways, 69 chairs, 58 drags) serving 600km of piste

Lift pass: Trois Vallées adult €145.50–215, child 5–13yrs €109.50–161, both for 6 days

Access: Chambéry airport 2hrs, Lyon airport 2½hrs, Geneva airport 3hrs, railway station at Moûtiers 25km

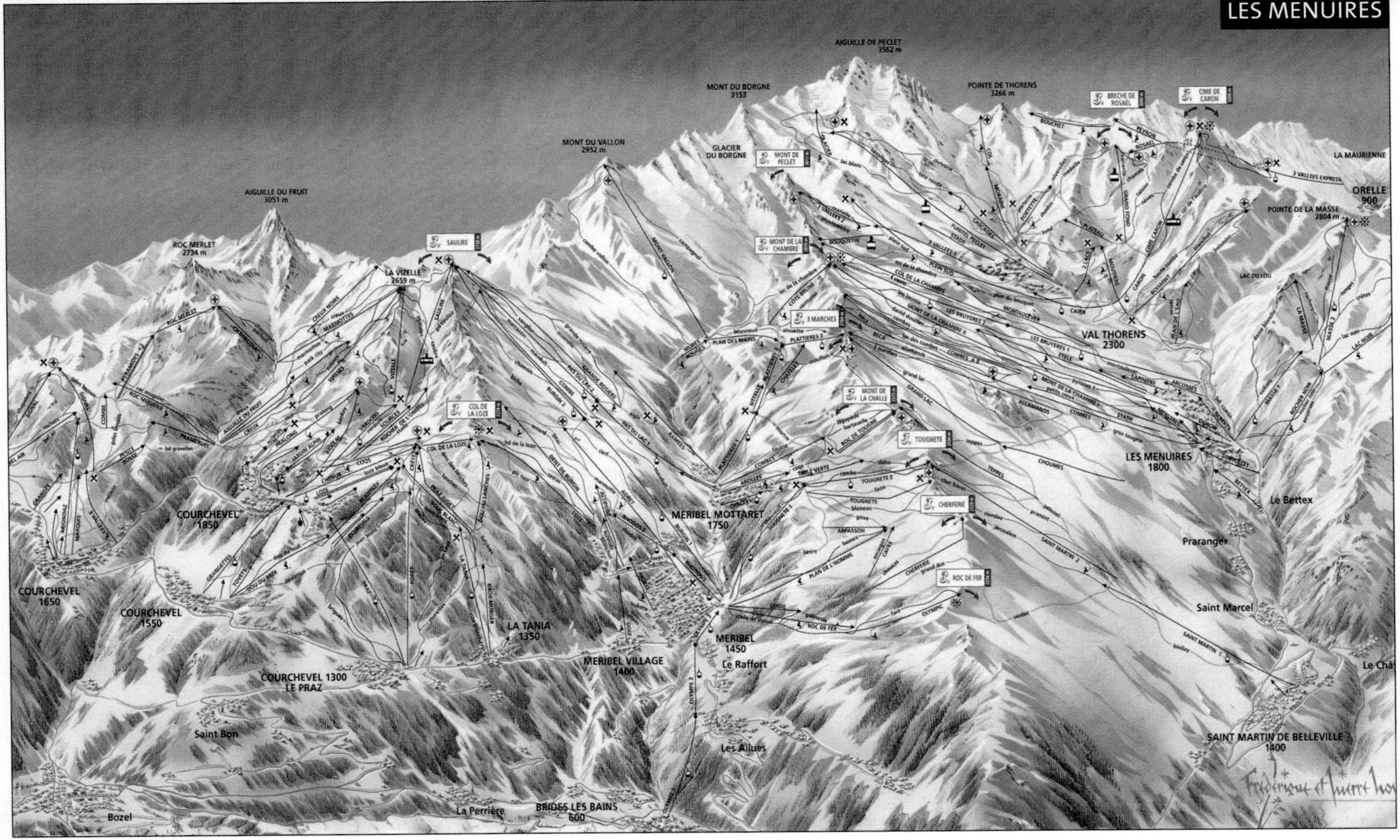
AIGUILLE DE PECLET
3562 m
MONT DU BORGNE
3153
POINTE DE THORENS
3266 m
BRECHE DE ROSAEL
CIME DE CARON
GLACIER DU BORGNE
MONT DE PECLET
MONT DU VALLON
2952 m
LA MAURIENNE
ORELLE
900
AIGUILLE DU FRUIT
3051 m
POINTE DE LA MASSE
2804 m
MONT DE LA CHAMBRE
ROC MERLET
2734 m
SAULIRE
LA VIZELLE
2659 m
LAC DU LOU
3 MARCHES
VAL THORENS
2300
COL DE LA LOZE
MONT DE LA CHALLE
TOUGNETE
LES MENUIRES
1800
Le Bettex
CHERFERIE
COURCHEVEL
1850
MERIBEL MOTTARET
1750
Praranger
ROC DE FER
COURCHEVEL
1650
COURCHEVEL
1550
Saint Marcel
LA TANIA
1350
MERIBEL
1450
MERIBEL VILLAGE
1400
Le Raffort
COURCHEVEL 1300
LE PRAZ
Saint Bon
Les Allues
SAINT MARTIN DE BELLEVILLE
1400
Bozel
La Perrière
BRIDES LES BAINS
600

a gleaming new MGM apartment block that has completely changed the aspect of the resort. The construction of a church also gave it physical, if not spiritual, soul providing a focal point for the real village that Les Menuires had finally become.

Much of the new development is concentrated on the pleasant satellites of Reberty, Les Bruyères and Preyerand, slightly higher up the hill, which have really become a resort in their own right with restaurants, shops, and bars (but no pharmacy – the only one is to be found in La Croisette).

Inevitably the downside of this grand metamorphosis is that Les Menuires is no longer the bargain basement it once was. However, accommodation prices remain significantly lower than in the more fashionable big-name resorts of the Trois Vallées. Val Thorens, St-Martin-de-Belleville and Méribel are easily reached on skis. A trip to the lower reaches of Courchevel is more of an expedition – a full day out with scarcely time to grab a quick lunch before beginning the journey home. Missing the last lift connections involves an expensive taxi ride.

Mountain

The skiing takes place on both sides of the valley. Les Menuires has its own challenging and usually uncrowded ski area on the 2805m Pointe de la Masse, reached from the village by gondola and chair. Runs down the front face include the infamous black Dame Blanche, which can be tricky in icy conditions. The summit is the starting point for several off-piste itineraries towards the Lac du Lou and Val Thorens, as well as down the valley towards St-Martin.

On the other side of Les Menuires, an assortment of gondolas and chairs take you up to Roc des 3 Marches and Mont de la Chambre above the Méribel Valley. The new Les Granges six-seater chair has replaced two old drag-lifts here. The enormous area of open slopes leading back down to Les Menuires provide the sunniest and some of the most enjoyable skiing in the Trois Vallées. A huge battery of snow-cannons usually manages to maintain cover on the lower slopes into April, although inevitably they suffer from their south-facing aspect. Riders have a new terrain park and a snowcross course in the Combes-Becca sector.

Learn

The **ESF**, **t** +33 (0)4 79 00 61 43, is the only ski school in Les Menuires. Most – but not all – instructors speak reasonable English.

Children

Village des Schtroumpfs, **t** +33 (0)4 79 00 63 79, cares for non-skiers from three months at La Croisette, and those from two-and-a-half years can go to the **Village des Piou Piou**, **t** +33 (0)4 79 00 69 50, in Bruyères. The **ESF**, **t** +33 (0)4 79 00 61 43, gives lessons from three years.

Lunch

Le Grand Lac, **t** +33 (0)4 79 08 25 78, is a new gourmet restaurant at the bottom of Les Granges chair. **Chalet 2000**, **t** +33 (0)4 79 00 60 57, at Reberty, is warmly recommended. **Chalet des Neiges**, **t** +33 (0)4 79 00 60 55, above St-Martin, has good food and a sunny terrace, and **Quatres Vents**, **t** +33 (0)4 79 00 64 44, at Les Bruyères, maintains a high standard.

Dine

Eateries include **La Marmite du Géant**, **t** +33 (0)4 79 00 74 75, and **Les Sonnailles**, **t** +33 (0)4 79 00 74 28, both in Les Bruyères.

La Trattoria, **t** +33 (0)4 79 00 74 23, in La Croisette and **La Ferme de Reberty**, **t** +33 (0)4 79 00 77 01, are also recommended.

Party

Après-ski in Les Menuires is fairly muted, with most French families keeping to their apartments. **The Tilbury**, **L'Oisans** and **Crazy Bar** are popular watering holes. **Le New Pop** at La Croisette and **Le Leeberty** at Les Bruyères are the late-night venues. Night-time tubing takes place on two 200m-long pistes equipped with a moving carpet. Swimming and skating are the other après-ski activities.

Sleep

Les Menuires is mainly apartment territory. All can be booked through the reservations office, **t** +33 (0)4 79 00 79 79.

Reberty/Les Bruyères:

- ★★★★**Les Montagnettes 3 Vallées**, **t** +33 (0)4 79 00 20 51, *www.montagnettes.com*, is a collection of spacious chalets and apartments.
- ★★★★**MGM Hameau des Marmottes**, **t** +44 (0)870 750 6820, *www.ernalow.co.uk*, are extremely comfortable apartments.
- ★★★★**Les Alpages de Reberty**, **t** +33 (0)4 79 01 35 35, is a smart Pierre et Vacances complex.
- ★★★**Les Bruyères**, **t** +33 (0)4 79 00 75 10, *www.latitudeshotels.com*, in Les Bruyères offers some good-value accommodation.
- ★★★**Hôtel Le Menuire**, **t** +33 (0)4 79 00 60 33, *www.le-menuire.fr*, has family-sized rooms with satellite TV.
- ★★★**L'Ours Blanc**, **t** +33 (0)4 79 00 61 66, *www.hotel-ours-blanc.com*, has a lounge with an open fireplace and a rustically decorated bar.
- ★★**Chalet 2000**, **t** +33 (0)4 79 00 60 57, *www.hotel-chalet2000.fr*, has double, triple and quadruple rooms.

Méribel

Profile

Méribel is a sprawling chalet-style resort built originally by an Englishman on the mountainside above the valley town of Moûtiers. The most central and convenient base for fully exploring the giant Trois Vallées ski area, it offers an enormous amount of intermediate skiing and the widest choice of luxury chalets of any resort in Europe

Resort

Méribel vies with Val d'Isère for the title of the most popular resort in Europe for English-speaking skiers. It was founded in the late 1930s by British skier Colonel Peter Lindsay who, like other international racers, had boycotted St Anton in Austria and was looking for a new resort when he stumbled upon the scenic Les Allues Valley.

The first lift was installed after the Second World War when Lindsay began developing the area in conjunction with French racer Emile Allais. He decreed that all buildings must be made of stone and

✻ BEST FOR

Beginners and intermediates, families, luxury chalets

ESSENTIALS

Altitude: 1400m (4,593ft)–2952m (9,685ft)
Further information: **t** +33 (0)4 79 08 60 01, *www.meribel.net*
Lifts in area: 167 in Trois Vallées (40 cableways, 69 chairs, 58 drags) serving 600km of piste
Lift pass: Trois Vallées adult €145.50–215, child 5–13yrs €109.50–161, both for 6 days
Access: Chambéry airport 2hrs, Lyon airport 2½hrs, Geneva airport 3hrs, Eurostar at Moûtiers, 18km

wood with slate roofs in order to blend into their beautiful mountain environment. Méribel today has grown into a ski city that he would not begin to recognize. It stretches in different *quartiers* up the mountain from Méribel Village at 1400m to the top of Méribel Mottaret at 1800m. But, miraculously, his building regulations have been vigorously adhered to and, with the exception of the original buildings of Mottaret, Méribel avoided the concrete architectural horrors of the 1960s. The main village is connected to the valley by a long gondola that climbs from the spa resort of Brides-les-Bains.

Heart of the resort is Méribel 1450, which houses most of the shops, restaurants, and the lift hub of La Chaudanne. The biweekly street market provides colour. Other communities are situated off the dead-end road leading to the Altiport and on the edge of the wooded pistes leading into the resort. Confusingly, Méribel Village is not the main village but a modern satellite situated a 2km drive away from 1450, but linked by chair-lift into the ski area.

Méribel Mottaret is a higher satellite situated at 1750m on the road above Méribel 1450, and is a convenient base for anyone wanting doorstep skiing and the best snow-cover. The different sectors of town are served by a ski-bus which reporters complain is oversubscribed. Some walking is inevitable. Before booking accommodation – particularly for families with young children – it's important to find out where your hotel or chalet is located.

From Méribel a mighty network of lifts links Courchevel, La Tania, Les Menuires and Val Thorens to form one of the world's greatest intermediate playgrounds. However, so many English-speakers congregate here during the winter months that you could be forgiven for thinking that this was some sloping suburb of southwest London rather than a top French ski resort.

Mountain

You need a whole season to explore every corner of the Trois Vallées, and Méribel is the best place to begin. From the Chaudanne lift centre at 1450 and from Méribel Mottaret higher up the valley, lifts rise on either side. To the east, gondolas take you up to 2738m at Saulire for a choice of descents towards Courchevel and La Tania. The mountain-side back down to the resort is crisscrossed with mainly blues, benign reds and an assortment of chairs. To the west, more gondolas and chairs rise to the long ridge that separates the valleys of Les Allues and Belleville. From the top you can ski towards Les Menuires, St-Martin-de-Belleville and Val Thorens. Alternatively you can explore the dozens of lifts and runs down to Méribel 1450 and Méribel Mottaret.

Accomplished skiers and riders head for the more challenging terrain off the Mont de la Chambre, Mont Vallon and the Col du Fruit at the head of the valley. The sheer volume of skiers funnelling into both 1450 and Mottaret at peak times means that some queuing is inevitable, but the lift system is extremely efficient. One of the greatest assets of the Trois Vallées is that anyone who can ski parallel can travel far afield without ever leaving blue runs, while better skiers can find a route to the same destination almost entirely on reds. The seemingly endless range of runs has produced a whole generation of skiers who never go anywhere else.

Méribel has good nursery slopes with easy green runs around the Altiport and back to the resort. The resort has two terrain parks: the 1200m Moon Park and the Snowpark des Plattières at Mottaret.

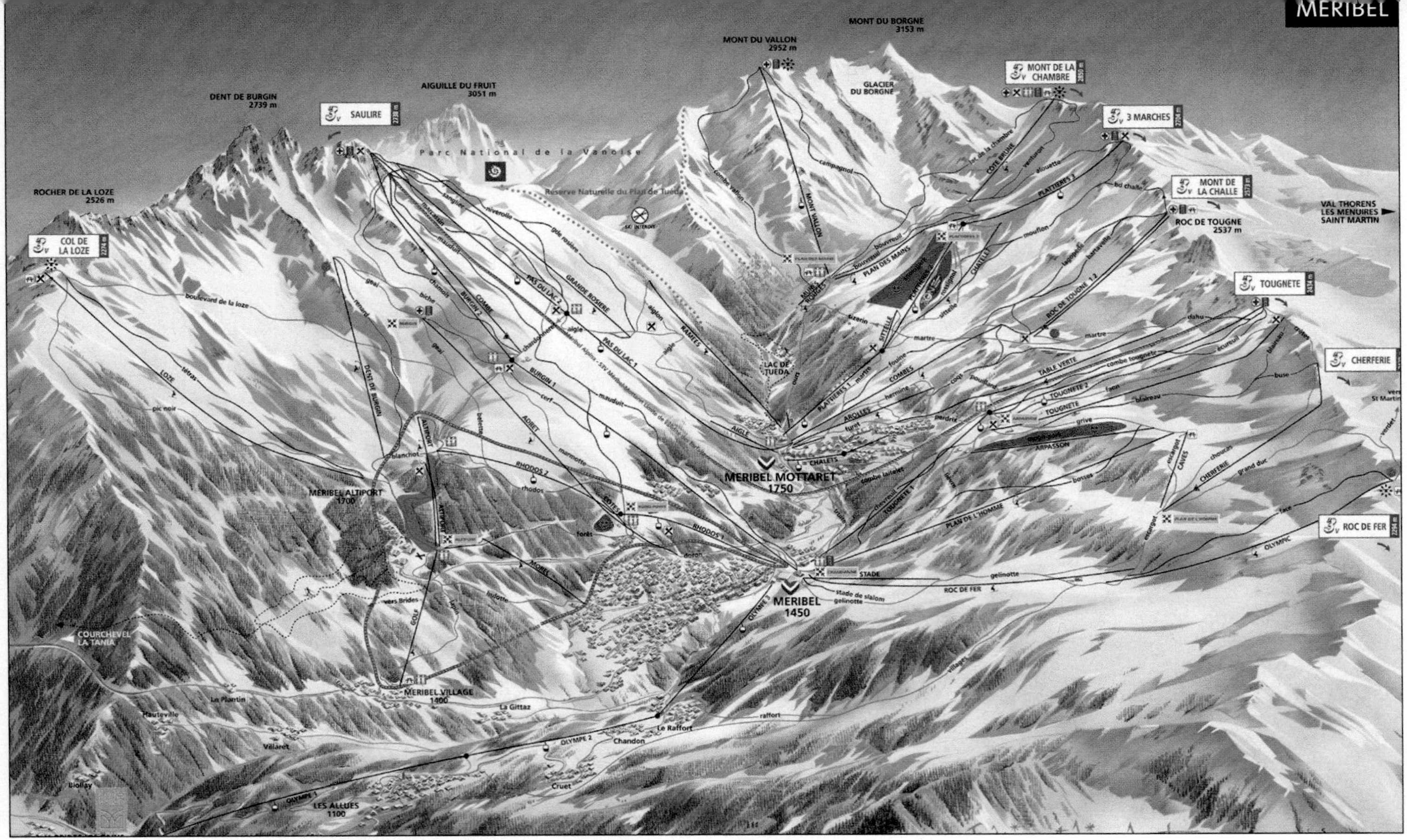
MONT DU BORGNE
3153 m
MONT DU VALLON
2952 m
GLACIER DU BORGNE
MONT DE LA CHAMBRE
3 MARCHES
MONT DE LA CHALLE
ROC DE TOUGNE
2537 m
VAL THORENS
LES MENUIRES
SAINT MARTIN
TOUGNETE
CHERFERIE
ROC DE FER
AIGUILLE DU FRUIT
3051 m
DENT DE BURGIN
2739 m
SAULIRE
ROCHER DE LA LOZE
2526 m
COL DE LA LOZE
Parc National de la Vanoise
Reserve Naturelle du Plan de Tueda
LAC DE TUEDA
MERIBEL MOTTARET
1750
MERIBEL
1450
MERIBEL ALTIPORT
1700
MERIBEL VILLAGE
1400
COURCHEVEL
LA TANIA
La Plantin
Hauteville
Villaret
La Gittaz
Le Raffort
Chandon
Cruet
Biollay
LES ALLUES
1100

Back

Learn

The **ESF**, **t** +33 (0)4 79 08 60 31, has 400 teachers and the standard of instruction varies enormously. Ian and Susan Saunders are BASI instructors who work for the ESF and have their own company, **Ski Principles**, **t** +33 (0)4 79 00 52 71. British-run **New Generation**, **t** +33 (0)4 79 01 03 18, is much praised by reporters. **Magic in Motion**, **t** +33 (0)4 79 08 53 36, is the other mainstream option. **Absolute Ski**, **t** +33 (0)6 68 51 74 94, is a small school with local instructors. **Ski Academy**, **t** +33 (0)4 79 08 11 99, teaches skiing and snowboarding and is geared towards English-speaking clients.

Children

Les Saturnins, **t** +33 (0)4 79 08 66 90, is the non-ski kindergarten for children aged 18 months to three years. The tourist office, **t** + 33 (0)4 79 08 60 01, also has a list of babysitters who will care for infants in your hotel or apartment. **Les P'tits Loups** ski kindergarten cares for children aged three to five years at **La Chaudanne**, **t** +33 (0)4 79 08 60 31, and at **Mottaret**, **t** +33 (0)4 79 00 49 49. The British ski school, **Parallel Lines**, **t** +44 (0)1702 589 580, has BASI instructors and small classes. **Snow Systems**, **t** +33 (0)4 79 00 40 22, receives praise. Off-piste guiding is through the **Bureau des Guides**, **t** +33 (0)4 79 00 30 38.

Lunch

Eating on the mountain is iniquitously expensive anywhere in the Trois Vallées. **Les Castors**, **t** +33 (0)4 79 08 52 79, is an old favourite at the foot of the Truite run in Méribel. **Les Rhododendrons**, **t** +33 (0)4 79 00 50 92, at the top of the Rhodos gondola and **Restaurant Le Rond Point**, **t** +33 (0)4 79 00 37 51, are both recommended. **Bibi Phoque**, **t** +33 (0)4 79 00 30 93, at Chaudanne, has reasonably priced pancakes. **The Altiport Hôtel**, **t** +33 (0)4 79 00 52 32, has a sunny terrace. **Chalet de Tougniat**, **t** +33 (0)4 79 00 45 11, at the top of the Combes chair out of Mottaret, is off the beaten track.

Dine

Most visitors here eat in their chalets, which accounts for the low number of good restaurants in proportion to the size of the resort. **Chez Kiki**, **t** +33 (0)4 79 08 66 68, specializes in meat cooked over an open fire. **La Taverne**, **t** +33 (0)4 79 00 32 45, in Hotel Le Roc offers pizzas and Savoyard cuisine. **Le Refuge**, **t** +33 (0)4 79 08 61 97, has a warm atmosphere and **Le Croix Jean-Claude**, **t** +33 (0)4 79 00 61 05, is good value with excellent food and wine. **Cactus Café**, **t** +33 (0)4 79 00 53 67, has reasonably priced Tex-Mex ('best value in the Trois Vallées').

In Mottaret, **Côte Brune**, **t** +33 (0)4 79 00 40 97, is an old favourite.Try **Au Temps Perdu**, **t** +33 (0)4 79 00 36 64, for a wide choice of crêpes, or **Pizzeria du Mottaret**, **t** +33 (0)4 79 00 40 50. **Le Ty Sable**, **t** +33 (0)4 79 00 43 32, is also recommended.

Party

In Méribel, **Jack's Bar** and **Le Rond Point** are busy in the late afternoon as the lifts close. **Le Saint Amour** and **Les Enfants Terribles** are wine bars with plenty of atmosphere. **Scott's** is an internet café with sofas and good bar food. **Le Loft**, located above the ice rink, and **Dick's Tea-Bar** are the late-night discos.

In Mottaret, **Le Rastro** is famous for its Tuesday rock parties, and **Zig Zig** beside it is popular as the lifts close. **Downtown Bar** has a pool table and occasional live music. The **Piano Bar** in Hotel Mont Vallon caters for an older age group. **Le Privilege** is the disco.

In Méribel Village, **Le Lodge du Village** has live après-ski music on Tuesdays and Thursdays.

Sleep

★★★★**Hôtel Le Grand Cœur**, **t** +33 (0)4 79 08 60 03, *www.legrandcoeur.com*, was one of Méribel's first hotels and remains its finest. Excellent food and service.

★★★★**Hôtel Le Mont Vallon**, **t** +33 (0)4 79 00 44 00, *www.hotel-montvallon.com*, is a stylishly decorated hotel in Mottaret, with family rooms, split-level suites, a swimming pool and fitness centre.

★★★★**Chalet Le Brames**, **t** +44 (0)20 7384 3854, *www.descent.co.uk*, set above the village, is the most sumptuous chalet here. It sleeps 20 and has a huge open-plan living room, gym, cinema and outdoor hot tub.

★★★★**Chalet Moguls**, **t** +44 (0)1264 738 257, *www.belvedereproperties.net*, is a charming home-from-home set in the exclusive Belvedere sector.

★★★**Chalet-Hôtel Marie Blanche**, **t** +33 (0)4 79 08 65 55, *www.marieblanche.com*, has wood-panelled bedrooms and a restaurant serving traditional Savoyard dishes.

★★★**Hôtel Le Yeti**, **t** +33 (0)4 79 00 51 15, *www.hotel-yeti.com*, has large, south-facing bedrooms and an attractive lounge with log fire.

★★★**Chalet-Hôtel Parc Alpin**, **t** +33 (0)4 79 08 29 63 has been completely rebuilt with 12 instead of 23 rooms and now has a pool and a sauna.

Montgenèvre

Profile

Sole French component of the otherwise Italian Milky Way circuit, an unpretentious French border town with lots of charm, but blighted by road traffic

Resort

Montgenèvre, the ancient village on the Italian frontier, is the only French part of the Milky Way ski area which last season successfully hosted the XX Winter Olympics. Away from the main arterial road it is a pleasant, unspoilt rural French town with tumbledown stone houses and a weekly market selling local produce. Unfortunately it is blighted by through traffic including heavy lorries en route from Turin to Briançon and beyond. However, reporters were impressed by the friendliness of the resort.

Mountain

Skiing takes place on both sides of the main road leading to the frontier. Montgenèvre's own area, beneath 2680m

* BEST FOR

Big ski area, beginners and intermediates, reasonable prices

ESSENTIALS

Altitude: 1860m (6,102ft)–2800m (9,186ft)
Further information: **t** +33 (0)4 92 21 52 52, *www.montgenevre.com*
Lifts in area: 86 in Milky Way (6 cableways, 38 chairs, 42 drags) serving 400km of piste
Lift pass: Milky Way (covers Montgenèvre, Sestriere, Sauze d'Oulx and other smaller resorts) adult €193, child 8–12yrs €137, both for 6 days
Access: Turin airport 1¼hrs

Le Chalvet, holds considerable charm and challenge, with runs for all standards leading back down to the village and over the border to Claviere. Snow-cannons were added to provide secure training slopes for the Olympic teams.

On the other side of the road, a gondola and a quad-chair provide direct access towards the Monti della Luna and the long runs to Cesana Torinese. Montgenèvre has a terrain park with a half-pipe in the Gondrans area. Reporters complain that the region has too many drag-lifts.

Learn

The **ESF, t** +33 (0)4 92 21 90 46, receives glowing reports ('staff spoke excellent English and were very attentive'). **Apeak, t** +33 (0)4 92 21 83 30, is the alternative.

Children

Halte Garderie, t +33 (0)4 92 21 52 50, is for six months to six years, **Club Piou Piou, t** +33 (0)4 92 21 90 46, introduces three- to five-year-olds to skiing, and **Apeak, t** +33 (0)4 92 21 83 30, runs a children's programme.

Lunch

Try **Les Chalmettes, t** +33 (0)4 92 21 93 04, **Les Anges t** +33 (0)6 14 61 97 52, and **La Bergerie, t** +33 (0)4 92 21 81 06.

Dine

Le Jamy, t +33 (0)4 92 21 92 62, has the best food and is renowned for its fondues. **La Ca del Sol, t** +33 (0)4 92 21 87 08, **Pizzeria Le Transalpin, t** +33 (0)6 63 48 38 15, and **Le Refuge, t** +33 (0)4 92 21 92 97, are all recommended. **Le Napoléon, t** +33 (0)4 79 21 94 60, is a warmly recommended pizzeria.

Party

Le Graal Café and **La Ca del Sol** are the resort meeting places. **Le Blue Night** is the disco. Montgenèvre has a natural skating rink at the bottom of the slopes.

Sleep

- ★★★**Hôtel Napoléon, t** +33 (0)4 92 21 92 04, *www.hotel-napoleon.com*, is the original inn.
- ★★★**Hôtel Valérie, t** +33 (0)4 92 21 90 02, *www.hotel-montgenevre.com*, near the church, is comfortable.
- ★★ **Hôtel Alpis Cottia, t** +33 (0)4 92 21 50 00, is reasonably priced.

Morzine and Les Gets

🏆 BEST FAMILY RESORT LES GETS 2007

Profile

These traditional resorts are two of the baker's dozen of small towns and villages that form the Portes du Soleil, a giant linked ski area that straddles the French border with Switzerland above Lac Léman. Morzine is a bustling market town, while Les Gets is a traditional Savoyard village

Resort

Morzine has been a ski resort since before the First World War, and during the mid-1920s it established a reputation as an important international holiday centre. Wealthy guests arrived to spend the winter at the comfortable Grand Hotel, which boasted central heating and fine cuisine. They passed their days ice-skating on the frozen lake and skiing on the rolling summer pastures of Pléney. The first cable-car was installed in 1934, but the Second World War put a stop to further development. It wasn't until 1960 that the winter sports industry began to eclipse the cattle and sheep farming which, together with forestry, still forms part of the local economy.

The catalyst for this was Jean Vuarnet, a young *Morzinois*, who was packed off to the USA that February with the expectations of the entire town on his shoulders. He came home from the VIII Winter Olympics in Squaw Valley clutching the gold medal for the downhill.

As a reward he was given the task of creating the more snow-sure satellite of Avoriaz on the clifftop above the town and of linking this new purpose-built village and Morzine to other resorts in the region – not only in France but also across the border with Switzerland.

The task proved every bit as difficult as beating Hanspeter Lanig of Germany and fellow Frenchman Guy Perillat down the mountain in California. But, with a winning combination of guile and charm, he finally persuaded the villages to bury differences which in some cases stretched back centuries, and create the Portes du Soleil. The first link was built in 1968 and the single lift pass – now electronic – was introduced in 1974. The ski area is named after a mountain pass above Les Crosets, on the Swiss side of the frontier, that catches the first rays of sunlight each morning. Ironically, Vuarnet is already better remembered for his sunglasses than his sunny ski area, which now has 206 lifts and 650km of piste.

Not every farmer was converted to harvesting the lucrative annual snow crop, and the attractive town of Morzine continues to be what it always was – a regional agricultural centre with a life that exists outside tourism.

✻BEST FOR

High-mileage cruisers, families, village ambience (Les Gets)

ESSENTIALS

Altitude: 1000m (3,280ft)–2466m (8,090ft)
Further information: **Morzine t** +33 (0)4 50 74 72 72, *www.morzine-avoriaz.com*; **Les Gets t** +33 (0)4 50 75 80 80, *www.lesgets.com*
Lifts in area: 206 in Portes du Soleil area (14 cableways, 82 chairs, 110 drags) serving 650km of piste
Lift pass: Portes du Soleil (covers 13 resorts) adult €152–179, child 5–16yrs €102–120, both for 6 days
Access: Geneva airport 1½hrs, railway stations at Thonon les Bains 31km, Cluses 25km

The town sits in a wooded basin marked by the confluence of several mountain streams and covers a large area on both sides of the river gorge. The principal street runs from the village centre up to the foot of Le Pléney where many of the hotels are located. The various sectors of the town, and the lift stations, are linked by a road-train and free buses.

Morzine's low altitude means that snow-cover in the village is by no means always reliable. Avoriaz usually has the best snow in the region, but this is not the best corner of the Alps for certain snow at Christmas or Easter. Avoriaz usually has the best skiing, but in these uncertain winters of global warming even its 2466m top station is simply not high enough. If only the mountains here were elevated by 1000m, the Portes du Soleil would be classed as one of the greatest circuits of the world.

Morzine is linked across 1550m Pléney to the traditional dairy farming village of Les Gets, a community that dates back to the 12th century. The two holiday bases are only 6km apart by road, but contrastingly different. Les Gets is a pleasing mix of old

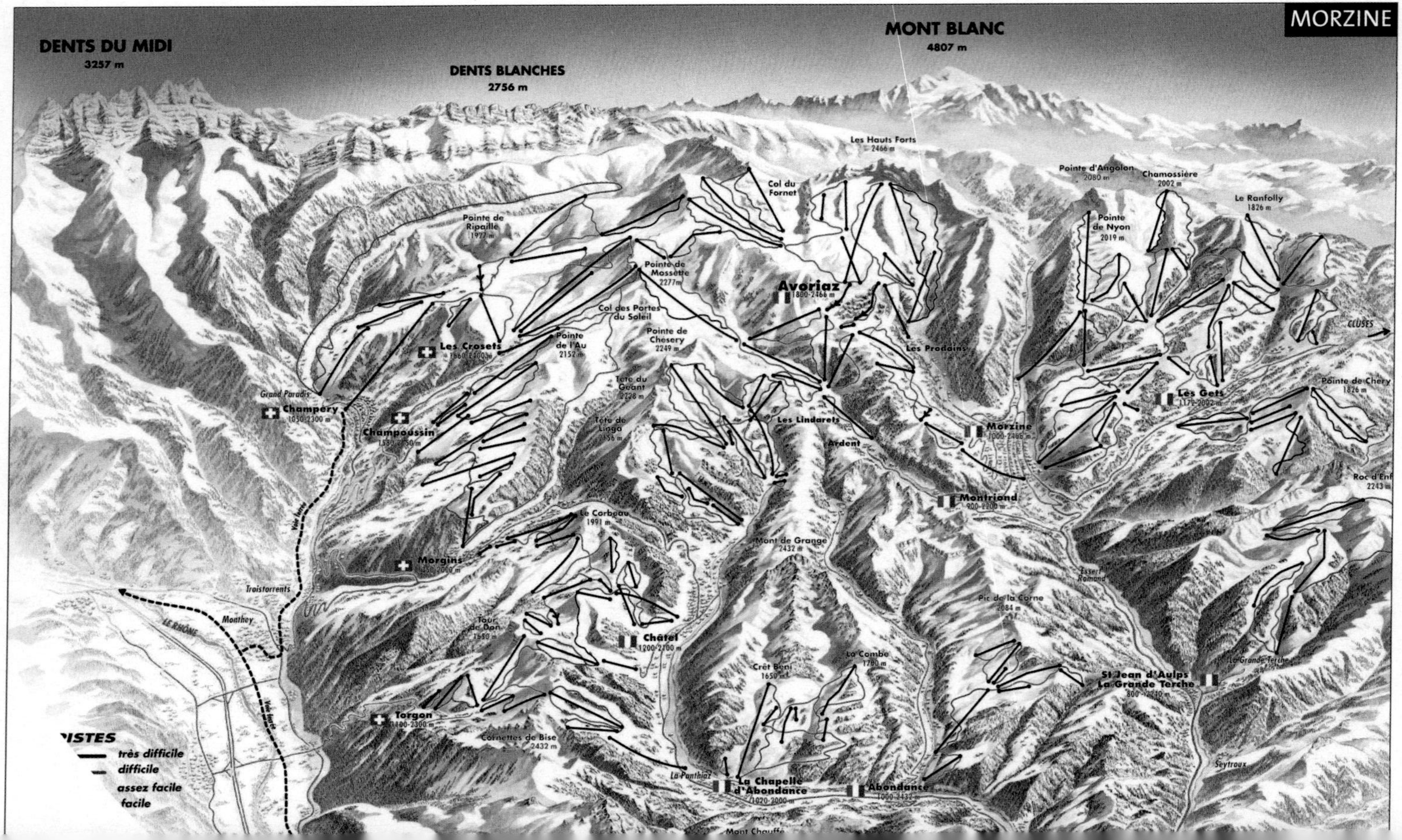
DENTS DU MIDI
3257 m
DENTS BLANCHES
2756 m
MONT BLANC
4807 m
Les Hauts Forts
2466 m
Pointe d'Angolon
2080 m
Chamossière
2002 m
Le Ranfolly
1826 m
Pointe de Nyon
2019 m
Col du Fornet
Pointe de Ripaille
1927 m
Pointe de Mossette
2277 m
Avoriaz
1800-2466 m
Col des Portes du Soleil
Pointe de Chesery
2249 m
Pointe de l'Au
2152 m
Les Crosets
1660-2400 m
Les Prodains
CLUSES
Pointe de Chery
1826 m
Les Gets
1172-2002 m
Grand Paradis
Champery
1050-2300 m
Champoussin
1580-2150 m
Tête du Géant
2228 m
Tête de Linga
Les Lindarets
Ardent
Morzine
1000-2466 m
Roc d'Enfer
2243 m
Montriond
900-2200 m
Le Corbeau
1991 m
Mont de Grange
2432 m
Morgins
1350-2000 m
Voie ferrée
Traistorrents
Essert Romand
Monthey
LE RHÔNE
Pic de la Corne
2084 m
Tour de Don
1650 m
Châtel
1200-2100 m
La Combe
1780 m
Crêt Beni
1650 m
La Grande Terche
St Jean d'Aulps
La Grande Terche
800-1750 m
Torgon
1100-2300 m
Cornettes de Bise
2432 m
Seytroux
PISTES
très difficile
difficile
assez facile
facile
La Panthiaz
La Chapelle d'Abondance
1020-2000 m
Abondance
1000-2432 m
Mont Chauffé

Savoyard chalets and more modern wooden-and-stone buildings constructed in keeping with their beautiful alpine surroundings. This is a family resort with a relaxed atmosphere and good links into the Portes du Soleil.

Mountain

A cable-car from the hamlet of Les Prodains, reached by free ski-bus from Morzine, provides the quickest and direct link to Avoriaz.

Alternatively, a gondola from Morzine takes you up to Super-Morzine where you can work your way up through the lift system to Avoriaz, or over to the pretty little goat-farming hamlet of Les Lindarets for access to Châtel and other resorts in the Portes du Soleil. The blue runs above Super-Morzine provide plenty of confidence-building cruising terrain.

From the other side of Morzine, linked by a free road-train, a side-by-side gondola and cable-car rise to Pléney. Blue, red and black runs served by a sequence of chair-lifts, all lead back over the undulating pastureland to the town. You can also drop off the backside of the ridge and follow a long, gentle blue run down into Les Gets.

Skiing takes place on the wooded slopes on both sides of the Les Gets valley, which is crisscrossed with further lifts that extend to 1850m Le Ranfoilly and 1665m La Rosta at the far end. On the north-western side of Les Gets, a gondola and a chair lead up to Mont Chéry. This is the location for dedicated slalom and snowcross courses, as well as a terrain park. Morzine has a large floodlit area with skiing, tubing and big-air that remains open until 10pm.

Off-piste is extensive in an area that continues to be underrated – last season it had some of the best snow-cover in Europe. We particularly enjoy the Combe d'Angolon, a spectacular powder bowl accessed from the top of the Chamossière chair-lift.

Anyone who can ski parallel can complete in a day the Portes du Soleil circuit, which takes you to most but not all the resorts. However, most of the time is spent on lifts rather than going downhill. It makes more sense to fully explore one sector at a time.

Learn

In Morzine, the **ESF**, **t** +33 (0)4 50 79 13 13, has a sound reputation for teaching modern technique in a friendly manner ('excellent-value two-hour lesson from a fluent English-speaker'). **British Alpine Ski and Snowboarding School**, **t** +33 (0)4 50 74 78 59 or **t** +44 (0)871 780 1500, is warmly recommended. **Ski, Snowboard et Aventures**, **t** +33 (0)4 50 79 05 16, has limited-size classes. Guiding is through **Bureau de la Montagne**, **t** +33 (0)4 50 79 03 55, and **Maison de la Montagne**, **t** +33 (0)4 50 75 96 65.

In Les Gets, the **British Alpine Ski and Snowboarding School**, **t** +33 (0)4 50 79 85 42 or **t** +44 (0)1485 572 596, receives equal praise. The **ESF**, **t** +33 (0)4 50 75 80 03, has a strong presence. **360 International**, **t** +33 (0)4 50 79 80 31, has a dedicated following. We recommend **ESI Ski Plus**, **t** +33 (0)4 50 75 86 01. Mountain guide **Marco Deshayes**, **t** +33 (0)6 86 95 43 74, has an intimate knowledge of off-piste in the Portes du Soleil.

Children

Morzine's **L'Outa**, **t** +33 (0)4 50 79 26 00, accepts little ones from three months to six years and was recommended by reporters. **Le Club des Piou-Piou**, **t** +33 (0)4 50 79 13 13, provides daycare with ski lessons for children from three to 12 years.

In Les Gets, which has the French government's *P'tits Montagnards* award for childcare, **Les Fripouilles**, **t** +33 (0)4 50 79 84 84, welcomes children from six months. The **ESF Jardins des Neiges**, **t** +33 (0)4 50 75 80 03, takes children from three to five years for a sensible mix of lessons and play. The **ESF Club des P'tits Montagnys**, **t** +33 (0)4 50 75 80 03, gives lessons to children aged four to 12 years. **Ile des Enfants** ski school, **t** +33 (0)4 50 75 84 47, gives lessons from three years.

Lunch

Try **Les Crêtes de Zorre**, **t** +33 (0)4 50 79 24 73, at Super-Morzine, **Les Mines d'Or**, **t** +33 (0)4 50 79 03 60, in the Vallée de la Manche and the **Belvédère**, **t** +33 (0)4 50 79 81 52, a welcoming mountain hut at Mont Chéry. **Chez Nannon**, **t** +33 (0)4 50 79 21 15, is a romantic hut half-buried (last year) on a blue piste beneath the Pointe de Nyon above Morzine.

Dine

In Morzine, **Le Tremplin**, **t** +33 (0)4 50 79 12 31, is rated by reporters. **L'Etale**, **t** +33 (0)4 50 79 09 29, serves regional cuisine in a mountain ambience, and **La Grange**, **t** +33 (0)4 50 75 96 40, is for a special occasion. **La Chamade**, **t** +33 (0)4 50 79 13 91, receives mixed reports: 'most delightful – the taste and presentation were special', and 'not so nice any more'. **Le Matafan**, **t** +33 (0)4 50 79 27 79, is said to be 'absolutely the best place for dinner'. **Le Mas de la Coutettaz**, **t** +33 (0)4 50 79 08 26, provides chalet-style communal dining in a centuries-old dining room. **L'Auberge de la Combe à Zore**, **t** +33 (0)4 50 79 15 06, is warmly recommended.

In Les Gets, **Le Flambeau**, **t** +33 (0)4 50 79 80 66, and **Le Tourbillon**, **t** +33 (0)4 50 79 70 34, are both recommended, along with **Le Vieux Chêne**, **t** +33 (0)4 50 79 71 93, and **Le Peau de Vache**, **t** +33 (0)4 50 75 86 64.

Party

Morzine has a large ice rink where you can skate and watch French league hockey matches. Other activities include tobogganing and snowmobiling. **Le Paradis du Laury's** is a popular disco. **L'Opéra**, the other late-night venue, becomes a teens-only haunt one evening each week during the school holidays. The **Cavern Bar** has a young and funky atmosphere and **The Boudha Café** is recommended for people-watching.

In Les Gets, the leisure centre has a swimming pool and a range of other facilities. **Bar Bush** and **Le Boomerang** are popular. For dancing, **The Iglu** is a small but fun nightclub.

Sleep

Morzine has a plentiful supply of hotels in each price bracket. In Les Gets, much of the accommodation is in chalets.

Morzine:

★★★**Hôtel Les Airelles**, **t** +33 (0)4 50 74 71 21, *www.les-airelles.com*, has been refurbished with comfortable rooms.

★★★**Hôtel Le Dahu**, **t** +33 (0)4 50 75 92 92, *www.dahu.com*, an old favourite, has tastefully decorated rooms and duplex family suites, along with delicious food.

★★★**Hôtel Neige Roc**, **t** +33 (0)4 50 79 03 21, *www.neige-roc.com*, at Les Prodains, is convenient for the cable-car to Avoriaz.

★★★**Hôtel Le Tremplin**, **t** +33 (0)4 50 79 12 31, *www.hotel-tremplin.com*, at the foot of the slopes, has a great view of the night-skiing and snowboarding.

★★**Hôtel Fleur des Neiges**, **t** +33 (0)4 50 79 01 23, *www.fleurdesneiges.com*, is rustic, has a heated pool, and a restaurant serving French country cuisine.

Le Mas de la Coutettaz, **t** +33 (0)4 50 79 08 26, *www.thefarmhouse.co.uk*, is an 18th-century manor house with eight delightful bedrooms.

Les Gets:

★★★★Ferme de Moudon, t +44 (0)20 7384 3854, *www.descent.co.uk*, is a 17th-century chalet three minutes' drive from the village centre. Inside, ancient timbers blend with modern design.

★★★★Ferme de Montagne, t +33 (0)4 50 75 36 79, *www.fermedemontagne.com*, is a luxuriously renovated farmhouse set above the village.

★★★Le Boomerang II, t +33 (0)4 50 79 80 65, *www.leboomerang2.com*, is a little piece of Australian outback in the French Alps.

★★★Chalet-Hôtel Les Alpages, t +33 (0)4 50 75 80 88, *www.hotel-alpages.com*, has a swimming pool and spa.

★★★Chalet-Hôtel Crychar, t +33 (0)4 50 75 80 50, *www.crychar.com*, on the piste, has cosy bedrooms, and a restaurant with a log fire and home-cooked food.

★★★Chalet-Hôtel La Marmotte t +33 (0)4 50 75 80 33, *www.hotelmarmotte. com* is a 1930s chalet on the edge of the village. Facilities include a swimming pool, spa and crèche.

★★★Hôtel Mont-Chéry, t +33 (0)4 50 75 80 75, *www.hotelmontchery.com*, in the town centre, has a swimming pool, and a restaurant serving 'inventive cuisine'.

★★★Hôtel Nagano, t +33 (0)4 50 79 71 46, *www.hotel-nagano.com*, has a swimming pool and is across the road from the ice rink.

★★Alpen' Sports Hôtel, t +33 (0)4 50 75 80 55, *www.alpensport-hotel.com*, has five simple chalets in its grounds sleeping from four to 17 people.

La Plagne

Profile

The giant ski area is made up of 10 mainly purpose-built villages set at different altitudes above the valley town of Aime. The skiing is linked by cable-car to Les Arcs and together they form Paradiski, one of the largest ski circuits in the world. Suits high-mileage cruisers, beginners, families and off-piste skiers. Alpine charm is in short supply in a couple of the higher villages

Resort

La Plagne tries and often succeeds in being all things to all people. The lower villages of Montchavin, Montalbert, Les Coches and Champagny-en-Vanoise have varying degrees of rustic farmland appeal, while the six higher holiday centres major on ski convenience. On paper, La Plagne is the perfect ski destination with a long vertical drop, snow-sure high-altitude runs, ski-in/ski-out hotels and apartments, and a sophisticated lift system. Runs below the treeline are delightful. However, the endless acres of exposed and often bland snowfields higher up and the architecture of some of the dormitory villages are not to everyone's taste.

Paradiski – its combined ski area with Les Arcs – is so vast that even an experienced skier will be hard put to travel from one end to the other and back in a single day. The double-decker Vanoise Express, which spans the Ponturin gorge that separates the two resorts, cost €16 million to build and is a remarkable feat of engineering.

✱BEST FOR

All levels of skier and rider, big ski area, off-piste

ESSENTIALS

Altitude: 1250m (4,100ft)–3250m (10,660ft)
Further information: t +33 (0)4 79 09 79 79, *www.la-plagne.com*
Lifts in area: 141 in Paradiski (1 mountain railway, 16 cableways, 66 chairs, 58 drags) serving 425km of piste
Lift pass: Paradiski (covers La Plagne/Les Arcs area and one day in each of Val d'Isère/Tignes, Pralognan-La-Vanoise, Les Saisies) adult €229, child 6–13yrs €172, both for 6 days
Access: Chambéry airport 2hrs, Geneva airport 2½hrs, Lyon airport 2½hrs, Eurostar station at Bourg-St-Maurice

However, both La Plagne and Les Arcs are so enormous in their own right that only a small proportion of visitors to either make use of it. Unless you plan more than two trips to Les Arcs during a one-week stay it is more economical to pay the daily supplement. The main beneficiaries are skiers who choose to stay in Montchavin or Les Coches. Instead of hiking up through the lift system on the La Plagne side, they can explore the equally rewarding terrain above Vallandry and Arc 1800.

The original high-altitude resort of Plagne Centre (1970m) is outwardly a monument to the alpine architectural atrocities of the 1960s but it has undergone a complete makeover down the years and functions well as a holiday centre. Aime-la-Plagne (2100m) resembles a battleship stranded on a white mountainside. Belle-Plagne (2050m) is easier on the eye with a pleasant village centre. Plagne-Bellecôte (1930m) is high-rise and plain. Plagne-Villages (2050m), Plagne-Soleil (2050m) and Plagne-1800 are much more agreeable wood-clad complexes built in sympathy with their glorious scenic surroundings.

Lower down the mountain, Montchavin and Champagny-en-Vanoise are rich in cowshed kitsch. These are old farming villages that have long since been won over to tourism, but they make excellent and attractive bases from which to explore the region.

Mountain

Wide-open motorway skiing above the treeline and gladed trails through the forest below it are the main features of the ski area. These are coupled with gentle beginner pistes and some truly outstanding off-piste if you know where to find it. You need a guide to discover the long, sweeping descent from the Glacier de Bellecôte down to Les Bauches, as well as the challenging Cul du Nant run from the back of the glacier into the Champagny-le-Haut valley.

The disadvantage of staying in the lower and much more pleasing villages is that you tend to spend an inordinate amount of time working your way up through the lift system before doing much actual skiing. Champagny (1250m) is the most convenient of these. Just two long lifts take you all the way to Plagne Centre, whereas from Montchavin you need to ride six to reach the same place.

We favour basing yourself in Plagne-Villages or Plagne-Soleil, the two villages that come closest to marrying charm with convenience. From here it is easy to reach the open skiing from the Roche de Mio and the Glacier de Bellecôte.

Scenic routes wind down through the forest to Montchavin, Les Coches, Champagny and Montalbert. Queues are generally not a feature of La Plagne, although the closure in bad weather of an arterial lift can have a knock-on effect across the entire area. The old, slow Arpette chair-lift out of Plagne-Bellecôte

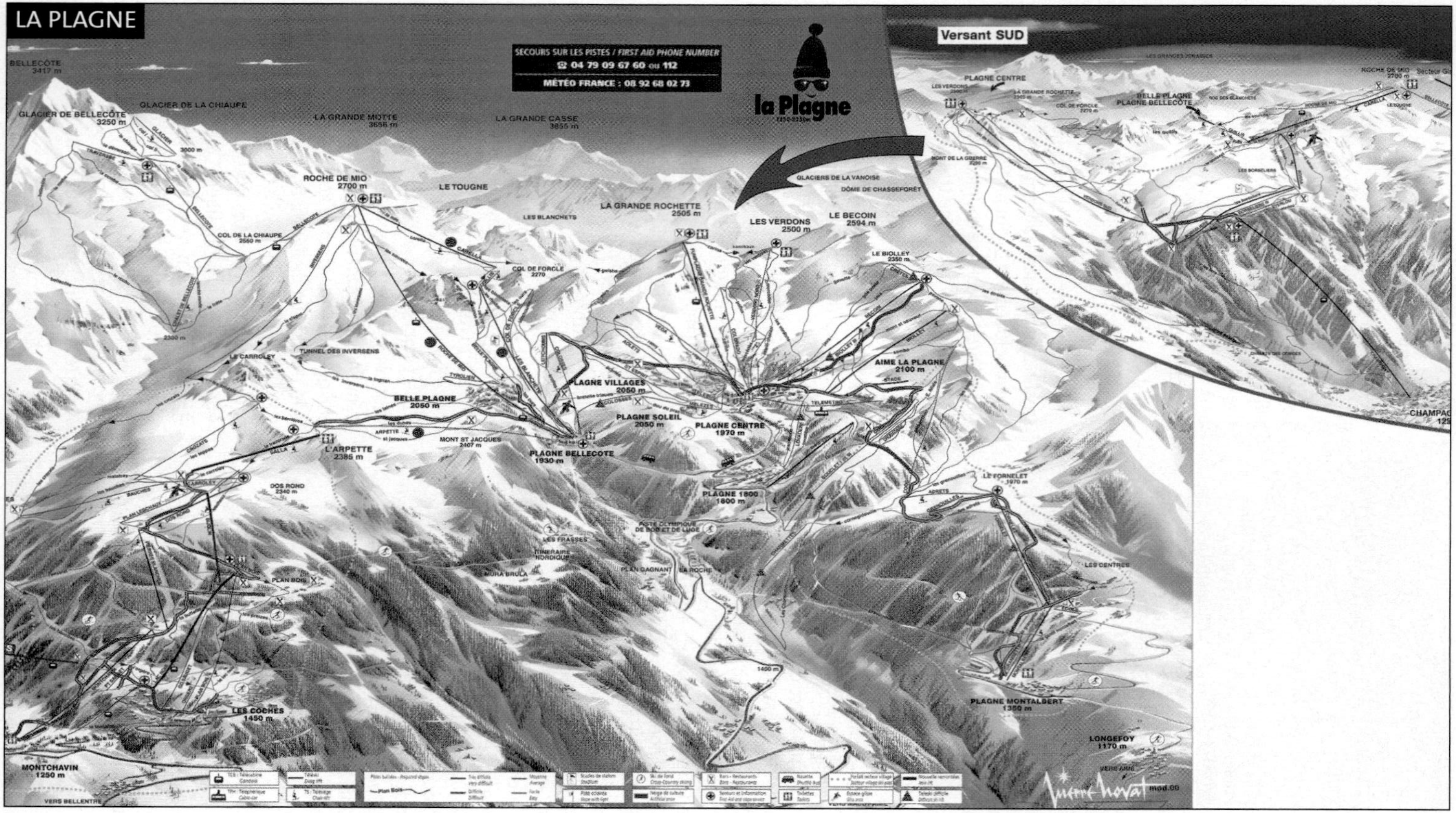

LA PLAGNE
SECOURS SUR LES PISTES / FIRST AID PHONE NUMBER
☎ 04 79 09 67 60 ou 112
MÉTÉO FRANCE : 08 92 68 02 73
la Plagne
Versant SUD
BELLECÔTE 3417 m
GLACIER DE LA CHIAUPE
GLACIER DE BELLECÔTE 3250 m
LA GRANDE MOTTE 3656 m
LA GRANDE CASSE 3855 m
ROCHE DE MIO 2700 m
LE TOUGNE
LES BLANCHETS
LA GRANDE ROCHETTE 2505 m
LES VERDONS 2500 m
LE BECOIN 2594 m
GLACIERS DE LA VANOISE
DÔME DE CHASSEFORÊT
LE BIOLLEY 2350 m
COL DE LA CHIAUPE 2560 m
COL DE FORCLE 2270
TUNNEL DES INVERSENS
LE CARROLEY
BELLE PLAGNE 2050 m
PLAGNE VILLAGES 2050 m
PLAGNE SOLEIL 2050 m
PLAGNE CENTRE 1970 m
AIME LA PLAGNE 2100 m
MONT ST JACQUES 2407 m
PLAGNE BELLECOTE 1930 m
L'ARPETTE 2385 m
DOS ROND 2340 m
PLAGNE 1800 1800 m
PISTE OLYMPIQUE DE BOB ET DE LUGE
LES FRASSES
ITINERAIRE NORDIQUE
PLAN GAGNANT
LA ROCHE
PLAN BOIS
LE FORNELET 1970 m
LES CENTRES
LES COCHES 1450 m
PLAGNE MONTALBERT 1350 m
LONGEFOY 1170 m
MONTCHAVIN 1250 m
VERS BELLENTRE
VERS AIME
PLAGNE CENTRE
BELLE PLAGNE
PLAGNE BELLECÔTE
ROCHE DE MIO 2700 m
CHAMPAG

la Plagne
1250-3250m
Travel with the number 1 ski specialist to France
Erna Low
UK REPRESENTATION
Res: 0870 750 6820
24 hrs: 020 7584 7820
E: info@ernalow.co.uk
www.ernalow.co.uk
paradiski
Savoie – France
AITO THE ASSOCIATION OF INDEPENDENT TOUR OPERATORS
ATOL PROTECTED 4179

SKI BEAT
LA PLAGNE
LA ROSIERE
LES ARCS
MERIBEL
LA TANIA
VAL D'ISERE
Quality holidays at affordable prices. Lovely chalets with spacious and comfortable living rooms, most bedrooms en-suite, superb food. Flexible travel, flights at civilised times. Free childcare available on certain dates. Online availability, booking and chalet videos.
01243 780 405
www.skibeat.co.uk
AITO THE ASSOCIATION OF INDEPENDENT TOUR OPERATORS
ATOL PROTECTED

has long been a notorious bottleneck, but it has been upgraded to an eight-person chair. Terrain parks are located at Plagne-Bellecôte, Montchavin-Les Coches and Champagny. Belle-Plagne now also has the Pro Snowpark with a big S reserved for expert riders.

Learn

The **ESF**, Plagne-Centre **t** +33 (0)4 79 09 00 40, Plagne-Villages **t** +33 (0)4 79 09 04 40, has around 500 instructors working from branches in each of the 10 villages.

In Plagne-Centre, **Oxygène**, **t** +33 (0)4 79 09 03 99, has a good reputation ('but gets crowded and disorganized at half-term'). **Evolution 2** in Montchavin, **t** +33 (0)4 79 07 81 85, and Les Coches, **t** +33 (0)4 79 04 20 83, is recommended. In Plagne-1800, **Reflex**, **t** +33 (0)4 79 09 16 07, is a small independent school. In Belle-Plagne, **El Pro**, **t** +33 (0)4 79 09 01 33, is the alternative to the ESF. **Antenne Handicap**, **t** +33 (0)4 79 09 13 80, in Aime-la-Plagne, teaches disabled skiers.

Children

Most villages have both non-ski and ski kindergartens. In Plagne-Centre, **Les P'tits Bonnets**, **t** +33 (0)4 79 09 00 83, cares for infants from 10 weeks to three years.

In Montchavin, **Le Chat Bleu**, **t** +33 (0)4 79 07 82 82, provides daycare. At Montalbert, **Les Bambins**, **t** +33 (0)4 79 09 77 24, looks after children from 18 months to six years. In Champagny, **Les Cabris**, **t** +33 (0)4 79 55 06 40, and **Garderie Marie-Christine**, **t** +33 (0)4 79 09 11 81, accept children from two years.

At Belle-Plagne, the **ESF nursery**, **t** +33 (0)4 79 09 06 68, cares for children from 18 months. At Plagne-Village, the **ESF nursery**, **t** +33 (0)4 79 09 04 40, accepts children from two years. In Aime-la-Plagne, **La Garderie des Lutins**, **t** +33 (0)4 79 09 04 75, takes children from two years. At Plagne-Bellecôte, **La Garderie Mini-club**, **t** +33 (0)4 79 09 05 91, cares for children from two years.

The **ESF**, **t** +33 (0)4 79 09 00 40, runs ski kindergartens in Montalbert, Champagny, Plagne-Centre, Plagne-Villages, Plagne-Soleil, Aime-la-Plagne, Plagne-Bellecôte, Belle-Plagne and Plagne-1800.

Lunch

You can eat well particularly if you are prepared to wait until the midday–2pm rush hour is over. Try **Au Bon Vieux Temps**, **t** +33 (0)4 79 09 20 57, below Aime-la-Plagne. **Le Forperet**, **t** +33 (0)4 79 55 51 27, is on the piste down to Montalbert. **Pappagone**, **t** +33 (0)4 79 55 18 87, next to the Roche de Mio gondola at Belle Plagne, is recommended for its pizzas. **Auberge de Montagne chez Pat du Sauget**, **t** +33 (0)4 79 07 83 51, is just above the Vanoise Express cable-car station. Nearby **Le Joli Bois**, **t** +33 (0)6 81 19 96 77, has 'great *lasagne*, but skip the *crêpes*'. **Loup Garou**, **t** +33 (0)4 79 09 20 17, and **Le Petit Chaperon Rouge**, **t** +33 (0)4 79 09 09 39, above 1800 are both recommended. **La Rossa**, **t** +33 (0)4 79 08 28 03, is at the top of the Champagny gondola. **Les Borseliers**, **t** +33 (0)6 07 54 96 19, in Champagny is known for *tartiflette* and other rustic Savoyard dishes.

Dine

In Montchavin, **La Boule de Neige**, **t** +33 (0)4 79 07 83 30, and **La Ferme de Cézar**, **t** +33 (0)4 79 07 85 31, are both recommended.

In Plagne-Centre, try **La Métairie**, **t** +33 (0)4 79 09 11 08, and **Le Refuge**, **t** +33 (0)4 79 09 00 13. In Belle-Plagne, **Le Matafan**, **t** +33 (0)4 79 09 09 19, is an old favourite. **Le Loup Blanc**, **t** +33 (0)4 79 09 13 61, in Plagne-1800 has good local cuisine at reasonable prices.

Party

La Plagne is not a place for a hectic nightlife. Bars such as **Monica's Pub** in Plagne-Soleil, **Le Mine** in Plagne-1800 and **No Blem Café** in Plagne-Centre are busy after skiing. Most of the action later on lies in Plagne-Centre at **Jet 37** and in Plagne-Bellecôte at **Saloon**. **Le Bleu Night** disco in Aime-la-Plagne is packed in high season. Champagny has **Le Galaxy** disco, and high-decibel **Oxygène** in rural Montchavin keeps the cows awake until the early hours.

La Plagne hosted the bobsleigh in the 1992 Winter Olympics and anyone can take a ride down the 1.5km serpentine track. A trip on an 80km/hr bob raft costs €35pp while a 100km/hr run on a real bobsleigh with a pro driver costs €105pp; for details, **t** +33 (0)4 79 09 12 73.

Sleep

- ★★★★**Résidence Aspen, t** +33 (0)4 79 55 75 75, in Plagne-Village receives glowing reports.
- ★★★★**Les Montagnettes apartments, t** +33 (0)4 79 55 12 00, are extremely comfortable.
- ★★★★**Les Balcons de Belle Plagne apartments, t** +33 (0)4 79 55 76 76, in Belle-Plagne are favourites among reporters.
- ★★★★**MGM's Les Hauts Bois apartments, t** +44 (0)870 750 6820 in Aime-la-Plagne are among the most luxurious in the resort. Residents have use of a stylish swimming pool, sauna and steam room.
- ★★★★**Les Chalets du Bouquetin, t** +33 (0)4 79 55 01 13, are in Champagny.
- ★★★**Paladien Terra Nova, t** +33 (0)4 79 55 79 00, in Plagne-Centre has 'a great location and good food, though a bit impersonal'.
- ★★**Hôtel Mercure, t** +33 (0)4 79 09 12 09, formerly the Eldorador, in Belle-Plagne has been refurbished.

Risoul

Profile

This convenient little resort is good value for money and is usually free of lift queues. There is little choice of nightlife, but Risoul now tends to attract students and school groups who have added to the liveliness of the place

Resort

Risoul shares its substantial ski area with Vars 1850 and they jointly market themselves as the Domaine de la Forêt Blanche. Risoul was purpose-built in the ski boom years of the 1970s as a budget-conscious no-frills family ski resort looking for a French rather than an international market. Its continued popularity at home and abroad is largely dependent on its reputation for low prices and reliable snow. When resorts elsewhere are suffering from a lack of cover at the beginning or towards the end of the season, Risoul usually has metres of the stuff from before Christmas until after Easter. The resort used to be extremely popular with the British, but the clientele has changed in recent years. Visitors from

*BEST FOR

Purpose-built convenience, value

ESSENTIALS

Altitude: 1850m (6,068ft)–2750m (9,020ft)
Further information: **t** +33 (0)4 92 46 02 60, *www.risoul.com*
Lifts in area: 53 (2 cableways, 15 chairs, 36 drags) serving 180km of piste
Lift pass: Forêt Blanche (covers Risoul and Vars) adult €143.50, child 5–11yrs €124.50, both for 6 days
Access: Grenoble airport 2½hrs, Marseille airport 3½hrs, railway station at Montdauphin-Guillestre 17km

Eastern Europe now outnumber the British among the 30 per cent of skiers and riders who are not French. The downside of Risoul is the airport transfer from Grenoble or Marseille, which in adverse winter weather conditions can be considerably longer than advertised. The silver lining of its isolated position is the absence of day-trippers and weekenders.

Accommodation is in appealing wood-and-stone apartment complexes, although the small shopping area suffers from a profusion of billboards and a lack of proper pavements. Other activities include snowmobiling, guided snowshoe excursions, parapente, winter horse-riding, and skating on the natural ice rink.

Mountain

Lifts rise from the village to 2571m Razi for connections to Vars-Sainte-Marie and Vars-Les-Claux, while a new six-seater chair takes you up to the second smaller ski area of Peyrefolle. The third sector of L'Homme de Pierre is reached by a sequence of drag-lifts – despite major improvements to the lift system in recent years the region still suffers from a predominance of these.

Risoul has a wide diversity of terrain. The green runs around the base area provide some of the best novice terrain in France, while more confident skiers will find that they can go far afield without ever being forced to stray from blue runs.

Experts will enjoy the ridge run reached by the Chabrières drag from the Col de Crévoux. This takes you to the starting point for the KL speed-ski track where a number of world records have been set over the years. Other descents from different points along the cornice are of sufficient gradient to test the nerve of even the most accomplished. The long runs down to Vars-Sainte-Marie from 2580m La Mayt are usually uncrowded and provide perfect cruising terrain.

Vars has also its own ski area on 2273m Peynier on the far side of the town but reached on skis from Vars-Les-Claux. The black Ecureuil, which follows the fall-line down the wooded slopes from the top, is one of the most enjoyable in the region. However, most of the 10 black runs are graded more for their lack of grooming than their gradient.

After a big dump, Risoul and Vars offer some outstanding off-piste opportunities between the trees. A natural half-pipe in the back bowl off the Col de Valbelle is an attraction for both skiers and riders. The Surfland terrain park on L'Homme de Pierre has a superpipe, jumps and rails, as well as a dedicated area for board novices.

Learn

The **ESF**, **t** +33 (0)4 92 46 19 22, and the rival **ESI**, **t** +33 (0)4 92 46 20 83, both have a sound reputation.

Children

Risoul has the French government's *P'tits Montagnards* award for good childcare. The **Garderie**, **t** +33 (0)4 92 46 02 60, cares for children from six months to six years, as does **Les Pitchouns**, **t** +33 (0)4 92 46 29 37.

Lunch

Serious mountain lunchers are in the wrong place. Try **Le Vallon**, **t** +33 (0)4 92 46 05 75, and **Le Tetras**, **t** +33 (0)4 92 46 09 83, or descend to either resort.

Dine

La Dalle en Pente, **t** +33 (0)4 92 46 05 40, has traditional mountain cuisine including fondue, raclette and *pierrade*. **Le Plante de Bâton**, **t** +33 (0)4 92 46 06 38 is also recommended. **La Cherine**, **t** +33

(0)4 92 46 01 80, under Les Mélèzes apartments, has good food at reasonable prices. **Snowboard Café, t** +33 (0)4 92 46 18 65, has cheap daily specials.

Party

Nightlife is limited to a few bars and the late-night **Le Morgan** disco. The resort centre can be extremely noisy and we advise families to choose accommodation in a quieter location away from the bars.

Sleep

Most visitors opt to stay in self-catering apartments.

★★★★**Balcons de Sirius, t** +33 (0)4 92 46 03 47, are new apartments.

★★**Au Bon Logis, t** +33 (0)4 92 45 14 47, *www.aubonlogis.fr*, is in the hamlet of Gaudissard, 10 minutes from Risoul.

★★**La Bonne Auberge, t** +33 (0)4 92 45 02 40, *www.labonneauberge-risoul.com*, is a chalet-style hotel that has been run by the same family for 30 years.

★★**Le Chardon Bleu, t** +33 (0)4 92 46 07 27, *http://lechardonbleu.free.fr*, is a clean and modern hotel overlooking the piste.

La Rosière

Profile

The French half of an intermediate ski area shared with La Thuile in Italy's Aosta Valley. A quiet village with uncrowded slopes, recommended for families

Resort

La Rosière is an important resort in the Haute Tarentaise above the valley town of Bourg-St-Maurice. It provides an easy winter link – on skis – to the Aosta Valley in Italy where it shares its ski area with La Thuile. Most probably the Carthaginian general Hannibal came this way in 247 BC en route to Rome. The current lift system would have no problem in ferrying his 26,000 men across the Petit-St-Bernard Pass by detachable quad-chair, but 38 war elephants might be quite another matter.

The lift company – it also owns Val d'Isère's mountain transport – is spending €33 million on improving facilities. First steps have been a remodelling of the base area and two new six-person lifts to provide swift mountain access.

*BEST FOR

Intermediates, families, big ski area

ESSENTIALS

Altitude: 1200m (3,937ft)–2650m (8,694ft)

Further information: **t** +33 (0)4 79 06 80 51, *www.larosiere.net*

Lifts in area: 37 (1 cableway, 17 chairs, 19 drags) serving 150km of piste

Lift pass: Area (includes La Thuile) adult €155, child 5–12yrs €108.50, both for 6 days

Access: Geneva and Lyon airports 2½hrs, railway station at Bourg-St-Maurice 30mins

Mountain

The skiing is on wide, open slopes and is best suited to adventurous intermediates. The 500m-long terrain park is reached by the Poletta drag.

Learn

The **ESF, t** +33 (0)4 79 06 86 21, has a worthy reputation and most instructors speak good English. The other choices are **ESI, t** +33 (0)4 79 06 81 26, and **Evolution 2, t** +33 (0)4 79 40 19 80.

Children

The **ESI, t** +33 (0)4 79 06 81 26, is recommended for its friendly instructors and we also have good reports of **Evolution 2, t** + 33 (0)4 79 40 19 80. The **ESF, t** +33 (0)4 79 06 86 21, is said to be excellent – 'our children loved the instructors' Harry Potter display after the torchlight descent'. **Le Club des Galopines** cares for skiers and non-skiers from 18 months and **Club Loisirs** from three years, both **t** +33 (0)4 79 06 89 67.

Lunch

Try **La Traversette, t** +33 (0)6 11 70 51 07, **Le Plan du Repos, t** +33 (0)4 79 06 87 92, and **L'Ancolie, t** +33 (0)4 79 06 86 71.

Dine

Le Relais du Petit-St-Bernard, t +33 (0)4 79 40 19 38, **L'Ancolie, t** +33 (0)4 79 06 86 71, and **Le Chalet, t** +33 (0)4 79 06 80 79, are recommended. **Le Turia, t** +33 (0)4 79 06 13 65, provides fine cuisine at reasonable prices.

Party

Le P'tit Relais and **Le Petit Danois** are busy as the lifts close. **Clay's** is a piano bar. **Le Pub** provides the late-night action.

Sleep

★★★★**Les Granges de La Rosière, t** +44 (0)870 750 6820, *www.ernalow.co.uk*, are smart MGM apartments.

★★★**Le Ruitor, t** +33 (0)4 79 06 82 07, *www.leruitor.com*, is 'cosy and comfortable, 350m from the lifts – but there is a free shuttle service'.

★★**Relais du Petit-St-Bernard, t** +33 (0)4 79 06 80 48, *www.petit-saint-bernard.com*, is well placed at the foot of the slopes.

★★**Le Solaret, t** +33 (0)4 79 06 80 47, *www.hotelsolaret.com*, is family-run.

Sainte-Foy

Profile

Burgeoning *station de ski* above an old village in the Haute Tarentaise, with lots of new chalets but as yet limited lifts. Renowned for its superb off-piste skiing

Resort

Sainte-Foy *station* is the purpose-built ski base above the old village of Sainte-Foy, on the road up to Tignes and Val d'Isère from Bourg-St-Maurice. In recent years it has been the centre of a speculative building boom, with a large development of attractive traditional-style chalets. Resort developer MGM is banking on the premise that the amount of new accommodation will force the French authorities to allow more lifts to be built. So far it appears to have worked. A new six-person chair at Camp Filleul, opening this winter to the west of the present ski area, should effectively double the resort's lift-accessed terrain.

Mountain

Sainte-Foy is a ski secret that has been long known to Val and Tignes habitués, who come here for the superb powder quality. Three quad-chairs take you up to 2612m Col de l'Aiguille, starting point for a choice of red or black pistes, while the second chair serves less demanding tree-lined terrain. Off-piste itineraries include the 1700m descent of the north face of Fogliettaz and a long powder run to the farming hamlet of Le Monal.

***BEST FOR**

Steep 'n' deep, off the beaten track

ESSENTIALS

Altitude: 1550m (5,084ft)–2620m (8,596ft)
Further information: **t** +33 (0)4 79 06 95 22, *www.saintefoy.net*
Lifts in resort: 4 (4 chairs) serving 50km of piste
Lift pass: adult €105, child 7–11yrs €81, for 6 days
Access: Chambéry airport 1hr, Geneva and Lyon airports 2hrs, railway station at Bourg-St-Maurice 20km

Learn

The **ESF**, **t** +33 (0)4 79 06 96 76, receives rave reviews from reporters ('instructors remember your names and care about sharing their passon with you').

Children

Les P'tits Trappeurs, **t** +33 (0)4 79 06 97 92, accepts children from three to 11 years.

Lunch

Try **Les Brevettes**, **t** +33 (0)6 88 21 08 79, and **Chez Léon**, **t** + 33 (0)6 09 57 23 88, at the top of the first chair,and **Maison à Colonnes**, **t** +33 (0)4 79 06 94 80, at the bottom of the lifts. **Chez Mérie**, **t** +33 (0)4 79 06 90 16, at Le Miroir serves hearty peasant fare.

Dine

La Bergerie, **t** +33 (0)4 79 06 25 51, is a gastronomic restaurant at the foot of the piste. **Maison à Colonnes**, **t** +33 (0)4 79 06 94 80, and **La Grange** in Hotel Le Monal, **t** +33 (0)4 79 06 90 07, are both good.

Party

The resort is quiet in the evening, with a choice of the **Pitchouli** for a drink after skiing, **L'Iceberg** and the bar of **Hôtel Le Monal**.

Sleep

★★★★**Les Fermes de Sainte-Foy**, **t** +33 (0)4 50 33 10 96, is a new MGM hotel complex of three- and four-room apartments opening this season.

★★★★**Yellow Stone Chalet**, **t** +33 (0)4 79 06 96 06, *www.yellowstone-chalet.com*, is run as a B&B for eight people. It has an indoor pool, a sauna and hot tub.

★★**Auberge sur la Montagne**, **t** +33 (0)4 79 06 95 83, *www.auberge-montagne.co.uk*, in the hamlet of La Thuile, is warmly recommended.

★★**Hôtel Le Monal**, **t** +33 (0)4 79 06 90 07, *www.le-monal.com*, is in the old village.

St-Gervais

Profile

Traditional spa town with modestly priced accommodation, linked by gondola and piste into the giant Megève ski area, 4km from a station and autoroute exit

Resort

This attractive small spa town has been a resort ever since the first tourists arrived here to take the waters in 1806. It lies at the head of a dramatic river gorge midway between Chamonix and Megève and serves as the gateway to two important ski areas encompassing the villlages of Le Fayet, Le Bettex and Saint-Nicolas-de-Véroce.

*** BEST FOR**
Big ski area, airport access

ESSENTIALS
Altitude: 860m (2,821ft)–2350m (7,708ft)
Further information: **t** +33 (0)4 50 47 76 08, *www.st-gervais.net*
Lifts in area: 122 in Evasion Mont Blanc (11 funiculars, 13 cableways, 38 chairs, 60 drags) serving 450km of piste; 729km in Mont Blanc ski area
Lift pass: Ski Pass Mont Blanc (covers all local resorts including Chamonix, Courmayeur, Les Houches) adult €252, child 5–15yrs €203, both for 6 days
Access: Geneva airport 45mins, TGV railway station at Sallanches 4km, regular buses to resort

Mountain

The main skiing to the east of the town, reached by a fast 20-person gondola from the outskirts, is linked across the slopes of Mont d'Arbois to Megève. The area has a terrain park and a half-pipe. On the other side of town, the venerable Mont Blanc Tramway, a rack-and-pinion railway dating back to 1904, takes you to the top of the neighbouring ski area of Les Houches.

Learn

Lessons are provided by the **ESF St-Gervais/Le Bettex, t** +33 (0)4 50 47 76 21, **ESF Saint-Nicholas-de-Véroce, t** +33 (0)4 50 93 21 61, and the **Mont Blanc Ecole de Ski, t** +33 (0)4 50 93 16 78, at Bettex.

Children

Garderie des Neiges, t +33 (0)4 50 93 14 81, cares for children aged six months to six years in Le Bettex. **Crèche Halte-Garderie, t** +33 (0)4 50 93 23 90, is for ages two to six years in Saint-Nicolas-de-Véroce. The two **ESF** branches provide lessons from four years.

Lunch

Try **Hôtel-Restaurant L'Igloo, t** +33 (0)4 50 93 05 84, at Mont d'Arbois and **Le Prarion, t** +33 (0)4 50 54 41 99, above Les Houches.

Dine

St-Gervais itself has some 35 restaurants. For crêpes try **4 Epices, t** +33 (0)4 50 47 76 08, and for pizzas **L'Eterle, t** +33 (0)4 50 93 64 30. **Le Four, t** +33 (0)4 50 93 14 16, and **A Robinson, t** +33 (0)4 50 93 59 00, serve local specialities.

Party

This is not a party town but there is a good selection of bars, a skating rink, casino and **La Nuit des Temps** disco.

Sleep

St-Gervais:

*****Hôtel Restaurant Le Carlina, t** +33 (0)4 50 93 41 10, *www.carlina-hotel.com*, is ski-in/ski-out with a traditional restaurant and an indoor pool.

*****Hôtel-Restaurant L'Igloo, t** +33 (0)4 50 93 05 84, *www.ligloo.com* is a chalet-style hotel set on the piste.

La Maison du Vernay, t +33 (0)4 50 47 07 55, *www.lamaisonduvernay.com*, is a B&B with five wood-panelled bedrooms, each with a different flower theme.

St-Martin-de-Belleville

🏆 BEST SMALL SKI HOTEL 2007: La Bouitte

🏆 BEST RESORT RESTAURANT 2007: La Bouitte

Profile

Offbeat and attractive old village with direct link in the huge Trois Vallées area. Excellent accommodation and restaurants, but limited après-ski

Resort

St-Martin-de-Belleville is a charming old village situated before Les Menuires on the road up from Moûtiers. It has an entirely different and more relaxed rural atmosphere than any of the better-known purpose-built resorts in the Trois Vallées. Most of the ancient stone and wood barns have been converted into chalets, but farmhouse cheese is still made here and you can still buy fresh milk by the pail.

*BEST FOR

Big ski area, rural ambience, ski gourmets

ESSENTIALS

Altitude: 1450m (4,757ft)–3300m (10,827ft)
Further information: **t** +33 (0)4 79 00 20 00, *www.st-martin-de-belleville.com*
Lifts in area: 167 in Trois Vallées (40 cableways, 69 chairs, 58 drags) serving 600km of piste
Lift pass: Trois Vallées adult €145.50–215, child 5–13yrs €109.50–161, both for 6 days
Access: Chambéry airport 2hrs, Lyon airport 2½hrs, Geneva airport 3hrs, Eurostar at Moûtiers, 20km away

Mountain

St-Martin's only fault used to lie in the inordinate amount of time that it took to link into the rest of the skiing in the Trois Vallées. But all that changed with the construction of a gondola and a fast chair that swiftly convey you up to the Tougnette Ridge for runs down to Les Menuires, or over the far side towards Méribel. In fresh powder conditions the runs from the ridge back to St-Martin are some of the best in the region – glorious acres of undulating pastures followed by tree-skiing.

Learn

There's an **ESF** branch, **t** +33 (0)4 79 00 61 43. **Compagnie des Guides**, **t** +33 (0)4 79 01 04 15, organizes off-piste excursions.

Children

Piou Piou, **t** +33 (0)4 79 08 91 15, cares for both non-skiing and skiing children from two-and-a-half years. Not all the staff speak English.

Lunch

Le Corbeley, **t** +33 (0)4 79 08 95 31, has a sunny terrace and good food, while **L'Etoile des Neiges**, **t** +33 (0)4 79 08 92 80, is a lunch-time favourite.

Dine

L'Eterlou, **t** +33 (0)4 79 08 94 07, is recommended, and **Le Montagnard**, **t** +33 (0)4 79 01 08 40, is in an old hayloft ('superb for an evening out'). **La Voûte**, **t** +33 (0)4 79 08 91 48, serves good pizzas. **L'Etoile des Neiges**, **t** +33 (0)4 79 08 92 80, uses fresh produce for its local specialities. Chef René Meilleur's **La Bouitte**, **t** +33 (0)4 79 08 96 77, at nearby

St-Marcel, has 'fabulous starters', a much-deserved Michelin star and an intimate farmhouse atmosphere.

Party

St-Martin has a few bars, including **Pourquoi Pas** piano bar, **Le Jokker** and **Brewski's**, but is a quiet place by night.

Sleep

- ★★★**Hôtel St-Martin**, **t** +33 (0)4 79 00 88 00, *www.hotelsaintmartin.com*, has rooms that have been individually decorated.
- ★★★**Alp'Hôtel**, **t** +33 (0)4 79 08 92 82, *www.alphotel.fr*, is comfortable and traditional.
- ★★★**Hôtel Edelweiss**, **t** +33 (0)4 79 08 96 67, *www.hotel-edelweiss73.com*, has 16 cosy rooms and a good restaurant.
- **La Bouitte**, **t** +33 (0)4 79 08 96 77, *www.la-bouitte.com*, in the nearby hamlet of St-Marcel, has five delightfully rustic suites tucked away in the eaves, up ladders and in other corners of the farmhouse. It also has an outdoor hot tub and a small spa.

Serre Chevalier

Profile

The collective name for a dozen linked villages that share a large ski area with the ancient garrison town of Briançon. Attractive tree-lined slopes and some varied off-piste. Suited to all standards of skier and rider looking for a combination of purpose-built and traditional resort with good-value accommodation and food

* BEST FOR

Big ski area, value, intermediates, snowboarders

ESSENTIALS

Altitude: 1200m (3,936)–2800m (9,184ft)
Further information: **t** +33 (0)4 92 24 98 98, *www.serre-chevalier.com*
Lifts in area: 68 (9 cableways, 20 chairs, 39 drags) serving 250km of piste
Lift pass: Grande Serre Che (covers all centres as well as 1 day in each of Alpe d'Huez, Les Deux Alpes, La Grave, Montgenèvre, Puy-St-Vincent) adult €176, child 6–12yrs €132, both for 6 days
Access: Turin airport 1½hrs, Grenoble airport 2hrs, Lyon airport 3hrs, railway station at Briançon, regular bus service to villages

Resort

Serre Chevalier is not a single resort but the collective marketing name adopted by a dozen villages that line the main Grenoble–Briançon road between the high mountain pass of the Col du Lautaret and the ancient town, close to the frontier with Italy. Accommodation and the main lifts are centred on Briançon and the quite separate villages of Chantemerle, Villeneuve-Le Bez and the sleepy little spa resort of Monêtier-Les-Bains. Where you choose to stay is dependent on your holiday priorities. The old walled town has considerable charm and a wonderful choice of restaurants. But, while it is directly linked to the mountain, it lacks the traditional atmosphere of a ski resort.

Chantemerle is the nearest village to Briançon, Villeneuve and the rustic hamlet of Le Bez beside it is the most convenient and charming village base with the most central access to the skiing that is spread along the wall of the valley.

Monêtier-Les-Bains (also known as Serre Chevalier 1500) is a picturesque spa village that has been a resort since Victorian times. Reporters say the baths are well worth a visit, but you must book – even to use the outdoor thermal pool, which is for soaking in rather than swimming.

The giant Milky Way area, venue last winter for the Winter Olympics, is a short drive away. La Grave and Les Deux Alpes can both be reached across the Col du Lauteret. Puy-St-Vincent, near Briançon, is also worth a visit.

Mountain

Lots of new lifts, including three six-packs last season, have been introduced in recent years as Serre Che continues to compete with its rivals further north in the alpine chain. The Clot Gautier chair above Villeneuve has been upgraded to a six-pack, as has the one from Aravet 2000 to Plateau Rouge.

The linked runs that stretch for more than 19km down the southern side of the valley provide a playground that will test the most advanced skier and rider. But at the same time there is an easy route down to the valley from each lift. Of the different sectors, Monêtier is the most appealing and usually the least crowded. This is the best end of the circuit for accomplished skiers and riders although the link with Villeneuve can sometimes suddenly close in bad weather and you may be forced to take the bus home if staying in Chantemerle or Briançon.

Isolée is an exciting black, which starts on the ridge from L'Eychauda at 2659m and plunges down towards Echaillon. Tabuc is a long black run through the woods with a couple of steep and narrow pitches. The Casse du Bœuf, a sweeping ridge through the trees back to Villeneuve, is one of our favourite runs.

This is considered one of the most friendly resorts in France for riders. The snowpark at Villeneuve has three tables and three boxes. The half-pipe at L'Aravet in Villeneuve is open until 9pm Tuesday–Friday during the French holidays. Chantemerle has a snowcross course with seven bends.

Learn

The **ESF** has branches in Chantemerle, **t** +33 (0)4 92 24 17 41, and Villeneuve, **t** +33 (0)4 92 24 71 99; they have a reputation for both friendliness and quality of instruction. In Chantemerle, **Evasion**, **t** +33 (0)4 92 24 02 41, and **Génération Snow**, **t** +33 (0)4 92 24 21 51, are recommended.

In Villeneuve, **Buissonnière ESI**, **t** +33 (0)4 92 24 78 66, is praised by reporters ('some beginner friends could not believe what could be achieved in a week'). **Altitude**, **t** +33 (0)6 08 02 51 82, provides the alternative. In Monêtier, **EurekaSki**, **t** +33 (0)6 89 31 66 56, or **t** +44 (0)1326 375 710, is a British-owned ski school, run by BASI instructors, with an excellent reputation.

Children

In Chantemerle, **Les Poussins**, **t** +33 (0)4 92 24 03 43, takes children from eight months. In Villeneuve, **Les Schtroumpfs**, **t** +33 (0)4 92 24 70 95, cares for children from six months. **Les Petits Aigles**, **t** +33 (0)4 92 24 29 31, also take non-skiing children from three years. In Monêtier, **Les Eterlous**, **t** +33 (0)4 92 24 45 75, accepts children aged from six months (18 months during French school holidays). The **ESF Jardin des Neiges**, **t** +33 (0)4 92 20 30 57, in Briançon, Chantemerle, **t** +33 (0)4 92 24 17 41, Villeneuve, **t** +33 (0)4 92 24 71 99, and in Monêtier, **t** +33 (0)4 92 24 42 66, provides a mix of tuition and play for children from three years. In Chantemerle, **Génération Snow**, **t** +33 (0)4 92 24 21 51, offers lessons to children aged seven to 11 years.

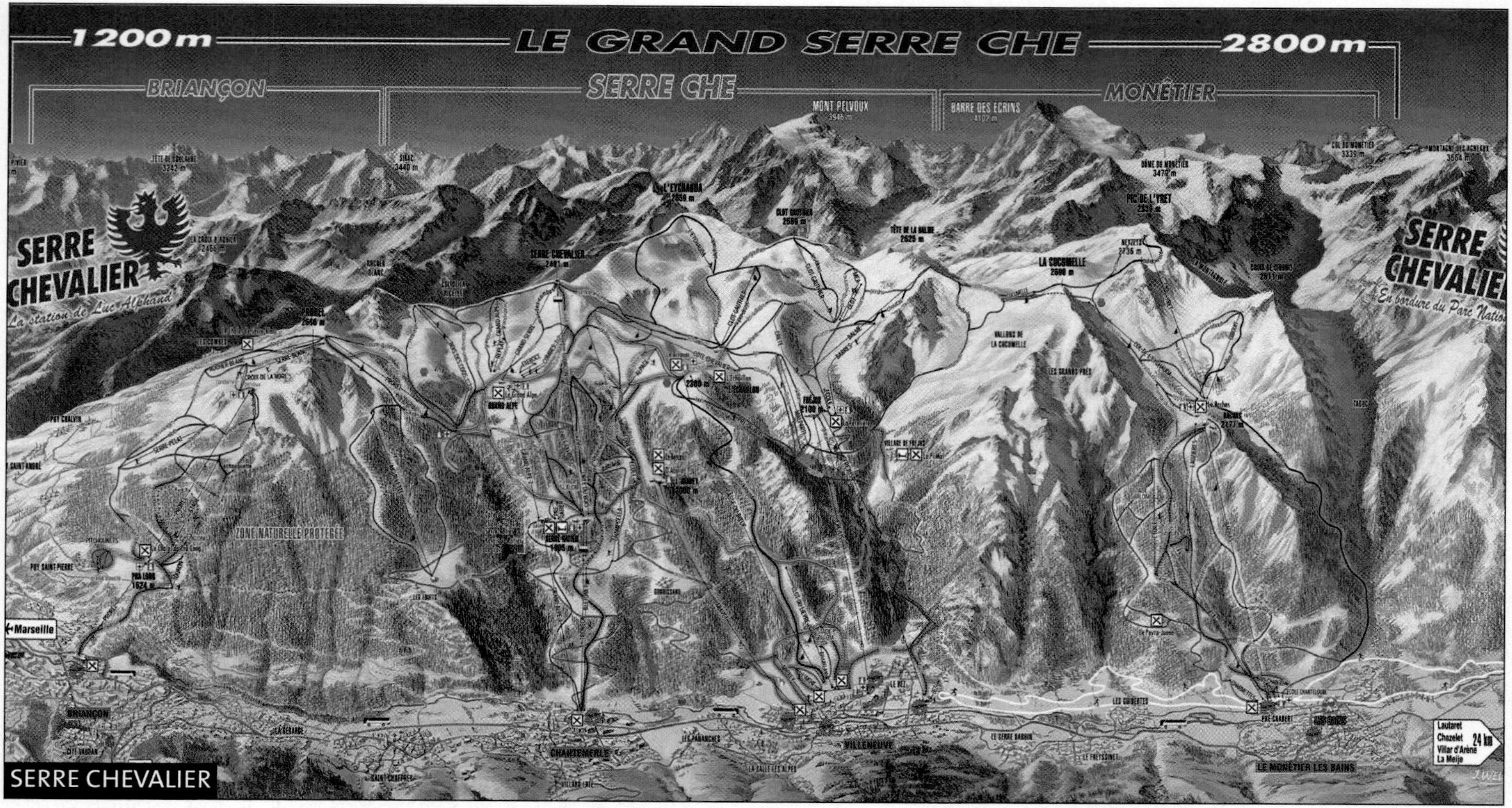

SERRE CHEVALIER

Lunch

Above Chantemerle, **Café Soleil, t** +33 (0)4 92 24 17 39, has carefully prepared food and a great atmosphere. **La Bergerie du Grand Alpe, t** +33 (0)6 81 34 34 14, serves local mountain cuisine.

Above Villeneuve, **The Pi Maï, t** +33 (0)4 92 24 83 63, has considerable charm, good food and attentive service as you sit by a roaring log fire. Remote **L'Echaillon, t** +33 (0)4 92 24 05 15, is also recommended. **D'Abord-L'Aravet 2000, t** +33 (0)4 92 24 97 67, is good value and has breathtaking views. **Le Bivouac de la Casse, t** + 33 (0)4 92 24 87 72, is at the top of the Casse du Bœuf chair-lift.

Above Monêtier, **Peyra Juana, t** +33 (0)6 81 11 40 26, is a mountain hut with some of the best food in the ski area. Try also **Le Bachas, t** +33 (0)4 92 24 50 66.

Dine

In Briançon, **Le Passé Simple, t** +33 (0)4 92 21 37 43, specializes in mountain dishes and cuisine from the seventeenth century. **Restaurant La Caponnière, t** +33 (0)4 92 20 36 77, is warmly recommended ('excellent dinner – very French').

In Chantemerle, **Le Loup Blanc, t** +33 (0)4 92 24 14 27, is praised by reporters. In Villeneuve, **La Pastorale, t** +33 (0)4 92 24 75 47, is recommended, **Le Bidule, t** +33 (0)4 92 24 77 80 in the hamlet of Le Bez has a warm atmosphere and enticing seafood and fish dishes. In Monêtier, **L'Antidote, t** +33 (0)4 92 4 40 02, in the Alliey Hotel is run by local celebrity chef Stéphane Froidevaux and has a Michelin star. **Chalet Auberge des Amis, t** +33 (0)4 92 24 43 27, is also recommended.

Party

This is not a party resort, with nightlife limited to local bars and the occasional very Gallic disco. **Le QG** in Chantemerle, **Le Bam Bam** and **La Baïta** in Villeneuve are the main focal points. **Le Lièvre Blanc** in Villeneuve is a riders' hang-out with weekly live music. **Le Yeti** in Chantemerle is strongly recommended. **Bar Alpin** is said to have a great atmosphere, as has the **Bar Le Que Tal**. In Chantemerle, the **Altiforme** fitness centre offers massage and beauty treatments. Villeneuve has a pool and fitness centre. **Les Bains de Monêtier** is a thermal spa with bath-temperature spring water.

Sleep

Most of Serre Chevalier's lodging is in apartments, and all accommodation can be booked through **Serre Chevalier Reservations, t** +33 (0)4 92 24 98 80.

Briançon:

- ****__Chalet Chez Bear, t__ +33 (0)4 92 21 11 70, in the hamlet of Belvoir just outside Briançon, is the area's most luxurious chalet, run by a British couple.
- ***__Hôtel Le Vauban, t__ +33 (0)4 92 21 12 11, *www.hotel-vauban.fr*, has a restaurant that uses fresh local produce. Specials include *foie gras* and *gigot d'agneau*.
- ***__Parc Hôtel, t__ +33 (0)4 92 20 37 47, *www.monalisahotels.com*, is 300m from the gondola. Its restaurant serves Alsace cuisine.

Chantemerle 1350:

- ***__Hôtel Plein Sud, t__ +33 (0)4 92 24 17 01, *www.hotelpleinsud.com*, is 250m from the lifts and has a pool.
- **__Grand Hôtel, t__ +33 (0)4 92 24 15 16, is more modest than its name, with a restaurant serving traditional mountain cuisine.

Villeneuve:

- ***__Hôtel du Mont Thabor, t__ +33 (0)4 92 24 74 41, *www.mont-thabor.com*, is fairly new, and has a swimming pool and games room.
- **__Chalet-Hôtel Le Pi Maï, t__ +33 (0)4 92 24 83 63, is in an isolated position up the

mountain at 1985m with a warm ambience and good food.

Monêtier:

****Hôtel Les Glaciers Bonnabel**, **t** +33 (0)4 92 24 42 21, *www.hotelbonnabel.com* is on the Col du Lautaret outside the town centre.

***Auberge du Choucas**, **t** +33 (0)4 92 24 42 73, *www.aubergeduchoucas.com*, is an ancient inn with a renowned restaurant serving delicious food.

Alliey & Spa Hôtel de Charme, **t** +33 (0)4 92 24 44 20, *www.alliey.com*, has an impressive wine cellar, two pools, and children are warmly welcomed.

Les Colchiques, **t** +33 (0)4 92 24 42 42, *www.les-colchiques.com*, has rooms for two to six people, and good food.

La Tania

Profile

Attractive low-level Trois Vallées alternative to Courchevel and Méribel. Recommended for families and skiers on a budget wanting to explore this giant ski area

*BEST FOR

Big ski area, families, value

ESSENTIALS

Altitude: 1350m (4,429ft)–3300m (10,825ft)
Further information: **t** +33 (0)4 79 08 40 40, *www.latania.com*
Lifts in area: 167 in Trois Vallées (40 cableways, 69 chairs, 58 drags) serving 600km of piste
Lift pass: Trois Vallées adult €145.50–215, child 5–13yrs €109.50–161, both for 6 days
Access: Chambéry airport 2hrs, Lyon airport 2½hrs, Geneva airport 3hrs, Eurostar at Moûtiers, 25km

Resort

La Tania was originally built as a dormitory for the 1992 Albertville Olympics. But the village, situated a couple of kilometres from Le Praz (Courchevel 1300) quickly evolved into a pleasant little family resort in its own right. It has the skiing of Courchevel and Méribel but without the high prices. Architecture is in traditional mountain style and Le Forêt, a collection of attractive Scandinavian-style chalets set in the woods above the village, contributes to the cosy mountain ambience.

Mountain

A jumbo gondola provides main mountain access and allows skiers to download when village snow-cover is limited. Lifts and pistes link to Courchevel 1850 as well as to Méribel via the Col de la Loze. When the light is flat, La Tania's own tree-lined skiing is the best place to be in the Trois Vallées.

Learn

The resort has a branch of the **ESF**, **t** +33 (0)4 79 08 80 39, as well as **Magic in Motion**, **t** +33 (0)4 79 01 07 85, and **Olivier Brané**, **t** +33 (0)4 79 08 24 21, an independent instructor who specializes in Trois Vallées tours.

Children

La Maison des Enfants, **t** +33 (0)4 79 08 40 40, is for non-skiers from three years, and **Le Jardin des Neiges**, **t** +33 (0)4 79 08 80 39, is for skiers from four years. Several tour operator chalets have crèches.

Lunch

Le Bouc Blanc, **t** +33 (0)4 79 08 80 26, at the top of La Tania gondola, provides tasty omelettes and good service. **Le Ski Lodge**, **t** +33 (0)4 79 08 81 49, in the village, offers great value for money.

Dine

La Tania has five restaurants including **La Taiga**, **t** +33 (0)4 79 08 80 33, and **La Ferme de La Tania**, **t** +33 (0)4 79 08 23 25, both of which offer inexpensive Savoyard specialities.

Party

Le Ski Lodge is the main resort rendezvous.

Sleep

★★★★**Chalet Titania**, **t** +44 (0)870 754 4444, *www.leski.com*, is in Le Forêt area and has a crèche on the ground floor. Other chalets include one for 22 with a crèche and another for 19 next door.

★★★**Hôtel Montana**, **t** +33 (0)4 79 08 80 08, in the village centre, is modern with a swimming pool ('the rooms are large and bright, but we were not impressed with either the food or the service').

★★**Hôtel Le Télémark**, **t** +33 (0)4 79 08 80 32, *www.hoteltelemark.com* is a rustic-style building set in the forest, with 12 rooms ranging from doubles to those sleeping seven.

The Mountain Centre Chalets, **t** +44 (0)1202 653 456, *www.themountaincentre.com* consist of two wooden chalets sleeping 32 and 40 in twin and triple rooms. Arrival and departure is on any day of the week, and dining arrangements are flexible.

Tignes

Profile

Part of the large well-linked Espace Killy ski area, shared with neighbouring Val d'Isère. Glacier skiing for most of the year and a reliable snow record. Convenient, but not suitable for those seeking a traditional alpine village ambience

Resort

This is France's most snow-sure resort, extremely popular with the French and a cosmopolitan melting pot of other nationalities. It remains open for skiing for 10 months of the year and is a mandatory summer destination for national ski teams in training – and for all those who can't last from season to season without snow beneath their feet. The glacier used to be open 365 days a year, but the combination of damage from global warming, and a falling interest in summer skiing over the past decade, has caused the resort to 'rest' from mid-May until mid-June and again from early September

*BEST FOR

Guaranteed snow-cover, all levels of skier and rider, off-piste, families

ESSENTIALS

Altitude: 2100m (6,888ft)–3456m (11,335ft)
Further information: **t** +33 (0)4 79 40 04 40, *www.tignes.net*
Lifts in area: 96 in Espace Killy (2 funiculars, 4 cableways, 45 chairs, 41 drags) serving 300km of piste
Lift pass: Espace Killy (Val and Tignes) adult €192.50, child 5–12yrs €144.50, both for 6 days.
Access: Chambéry airport 2hrs, Grenoble airport 2hrs, Lyon airport 2½hrs, Geneva airport 3hrs, railway station at Bourg-St-Maurice 26km

until October. During the summer months 13 lifts serve 20km of high-altitude pistes with a respectable vertical drop of 750m.

Tignes is divided into four main areas with the main village also sub-divided into different *quartiers*. The resort lies at the head of the Haute Tarentaise, a 40-minute drive up the valley from Bourg-St-Maurice, and is connected by lifts and pistes to Val d'Isère. Together they form a 96-lift area with 300km of piste that is known as L'Espace Killy and has few equals for the diversity of its skiing and riding.

The main resort, built at 2100m, was a monument to the architectural horrors of the 1960s, a concrete jungle completely out of keeping with its beautiful setting beneath the twin peaks of La Grande Motte and La Grande Casse. However, huge investment in recent years has transformed Tignes into a much more aesthetically pleasing place. New buildings have been constructed in a sympathetic mountain style and the older beasts are either being reclad or torn down one by one for redevelopment.

Tignes itself divides into Le Lavachet with its high-rise apartment blocks, and more agreeable and convenient Tignes-le-Lac on the edge of a small lake. Le Lac has undergone a complete makeover in recent years and a tunnel acts as a bypass for through traffic to the principal lift station still higher up at Val Claret.

This is the most convenient base for the skiing with immediate access to the underground funicular and the link lift to Val d'Isère. The much lower villages of Tignes-les-Boisses and the valley farming community of Tignes-les-Brévières provide a much more rural environment. They are well linked into the lift system and cannon-assisted snow-cover usually remains sufficient in late April. However, it is a long way up through the lift system to reach La Grande Motte and Val d'Isère.

Significant plans are proposed for the redevelopment of Tignes-les-Boisses, including the rerouting of the road, real estate and replacement lifts.

Mountain

The focal point is the 3656m Grande Motte, reached from Val Claret by an efficient but claustrophobic funicular or by a long two-stage quad-chair. The train takes six minutes to reach the Panoramic mountain restaurant; from there a cable-car takes you to 3456m for the start of some spectacular glacial terrain. You need a local guide to explore the considerable powder opportunities such as the magnificent North Face leading through the *séracs*. Wide pistes for all standards lead back down to Val Claret. From mid-November until the lifts close in May this involves a vertical drop of 1400m. The terrain off to the sides appears benign but is dotted with crevasses and great care should be taken. A number of steep chutes, including the infamous Couloir Deux, can be reached from the funicular.

From Val Claret and the main village of Tignes other lifts lead up to the Col du Palet, where you can ski off-piste with a guide all the way to Les Arcs and linked La Plagne. The route off the back of the col is prone to avalanche and should only be attempted with a guide. Lifts also bring you up to the 2748m Aiguille Percée, the unusual rock formation that appears on almost every postcard of Tignes. The black La Sache run, which leads from here all the way to Tignes-les-Brévières at 1500m, is wonderful when groomed but otherwise offers a long mogul run for bump enthusiasts only.

The terrain park at Tignes-le-Lac has a beginner half-pipe as well as an expert one, a snowcross course and assorted obstacles. There is a summer terrain park on the glacier and Tignes has two

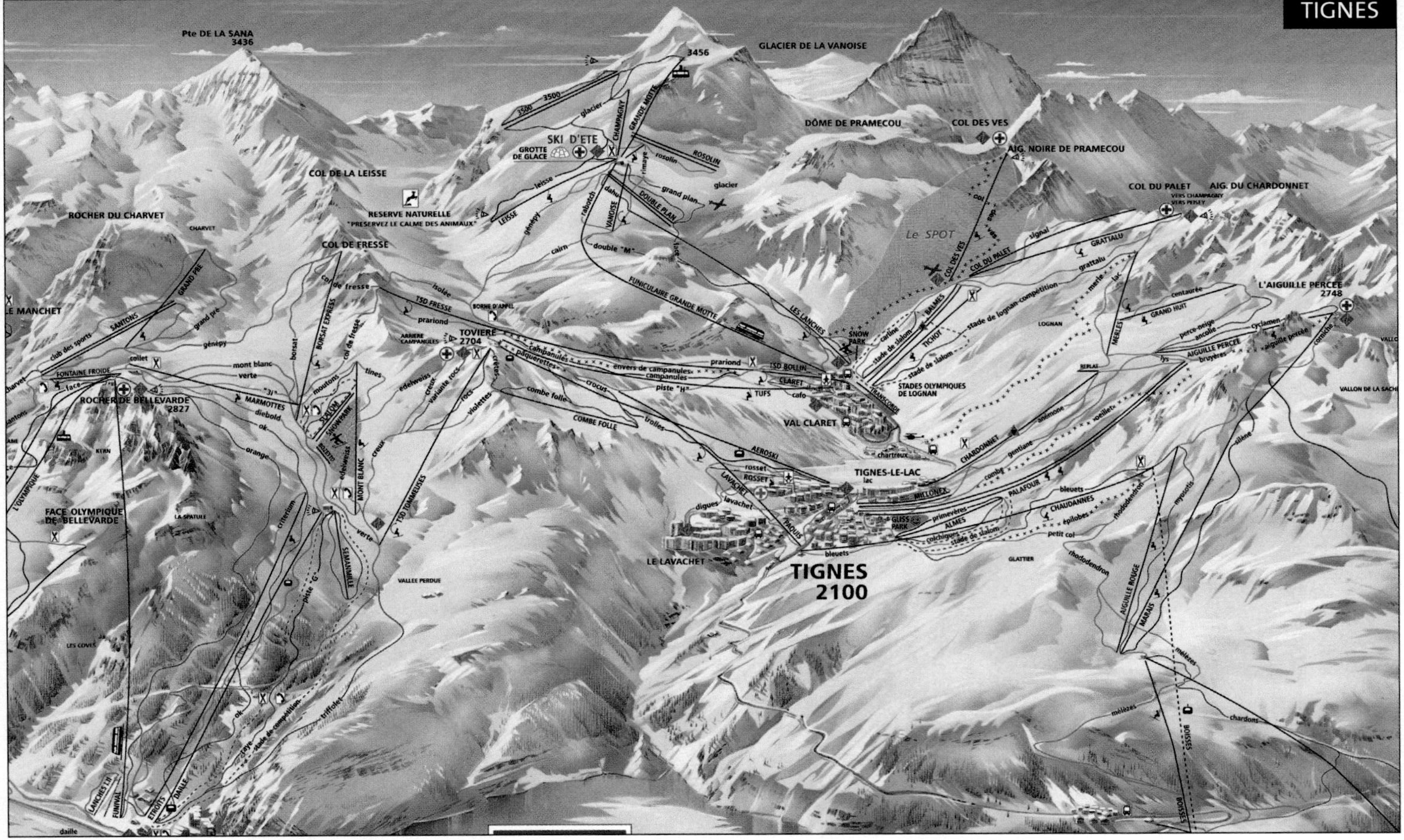
Pte DE LA SANA
3436
3456
GLACIER DE LA VANOISE
DÔME DE PRAMECOU
COL DES VES
AIG. NOIRE DE PRAMECOU
COL DU PALET
AIG. DU CHARDONNET
SKI D'ETE
GROTTE DE GLACE
COL DE LA LEISSE
RESERVE NATURELLE
"PRESERVEZ LE CALME DES ANIMAUX"
ROCHER DU CHARVET
COL DE FRESSE
Le SPOT
L'AIGUILLE PERCEE
2748
LE MANCHET
TOVIERE
2704
SNOW PARK
STADES OLYMPIQUES DE LOGNAN
FUNICULAIRE GRANDE MOTTE
ROCHER DE BELLEVARDE
2827
VAL CLARET
TIGNES-LE-LAC
LE LAVACHET
FACE OLYMPIQUE DE BELLEVARDE
TIGNES
2100
VALLEE PERDUE
VALLON DE LA SACHE
BOISSES

dedicated freeride zones – each known as Le Spot. One of these has fixed locations and equipment to practise the use of avalanche equipment.

Learn

The **ESF Tignes le Lac, t** +33 (0)4 79 06 30 28, and **ESF Val Claret, t** + 33 (0)4 79 06 31 28, are both praised by reporters. **Ecole Henri Authier, t** +33 (0)4 79 06 36 38, is another alternative. **Evolution 2, t** +33 (0)4 79 40 09 04, received some unfavourable comments from reporters. **Snow Fun, t** +33 (0)4 79 06 46 10, is commended for its small classes. **British Alpine Ski & Snowboard School, t** +33 (0)6 79 51 24 05, or **t** +44 (0)709 220 6321, specializes in teaching English-speaking pupils.

ESI, t +33 (0)4 79 06 36 15, and **333, t** +33 (0)4 79 06 20 88, at Val Claret, are the ski and snowboard alternatives. **Snocool, t** +33 (0)4 79 40 08 58, **Surf Feeling, t** +33 (0)4 79 06 53 63, and **Kébra Surfing, t** +33 (0)4 79 06 43 37, are the dedicated board schools, **Tetra Hors Piste, t** +33 (0)4 79 41 97 07, at Le Lac, specializes in off-piste. **Bureau des Guides, t** +33 (0)4 79 06 42 76, offers guiding.

Children

Les Marmottons Tignes le Lac, t +33 (0)4 79 06 51 67, and **Les Marmottons Val Claret, t** +33 (0)4 79 06 37 12, accept children from three and a half years, but staff are said to be rather Gallic in attitude. The **ESF, t** +33 (0)4 79 06 30 28, offers lessons from four years, and the **ESI, t** +33 (0)4 79 06 36 15, from five. **Evolution 2, t** +33 (0)4 79 06 43 78, accepts children from three years and provides free helmets.

Lunch

Upstairs at L'Arbina, t +33 (0)4 79 06 34 78, in Le Lac, is a gastronomic experience with a good-value daily *formule skier* menu. Specialities include *rognons de veau* and *coquilles St Jacques*, but you must book in advance.

Le Panoramic, t +33 (0)4 79 06 60 11, at the top of the Grande Motte funicular, has a good restaurant as well a large self-service with reasonable fare. **La Pignatta, t** +33 (0)4 79 06 32 97, in Val Claret has good pizzas, fresh pasta and a sunny terrace. Nearby **Le Dahu, t** +33 (0)4 79 06 50 98, offers a friendly welcome in a wood-panelled dining room. In Tignes-les-Boisses the newly refurbished **Hôtel Le Marais, t** +33 (0)4 79 06 40 06, has a welcoming restaurant, conservatory and terrace with good-quality local dishes.

Dine

In Val Claret, **Le Caveau, t** +33 (0)4 79 06 52 32, has 'very good food and very reasonable prices'. For Savoyard setting and food, try **Grattalu, t** +33 (0)4 79 06 30 78, and **Brasserie du Petit Savoyard, t** +33 (0)4 79 06 36 23. **Daffy's Café, t** +33 (0)4 79 06 38 75, is a popular Tex-Mex. **Le Ski d'Or, t** +33 (0)4 79 06 51 60, offers gourmet cuisine, and **Myako, t** +33 (0)4 79 06 34 79, is a sushi restaurant. **La Pizzeria 2000, t** +33 (0)4 79 06 38 49, has great pizzas, fondue and raclette.

In Le Lac, **Upstairs at L'Arbina, t** +33 (0)4 79 06 34 78, continues to be the best gourmet restaurant in the area.
Le Clin d'Œil, t +33 (0)4 79 06 59 10, is small and intimate. **Le Brasero, t** +33 (0)4 79 06 30 60 ,serves meat dishes.
Le Grenier, t +33 (0)4 79 06 37 79 is a typical Savoyard restaurant.

Party

In Val Claret, **Crowded House** lives up to its name. **The Fish Tank** is also popular. **Move Café** has live music. **Grizzly's Bar**, decorated with carved bears, has lots of character and doubles as a smart boutique. **Melting Pot** and **Blue Girl** are the late-night venues.

In Le Lac, try **Loop Bar**, **L'Embuscade**, **Grotte du Yeti**, **The Red Lion**, and **Alpaka**. **Angel Bar** is a popular internet café. **Red Z Winter** and **Jack's** are the nightclubs.

In Lavachet, Harri's Bar has become **Scotties** – run by Mark Warner. **TC's** is ever popular.

Sleep

Le Lac:

★★★★**Les Suites de Montana**, **t** +33 (0)4 79 40 01 44, are sumptuously decorated apartments with an outdoor heated pool and a games room.

★★★**Hôtel Alpaka Lodge**, **t** +33 (0)4 79 06 45 30, *www.alpaka.com*, is comfortable. Its bar offers 'an unbelievable array of cocktails'.

★★★**Les Campanules**, **t** +33 (0)4 79 06 34 36, *www.campanules.com*, is chalet-style and has been owned by the same family since 1958.

★★★**Hôtel Le Lévanna**, **t** +33 (0)4 79 06 32 94, *www.levanna.com*, is a new family hotel that opened two winters ago.

★★**Hôtel L'Arbina**, **t** +33 (0)4 79 06 34 78, *www.arbina.net*, is well positioned and has a wonderful restaurant.

Val Claret:

★★★★**L'Ecrin des Neiges**, **t** +44 (0)870 750 6820, *www.ernalow.co.uk*, are comfortable and convenient apartments, with a mini spa complex and swimming pool.

★★★★**Hôtel Le Ski d'Or**, **t** +33 (0)4 79 06 51 60, has a gastronomic restaurant, thalasso spa and gym.

★★**Hôtel La Vanoise**, **t** +33 (0)4 79 06 31 90, *www.hotelvanoise.com*, has doorstep skiing and inviting rooms.

Val d'Isère

Profile

Its dedicated fans – and they are legion – consider that Val and adjoining Tignes have the best off-piste skiing in Europe. This high-altitude glacial resort has a reliable snow record and modern lift system. Recommended for complete beginners, strong intermediates and experts – but not for wobbly second-weekers. Busy nightlife, but light on gourmet restaurants for a resort of this size and sophistication

Resort

Val d'Isère combines with neighbouring Tignes to form one of the principal winter playgrounds of Europe. More British skiers go here than to any other resort in the world and amount to 36 per cent of the population during the winter months. Fortunately the French also favour it and prevent it from become altogether anglicized by providing counterbalance.

*BEST FOR

Big ski area, strong intermediates and experts, off-piste, luxury chalets

ESSENTIALS

Altitude: 1850m (6,068ft)–3456m (11,335ft)
Further information: **t** +33 (0)4 79 06 06 60, *www.valdisere.com*
Lifts in area: 86 in Espace Killy (2 funiculars, 4 cableways, 44 chairs, 36 drags) serving 300km of piste
Lift pass: Espace Killy (Val and Tignes) adult €192.50, child 5–12yrs €144.50, both for 6 days
Access: Chambéry airport 2hrs, Lyon airport 2½hrs, Geneva airport 2½hrs, Grenoble airport 2½hrs, railway station at Bourg-St-Maurice 30km

Val is a cultural and social melting pot for dedicated skiers and riders from all over the world who are drawn by the high, rugged mountains at the head of the beautiful Tarentaise Valley.

The village, which stretches along the road from purpose-built La Daille to the farming outpost of Le Fornet, has smartened its appearance in recent years and can now be described as attractive. Wide pavements have been created where there were previously none. Mature trees have been transplanted to line the main commercial area, and the worst of the concrete edifices of the 1960s have been reclad in soothing wood.

Focal point is Val Village, a cluster of 'old' buildings housing smart boutiques. This was created for the 1992 Winter Olympics around the 11th-century church and the handful of genuine old farmhouses dating back to when the settlement was a hunting lodge for the Ducs de Savoie.

Val has grown in all directions in recent years and even the central area is now divided into different *quartiers*. Of the two satellites, La Daille has purpose-built ski convenience but little character. By contrast, burgeoning Le Fornet is becoming an increasingly attractive place in which to base yourself, although it's a long walk home to both from the nightlife that is entirely confined to the centre.

The Train Rouge, the resort's free bus service, runs with startling efficiency every few minutes during the day from one end of the resort to the other. Buses between Val and Tignes are neither as frequent or as cheap as you might expect. Parking is difficult, but having a car is useful for visiting Sainte-Foy or for trips to Paradiski and La Rosière.

Val's biggest plus point is its altitude and geographical situation that create a snow-sure microclimate. You can ski here from late November until early May and book a holiday in the certainty that you will not find green fields on arrival. The piste-skiing is good, but to its ardent followers it is the easily accessible deep snow terrain that beckons. This is a high-mountain area that carries an ever-present risk of avalanche and should always be treated with the utmost respect. Fatal accidents – they happen each winter – are usually caused by inexperienced or ignorant skiers and riders ignoring warnings and venturing off-piste when it's not safe to do so on the principle that 'it can't happen to me'. It can.

The ski area often takes a full day to fully reopen after a serious dump, and wise skiers head off for a day in the more sheltered and secure powder of Sainte-Foy. Conversely, the snowmaking facilities are world-class and even the Pissaillas Glacier has now been fitted out, ensuring good snow in early season as well as for summer skiing in July. Radio Val d'Isère on 96.1FM gives bilingual weather and piste-grooming updates.

Mountain

No fewer than eight entry points give access to the mountain, thus ensuring that even during high-season weeks, when French families are on holiday, queuing is never a serious problem.

The most convenient and quickest way into the system is to catch either the Funival underground funicular from La Daille or the 30-person jumbo gondola that also rises to the top of Bellevarde from near the swimming pool at the foot of the nursery slopes.

From here a network of pistes and lifts fan out towards the Rocher du Charvet in one direction and towards Tignes in the other. The Tommeuse chair provides a efficient link to 2704m Tovière, starting point for a choice of runs down to Tignes.

Bellevarde is also the start of the OK downhill course (named after two of Val's Olympic champions, Henri Oreiller and Jean-Claude Killy), which brings you over

Inspirational
Luxury ski holidays since 1986
IATA

espace killy
le plus bel espace de ski du monde
DE LA GALISE 3343
Gde AIGUILLE ROUSSE 3482
Pte DU MONTET 3488
OUILLE NOIRE
MEAN MARTIN 3330
Pte DE LA SANA 3436
LA GRANDE MOTTE 3656
LA GRANDE CASSE 3852
AIG. PERS
GLACIER DES SOURCES DE L'ISERE
SIGNAL DE L'ISERAN 3241
GLACIER DE PISSAILLAS
REFUGE DU PRARIOND
SKI D'ETE
COL DE L'ISERAN 2762
ARCELLE
REF. DES FOURS
GLACIER DE LA VANOISE
DÔME DE PRAMECOU
COL DES VES
AIG. NOIRE DE PRAMECOU
GORGES DE MALPASSET
COL DE LA LEISSE
RESERVE NATURELLE
"PRESERVEZ LE CALME DES ANIMAUX"
GROTTE DE GLACE
COL DU PALET
ROCHER DU CHARVET
COL DE FRESSE
RESERVE NATURELLE
PONT ST CHARLES
LE MANCHET
TOVIÈRE 2704
SOLAISE 2560
ROCHER DE BELLEVARDE 2827
STADES OLYMPIQUES DE LOGNAN
VAL CLARET
LE FORNET 1930
SANTELEINA 3605
LE CHATELARD
FACE OLYMPIQUE DE BELLEVARDE
TIGNES-LE-LAC
LE LAVACHET
TIGNES 2100
LE JOSERAY
VAL D'ISERE 1850
LE LAISINANT
LE DÔME 3026
LE CRÊT
LA DAILLE 1785
LAC DU CHEVRIL
TIGNES LES BOISSES 1850
LE VILLARET DU NIAL
LE CHEVRIL
Val d'Isère
TIGNES
mod 83 ©
04

some moderately demanding but wonderfully enjoyable terrain all the way to the Funival station at La Daille.

From the other side of the nursery area in Val, a choice of cable-car or a detachable-chair takes you up Solaise and on towards Le Fornet. From the top of the Manchet chair the long red Mattis run brings you down to the hamlet of Le Laisanant. A new chair-lift last season means you can continue on to Le Fornet without having to take a bus. The high summer ski area at the top of Le Fornet has guaranteed snow-cover, thanks to the aforementioned snowmaking infrastructure.

Dramatic improvements to the lifts at this end of Espace Killy means that you can now ski from Le Fornet to the far corners of Tignes in a single morning. It is important to note that the official piste grading in Val is markedly stiffer than you will find elsewhere. For blue, read red. Intermediates should treat runs that are marked black with considerable caution until they know what is involved.

The nursery slopes in the middle of the village are both good and free, but their position, just off the main descent from Solaise, means that fast-moving traffic often needs to be negotiated when going to and from the novice lift.

Val's *tour de force* lies in its potential for serious off-piste. Try the Face du Charvet, a steep powder classic accessed from the Grand Pré chair. Danaides, reached from the Solaise Express chair, brings you steeply down through the forest above the town.

No good skier or rider should miss a day-trip to Bonneval-sur-Arc, an attractive little village in the neighbouring Haute Maurienne. The itinerary starts with a 20-minute hike from the top of Le Fornet, followed by a choice of sweeping powder descents over the far side of the ridge. The return journey is best accomplished by a pre-arranged, four-minute helicopter ride for €90 per person. The alternative is a five-hour taxi journey.

Espace Killy is popular with freeriders who will find lots of natural gullies and cliffs. La Daille terrain park has a half-pipe and a host of obstacles, as well as two snowcross courses. Riders and twin-tippers also congregate on the Grande Motte above Tignes.

Learn

Val has a dozen ski schools as well as 20 independent individual private instructors. Choosing the right one for your requirements is no easy task.

The **ESF**, **t** +33 (0)4 79 06 02 34, has a strong presence and offers cutting-edge tuition. But it obstinately maintains a firmly focused Gallic outlook (it only employs one British instructor) despite the fact that 36 per cent of skiers here are Anglo-Saxon.

We strongly recommend **Top Ski**, **t** +33 (0)4 79 06 14 80, a cult school run by ex-French racer Pat Zimmer, that specializes in teaching and guiding off-piste as well as giving regular lessons and telemark instruction.

We also recommend **The Development Centre**, **t** + 33 (0)6 15 55 31 56, run by British instructors. **Mountain Masters t**+ 33 (0)4 79 06 05 14, and **Alpine Experience**, **t** +33 (0)4 79 06 28 81, also have established reputations for teaching off-piste.

The other schools include **Snow Fun**, **t** +33 (0)4 79 06 22 24, **Ski Concept**, **t** +33 (0)4 79 40 19 19, **Ogier**, **t** +33 (0)4 79 06 18 93, **Misty Fly**, **t** +33 (0)4 79 40 08 74, **Tetra Hors Piste**, **t** +33 (0)4 79 41 97 07, and **Val Glisse**, **t** +33 (0)4 79 06 00 72. Guiding can be arranged through the **Bureau des Guides**, **t** +33 (0)4 79 06 94 03, and through ski schools.

Children

For tuition, we recommend **Oxygène**, **t** +33 (0)4 79 41 99 58, and **Evolution 2**, **t**+ 33 (0)4 79 41 16 72. **Le Village des**

Enfants, t +33 (0)4 79 40 09 81, cares for children from three to eight years with a mix of play and ski lessons. **Le Petit Poucet, t** +33 (0)4 79 06 13 97, collects and delivers children from three years from wherever they are staying. The main ski schools all run courses for children. The Tourist Office, **t**+ 33 (0)4 79 06 06 60, has a list of recommended babysitters.

Lunch

L'Edelweiss, t + 33 (0)6 10 28 70 64, on the blue Mangard piste above Le Fornet, is a fairly new mountain hut with a log fire and good meat and fish. **La Fruitière, t** +33 (0)4 79 06 07 17, situated on the OK run, has excellent spaghetti Bolognese and lamb dishes. The name means 'dairy' and it is suitably decorated with milk churns. **Le Trifollet, t** +33 (0)4 79 41 96 99, and **Les Tufs, t** +33 (0)4 79 06 25 01, further down and at the foot of the OK, are friendly pizza-and-steak alternatives. **Le Signal, t** +33 (0)4 79 06 03 38, at the top of Le Fornet cable-car, has an enthusiastic welcome, excellent food and good service, all upstairs. Downstairs there is a competent self-service. **Bananas, t** +33 (0)4 79 06 04 23, at the foot of Bellevarde, has good burgers and Tex-Mex, but better bacon-and-eggs. Best lunch in the region is upstairs at **L'Arbina, t** +33 (0)4 79 06 34 78 in Tignes-le-Lac. Specialities include *rognons de veau* and *coquilles St Jacques*. Sensibly priced lunch menu.

Dine

Much the best restaurant in Val is no more: Le Chalet du Crêt has been sold as a private home. For a resort of this quality Val is short on gourmet eateries. **La Grande Ourse, t**+ 33 (0)4 79 06 00 19, by the nursery slopes, heads the list. **Le Blizzard, t** +33 (0)4 79 06 02 07, in the hotel of the same name, also has reasonable food in a pleasant atmosphere. **Le 1789, t** +33 (0)4 79 06 17 89, next to the Galérie des Cimes, has an open fire and offers a warm welcome. **La Taverne d'Alsace, t** +33 (0)4 79 06 48 49, provides traditional French cuisine at reasonable prices. A new and interesting entry is **L'Atelier d'Edmond, t** +33 (0)4 79 00 00 82, in Le Fornet with a lovely rustic interior and fixed-price well-balanced menu at around €60. **Hôtel L'Aigle des Neiges, t** +33 (0)4 79 06 18 88, also has an interesting new complex of three restaurants at different price levels called Up, Side and Down.

Party

Le Graal was the new nightclub last season, a replacement for defunct Club 21. **Dick's Tea Bar** remains the most celebrated disco in the Alps. Alternative après-ski centres around **Café Face, Le Petit Danois**, the **Pacific Bar, Le Pub** and the **Saloon Bar** beneath the Hotel Brussels. British teens gather downstairs at **Bananas**.

Sleep

Val is primarily a chalet resort but has a few decent hotels.

*****deluxe* **Hôtel Les Barmes de l'Ours, t** +33 (0)4 79 41 37 00, *www.hotel-les-barmes.com*, is stylish and comfortable, but overpriced.

*****deluxe* **Eagle's Nest** and **Big Yeti, t** +44 (0)20 8682 5050, *www.scottdunn.com*, are extraordinarily smart chalets in the Les Carats *quartier*.

******Hôtel Le Blizzard, t** +33 (0)4 79 06 02 07, *www.hotelblizzard.com*, has a fine bar area and restaurant, but the bedrooms are disappointing.

******Hôtel Christiania, t** +33 (0)4 79 06 08 25, *www.hotel-christiania.com*, has plenty of atmosphere.

- ★★★★**Hôtel L'Aigle des Neiges, t** +33 (0)4 79 06 18 88, *www.latitudes-hotels.com*, was formerly Les Latitudes in the heart of the old village. It has been refurbished in contemporary style.
- ★★★★**Aspen Lodge, t** +44 (0)20 8875 1957, *www.vip-chalets.com*, is an extremely comfortable catered apartment block on the main street.
- ★★★**Hôtel La Savoyarde, t** +33 (0)4 79 06 01 55, *www.la-savoyarde.com*, has a strong following and is conveniently located.
- ★★★**Hôtel Le Tsanteleina, t** +33 (0)4 79 06 12 13, *www.hoteltsanteleina.com*, enjoys a loyal British following.

A number of sumptuous private homes as well as more basic apartments are also available to let by the week through **Val d'Isère Agence, t** +33 (0)4 79 06 73 50, *www.valdisere-agence.com*.

British-owned **Mountain Rooms and Chalets, t** +33 (0)4 79 41 17 43, *www.mrooms.co.uk*, also has a good choice of accommodation.

Valmorel

Profile

Pleasant purpose-built unsophisticated resort with good nursery slopes and modest intermediate skiing. Suits families with young children

Resort

Valmorel is an attractive ski resort that was developed in 1976 almost in architectural protest at the concrete horrors perpetrated a decade earlier elsewhere. It was constructed in a style sympathetic to its mountain setting and over the years it has matured into a family-friendly resort. The large ski area extends into the Maurienne Valley and to the not-so-attractive resort of St-François-Longchamp. It is also linked with the little beginner resort of Doucy-Combelouvière.

* BEST FOR

Beginners, families, value

ESSENTIALS

Altitude: 1400m (4,592ft)–2550m (8,364ft)

Further information: t +33 (0)4 79 09 85 55, *www.valmorel.com*

Lifts in area: 52 in Grand Domaine (2 cableways, 14 chairs, 36 drags) serving 151km of piste

Lift pass: Grand Domaine (covers Valmorel, Doucy-Combelouvière and Saint-François-Longchamp) adult €171, child 5–8yrs €111, 8–13yrs €145.50, all for 6 days

Access: Chambéry airport 90km, railway station at Moûtier 15km

Mountain

The skiing stretches in one direction to the 1981m Col du Gollet and to the other across a gorge to mainly intermediate terrain in the Maurienne. The nursery slopes are exceptionally good. The area also lends itself to some excellent off-piste that remains untracked for days after a fresh fall. The snowpark has a half-pipe and boardercross course.

Learn

ESF, t +33 (0)4 79 09 81 86, is the main school, which has a solid reputation, and most instructors speak English ('achieved the fine and crucial balance between improving our technical prowess and seeing as many different runs as were within our reach'). Independent instructors include **Marie-Thérèse Hemart, t** +33 (0)4 79 09 84 67.

Valmorel la Belle, Grand Domaine

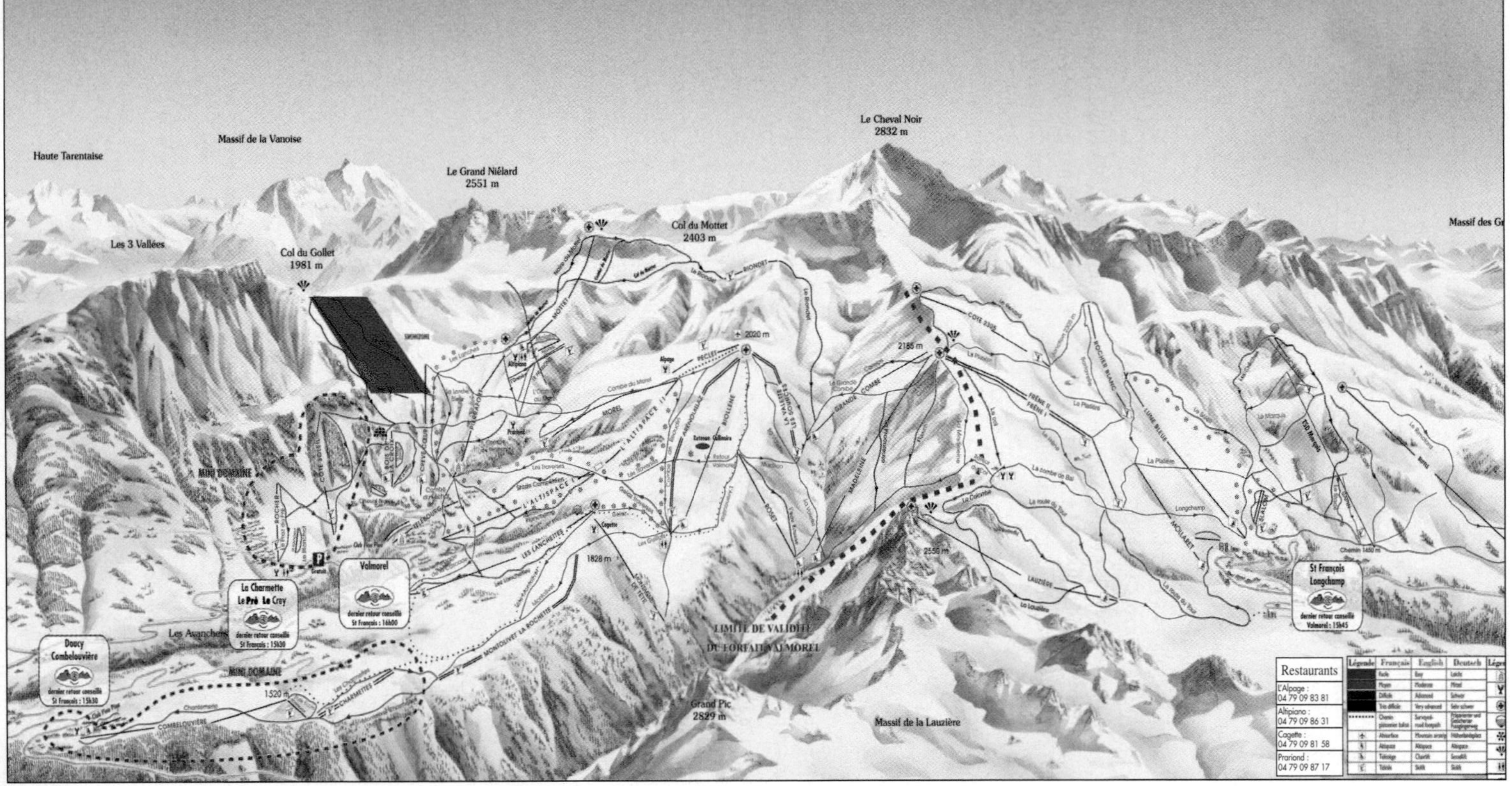

Children

Les Piou Piou is a children's club run by the **ESF**, which accepts non-skiers from 18 months and skiers from three to six years.

Lunch

L'Altipiano, **t** +33 (0)4 79 09 86 31, has à la carte specialities, while **Banquoise** 2000, **t** +33 (0)4 79 59 10 60, is rustic with a log fire. **Les Mazots**, **t** +33 (0)4 79 59 10 01, has Savoyard specials including croûte au fromage, and **L'Alpage**, **t** +33 (0)4 79 09 83 81, is a recommended self-service.

Dine

La Grange, **t** +33 (0)4 79 09 82 51, offers grilled Savoyard cuisine, and **La Marmite**, **t** +33 (0)4 79 09 83 19, has a cosy atmosphere. **L'Aigle Blanc**, **t** +33 (0)4 79 09 83 76, in the forest outside the village, has local dishes. **Le Jimbo Lolo**, **t** +33 (0)4 79 09 82 13, serves tapas and Tex-Mex in a South American atmosphere, **Chez Albert**, **t** +33 (0)4 79 09 81 77, offers wood-fired pizzas, and **Le Petit Savoyard**, **t** +33 (0)4 79 06 90 22, has more sophisticated fare.

Party

As one reporter put it, 'not a resort for young people who want a lively nightlife'. **Le Ski Roc** is a wine bar, and **La Cordée** has music. **Les Nuits Blanches** is a disco with two separate rooms called **Le Before** and **L'After**.

Sleep

★★★**Hôtel Club du Soleil La Fontaine**, **t** +33 (0)4 79 09 87 77, is family friendly.

★★**Hôtel du Bourg**, **t** +33 (0)4 79 09 86 66, *www.hoteldubourg.com*, is in the village centre and has been recently renovated ('warm, convenient, but very basic').

Chalet-Hôtel Edelweiss, **t** +33 (0)4 79 09 88 08, *www.chalethoteledelweiss.com*, is a gîte, with 10 bedrooms and bathrooms.

Val Thorens

Profile

The highest ski village in Western Europe, which has guaranteed snow-cover from before Christmas until after Easter, is part of the giant Trois Vallées area. Not recommended for non-skiers

Resort

This high *station de ski* in the Trois Vallées has grown in a generation from a bland and soulless lift-station-with-apartments into a rather charming village at the end of the 25km road up from Moûtiers. It sits surrounded by a horseshoe of peaks at the end of the Belleville Valley, with links across the 2850m Mont de la Chambre towards Méribel and Courchevel beyond. However, there is sufficent skiing for all levels to deter most one-week visitors from venturing elsewhere.

* BEST FOR

Snow-sure, big ski area, off-piste

ESSENTIALS

Altitude: 2300m (7,544ft)–3300m (10,827ft)

Further information: **t** +33 (0)4 79 00 08 08, *www.valthorens.com*

Lifts in area: 167 in Trois Vallées (40 cableways, 69 chairs, 58 drags) serving 600km of piste

Lift pass: Trois Vallées adult €145.50–215, child 5–13yrs €109.50–161, both for 6 days

Access: Chambéry airport 2hrs, Lyon airport 2½hrs, Geneva airport 3hrs, Eurostar at Moûtiers, 25km

These days, the Trois Vallées is a misnomer because the lift system stretches over the 3200m Cime de Caron all the way down to Orelle in the Maurienne Valley. The 3 Vallées Express gondola from here provides a convenient backdoor into the system. Italians can reach Orelle by the Fréjus Tunnel in two hours from Turin or in less than an hour from Sestriere and the resorts of the Milky Way.

New hotels and apartment *résidences* have been designed more in keeping with their mountain environment than the original buildings. Val Thorens is a strictly pedestrian resort – you are allowed in to unload but must then park in one of the car parks on the edge of town.

On a sunny day after a fresh snowfall, few places are more inviting than Val Thorens. But when the weather closes in you quickly realize why the locals never chose to build a farming community at this altitude. In flat light the treeless pistes lack any point of reference.

Mountain

A chair-lift and the swift Bouquetin gondola provide the link to the Col de Chambre and the long run down to Méribel-Mottaret. Pistes lead from the village to the Péclet Funitel gondola, which takes you up to the glacier and to a network of fast chairs and gondolas that crisscross the mountainside below the ridge separating the Belleville and Maurienne valleys. A gondola and a cable-car, reached by a blue piste below the resort, rise to the 3200m Cime de Caron. This is the starting point for the Combe de Caron, one of the most testing black runs in the area. Wonderful long continuations lead down through 1400m vertical to Les Menuires. For other even longer off-piste runs, like the scenic Itinéraire du Lou, you need the services of a local guide.

From the far side of the Cime de Caron, two chair-lifts take you up to the 2300m Sommet des Pistes, which accesses two high-altitude runs down the Glacier de la Pointe Renod and a snowcross course. Val Thorens' main snow park is on the 2 Lacs piste just above the resort. It has a 110m half-pipe and an assortment of rails and other obstacles. Val Thorens has France's only toboggan course with a 700m verticial drop, reached by the Péclet gondola.

Learn

ESF, **t** +33 (0)4 79 00 02 86, and the **ESI**, **t** +33 (0)4 79 00 01 96, are the main schools. Reporters favour **Ski Cool**, **t** +33 (0)4 79 00 04 92, and **Pros-Neige**, **t** +33 (0)4 79 01 07 00. A number of other little schools offer specialist courses and guiding. These include **Stages Patrick et Eric Berthon**, **t** +33 (0)4 79 00 06 16, which offers bumps and freeride training.

Children

The **ESF**, **t** +33 (0)4 79 00 02 86, at Village Le Montana and Le Village Roc, cares for children from three months, with lessons from three years. **Stages Zig Zag – Fabienne Pander**, **t** +33 (0)4 79 00 02 66, takes groups of up to eight children (who have at least the ESF Three Star qualification) to a different valley each day.

Lunch

Try **La Chaumière**, **t** +33 (0)4 79 00 01 13, **Chalet Les 2 Ours**, **t** +33 (0)4 79 01 14 09, and **Chalet Génépi**, **t** +33 (0)4 79 00 03 28.

L'Oxalys, **t** +33 (0)4 79 00 20 51 offers the kind of full-blown gastro lunch that precludes afternoon skiing. **Etape 3200**, **t** +33 (0)6 07 31 04 14, at the top of the Cime de Caron, has great views.

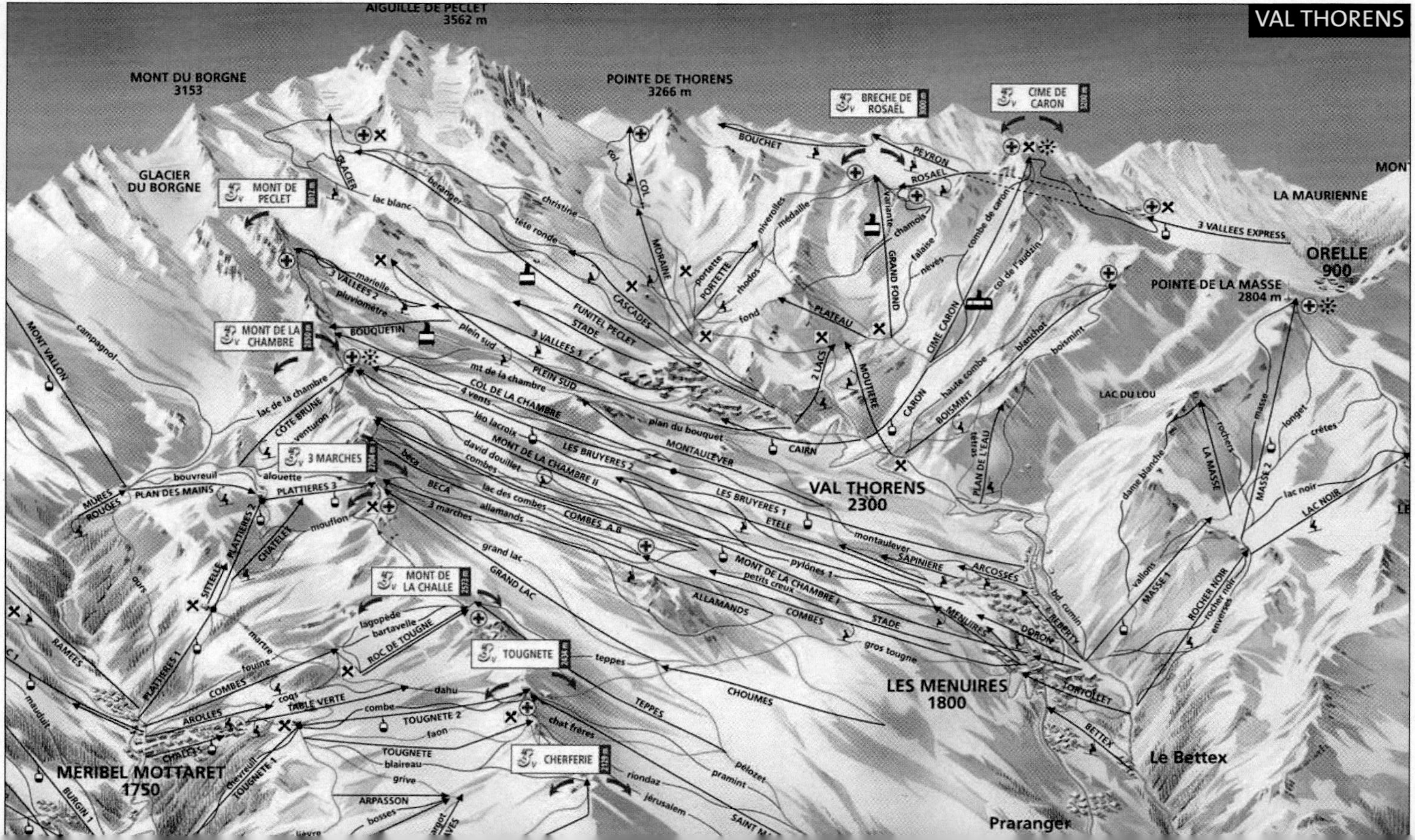
VAL THORENS
AIGUILLE DE PECLET
3562 m
MONT DU BORGNE
3153
GLACIER
DU BORGNE
POINTE DE THORENS
3266 m
BRECHE DE
ROSAËL
CIME DE
CARON
LA MAURIENNE
ORELLE
900
POINTE DE LA MASSE
2804 m
MONT DE
PECLET
MONT DE LA
CHAMBRE
3 MARCHES
MONT DE
LA CHALLE
TOUGNETE
CHERFERIE
VAL THORENS
2300
LES MENUIRES
1800
MERIBEL MOTTARET
1750
Le Bettex
Praranger
LAC DU LOU
GLACIER
lac blanc
beranger
christine
tête ronde
COL
col
MORAINE
CASCADES
FUNITEL PECLET
STADE
3 VALLEES 1
3 VALLEES 2
3 VALLEES EXPRESS
BOUCHET
PEYRON
ROSAEL
variante
chamois
falaise
névés
GRAND FOND
combe de caron
col de l'audzin
CIME CARON
PLATEAU
2 LACS
MOUTIERE
CARON
CAIRN
BOISMINT
haute combe
blanchot
boismint
PLAN DE L'EAU
tétras
portette
PORTETTE
rhodos
niverolles
médaille
fond
marielle
pluviomètre
BOUQUETIN
plein sud
PLEIN SUD
mt de la chambre
COL DE LA CHAMBRE
4 vents
léo lacroix
MONT DE LA CHAMBRE II
david douillet
combes
plan du bouquet
MONTAULEVER
LES BRUYERES 2
LES BRUYERES 1
ETELE
montaulever
SAPINIERE
ARCOSSES
pylônes 1
MONT DE LA CHAMBRE I
petits creux
ALLAMANDS
COMBES
STADE
MENUIRES
DORON
REBERTY
bd. cumin
TORTOLLET
BETTEX
gros tougne
CHOUMES
TEPPES
teppes
grand lac
GRAND LAC
COMBES A.B
lac des combes
allamands
BECA
beca
3 marches
lac de la chambre
CÔTE BRUNE
venturon
alouette
bouvreuil
PLAN DES MAINS
MURES ROUGES
PLATTIERES 3
PLATTIERES 2
PLATTIERES 1
CHATELET
mouflon
SITTELLE
ours
campagnol
MONT VALLON
RAMEES
maudiut
BURGIN 1
lagopède
bartavelle
ROC DE TOUGNE
martre
fouine
COMBES
coqs
TABLE VERTE
dahu
combe
TOUGNETE 2
faon
TOUGNETE
blaireau
grive
ARPASSON
bosses
ARROLLES
CHALLES
chevreuil
TOUGNETE 1
chat frères
pélozet
pramint
riondaz
jérusalem
SAINT M
rochers
LA MASSE
masse
longet
crêtes
MASSE 2
dame blanche
vallons
MASSE 1
lac noir
LAC NOIR
ROCHER NOIR
rocher noir
enverses

Dine

Celebrity chef Jean-Michel Bouvier's **L'Oxalys**, **t** +33 (0)4 79 00 20 51, and **La Table du Roy**, **t** +33 (0)4 79 00 04 78, in the Hotel Le Fitz Roy, are the most gastronomic establishments in town – during high season you need to book in advance. **Auberge du Sherpa**, **t** +33 (0)4 79 00 00 70, in Hotel du Sherpa and **Le Bellevillois**, **t** + 33 (0)4 79 00 04 33, in Hotel Le Val Thorens are both recommended. **La Cabane**, **t** +33 (0)4 79 00 83 84, is an old-style chalet with a warm atmosphere. **La Grange de Pierrette**, **t** +33 (0)4 79 00 00 88, is also praised along with **Le Panoramic**, **t** +33 (0)4 79 00 04 77 in Hotel Le Bel Horizon. **Le Blanchot**, **t** +33 (0)4 79 00 55 78, is a wine bar with a small number of tables and 'exceptionally good food – quite a little gem for the chalet staff's night off'.

Party

Popular bars include **Le Tango**, **Ski Rock Café**, **The Viking Pub** and **The Frog and Roast Beef**. **Le Malaysia** and **The Underground** are the late-night venues. **New Generation sports centre**, **t** +33 (0)4 79 00 00 18, has tennis and squash courts, a swimming pool, a gym and a spa.

Sleep

★★★★*deluxe* **L'Oxalys**, **t** +33 (0)4 79 00 20 51, *www.valthosport.com*, is a chalet complex with a gastronomic restaurant.

★★★★**Le Fitz Roy**, **t** +33 (0)4 79 00 04 78, is a magnificent chalet-style hotel with swimming pool and fitness centre.

★★★**Le Val Thorens**, **t** +33 (0)4 79 00 04 33, has three restaurants and a lounge with fireplace.

★★★**Le Sherpa**, **t** +33 (0)4 79 00 00 70, is value-for-money and offers good food.

★★★**Le Portillo**, **t** +33 (0)4 79 00 00 88, has individually decorated rooms and a gourmet restaurant.

★★★**Le Bel Horizon**, **t** +33 (0)4 79 00 06 08, is a good-value family option.

★★**Le Val Chavière**, **t** +33 (0)4 79 00 00 33, in the resort centre, is reasonably priced.

Vaujany

Profile

Rural farming village with direct links into the extensive Alpe d'Huez ski area. Excellent for families, intermediates, gourmets and off-piste enthusiasts

Resort

In the late 1980s, Vaujany became unexpectedly wealthy through land sold for France's largest hydroelectric scheme. The villagers swapped tractors for piste-bashers, and converted cowsheds to chalets after Vaujany became a ski resort by building a giant cable-car linking into the giant Alpe d'Huez ski area. A welcome improvement last season was an escalator connecting the lift area

* BEST FOR

Rural village atmosphere, big ski area, families, value

ESSENTIALS

Altitude: 1250m (4,101ft)–3330m (10,922ft)
Further information: **t** +33 (0)4 76 80 72 37, *www.vaujany.com*
Lifts in area: 86 (16 cableways, 25 chairs, 45 drags) serving 240km of piste
Lift pass: Area (covers linked resorts, 2 days in Les Deux Alpes, 1 day in La Grave, The Milky Way, Puy-St-Vincent, and Serre Chevalier) adult €192, child 5–15yrs €137, both for 6 days
Access: Grenoble airport 1½hrs, Lyon airport 2hrs

with accommodation at the top of this steep village.

Mountain

Vaujany's hayricks-to-riches story explains the presence of a 160-person cable-car in this picturesque but no longer sleepy mountain village. The second stage goes up to Dôme des Petites Rousses at 2800m giving direct access to Alpe d'Huez and lifts going up to the 3330m Pic Blanc. A gondola also connects the village to Montfrais.

Learn

The **ESF**, **t** +33 (0)4 76 80 71 80, is the main ski and board school. **Le Massif**, **t** +33 (0)6 07 97 38 11, **Christelle Morin**, **t** +33 (0)6 83 14 05 74, and **V.O. Coaching**, **t** +33 (0)6 60 27 60 32, also provide lessons.

Children

La Garderie, **t** +33 (0)4 76 80 77 53, offers daycare for children aged six months to five years, and British tour operator **Ski Peak** provides a native English-speaking nanny. The **ESF**, **t** +33 (0)4 76 80 71 80, runs all English-speaking classes during school holidays.

Lunch

Les Airelles, **t** +33 (0)4 76 80 79 78, at the top of the Montfrais nursery slope, is a family favourite. **Auberge de L'Alpette**, **t** +33 (0)47 6 80 70 00, has wonderful omelettes and salads.

Dine

Hôtel Rissiou, **t** +33 (0)4 76 80 71 00, has fine food and wine. **La Remise**, **t** + 33 (0)4 76 80 77 11, has great pizzas and fondues. **Le Chardon Bleu**, **t** +33 (0)4 76 11 03 95, at La Villette is simple but well worth the 1km walk.

Party

The **Swallow Bar** is the mandatory resort meeting place for teenagers and twenty-somethings, as well as the **L'Etendard** bar. **Arsen's** Internet café is also popular. The skating rink and a giant swimming pool with flumes provide après-ski entertainment.

Sleep

Accommodation is mainly in apartments and in comfortable chalets in Vaujany and in the neighbouring hamlet of La Villette, 1km away.

****Chalet Saskia, t** +44 (0)1428 608070, *www.skipeak.com*, is a charming stand-alone chalet at the lower end of the village, with exquisite food.

***Résidence La Perle L'Oisans, t** +44 (0)1428 608070, *www.skipeak.com*, on the higher level of the village, has the most spacious and convenient apartments.

Hôtel Le Rissiou, t +33 (0)4 76 80 71 00, *www.skipeak.com*, offers the best hotel accommodation in the village.

Les Cimes, t +33 (0)4 76 79 86 50, has small but pleasant rooms.

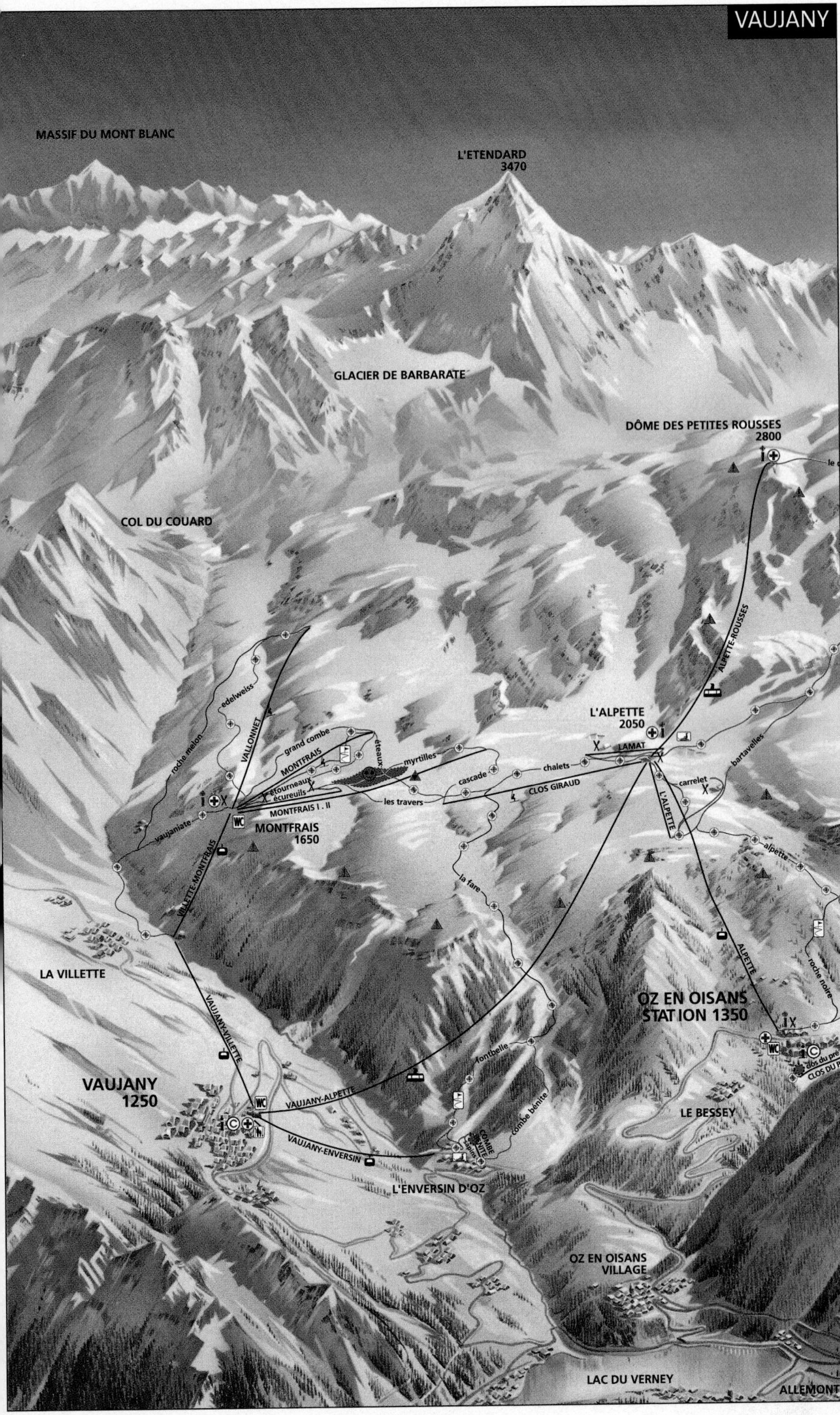
MASSIF DU MONT BLANC
L'ETENDARD
3470
GLACIER DE BARBARATE
DÔME DES PETITES ROUSSES
2800
COL DU COUARD
ALPETTE-ROUSSES
edelweiss
VALLONNET
roche melon
grand combe
MONTFRAIS
éteaux
myrtilles
étourneaux
écureuils
les travers
cascade
chalets
CLOS GIRAUD
L'ALPETTE
2050
LAMAT
carrelet
bartavelles
L'ALPETTE
vaujaniate
MONTFRAIS I . II
MONTFRAIS
1650
VILLETTE-MONTFRAIS
alpette
la fare
LA VILLETTE
ALPETTE
roche noire
OZ EN OISANS
STATION 1350
VAUJANY-VILLETTE
clos du pré
CLOS DU PRÉ
fontbelle
VAUJANY
1250
VAUJANY-ALPETTE
LE BESSEY
combe bénite
COMBE BÉNITE
VAUJANY-ENVERSIN
L'ENVERSIN D'OZ
OZ EN OISANS
VILLAGE
LAC DU VERNEY
ALLEMONT

06

The Top Resorts: Italy

Arabba

***BEST FOR**

Steep skiing, village atmosphere

ESSENTIALS

Altitude: 1600m (5,248ft)–2949m (9,676ft)
Further information: t +39 0436 179130, *www.arabba.it*
Lifts in area: 22 (4 cableways, 13 chairs, 5 drags) serving 54km of piste; 450 lifts in Dolomiti Superski
Lift pass: Dolomiti Superski adult €155–254, child 8–16yrs €109–178, both for 6 days
Access: Verona airport 3hrs, railway stations at Belluno 75km, Brunico 45km

Profile

Best base for the steepest pistes in the otherwise intermediate Sella Ronda ski area. Small village with limited nightlife, unsuitable for non-skiers

Resort

Arabba guards the gateway to the 3342m Marmolada and is the best place in the Sella Ronda for committed skiers and riders.

Mountain

The village's reputation as a base for serious skiers is built upon the steep north-facing slopes of 2478m Porta Vescovo. An often oversubscribed cable-car serves a choice of challenging black runs, as well as much gentler alternatives leading back to the resort. The Marmolada tour takes you down to the town of Malga Ciapela. A three-stage cable-car rises to Punta Rocca at 3269m for a glorious 12km descent all the way back to Malga Ciapela.

Learn

The choice lies between **Arabba Ski School**, **t** +39 0436 79160 and **Rocca-Marmolada**, **t** +39 0437 722060.

Children

Snow White Village, run by the Arabba Ski School, accepts kids from two years of age on weekdays, **t** +39 0437 722277.

Lunch

Rifugio Capanna Bill, **t** +39 0437 722100, near Malga Ciapela offers home-made pasta and grilled meat. **Miky's Grill**, **t** +39 0436 79119, in the Hotel Mesdi, offers simple lunch-time fare. **Rifugio Plan Boé**, **t** +39 0436 79339, on the anti-clockwise route, has a suitably rustic atmosphere. **Bec de Roces**, **t** +39 0436 79193, has a self-service area and an upstairs pizzeria.

Dine

Pizzeria 7 Sass, **t** +39 0436 780135, is recommended. **Al Tablé**, **t** +39 0436 79302, specializes in local game. **Al Forte**, **t** +39 0436 79329, is housed in a late 19th-century Austro-Hungarian fort and has live music on Wednesdays. **Ru de Mont**, **t** +39 0436 780020, in the satellite village of Renaz, has good pizzas.

Party

Nightlife is muted. **Peter's Bar**, the Sporthotel's **Bacchus Cellar Bar** and **La Treina** are the main bars.

Sleep

******Sporthotel Arabba**, **t** +39 0436 79321, *www.sporthotelarabba.com*, has a large

MARMOLADA
MARMOLATA
3342 m
Piz Boè
3152 m
Col di Lana
2462 m
P.so Campolongo
1875 m
ARABBA
P.so Falzarego
2105 m
Lavarella
3055 m
Conturines
3064 m
Cortina
VAL BADIA
S.CASSIANO
LA VILLA
PEDRACES
CORVARA
GARDENACIA
P U E Z
S E L L A G R U P P E
P.so Pordoi
Pordoi Joch
2239 m
P E C O L
Col Rodela
2484 m
CANAZEI
CAMPITELLO
P.so Gardena
Grödnerjoch
2121 m
P.so Sella
Sella Joch
2244 m
Dantercepies
2300 m
Piz Setëur
2064 m
Plan de Gralba
1800 m
S T E V I A
SECEDA
Seceda
2518 m
Col Raiser
2103 m
Cuca
Cucasattel
Piz Sella
2284
SASSOLUNGO
LANGKOFEL
3181 m
SASSOPIATTO
PLATTKOFEL
2956 m
Ciampinoi
2254 m
SELVA GARDENA
WOLKENSTEIN
1564 m
Mont de Sëura
2117 m
Val Gardena Ronda Express
Monte Pana
1636 m
Saslong
S.CRISTINA
ST.CHRISTINA
1428
Saltria
1700 m
Denti di Terrarossa
Rosszähne
2657 m
Punta d'Oro - Goldknopf
2210 m
Monte Piz
2109 m
A L P E D I S I U S I
S E I S E R A L M
SCILIAR
SCHLERN
Bullaccia
Puflatsch
2130m
PUNTA SANTNER
SANTNER SP.
2413 m
Rasciesa Dafora
Ausserraschötz
2281 m
R A S C I E S A
R A T S C H Ö T Z
S. Giacomo
St. Jacob
1569 m
ORTISEI
ST. ULRICH
1236
Pufels
1484 m
BOLZANO
BOZEN
S. Pietro
St. Peter
Laion
Lajen

pool and a spa offering a full range of treatments.

★★★★**Hotel Griffone, t** +39 0436 780034, *www.hotelgrifone.com*, is situated outside town on Passo Campolongo.

★★★**Hotel Portavescovo, t** +39 0436 79139, *www.portavescovo.it*, has a children's playroom, swimming pool and gym.

★★★**Hotel Evaldo, t** +39 0436 79109, *www.hotelevaldo.com*, is traditional, with an attractive swimming pool, wellness area and nearby self-catering apartments.

★★★**Hotel Garni Royal, t** +39 0436 79293, *www.hotel.garniroyal.com*, has good-sized bedrooms, sauna, steam room and hot tub, and is warmly recommended.

★★★**Hotel Mesdi, t** +39 0436 79119, *www.hotelmesdi.com*, is fairly new and has an impressive wellness centre.

★★★**Hotel Olympia, t** +39 0436 79135, *www.hotel-olympia.com*, contains apartments and a restaurant.

Chalet Barbara, t +39 0436 780155 is a new all-wood B&B, furnished in cosy alpine style.

Bormio

Profile

Large historic spa town with lots of atmosphere and a small high-altitude ski area. A wide choice of ski and snowboard tuition is available

Resort

Bormio is a large town dating back to Roman times, with a charming pedestrianized centre and a somewhat limited ski area. It has far more of an authentic Italian atmosphere than many comparable resorts and is best suited to couples and families.

* BEST FOR

Families, authentic Italian ambience

ESSENTIALS

Altitude: 1225m (4,018ft)–3012m (9,879ft)

Further information: t +39 0342 903300, *wwwbormioski.it*

Lifts in area: 17 (3 cableways, 7 chairs, 7 drags) serving 40km of piste

Lift pass: 4 Valleys (covers Bormio, Santa Caterina, Le Motte and Oga) adult €102–155, child from 6yrs €71–110, both for 6 days

Access: Bergamo and Milan airports 3hrs

Mountain

The resort's greatest plus point is its high altitude that allows skiing to continue until after Easter. New lifts are an enduring legacy of the successful 2005 Alpine Skiing World Championships. Main mountain access is by a two-stage cable-car from the edge of town that takes you up to the Cima Bianca top station via Bormio 2000, a mid-station with a family hotel and a shopping mall. A gondola and quad-chair offer an alternative route. The long descents provide ideal cruising territory for intermediates.

Learn

Of the seven ski schools, **Bormio Alta Valtellina, t** +39 0342 911020, is highly recommended for its friendly, English-speaking instructors.

Children

The ski schools take children from four years, while the crèche at the **Scuola Sci Contea, t** +39 0342 911605, accepts children from three years.

Lunch

Try **La Rocca, t** +39 0342 905083, an old-fashioned hut on the main trail down to

Bormio 2000, and **Rododendri Chalet**, **t** +39 0342 905034, just above 2000.

Dine

La Rasiga, **t** +39 0342 901541, is a stylishly converted sawmill. **Vecchia Combo**, **t** +39 0342 901568, **Al Filo**, **t** +39 0342 904771, **Osteria dei Magri**, **t** +39 0342 910456, and **Kuerc**, **t** +39 0342 904738, are also recommended.

Party

Braulio is a microbrewery and a wine bar. **Lord Byron** attracts a young crowd. **Gordy's Pub** and **Sotto-Sotto** are popular alternatives. The late-night focus is the **King's Club** disco. The **Rezia Hotel** has a jazz café, and **Shangri-la** has a good choice of cocktails.

Sleep

★★★★**Hotel Baita dei Pini**, **t** +39 0342 904346, *www.baitadeipini.com*, is an excellent hotel, 400m from the gondola.

★★★★**Hotel Palace**, **t** +39 0342 903131, *www.palacebormio.it*, is recently renovated and close to the town centre.

★★★★**Hotel Posta**, **t** +39 0342 904753, *www.hotelposta.bormio.it*, is a former staging inn with an attractive interior.

★★★★**Hotel Rezia**, **t** +39 0342 904721, *www.reziahotel.it*, is in the pedestrianized centre. Its restaurant serves local Valtellina dishes.

★★★**Hotel Funivia**, **t** +39 0342 903242, *www.hotelfunivia.it*, is close to the lifts and has spacious bedrooms.

★★★**Hotel Nevada**, **t** +39 0342 910888, *www.anzibormio.com*, is at the foot of the Bormio 2000 cable-car and has comfortable rooms.

Canazei

Profile

An attractive little town that acts as a mass-market base for skiers and riders wanting to explore the Sella Ronda. The remainder of the Fassa valley has less crowded skiing and rural villages

Resort

Canazei and adjoining Campitello are the main resorts in the 20km Val di Fassa, a key player in the Sella Ronda circuit, which forms the core of the Dolomiti Superski, the world's largest area lift pass. The valley has been heavily developed for tourism, but with its backdrop of high mountain peaks and heavily wooded lower slopes, it is by no means unattractive.

It takes around two hours to complete the 40km circuit that links Canazei with Selva Gardena, Arabba and Corvara – the principal compass points. It can be skied in either direction. You take 13 lifts clockwise and 15 lifts anticlockwise. How much time is actually spent skiing depends on your level of proficiency. In planning your day, you must also allow for

*** BEST FOR**

High-mileage intermediates, night-owls

ESSENTIALS

Altitude: 1460m (4,790ft)–2949m (9,676ft)
Further information: **t** +39 0462 602466, *www.fassa.com*
Lifts in area: 78 (13 cableways, 39 chairs, 26 drags) serving 200km of pistes; 450 lifts in Dolomiti Superski
Lift pass: Dolomiti Superski adult €155–254, child 8–16yrs €109–178, both for 6 days
Access: Verona airport 2hrs, railway station at Bolzano 1hr

possible lift queues. It makes sense to start before 10am and to reach the last of the four main passes by 3.30pm. The lifts close at 5pm – or earlier – in bad weather conditions. Skimap Sella Ronda, available from lift stations and tourist offices, clearly indicates the route and the signposting is good. However, the number of variations and tangental links to other ski areas off the main circuit can be both tempting and confusing.

Other villages in the Val di Fassa, including Alba, Pozza, Moena and Vigo di Fassa, have their own small and much quieter ski areas that tend to attract multi-generational Italian families rather than an international clientele.

Canazei itself is a hotchpotch of narrow cobbled lanes flanked by old barns, modern hotels, a good choice of restaurants and a surprisingly wide range of shops. Visitors are reliant upon the ski-bus or postbus for reaching the lifts from most of the accommodation, but services throughout the valley are efficient. If one of the main access lifts is crowded, you can always stay on the bus and travel to the next.

Mountain

A modern gondola on the edge of Canazei provides the only means of access to the mid-station at Pecol. The seven-minute journey leaves you with a choice of a chair or an 80-person cable-car for formal entry into the Sella Ronda. In theory an intermediate can ski back down to Canazei, but conditions of the south-facing slopes usually limit the opening of this piste to the middle weeks of the season.

Campitello 1440m acts as an alternative access point. A cable-car takes you up to Col Rodella, from where you either work your way through a sequence of chair-lifts to Passo Sella and Val Gardena beyond, or ski down a pleasant and long intermediate run to Plan Frataces to catch the connection to Passo Pordoi and the anticlockwise route to Arabba.

Passo Pordoi, midway between Canazei and Arabba, has the steepest piste skiing in the Dolomites and is accessed by the ancient Sass Pordoi cable-car. But this is a variation off the Sella Ronda strictly reserved for truly accomplished skiers.

From the top, you can either return down a truly challenging itinerary run to Passo Pordoi, or follow the difficult Val Lasties to Canazei. Alternatively, you can – with a guide – explore the Val Mesdi. This cuts across the Sella, the giant rounded stump of a mountain at the heart of the famous ski circuit, and brings you down to Colfosco. All these off-piste descents require good snow and stable weather conditions as well as a level of expertise not necessarily required elsewhere in the Sella Ronda.

Canazei- and Pozza-based skiers also have the chance to explore Sella Brunech, the lesser-known ski area on the far side of the Fassa Valley, reached by a cable-car from Alba and a gondola from Passa. This is a pleasant and nearly always uncrowded intermediate playground that is augmented by other lifts on Ciampedie on the other side of the valley at Vigo. The further reaches of the valley have other ski opportunities beginning from Carezza and Passo Costalunga as well as from Ronchi above Moena. From here it is possible to delve on skis still further to Passo San Pellegrino and also into the intricate lift system of the Val di Fiemme. Not all links are seamless and the occasional bus journey is necessary.

Learn

None of the teaching establishments in the valley stands out for its cutting-edge tuition and by no means every instructor speaks fluent English. The schools are **Canazei-Marmolada, t** +39 0462 601211, **Campitello, t** +39 0462 750350, **Moena-Dolomiti, t** +39 0462 573770, **Vajolet Pozza di Fassa, t** +39 0462 763309, and **Vigo di Fassa-Passo Costalunga, t** +39 0462 763125.

Children

Childcare is limited. **Baby Park Ciampedie** in Vigo (at the top of the cable-car), run by the Vigo di Fassa school, and **Babylandia-Alpe di Lusia** (at the top of the Lusia cable-car), run by the Moena-Dolomiti school, both offer daycare and lessons. **Park Bimbo Neve, t** +39 0462 763309, in Pozza, is operated by the Vajolet Pozza di Fassa ski school for children over three years. **Kinderland e Fantaski, t** +39 0462 601211, is run by the Canazei-Marmolada ski school and offers daycare for three years and over, and lessons for the over-fours.

Lunch

The mountainside is dotted with privately owned huts, and from midday onwards enticing aromas signal the start of lunch, which the Italians see as an essential component of the skiing day. Try **Rifugio Maria, t** +39 0462 601178, on top of Sass Pordoi, which specializes in Trentino cuisine. From its sun terrace it offers some of the best views in the Dolomites. **Refuge Frederich August, t** +39 0462 750133, is on the Col Rodella.

Baita Checco, t +39 335 6563512, above Vigo, and **Bellavista, t** +39 0462 763200, 30m from the base cable-car station at Viga, are both worthy lunch spots. **Tobia del Giagher, t** +39 0462 602385, above Alba, and **Buffaure, t** +39 0462 764101, on the piste above Pozza, are also recommended.

Dine

In Canazei most of the best evening restaurants are in hotels. **La Cacciattora, t** +39 0462 601411, has fresh fish shipped in every day. **La Perla's, t** +39 0462 602453, signature dish is *pappardelle* (broad ribbons of pasta) with a game sauce. In Campitello, **La Cantinetta, t** +39 0462 750405, is renowned for its polenta with mushrooms and venison. In Pozza, **Al Crocefisso, t** +39 0462 764260, is known for its roast lamb shanks and porcini dumplings. Try the house antipasto and grilled venison cutlets at **Al Vecchio Mulino, t** +39 0462 764477. **El Pael, t** +39 0462 601433, is another good choice.

In Moena, **Malga Panna, t** +39 0462 573489, is one of the truly outstanding restaurants in the region. Signature dishes include rabbit ravioli with rosemary. **Le Giare, t** +39 0462 764696, is in Pozza. In Vigo, **Hotel Andes, t** +39 0462 764575, has a popular pizzeria and restaurant with fresh pasta dishes.

Party

Nightlife centres around bars in Canazei and Campitello including **Frogs** in Alba, **La Stüa dei Ladins, Rosengarten, The Esso Bar, The Husky Bar** and **Kusk** in Canazei, with **da Gulio** and **Ton Tin** in Campitello. The new **Snow Tube** at Alba makes for some fun evening entertainment, and there is a floodlit slope at Pozza.

Sleep

Canazei:
★★★★**Hotel Astoria, t** +39 0462 601302, *www.hotel-astoria.net*, has been run by the same family since the Second World War and provides comfortable rooms and good food.
★★★★**Hotel Croce Bianca & Spa Vivenes, t** +39 0462 60111,

www.hotelcrocebianca.com, has been in the same family since 1869 and now houses an impressive spa and the popular Husky Pub.

★★★★**Hotel La Perla**, **t** +39 0462 602453, *www.hotellaperla.net*, is popular with British guests and also has an exotic wellness area.

★★★★**Hotel La Cacciatora**, **t** +39 0462 601411, *www.lacacciatora.it*, situated in Alba just 100m from the Ciampac cable-car, has been completely renovated.

★★★**Park Hotel Faloria**, **t** +39 0462 601118 has small rooms but is reasonably priced with a fine restaurant.

Campitello:

★★★★**Hotel Medil**, **t** +39 0462 750088, *www.hotelmedil.it*, offers the smartest accommodation, and has a bar with live music.

★★★**Hotel Alpi**, **t** +39 0462 750400, *www.hotelalpi.it*, is located 400m from the cable-car and has a ski-bus stop outside the door.

Hotel Panorama, **t** +39 0462 750112, *www.panoramahotel.it*, is at the far end of the village but convenient for the Col de Lin nursery slope.

Moena:

★★★★**Garden Hotel**, **t** +39 0462 573314, *www.gardenhotel.biz*, has an indoor swimming pool, and a piano bar.

Pozzo and Vigo di Fassa:

★★★★**Corona Sport & Wellness Hotel**, +39 0462 764211, *www.hotelcorona.com*, in Vigo, is impressive and was used by former Olympic slalom skier Alberto Tomba as his training base.

★★★★**Hotel Ladinia**, **t** +39 0462 764201, *www.hotelladinia.com*, in Pozzo, is recommended.

Cavalese

Profile

Small town in the beautiful Val di Fiemme, an excellent base for anyone looking for genuine Dolomite atmosphere coupled with good alpine and cross-country skiing

Resort

Cavalese is the capital of the Val di Fiemme, a heavily wooded valley north of Trento with nine separate ski areas. The spruce is prized by furniture makers and, back in the 1700s, Stradivari strolled through these woods selecting the raw material for his violins.

Fiemme is otherwise best known for its 70km cross-country race each January for 6,000 pro-am skiers. The pick of the skiing is found at Cavalese, and at Predazzo, the other main town.

Mountain

Rifugio Paion, the high point of Alpe Cermis, can be accessed either by a gondola and chair-lift or by a couple of chairs. These lifts, together with a further drag, combine to form a pleasant ski area that is more scenic than challenging. Mainly blue and easy red runs with a vertical drop of 1400m lead down over summer pastureland and through the woods to Cavalese.

Predazzo is a starting point for the more complex 17-lift area of Ski Center Latemar, which extends through Pampeago to San Floriano. Passo Rolle at 1980m is the setting for a compact five-lift complex above the much larger ski area of San Martino di Castrozza.

* BEST FOR

Italian atmosphere, easy alpine and scenic cross-country skiing

ESSENTIALS

Altitude: 900m (2,953ft)–2250m (7,382ft)
Further information: +39 0462 241199, *www.valdifiemme.info*
Lifts in area: 46 (7 cableways, 28 chairs, 11 drags) serving 107km of piste; 450 lifts in Dolomiti Superski
Lift pass: Dolomiti Superski adult €155–254, child 8–16yrs €109–178, both for 6 days
Access: Verona airport 2hrs, railway station at Bolzano 1hr

Learn

The schools are **Alta Val di Fiemme, t** +39 0462 502999, **Cermis Cavalese, t** +39 0462 341303, **Alpe di Pampeago, t** +39 0462 813337, and **Passo du Lavaze, t** +39 0462 231830.

Children

Kinderheim Gardone, t +39 0462 502999, at Predazzo, **Cermislandia, t** +39 0452 235311, at Alpe Cermis and **Asilo della Neve Pampeago, t** +39 0462 813337, all accept children from three years.

Lunch

Try **Rifugio Paion, t** +39 0462 341616, at Alpe del Cermis. **Eurotel Alpe Cermis, t** +39 0462 340572, at the top of the cable-car, has a sunny terrace. **Baita Dosso Larica, t** +39 0462 235411, at Doss dei Laresi, specializes in game. **Baita Gardone, t** +39 0462 503110, at Predazzo, is recommended.

Dine

In Cavalese, **Cantuccio, t** +39 0462 235040, is famous for its lamb dishes. **El Molin, t** +39 0462 340074, housed in an old cow shed, has a huge range of pasta. **Ristorante des Alpes, t** +39 0462 231117, is renowned for its *tortellini*. In Predazzo, **Hotel Ancora, t** +39 0462 501651, has a fine restaurant. **Saronch, t** +39 0462 503161, specializes in fresh fish.

Party

The **Igloo Bar** at Gardone, the **Siglu** at Doss dei Laresi, and the **Ganischger Alm** at Pampeago are three of the après-hotspots. Later on, the action moves to **Mardok** and **El Calderon** pubs in Cavalese, and to **Poldo's** and the **Al Santo** wine bar in Predazzo.

Sleep

Cavalese:

★★★★**Hotel Grünwald, t** +39 0462 340369, *www.hotelgrunwald.it*, has a piano bar and swimming pool.

★★★★**Hotel La Roccia, t** +39 0462 231133, *www.hotellaroccia.it*, has a spa.

★★★**Hotel Excelsior e Molin, t** +39 0462 340403, *www.excelsiorcavalese.com*, is comfortable and friendly.

★★★**Orso Grigio, t** +39 0462 341481, *www.hotelorsogrigio.it*, is the building in which Emperor Franz Joseph used to stay in the 19th century.

Predazzo:

★★★★**Hotel Ancora, t** +39 0462 501651, *www.ancora.it*, offers some of the best accommodation in the valley.

★★★**Hotel Sole, t** +39 0462 576299, *www.hsole.it*, outside the town at Bellamonte, is child-friendly.

Cervinia

Profile

High-altitude resort with guaranteed snow-cover during a long season. Suits beginners as well as intermediates who will enjoy the long, flattering runs. It is linked to Zermatt in Switzerland and they share a lift pass

*BEST FOR

Beginners, long intermediate runs, guaranteed snow-cover

ESSENTIALS

Altitude: 2050m (6,726ft)–3883m (12,740ft)
Further information: t +39 0166 949136, *www.montecervino.it*
Lifts in area: 57 with Zermatt (2 funiculars, 19 cableways, 20 chairs, 16 drags) serving 200km of piste in Cervinia, 313km with Zermatt
Lift pass: Area (covers Cervinia, Valtournenche, Zermatt) adult €183–228, child 9–13yrs €91.50–114, both for 6 days
Access: Geneva and Turin airports 2hrs, railway station at Châtillon 27km, regular buses to resort

Resort

Cervinia is a high-altitude resort with fabulous long runs and virtually guaranteed snow conditions throughout the winter. It's somewhere Italy should be proud of. Il Duce, Benito Mussolini, felt exactly the same about this and decreed in the 1930s that the then embryo resort should change its name from the Swiss-German-sounding Breuil to Cervinia to reflect the Italianate glory of the mountain above it. Unfortunately most of us think of the Matterhorn rather than Il Cervino when we view the angular peak that adorns more postcards than any other in the world. From the Italian side the peak first climbed by Edward Whymper in 1865 looks unremarkable.

The nucleus of pre-Second World War buildings reflect the austere imperial style of the time, but all that was a long time ago. Cervinia today is a modern ski resort with a hotch-potch of mainly unenterprising architecture created over the past half-century by those who believe that this is Italy's greatest resort.

Actually, it's not. It's a wonderfully ski-friendly playground, dictated by the easy gradient of its seemingly never-ending slopes. These allow beginners and wobbly intermediates to gain enormous confidence in the extensive high-mountain area. At the same time boy- and girl-racers will enjoy the length of the perfectly groomed runs – and if they are bored by the benign gradient, they can always cross the Klein Matterhorn for the more severe pistes of Zermatt.

Valtournenche is an old village 9km by road from Cervinia, but linked into the same ski area.

Mountain

Cervinia's biggest asset is altitude. At 2050m, with slopes rising to 3883m, it is one of Europe's most snow-sure resorts, set against a superb glacial backdrop. It's a place where long runs right down to village level are virtually guaranteed from the beginning of December until early May. Summer skiing continues on the glacier throughout the year. Seven lifts serve 21km of prepared piste with an enormous out-of-season vertical drop of 1000m in the right conditions. A terrain park, with a superpipe and a half-pipe, is open from July until October.

The link to Zermatt and the joint lift pass, engineered after a decade of talks between the two resorts, are of benefit to both parties.

SKIRAMA BREUIL-CERVINIA VALTOURNENCHE-ZERMATT

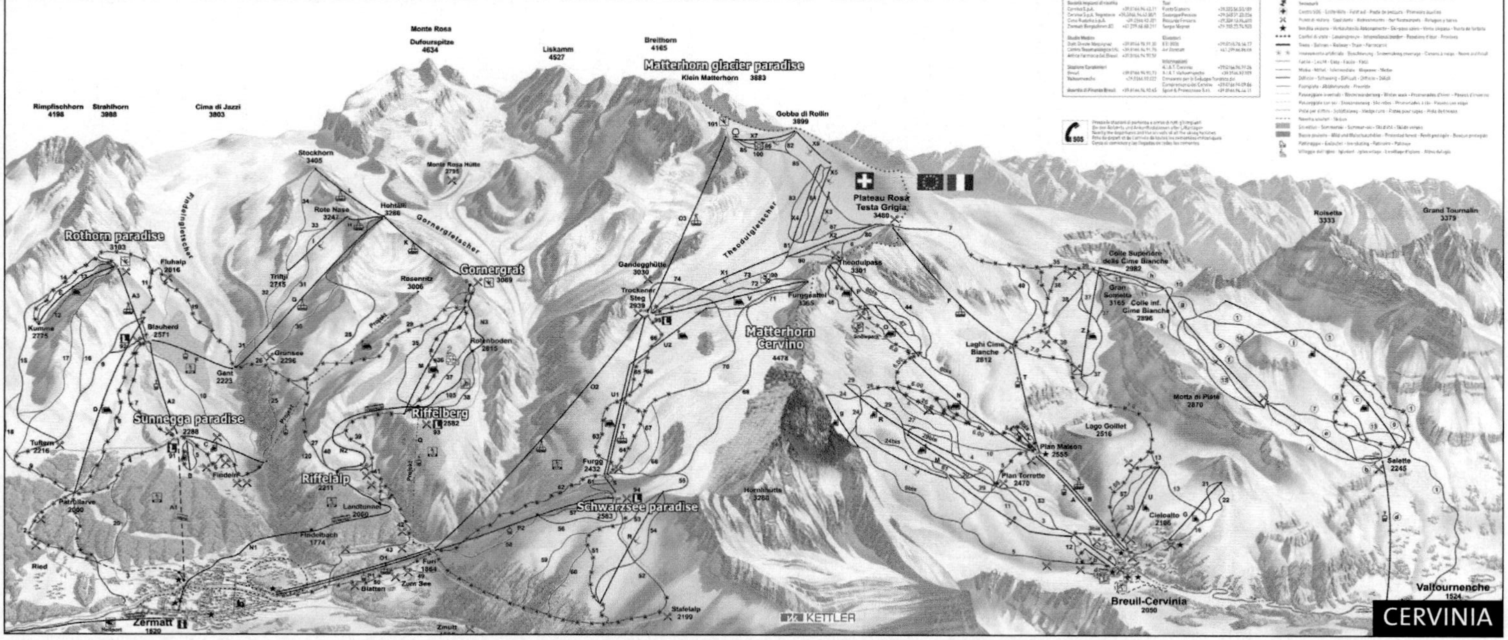

However, don't make the mistake of thinking that by staying in Cervinia you can fully enjoy Zermatt on the cheap – the distances are too great to be able to do any more than sample what the Swiss have to offer.

Beginners and lower intermediates will find themselves content with the 28 lifts on the Italian side that extend down to Valtournenche at 1524m. If they want to visit Switzerland during their stay they can invest in a one-day supplement to the local lift pass. It is important to allow plenty of time to make the long journey back up the Klein Matterhorn and over to Italy at the end of the day. The high-altitude link is prone to sudden rupture in adverse weather conditions. The taxi journey from one resort to the other takes six hours – it's better to bivouac for the night in the wrong country.

A six-pack and two fixed-grip quads are planned for this season. A gondola and parallel cable-car take skiers up from Cervinia to the mid-mountain hub of 2559m Plan Maison. The base station is an annoying walk up from much of the accommodation. The lazy but rather longer alternative is to work your way up the lift system by drag-lift from the nursery slopes.

From Plan Maison, a network of modern multiple chairs, a gondola and finally a cable-car bring you up to the summer ski area of Plateau Rosa at 3480m. From here you can ski down the Theodulgletscher to Trockener Steg in Switzerland, or return to Cervinia on the 8km Ventina (no.7 on the resort's piste map). This is one of the classic runs of the Alps. For the second- or third-week skier fresh from the nursery slopes, the easy gradient should present no problems. Its completion will give an enormous sense of achievement. For the advanced skier or a rider, a couple of these at the start of the day when the pistes are deserted should reduce the fittest legs to *lasagne*. If you are still hungry, try the descent from the Plateau Rosa to Valtournenche – it's more than twice as long.

The lack of pitch throughout the ski area on the Italian side can be irksome for strong skiers. They will quickly discover that Cervinia has no steep piste skiing at all, just kilometre upon kilometre of blue and red cruising runs. However, it is ideal for novices who can explore the entire mountain after just a week on skis.

In powder conditions there's plenty of good off-piste to be discovered on the shoulder above Cieloalto. Local guides can provide access from the lift system to an enormous number of enjoyable high-altitude descents that can be exceedingly demanding. Heli-skiing is also possible on the Monte Rosa.

The terrain park that is served by the Fornet chair has both a half-pipe and a snowcross course.

Learn

The choice of schools here lies between the traditional **Cervino, t** +39 0166 949034, **Breuil, t** +39 0166 940960, and newer **Matterhorn Cervinia, t** +39 0166 949523. **Valtournenche** has its own ski school, **t** +39 0166 92515. Mountain guides from the local bureau in Cervinia are much more reasonably priced than their Swiss counterparts, but have equal expertise on the border peaks. Go with **Guide del Cervino, t** +39 0166 948169, or **Heliski Cervinia, t** +39 0166 949267.

Children

Mini Club Biancaneve, t +39 0166 940201, is a non-ski kindergarten taking children from newborn to eight years old. **Kid Zone, t** +39 0166 940960, is a play area at Plan Maison. Children must be accompanied by an adult. All the ski schools run classes for children from four or five years.

Lunch

Chalet Etoile, **t** +39 0166 940220, near the Rocce Nere chair-lift, is the best restaurant on the mountain, renowned for its spaghetti with lobster. **Ventina**, **t** +39 338 6642596, on the way down from Plateau Rosa, has home cooking. **Bontadini**, **t** +39 335 250312, on the slope of the same name, also received good reviews. **Le Pousset**, **t** +39 339 6946228, below Laghi Cime Bianche, serves local specialities, as does **Baita Cretaz**, **t** +39 0166 949914, on the nursery slopes.

Dine

Hermitage, **t** +39 0166 948998, has outstanding 'international cuisine' served in an elegant dining room. **Le Bistrot de l'Abbé**, **t** +39 0166 949060, is smaller and more rustic, but a worthy runner-up. **La Nicchia**, **t** +39 0166 949842, is smart with rich food. **La Tana, t** +39 0166 949098, is singled out for its game and mushroom dishes. **Copa Pan**, **t** +39 0166 949140, is expensive, has a rustic decor, and is rated for its food. **La Maison de Saussure**, **t** +39 0166 948259, is typical, serving Valdostana specialities in wood-panelled surroundings. Eat tasty pizzas at **Al Solito Posto**, **t** +39 0166 949126, and at the classical pizzeria, **Matterhorn**, **t** +39 0166 948518, another good dining option.

Party

Nightlife is more muted than you might expect in an Italian resort of this calibre. **Lino's Bar**, beside the ice rink, is everyone's favourite when the lifts close. Cocktails in the **Hotel Edelweiss** are ingenious and intoxicating. **Lo Yeti, Copa Pan** and **Hostellerie des Guides** are popular, as well as the infamous and ever-crowded **Dragon Bar**.

Sleep

★★★★**Hotel Hermitage**, **t** +39 0166 948998, *www.hotelhermitage.com*, situated on the edge of town, has the relaxed atmosphere of a country house.

★★★★**Petit Palais**, **t** +39 01669 49371, is renowned for the quality of its half-board cuisine.

★★★★**Hotel Punta Maquignaz**, **t** +39 0166 949145, *www.puntamaquignaz.com*, is an attractive hotel close to the drag-lifts,

★★★★**Sertorelli Sport Hotel**, **t** +39 0166 949797, *www.sertorelli-cervinia.it*, maintains a consistently high standard.

★★★**Hotel Breuil**, **t** +39 0166 949537, is rated 'clean, spacious and very acceptable'.

★★★**Albergo Grandes Murailles**, **t** +39 0166 932956, *www.hotelgmurailles.com*, is a homely little hotel in Valtournenche village centre, with 16 large rooms decorated with warm rugs and wrought-iron beds.

★★★**Hotel Jumeaux**, **t** +39 0166 949044, *www.hotel-jumeaux.com*, is pleasant, and furnished with antiques and period prints.

★★★**Hotel Mignon**, **t** +39 0166 949344, *www.mignoncervinia.com*, is centrally placed and cosy, with a good restaurant.

Les Neiges d'Antan, **t** +39 0166 948775, *www.lesneigesdantan.it*, is a few minutes' drive from the lifts by hotel bus. Downstairs the decoration is traditional, while upstairs both the bedrooms and the bathrooms have been tastefully revamped.

Champoluc

Profile

A linked circuit of unspoilt ski villages in a rustic corner of the Val d'Aosta with plenty of intermediate skiing in Champoluc and Gressoney as well as truly rugged off-piste above Alagna

* BEST FOR

Small village atmosphere, big intermediate ski area, rugged off-piste (Alagna)

ESSENTIALS

Altitude: 1568m (5,144ft)–3370m (11,056ft)
Further information: t +39 0125 303111, Alagna only: t +44 (0)8701 622 273, *www.monterosa-ski.com*
Lifts in area: 31 (8 cableways, 18 chairs, 5 drags) serving 180km of piste
Lift pass: Aosta Valley (includes Courmayeur, La Thuile, La Rosière, Champoluc-Gressoney-Alagna) adult €186, child 8–12yrs €139.50, , child under 8yrs €46.50, all for 6 days
Access: Turin airport 1½hrs

Resort

Champoluc and the linked villages of Gressoney-La-Trinité, Stafal and Alagna form an area known as Monterosa Ski at the northeastern end of the wide Aosta Valley beneath the towering peak of Monte Rosa. Champoluc and Gressoney are best suited to families, while Alagna is more of a raw mountain experience, a glacial high-altitude ski area that rivals Argentière for its demanding off-piste opportunities. Catch it while you can – every season this resort that is so revered by powderhounds is becoming increasingly commercial.

However, most of Monterosa Ski is given over to easy blue and gentle red pistes that are well connected by a predominantly modern lift system. It's worth noting that, while the different resorts are close on the map and easily reached on skis from one to the other, the journey by road between any two of them is at least two hours.

Champoluc dates from the 15th century and still has some lovely old houses. It has expanded along the river bank in recent years with a blossoming of modern hotels and restaurants, but fortunately it has managed to retain its village atmosphere.

Gressoney-La-Trinité and larger Gressoney-St-Jean in the neighbouring valley are also mountain communities that have jumped from farming and forestry to feeding foreigners in the course of a single generation. Stafal is a modern purpose-built outpost above Gressoney-La-Trinité. Alagna, which lies in Piedmont just beyond the Aosta Valley, is even more rustic with little wooden houses with built-in hay frames.

Mountain

Wherever you choose to stay you must contend with one of the worst lift maps in Europe and finding your way around relies more on luck than map-reading skills. All lifts eventually lead you to Stafal, the focal point of the ski area, where you turn west for 2971m Monte Bettaforca and Champoluc beyond. East takes you to Passo dei Salati and to Alagna.

Both Gressoney and Champoluc offer intermediate cruising and the beauty of the area is that you feel you are going somewhere each day. Each resort has a dedicated novice area. Best black itinerary is the 7km descent from Punta Indren towards Alagna.

The area suits all standards, although more accomplished skiers and riders are advised to stay in, or within easy reach of, Alagna. Given good snow conditions, this whole area provides some extraordinary freeriding and couloir skiing, and heli-

CERVINO (MATTERHORN) 4475
BREITHORN OCCIDENTALE 4165
BREITHORN CENTRALE 4160
BREITHORN ORIENTALE 4139
ROCCIA NERA 4062
POLLUCE 4094
CASTORE 4226
LYSKAMM OCCIDENTALE 4477
LYSKAMM ORIENTALE 4532
PUNTA DUFOUR 4633
Rifugio Margherita 4559
PIRAMIDE VINCENT 4215
PUNTA GIORDANI 4046
Rifugio Gnifetti 3611
Rifugio Mantova 3498
Capanna Resegotti 3624
PUNTA TRE AMICI 3425
PLATEAU ROSA 3480
GOBBA DI ROLLIN 3899
Capanna Quintino Sella 3585
Rifugio Guide di Ayas 3425
Rifugio Mezzalama 3036
CRESTA ROSSA 3670
Capanna Valsesia 3212
PUNTA VITTORIA 3439
PUNTA GROBER 3498
COLLE CIME BIANCHE 3004
BETTOLINA 2904
MONTE ROISETTA 3334
PALON DI RESY 2676
TELCIO 2833
Punta Indren mt. 3260
Passo Salati mt. 2971
CIMALEGNA
BOCCHETTA DELLE PISSE
MONTE TAGLIAFERRO 2964
Colle Bettaforca mt. 2727
Stafal mt. 1818
Gabiet mt. 2318
Col d'Olen mt. 2881
GRAND TOURNALIN 3379
STAFAL TSCHAVAL
PASSO ZUBE 2874
Lago Gabiet
WOLD
Ciarcerio mt. 1992
Mont Ros mt. 2457
SAINT-JACQUES
FRACHEY 1623
Seehorn mt. 2390
Pianalunga mt. 2046
ORSIA
Sant'Anna mt. 2180
ALAGNA VALSESIA 1212
BEC DE NANA 3010
TESTA GRIGIA 3314
Punta Jolanda mt. 2278
CORNO BIANCO 3320
COLLE VASCOCCIA 2558
Sarezza mt. 2702
Pian Pera mt. 2307
CHAMPOLUC 1579
COLLE PINTER 2777
Area del Pino mt. 1780
Ostafa mt. 2420
GRESSONEY-LA-TRINITE' 1637
RIVA VALDOBBIA
Crest mt. 1980
COLLE PERRIN 2655
CORNO BUSSOLA 3023
ANTAGNOD 1720
COLLE PALASINAZ 2670
COLLE VALDOBBIA 2480
MONTE ZERBION 2727
GRESSONEY-SAINT-JEAN 1387
CORBET
Litteran mt. 2235
Weissmatten mt. 2023
CORNO ROSSO 2979
BIELCIUCKEN 1348
COLLE RANZOLA 2170
Champeille mt. 1736
EXTREPIERAZ
ESTOUL 1805
COLLE DI JOUX
VOLLON
BRUSSON 1332
monterosa ski
ANTAGNOD
N. IMPIANTO / LIFT
BOUDIN
ANTAGNOD PIAN PERA
TAPIS ROULANT ANTAGNOD 1
TAPIS ROULANT ANTAGNOD 2
N. PISTA / SLOPE
A1 MINIERA
A2 CIAMP SEC
A3 VASCOCCIA
A4 BOUDIN
A6 BABY SNOW PARK ANTAGNOD
BRUSSON
N. IMPIANTO / LIFT
ESTOUL BABY
PALASINAZ 1 E 2
CHAMPEILLE - LITTERAN
N. PISTA / SLOPE
E1 CHAMPEILLE
E4 PALASINAZ
E5 ARPETTE
E7 CHANLOSSERRE
E8 FONTANE
CHAMPOLUC - FRACHEY
N. IMPIANTO / LIFT
8 CHAMPOLUC - CREST
9-10 TAPIS ROULANT FONTANEY 1 E 2
11 OSTAFA 3
12 TAPIS ROULANT OSTAFA
13 OSTAFA - COLLE SAREZZA
14 CIARCERIO - BELVEDERE
15 FRACHEY - ALPE CIARCERIO
16 PIAN TZECCON
17 ALPE MANDRIA
N. PISTA / SLOPE
C1 DEL BOSCO
C2 CAMPO SCUOLA CREST
C3 OSTAFA 2
C4 OSTAFA 1
C5 SAREZZA
C6 SAREZZA-CONTENERY
C7 BELVEDERE
C8 CIOSAL
C9 CONTENERY
C10 DEL LAGO
C11 DEL MONTE
C13 LIAISON
C14 DEL COLLE
C15 DEI LARICI
C16 PIAN DE LA SAL
C17 BABY SNOW PARK OSTAFA
GRESSONEY-LA-TRINITE'
N. IMPIANTO / LIFT
19 S. ANNA - COLLE BETTA
20 STAFAL - SANT'ANNA
21 TAPIS ROULANT STAFAL
22 STAFAL - GABIET
23 CASTORE
24 ORSIA - BEDEMIE
25 BEDEMIE - SEEHORN
26 PUNTA JOLANDA
27 TAPIS ROULANT EDELBODEN
N. PISTA / SLOPE
B1 PISTONE BETTA
B2 BETTA 1
B3 NERA
B4 S. ANNA
B5 DIRETTA STAFAL
B6 SW DELLE MARMOTTE
B7 BABY SNOW PARK STAFAL
G1 BABY SNOW PARK EDELBODEN
G2 ORSIA
G3 JOLANDA
G4 JOLANDA 1
G5 ALPE RICKA
G6 MOOS
G7 SALATI
G8 SALATI 1
G9 CASTORE
G10 SW CHAMOIS
G11 SW COLLEGAMENTO GABIET
G12 SW COLLEGAMENTO RICKA
GRESSONEY-SAINT-JEAN
N. IMPIANTO / LIFT
29 WEISSMATTEN
30 RONKEN
31 SONNE
N. PISTA / SLOPE
W1 LARICI
W2 LEONARDO DAVID
W3 LEONARDO DAVID S.G.
W4 LEONARDO DAVID SL.
W5 WELDE
W6 BABY RONKEN
W7 BABY SONNE
ALAGNA
N. IMPIANTO / LIFT
32 PIANALUNGA - CIMALEGNA - SALATI
33 ALAGNA - PIANALUNGA
34 PIANALUNGA - BOCCHETTA
35 BOCCHETTA - INDREN
N. PISTA / SLOPE
V1 ALAGNA
V2 MULLERO
V3 OLEN
V4 CIMALEGNA
V5 BODWITCH
V6 WOLD 1
V7 WOLD 2
FACILE / EASY
MEDIA / INTERMEDIATE
SW PERCORSO DI RIENTRO / SKI WEG
DIFFICILE / DIFFICULT
PISTA CON INNEVAMENTO ARTIFICIALE
SLOPE WITH SNOW-MAKING MACHINES
Versione aggiornata a Luglio 2005
Last updated map: July 2005
www.monterosa-ski.com
STAZIONE METEO / WEATHER SENSORS
PISTA DI GARA / RACE SLOPE
BOARDER-CROSS / SNOW PARK
PUNTO DI RISTORO / RESTAURANT
PUNTO DI SOCCORSO / FIRST AID STATION
ATTENZIONE! PRECIPIZIO / CAUTION! PRECIPICE
WEBCAM
SKI-LIFT
TELECABINA / GONDOLA
SEGGIOVIA / CHAIRLIFT
FUNIVIA / CABLEWAY
BABY SNOW PARK
POLIZZA ASSICURATIVA
Snowcare
2€ AL GIORNO
www.24hassistance.com

skiing is also possible. However, avalanche danger is ever present and this should not be attempted without a local guide.

Learn

The schools are **Gressoney-St-Jean, t** +39 0125 355291, **Gressoney Monte Rosa, t** +39 0125 366015, **Alagna, t** +39 0163 922961, **Antagnod, t** +39 0125 306641, **Brusson, t** +39 0340 5410632, and **Champoluc, t** +39 0125 307194. All are generally good, but English is by no means widely spoken. **Ski 2, t** +44 (0)1962 713 330, has its own British ski school in Champoluc with BASI instructors. Mountain guiding is with **Champoluc, t** +39 0348 5186479, **Gressoney, t** +39 0125 366139, and **Alagna, t** +39 0163 91310.

Children

Ski 2, t +44 (0)1962 713 330, runs a crèche with British-qualified nannies for its clients in Champoluc, close to Hotel Relais des Glaciers. It accepts children from three months to skiing age, seven days a week. The operator also runs its own ski school with BASI instructors for five hours a day for kids aged four to 12 years. **Champoluc ski school, t** +39 0125 307194, takes children from five years.

At Stafal, **Hotel Monboso, t** +39 0125 366302, cares for children from four to eight years. In Gressoney, skiers over six years must join the adult classes. **Alagna ski school, t** +39 0163 922961, accepts children from three years.

Lunch

Try **Albergo del Ponte, t** +39 0125 806667, a mountain hut with rooms above Gabiet that serves delicious pasta. **Rifugio Guglielmina, t** +39 0163 91444, between the Alagna and Gressoney valleys, has good food and even better views. **The Belvedere, t** +39 0349 4915130 (at the top of lift 12), has excellent views and traditional cooking. **Bar Ostafa, t** +39 339 8180709, at the top of the new gondola that has replaced chairs 8 and 9, is known for its home-made pasta. It's 'cheerful and convenient for a hot dog and chips'.

Dine

In Champoluc, **Le Sapin, t** +39 0125 307598, has good food at reasonable prices. **Favre, t** +39 0125 307131, features local game. **Hotel Villa Anna Maria, t** +39 0125 307128, has reasonable mountain food and an exceptional wine list. **Le Petit Coq, t** +39 0125 307997, at Frachey is elegant-rustic. In Gressoney-St-Jean, **Lo Stambecco, t** +39 0125 355201, has fine grilled steaks and lamb. In Stafal, **Capanna Carla, t** +39 0125 366130, serves regional cuisine at reasonable prices in a warm atmosphere. In Alagna, **Fum D'ss, t** +39 0163 922923, has local game with polenta. **Ristorante Unione, t** +39 0163 922930, and **Stolemberg, t** +39 0163 923201, are recommended.

Party

The nightlife is what you make it. For families and serious skiers this usually means an early bath and bed. Bars such as **Hirsch Stube** and the **Petit Bar** in Gressoney provide some entertainment. **Disco Gram Parsons** is in Hotel California.

Sleep

Champoluc:

- ********Hotel Breithorn, t**** +39 0125 308734, *www.breithorn.com*, is smart-rustic with a good spa.
- *******Hotel Villa Anna Maria, t**** +39 0125 307128, *www.hotelvillaannamaria.com*, has 20 individually decorated bedrooms.

*****Hotel Castor**, **t** +39 0125 307117, *www.hotelcastor.it*, is run by a local Englishman and is warmly recommended.

*****Hotel California**, **t** +39 0125 307977, *www.wrpub.it*, is decorated with 1960s music memorabilia. Choose the Bob Dylan Room or the Doors Room.

*****Hotel de Champoluc**, **t** +39 0125 308088, *www.hoteldechampoluc.net*, is recommended.

****Hotel Favre**, **t** +39 0125 307131, *www.tako.it*, is small and well managed with friendly staff.

Alagna:

******Hotel Cristallo**, **t** + 39 0163 91285, *www.hotelcristalloalagna.com*, is in the centre near the 16th-century church.

*****Pensione Genzianella**, **t** +39 0163 923921, *www.monterosa4000.it*, has recently been refurbished.

*****Albergo Monte Rosa**, **t** +39 0163 923209, *www.albergomonterosa.com*, was built in 1908 and is still run by the same family.

*****Hotel Mirella**, **t** +39 0163 922965, is a B&B with rooms over a cake shop.

Gressoney valley:

******Hotel Monboso**, **t** +39 0125 366302, *www.igrandiviaggi.it*, at Stafal, is recommended.

*****Hotel Gasthaus Lysjoch**, **t** +39 0125 366150, *www.hotellysjoch.com*, in Gressoney-La-Trinité, is a cosily old-fashioned Tyrolean-style chalet.

*****Hotel La Gran Baita**, **t** +39 0125 356441, near Gressoney Weissmatten, is a lovingly restored ancient Walser house.

*****Hotel Lo Scoiattolo**, **t** +39 0125 366313, *www.htlscoiattolo.com*, in Gressoney-La-Trinité, is comfortable with a warm ambience.

Cortina d'Ampezzo

***BEST FOR**

Sophisto-cats, ski gourmets, all levels of skier and rider

ESSENTIALS

Altitude: 1224m (4,015ft)–3243m (10,640ft)
Further information: **t** +39 0436 3231, *www.cortina.dolimiti.com*, *www.infodolomiti.it*
Lifts in area: 36 (6 cableways, 24 chairs, 6 drags) serving 170km of piste; 450 lifts in Dolomiti Superski
Lift pass: Dolomiti Superski adult €155–254, child 8–16yrs €109–178, both for 6 days
Access: Venice airport 2hrs, railway station at Calalzo-Pieve di Cadore 35km

Profile

Italy's top ski town reigns supreme in a beautiful setting against the backdrop of the craggy peaks of the Dolomites. It suits all levels of skiers, riders and non-skiers who are prepared to swap ski convenience and modern lifts systems for old-world charm

Resort

Italy's smartest winter destination, dominated by its magnificent green-and-white bell tower and a glittering confection of grand 19th-century mansions, sits in splendid linguistic defiance of its neighbours, a two-hour drive from Venice.

Despite being variously occupied over the centuries by foreign invaders that have included Bavaria, France, Austria, Italy, Germany and even the Americans in 1945, Cortina has stubbornly maintained a spiritual independence of its own. While the residents of surrounding towns and villages primarily speak Italian or German, native Cortinese cling to their ancient Ladino language when they converse among themselves.

The town is surrounded by soaring cathedrals of dolomitic limestone that rise to over 3000m. These distinctive mountains, named after French geologist Deodat de Dolomieu, turn a surreal shade of pink in the final rays of the setting sun. Encroaching twilight is the signal for Cortina to come out to play. A colony of voluminous fur coats and designer ski wear gathers noisily in the Piazza Venezia at the start of the evening *passeggiata*.

The actual business of skiing plays second fiddle to the social sport of seeing and being seen in the elegant boutiques and antique shops that line the Corso Italia, the pedestrianized main street. Much later, the perpetual party atmosphere is transferred to intimate wine bars, expensive restaurants and a smattering of softly lit nightclubs.

The skiing has plenty of appeal for all standards. But one reason for the resort's failure to attract a significant international clientele in recent decades is inevitably related to the lack of regular investment in high-speed mountain transport. However, three new detachable-chairs have been added in the past two seasons – one in each of the Cristallo, Faloria and Tofana areas. This is at least a start, but still a question of too little, too late.

Cortina Adrenalin Center, t +39 0436 860808, offers alternative snow sports such as bobsleigh and ice-climbing. **Adrenalin Park** behind the bob run has zip-wires with 40 platforms in the trees and is open in the evening.

Mountain

The main skiing is divided into two separate ski areas of Faloria/Staunies and Tofana/Socrepes that can both be reached by old-fashioned cable-cars from either side of town. A busy ski-bus service provides a link to the lifts, but skiing convenience is not a strong feature in Cortina. These two are supplemented by a diverse handful of smaller, unconnected areas as well as a direct link into the Sella Ronda via another ancient cable-car at Passo Falzarego, a 20-minute free bus ride away.

Tofana, the 3243m highest point in the ski area, provides spectacular views. Two chairs from the second stage of the cable-car give access to a collection of blue and red runs. An easy black run links into the more demanding Socrepes sector that can otherwise be reached by a blue run from the top of the first stage of the cable-car.

The bottom of Socrepes is devoted to a benign and scenic nursery area, served by four chairs and three drag-lifts, that curiously resembles a sloping Kensington Gardens. These beginner runs can be reached by bus from the town at Lacedel on the outskirts and at the top of the nursery area at Pocol, 6km from Cortina.

Faloria, reached by a relic of a cable-car, which spans a cliff face on the other side of Cortina, has plenty of intermediate appeal. You can work your way along the mountainside through a sequence of chair-lifts and blue/red runs down to the road at Rio Gere. A modern chair-lift on the far side brings you up to Son Forca and one of the most dramatic runs in the Dolomites. The steep, black Staunies and the fast, red Padeon that it becomes in the lower stages is sandwiched dramatically between two mighty pillars of rock.

Cinque Torri, on the road up to Passo Falzarego, is the pick of the smaller ski areas. The lifts here are mainly modern – another detachable-quad was installed two seasons ago – and at peak times Cinque Torri offers some of the best and usually least crowded skiing in the region.

Passo Falzarego is the base station for the cable-car that takes you up to Lagazuoi at 2800m for the scenic Hidden Valley run down to Armentarola and a link into the Sella Ronda.

The old lift climbs a cliff face dotted with windows into a rabbit warren of First World War tunnels that connected gun emplacements and observation posts. These can be explored with a guide in summer, but not in winter.

With skiers arriving from both sides of the pass, the queue for the cable-car can last an hour. But the reward is an 8km red roller coaster that takes you down past a spectacular frozen turquoise waterfall to Armentarola. You have to return to Passo Falzarego and to Cortina by bus.

Learn

Azzurra, **t** +39 0436 2694, and **Ski Cortina**, **t** +39 0436 2911, are both recommended by reporters. The others are **Cristallo-Cortina**, **t** +39 0436 870073, and **Dolomiti-Cortina**, **t** +39 0436 862264, **Scuola Fondo Ski Cortina**, **t** +39 0436 2911, and **Morotto**, **t** +39 0436 862201, are both based at the Fiames Nordic Centre and teach cross-country.

Children

As in most resorts, specialist childcare facilities are minimal because Italians tend to take granny with them on holiday. **Gulliver Park Kindergarten**, **t** +39 340 055 8399, in the Pocol sector cares for children aged from three months to three years.

Lunch

Lunch at **Rifugio Averau**, **t** +39 0436 4660, in Cinque Torri, heads the list and is famous for its home-made pasta including *pappardelle con funghi* (broad ribbons of pasta with mushrooms). Don't confine your choice to one type of pasta – on request, three are served on a single plate.

Rifugio Duca d'Aosta, **t** +39 0436 2780, in the Tofana/Socrepes sector is also recommended along with nearby **Rifugio Pomedes**, **t** +39 0436 862061. **El Sorei**, **t** +39 0436 877017, also has good food.

Dinner

Dine at Michelin-starred **Tivoli**, **t** +39 0436 866400, in an intimate ambience enhanced by panelled walls decorated with copper pans and a wood-burning stove in one corner. **El Toula**, **t** +39 0436 3339, is a converted three-storey hay barn with a rustic atmosphere created by locally carved furniture and sprigged tablecloths. **Leone & Anna**, **t** +39 0436 2768, is a tiny, romantic Sardinian restaurant that has been pleasing the palates of Cortina for 30 years. **Zanvor**, **t** +39 0436 860789, and **La Tavernetta**, **t** +39 0436 868102, are also recommended. **Pizzeria Vienna**, **t** +39 0436 866944, has a great choice of pizzas.

Party

Party in the early evening at the **Enoteca** wine bar, in the bar of the Hotel de la Poste. **DOK-LP26** is a curious mixture of *prosciutteria* and cocktail bar with live music. It is owned by a millionaire Italian builder who constructed most of Val d'Isère and the new village in Les Arcs – which also has a sister LP26. Other popular bars are **Villa Sandi**, **Brio di Vino** and **El Becalen**. The **VIP Club** at the Hotel Europa and the **BLV Room** liven up after midnight, along with the **Bilbo Club**. **Disco Belvedere** at Pocol has a youthful following.

Sleep

A new airport transfer service was introduced last winter from Venice and Treviso (to connect with Ryanair). The service is free of charge to some hotels and at a rate of €20 return to others.

★★★★★**Hotel Cristallo**, **t** +39 0436 881111, *www.cristallo.it*, is situated a five-minute uphill walk from the centre. Rooms are decorated in Gustavian style with hand-painted woodwork and delicate frescoes.

★★★★★**Miramonti Majestic Grand**, **t** +39 0436 4201, *www.geturhotels.com*, situated 2km out of town is an imposing *fin de siècle* palace. It has a wellness centre and a large indoor pool.

★★★★**Hotel Ancora**, **t** +39 0436 3261, *www.hotelancoracortina.com*, situated in the heart of the Corso Italia, is convenient for the nightlife. Its Terrazza Viennese is a resort meeting place.

★★★★**Hotel de la Poste**, **t** +39 0436 4271, *www.delaposte.it*, in the pedestrianized centre, is an old coaching inn and another resort rendezvous that has been run for generations by the Manaigo family. Some of the rooms are rather small, but the bathrooms are large.

★★★★**Parc Hotel Victoria**, **t** +39 0436 3246, *www.hotelvictoriacortina.com*, has a solid reputation and is conveniently situated at the beginning of the Corso Italia.

★★★**Hotel Aquila**, **t** +39 0436 2618, *www.aquilacortina.com*, at the far end of the Corso Italia, is family-run and friendly with an indoor swimming pool.

★★★**Hotel Menardi**, **t** +39 0436 2400, *www.hotelmenardi.it*, is a mid-19th-century farmhouse. Its original decoration incorporates the Menardi family's memorabilia.

★★★**Hotel Olimpia**, **t** +39 0436 868524, *www.hotelolimpiacortina.com*, is a reasonably priced and centrally situated B&B.

Corvara

Profile

Attractive, sophisticated village with great hotels and superb restaurants that acts as a convenient base for exploring the Sella Ronda

Resort

Corvara is a sprawling but sophisticated village that makes one of the most convenient bases from which to explore the Sella Ronda. It has on-mountain links towards Arabba in one direction and Selva in the other, while off the circuit you can ski to La Villa, San Cassiano and Armentarola.

Mountain

The modern Boè gondola takes you towards Arabba on the clockwise circuit of the Sella Ronda. It is also the most efficient means of reaching Corvara's own ski area as well as the extensive sunny slopes that it shares with San Cassiano, Armentarola and La Villa.

From near the gondola base, a quad-chair takes you on the anticlockwise route towards Colfosco and Selva. The easy blue and reds around Corvara are perfect for intermediates. However, many of the lifts away from the circuit are frustratingly slow.

Learn

Corvara-Ladinia, **t** +39 0471 836126, and **Colfosco**, **t** +39 0471 836218, schools both have good reputations.

Children

Skikinderland, **t** +39 0471 836126, cares for children from two years.

Lunch

Try **Capanna Nera/Neger Hütte**, **t** +39 0471 836138, at the bottom of the Pralongia piste, **Baita La Marmotta**, **t** +39 0471 836125, and **Punta Trieste**, **t** +39 0471 836643, both on Pralongia, or **Mesoles**, **t** +39 0471 836023, near Colfosco.

Dine

Stüa di Michil, **t** +39 0471 836132, is the Michelin-starred restaurant in Hotel La Perla. The 16th-century **Stüa dl'Jagher**, **t** +39 0471 836085, in Hotel Sassongher has the atmosphere of the hunting lodge it once was. **La Tambra**, **t** +39 0471 836281, specializes in Mediterranean cuisine. **Hotel Alisander**, **t** +39 0471 836055, is renowned for fresh fish. **Stüa Ladina** in the Sporthotel Panorama, **t** +39 0471 836083, provides local cuisine.

Party

Grillkeller Adler and the **Veranda Keller** are noisy. Piano bars in **Hotel Sassongher**, **La Perla** and **Table** are more sophisticated. Popular **Posta Zirm Taverna** is the late-night spot.

*BEST FOR

High-mileage skiers and riders, ski gourmets, comfort-lovers

ESSENTIALS

Altitude: 1568m (5,144ft) – 2949m (9,676ft)
Further information: **t** +39 0471 836176, *www.altabadia.org*
Lifts in area: 52 in Alta Badia (9 cableways, 29 chairs, 14 drags) serving 130km of piste; 450 lifts in Dolomiti Superski area
Lift pass: Dolomiti Superski adult €155–254, child 8–16yrs €109–178, both for 6 days
Access: Verona airport 2½hrs

Sleep

★★★★**La Perla**, **t** +39 0471 831000, *www.romantiklaperla.it*, has walls adorned with carved angels and floors covered with Oriental rugs.

★★★★**Posta Zirm Hotel**, **t** +39 0471 836175, *www.postazirm.com*, is a resort meeting place, with a spa and pool designed to feng shui principles.

★★★★**Hotel Sassongher**, **t** +39 0471 836085, *www.sassongher.it*, is traditional with a sound reputation.

★★★**La Plaza**, **t** +39 0471 836011, *www.laplaza.it*, is recommended.

★★★**Hotel Grand Ciasa**, **t** +39 0471 836138, *www.granciasa.com*, in Colfosco, is also recommended.

Courmayeur

Profile

Lovely old town on the Italian side of the Mont Blanc Tunnel, with dramatic scenery but limited piste skiing. Suits novices, low intermediates and experts. Superb restaurants both on and off the slopes and a lively nightlife

Resort

Courmayeur is one of the great ski and climbing villages of the Alps, an ancient community situated just below the Italian end of the Mont Blanc Tunnel at the foot of the mightiest mountain in Western Europe. Like nearby Chamonix, its proximity by autoroute to Geneva airport makes it popular with weekenders from other countries, while Italians from Turin arrive in numbers on Friday evenings. Despite being no more than a 20-minute drive from Chamonix, Courmayeur has an entirely different weather pattern thanks to the towering intervening presence of Mont Blanc. The snow is not always as good on the Italian side, but Courmayeur gets much more sunshine during the course of the winter.

The heart of the old village is the cobbled and pedestrianized Via Roma that is lined with boutiques, bars, delicatessens and expensive interior decoration and antique shops. Steep and narrow cobbled alleyways lead off on either side. Eating is the alternative occupation to skiing, with Courmayeur boasting the best mountain restaurants of any Italian resort as well a delightful choice of evening eateries. Its downside is the main arterial road that separates the town from the ski area. Choose where you stay with care to avoid the midnight chorus of gear changes from trucks and cars trundling to and from the tunnel. To get the best out of the skiing in the region you need a car. It's best to invest in the more expensive regional lift pass that also covers other resorts in the Aosta Valley such as Pila, Champoluc and Gressoney, as well as La Thuile and linked La Rosière in France.

✻ BEST FOR

All levels of skier and rider, romantics, serious lunchers, night-owls

ESSENTIALS

Altitude: 1200m (3,937ft)–2624m (8,609ft)

Further information **t** +39 0165 842060, *www.aiat-monte-bianco.com*

Lifts in area: 19 (8 cableways, 8 chairs, 3 drags) serving 36km of piste

Lift pass: Aosta Valley (includes Courmayeur, La Thuile, La Rosière and Champoluc-Gressoney-Alagna) adult €186, child 8–12yrs €139.50, child under 8yrs €46.50, all for 6 days

Access: Geneva airport 1½hrs, Turin airport 2hrs, railway station at Pré-St-Didier 5km, regular buses from station

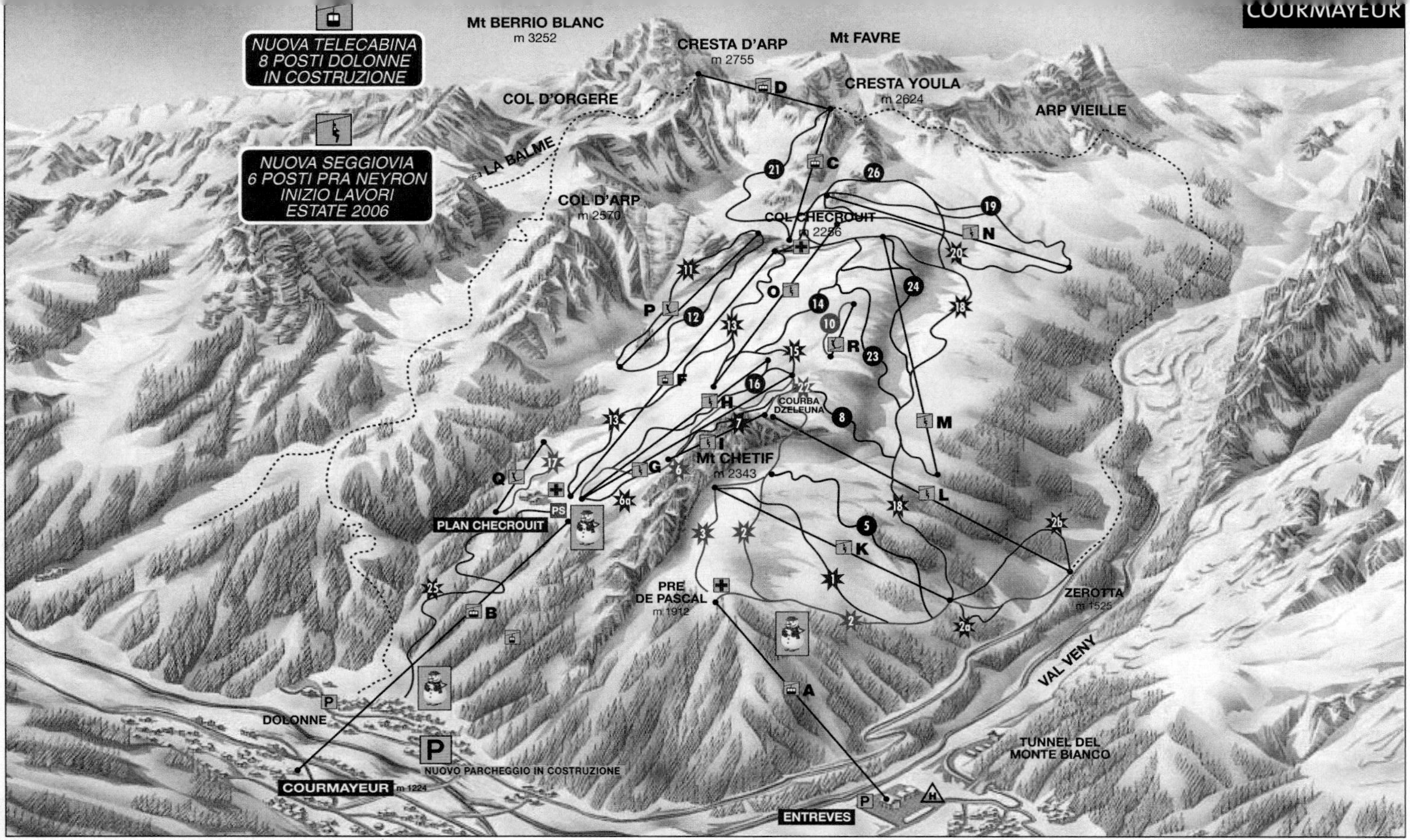
NUOVA TELECABINA
8 POSTI DOLONNE
IN COSTRUZIONE
NUOVA SEGGIOVIA
6 POSTI PRA NEYRON
INIZIO LAVORI
ESTATE 2006
Mt BERRIO BLANC
m 3252
CRESTA D'ARP
m 2755
Mt FAVRE
CRESTA YOULA
m 2624
ARP VIEILLE
COL D'ORGERE
LA BALME
COL D'ARP
m 2570
COL CHECROUIT
m 2256
COURBA
DZELEUNA
Mt CHETIF
m 2343
PLAN CHECROUIT
PRE
DE PASCAL
m 1912
ZEROTTA
m 1525
VAL VENY
TUNNEL DEL
MONTE BIANCO
DOLONNE
NUOVO PARCHEGGIO IN COSTRUZIONE
COURMAYEUR
m 1224
ENTREVES

Mountain

A cable-car from Courmayeur provides mountain access to Plan Chécrouit, the main hub of this moderately compact ski area facing Mont Blanc. A blue piste brings you down again to the valley – not to the cable-car but to Dolonne on the far side of the main road from where you must take a bus to return to Courmayeur. Therefore it is better to download by cable-car at the end of the day, but skis and boots can be left at Plan Chécrouit. You can also reach the mountain by another cable-car from Entrèves, nearer to the tunnel.

From Plan Chécrouit, a small network of lifts takes you up to Col Chécrouit at 2256m. Two ancient cable-cars rise to higher Cresta Youla and Cresta d'Arp. The latter is the 2755m starting point for some outstanding off-piste runs that take you down through 1500m of vertical to Dolonne or through the scenic Vallon de Youla to the village of La Balme just outside La Thuile at the foot of the Petit-St-Bernard pass. These itinerary runs require no special technical skills, but it's easy to get lost and the risk of avalanche is ever present. It makes sense to ski them with a local guide.

Other lifts from Plan Chécrouit bring you to the shoulder of 2343m Mont Chétif for the pick of Courmayeur's piste skiing – mainly red and black runs leading down towards the Val Veny with magnificent views of Mont Blanc.

A dedicated nursery slope served by the Chiecco drag-lift at Plan Chécrouit is in a secluded position on the edge of the piste. But novices and wobbly second-weekers must otherwise contend with a heavy amount of traffic converging on the mid-mountain station. More easy slopes are to be found at the top of the Maison Vieille chair-lift.

In the right snow conditions, Val Veny slopes offer hours of entertainment, with a few surprisingly challenging pistes such as the black Pista dell'Orso and Diretta. However, accomplished skiers and riders will soon tire of the limited piste skiing available from Plan Chécrouit.

They should head to the other side of Courmayeur to ride the three-stage Mont Blanc cable-car at La Palud, near the village of Entrèves. This takes you all the way up to Punta Helbronner at 3462m where you can descend the Vallée Blanche to Chamonix – without having to negotiate the infamous ice-steps on the French side.

A number of descents of varying difficulty and danger are possible on the Italian side of Mont Blanc and you are strongly recommended to use a local guide. Spectacular heli-skiing is also possible from a number of fixed drops above the Val Veny. There is a snowcross course served by the Plan de la Grabba chair and a new rail park by the Le Greye drag above Plan Chécrouit. Val Ferret, at the foot of the Grandes Jorasses a few minutes' drive from Courmayeur, is the setting for 20km of spectacular cross-country trails.

Learn

Monte Bianco, t +39 0165 842477, and **Courmayeur, t** +39 0165 848254, are the main schools. Both have a sound reputation for teaching modern technique. However, not all instructors are fluent English speakers. **Interski, t** +44 (0)1623 456 333, is a British tour operator with its own school. Guiding is available from **Società delle Guide Alpine di Courmayeur, t** +39 0165 842064, and heli-skiing with **Air Vallée, t** +39 0165 869814.

Children

Kinderheim, t +39 0165 842477, at Plan Chécrouit cares for children from

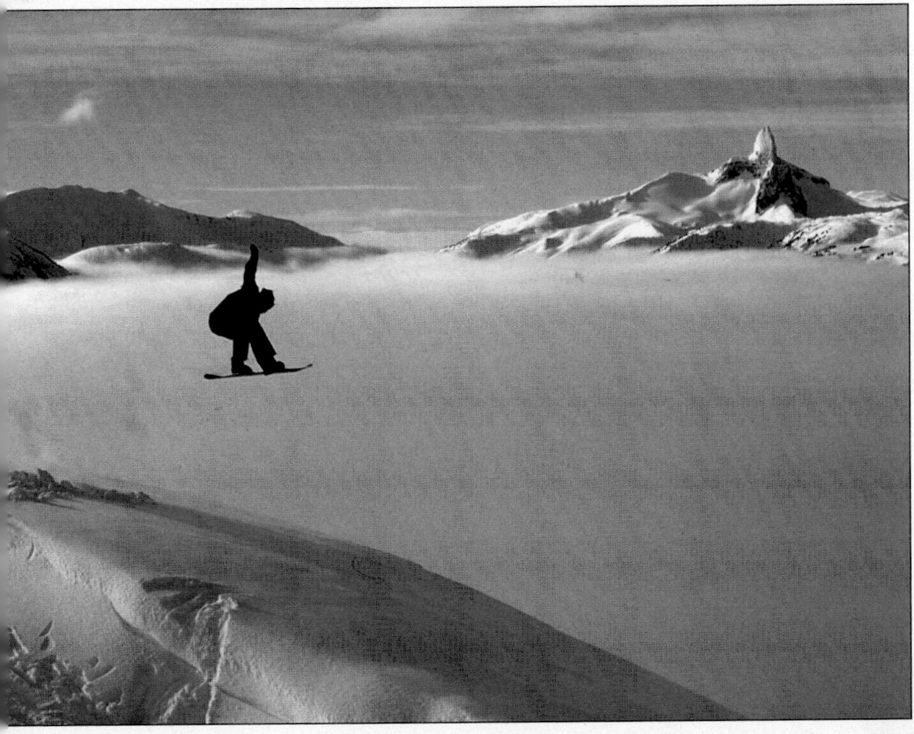

newborn to 12 years with an alternative pick-up and drop-off point at the foot of the cable-car. Both Italian ski schools give lessons to children from four years.

Lunch

Courmayeur has the best value-for-money mountain eateries anywhere in the world. **Rifugio Maison Vieille, t** +39 337 230979, serves grilled meat and fine pasta and has a big wood-burning stove. **Hotel Christiania, t** +39 0165 843572, at Plan Chécrouit is a gastronomic delight. **Chiecco, t** +39 338 7003035, is warmly recommended. **La Grolla, t** +39 0165 869095, on the Val Veny side, has lots of atmosphere and fine cuisine. On the Mont Blanc side, **Rifugio Pavillon, t** +39 0165 844090, at the top of the first stage of the cable-car, has a sunny terrace and great food. **Rifugio Torino, t** +39 0165 844034, at the second stage, is also recommended.

Dine

Pierre Alexis 1877, t +39 0165 843517, is still the top eatery in town and has a particularly extensive wine list. **Cadran Solaire, t** + 39 0165 844609, is a close contender for cuisine and atmosphere. **Mont Fréty, t** +39 0165 841786, and **La Terrazza, t** +33 0165 843330, are also recommended. **La Maison de Filippo, t** +39 0165 869797, in the suburb of Entrèves, is an exercise in unparalleled gluttony; it offers a fixed-price menu of more than 30 courses.

Party

The American Bar and the **Bar Roma**, with its comfortable sofas and armchairs, are busy throughout the evening. **Cadran Solaire** attracts the smart crowd while the **Red Lion** is a more basic pub. **Les Privé, Bar Posta** and **Bar delle Guide** both have lots of atmosphere. **I Maquis** in Entrèves is the best nightspot. **Jimmy Night Café, Planet** and **Poppy's** are the others.

Sleep

★★★★Gran Baita, t +39 0165 844040, *www.sogliahotels.com*, is comfortable but inconveniently positioned outside the town.

★★★★Hotel Pavillon, t +39 0165 846120, *www.pavillon.it*, has a swimming pool and a sauna.

★★★★Royal e Golf, t +39 0165 831611, *www.royalegolf.com*, is close to the centre of town.

★★★Hotel Courmayeur, t +39 0165 846732, *www.hotelcourmayeur.com*, is welcoming, with a open fire in the sitting room.

★★★Bouton d'Or, t +39 0165 846729, *www.hotelboutondor.com*, is a firm favourite in a quiet location close to the centre. It doesn't have a restaurant but arranges half-board in a choice of restaurants.

★★★Auberge de la Maison, t +39 0165 869811, *www.aubergemaison.it*, in the quiet little hamlet of Entrèves, has attractively decorated rooms, and friendly owners.

★★★Hotel Dolonne, t +39 0165 846674, *www.hoteldolonne.com*, is a luxury family hotel in the hamlet of the same name. It has some interesting antiques and log fires.

★★★Hotel Meublé Laurent, t +39 0165 846687, *www.meublelaurent.com*, is traditional, cosy and clean.

Kronplatz

***BEST FOR**
High-mileage intermediates, snowboarders

ESSENTIALS
Altitude: 900m (2,953ft)–2275m (7,464ft)
Further information: t +39 0474 555447, *www.kronplatz.com*
Lifts in area: 32 (20 cableways, 6 chairs, 6 drags) serving 103km of piste; 450 lifts in Dolomiti Superski area
Lift pass: Dolomiti Superski adult €155–254, child 8–16yrs €109–178, both for 6 days
Access: Innsbruck airport 1¾hrs, railway station at Bruneck 10mins

Profile

A ski area rather than a single resort in the South Tyrol that has the most sophisticated network of gondolas in the world, but is largely unknown outside Italy and Germany

Resort

Until now Kronplatz has been one of the great secrets of the South Tyrol. It is the top Italian ski resort for Germans, but has remained virtually unknown elsewhere. However, a new gondola scheduled to open this season will link it (with a short bus ride) into the main Alta Badia lift system with connections into the Sella Ronda. The dome-shaped mountain, which is also known as Plan de Corones, is a ski area rather than a single centre. Accommodation is in the nearby town of Bruneck (Brunico) and in a dozen small villages around the mountain base. Only St Vigilio di Marebbe is Italian- and Ladin-speaking.

Mountain

Kronplatz has a remarkable 20 gondolas – most of them state-of-the-art. Along with 12 chairs and drags they are capable of ferrying enormous numbers of skiers to the summit. Most of the descents are undemanding, but the black Sylvester and the Herrneg roller coaster provide challenge. Mountain access by gondola is from Olang, Bruneck/Reischach or St Vigilio.

Learn

Valdaora/Rasen, **t** +39 0474 592091, teaches new technique in a friendly manner. The other schools are **Kronplatz/Plan de Corones**, **t** +39 0474 548474, **San Vigilio**, **t** +39 0474 501049, **Sporting Al Plan**, **t** +39 0474 501448, and **Cima**, **t** +39 0474 497216.

Children

Croniworld, **t** +39 0474 548474, on the summit, cares for children from three to eight years. The villages of Olang-Rasen and St Vigilio both have kindergartens.

Lunch

Herzlalm, **t** +39 0474 550723, is a rustic hut with waiter service, reached by the Pramstall piste. **Bergfreunder Hütte**, **t** +39 0474 548049, by the valley station of the Gipfelbahn, is recommended. **Berggasthof Graziani**, **t** +39 0474 501158, on piste no.12 has a welcoming atmosphere and traditional cuisine. **Oberegger Alm**, **t** +39 347 5220122, a 17th-century farmhouse on the run down to Olang, is renowned for it dumplings and *Speck*-and-cabbage salad.

Dine

In Olang, **Pizzeria Petrus, t** +39 0474 496202, and **Christl, t** +39 0474 498212, are praised. In San Vigilio, **Fana Ladina, t** +39 0474 501175, specializes in Ladino cuisine. In Bruneck, **Zum Goldenen Löwen, t** +39 0474 555834, is popular.

Party

In Reischach, German-style après-ski begins before the lifts close at **Après Ski Tenne, Igli Bar Gigger, K1** and **Pub Hardimitz'n**. Olang has a similar scene at **Ski Toni** and **Skistadl**. Lively **Igloo** is in St Vigilio. Bruneck has a more cosmopolitan choice of bars and discos.

Sleep

Bruneck:
★★★★**Royal Hotel Hinterhuber, t** +39 0474 541000, *www.royal-hinterhuber.com*, is traditional.
★★★★**Hotel Petrus, t** +39 0474 548263, *www.hotelpetrus.com*, has a warm atmosphere.
Olang:
★★★★**Hotel Mirabell, t** +39 0474 496191, *www.mirabell.it*, has a first-rate spa.
★★★★**Hotel Post, t** +39 0474 496127, *www.post-tolderhof.com*, has comfortable rooms and a separate six-bedroom Art Nouveau villa.
St Vigilio:
★★★★**Wellness Hotel Almhof Call, t** +39 0474 501043, *www.almhof-call.com*, has a swimming pool built into the rocks.
★★★★**Parc Hotel Posta, t** +39 0474 501010, *www.parchotel-posta.com*, is family-friendly.

Livigno

Profile

Most remote and cheapest of all alpine resorts, with good beginner and limited intermediate skiing. The town's duty-free status encourages an alcohol-fuelled nightlife

Resort

Duty-free Livigno is the cheapest and also the most inaccessible of all mainstream resorts in the Alps. Its fiscal privileges date back to 1600 and were confirmed by Napoleon in 1805 and the EC in 1960. The resort can compete comfortably on price with Andorra, although the Pyrenean principality has the edge on skiing and accessibility.

Nevertheless, Livigno is a great beginner area for anyone who wants to discover skiing or snowboarding without huge financial commitment.

The village is divided into the four hamlets of Santa Maria, San Antonio, San Rocco and Trepalle. Of these, San Antonio is the main resort rendezvous with the majority of hotels, bars and restaurants.

Mountain

On southeast-facing Carosello, a gondola rises to 3000m and five chairs, including the new Federia, serve undulating slopes above the treeline. The area is ideally suited to beginners who take their first slide on skis on a dozen nursery drags on Carosello. Intermediates will enjoy the steeper slopes on Monte Sponda and Il Mottolino.

* BEST FOR
First-timers, value, wild nightlife

ESSENTIALS
Altitude: 1820m (5,970ft)–2797m (9,177ft)
Further information: t +39 0342 052200, *www.livignoweb.com*
Lifts in area: 32 (3 cableways, 15 chairs, 14 drags) serving 115km of piste
Lift pass: adult €138–163, child under 15yrs €97–113, both for 6 days
Access: Zurich airport 5hrs, Bergamo airport 4hrs, railway station at Tirano 2¼hrs

Learn

The ski schools are **Top Club Mottolino**, t +39 0342 970822, **Azzura Livigno**, t +39 0342 996683, **Inverno/Estate**, t +39 0342 996276, and **Livigno Italy**, t +39 0342 996767. **Madness**, t +39 0342 997792, is the specialist snowboard school.

Children

Peribimbi, t +39 0342 970711, cares for non-skiers from 18 months to three years. **M'eating Point**, t +39 0342 9997408, accepts children from three years. The ski schools provide lessons from four years.

Lunch

Try **La Costaccia**, t +39 0342 997264, for its outdoor barbecue. **Tea da Borch**, t +39 0342 997016, below Carosello, is also recommended.

Dine

The Michelin-rated **La Pioda**, t + 39 0342 997610, is close to San Rocco church. **La Rusticana**, t +39 0342 996047, is renowned for its pizzas. **La Vecchia Lanterna**, t +39 0342 996103, has lots of atmosphere and is good value. **Bellavista**, t +39 0342 997334, is praised by one reporter who has spent 20 holidays in Livigno.

Party

Tea del Vidal and **Galli's** are the busiest bars. **Kokodi** and **Il Cielo** provide the late-night entertainment.

Sleep

★★★★**Hotel Amerikan**, t +39 0342 996521, *www.amerikan.it*, has a wellness centre.
★★★★**Hotel Concordia Lungolivigno**, t +39 0342 990100, *www.lungolivigno.com*, has attractive rooms.
★★★★**Hotel Intermonti**, t +39 0342 972100, *www.valfin.it*, is in four chalets on the hillside.
★★★★**Hotel Spöl Charme and Relax**, t +39 0342 996105, *www.hotelspol.it*, is in the town centre with a good spa.
★★★**Hotel Compagnoni**, t +39 0342 996100, is 'comfortable and conveniently situated in the centre of town'.
★★★**Hotel Villaggio San Carlo**, t +39 0342 972000, *www.valfin.it*, is set in seven chalets linked by internal corridors.

Madonna di Campiglio

Profile

Smart, traditional resort with good snowboarding that attracts wealthy skiers from Verona, Venice and Milan. Excellent hotels, good restaurants and a lively nightlife, but lack of kindergarten means it is not suited to families with small children

***BEST FOR**

Sophisto-cats, intermediate skiers, snowboarders

ESSENTIALS

Altitude: 1520m (4,987ft)–2505m (8,219ft)
Further information: t +39 0465 447501, *www.campiglio.it*
Lifts in area: 22 (5 cableways, 12 chairs, 5 drags) serving 90km of piste; 140 lifts in Skirama region serving 340km of piste
Lift pass: Super Skirama Dolomiti (includes Madonna di Campiglio, Marilleva/Folgarida, Peio, Monte Bondone, Pinzolo, Paganella, Folgaria Lavarone and Passo Tonale) adult €167–188, child from 8yrs €135–151, both for 6 days
Access: Verona airport 2½hrs, railway station at Trento 80km

Resort

Madonna has a traditional charm and village ambience that attracts a curious combination of older skiers and young snowboarders who return here year after year – one in search of easy cruising and bodily comforts, the other for some of the best riding in Italy. The first chair-lift opened for business here in 1948 and it has been a popular resort with an international clientele since the 1960s. In what is already considered an expensive resort by Italian standards, prices have steadily risen since the introduction of the euro.

The village fathers have now solved the problem of through traffic that used to plague the resort. A bypass has returned it to the congenial little mountain community that it used to be. New buildings blend well with the old. Its wealthy guests demand and get a high standard of hotels. You can eat well here and, for those who live life in the fast track, the nightlife is livelier than in most other Italian resorts. Racing driver Michael Schumacher is a regular visitor who beats his minders around the resort's go-kart track when not skiing.

The resort is situated in the Brenta Dolomites, well to the west of the Sella Ronda, and is not included in the giant Dolomiti Superski lift pass. It is reached by a 75km serpentine climb from the Brenner–Verona autostrada through galleried tunnels and past spectacular drops. Along with Cortina d'Ampezzo, Madonna attracts more glitterati than any other resorts in Italy. Like Cortina, not all its smart visitors venture onto the slopes. Shopping and eating out have both been raised to an art form, while skating on the scenic little lake provides an alternative activity. Madonna is much smaller than Cortina, but has a considerably more modern lift system and far better snowboarding facilities. The first terrain park was created here as long ago as 1993, and committed riders from all over the country gather each winter in the current park in the Grosté area.

Mountain

Madonna is officially rated the top resort in Italy for piste-grooming. This makes it popular with its slightly older than average clientele who revel in some of the most flattering slopes of the Dolomites. What at first sight appear to be three entirely separate ski areas covering the slopes on three sides of the village are in fact cunningly linked at valley level. The link is created by a snow-cannon-maintained piste that winds from one area to the other beneath a series of road bridges. A link to neighbouring Pinzolo is also being built.

The first area, 5 Laghi, is reached by a five-minute cable-car ride from the centre of the village. This takes you up to a *rifugio* of the same name, the starting point for an easy blue run that brings you to the Patascoss quad-chair. The 3-Tre piste from the top has a couple of sharp bends and dramatic changes in gradient.

On the lower half of the mountain this red run turns a wicked shade of black as it becomes the notorious Canalone Miramonti, which used to be used as a World Cup course. The bottom half can also be reached by a double chair-lift. The run is floodlit for night-skiing.

From the northern end of town, a modern 12-person gondola takes you up to Pradalago at 2100m, the largest of the three ski areas. It is linked to the neighbouring resorts of Marilleva and Folgarida. Direct return to the resort is by the always challenging Amazzonia black, which crosses beneath the gondola. Less accomplished skiers and riders take the blue Pradalago Facile run, which follows a much gentler line around the shoulder. Two quad-chairs and a couple of drags access a pleasant mixture of easy and intermediate runs on Pradalago. Skiers heading for Marilleva and Folgarida, in the larger Skirama area, follow the red Genziana piste down to Malga Vigo.

The third area of Monte Spinale/Grosté is on the opposite side of the valley and is reached by a two-stage gondola from the east side of town. At 2443m this is the high point of the ski area. Cima Grosté and Corna Rossa, two short red pistes at the top, are served by a new six-person chair. The linked area of Monte Spinale can also be reached by gondola from the resort. Spinale direttissima, beneath the gondola, is one of the most enjoyable black runs in the resort.

Learn

The seven schools here all compete vigorously with each other for customers but none stands out as being better than any of the rest. In general, the standard of teaching in Italian resorts does not reflect the enormous advances in equipment that has led to basic changes in technique. The schools are **Adamello Brenta**, **t** +39 0465 443412, **Campo Carlo Magno**, **t** +39 0465 443222, **5 Laghi**, **t** +39 0465 441650, **Des Alpes**, **t** +39 0465 442850, **Nazionale**, **t** +39 0465 443243, **Professional Snowboarding**, **t** +39 0465 443251, and **Rainalter**, **t** +39 0465 443300.

Children

All the ski schools offer lessons for children, but there is currently no kindergarten. Babysitting can be arranged through the tourist office.

Lunch

Try **Cascina Zeledria**, **t** +39 0465 440303, just above the woods on Pradalago below Piste No.7. Artini, the owner, is a well-known local chef specializing in regional Trentino dishes. If you're lucky, you'll get a tow by snowmobile back up to the piste. **Giorgio Graffer**, **t** +39 0465 440539, on the blue run down from the top of Grosté, is a classic mountain refuge with home-made local dishes. **Rifugio Malga Montagnoli**, **t** +39 0465 443355, at the bottom of Marchi black run on Monte Spinale, is one of the better self-service mountain restaurants in the area.

Dine

Dine at **Da Alfiero**, **t** +39 0465 440117, which is known for its home-made spaghetti dishes and for lamb cutlets in balsamic vinegar with asparagus. **Al Sottobosco**, **t** +39 0465 440737, is a kilometre from town, but worth the journey for its *pappardelle ai mirtilli e funghi porcini* (broad ribbons of pasta with blueberries and porcini mushrooms). **Artini**, **t** +39 0465 440122, is famed for its *risotto ai funghi* and its chocolate crêpes. **Al Sarca**, **t** +39 0465 440287, has wonderful home-made salami, grilled alpine trout, and *panna cotta* with woodland fruits. **Antico Focolare**, **t** +39

0465 441686, has a warm ambience and serves typical Trentino dishes including venison and polenta with gorgonzola and mushrooms. **La Locanda degli Artisti**, t +39 0465 442980, has lots of atmosphere and good food at low prices.

Le Roi, t +39 0465 443075, and **Belvedere**, t +39 0465 440396, are both warmly recommended by reporters. You can take a ride by snowcat at night to eat in **Cascina Zeledria** or three other cow sheds that have been converted into mountain restaurants – **Malga Montagnoli**, t +39 0465 443355, **Boch**, t +39 0465 440465, and **Malga Ritorto**, t +39 0465 442470.

Party

Bar Suisse, **La Cantina del Suisse** and the **Franz-Josef Stube** are the main après-ski haunts. **The Zangola**, situated in a converted cow shed 3km out of town, is one of the most famous discos in the Alps.

Sleep

★★★★**Alpen Suite Hotel**, t +39 0465 440100, *www.alpensuitehotel.it*, has 28 one-bedroom suites, each with its own sitting room.

★★★★**Hotel Bertelli**, t +39 0465 441013, *www.hotelbertelli.it*, dates back to the 1930s. Completely rebuilt in 1999, it is a traditional family hotel situated just 50m from the Pradalago cable-car.

★★★★**Biohotel Hermitage**, t +39 0465 441558, *www.chalethermitage.com*, has been in the Maffei family for over 100 years and has been refurbished as an eco hotel. It is situated over a kilometre from the resort but operates a bus service to the lifts and shops. Local dishes and home-made pasta are a speciality of the restaurant.

★★★★**Hotel Relais Club des Alpes**, t +39 0465 440000, *www.relaisdesalpes.it*, is also in a ski-in/ski-out position in the middle of the resort.

★★★★**Hotel Lorenzetti**, t +39 0465 441404, is on the edge of the piste and on the outskirts of the village.

★★★★**Palace Hotel**, t +39 0465 441004, *www.savoiapalace.com*, 50m from the 5 Laghi cable-car, is a favourite with British visitors.

★★★★**Spinale Club Hotel**, t +39 0465 441116, *www.editeltn.it/hotelspinale*, is situated close to the resort centre and the skiing.

★★★★**Hotel Carlo Magno Zeledria**, t +39 0465 441010, which has been run by the same family since 1947, is warmly praised ('entirely refurbished with a lovely wellness centre').

★★★**Hotel Bellavista**, t +39 0465 441034, *www.bellavistacampiglio.it*, has a friendly atmosphere and is opposite the Pradalago cable-car station.

★★★**Grazia Hotel Plaza**, t +39 0465 443100, is comfortable and conveniently located in the village centre.

Ortisei

Profile

Lowest and one of the most attractive of the Val Gardena villages, with links into both the Sella Ronda and the scenic Alpe de Siusi ski areas

Resort

Ortisei in the Val Gardena is a pretty alternative to nearby Selva. You can enjoy the skiing of the Sella Ronda but also have direct access to the more secluded Alpe di Siusi. Pastel-painted and ornately frescoed buildings flank the pedestrianized main street and central piazza. Escalators and walkways provide easy access to the lifts.

Mountain

A long gondola, followed by a cable-car, takes you up over a dramatic cliff face to 2518m Seceda. From here, you can either return to the village, or continue to Pla da Tieja above Santa Cristina. This is the terminal for the new underground funicular that effectively links Ortisei into the Sella Ronda and beyond.

On the southern edge of Ortisei, reached by a new pedestrian bridge, a gondola acts as the gateway to the Alpe di Siusi, From the top station, you can reach Compatsch on the Alpe di Siusi plateau where a handful of modern hotels have sprung up in recent years.

Learn

Ortisei, **t** +39 0471 796153, and **Saslong**, **t** +39 0471 786258, schools provide adequate instruction.

Children

Ortisei Ski School Miniclub cares for children from two years. **Hotel Cavallino Bianco Miniclub**, **t** +39 0471 783333, cares for children from one month to 12 years.

Lunch

Try **Sofie Hütte**, **t** +39 335 5271240, at Seceda and **Rifugio Col Raiser**, **t** +39 0471 796302, above Pla da Tieja. On the Alpe di Siusi side, stop at the **Sanon Hütte**, **t** +39 0471 727002, or **Mont Seuc** at the top of the gondola.

Dine

Anna Stuben, t +39 0471 796315, in the Hotel Gardena-Grödnerhof, serves local specialities. **Tubladel**, **t** +39 0471 796879, is in a converted hay barn. **La Rosticceria**, **t** +39 335 6174467, is renowned for its grilled meat and fish. **Concordia**, **t** +39 0471 796276, smokes its own game and ham. **Vedl Mulin**, **t** +39 0471 796089, is a popular pizzeria.

*BEST FOR

Italian ambience, high-mileage skiers and riders

ESSENTIALS

Altitude: 1236m (4,055ft)–2949m (9,676ft)
Further information: **t** +39 0471 796328, *www.valgardena.it*
Lifts in area: 83 (10 cableways, 36 chairs, 37 drags) serving 176km of piste; 450 lifts in Dolomiti Superski
Lift pass: Dolomiti Superski adult €155–254, child 8–16yrs €109–178, both for 6 days
Access: Verona airport 2hrs, railway station at Bolzano 1hr

Party

Seceda and **Siglu**, at the Cavallino Bianco, are the main après-ski rendezvous.

Sleep

★★★★★**Hotel Gardena-Grödnerhof**, **t** +39 0471 796315, *www.gardena.it*, was completely rebuilt in 2001.

★★★★**Hotel Adler**, **t** +39 0471 775050, *www.hotel-adler.com*, is an elegant place with an impressive spa.

★★★★**Hotel Cavallino Bianco**, **t** +39 0471 783333, *www.cavallino-bianco.com*, was refurbished last winter and still has the most comprehensive child facilities of any ski resort.

★★★★**Hotel Hell**, **t** +39 0471 796785, *www.hotelhell.it*, is situated in a heavenly ski-in/ski-out position.

★★★**Hotel Arnaria**, **t** +39 0471 796649, *www.arnaria.com*, is a family-run pension.

★★★**Hotel Digon**, **t** +39 0471 797266, *www.hoteldigon.com*, has recently been renovated.

Passo Tonale

***BEST FOR**

Reliable snow-cover, long season, intermediates

ESSENTIALS

Altitude: 1883m (6,178ft)–3069m (10,069ft)
Further information: t +39 0364 903838, *www.valdisole.net*
Lifts in area: 27 (1 cableway, 19 chairs, 7 drags) serving 100km of piste
Lift pass: Super Skirama Dolomiti (includes Madonna di Campiglio, Marilleva/Folgarida, Peio, Monte Bondone, Pinzolo, Paganella, Folgaria Lavarone and Passo Tonale) adult €167–188, child from 8yrs €135–151, both for 6 days
Access: Verona airport 2½hrs, railway station at Edolo 30mins

Profile

Unprepossessing high-altitude village with snow-sure skiing from late October until early May, as well as year-round summer skiing on the Presena Glacier

Resort

Passo Tonale is situated at the western end of the Val di Sole and its high altitude makes it one of the most snow-sure resorts in Italy. Some 11 new lifts have transformed mountain access in recent years. National ski teams train here and it has a strong international following. The resort opens from late October until the beginning of May, but summer skiing continues throughout the year on the Presena Glacier.

Mountain

Passo Tonale has plenty of beginner and intermediate terrain, with access by cable-car to Passo Paradiso, where a chair and three drags bring you to the 3069m summit. From here, long runs lead back to the village over high-altitude terrain. On the other side of the main road, the south-facing slopes are served by a sequence of chairs and drags over undulating pastures. One chair takes you to the old smuggling route of Passo Contrabbandieri at 2681m. The resort is linked by two-stage gondola to the village of Ponte di Legno.

Learn

Tonale-Presena, t +39 0364 903991, **Pontedilegno-Tonale, t** +39 0364 903943, and **Castellaccio, t** +39 0364 900302, have good reputations. **6punto9, t** +39 335 803604, is the snowboarding specialist.

Children

Miniclub, t +39 0364 900501, in Hotel Miramonti cares for non-resident children from newborn to three years. It will also offer free daycare for older children if they are hotel guests. **Fantaski, t** +39 0364 903991, is the ski kindergarten.

Lunch

Ristorante Erica, t +39 0364 91460, at the foot of the Paradiso cable-car and **Capanna Presena, t** +39 0463 758299, at the top are both recommended.

Dine

Try **Ristorante Rododendro, t** +39 0364 900259, and **Serodine, t** +39 0364 903724. Reporters praised pizzeria **Antares, t** +39 0364 903789, and **Il Focalare, t** +39 0364 903790.

Party

The resort is friendly and unpretentious. Try the **Umbrella Bar** after skiing. **Baita**

Faita and **Nico's** are popular resort rendezvous. **Disco-Pub Miramonti** and **Heaven** are usually crowded. **Antares** has live music, and **Bar Paninoteca Cantuccio** stays open until 6am.

Sleep

- ****Grand Hotel Miramonti, t** +39 0364 900501, *www. miramonti.com*, is the best hotel in town.
- ***Hotel La Mirandola, t** +39 0364 903933, is an old hospice up the mountain with snowmobile transport until 2am.
- ***Hotel Orchidea, t** +39 0364 903935, *www.hotelorchidea.net* is a comfortable family-run establishment.
- ***Hotel Panorama Edelweiss, t** +39 0364 903789, *www.panoramaedelweiss.com*, offers good food.
- ***Hotel La Torretta, t** +39 0364 903978, *www.hotellatorretta.com*, is 'in a perfect location and has mouth-watering pizzas'.

San Cassiano

Profile

Small, sophisticated village that shares its intermediate ski area with larger La Villa. Both are renowned for their designer hotels and gourmet restaurants

Resort

San Cassiano is a quiet village just off the main Sella Ronda circuit. Larger La Villa shares its immediate ski area, which is linked to Armentarola and Corvara. They make an attractive holiday base but links with the Sella Ronda from San Cassiano are frustratingly slow.

* BEST FOR

Comfort-lovers, quiet backdoor into Sella Ronda

ESSENTIALS

Altitude: 1537m (5,043ft)–2949m (9,676ft)
Further information: **t** +39 0471 849422, *www.altabadia.org*
Lifts in area: 52 in Alta Badia (9 cableways, 29 chairs, 14 drags) serving 130km of piste; 450 lifts in Dolomiti Superski
Lift pass: Dolomiti Superski adult €155–254, child 8–16yrs €109–178, both for 6 days
Access: Verona airport 2½ hrs

Mountain

Mountain access from San Cassiano and La Villa is by gondola and, even during peak season, queues are rare. In San Cassiano the lift station is a 10-minute walk from the centre but the main hotels operate a courtesy minibus service. The immediate ski area consists of gentle pistes above and below the treeline that are ideally suited to beginners and to intermediates who want the feeling of 'going somewhere' each day.

Learn

The choice lies between **San Cassiano, t** +39 0471 849491, **La Villa, t** +39 0471 847258, **Pedraces, t** +39 0471 839648, and **Dolomites, t** +39 0471 844018, ski schools.

Children

La Villa ski school runs a kindergarten and miniclub. **Dolomites ski school** has a playground on Piz La Villa. **Casa Bimbo, t** +39 0471 838096, in Pedraces, cares for babies and children up to 11 years.

Lunch

Try **Rifugio Scotoni, t** +39 0471 847330, above Armentarola for barbecued meat.

Marmolada 3342 m
Sassolungo - Langkofel 3181 m
PASSO PORDOI
PORDOI - PASS
2239 m
CAMPITELLO
ALBA
CANAZEI
PASSO SELLA
SELLA - PASS
2242 m
PLAN DE GRALBA
SELVA VALGARDENA
WOLKENSTEIN
1566 m
Piz Sella
PASSO GARDENA
GRÖDNERJOCH
2121 m
CAPRILE
BELLUNO
ARABBA
PASSO CAMPOLONGO
CAMPOLONGO - PASS
1875 m
COLFOSCO
1645 m
CORVARA
1568 m
PASSO FALZAREGO
FALZAREGO - PASS
2105 m
PASSO VALPAROLA
VALPAROLA - PASS
2168 m
LAGAZUOI
2778 m
LA VILLA
1433 m
PEDRACES
1324 m
SAN CASSIANO
1537 m
ARMENTAROLA
CENTRO FONDO
LANGLAUFZENTRUM
S.LEONARDO
1371 m
Brunico - Bolzano
Bruneck

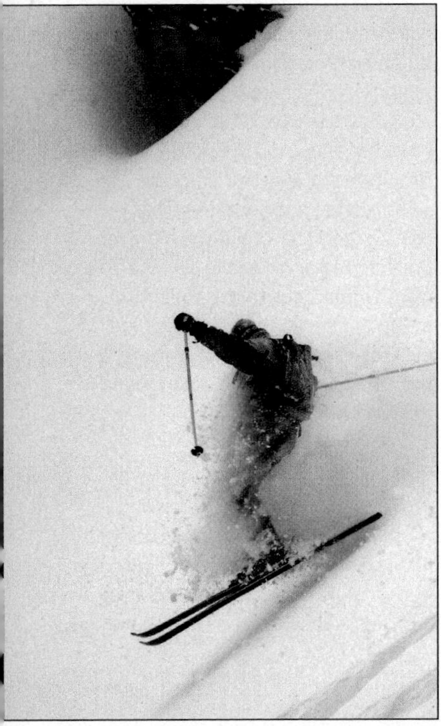

Also recommended is the nearby **Capanna Alpina, t** +39 0471 847330. **Malga Saraghes, t** +39 335 7897164, above San Cassiano, has outstanding home-made pasta.

Dine

In San Cassiano, **St Hubertus, t** +39 0471 849500, and **La Siriola, t** +39 0471 849445, have Michelin stars. In La Villa, **Ciastel Colz, t** +39 0471 847511, serves South Tyrol cuisine with gourmet flair.

Party

The **Rosa Alpina** and **Siriola** both have wine bars. **Franz de la Vedla** and **Hug's bar** are both popular meeting places. In La Villa the evening action is centred around **Durni's Pub** and **La Bercia**.

Sleep

San Cassiano:
- ★★★★**Rosa Alpina, t** +39 0471 849500, *www.rosaalpina.it*, epitomizes the new wave of first-rate hotels being established in the Dolomites.
- ★★★★**Dolomiti Wellness Hotel Fanes**, **t** +39 0471 849470, *www.hotelfanes.it*, offers good child reductions.
- ★★★**Hotel Conturines-Posta, t** +39 0471 849464, *www.conturines.it*, is family-run.

La Villa:
- ★★★★**Ciastel Colz, t** +39 0471 847511, *www.colz.siriolagroup.it*, is a magnificently restored early 16th-century castle with four bedrooms.
- ★★★**La Majun, t** +39 0471 847030, *www.lamajun.it*, has quirky interior design and a swimming pool lined with flagstones.
- ★★★**Hotel La Villa, t** +39 0471 847035, *www.hotel-lavilla.it*, has a wellness area.

Sauze d'Oulx

Profile

Important value-for-money component of the giant Milky Way ski area with plenty of high-mileage cruising, decent restaurants and wild nightlife. Suits 20- and 30-somethings in search of piste and party

Resort

Sauze d'Oulx has a longstanding and justified reputation as one of the winter party capitals, a place where pub culture takes precedence, despite valiant attempts over many years by the village fathers to engineer a more family-oriented environment. Sauze is one of the main resorts of the 86-lift Milky Way circuit that straddles the border with France and provides a mighty 400km of groomed runs. Much the best skiing in the region is found here, although holidays for many readers were blighted last season by lack of snow and lift closures in the run-up to the Winter Olympics.

The original medieval town has considerable charm but the more recent buildings adjacent to the slopes are far from sympathetic to their beautiful mountain environment. Skiing here inevitably involves a lot of walking, and the resort bus service is not included in the weekly lift pass.

Mountain

From the village, a sequence of chair-lifts takes you up to the mid-mountain hub of Sportinia for access to Cesana and Sestriere. Other lifts rise from the village

*** BEST FOR**

High-mileage cruising, party-goers, families

ESSENTIALS

Altitude: 1509m (4,951ft)–2507m (8,225ft)
Further information: t +39 0122 850700, *www.comune.sauzedoulx.to.it*
Lifts in area: 86 in Milky Way (6 cableways, 38 chairs, 42 drags) serving 400km of piste
Lift pass: Milky Way (covers Montgenèvre, Sestriere, Sauze d'Oulx and other smaller resorts) adult €193, child 8–12yrs €137, both for 6 days
Access: Turin airport 1hr, railway station at Oulx 5km, regular buses to resort

to Clotes and the open slopes of Pian della Rocca, as well as to the secluded and nearly always uncrowded sector beneath 2540m Monte Genevris. On busy high-season weekends, this is where you will find the locals. The Sauze d'Oulx slopes face west and north, and the majority of them are below the treeline. Sportinia is in effect a higher satellite with hotels, restaurants and good nursery slopes.

The resort quite wrongly has a 'novice' label attached to it. In fact, the majority of the runs are graded intermediate, and it's an excellent playground for accomplished skiers and riders looking for high mileage. Some of the best skiing is found between Sportinia and Sansicario. Good skiers will also want to journey on across the Monti della Luna to Montgenèvre in France. The new gondola linking Sestriere with Monte Fraiteve also allows for a swift return from Sestriere to Sauze.

Learn

Scuola Sauze d'Oulx, **t** +39 0122 858084, has an excellent reputation for teaching up-to-date technique. The others are **Sauze Project**, **t** +39 0122 858942, and **Sauze Sportinia**, **t** +39 0122 850218. Not all instructors speak good English. **Guide Alpine Valsusa**, **t** +39 0335 398984, and **Elisusa Heli-skiing**, **t** +39 0122 623162, are the off-piste specialists.

Children

Piccolo Dumbo, **t** +39 347 6913531, and **La Cinciarella**, **t** + 39 328 6445146, accept children from 13 months. All the ski schools offer lessons from four years.

Lunch

Chalet Il Capricorno, **t** +39 0122 850273, at the top of the Clotes piste, is renowned for chef Maria Rosa Sacchi's handmade ravioli and is much the best restaurant on the mountain. **Ciao Pais**, **t** +39 0122 850280, at Clotes, is recommended. **Capanna Kind**, **t** +39 0122 850206, and **La Tana dell'Orso**, **t** +39 0122 850226, at Sportinia, are favourites with reporters.

Dine

Del Falco, **t** +39 0122 858063, and **Del Borgo**, **t** + 39 0122 858318, have a warm atmosphere and good food. **Gran Villar**, **t** + 39 0122 858822, and **La Griglia**, **t** + 39 0122 850344, are also recommended.

Party

The New Scotch Bar at the foot of the slopes is a resort institution.

Wine Bar Gran Trun and **Village Café** have live bands. **The Grotto**, the bar of Hotel Derby, and **The Cotton Club** are ever popular. **Osteria dei Vagabondi** has live music. **Schuss Disco**, **Gina-Il Bandito**, **Paddy McGinty's** and **Queen's Lounge** are the late-night venues.

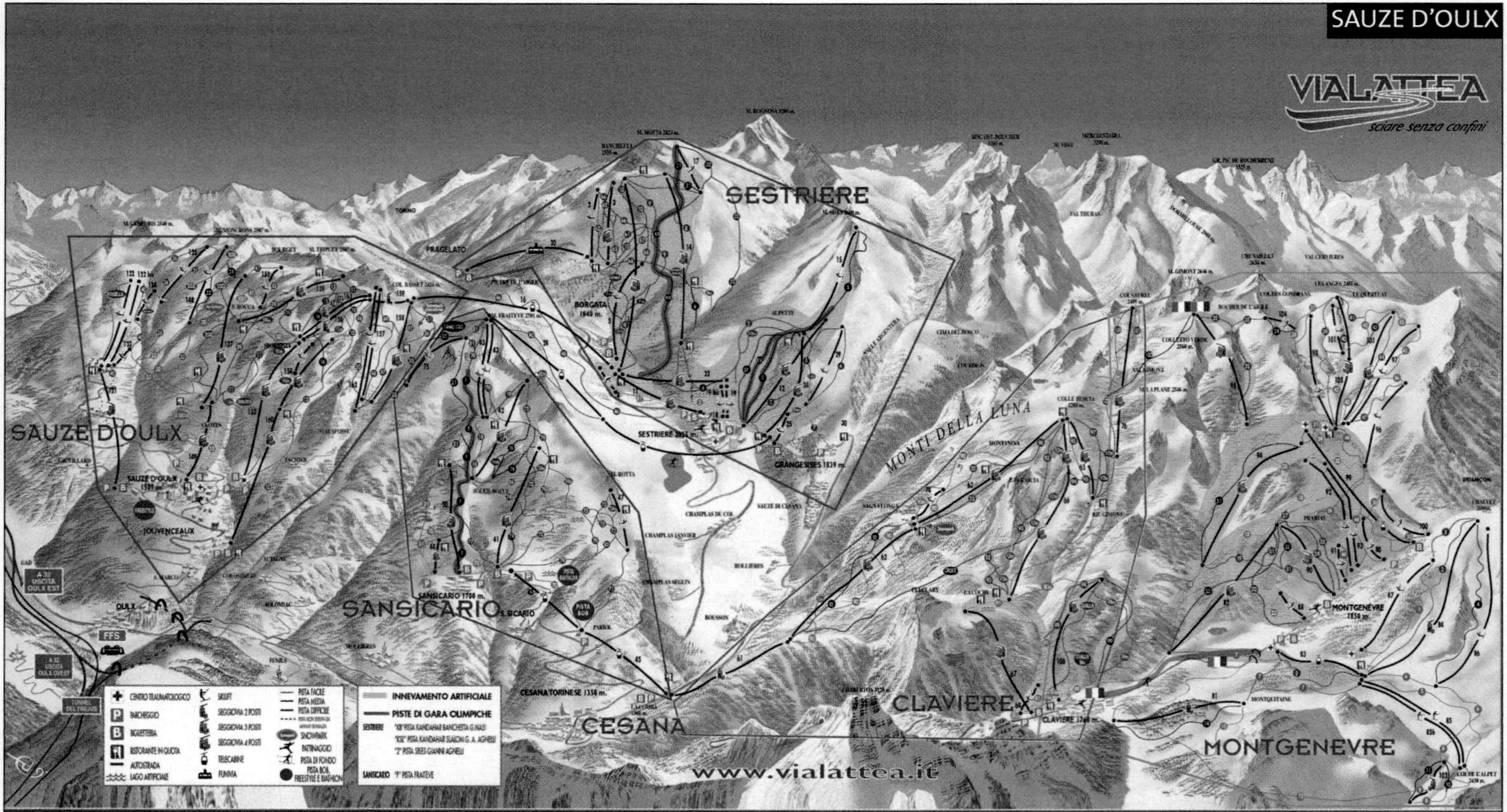

LE LINEE COLORATE PERMETTONO DI INDIVIDUARE GLI IMPIANTI UTILIZZABILI CON I SINGOLI BIGLIETTI DI AREA - THE COLOURED LINES INDICATE UNDER WHICH AREA EACH LIFT IS INCLUDED - LES LIGNES COLORÉS PERMETTENT DE REPÉRER LES REMONTÉES UTILISABLES AVEC LES FORFAIT DE ZONE.

Sleep

★★★★**Il Capricorno, t** +39 0122 850273, is a comfortable boutique hotel in an isolated position on the Clotes piste.

★★★★**Gran Baita, t** +39 0122 850183, is praised as 'excellent – very clean, the staff are pleasant'.

★★★★**Hotel Relais des Alpes, t** + 39 0122 859747, *www.gestioniabc.it*, in the resort centre, was recently renovated.

★★★★**La Torre, t** +39 0122 859816, is one of Sauze's most comfortable establishments, although we have mixed reports of the half-board food.

★★★**Hotel Miravalle, t** +39 0122 858530, *www.gestioniabc.it*, has been recently refurbished and has excellent cuisine.

★★★**Hotel Sauze, t** +39 0122 850285, *www.gestioniabc.it*, near the Clotes piste, has been completely refurbished.

★★★**Hotel Splendid, t** +39 0122 850172, *www.gestioniabc.it*, is in a quiet position, with a swimming pool.

★★★**Hotel Stella Alpina, t** +39 0122 858731, *www.stellalpinahotel.it*, is slope-side with a good atmosphere. The owner's wife is British.

★★★**Parc Hotel Gran Bosco, t** +39 0122 850166, *www.sauzedoulx.org/granbosco*, 1km out of town, has a courtesy bus, good food and friendly staff.

★★**Hotel Meublé Gran Trun, t** +39 0122 850016, has simple rustic-style rooms above the wine bar of the same name, and suits night-owls but not families.

★★**Hotel Hermitage, t** +39 0122 850385, *www.sauzedoulx.org/hermitage*, on the piste at Clotes, is clean and comfortable.

★★**Hotel Miosotis, t** +39 0122 850288, *www.gestioniabc.it*, is conveniently situated for lifts to Clotes and Sportinia.

Chalet Faure, t +39 0122 859760, *www.chaletfaure.it*, is full of atmosphere, with some split-level bedrooms and a spa.

Selva Gardena

Profile

One of the best-known resorts of the vast Sella Ronda ski circuit. The resort has good family facilities and some good mountain restaurants

Resort

Selva, also known as Wolkenstein, is a rather bland resort that stretches without a heart along the busy road between Bolzano and Corvara and links almost seamlessly to neighbouring villages of Santa Cristina and Ortisei. However, the high number of hotel beds and rental

✱ BEST FOR

High-mileage intemediates, families, serious lunchers

ESSENTIALS

Altitude: 1563m (5,128ft)–1800m (5905ft)
Further information: t +39 0471 795122, *www.valgardena.it*
Lifts in area: 83 in Selva Val Gardena (1 funicular, 9 cableways, 36 chairs, 37 drags) serving 175km of piste. 450 in Dolomiti Superski area
Lift pass: Dolomiti Superski adult €155–254, child 8–16yrs €109–178, both for 6 days
Access: Innsbruck airport 120km, Verona airport 2½hrs

chalets coupled with direct access into the Sella Ronda make it a popular and convenient base from which to explore the core of the Dolomites.

Selva is the setting each December for the Val Gardena Downhill, traditionally one of the earliest European venues of the season for the Men's World Cup. Britain's Konrad Bartelski famously took second place on the podium here back in 1981.

This does much to publicize the resort but gives a false impression that the skiing here is demanding. In fact, the area is best suited to beginners, intermediates and to families looking for a bustling resort with a moderate amount of nightlife and plenty of alternative activities.

Mountain

Selva is one of the four compass points of the Sella Ronda, the 40km circuit around the Gruppo Selle massif. It takes around two hours of lifts to complete in either direction, plus or minus the joker factor of any queues. You take 13 lifts on the clockwise route and 15 lifts on the anticlockwise. The amount of time actually spent skiing can be remarkably short – depending on your level of proficiency. You really don't need to be an accomplished skier to complete it. Anyone who has skied for three weeks should be able to achieve it, but you do need a moderate level of fitness.

Skiers travelling clockwise from Selva take a chair-lift followed by a long gondola up to 2300m Dantercepies to begin the long descent towards Colfosco and Corvara beyond. anticlockwise skiers and riders take the Ciaminoi gondola for the easy piste down to Plan de Gralba in the direction of Passo Pordoi and Arabba. You can also leave the circuit to explore the Val di Fassa.

The Ciaminoi downhill course – it is an intermediate piste when not prepared for racing – brings you down to Santa Cristina and the terminal for the new Val Gardena Ronda Express, an underground funicular that gives skiers direct access to Ortisei's ski area. Ciaminoi and the adjoining Mont de Seura sector – reached by a new quad-chair – provide some of the most scenic and enjoyable skiing in the valley.

Nursery slopes served by half-a-dozen short drags just above the resort provide a near-perfect playground for the large number of beginners who come to Selva.

Learn

In Selva, the choice lies between **2000**, **t** +39 0471 773125, and **Ski & Boarders' Factory**, **t** +39 0471 794257. We have mixed reports of both of these. In Santa Cristina, **CIR**, **t** +39 0471 790184, and **Santa Cristina**, **t** +39 0471 792045, are less internationally oriented.

Children

Casa Bimbo, **t** +39 348 8700661, run by the Santa Cristina school cares for children from 18 months. All the schools offer children's classes. Reporters praise the nursery slopes as 'brilliant'.

MARMOLADA
MARMOLATA
3342 m
Piz Boè
3152 m
P.so Campolongo
1875 m
Col di Lana
2462 m
P.so Falzarego
2105 m
Lavarella
3055 m
Conturines
3064 m
Cortina
VAL BADIA
LA VILLA
PEDRAGES
CORVARA
GARDENACIA
P U E Z
SELLA GRUPPE
P.so Gardena
Grödnerjoch
2121 m
P.so Pordoi
Pordoi Joch
2239 m
Col Rodela
2484 m
CANAZEI
CAMPITELLO
P.so Sella
Sella Joch
2244 m
Dantercepies
2300 m
Piz Seteur
2064 m
Plan de Gralba
1800 m
Piz Sella
2284
SASSOLUNGO
LANGKOFEL
3181 m
SASSOPIATTO
PLATTKOFEL
2956 m
Ciampinoi
2254 m
S E C E D A
Seceda
2518 m
Col Raiser
2103 m
Cuca
Cucasattel
SELVA GARDENA
WOLKENSTEIN
1564 m
Val Gardena Ronda Express
Monte Pana
1636 m
Mont de Seura
2117 m
Saslong
S.CRISTINA
ST.CHRISTINA
1428
Rasciesa Dafora
Ausserraschötz
2281 m
R A S C I E S A
R A T S C H Ö T Z
ORTISEI
ST. ULRICH
1236
BOLZANO
BOZEN
Saltria
1700 m
Monte Piz
2109 m
A L P E   D I   S I U S I
S E I S E R   A L M
Bullaccia
Puflatsch
2130 m
Denti di Terrarossa
Rosszähne
2657 m
SCILIAR
SCHLERN
PUNTA SANTNER
SANTNER SP.
2413 m

Lunch

Try **L'Medel, t** +39 0471 795235, on the piste of the same name. It is decorated with local mountain antiques. **Piz Sella, t** +39 0471 794115, is a wood-panelled restaurant with a warm atmosphere. **Rifugio Emilio Comici, t** +39 0471 794121, above Plan de Gralba, specializes in fresh fish. **Baita Panorama, t** +39 0471 795372, on the Dantacepies piste above Selva, has good homely fare.

Dine

Le Stuben, t +39 0471 795555, in Hotel Alpenroyal, offers a choice of five dining rooms, each with a different ambience ranging from alpine hut to formal 17th-century country house. **Armin's Grillstube** in the Hotel Armin, **t** +39 0471 795347, has fine steaks. **Al Cervo, t** +39 0471 795086, **La Bula, t** +39 0471 795208, **Rino,** and **Stübele** are popular pizzerias. In Santa Cristina, **Bistro Susi, t** +39 0471 793703, is warmly recommended, along with **Da Peppi, t** +39 0471 793335.

Party

Laurinkeller, t +39 0471 795059, is the long-established resort rendezvous. **Umbrella Bar, t** +39 0471 772200, in front of Hotel Wolkenstein, and **Igloo Bar, t** +39 0471 795135, are ever crowded. In Santa Cristina, **Crazy Pub, t** +39 338 6370581, and **Bar 2000, t** +39 0471 793693, are the liveliest bars.

Sleep

Selva:

*****Alpenroyal Sporthotel Gourmet & Relax, t** +39 0471 795555, *www.alpenroyal.com*, has giant swimming pool housed in an all-glass conservatory. The Eghes Spa offers an exhaustive range of treatments.

****Acadia Beauty & Relax, t** +39 0471 774444, *www.acadia.it*, has been run by the Prinoth family for four generations.

****Granvara Sport & Wellness Hotel, t** +39 0471 795250, *www.granvara.com*, is in a quiet position on the edge of piste. The owner also runs the 2000 ski school.

****Sporthotel Gran Baita, t** +39 0471 795210, *www.hotelgranbaita.com*, has been looking after skiers since 1953.

****Sporthotel Maciaconi, t** +39 0471 793500, *www.hotelmaciaconi.com*, has a large pool, sauna and solarium.

***Hotel Armin, t** +39 0471 795347, *www.hotelarmin.com*, is friendly.

***Albergo Gruppo Sella, t** +39 0471 795182, *www.grupposella.com*, situated a couple of kilometres outside Selva at Plan de Gralba, is owned by a former Italian World Cup racer.

***Hotel Wolkenstein, t** +39 0471 772200, *www.wolkenstein.it*, is strong on après-ski which can last deep into the night.

Santa Cristina:

****Alpenhotel Plaza, t** +39 0471 793463, *www.alpenhotelplaza.com*, is a new hotel in the centre of the village.

****Hotel Diamant Port & Wellness,** +39 0471 796780, *www.hoteldiamant.it*, is set in an extensive private park.

***Charme-Hotel Uridi, t** +39 0471 793215, *www.uridi.it*, is recommended.

Sestriere

Profile

Setting for the main alpine events in the Turin Winter Olympics in 2006, a slightly austere high-altitude ski village in the Milky Way. Suits intermediates in search of high-mileage cruising

✻ BEST FOR

High-mileage intermediates, Italian atmosphere, lively nightlife at weekends

ESSENTIALS

Altitude: 2035m, 6,675ft)–2823m, (9,262ft)
Further information: t +39 0122 353099, *www.sestriere.it*
Lifts in area: 86 in Milky Way (6 cableways, 38 chairs, 42 drags) serving 400km of piste
Lift pass: Milky Way (covers Montgenèvre, Sestriere, Sauze d'Oulx and other smaller resorts) adult €193, child 8–12yrs €137, both for 6 days
Access: Turin airport 1½hrs, railway station at Oulx 30 mins, buses to resort

Resort

Sestriere was purpose-built as a ski resort in 1934 by the Agnelli family, which founded Fiat. Last winter it hosted with considerable success the lion's share of the alpine events in the Winter Olympics.

Sestriere is the capital of the Milky Way – or Via Lattea – an alliance of villages that straddles the Italian/French frontier between Turin and Briançon. The Olympic venue has the highest and most challenging skiing in the region, along with a level of sophistication that is lacking in neighbouring Sauze d'Oulx. When Giovanni Agnelli originally built the resort, the high-altitude site he chose had a good snow record. However, in these times of climate change, cover is not as reliable as it used to be. The village is dominated by the twin towers of the original smart Torre and Duchi d'Aosta hotels.

Mountain

The Milky Way in general and Sestriere in particular have benefited from the Olympics. A new eight-person gondola connects Cesana to Sansicario in only eight minutes instead of 30 on the old Pariol and Forte chairs. A 60-person cable-car now links the ancient outlying town of Pragelato with Borgata.

The old, slow Trebials chair between Borgata and Sestriere has been upgraded to a detachable-quad. The Garnel drag-lift has by replaced by a chair from the Olympic Village up to Alpette, with a tunnel beneath the giant-slalom piste. At Claviere, a new detachable-quad connects La Coche to Colle Bercia and lots more snow-cannon have been installed.

Sestriere's skiing is split into the Monte Motta and Monte Sises sectors. Both are reached by quad-chairs and offer skiing for all standards. The beginner slopes just above the village are particularly good, and Sestriere has a terrain park with a half-pipe and a snowcross course.

Best powder run in the Milky Way is the Rio Nero, which follows a river gully down to the Oulx–Cesana road from Monte Fraiteve. Heli-skiing is possible on the top of Valle d'Argentera and Val Thures.

Learn

Sestriere has four ski schools of which **Scuola Sci Sestriere**, **t** +39 0122 77060, is much the largest, with focus on making lessons enjoyable. The others are **Borgata**, **t** +39 0122 77497, **Extrème**, **t** +39 0122 76214, and **Olimpionica**, **t** +39 0122 76116. Guiding can be arranged through **Guide Alpine Sestriere**, **t** +39 335 6601940.

Children

Asilo Neve, **t** +39 0122 755444, cares for children from two years and over.

Lunch

Try **Rifugio Alpette**, **t** +39 0122 755505, for fresh pasta. **Chisonetto**, **t** +39 0122 76094, is renowned for its polenta. **La Brua**, **t** +39 0122 76000, at Grangesises is good, **La Gargotte**, **t** +39 0122 76888, is

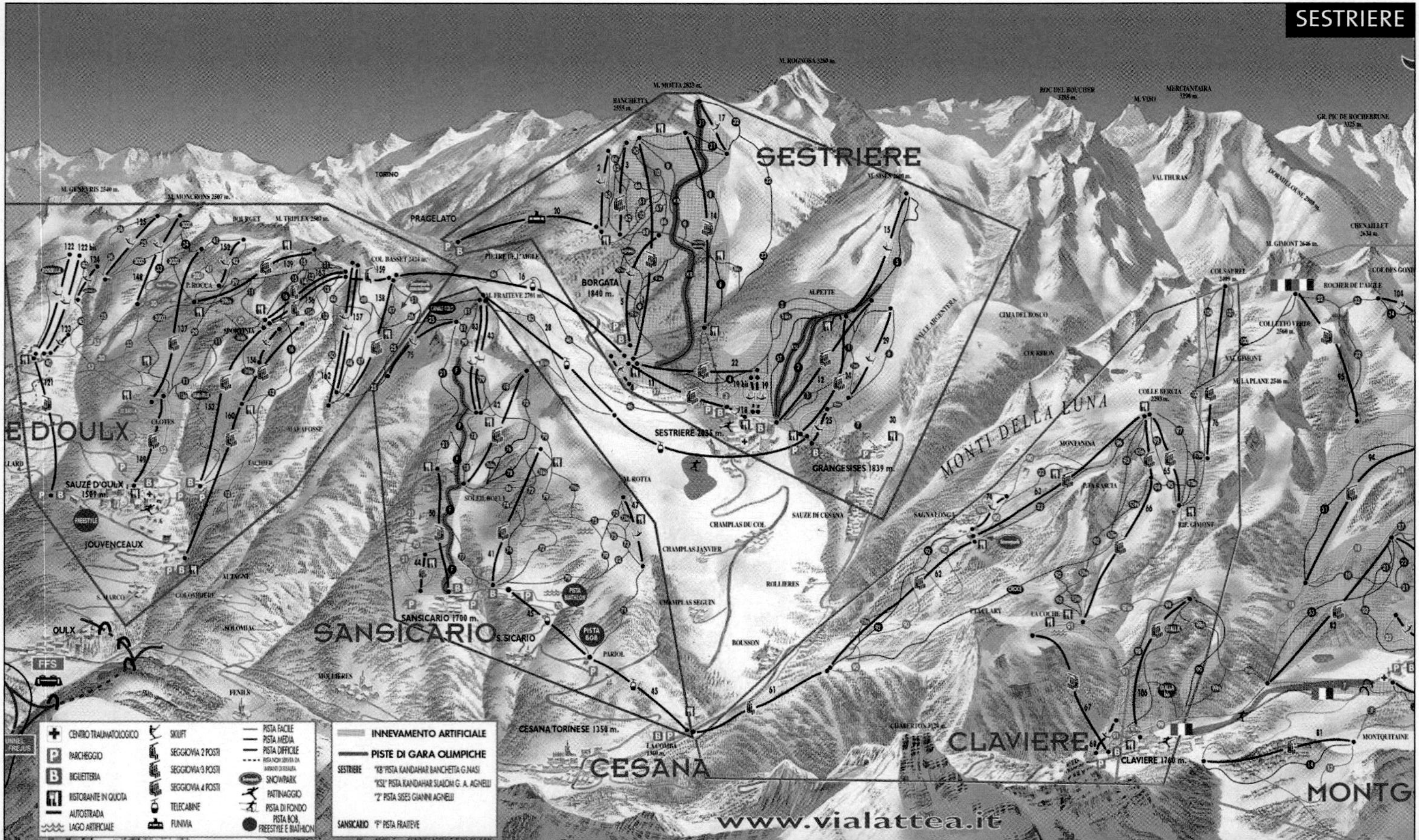
SESTRIERE
SANSICARIO
CESANA
CLAVIERE
MONTG
E D'OULX
MONTI DELLA LUNA
SESTRIERE 2035 m.
BORGATA 1840 m.
GRANGESISES 1839 m.
SANSICARIO 1700 m.
CESANA TORINESE 1350 m.
CLAVIERE 1760 m.
SAUZE D'OULX 1509 m.
PRAGELATO
JOUVENCEAUX
OULX
TORINO
M. ROGNOSA 3280 m.
M. MOTTA 2823 m.
BANCHETTA 2555 m.
M. GENEVRIS 2540 m.
M. MONCRONS 2507 m.
M. TRIPLEX 2507 m.
COL BASSET 2424 m.
M. FRAITEVE 2701 m.
ROC DEL BOUCHER 3255 m.
MERCIANTAIRA 3290 m.
M. VISO
GR. PIC DE ROCHEBRUNE 3325 m.
CHENAILLET 2634 m.
M. GIMONT 2646 m.
COLLE BERCIA 2293 m.
COLLETTO VERDE 2560 m.
ROCHER DE L'AIGLE
M. LA PLANE 2546 m.
CHAMPLAS DU COL
CHAMPLAS JANVIER
CHAMPLAS SEGUIN
SAUZE DI CESANA
ROLLIERES
BOUSSON
PARIOL
S. SICARIO
M. ROTTA
SAGNA LONGA
MONTANINA
LA COCHE
MONTQUITAINE
CENTRO TRAUMATOLOGICO
PARCHEGGIO
BIGLIETTERIA
RISTORANTE IN QUOTA
AUTOSTRADA
LAGO ARTIFICIALE
SKILIFT
SEGGIOVIA 2 POSTI
SEGGIOVIA 3 POSTI
SEGGIOVIA 4 POSTI
TELECABINE
FUNIVIA
PISTA FACILE
PISTA MEDIA
PISTA DIFFICILE
SNOWPARK
PATTINAGGIO
PISTA DI FONDO
PISTA BOB, FREESTYLE E BIATHLON
INNEVAMENTO ARTIFICIALE
PISTE DI GARA OLIMPICHE
SESTRIERE "KB" PISTA KANDAHAR BANCHETTA G.NASI
"KSL" PISTA KANDAHAR SLALOM G. A. AGNELLI
"2" PISTA SISES GIANNI AGNELLI
SANSICARIO "F" PISTA FRAITEVE
www.vialattea.it

expensive but worth it. **Lou Brachettes**, **t** +39 0122 77598, and **La Tana della Volpe**, **t** +39 335 362054, at the top of the Banchetta cable-car, is also recommended. Try also **Raggio di Sole**, **t** +39 0122 70170, **Valuncro**, **t** +39 0122 70286, and **Il Capret**, **t** +39 0122 70215.

Dine

Ristorante Du Grand-Père, **t** +39 0122 755970, in the hamlet of Champlas Janvier, specializes in local Piedmont dishes. **Antica Osteria**, **t** +39 0122 785300, in Pragelato, close to the site of the new cable-car, is a converted cow shed with a vaulted ceiling. **Le Lanterne**, **t** +39 0122 795283, in Grangesises, and **Pinky Pizzeria**, **t** +39 0122 76441, are recommended.

Party

Après-ski is quiet during the week but picks up at weekends when young and wealthy *Torinos* are in town. The **Kandahar** bar beneath the Hotel du Col is stylish and friendly. The infamous **Irish Igloo** and **Tabata** provide the late-night entertainment, spliced by inevitable vodka-and-Red Bull.

Sleep

- ★★★★**Grand Hotel Sestriere**, t +39 0122 76476, *www.grandhotelsestriere.it*, has been recently restored with a fine spa.
- ★★★★**Hotel Cristallo**, **t** +39 0122 750707, *www.newlinehotels.com*, has small rooms but a large new swimming pool.
- ★★★★**Il Fraitevino**, **t** +39 0122 76022, *www.hotelilfraitevino.it*, is in the centre of town.
- ★★★★**Pragelato Village Resort & Spa**, **t** +39 0122 740011, is a luxurious new development in Pragelato, linked by cable-car to Borgata.
- ★★★**Hotel Biancaneve**, **t** +39 0122 755176, *www.newlinehotels.com* suits families.
- ★★★**Hotel Banchetta**, **t** +39 0122 70307, *www.sestriere2000.com*, in the satellite of Borgata, is in a peaceful position 200m from the lift.

La Thuile

Profile

The Italian half of a large intermediate ski area shared with La Rosière in France, renowned for the quality of its snow and its restaurants

Resort

La Thuile is situated in a remote corner of the Aosta Valley at the foot of the Petit-St-Bernard Pass to France, which is closed in winter. It was once a grim mining town that has embraced tourism with enthusiasm, although not all its new buildings are sympathetic to their beautiful mountain environment. The good snow record can sometimes provide outstanding off-piste skiing when other

*** BEST FOR**

Uncrowded and usually snow-sure pistes, outstanding off-piste, value

ESSENTIALS

Altitude: 1441m (4,728ft)–2641m (8,665ft)
Further information: **t** +39 0165 884179, *www.lathuile.it*
Lifts in area: 37 (1 cableway, 17 chairs, 19 drags) serving 150km of piste
Lift pass: Aosta Valley (includes Courmayeur, La Thuile, La Rosière, and Champoluc-Gressoney-Alagna) adult €186, child 8–12yrs €139.50, child under 8yrs €46.50, all for 6 days
Access: Turin and Geneva airports 2hrs, railway station at Pré-St-Didier 15mins, regular buses from station

resorts have little to offer. The skiing is linked to La Rosière in France.

Mountain

A cableway and a parallel chair rise over wooded terrain to the mid-mountain station of Les Sucres at 2200m. A network of further lifts climb to the French border. This is a demanding ski area, with a predominance of steep reds and the occasional black. Heli-skiing is possible on the Ruitor Glacier. La Thuile has good nursery slopes, a terrain park and a half-pipe.

Learn

Instruction is restricted to **La Thuile** ski school, **t** +39 0165 884123, which was founded in 1964. We have mixed reports: the standard of tuition appears to be high, but language skills and attitudes are variable.

Children

Il Grande Albero, **t** +39 0165 884986, accepts children from newborn to three years. Ski school **Miniclub**, **t** +39 0165 884123, takes children from four years.

Lunch

Try **Rifugio Lo Riondet**, **t** +39 0165 884006, on the piste from the pass. **La Bricole**, **t** +39 0165 884149, is in an attractive old house at the bottom of the lifts. **L'Eden**, **t** +39 0165 885348, provides outstanding food, and **La Meleze**, **t** +39 0165 885553, above the gondola station, is new.

Dine

A La Lune, **t** +39 0165 884964, has Tuscan cooking. **Le Rascard**, **t** +39 0165 88499, serves innovative cuisine including chocolate pizza. **La Fordze**, **t** +39 0165 884800, specializes in grilled meat and game. **La Bricole**, **t** +39 0165 884149, is traditional, **La Lisse**, **t** +39 0165 884167, serves local specialities, and **La Raclette**, **t** +39 0165 884541, is recommended. **La Grotta**, **t** +39 0165 884474, has 'a great atmosphere and offers value for money'. **Taverna Coppa Pan**, **t** +39 0165 884797, is praised ('food and service are excellent').

Party

'Do not go out in search of entertainment,' warned a reporter, 'because you will be disappointed.' Another said: 'Great place for skiing, but if you enjoy a few beers afterwards go elsewhere.' What there is includes **Bar La Buvette**, **La Bricolette**, **La Cage aux Folles** and **La Bricole** for dancing.

Sleep

****__Planibel Hotel and Aparments__, **t** +39 0165 884541, *www.tivigest.com*, is a giant complex with pool, disco and shops.

***__Chalet Alpina__, **t** +39 0165 884187, is a rustic hotel 200m from the lifts.

***__Chalet Eden__, **t** +39 0165 885050, is renowned for its food.

***__Hotel du Glacier__, **t** +39 0165 884137, is convenient and has been refurbished ('always assured of a warm welcome').

***__Les Granges__, **t** +39 0165 883048, 3km out of town, has home cooking.

__Entrèves__, **t +39 0165 884134, is a recently restored family hotel.

07 The Top Resorts: Scandinavia

Åre, Sweden

***BEST FOR**

All levels of skier and rider, snowmobiling, reindeer- and dog-sledding

ESSENTIALS

Altitude: 384m (1,259ft)–1420m (4,659ft)
Further information: t +46 (0)647 17700, *www.skistar.com*
Lifts in area: 43 (1 funicular, 2 cableways, 9 chairs, 31 drags) serving 93km of piste
Lift pass: adult SEK1,545, child 8–15yrs SEK1,235, both for 6 days
Access: Östersund/Frösö airport (via Stockholm/Arlanda airport) 60mins, Trondheim airport 2hrs, railway station in resort

Profile

Scandinavia's only truly world-class downhill ski resort, suited to all standards of skier and snowboarder, as well as families who are not on a strict budget

Resort

Åre is the largest resort in Scandinavia, with skiing that matches many resorts in the Alps for the length of its runs, the gradient and the extent of the terrain. It is the setting for the World Skiing Championships this season and a new downhill course is being created. The skiing is spread across different villages that are linked on-mountain and by ski bus. Confusingly, two of these – Duved and Åre Björnen – seek resort status in their own right, but Åre Village is the international player.

Mountain

A detachable-quad and a six-seater chair take skiers from the valley to the top station in under four minutes. From here a network of lifts crisscrosses the mountainside both above and below the treeline. A tow behind a snowcat brings experienced skiers and riders to the 1420m summit of Åreskutan, starting point for a rewarding off-piste descent. The Olympia lift is to be replaced this season by Scandinavia's first 'chondola' – a combination of chair and gondola – which will greatly ease mountain access at peak times. Slopes are open for night-skiing until 8pm for much of the season. Cross-country skiing is also a popular pastime with 56km on trails on the shores of the lake.

Learn

Beginners are well served by the **Åre ski school**, +46 (0)771 840000, which enjoys a sound reputation and is staffed entirely by fluent English-speakers.

Children

The **village crèche, t** +46 (0)647 17700, cares for non-skiing children from three to five years. The ski school kindergarten offers tuition from three years.

Lunch

Try **Ullådalsstugan, t** +46 (0)647 53171, and **Hummelstugan, t** +46 (0)647 53284. You can buy reindeer burgers from Lapps in front of their teepees at Stendalen.

Dine

Villa Tottebo, t +46 (0)647 50620, is an old hunting lodge specializing in reindeer steaks. **Marmite, t** +46 (0)647 50240, has gourmet cuisine. **Liten Krog, t** +46 (0)647 52200, is recommended for its reasonably priced pizzas. **Easy Kitchen, t** +46 (0)647 12000, in Holiday Club Åre, features stir-fry wok dishes, pizzas and salads. **Carins Krog, t** +46 (0)647 10450, outside the village, serves reindeer tartare. Other dishes include fish caught by the owner and mushrooms picked by his wife.

Party

Skiers' Bar at Hotel Diplomat, **Fjällgården** ('amazing place stuffed full of people dancing on tables at 4pm') and **Werséns Bar** are packed when the lifts close. **Bygget** at Arefjällby is one of the best nightspots. Another popular nightclub, **Country Club**, is located in Hotel Diplomat Åregården.

Sleep

Accommodation can be booked through a central office, **t** +46 (0)647 17700.

Luxury:

★★★★**Hotel Diplomat Åregården**, **t** +46 (0)647 17800, *www.diplomathotel.com*, is close to the lifts and has 18 single rooms among its 54 rooms and suites.

★★★★**Totthotell**, **t** +46 (0)647 15000, *www.totthotell.com*, contains minimalist modern bedrooms and apartments, and a huge spa with 17 treatment rooms.

Moderate:

Diplomat Ski Lodge, **t** +46 (0)647 17800, *www.diplomathotel.com*, is recently refurbished, within walking distance of the lifts, and has a large number of family rooms.

Holiday Club Åre, **t** +46 (0)647 12000, *www.holidayclub.se*, is one of the biggest ski hotels in Sweden, with four restaurants, bowling and an adventure pool with 67m of winding waterslide.

Hotell Fjällgården, **t** +46 (0)647 14500, *www.fjallgarden.se*, is slope-side, with a good restaurant, and 'very buzzy'.

Geilo, Norway

Profile

Traditional resort with impressive cross-country skiing and limited but relaxed downhill skiing for beginners to intermediates

Resort

Geilo is one of the best family resorts in Scandinavia, a village well known to avid cross-country skiers as one of the centres of the famous Hardangervidda Plateau, with a total of 220km of loipe in the immediate area of the resort. Geilo is also known as the European capital of kite-surfing and is a past host of the world championships.

Mountain

With a vertical drop of only 373m, the resort is best suited to beginners, low intermediates and families. The two main ski areas are inconveniently situated on either side of a wide valley, with the resort in the centre.

Most of the skiing is at Geilohovda, while the Vestlia area is best for novices. A third area at Kikut has a quad-chair and a drag-lift. Reporters enthuse about the friendliness of the locals and the fact that the slopes are uncrowded. Geilo has a terrain park at Fugleleiken and a smaller one at Vestlia.

*BEST FOR

Beginners and low intermediates, families, cross-country

ESSENTIALS

Altitude: 800m (2,624ft)–1178m (3,864ft)
Further information: t +47 3209 5900, *www.geilo.no*
Lifts in area: 19 (5 chairs, 14 drags) serving 40km of piste
Lift pass adult Kr1,070–1,225, child 7–15yrs Kr 800–920, both for 6 days
Access: Fagernes airport 2hrs, Oslo airport 4½hrs

Learn

Per Bye, **t** +47 3209 0650, and **Geilolia**, **t** +47 3209 0000, are the two excellent schools. 'This is a top resort for novice instruction' enthused one reporter. 'No arrogant show-off instructors here – just honest, nice and well qualified people who actually want you to get better.'

Children

The much-praised **Trollklubben** kindergarten, **t** +47 3209 5518, at Vestlia, cares for children from newborn to seven years.

Lunch

Six cafés and kiosks up the mountain serve basic fare, but no alcohol until after 3pm. The sun terrace of the stately **Dr Holms Hotel**, **t** +47 3209 5940, is a lunch-time rendezvous.

Dine

The rustic-style **Hallingstuene**, **t** +47 3209 1250, specializes in game. **Peppe's Pizza**, **t** +47 3209 1815, is the cheaper alternative.

Party

Jegerbaren and **Lille Blå** are popular and lively. **Recepten Pub** in the Dr Holms Hotel and the **Pianobaren** in the Highland have plenty of ambience. **Highdance** is the disco.

Sleep

All accommodation can be booked through a central number, **t** +47 3209 5940.

Luxury:

Dr. Holms Hotel, **t** +47 3209 5700, *www.drholms.no*, has been the focal point of the resort for 100 years.

Moderate/Budget:

Bardøla Hyttegrend are 22 log cabins set in the woods, each with four bedrooms, two bathrooms, and a cosy sitting room.

Lia Fjellstue, **t** +47 3208 7400, *www.liafjellstue.no*, is in Skurdalen, 14km from Geilo, with magnificent views of Hardangervidda. There are eight new luxury suites and traditional Norwegian food is served.

Park Inn Highland, **t** +47 3209 6100, *www.highland.no*, is recommended for families.

Vestlia Resort, **t** +47 3208 7200, *www.vestlia.no*, in the Vestlia ski area, has excellent food.

Ustedalen Hotel, **t** +47 3209 6700, *www.ustedalen.no*, is a comfortable family-run establishment 700m from the resort centre.

Hemsedal, Norway

Profile

Suited to all standards of skier as well as families. Has an excellent terrain park for snowboarders and twin-tip skiers

Resort

Hemsedal has the most challenging downhill skiing in Norway. The resort is divided into the self-contained Skisenter at the base of the mountain and the original community of Hemsedal two miles away. Plans are on the drawing board to link the two by gondola. At the moment they are connected by a free ski-bus.

Mountain

The skiing is suited to all standards with some genuinely steeper terrain served by an eight-seater chair, including the Hjallerløypa run, which deserves its double-black classification. Reidarskaret is a challenging off-piste itinerary that evolves from a precipitous couloir. You are advised to take a guide who will arrange for a taxi to bring you back to the resort. However, there is also plenty of benign terrain for novices and intermediates. Night-skiing until 9pm is possible four days a week until mid-March.

The resort now has two terrain parks. The 600m main park, considered to be one of the best in Europe, has two half-pipes and a quarter-pipe. The recently extended second one in the Trollskogen area is aimed at new riders.

*BEST FOR
All levels of skier, snowboarders

ESSENTIALS
Altitude: 650m (2,133ft)–1497m (4,911ft)
Further information: t +47 3205 5030, *www.hemsedal.com*
Lifts in area: 21 (6 chairs, 15 drags) serving 43km of piste
Lift pass: adult Kr1,320, child 7–15yrs Kr1,060, both for 6 days
Access: Oslo airport 3½hrs

Learn

Hemsedal Ski School, t +47 3205 5067, has a good reputation. **Solheisen Ski and Snowboard School, t** +47 4130 5094, is an alternative learning centre at Solheisen, a 10-minute drive away. Its three lifts are included in the Hemsedal lift pass.

Children

A large new children's area with five easy runs makes this one of the best resorts in Scandinavia for kids. Ski passes and helmet rental are free for under sevens. The **Trollia crèche, t** +47 3205 5320, beside the slopes cares for childen from three months.

Lunch

Try **Harahorn, t** +47 3206 2380, mid-mountain. Cafés at Hemsedal Village include **Kremen Kafe, t** +47 3206 0237, and **Café Kakaotwo, t** +47 9509 5811.

Dine

The restaurant at **Hotel Skarsnuten, t** +47 3206 1700 serves gourmet food. **Norlandia Skogstad Hotel, t** +47 3205 5000, **Peppes Pizza, t** +47 3205 9557, and the **Hemsedal Café, t** +47 3205 5410, are recommended.

Party

Garasjen is the main meeting place. The **Skogstad Piano Bar** and **Hemsedal Café** are also always crowded.

Sleep

For accommodation contact Hemsedal Booking, **t** +47 3205 5060.

Luxury:

Skarsnuten Hotell, t +47 3206 1700, *www.skarsnutenhotel.no*, is at 1000m, linked by chair to the Mountain Village.

Norlandia Skogstad Hotell, t +47 3205 5000, *www.norlandia.no/skogstad*, in Hemsedal village, has a nightclub and swimming pool and is the centre for nightlife.

Moderate:

Hemsedal Hotell, t +47 3205 5400, *www.gohemsedal.com*, is situated at Tuv, midway between Hemsedal and the lifts.

Flaget Farm, t +47 3206 2400, is where you spend the night in a Lavvo – a wigwam-style home used by Sami herdsmen. You bathe in a hot tub and sleep on reindeer skins around a central oven. Dinner is served around an open fire.

Levi, Finland

Profile

Offbeat resort in the Arctic Circle with a long snow-sure season. Suits beginners and intermediates, with a wide choice of non-skiing activities, but limited nightlife

Resort

Finland's only truly international ski resort has guaranteed snow from mid-October until mid-May, which explains why Rossignol has one of its four worldwide equipment test centres here.

Levi is situated in magical surroundings in a pine forest 161km from Rovaniemi, the capital of Finnish Lapland.

From November to January the sun fails to make it over the horizon, and when not pitch dark the resort is bathed in soft twilight. Some 15 runs are floodlit from 10am to 8pm by sodium lamps, which give the winter landscape a surreal tint. By night, the Northern Lights dance across the sky. After New Year the hours of daylight increase, and in spring the ski area is open without lights until 8pm.

Mountain

This is a modest ski area with short runs down all sides of the dome-shaped mountain, best suited to beginners, low intermediates and families. A modern gondola acts as the backbone of the 26-lift system. The resort has a superpipe and a separate terrain park with half-pipe and a snowcross course.

Other activities include 230km of cross-country skiing, a visit to a Lapp farm for reindeer rides, snowmobiling, dog-sledding and ice-diving.

*BEST FOR

Beginners, low intermediates, families, reindeer- and dog-sledding

ESSENTIALS

Altitude: 400m (1,312ft)–531m (1,742ft)
Further information: **t** +358 (0)16 641 246, *www.levi.fi*
Lifts in area: 26 (1 cableway, 25 drags) serving 45km of piste
Lift pass: adult €68–137, child under 12yrs €41–82, both for 6 days
Access: Kittilä airport 10mins

Learn

Levi Ski School, **t** +358 (0)16 641 655, has an excellent reputation and lessons include the use of lifts.

Children

Tenavatokka, t +358 (0)16 641 377, cares for skiing and non-skiing kids from newborn to six years. Adjoining **Children's Land** has three baby-lifts. Children under seven wearing helmets can ski free.

Lunch

Try **Battery Grilli, t** +358 (0)16 641 346, **Carlsberg Pub, t** +358 (0)16 641 313, **Alpine Café Paulig, t** +358 (0)16 641 314, and **Luvattumaa, t** +358 (0)407 400 925.

Dine

Most guests eat in their hotels where reindeer rules the menu. **Fun Action Fondue, t** +358 (0)400 503 278, is what it says it is. **Levin Gastro, t** +358 (0)16 644 884, is a gourmet experience. **Levin Bistro, t** +358 (0)16 644 125, is a pizzeria.

Party

The Seika nightclub and **Joiku Karaoke Bar** are both in Spa Hotelli Levitunturi. **Disco Beige** is the alternative.

Sleep

Accommodation can be booked through a central office, **t** +358 (0)16 639 3300.

Luxury:

Hotelli K5 Levi, t +358 (0)16 639 1100, *www.k5levi.fi*, has 35 no-smoking rooms, minimalist decoration and private saunas or hot tubs in each room.

Spa Hotelli Levitunturi, t +358 (0)16 646 301, *www.hotellilevitunturi.fi*, has a swimming pool, five restaurants, a nightclub and a sports hall with tennis, badminton and basketball courts.

Moderate:

Hotel Hullu Poro, t +358 (0)16 651 0100, *www.hulluporo.fi*, meaning 'crazy reindeer', has a new extension with comfortable a rooms – some with private saunas.

08

The Top Resorts: Spain

Baqueira–Beret

🏆 BEST LUXURY SKI HOTEL 2007 (LA PLETA)

🏆 BEST SMALL RESORT 2007

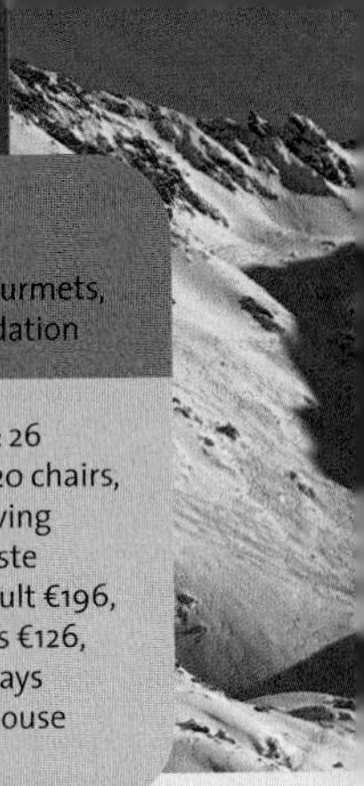

*** BEST FOR**

All levels of skier and rider, ski gourmets, party-goers, comfortable accommodation

ESSENTIALS

Altitude: 1500m (4,920ft)–2510m (8,235ft)

Further information: t +34 973 63 90 10, *www.baqueira.es*

Lifts in area: 26 (1 gondola, 20 chairs, 5 drags) serving 104km of piste

Lift pass: adult €196, child 6–11yrs €126, both for 6 days

Access: Toulouse airport 2hrs

Profile

Spain's smartest resort set amid dramatic Pyrenean scenery and patronized by King Juan Carlos. A wide choice of restaurants and nightlife

Resort

Seaside and sangria rather than slalom and snow are more familiarly associated with Spanish holidays, but the country does in fact offer surprisingly good skiing.

For years, Baqueira–Beret in the Pyrenees has remained Europe's best-kept ski secret, shared by a small but knowledgeable band of international skiers who have found a truly viable alternative to the over-commercialized resorts of the Alps. The trouble with nearly all such so-called 'alternatives' to the big-name resorts is that they usually lack either the variety of terrain or the sophisticated infrastructure of the Alps – or both. Not so Baqueira in the Val d'Aran, a cross-cultural pocket of the Pyrenees where Spanish, Catalan and Aranese are all spoken. French is also widely understood.

As a holiday destination it has serious chic status. The Spanish monarch has a majestic home here. King Juan Carlos no longer skis, but his children and their families visit most weekends during the season. Even Victoria Beckham and children stayed here last season.

For the past 42 years since the resort opened above the ancient town of Vielha, Baqueira has been content to offer its slopes to a predominantly Spanish market. However, it is now actively seeking an international image as the ski area expands into neighbouring valleys. Two major new hotels just below the resort are under construction, and the first stage of a new gondola from the centre of the village provides hugely improved mountain access. The second stage, due to be built next year, will provide doorstep skiing from the new hotels which have already sparked interest among the mainstream British ski specialists.

Baqueira seems set to realize a major international profile. For those of us who have quietly enjoyed its skiing over the years, this is a shame – but in today's competitive market ski resorts must evolve or die. The window between unspoilt mountainsides and commercial exploitation is sadly a narrow one.

Pretty it is not. The original purpose-built edifices are made of functional concrete. However, more recent additions are in a much more pleasing style, in keeping with the resort's dramatically beautiful setting on the the road that leads up to the high Bonaigua Pass.

Anyone not used to the Spanish way of doing things needs to understand the timetable in order to survive. For indigenous guests, skiing is an activity you rarely contemplate before 10.30am. Lunch is at 2pm or even 3pm, followed by a last run to the base area. Rioja-and-tapas last until 7pm when the bars empty – and everyone goes to bed. The Spanish summer siesta habit remains unbroken in winter. Dinner *en famille* is at 10pm or at 11pm for grown-ups, and the nightclubs start to warm up around 2am.

Mountain

Statistics tell you the resort has 26 lifts, 104km of piste, and a 1000m vertical drop, but that's only a small part of the story. The skiing truly suits all standards with plenty of easy cruising terrain, as well as steeper slopes for advanced inter-mediates. Easily accessible off-piste in the Bonaigua and Beret sectors rivals the best of Switzerland and France. You can even heli-ski here at a modest £50 a drop.

The new gondola provides the main means of mountain access, replacing a strange quad-chair that you rode without skis (you slotted them into the back of the chair in front). It begins from just below the chair – with an altered piste to accommodate it – and ends at the same mid-mountain station at 1800m. At first glance such expenditure seems unnecessary. The Spanish are slow to ski each morning and rush-hour queues are almost unheard of. However, the gondola is designed to cope with the extra traffic envisaged from the two new hotels. A second phase of the gondola from hotels to ski base should be in position by the start of this season.

Snow-cannons installed last season on the front have greatly assisted piste maintenance – although Baqueira has notched up an outstanding record for good snow-cover in recent years.

The moderately extensive ski area covers four linked mountains that offer a substantial vertical drop of 1000m. Most is given over to comfortable cruising terrain, but there are all sorts of variants, with some sharp little drop-offs at the edge of runs, and plentiful off-piste opportunities with a guide. Where Goats Tumble, Baqueira's most infamous couloir, can test even experienced powderhounds to the full. There is a half-pipe at Beret.

Learn

Baqueira Ski School, **t** +34 973 63 90 10, has 200 ski instructors, but don't expect many of them to speak fluent English. **Ski Miquel**, **t** +44 (0)1457 821 200, runs its own BASI ski school with British instructors.

Children

Baqueira has **Snowparks** for kids of three months to three years opposite the Bosque ski-lift at 1800, **t** +34 606 54 41 32, opposite the control tower in Beret, **t** +34 606 54 41 34, and next to the Hotel Montarto at 1500, **t** +34 973 64 54 48.

Lunch

Lunch at **Restaurante Salad Bar 2200m**, **t** +34 973 63 90 90, is more interesting than its name – it serves a variety of grilled-to-order meats along with the lettuce leaves. **Cap del Port**, **t** +34 973 25 00 82, a gothic folly, offers haute cuisine 200m from Bonaigua village. **Restaurant 1800**, **t** +34 973 64 52 02, is at the foot of the Baqueira Plain chair and serves Aranese and Catalan cuisine. The cut-price alternative is to settle for £7-a-head tapas and Rioja back in town at **Tamarro's**, **t** +34 973 64 43 22.

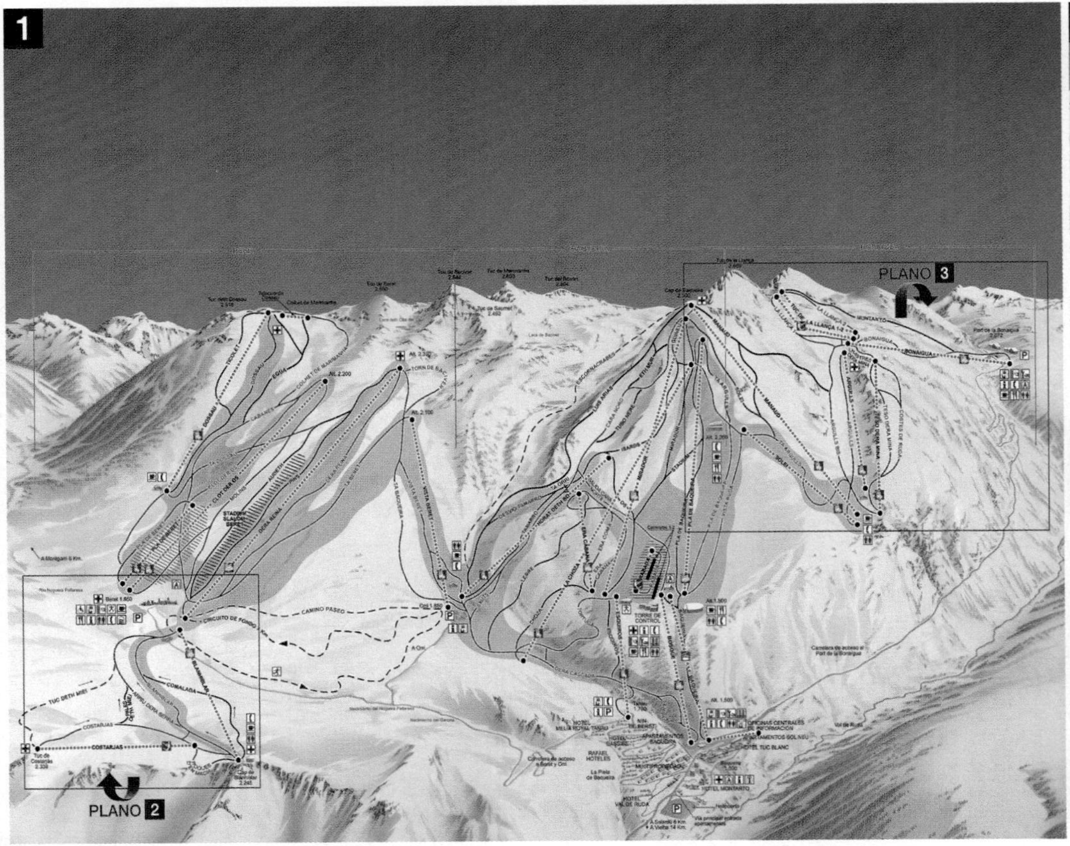
1
PLANO 3
PLANO 2
CAMINO PASEO
CIRCUITO DE FONDO
COSTARJAS
COMALADA
TUC DETH MIEI
TORRE DE CONTROL
HOTEL TUC BLANC
HOTEL MONTARTO
HOTEL VAL DE RUDA
RAFAEL HOTELES
OFICINAS CENTRALES DE INFORMACION
STADIUM BLANCA BERET
COSTES DE RUDA
TESO DERA MINA
ARGULLS
BONAIGUA
MONTANTO
MANAUD
VISTA BERET
TORN DE BACIVER
DOSSAU
TRIOLET
EGUA

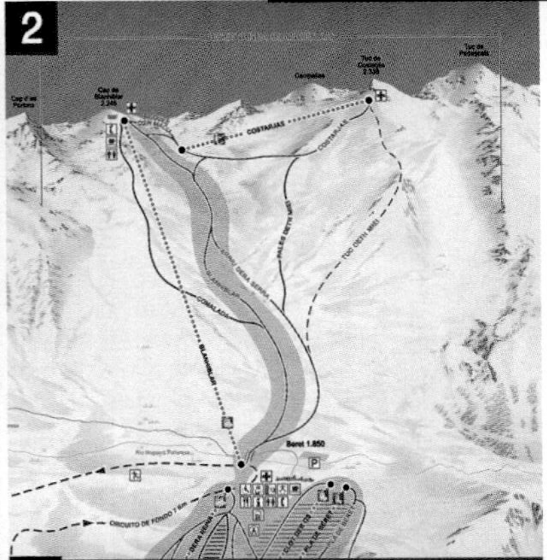
2
Beret 1.850
COSTARJAS
CIRCUITO DE FONDO 7 Km.

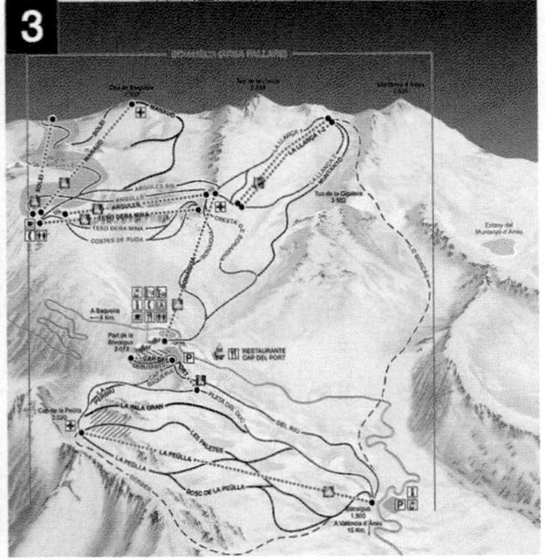
3
RESTAURANTE CAP DEL PORT
LA PEÜLLA
BOSC DE LA PEÜLLA
LES PLEITES
LA PALA GRAN
ARGULLS
TESO DERA MINA
COSTES DE RUDA

Dine

Gastronomically we rate it among the top 10 ski resorts in the world for haute cuisine at sensible prices – with a couple of dozen restaurants quite literally fit for a king. **La Pleta, t** +34 973 645550, in the hotel of the same name, has the best table in the resort itself. **Esquiro, t** +34 973 645430, specializes in hearty Aranese dishes. **La Borda Lobato, t** +34 973 645708, majors in roast suckling pig and whole baby lamb carved at the table. **Urtau, t** +34 973 641815, in nearby Arties, is warmly recommended for its variety of duck dishes and crêpes. **Casa Irene, t** +34 973 644364, also in Arties, has excellent fresh fish and grilled meat.

Party

Nightlife starts late in Spain. **Tiffany's** and **Pacha** are the popular nightclubs. Others include **Tuc Nere**, and **Vielha Dance Club** in Vielha.

Sleep

★★★★★**Rafaelhoteles La Pleta, t** +34 973 64 55 50, *www.rafaelhoteles.com*, with its bell tower and Aranese design, has a swimming pool and a shuttle service to the lift ('a truly outstanding modern hotel with a fine spa and the best gastronomic cuisine in the resort').

★★★★★**Melia Royal Tanau Boutique Hotel, t** +34 973 64 44 46, *www.solmelia.com*, has a chair-lift to the slopes.

★★★★**Parador de Arties, t** +34 973 64 08 01, *www.paradores-spain.com*, is in the hamlet of Arties; traditional design with wooden beams in all bedrooms.

★★★★**Hotel Casa Irene, t** +34 973 64 43 64, *www.innsofspain.com*, is also in Arties. It has spacious and rustic rooms and a good restaurant serving local specialities.

★★★★**Hotel Chalet Bassibe, t** +34 973 64 51 52, *www.valderuda-bassibe.com*, is up at Baqueira 1700.

★★★★**Hotel Montarto, t** +34 973 63 90 01, *www.montarto.com*, boasts two restaurants, a swimming pool and children's entertainment.

★★★**Hotel Orri, t** +34 973 64 60 86, *www.husa.es*, located in the small village of Tredós 2km from Baqueira, offers free transport to the slopes.

★★**Hotel Tuc Blanc, t** +34 973 64 43 50, *www.hoteltucblanc.com*, is conveniently set at the foot of the slopes.

09

The Top Resorts: Switzerland

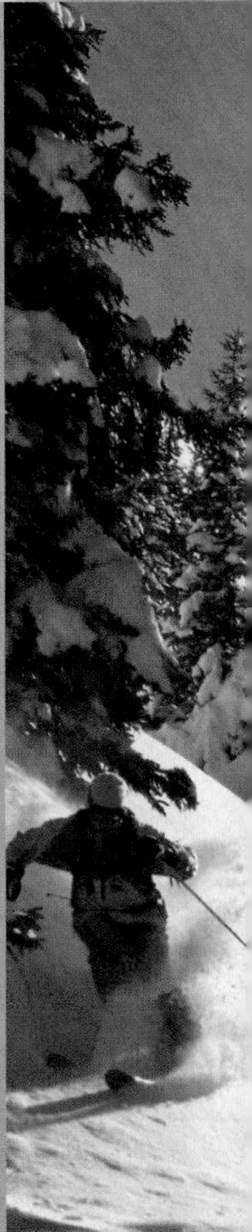

Invest in Switzerland
New releases of fabulous projects in the Swiss Alps
www.investorsinproperty.com
SKI PROPERTY SPECIALISTS SINCE 1986
tel: +44 (0) 20 8905 551
Aletsch Glacier – the "Glacier Village" - newly renovated 3 bedroom chalets from £275,000
Saas Fee – "Residence Mountain Village" - new 3 bedroom apartments from £310,000
Verbier ski area – 4 bedroom chalets from £350,000 in Mayens de Riddes, new project coming up in Les Collons.
Villars – "Le Closel" - 3 bedroom apartments from £325,000 and 4 bedroom chalets from £560,000
Wengen – "Racers Retreat" 3 bedroom duplex apartments from £260,000 near the chairlift at the foot of the Lauberhorn downhill

Andermatt

*BEST FOR

Steep 'n' deep, off the beaten track

ESSENTIALS

Altitude: 1445m (4,740ft)–2965m (9,725ft)

Further information: t +41 (0)41 887 1454, *www.andermatt.ch*

Lifts in area: 35 in Gottard–Oberalp (1 funicular, 3 cableways, 10 chairs, 21 drags) serving 166km of piste

Lift pass: Gottard–Oberalp (covers Andermatt, Oberalp, Sedrun and Disentis) Adult CHF230, youth 13–17yrs CHF173, child 6–12yrs CHF115

Access: Zurich airport 1½hrs, railway station in resort

Profile

Quaint and picturesque non-mainstream resort that is the reserve of serious skiers and riders looking for steep pistes and plenty of challenging powder runs

Resort

Andermatt has a low profile as an international resort, but all that may be about to change. Outside Switzerland it is known only to that dedicated three per cent of skiers whose enjoyment of the sport lies mainly in exploring ungroomed slopes well away from the resort. Its isolated position in the Urseren Valley by the Gotthard pass and road tunnel makes it an unlikely winter destination. However, a wealthy Egyptian businessman has announced plans to build a year-round resort here of a kind never before seen in the Alps. It will include 800 hotel rooms, a golf course, and a pool with a sandy beach. Samih Sawiris, the entrepreneur behind the giant El Gouna resort on the Red Sea, has the backing of the majority of the villagers. However, lengthy planning and environmental hurdles have to be overcome before the idea is transformed into reality.

The Swiss government adopted Andermatt over many years as a major training centre for its alpine troops, who are never likely to fight a war against any of its neighbours. These days, the army presence is much more muted and the military authorities have expressed a willingness to hand over 600,000 square metres of land for Sawaris' scheme.

Mountain

The Gemsstock is the main ski area reached from Andermatt by a two-stage cable-car that takes you up to the top of the Gurschengletscher at 2963m. From here a famous Bernard Russi-designed run brings you all the way back down to Andermatt. Another marginally easier piste takes you down the St Anna glacier to the mid-mountain station, Gurschen.

The separate ski area of Gütsch, reached by a two-stage chair-lift on the other side of the resort and by a train that goes up to the 2044m Oberalppass, is overall less challenging but still has some demanding slopes. Two other areas, Hospental and Realp, provide further advanced and intermediate terrain.

Learn

Snowsports School Andermatt, **t** +41 (0)41 887 1240, is the only learning academy. **Bergschule Uri**, **t** +41 (0)41 872 0900, **Bergschule Montanara**, **t** +41 (0)41 878 1259, and **Alpine Sportschule Gotthard**, **t** +41 (0)41 883 1728, all provide guiding.

Children

Snowsports School Andermatt accepts children from four-and-a-half years.

Lunch

Try **Bergrestaurant Gurschen, t** +41 (0)41 887 1618, for wholesome fare at reasonable prices, and **Bergrestaurant Nätschen-Gütsch, t** +41 (0)41 887 1352.

Dine

The Bahnhofbuffet, t +41 (0)41 888 0050, is recommended. **Tre Passi, t** +41 (0)41 887 0088, is good for venison and wild boar. **Postillion, t** +41 (0)41 887 1044, and **Spycher, t** +41 (0)41 887 1753, are also praised. In Hospental, try **Zum Dörfli, t** +41 (0)41 887 0132.

Party

Baroko Music Bar and **Dancing Gotthard** are the liveliest spots. Others to try are **Ochsen, Barry Bar, Piccadilly Pub** and **Bar La Curva**.

Sleep

- ★★★**Activ Kronen Hotel Andermatt, t** +41 (0)41 887 0088, *www.kronenhotel.ch*, is a family-run hotel.
- ★★★**Drei Könige & Post, t** +41 (0)41 887 0001, *www.3koenige.ch*, is a quiet, central hotel, with a wellness centre.
- ★★★**Monopol-Metropol, t** +41 (0)41 887 1575, *www.monopol-andermatt.ch*, has simple rooms, some with kitchenettes.
- ★★★**Hotel Schweizerhof, t** +41 (0)41 887 1189, *www.schweizerhof-andermatt.ch*, is central and its restaurant specializes in Italian cooking and fondues.
- ★★★**Hotel Sonne, t** +41 (0)41 887 1226, *www.hotelsonneandermatt.ch*, is two minutes' walk from the Gemsstock cable-car.

Crans-Montar

Profile

Large town with smart hotels and elegant boutiques. Suits epicurean intermediates in search of certain snow, and is one of the best resorts for snowboarders

Resort

Skiing began in 1911 in Crans and the adjoining village of Montana when British pioneer Sir Arnold Lunn organized the first genuine downhill in skiing history. He chose this scenic little resort, partly because of its long vertical drop from the Plaine Morte glacier. More importantly, his father Henry had been running golf holidays for the previous five years and had already established the necessary local contacts.

Crans-Montana had already built a reputation from the 1890s as a centre for tuberculosis clinics. During the early days, invalid and sportsman sat uneasily side by side in the resort's cafés and restaurants. Today a large proportion of the hotels still offer health treatments with dietary restaurants and doctors on hand to prescribe treatments, much to the bemusement of young snowboarders who congregate here for some of the best riding facilities in Switzerland.

Crans, Montana and neighbouring Aminona are in an enviable position on a sunny plateau above the Rhône Valley dotted with larches and lakes. However, they have grown together in an urban sprawl along several kilometres of main road that is often clogged with traffic.

✱ BEST FOR
Intermediates, snowboarders, shoppers, ski gourmets

ESSENTIALS
Altitude: 1500m (4,920ft)–3000m (9,840ft)
Further information: t +41 (0)27 485 0404, *www.crans-montana.ch*
Lifts in area: 33 (6 cableways, 6 chairs, 21 drags) serving 140km of piste
Lift pass: adult CHF274, youth 16–19yrs CHF233, child 6–15yrs CHF164, all for 6 days
Access: Sion airport 30 mins, Geneva airport 1½hrs, railway station at Sierre 15km, bus to resort

The fresh alpine air, for which it originally won acclaim, carries more than a healthy share of carbon monoxide. However, a funicular from the valley town of Sierre takes only 12 minutes to reach Crans and has done much to alleviate the traffic problem, particularly at weekends.

Mountain

Crans-Montana is a pleasant family ski area that suits intermediates who are happy to take a few cruising runs amid spectacular scenery before settling down to a long lunch on a sunny terrace. Former 007 Roger Moore, a long-time resident, falls happily into this bracket. It also has good nursery slopes, but advanced skiers will soon tire of the lack of challenging gradients. The only officially graded black run is a bumpy fall-line pitch under the Toula chair that does not really justify its colour. Possible itinerary routes from the Plaine-Morte glacier include an enjoyable run down to the lake at Zeuzier. By walking through tunnels – a torch is needed – and skiing down a summer road, you can reach the ski area of the neighbouring purpose-built resort of Anzère. Novice skiers get a carefree introduction to the sport on nursery slopes served by three drag-lifts on the golf course at Crans.

Crans-Montana and Aminona have terrain parks, and there is a half-pipe at Cry d'Err.

Learn

Swiss Snowsports Schools in Crans, **t** +41 (0)27 485 9370, and Montana, **t** +41 (0)27 481 1480, both have worthy reputations. **Ski & Sky**, **t** +41 (0)27 485 4250, is a much-praised alternative. **Stoked**, **t** +41 (0)27 480 2421, used to be just a dedicated riding academy but now also teaches skiing. **Air Glacier**, **t** +41 (0)27 329 1415, and **Helicopter Services**, **t** +41 (0)27 327 3060, offer heli-skiing.

Children

Fleurs des Champs, **t** +41 (0)27 481 2367, the kindergarten next to Hotel Eldorado in Montana, accepts children from three months to seven years on weekdays only and is recommended. **Zig-Zag**, **t** +41 (0)27 481 2205, also in Montana, takes children from 18 months. The **Jardin des Neiges**, **t** +41 (0)27 481 1480, is at the Grand Signal mid-station, and **Crans Ski School kindergarten**, **t** +41 (0)27 485 9370, is beside the tubing slope.

Lunch

The resort has 13 mountain eateries, including the delightful but expensive **Merbé**, **t** +41 (0)27 481 2297, and **Plumachit**, **t** +41 (0)27 481 2532, which has great atmosphere and food at better prices. **Cabane des Violettes**, **t** +41 (0)27 481 3919, is a genuine touring hut which provides simple meals.

Dine

In Crans try **Nouvelle Rôtisserie**, **t** +41 (0)27 481 1885, and **La Bergerie du Cervin**, **t** +41 (0)27 481 2180, which specializes in raclette, fondue and other cheesy dishes. In Montana, **Gastronomique l'Ours**, **t** +41 (0)27 485 9333, has lots of atmosphere and good food. **La Diligence**, **t** +41 (0)27 485 9985, is renowned for its Middle Eastern cuisine, and **Au Gréni**, **t** +41 (0)27 481 2443, a Roger Moore favourite, serves gourmet fare at film-star prices. **Rhapsodie**, **t** +41 (0)27 481 1155, is new.

Party

Bars include **Punch Bar Cubain**, which has salsa and samba music. **Monk'is Bar** and **Amadeus** are popular, and **New Pub** is on the edge of the lake. Teenagers flock to Montana's **Number Two** for late drinking. **Absolut** and **Le Barocke** are the discos, while **Sporting Club** has dancing.

Sleep

Crans:

★★★★★**Hostellerie du Pas de l'Ours**, **t** +41 (0)27 485 9334, *www.relaischateaux.com*, is a stylish hotel.

★★★★★**Hôtel Royal**, **t** +41 (0)27 481 3931, *www.hotel-royal.ch*, has a wellness centre with a good pool.

★★★★★**Grand Hôtel du Golf**, **t** +41 (0)27 481 4242, *www.grand-hotel-du-golf.ch*, is elegant and discreet.

★★★**Hôtel Mont-Blanc**, **t** +41 (0)27 481 3143, on a hill above Crans, has striking views and 13 spacious bedrooms.

Domaine de la Baronne, **t** +44 (0)870 787 1785, *www.oxfordski.com*, built in the 1950s outside the village, is more Florentine palazzo than Heidi chalet. It sleeps 14 in splendour.

Montana:

★★★**Hôtel St-George**, **t** +41 (0)27 481 2414, *www.hotel-st-george.ch* offers good food and service but small rooms.

★★★**Hôtel de la Prairie**, **t** +41 (0)27 481 4421, is chalet-style with lovely views from the breakfast table.

Davos

Profile

Glorious pistes amid spectacular scenery in the place where alpine skiing began over a century ago. The large town shares its Parsenn ski area with Klosters. Good for snowboarders, and suits all standards of skier

Resort

Davos is a spa town that has a life beyond skiing. Each winter it receives worldwide exposure when global movers and shakers, along with a small army of protesters, gather for the World Economic Forum. While the likes of Blair, Bush and Bill Gates are airing their predictions in the conference centre, skiers and riders are just as importantly engaged on the mighty mountain above.

The Parsenn is one of Europe's classic ski areas, where the sport first developed in the early 1880s when a local businessman imported a pair of the new 'Norwegian snowshoes' from Oslo. They quickly became the teenage rage and a local carpenter busily carved copies. A British

*BEST FOR

Cosmopolitan sophistication, intermediates and experts, off-piste

ESSENTIALS

Altitude: 1560m (5,117ft)–2844m (9,328ft)
Further information: **t** +41 (0)81 415 2121, *www.davos.ch*
Lifts in area: 62 in Davos/Klosters area (4 funiculars, 11 cableways, 9 chairs, 38 drags) serving 370km of piste
Lift pass: adult CHF282, child 6–17yrs CHF94, both for 6 days
Access: Zurich airport 2½hrs, railway station in Davos Dorf and Davos Platz

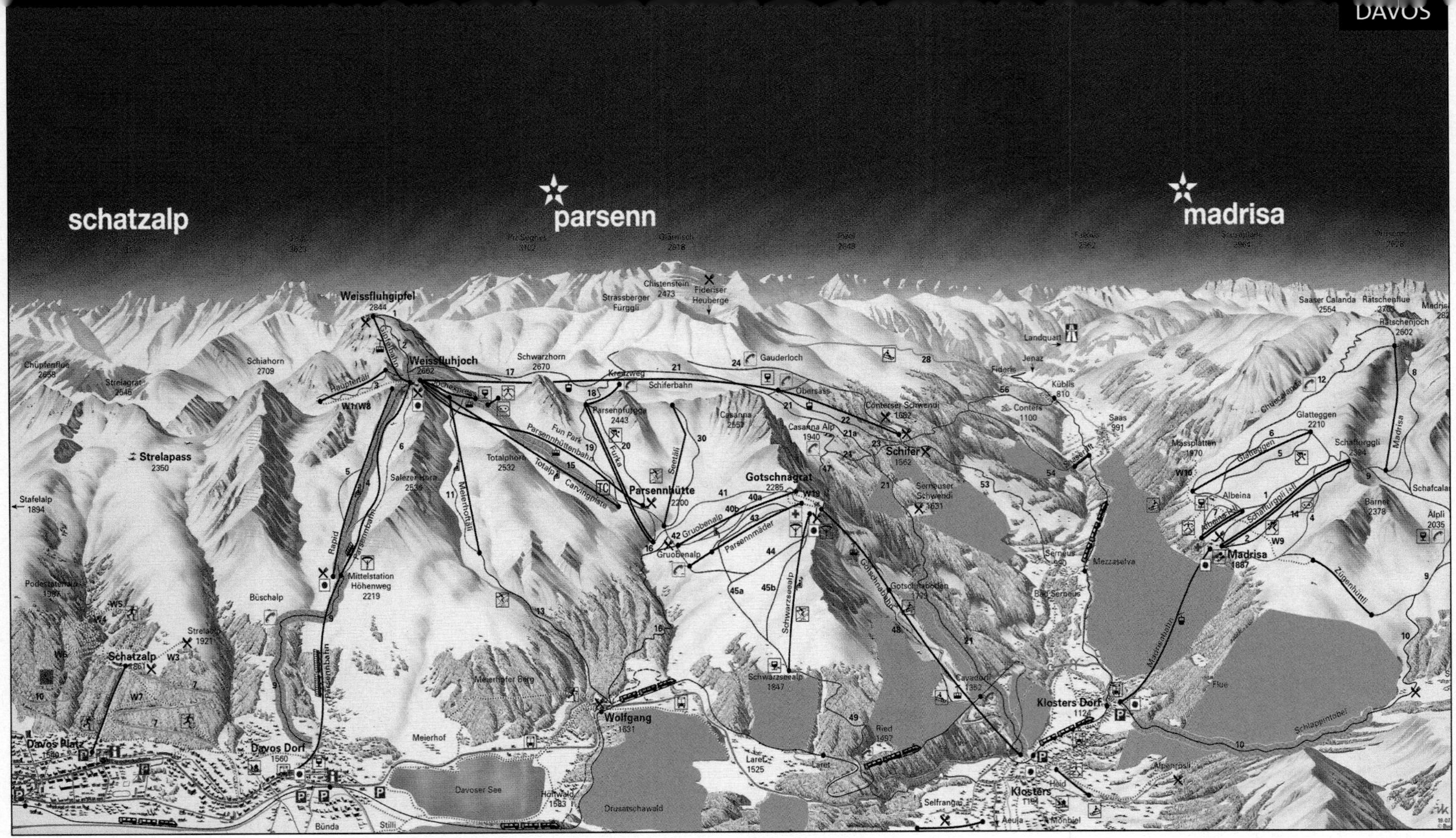
schatzalp
parsenn
madrisa
Weissfluhgipfel
2844
Weissfluhjoch
2662
Schwarzhorn
2670
Schiahorn
2709
Chüpfenflue
2658
Strelagrat
2546
Strelapass
2350
Stafelalp
1894
Schatzalp
1861
Strelaböden
1921
Mittelstation Höhenweg
2219
Büschalp
Salezer Horn
2536
Totalphorn
2532
Parsennfurgga
2443
Parsennhütte
2200
Gotschnagrat
2285
Gruobenalp
Schwarzseealp
1847
Casanna
2557
Casanna Alp
1940
Gauderloch
Obersäss
Kreuzweg
Schiferbahn
Schifer
1562
Conterser Schwendi
1682
Serneuser Schwendi
1631
Gotschnaboden
1772
Cavadürli
1352
Strassberger Fürggli
Chistenstein
2473
Fideriser Heuberge
Landquart
Jenaz
Fideris
Küblis
810
Conters
1100
Saas
991
Serneus
985
Bad Serneus
Mezzaselva
Klosters Dorf
1124
Klosters
1191
Selfranga
Aeuja
Monbiel
Alpenrösli
Flue
Schlappintobel
Madrisa
1887
Albeina
Mässplätten
1970
Glatteggen
2210
Schaffürggli
2394
Bärnet
2378
Älpli
2035
Saaser Calanda
2554
Rätschenflue
Rätschenjoch
2602
Zügenhüttli
Madrisabahn
Gotschnabahn
Parsennbahn
Parsennhüttenbahn
Rapid
Gipfelbahn
Hauptertäli
Meierhoftäli
Fun Park
Carvingpiste
Furka
Seetäli
Parsennmäder
Schwarzseealp
Wolfgang
1631
Meierhof
Davoser See
Hohwald
1583
Drusatschawald
Laret
1525
Ried
1497
Davos Platz
1560
Davos Dorf
1560
Bünda
Stilli
Podestatenalp
1987

woman resident who had lived in Norway showed them how to turn the planks. The trend soon caught the attention of the large foreign community in Switzerland's top sanatorium resort for victims of tuberculosis.

It might have ended there but for the timely presence of the man who was about to become Britain's first ski writer. Arthur Conan Doyle, who created Sherlock Holmes, had brought his terminally ill wife to Davos in the hope of a cure. During the many months of her treatment he became hooked on skiing. He wrote about his experiences in *Strand* magazine and encouraged a whole generation of well-to-do Brits to come out and try skiing for themselves. The Davos English Ski Club built its first refuge for members in 1906.

Many years slipped by before the first mountain railway was built and then in 1934 a local man came up with the invention of the drag-lift within weeks of a similar contraption being designed in Alpe d'Huez in France. Davos never looked back. As antibiotics put the sanatorium business into decline, winter sports became increasingly big business.

The town – the highest in Western Europe – is by no means attractive. Large hotels that are urban rather than alpine in construction and character straggle along the roadside for a couple of kilometres from the railway half of Davos Dorf to Davos Platz. Where you stay is of crucial important to ski convenience. Of the two sectors Davos Dorf is best for skiing, while Davos Platz has most of the shops, restaurants and nightlife. Regular buses run the loop of the one-way system, but it can be a long walk home to Davos Dorf late at night.

Mountain

The Parsenn is the largest and the most famous – but not the only – ski area. Jakobshorn, reached from Davos Platz, is popular with snowboarders. It has two half-pipes, a snowcross course and night-riding. The outlying areas of Pischa and Rinerhorn are both worth visiting when the Parsenn is crowded during peak weeks of the season. This winter, Pischa repositions itself as a dedicated freeride zone with an avalanche training centre and only two prepared pistes.

However, the Parsenn is the main course. Take the recently rebuilt first stage of the Parsennbahn funicular from Davos Dorf, followed by the six-person chair to the Weissfluhjoch for the start of the first run of the day. The alternative slow second stage of the train has yet to be refurbished and should be avoided. From Weissfluhjoch a short cable-car also takes you up a further 180m vertical to the 2844m Weissfluhgipfel, the highest point in the area. A network of lifts and mainly intermediate runs stretches across the mountainside to Klosters. All the different lift companies in the area are now amalgamated and one electronic pass serves the whole region.

From the Weissfluhgipfel you can ski 12km with a 2000m vertical drop down to the farming hamlets of Küblis and Serneus from where you can return to Klosters and then to Davos by train. Anyone who can ski parallel can do it, and in mid-season, when the snow is at its best, it's a great way to end the day.

This is not an ideal resort for complete beginners. Madrisa is too far away (suitable only for Klosters-based skiers). The Bolgen beginner slopes at the bottom of the Jakobshorn are the best bet. Bünda in Davos Dorf is steeper. At the other end of the scale of expertise, the best black run starts from the top of the Parsenn and descends through the Meierhofer Tälli to the hamlet of Wolfgang between Klosters and Davos. Still more demanding itinerary routes on the other side of the Parsenn take you down to Klosters.

In the right snow conditions off-piste opportunities abound and this is a great area for ski-touring. Conan Doyle wrote vividly of crossing the Maienfeld Furka Pass to Arosa, and you can follow in his tracks if you are prepared for a four-hour climb and a three-hour train journey home again. Davos is also big on cross-country skiing with 75km of trails at Jakobshorn as well as in the Dischma and Sertig valleys. Shopping is a major après-ski activity with a wide range of shops as befits a rich town of this international calibre.

Learn

Swiss Snowsportschool, **t** +41 (0)81 416 2454, offers ski and board. **New Trend**, **t** +41 (0)81 413 2040, specializes in off-piste tours with emphasis on the use of safety equipment. **Top Secret Ski & Board Freestyle School**, **t** +41 (0)81 413 4043, and British-run **White Heat**, **t** +44 (0)20 8989 3281, both also concentrate on off-piste instruction.

Children

Swiss Snowsportschool, **t** +41 (0)81 416 2454, is praised for its children's classes from three years on Bolgen and Bünda, with lunch and lifts included in the price, and a **Bobo Wonderland playground**, in both areas. **New Trend**, **t** +41 (0)81 413 2040, accepts children from four years. **Kinderschatzalp**, **t** +41 (0)81 415 5151, and **Wallis Kidsclub**, **t** +41 (0)81 417 9333, are both for kids from three years.

Lunch

Chalet Güggel, **t** +41 (0)81 413 5148, on Jakobshorn is a welcoming mountain hut with the best *Rösti* in the region. **Hotel Kulm**, **t** +41 (0)81 417 0707, built in 1864 in the hamlet of Wolfgang, is a favourite of Prince Charles. **Gallo Rosso** at the Weissfluhjoch, **t** +41 (0)81 417 6611, and **Bruhin's Weissfluhgipfel**, **t** +41 (0)81 417 6644, are both praised.

Dine

Hubli's Landhaus, **t** +41 (0)81 417 1010, which has a Michelin star, the **Magic Mountain**, **t** +41 (0)81 415 3747, in the Waldhotel Bellevue, and the **Stübli**, **t** +41 (0)81 410 1717, in Hotel Flüela, are the gourmet choices. Also try **Zauberberg**, **t** +41 (0)81 415 4201, in Hotel Europe. The **Goldener Drachen**, **t** +41 (0)81 414 9797, is a Chinese eatery in the Hotel Bahnhof Terminus, and **Ahaan-Thai**, **t** +41 (0)81 413 6044, is another Oriental offering in Hotel Stela at Davos Platz. The **Pöstli**, **t** +41 (0)81 415 4500, in the Morosani Posthotel, serves light Swiss cuisine and fish dishes.

Party

Popular bars include **Chämi** and **Ex-Bar**. **Café Schneider** in Davos Platz and **Café Weber** in Davos Dorf are traditional coffee houses with tasty cakes. Europe's largest natural ice rink at Davos Dorf attracts a large après-ski crowd. Swiss league and international ice hockey matches are staged at the Sports Centre. The **Cabanna Club** is the late-night venue. Riders like the disco of the **Hotel Bolgenschanze**.

Sleep

★★★★★**Hotel Steigenberger Belvédère**, **t** +41 (0)81 415 6000, *www.davos.steigenberger.ch*, above Platz, is traditional.

★★★★**Arabella Sheraton Hotel Waldhuus**, **t** +41 (0)81 415 3747, in Platz is chalet-style and family-friendly.

★★★★**Arabella Sheraton Seehof**, **t** +41 (0)81 415 9444, has the fastest internet connection in Switzerland – Bill Gates stays here.

★★★★**ArtHaus Hotel Quisisana**, **t** +41 (0)81 413 5104, *www.arthaushotel.ch*, is inspired by the owner's art collection. All the rooms are individually decorated.

★★★★**Hotel Flüela**, **t** +41 (0)81 410 1717, *www.fluela.ch*, opposite Dorf railway station, has a spa, swimming pool and piano bar.

★★★★**Hotel Sunstar Park**, **t** +41 (0)81 413 1414, *www.sunstar.ch*, receives much repeat booking – the guest book reveals people who have been back eight times.

★★★★**Turmhotel Victoria**, **t** +41 (0)81 417 5300, *www.victoria-davos.ch*, in Dorf, is recommended for its health centre and good food.

★★★★**Waldhotel Bellevue**, **t** +41 (0)81 415 37 47, *www.waldhotel-bellevue.ch*, is a traditional hotel in Platz ('helpful, friendly, and excellent cuisine').

★★★**Hotel Dischma**, **t** +41 (0)81 410 1250, *www.dischma.ch*, is a small, family-run hotel that is 'one bus stop from the Parsennbahn and has excellent food'.

Chalet-Hotel Larix, **t** +41 (0)81 413 1188, *www.hotel-larix.ch*, is an attractive chalet-style hotel run by a British couple. Bedrooms are all individually designed.

Engelberg

Profile

High-altitude snow-sure resort in Central Switzerland within easy reach of Zurich and Luzern that is popular with snowboarders and younger skiers

✱ BEST FOR

Reliable snow-cover, intermediates, off-piste, airport access

ESSENTIALS

Altitude: 1020m (3,346ft)–3028m (9,934ft)
Further information: t +41 (0)41 639 7777, *www.engelberg.ch*
Lifts in area: 25 (1 funicular, 9 gondolas, 8 chairs, 7 drags) serving 82km of piste
Lift pass: adult CHF250, child 6–15yrs CHF100, both for 6 days
Access: Zurich airport 2hrs, railway station in resort

Resort

Engelberg, above the beautiful lakeside city of Luzern, is better known in Calcutta than it is in London or New York. In recent years it has become a location for Bollywood movies. Thousands of Indian fans flock here each summer to tread in the footsteps of their heroes on the flower-decked lower slopes of the 3238m Titlis.

In winter, Engelberg puts away its poppadoms and returns to the familiar guise of traditional ski resort that it first adopted before and immediately after the Second World War when it was one of the most fashionable ski centres in Europe. Engelberg has seen renewed success in recent years – thanks to new lifts, a good snow record, and a concerted effort to attract young snowboarders and freeriders.

Mountain

Beginners and families with small children head for the sunny slopes of Brunni, reached by a cable-car followed by fixed-grip chair from just above the town.

The main Titlis ski area on the other side of town is reached by a modern gondola or a parallel, high-season combination of funicular and cable-car. The second stage of the gondola rises over sheer cliffs to Trübsee at 1800m where a chair-lift conveys you over the frozen lake towards Jochstock at 2564m and the terrain park.

Alternatively you continue on up by cable-car towards the summit of Titlis. The last stage is completed in the Rotair revolving cable-car with panoramic views. Off-piste itineraries include the Laub, a powder bowl with a leg-burning 1120m vertical drop.

Learn

The excellent **Skischule Engelberg-Titlis**, **t** +41 (0)41 639 5454, has the monopoly. **Snowboard School Engelberg**, **t** +41 (0)41 639 5455, and **Boardlocal Snowboard Engelberg**, **t** +41 (0)41 637 0000, are for riders.

Children

Skischule Engelberg-Titlis, **t** +41 (0)41 639 5454, accepts skiers from three years. **Hotel Edelweiss**, **t** +41 (0)41 639 7878, and **Hotel Ramada**, **t** +41 (0)41 639 5858, both have crèches.

Lunch

Titlis-Stübli, **t** +41 (0)41 639 5080, has high-altitude gourmet cuisine, **Untertrübsee**, **t** +41 (0)41 637 1226, and **Ritz**, **t** +41 (0)41 637 2212, at Gerschnialp are both rated for standard cheesy mountain fare. **Brunnihütte**, **t** +41 (0)41 637 3732, at Brunni, produces some good home cooking.

Dine

Spannort, **t** +41 (0)41 637 2626, is traditionally Swiss. **Axels**, **t** +41 (0)41 639 5087, serves French cuisine. **Alpenclub**, **t** +41 (0)41 637 1243, is highly recommended.

Party

Head for **The Spindle**, **The Yucatan** or the smarter **Hotel Eden**.

Sleep

******Ramada Hotel Regina Titlis**, **t** +41 (0)41 639 5858, *www.treff-hotels.de*, is a modern hotel with a swimming pool.

******Hotel Waldegg**, **t** +41 (0)41 637 1822, *www.waldegg-engelberg.ch*, is set well above the town and houses one of the resort's leading restaurants.

*****Hotel Europe – Europaischer Hof**, **t** +41 (0)41 639 7575, *www.hoteleurope.ch*, is in a 1905 Art Nouveau building.

*****Hotel Spannort**, **t** +41 (0)41 637 2626, *www.spannort.ch*, is family-run.

*****Hotel Terrace**, **t** +41 (0)41 639 6666, *www.terrace.ch*, was built in 1904 above the town.

Grindelwald

Profile

Busy and sophisticated village beneath the mighty Eiger that attracts a cosmopolitan crowd to its large and mainly intermediate ski area

Resort

Grindelwald is one of the world's oldest and most cosmopolitan ski resorts. The first British ski pioneers came to this corner of the Bernese Oberland in the 1880s. They were drawn by the awesome beauty of the Eiger, the Schreckhorn and the Wetterhorn that tower above it – and by the newly built rack-and-pinion mountain railway that not only provided easy access but acted as the first ski-lift. Despite its network of cableways, chair- and drag-lifts, the railway still today forms the backbone of the lift system in the linked Jungfrau region that Grindelwald shares with Wengen and Mürren.

***BEST FOR**

Beginners and intermediates, off-piste, mountain scenery

ESSENTIALS

Altitude 943m (3094ft)–2501m (8,206ft)
Further information: t +41 (0)33 854 1212, *www.grindelwald.ch*
Lifts in area: 40 in Jungfrau Top Ski Region (5 funiculars, 5 cableways, 16 chairs, 14 drags) serving 221km of piste
Lift pass: Jungfrau (covers Grindelwald, Mürren, Wengen) adult CHF295, child 6–19yrs CHF148, both for 6 days
Access: Zurich airport 2hrs, Geneva airport 3hrs, railway station in resort

Visitors from all over the world – and Japan in particular – come here to ride the train that rises though the north face of the Eiger to the 3454m Jungfraujoch, the highest station in Europe. Trains run with typical Swiss precision to a printed timetable. New rolling stock is being introduced, but reporters complain that rail is an annoyingly slow means of uphill transport that cuts into skiing time.

Mountain

Grindelwald has its own ski area of First that is reached by gondola from the village. It takes you up to the sunny mid-mountain station of Bort. From Schreckfeld, two drags provide high-altitude novice terrain and a couple of chairs continue up to Oberjoch at 2501m. Most of the skiing is easy intermediate, but a long black run from the top of the Egg drag-lift follows the line of the gondola back to the resort and is of considerable challenge. However, the main ski area is Kleine Scheidegg beneath the north face of the Eiger. Grindelwald shares these intermediate slopes with Wengen and a train runs from the base station at Grund up the mountain and over the shoulder to Wengen on the far side. Halts along the way provide access to runs on both sides. From Kleine Scheidegg itself, on top of the shoulder, a further train or a drag-lift brings you up to the Eigergletscher, the high point of the joint ski area and starting point for two notorious black runs – Blackrock and Oh God. Off-piste opportunities abound, with high-altitude drops possible on the surrounding glaciers and peaks by helicopter and fixed-wing aircraft. This is high alpine terrain and a guide should be used at all times.

A gondola also rises from Grund to the 2230m Männlichen ridge that separates the two resorts. From here you can work your way through a sequence of chair-lifts and easy pistes to the Lauberhorn, starting point for one of the classic World Cup downhill courses. Grindelwald has a terrain park at Bargelegg.

Learn

Grindelwald should be a perfect location for complete novices, but we cannot recommend it because of the restrictive lessons offered by the mainstream **Swiss Ski & Snowboard School, t** +41 (0)33 854 1280. It gives mornings-only group lessons from Sunday to Friday. The other schools are **Offizielle Private Buri Sport, t** +41 (0)33 853 3353, **Kleine Scheidegg, t** +41 (0)33 855 1445, **Privat-Ski.ch, t** +41 (0)79 445 0322, and **Felix Skischule, t** +41 (0)33 853 1288. Guiding is through **Swiss Snowsports and Mountaineering School Grindelwald, t** +41 (0)33 854 1280.

Children

Kinderclub Bodmi, t +41 (0)33 853 5200, cares for non-skiing children from three years in its play area by the nursery slopes. **Kinderhort Sunshine, t** +41 (0)79 632 8178, accepts children from one month old at Männlichen. **Kinderhort Murmeli, t** +41 (0)33 853 0440, at First accepts

Wetterhorn
3701 m 12143 ft
Schreckhorn
4078 m 13380 ft
Eiger
Mönch
Jungfraujoch
Top of Europe
3454 m 11333 ft
Jungfrau
Breithorn
3782 m 12408 ft
Tschingelhorn
Gspaltenhorn
Schilthorn
Piz Gloria
2971 m 9748 ft
Schwarzhorn
2928 m 9607 ft
Gemsberg
Wildgerst
Eismeer
3160 m 10368 ft
Jungfraubahn
Eigerwand
2865 m 9400 ft
Eigergletscher
2320 m 7612 ft
Birg
2676 m
Gr. Scheidegg
1962 m 6434 ft
Stepfi
Pfingstegg
Kl. Scheidegg
2061 m 6762 ft
berjoch
2501 m 8206 ft
Schilt
Hohwald
Bärgelegg
Grindel
First
2168 m 7113 ft
Schreckfeld
Egg
Bort
Waldspitz
Firstbahn
Faulhorn
2681 m 8796 ft
Bussalp
1800 m 5906 ft
Grindelwald
1034 m 3393 ft
Grund
Schwendi
Burglauenen
Lütschental
Alpiglen
Wengernalpbahn
Arven
Lauberhorn
Jumpers Corner
Fallboden
Wixi
Wengernalp
1873 m 6145 ft
Lauberhorn
2473 m 8111 ft
"Lauberhorn Live" Rennstrecke
Brandegg
Hönegg
Gummi
Tschuggen
Männlichen
2230 m 7317 ft
Holenstein
Lager
Männlichenbahn GGM
Männlichen-Gipfel
Männlichenbahn LWM
Allmend
Innerwengen
Slalom Strecke
Bumps
Trümmelbach
Wengen
1274 m 4180 ft
Wengiboden
Wengwald
Schilthornbahn
Engetal
Muttleren
Stellifluh
2232 m
Kandahar
Gimmeln
Schiltgrat
Gimmelwald
1400 m 4593 ft
Allmendhubel
1912 m 6273 ft
Mürren
1634 m 5361 ft
Maulerhubel
Winteregg
Stechelberg
922 m 3025 ft
Schwalmeren
Lauterbrunnen
796 m 2612 ft
Mürrenbahn
Grütschalp
1486 m 4879 ft
Isenfluh
Schynige Platte
1967 m 6454 ft
Zweilütschinen
653 m 2142 ft
Breitlauenen
1542 m 5058 ft
Saxeten
Gsteigwiler
Wilderswil
584 m 1916 ft
Matten
Heimwehfluh
Interlaken West
Interlaken
567 m 1860 ft
Interlaken Ost
Bönigen
Därligen
Leissigen
THUNERSEE
Beatushöhlen
Unterseen
Goldswil
Harder Kulm
Ringgenberg
BRIENZERSEE
Iseltwald
Niederried
Habkern
Waldegg
Vorsass
Beatenberg
1200 m 3940 ft
Beatenbucht
Meiringen - Grimsel - Sustenpass
Brünig - Luzern
Thun - Bern - Lötschberg - Brig - Milano

children from six months. **Felix Skischule** takes children from three years.

Lunch

Brandegg on Kleine Scheidegg, **t** +41 (0)33 853 1057, is world renowned for its apple fritters. **Jagerstübli**, **t** +41 (0)33 853 1131, below Männlichen, is a farmhouse with a cosy atmosphere. **Hotel Aspen**, **t** +41 (0)33 854 4000, above Grund is 'sunny and welcoming'. **Berghaus**, **t** +41 (0)33 853 3651, at Bort, is reasonably priced. **Hotel Wetterhorn**, **t** +41 (0)33 853 1218, on the way down to Grindelwald, is recommended.

Dine

Adlerstube, **t** +41 (0)33 854 7777, in the Sunstar, is family friendly, with a large play area. **La Marmite**, **t** +41 (0)33 853 3553, in Hotel Kirchbühl, **The Derby-Bahnhof**, **t** +41 (0)33 854 5461, and **Schmitte**, **t** +41 (0)33 853 2202, in Hotel Schweizerhof, are recommended. Kreuz & Post's **Challi-Stübli**, **t** +41 (0)33 854 5492, and **Gade**, **t** +41 (0)33 854 1020, in Hotel Eigerblick, are also praised.

Party

'Nightlife is grim', said one reporter. **Downtown Park** has DJs and regular live bands. **Challi-Bar**, **Cava-Bar** and **Espresso** are resort meeting places. **Gepsi-Bar** has live music and attracts an older clientele. **Mescalero** and the **Plaza** are the late-night venues.

Sleep

*****__Grand Regina Alpin WellFit Hotel__, **t** +41 (0)33 854 8600, *www.grandregina.ch*, is decorated with antiques and has a spa.

****__Romantik Hotel Schweizerhof__, **t** +41 (0)33 853 2202, *www.hotel-schweizerhof.com*, was built in 1892 and retains its traditional character.

****__Hotel Kreuz & Post__, **t** (0)33 854 5492, *www.kreuz-post.ch*, has a wellness centre, dancing-bar and good food.

****__Hotel Spinne__, **t** +41 (0)33 854 8888, *www.spinne.ch*, contains three restaurants and a disco.

****__Sunstar-Hotel__, **t** +41 (0)33 854 7777, *www.sunstar.ch/grindelwald*, is opposite the First gondola, has a spa and sleeps 400.

***__Hotel Alpenhof__, **t** +41 (0)33 853 5270, *www.alpenhof.ch*, is piste-side and three minutes' walk from the centre.

***__Hotel Bodmi__, **t** +41 (0)33 853 1220, *www.bodmi.ch*, on the nursery slopes, only accepts individual bookings and no groups ('good for kids, excellent food and friendly staff').

***__Hotel Derby__, **t** +41 (0)33 854 5461, *www.derby-grindelwald.ch*, is family-run and in the town centre.

***__Chalet-Hotel Gletschergarten__, **t** +41 (0)33 853 1721, *www.hotel-gletschergarten.ch*, is close to the piste, with wood-panelled public rooms and suites, and comfortable modern bedrooms.

***__Hotel Hirschen__, **t** +41 (0)33 854 8484, *www.hirschen-grindelwald.ch*, has been in the same family since 1870 and is known for its cooking.

Gstaad

✱ BEST FOR

Wealthy sophisto-cats, ski gourmets, beginners and intermediates

ESSENTIALS

Altitude: 1050m (3,445ft)–2979m (9,744ft)
Further information: t +41 (0)33 748 8737, *www.mountainrides.ch/www.gstaad.ch*
Lifts in area: 62 (15 cableways, 17 chairs, 30 drags) serving 250km of piste
Lift pass: regional Top Card adult CHF266, youth 16–19yrs accompanied by parent CHF171, child 9–15yrs CHF139, all for 6 days
Access: Geneva airport 1½hrs, railway station in resort

Profile

Quaint village with an exclusive hotel and smart chalets that were once the haunt of celebrities, but its low altitude limits snow-cover in these uncertain winters of global warming

Resort

This was once the winter home of the rich and the famous. In the 1970s you could easily find yourself sharing a chair-lift with Liz Taylor, Richard Burton, Julie Andrews or Roger Moore. But times – and more significantly, climates – change. By the standards of 21st-century ski resorts, the skiing is limited in challenge. Nearly half of it is graded as easy. Uncertain snow-cover at this low altitude – last season was a welcome exception – has driven the next generation of celebrities to seek fresh pastures. The village understandably argues that the volume of skiing covered by the regional lift pass compensates for the absence of demanding gradient. Nearby Les Diablerets glacier, which has a top height of 2979m, always provides limited skiing even in the driest winters. Rougemont offers some challenging skiing.

Mountain

Gstaad's own skiing takes place in the separate Wispile and Eggli areas on either side of the village with a top height of less than 2000m. The mainly easy blue runs here and on the other nearby pastures offer limited challenge – and limited snow-cover for much of the winter. Two new chair-lifts at St Stephan and the Chalberhöni speed up the journey.

Ski-buses to the surrounding villages of Saanenmöser and Schönried St Stephan, Zweisimmen, Lauenen, Gsteig, Saanen and Château d'Oex are all included in the regional lift pass.

Terrain parks are located on Eggli, at Hornberg above Saanenmöser, and at Rinderberg above Zweisimmen. More than 140km of cross-country tracks line the valley floor.

Learn

The choice lies between **Gstaad Snowsports, t** +41 (0)33 744 1865, **Snowsports Saanenland, t** +41 (0)33 744 3665, and **Alpinzentrum Gstaad Snowsports, t** +41 (0)33 744 1044.

Children

All the ski schools offer lessons. Babysitting is available through the tourist office.

Lunch

Try the rustic **Chemistube, t** +41 (0)33 722 2240, at the Lengebrand mid-station above St Stephan, **Gobeli, t** +41 (0)33 722 1219, at Rinderberg, **Kübelialp, t** +41 (0)33 744 9898, near the mid-station at

Saanersloch, **Berghaus Rellerli, t** +41 (0)33 748 8722, above Schönried, and **Berghaus Wasserngrat, t** +41 (0)33 748 9622, at Wasserngrat.

Dine

In Gstaad, Robert Speth, former Gault Millau Swiss Chef-of-the-Year, presides over the kitchen in the **Chesery, t** +41 (0)33 744 2451, built in 1962 by the Aga Khan. **Rooster Bar, t** +41 (0)79 481 6561, in Hotel Gstaaderhof, serves Thai food. **Spoon de Neige**, in the sixteenth-century Chlösterli, **t** +41 (0)33 748 7979, is warmly recommended. **Hüsy, t** +41 (0)33 722 1056, in Zweisimmen specializes in fresh fish. Erich Baumer's **Sonnenhof, t** +41 (0)33 744 1023, in Saanen has great food and a warm ambience.

Party

In Gstaad, the Palace Hotel's **GreenGo** nightclub is the place to see and be seen. The locals meet at **Richi's Pub**. Other haunts include **Hush**, managed by Roger Moore's son, Geoffrey, **Stall-Bar Chlösterli**, **La Cave** and **Rialto Bar.**

Sleep

- ★★★★★**Palace Hotel, t** +41 (0)33 748 5000, made famous by Peter Sellers in *The Pink Panther* looks likes a fairy-tale castle.
- ★★★★★**Grand Hotel Park, t** +41 (0)33 748 9800, is the opulent alternative.
- ★★★★**Hotel Bernerhof, t** +41 (0)33 748 8844, is conveniently close to the train station.
- ★★★★**Hotel Christiania, t** +41 (0)33 744 5121, has individually designed bedrooms.
- ★★**Hotel Olden, t** +41 (0)33 744 3444, is family-run and cosy.
- **Posthotel Rössli, t** +41 (0)33 748 4242, *www.posthotelroessli.ch*, is in the village centre and has pine-panelled rooms and a restaurant which serves traditional local fare.

Klosters

Profile

Attractive traditional resort that shares the Parsenn ski area with Davos. Well-groomed slopes for intermediates and tough off-piste, along with some memorable mountain restaurants

Resort

Despite its high international profile largely created by the annual visits of Prince Charles and his sons, Klosters clings tenaciously to its roots as a typical Swiss alpine village that combines tourism with the more serious business of farming. Unlike Davos, its much larger and more cosmopolitan sister that shares the Parsenn ski area, Klosters entertains fame and embraces fortune but has never knowingly sought either. Of course, this unassuming air is exactly what attracts people like Prince Charles and the wealthy bankers from Zurich's Bahnhofstrasse who form an important part of its up-market clientele. The farming community has been welcoming tourists ever since the first British skiers showed up here in 1904, drawn by the steeper ski slopes at this end of the Parsenn.

Like Davos, the resort is divided into two sectors. Klosters Platz around the main railway station is the village centre, with most of the hotels, shops and restaurants, and access to the Parsenn. Klosters Dorf, also on the railway line but a couple of kilometres away, is a more remote outpost around the base of the Madrisa gondola. A regular bus service connects the two. The regional lift pass also includes the outlying and separate ski areas of Rinerhorn, Jakobshorn and

* BEST FOR

All levels of skier and rider, off-piste, mountain restaurants

ESSENTIALS

Altitude: 1192m (3,911ft)–2844m (9,328ft)
Further information: **t** +41 (0)81 410 2020, *www.klosters.ch*
Lifts in area: 53 in Davos/Klosters area (2 funiculars, 13 cableways, 9 chairs, 29 drags) serving 370km of piste
Lift pass: adult CHF282, child 6–17yrs CHF94, both for 6 days
Access: Zurich airport 2½hrs, railway stations in Klosters Dorf and Klosters Platz

Pischa. The latter has repositioned itself this season as a dedicated freeride zone with only two of the pistes being groomed on a regular basis. Trains between Klosters and Davos are also included in the pass.

Mountain

Klosters' own area, Madrisa, has some of the best beginner slopes in this part of Switzerland but is too often dismissed as just a novice ski area. A painfully slow gondola followed by two more lifts brings you to the start of Prince Charles' favourite run – follow the piste to the Alpi hut, fork left on to the steep black No.10 on the map. A long path by a dramatic river gully brings you back to the gondola base. From the top of Madrisa you can ski, with a guide, to Gargellen in Austria.

For most skiers and riders the Parsenn is the main course. Mountain access from Klosters Platz is by the two-stage Gotschna cable-car. Much the most challenging pistes and itinerary routes are to be found at this end of the Parsenn. Several spectacular and demanding runs such as the usually wickedly mogulled Drostobel lead down through the trees to Klosters.

A network of lifts and pistes takes you across the Parsenn to the Weissfluhjoch above Davos and the still higher 2844m Weissfluhgipfel. From here you can ski 12km through 2000m vertical down to the outlying villages of Küblis and Serneus. It's a fine way to end the day, with a drink at the bottom before catching the train back up the valley to Klosters.

Snowboarders find a frustrating number of flats in the centre of the Parsenn. They congregate in the separate Davos ski area of Jakobshorn which has a terrain park, two half-pipes and a snowcross course.

Learn

Saas Ski and Snowboard School, **t** +41 (0)81 420 2233, has mainly young instructors speaking fluent English. **Swiss Snowsports School**, **t** +41 (0)81 410 2828, is the competition. **Boardriding Klosters**, **t** +41 (0)81 420 2662, and **Bananas**, **t** +41 (0)81 422 6660, are the boarding specialists. Guiding is with **Adventure Skiing**, **t** +41 (0)81 422 4825, **Berger Jürg**, **t** +41 (0)81 422 3636, and through the ski schools.

Children

Kids Land t +41 (0)81 410 2170 at Madrisa is for non-skiers from two years, while the **Snow Garden**, **t** +41 (0)81 410 2828, based in the Sports Centre at Klosters Platz, is for skiers over four years.

Lunch

Berghaus Erika, **t** +41 (0)81 422 1117, in the hamlet of Schlappin on the black run down from Madrisa, is warmly recommended for its *Rösti*. Reporters complain that the famous Schwendi Houses, rustic huts on the Parsenn, have dropped their standards and are overpriced. Best bet is the **Schwendi Ski und Berghaus**, **t** +41 (0)81 422 1289. **Gotschna**, **t** +41 (0)81 422 1428, at Serneus, is a welcome sight after the long run down. **Schifer Berghaus**, **t** +41 (0)81 332 1533, has good food and a cheerful atmosphere.

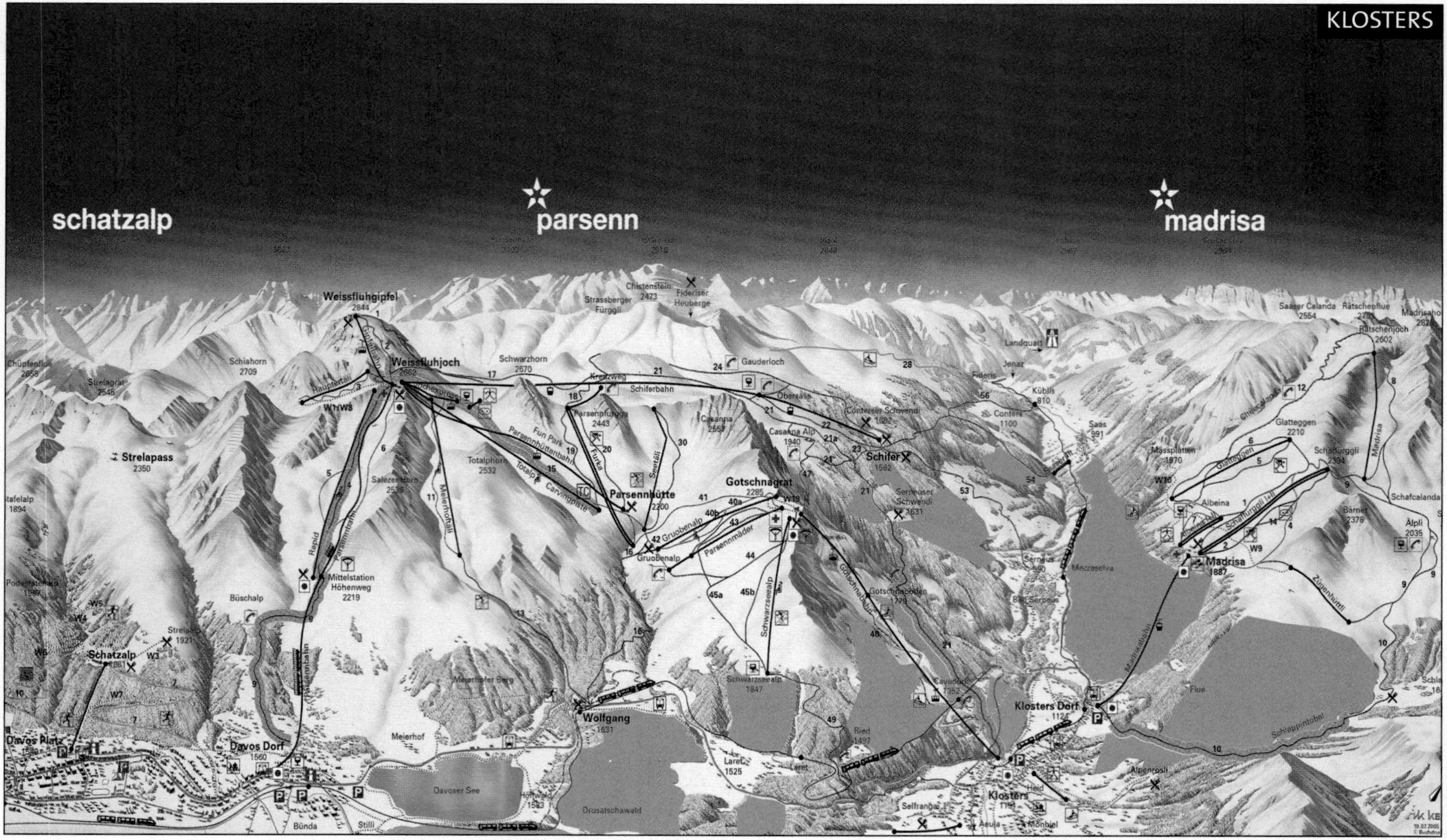
schatzalp
parsenn
madrisa
Weissfluhgipfel
2844
Weissfluhjoch
2662
Schiahorn
2709
Strelagrat
2546
Strelapass
2350
Schwarzhorn
2670
Strassberger Fürggli
Chistenstein
2473
Fideriser Heuberge
Gauderloch
Kreuzweg
Schiferbahn
Parsennfurgga
2443
Casanna
Casanna Alp
1940
Conterser Schwendi
Schifer
1662
Fun Park
Parsennhüttenbahn
Totalphorn
2532
Totalp
Carvingpiste
Furka
Parsennhütte
2200
Gotschnagrat
2285
Gruobenalp
Parsennmäder
Schwarzseealp
1847
Serneuser Schwendi
Gotschnaboden
Gotschnabahn
Cavadürli
Klosters Dorf
1124
Klosters
Selfranga
Aeuja
Monbiel
Alpenrösli
Landquart
Jenaz
Fideris
Küblis
810
Conters
1100
Saas
991
Serneus
Mezzaselva
Madrisabahn
Madrisa
1887
Albeina
Mässplatten
1970
Glatteggen
2210
Schaffürggli
2394
Saaser Calanda
2564
Rätschenflue
Rätschenjoch
2602
Schafcalanda
Bärnet
2378
Älpli
2035
Zügenhüttli
Schlappintobel
Flue
Mittelstation Höhenweg
2219
Rapid
Parsennbahn
Salezer Horn
Meierhoftäli
Büschalp
Schatzalp
1861
Strelaalp
1921
Davos Platz
Davos Dorf
1560
Meierhofer Berg
Meierhof
Davoser See
Wolfgang
1631
Drusatschawald
Laret
1525
Ried
1497
Bünda
Stilli
Hörnli
Chüpfenflue
2658
Podestatenalp
tafelalp
1894
Obersäss
Seetäli
Hauptertäli

Dine

Celebrity chef Beat Bolliger runs his Michelin-starred restaurant in **Hotel Walserhof**, **t** +41 (0)81 410 2929, which is the top dining spot in town. In high season you must book well in advance. **Chesa Grischuna**, **t** +41 (0)81 422 2222, maintains a high standard. The **Wynegg**, **t** +41 (0)81 422 1340, serves wholesome mountain fare in pleasant surroundings.

Party

The **Gotschnabar**, next to the cable-car station, has been totally rebuilt and is the latest après-ski meeting point. **Steinbock Bar**, **Chesa Grischuna**, and the **Piano Bar** in the Silvretta Parkhotel are usually lively. Later on, Prince Harry's favourite, **Casa Antica**, is the hotspot. Try also **Kir Royal**, the **Rössli Bar**, and the **Mountain Pub** in Klosters Dorf.

Sleep

******Hotel Alpina**, **t** +41 (0)81 410 2424, *www.alpina-klosters.ch*, is a well-positioned hotel with a small swimming pool and a restaurant serving 'creative cooking'.

******Chesa Grischuna**, **t** +41 (0)81 422 2222, *www.chesagrischuna.ch*, has been welcoming guests since 1938, and retains its rustic style.

******Eugenia**, **t** +44 (0)20 7384 3854, *www.descent.co.uk*, is a handsome villa with vast bedrooms, oak-panelled walls, beautiful marble and stripped wood floors, and impressive pillared fireplaces.

******Hotel Pardenn**, **t** +41 (0)81 423 2020, *www.pardenn.ch*, is central yet quiet, with a swimming pool and a restaurant that has vegetarian options.

******Hotel Vereina**, **t** +41 (0)81 410 2727, *www.vereinahotel.ch*, has more suites than bedrooms, a huge pool and exquisite basement spa.

******Hotel Walserhof**, **t** +41 (0)81 410 2929, *www.walserhof.ch*, has an excellent restaurant and royal patronage.

******Silvretta Parkhotel**, **t** +41 (0)81 423 3435, *www.silvretta.ch*, has large rooms, a wellness centre and children's Flipper Club.

*****Hotel Rustico**, **t** +41 (0)81 410 2288, *www.the-rustico-klosters.ch*, has bedrooms that are individually decorated and serves Asian-Japanese food in its restaurant.

Hotel Wynegg, **t** +41 (0)81 422 1340 is a cosy old hotel run along the lines of a large chalet for its mainly British guests.

Laax

Profile

One of Switzerland's largest and most snow-sure ski areas that is virtually unknown internationally. Good choice of hotels, popular with snowboarders, but not the best resort for non-skiers

Resorts

Flims and neighbouring Laax in the Graubunden have been spa resorts since the 1880s and ski resorts since 1962 when

* BEST FOR

High-mileage skiers and riders, families, big vertical drop

ESSENTIALS

Altitude: 1100m (3,609ft)–3018m (9,902ft)
Further information: **t** +41 (0)81 927 7001, *www.laax.com*
Lifts in area: 27 (11 cableways, 8 chairs, 8 drags) serving 220km of piste
Lift pass: CHF309, child 6–17yrs CHF103, both for 6 days
Access: Zurich airport 1½hrs

the glacier above them was first developed for skiing. Together with the picturesque farming village of Falera, they form what is now called LAAX, one of the largest ski circuits in the Alps.

Flims is made up of the two quite separate hamlets of Flims Dorf ('ski convenient') and Flims Waldhaus ('isolated from the ski area, but better choice of hotels'). Laax is also a bus ride away from the lifts but has Laax Murschetg, a more ski-friendly satellite built around the base station. Murschetg has become a serious destination for snowboarders who congregate at the Riders' Palace hotel. Falera is a much smaller and more rural community, but with a direct lift link into the system. A ski-bus connects all the accommodation and base stations.

Mountain

The skiing takes place on the 3018m Vorab Glacier and on the slopes of four other interconnected peaks. Much of it is above the treeline and suited to skiers of all standards, but particularly intermediates in search of long cruising runs. There is also plenty of steeper terrain, divided by bands of rock and steep gullies in the Siala and Cassons sectors. A long itinerary from the glacier descends 2000m to the remote hamlet of Ruschein Ladir.

The top of the glacier is the starting point for the annual Weisse Schuss, a 14km pro-am downhill race that ends in Flims Dorf. The undulating FIS downhill course from Crap Sogn Gion down to Laax–Murschetg provides plenty of scope for boy and girl races, but no great technical difficulty when not prepared for racing. A more challenging descent is the Platt'Alva itinerary from Nagens or the black Sattel from Voralb down to Alp Ruschein.

Laax attracts a high percentage of snowboarders who gather at the terrain parks and half-pipes on the glacier and at Crap Sogn. It is also a major centre for cross-country skiing with trails along the valley from Flims and through the nearby villages of Trin and Sagogn. Higher-altitude loipe are also located in the Bargis Valley.

Learn

The mainstream **Snowsports School**, t +41 (0)81 927 7171, and **Snowboard Fahrschule**, t +41 (0)81 927 7155, have branches in Flims, Laax and Falera.

Other schools in Flims Dorf are **Alpine Action Unlimited**, t +41 (0)81 936 7474, **EuroBoard**, t +41 (0)81 281 8183, **EuroSki**, t +41 (0)79 683 5642, **Rock and Snow**, t +41 (0)78 679 7153, **Roland Tuchschmid**, t +41 (0)79 742 6677, **Touchdown** t +41 (0)78 830 5960, and **Yetis**, t +41 (0)79 635 3767.

Other schools in Flims Waldhaus are **Mountain Fantasy**, t +41 (0)81 936 7077, and **Swissraft**, t +41 (0)81 911 5250. In Laax, **Inspiraziun Grischun**, t +41 (0)76 391 6894, is recommended.

Children

Swiss Snowsports School, t +41 (0)81 927 7171, runs a kindergarten for children from two years, with ski lessons from four years. **Park Hotels Waldhaus**, t +41 (0)81 928 4848, and **Hotel Adula**, t +41 (0)81 928 2828, both run crèches for guests. In Flims Dorf, **Annina Hägler**, t +41 (0)79 791 5221, runs a non-ski kindergarten.

Lunch

Try **Startgels Alpenrose**, t +41 (0)81 911 5848, **Naraus Enzian**, t +41 (0)81 911 5878, **Segneshütte**, t +41 (0)81 927 9925, and **Cassonsgrat Edelweiss**, t +41 (0)81 911 5898. **Capalari Mountain Hostel**, t +41 (0)81 927 7373, at Crap Sogn Gion is recommended. **Elephant**, **t** +41 (0)81 927 7390, at Crap Masegn and **Tegia Larnags**, **t** +41 (0)81 927 9910, are the gourmet choices.

Dine

Recommended restaurants include **La Clav**, **t** +41 (0)81 928 2828, in Hotel Adula, and **Clavau Vegl**, **t** +41 (0)81 911 3644, in Flims Dorf, for regional specialities. Pizzeria **Pomodoro**, **t** +41 (0)81 911 1062, and **Pizzeria La Dolce Vita**, **t** +41 (0)81 928 1440, in Flims Waldhaus, are singled out. In Laax, **Romana**, **t** +41 (0)81 921 5055, specializes in Balkan cuisine and **Riva**, **t** +41 (0)81 921 5353, has good cheese dishes. **Casa Seeli**, **t** +41 (0)81 921 30 48, in Falera, is praised.

Party

In Flims Dorf, **Iglu Music Bar** and **Legna Bar** are the main rendezvous. **Living-room Flims** is less frenetic. In Flims Waldhaus, **Bellavista Bistro Bar** is popular. In Laax, **Casa Veglia** is the disco favourite with occasional live concerts. **Riders Palace Club and Lobby** at the Riders Palace DesignHotel is where snowboarders congregate for parties, concerts and shows. The **Crap Bar** is also rated.

Sleep

Flims:

*****Park Hotel Waldhaus**, **t** +41 (0)81 928 4848, *www.parkhotel-waldhaus.ch*, is a giant hotel complex set in five buildings linked by underground walkways.

****Hotel Adula**, **t** +41 (0)81 928 2828, *www.adula.ch*, in Flims Dorf, has good children's facilities and La Mira spa.

****Albana Sporthotel**, **t** +41 (0)81 927 2333, *www.albana-flims.ch*, is convenient for the slopes.

****Sunstar Hotel Surselva**, **t** +41 (0)81 928 1800, *www.sunstar.ch/flims*, in Waldhaus, has a swimming pool and wellness centre. Children under 16 years pay only CHF1 per year of age per night.

***Ayurveda-Wohlfühlhotel Fidazerhof**, **t** +41 (0)81 920 9010 in Fidaz, has minimalist-design rooms and a spa offering Ayurvedic treatments.

Laax:

***Hotel Posta Veglia**, **t** +41 (0)81 921 4466, *www.poestlilaax.ch*, has panelled rooms with hand-painted furniture.

***Hotel La Siala**, **t** +41 (0)81 927 2222, *www.lasiala.ch*, in the farming hamlet of Falera, has an indoor swimming pool.

***Riders Palace DesignHotel**, **t** +41 (0)81 927 9700, *www.riderspalace.com*, is an unusual blend of designer hotel and backpacker hostel with different rooms for different budgets.

Mürren

Profile

Chocolate-box pretty, car-free village with some steep skiing for strong intermediates and advanced skiers. Not the ideal resort for beginners

*BEST FOR

Car-free village, mountain scenery, intermediates and advanced skiers

ESSENTIALS

Altitude: 1650m (5,412ft)–2971m (9,748ft)
Further information: **t** +41 (0)33 856 8686, *www.wengen-muerren.ch*
Lifts in area: 13 (2 railways, 2 cableways, 5 chairs, 4 drags); 40 in Jungfrau Top Ski Region serving 221km of piste
Lift pass: Jungfrau (covers Grindelwald, Mürren, Wengen) adult CHF295, child 6–19yrs CHF148, both for 6 days
Access: Zurich airport 3hrs, Geneva airport 4hrs, railway station in resort

Resort

Back in 1911, Henry Lunn, an entrepreneurial lawn tennis equipment salesman, launched a new career for himself as the first ski package tour operator in this delightful Swiss village located high above Lauterbrunnen in the Bernese Oberland.

He persuaded the Jungfrau Railway to keep the line open during the winter, rented the Palace Hotel and asked the 'right' sort of Englishmen – those who had been privately educated – to come and join him. He never actually skied himself. His son Sir Arnold, founder of modern ski racing – and, in turn, his son Peter – continued the association. Sir Arnold's Kandahar Ski Club made its home here in 1922 and a strong relationship with Britain has continued until the present day.

The car-free village is the perfect example of a quaint Swiss alpine community with Heidi-esque chalets and dramatic views of the Eiger, the Mönch and the Jungfrau. The village is perched on a balcony 550m above the valley and is reached either by a funicular and mountain railway from Lauterbrunnen, or by cable-car from Stechelberg and Gimmelwald. Mürren shares its lift pass with Wengen and Grindelwald, which can be reached by train. However, distances are big and the trains are slow. Most Mürren-based skiers tend to remain in their own 13-lift territory dominated by the 2970m Schilthorn.

Mountain

The skiing here suits most standards – but, despite the vociferous protestations of committed Mürrenites, there is not much of it. A chair-lift from the edge of the village and a drag above serve undulating intermediate runs on the 2145m Schiltgrat. A funicular from the village gives access to a nursery slope at Allmendhubel and further reds as well as an easy blue back to the village. The Winteregg sector, reached by train from Mürren or by piste and chair from Allmendhubel, has easy, open pistes. In good snow conditions it is possible to ski all the way down to Lauterbrunnen.

Serious skiers and riders take the cable-car from the village up to Birg and then the final stage to the Piz Gloria revolving restaurant on the 2970m summit of the Schilthorn. The black descent is one of the classic runs of the Alps and starting point for the annual pro-am Inferno Race, which goes down to Winteregg or even Lauterbrunnen when conditions permit. The top section can become heavily mogulled later in the day. The Muttlern and Kandahar chairs beneath Obere Hubel, allow further skiing without having to descend to the cable-car.

Off-piste opportunities abound, but it's essential to take a guide. Tschingel-Chrachen off the Schilthornbahn is steep and technically demanding, but prone to avalanche. Others include Hidden Valley from the summit of the Maulerhubel to Grutsch, and the Blumental.

Learn

The **Swiss Ski and Snowboard School**, **t** +41 (0)33 855 1247, has no competition, but the level of instruction is surprisingly high. Group ski lessons are limited to two hours each morning from Monday to Saturday. Snowboard group lessons are afternoon-only, from Monday to Friday.

Children

Snowgarten, t +41 (0)33 856 8686, behind Hotel Jungfrau, cares for non-skiing children from 18 months to five years with free nappies and a pick-up service from hotels on request.

Wetterhorn
Schreckhorn
Eiger
Mönch
Jungfraujoch
Top of Europe
3454 m 11333 ft
Jungfrau
Breithorn
Tschingelhorn
Gspaltenhorn
Schilthorn
Piz Gloria
2971 m 9748 ft
Schwarzhorn
2928 m 9607 ft
Gemsberg
Wildgerst
Eismeer
Eigerwand
Eigergletscher
2320 m 7612 ft
Birg
2676 m
Gr. Scheidegg
1962 m 6434 ft
berjoch
2501 m 8206 ft
Schilt
Stepfi
Pfingstegg
Kl. Scheidegg
2061 m 6762 ft
Salzegg
Alpiglen
Wengernalpbahn
Brandegg
First
2168 m 7113 ft
Schreckfeld
Hohwald
Bort
Waldspitz
Faulhorn
2681 m 8796 ft
Egg
Firstbahn
Lauberhorn
2473 m 8111 ft
"Lauberhorn Live" Rennstrecke
Fallboden
Wixi
Wengernalp
1873 m 6145 ft
Tschuggen
Männlichen
2230 m 7317 ft
Holenstein
Läger
Männlichenbahn GGM
Männlichen-Gipfel
Männlichenbahn LWM
Allmend
Innerwengen
Slalom Strecke
Trümmelbach
Wengen
1274 m 4180 ft
Wengiboden
Wengwald
Bussalp
1800 m 5906 ft
Grindelwald
1034 m 3393 ft
Grund
Schwendi
Burglauenen
Lütschental
Schynige Platte
Gimmelwald
1400 m 4593 ft
Mürren
1634 m 5361 ft
Stechelberg
922 m 3025 ft
Allmendhubel
1912 m 6273 ft
Maulerhubel
Winteregg
Schwalmeren
Stellifluh
Muttleren
Engetal
Schilthornbahn
Lauterbrunnen
796 m 2612 ft
Mürrenbahn
Grütschalp
1486 m 4379 ft
Isenfluh
Zweilütschinen
653 m 2142 ft
Breitlauenen
Saxeten
1102 m 3615 ft
Gsteigwiler
Wilderswil
584 m 1916 ft
Heimwehfluh
Matten
Interlaken West
Interlaken
567 m 1860 ft
Interlaken Ost
Därligen
Leissigen
Beatushöhlen
THUNERSEE
Beatenberg
1200 m 3940 ft
Vorsass
Waldegg
Unterseen
Harder Kulm
Goldswil
Bönigen
Iseltwald
BRIENZERSEE
Ringgenberg
Niederried
Habkern
Meiringen - Grimsel - Sustenpass
Brünig - Luzern
Thun - Bern - Lötschberg - Brig - Milano

Lunch

The revolving **Piz Gloria**, **t** +41 (0)33 826 0007, on the summit of the Schilthorn, was made famous in the 1968 Bond film, *On Her Majesty's Secret Service*, and is worth a visit even if the views are more spectacular than the cuisine. The **Schilthornhütte**, **t** +41 (0)78 788 5767, on the way down, serves simple mountain fare. **Gimmelen**, **t** +41 (0)33 855 1366, is renowned for its cheesy dishes and *Apfelkuchen*. **Sonnenberg**, **t** + 41 (0)33 855 1127, is praised for its *Rösti*. **Suppenalp**, **t** +41 (0)33 855 1726, has a sunny terrace and good food.

Dine

Hotel Eiger Stübli, **t** + 41 (0)33 856 5454, **Hotel Alpenruh**, **t** +41 (0)33 856 8800, and the **Eiger Guesthouse**, **t** +41 (0)33 856 5460, are all recommended, along with **Hotel Edelweiss**, **t** +41 (0)33 856 5600, and the **Stägerstübli**, **t** +42 (0)33 855 1316. **Kandahar Snack**, **t** +41 (0)33 855 8695, offers good light meals.

Party

The **Ballon Bar** in the Anfi Palace, **The Pub** in the Eiger Guesthouse and the **Tächi Bar** in Hotel Eiger are the main evening meeting places. The **Blüemlichäller** disco in Hotel Blumental and **The Inferno** disco in the Anfi Palace are crowded in high season.

Sleep

★★★★**Anfi Palace**, **t** +41 (0)33 856 9999, *www.muerren.ch/palace*, dates back to the Edwardian days of Henry Lunn, when it housed its first tourists.

★★★★**Hotel Eiger**, **t** +41 (0)33 856 5454, *www.hoteleiger.com*, across the road from the railway station, is the only hotel with its own indoor pool.

★★★**Hotel Alpenruh**, **t** +41 (0)33 856 8800, *www.hotelschilthorn.ch*, at the Schilthornbahn end of the village, has a good restaurant and great views.

★★★**Hotel Blumental**, **t** +41 (0)33 855 1826, *www.muerren.ch/blumental*, has been recently renovated.

★★★**Hotel Edelweiss**, **t** +41 (0)33 856 5600. *www.edelweiss-muerren.ch*, is friendly and well positioned ('excellent views and food').

★★★**Hotel Jungfrau**, **t** +41 (0)33 856 6464, *www.hoteljungfrau.ch*, is a friendly place, with an annexe called Haus Mönch across the road.

★**Eiger Guesthouse**, **t** +41 (0)33 856 5460, formerly the Belmont, has Swiss-Scottish owners, low prices and a relaxed atmosphere.

Saas-Fee

Profile

Traditional village offering year-round glacier skiing. Terrain is best suited to beginners, low intermediates and ski tourers. Popular resort for snowboarding

Resort

Saas-Fee is an ancient village in a supreme high-altitude setting, surrounded by a horseshoe of no less than 13 peaks of 4000m. Blackened chalets interspersed with modern hotels, fashion boutiques and ski shops line its narrow car-free streets. Its high altitude allows skiing on the glacier from the beginning

*BEST FOR

Guaranteed snow-cover, beginners to low intermediates, snowboarders

ESSENTIALS

Altitude: 1800m (5,905ft)–3600m (11,810ft)
Further information: t +41 (0)27 958 1858, *www.saas-fee.ch*
Lifts in area: 22 (1 funicular, 7 cableways, 1 chair, 13 drags) serving 100km of piste
Lift pass: Saasertal (covers Saas-Fee, Saas-Grund, Saas-Almagell, and Bahlen) adult CHF341, child 6–16yrs CHF208, both for 6 days
Access: Geneva airport 4hrs, Sion airport 1½hrs, railway station at Visp or Brig, hourly bus connection

of July through to the start of the winter season in November. Despite its year-round tourism, Saas-Fee somehow manages to maintain an innocent charm often lacking in major resorts. The handful of powerful village families who still run it have been known to favour image over commercial gain. The resort once famously reneged on its lucrative contract to stage the British University Ski Championships over worries that the alcoholic après-ski intake of contestants and supporters might upset the sensibilities of older guests. You can still buy fresh milk by the pail, the lift system is modern and efficient, and it has some of the best nursery slopes in Switzerland.

However, such alpine bliss has its drawbacks. The glacial terrain is as hostile as it is beautiful. Much of the mountainside is littered by giant *séracs* and wide crevasses that beckon anyone who is foolish enough to leave the marked piste without a local guide. Such treacherous topography means that the pistes themselves are inevitably limited in scope and reporters complain that for a resort of this size there is simply not enough skiing or riding for a whole week. The separate outlying hamlets of Saas-Almagell and Saas-Grund provide a little more variety. Saas-Fee also has a whole mountain, served by a gondola, that is reserved for tobogganing. Cars must be left in car parks on the outskirts of the resort and transport is confined to electric ski-buses and taxis.

Mountain

Access is by cable-cars from either end of the resort, which take you to the mid-mountain station of Morenia. A further cable-car continues to 3000m Felskinn, starting point for the Metro-Alpin, the world's highest underground funicular. This brings you up to Allalin at 3500m, just below the highest point of the ski area. A gondola from the village, followed by a cable-car and a sequence of drag-lifts, provides a slower alternative passage to the top of the mountain. Despite the full range of colour codings, neither of the main routes back down offers much challenge. A network of other lifts – mainly drag-lifts because of the itinerant nature of the glacier – gives access to more short runs. The separate Plattjen sector, reached by gondola from the village, provides more intermediate skiing and a floodlit piste for night-skiing. Saas-Fee has a terrain park and half-pipe served by the Mittaghorn drag reached from Morenia. There is also a half-pipe and snowcross course in the summer ski area.

Learn

In the past, the overtly staid **Swiss Ski and Snowboard School**, **t** +41 (0)27 957 2348, has had the monopoly for skiing, but the **Eskimo Snowboard School**, **t** +41 (0)27 957 4904, now has a ski division which is warmly recommended. The Swiss school has been heavily criticized for being old-fashioned and not keeping abreast of modern technique. However, the standard of teaching is said to be much improved and most instructors speak good English.

Children

Murmeli, t +41 (0)27 957 4057, in Hotel Artemis offers daycare for children aged one month to six years, and **Glückskäfer**, t +41 (0)79 225 8154, provides babysitting in your hotel or apartment.

Lunch

The **Metro-Alpin** revolving restaurant, t +41 (0)957 1771, at Mittelallalin, has great views and average food. **Berghaus Plattjen**, t +41 (0)79 566 6926, serves fine *Rösti*. Try also **Egginer Morenia**, t +41 (0)957 1881, **Längfluh**, t +41 (0)957 2132, and the **Gletschergrotte**, t +41 (0)957 2160. Many skiers return to the village at lunch-time.

Dine

Vernissage, t +41 (0) 27 958 1904, restaurant and après-ski complex was opened last season by avant-garde Zermatt artist and designer Heinz Julen. **Cheminée**, t +41 (0) 27 957 2748, **Cäsar Ritz**, t +41 (0)27 958 1900, in the Ferienart Resort, and the Michelin-rated **Fletschhorn Waldhotel**, t +41 (0)27 957 2131, are warmly recommended. **Boccalino**, t +41 (0)27 957 1731, and **Don Ciccio**, t +41 (0)27 957 4020, are good pizzerias.

Party

Après-ski is wild. Busy bars include **Alpen-Pub**, **Happy Bar**, **Metro-Bar**, **Nesti's Ski-Bar** and **Hozwurm**. Later on the action switches to **Vernissage**, **Crazy Night**, **John's Pub** and **Popcorn The Snowboard Joint** in Hotel Dom.

Sleep

- ★★★★★**Ferienart Resort & Spa**, t +41 (0)27 958 1900, has six restaurants and a new health-and-fitness centre.
- ★★★★**Hotel Metropol**, t +41 (0)27 957 1001, is run on Feng-Shui principles with bio and Finnish saunas as well as a disco.
- ★★★★**Gourmet & Wellnesshotel Schweizerhof**, t + 41 (0)27 958 7575, has a waterfall in the lounge and reception rooms decorated in *belle epoque* style.
- ★★★★**Allalin Relais du Silence**, t +41 (0)27 957 1815, is in a peaceful setting and has lots of atmosphere.
- ★★★**Fletschhorn Waldhotel**, t +41 (0)27 957 2131, *www.fletschhorn.ch*, set in the woods above Saas-Fee, houses both a modern art gallery and an outstanding wine cellar.
- ★★★**Unique Hotel Dom**, t +41 (0)27 957 5101, is a central snowboarders' rendezvous, with a state-of-the-art Sony sound system in every room.

St Moritz

Profile

One of the world's most famous resorts with beautiful scenery, great hotels, gourmet restaurants, superb shops and a wide range of other winter sports

Resort

The first home of winter sports in the Alps has been an important spa town since the Middle Ages and has never knowingly lost an opportunity to market itself internationally. The brand name, synonymous with wealth and high-living, is protected by trademark in 50 countries around the world. As long ago as 1519,

✱ BEST FOR

All levels of skier and rider, wealthy sophisto-cats, ski gourmets, non-skiers

ESSENTIALS

Altitude: 1800m (5,904ft)–3303m (10,834ft)
Further information: t +41 (0)81 837 3333, *www.stmoritz.ch*
Lifts in area: 56 (1 funicular, 10 cableways, 18 chairs, 27 drags) serving 350km of piste
Lift pass: Upper Engadine (covers Celerina, Pontresina, St Moritz, Sils Maria, Silvaplana and 1 day in Livigno) adult CHF265–339, child 6–12yrs CHF90–115, both for 6 days
Access: Zurich airport 3–4hrs, railway station in resort

Pope Leo X was offering full absolution for every Christian who visited the healing mineral springs.

Reliable weather in the Engadine Valley brought summer visitors, but it wasn't until 1864 that hotelier Johannes Badrutt hit upon the idea of a creating a winter season. That September he overheard four Englishmen lamenting the fact that they must soon return to London for the winter and would be back again the following July. He suggested they returned in January and wagered that if they experienced fewer sunny days in winter than in summer he would pay for their accommodation. Johannes was on a statistical winner – and the rest is history.

They skated on the frozen lake and tobogganed on a steep slope that was to become the Cresta Run. Today it remains the most macho and dangerous of all winter sports. The private and still British-run St Moritz Tobogganing Club continues to maintain a sexist men-only stance as it has done for more than 100 years.

Socially well-connected beginners can launch themselves head first down the ice on a heavy metal skeleton toboggan on four mornings a week from Christmas to the end of February. They achieve speeds of around 100kph.

The Cresta should not be confused with bobsleigh. St Moritz has the one remaining natural ice run that is rebuilt each winter with nine serpentine bends snaking down to Celerina. Skating and curling are also important activities that take place on the frozen lake. Not all alternative sports involve sliding – golf, polo, horse-racing, showjumping, greyhound racing and even cricket are played and watched by St Moritz's hedonistic clientele.

The resort is divided into two communities. St Moritz Bad lies along the shore of the lake, while St Moritz Dorf is the higher town centre. Surprisingly for a place with such an impeccable pedigree, the architecture is far from being aesthetically pleasing. The beauty of the place lies not in the views of the resort itself but in the vista from it.

Mountain

Skiing is only one of the many winter activities offered by St Moritz, but the area is extensive, with sufficient variety and challenge to please most skiers and riders. The regional lift pass covers 57 lifts in villages scattered across the Upper Engadine. These include Celerina, Pontresina, Silvaplana and Sils Maria. They are by no means all connected.

St Moritz's own skiing takes place on Corviglia, reached by a cable-car from St Moritz Bad or by a funicular from St Moritz Dorf. It can also be accessed by chair from Suvretta and by gondola from Celerina. A 100-person cable-car continues on up to Piz Nair at 3057m.

Corvatsch, on the other side of the valley, and reached by bus, is of greater interest to advanced skiers and riders. It is reached from Sils Maria, Silvaplana and Surlej.

The third outlying main area of Diavolezza-Lagalb rises to a snow-sure

ST MORITZ

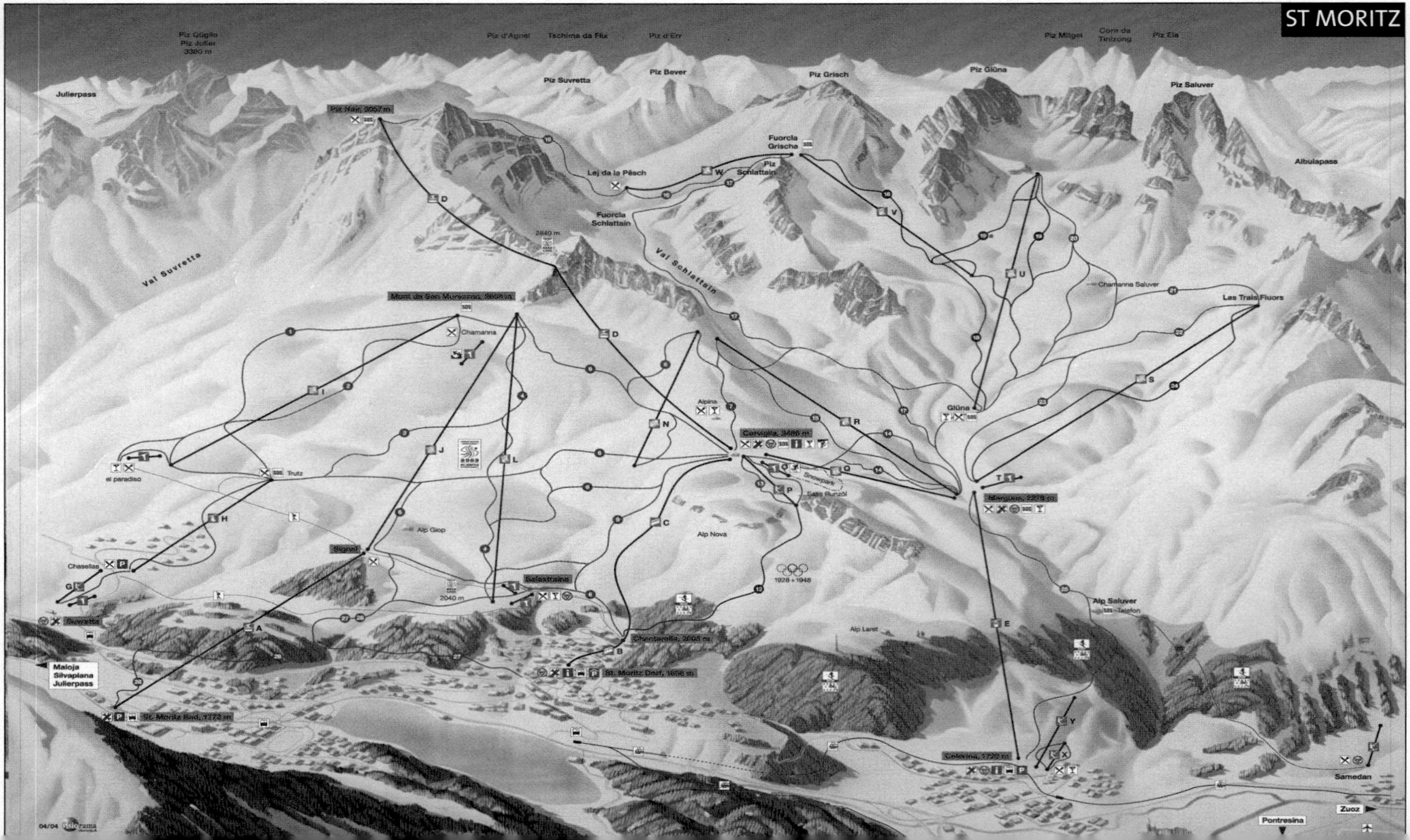

Piz Güglia
Piz Julier
3380 m
Piz d'Agnel
Tschima da Flix
Piz d'Err
Piz Mitgel
Corn da Tinizong
Piz Ela
Julierpass
Piz Suvretta
Piz Bever
Piz Grisch
Piz Glüna
Piz Saluver
Albulapass
Fuorcla Grischa
Piz Schlattain
Lej da la Pêsch
Fuorcla Schlattain
2840 m
Val Schlattain
Val Suvretta
Chamanna Saluver
Las Trais Fluors
Chamanna
Alpina
Glüna
Trutz
el paradiso
Snowpark
Sass Runzöl
Alp Nova
Alp Giop
1928 + 1948
Chasellas
2040 m
Alp Laret
Alp Saluver
Telefon
Maloja
Silvaplana
Julierpass
Samedan
Zuoz
Pontresina
04/04

3000m and is reached from St Moritz by bus or train. A long itinerary run from the top of Diavolezza, considered to be one of the alpine classics, winds down over heavily crevassed glacial terrain to Morteratsch.

High prices restrict the number of young riders who can afford to come to St Moritz, but those that do find some outstanding terrain. Diavolezza is great for freeriding. The terrain park and half-pipe at Corviglia is accessed by the Munt da San Murezzan chair.

Cross-country skiing is as popular as the downhill variety, with tracks through the pine forest and along the shores of the lake. The annual pro-am 42km Engadine Marathon attracts thousands of *langläufers* and is a highlight of the European cross-country calendar.

Learn

Swiss Snowsports School, **t** +41 (0)81 830 0101, and **Suvretta**, **t** +41 (0)81 836 3600, are both recommended, along with **Wave Snowboard School**, **t** +41 (0)81 837 5353, in Celerina. A high number of the resort's wealthy guests book private guides, which has resulted in the establishment of a number of specialist organizations: **Private Ski Instructor Association St Moritz/Engadin**, **t** +41 (0)81 852 1885, **AAA**, **t** +41 (0)81 832 2233, **Bergsteigerschule Pontresina**, **t** +41 (0)81 838 8333, and the **St Moritz Experience**, **t** +41 (0)81 833 7714. **Heli Bernina**, **t** +41 (0)81 852 4677, and **Heliswiss**, **t** +41 (0)81 852 3535, can arrange heli-skiing.

Children

Hotel Schweizerhof, **t** +41 (0)81 837 0707, has daycare for children over three years, as does **Badrutt Palace Hotel**, **t** +41 (0)81 837 1000. **Suvretta House's Teddy Bear Club**, **t** +41 (0)81 836 3636, has a kindergarten for small guests from 12 months old, and a children's restaurant. **Kempi Kids Club**, **t** +41 (0)81 838 3838, in the Grand Hotel des Bains Kempinski officially takes children from three years, although it will also care for guests' babies. All the ski schools take children from four years.

Lunch

On Corviglia, La Marmite, which has a justified reputation as the best (and most expensive) high-altitude lunching experience in the Alps, is now known as **Mathis Food Affairs**, **t** +41 (0)81 833 6355. Owner Reto Mathis continues to serve caviar and truffle-rich dishes in the stately style pioneered a generation ago by his father Hartly. **Chasellas**, **t** +41 (0)81 833 3854, **Trutz**, **t** +41 (0)81 833 7030, and **Chamanna**, **t** +41 (0)79 682 5080, are all owned by the Suvretta House Hotel and are warmly recommended along with **Salastrains**, **t** +41 (0)81 833 3867.

Dine

Chesa Veglia, **t** +41 (0)81 837 2800, serves Engadine specialities and fine pizzas. **Jöhri's Talvo** at Campfer, **t** +41 (0)81 833 4455, is renowned for its local venison and game. **Nobu**, **t** +41 (0)81 837 2624, has opened in Badrutt's Palace Hotel for gourmet sushi and other Japanese cuisine, and **The Sunny Bar** at the Kulm, **t** +41 (0)81 836 8000, also serves sushi. **Trutz**, **t** + 41 (0)81 833 7030, is open for evening fondue and raclette. **The Grischuna** at the Hotel Monopol, **t** +41 (0)81 837 0404, is warmly recommended.

Party

Hanselmann's in St Moritz Dorf is a 100-year-old coffee house that is a resort meeting place after skiing, serving pastries and delectable ice cream. Moroccan-themed **King's Club**, **t** +41 (0)81 837 1000, is the top nightclub. **Diamond** is the latest hotspot, with a lounge, restaurant and club. **Vivai**, **Cascade** and **Cava** in the Hotel Steffani are rated. **Devil's Place** bar at Hotel Waldhaus am See has the world's biggest range of malt whisky and receives a mention in *Guinness World Records*. The **Stübli** at the Schweizerhof has late-night dancing on tables, and after 10pm is 'so crowded that you could not possibly fall off'. The **Muli Bar** hosts country-and-western music, **Bobby's Bar** is for the under-20s.

Sleep

*****__Grand Hotel des Bains Kempinski__, **t** +41 (0)81 838 3838, in St Moritz Bad, has a renowned spa, the smartest wine bar in town, and a casino.

*****__Badrutt's Palace Hotel__, **t** + 41 (0)81 837 1000, with its landmark tower, is the most famous establishment housing seven restaurants and the King's Club.

*****__Kulm Hotel__, **t** +41 (0)81 836 8000, is the customary choice of Cresta riders.

*****__Suvretta House__, **t** +41 (0)81 836 3636, has a spa, skating-rink, nursery slope, its own ski-lift and ski school.

*****__Hotel Carlton__, **t** +41 (0)81 836 7000, is the smallest of the five-stars with a more intimate country-house atmosphere.

****__Hotel Schweizerhof__, **t** +41 (0)81 837 0707, is renowned for its Acla and Clavadatsch restaurants and its basement Hofkeller.

****__Hotel Steffani__, **t** +41 (0)81 836 9696, is a traditional family-owned hotel in the centre of town with the resort's oldest restaurant.

***__Hotel Waldhaus am See__, **t** +41 (0)81 833 7676, is comfortable and world famous for its whisky collection, but is a brisk walk from the town centre.

***__Hotel Arte__, **t** +41 (0)81 837 5858, in St Moritz Dorf, has nationally themed bedrooms including Engadine, Australian, Japanese, Venetian and Mexican.

Verbier

🏆 BEST SKI RESORT 2007

Profile

Switzerland's overall most challenging skiing both on and off-piste. Some excellent chalet accommodation, and a magnet for party-goers and snowboarders

Resort

Verbier may lack the Edwardian pedigree of Davos or the aristocratic authority of the Bernese Oberland, but it has the panache and the high mountain terrain to attract the cream of international skiers and riders. The first lift, a Heath Robinson petrol-driven affair that pulled a sledge 200 vertical metres, wasn't opened until

* BEST FOR

Strong intermediates and experts, cosmopolitan sophistication, party-goers

ESSENTIALS

Altitude: 1500m (4,920ft)–3330m (10,925ft)
Further information: **t** +41 (0)27 775 3888, *www.verbier.ch*
Lifts in area: 84 in Four Valleys (1 mountain railway, 16 cableways, 25 chairs, 42 drags) serving 412km of piste
Lift pass: Four Valleys (covers Bruson, Nendaz, Thyon, Verbier, Veysonnaz) adult CHF325, youth 15–18yrs CHF276, child 6–15yrs CHF228, all for 6 days
Access: Geneva airport 2–3hrs, railway station at Le Châble 30mins by car or 10mins by cableway

1946. In those austere times, British and, indeed, German skiers were still otherwise engaged. Another 11 years passed before the Attelas cable-car was built, and only then could Verbier could propertly describe itself as a ski resort.

Verbier today is a thriving modern resort with an improved lift system and some extraordinarily challenging pistes, as well as a clutch of stomach-churning steep couloirs and limitless powder terrain. It's a hugely popular weekend destination for wealthy Swiss from Geneva and avid skiers from London – many of whom rent apartments for the season and commute on Friday and Sunday evenings. As a result the nightlife is rivalled by few other resorts in the Alps.

Verbier is linked by lift and and an expensive electronic pass to neighbouring Thyon, Veysonnaz and Nendaz. Together they form the Four Valleys, an uneasy alliance that should not be compared to the French Trois Vallées. In practice, few Verbier-based skiers bother to journey into the far corners of the area where the lifts are primitive. More importantly, the pick of the slopes are found close to home on Mont Fort and Mont-Gelé.

The village itself, situated above the valley town of Le Châble, 10km from Martigny, is a pleasing collection of chalets centred around a *place centrale* and dominated by a 1962 church with a 20m spire. Only 1,170 of the 12,000 beds are in hotels and little of the accommodation offers doorstep skiing. You can learn to ski or ride here and enjoy some easy intermediate runs, but overall the resort best suits accomplished skiers and riders looking for steep slopes and a bottomless nightlife.

Mountain

Access to Verbier's main ski area is a bus ride from Médran or a short walk from the Place Centrale. From here two gondolas rise to the 2200m mid-mountain hub of Les Ruinettes. A gondola also comes up from Le Châble and day-visitors are encouraged to use this rather than drive up to the resort.

A long-awaited new lift opened last winter, linking Les Attelas to 2260m La Chaux where the Jumbo cable-car rises to 2950m Col des Gentianes and finally to Mont Fort, the top of the ski area at 3330m. This allows skiers from Geneva arriving at Le Châble rail station to reach Mont Fort in 50 minutes.

The alternative route from Les Ruinettes is to take the Funispace gondola up to 2740m Attelas. From here, you either take the cable-car up to the demanding slopes of Mont-Gelé, descend towards Les Ruinettes, or continue on into the Lac des Vaux sector. The black piste from the top of Mont Fort demands considerable concentration, particularly in icy conditions. Verbier is also famous for its ski itineraries that are patrolled but not groomed. Most notorious of these is Tortin, a steep, wide slope that is often dangerous to access because of exposed rocks at the top.

The standard of skier and rider in Verbier is high. Within hours of a fresh snowfall you will find tracks on even the most impossible-looking slopes, and runs such as Stairway to Heaven and Hidden Valley give the appearance of having been pisted. The north face of Mont Fort, with its B52 and Poubelle variants, is routinely skied, despite its hair-raising entry.

Not all the skiing is so radical. Les Ruinettes offers plenty of easier blue runs as does the resort's second ski area of Savoleyres, reached by gondola from the other side of town. The skiing here has been improved with a detachable six-person chair. It benefits from sunny south-facing slopes towards Verbier and longer, better runs down its back side to La Tzoumaz.

4 Vallées
Mont Collon 3637 m.
Pigne d'Arolla 3796 m.
Mont-Blanc de Cheilon 3870 m.
La Ruinette 3875 m.
Mont Fort 3330 m.
Grand Combin 4314 m.
Petit Combin 3672 m.
Mont Vélan 3734 m.
Super-St-Bernard 2800 m.
Hospice 2469 m.
Italie
Grande Dixence
Col des Gentianes 2950 m.
Bec des Rosses 3222 m.
Mont-Gelé 3023 m.
Mont Rogneux 3084 m.
Six Blanc 2245 m.
Bourg-St-Pierre
La Breya 2188 m.
La Fouly 1600 m.
Vichères 1423 m.
Orsières
Champex-Lac 1470 m.
L'Etéygeon
Greppon Blanc 2700 m.
Mont-Rouge 2491 m.
Lac de Cleuson
Combatzeline 2238 m.
Tortin 2050 m.
Chassoure 2740 m.
Attelas 2727 m.
La Chaux 2260 m.
2482 m.
Lourtier
Champsec
Ethérolla 2450 m.
EVOLÈNE
Plan-du-Fou 2430 m.
Les Ruinettes 2200 m.
Col des Mines
SIVIEZ 1730 M.
Dent de Nendaz 2463 m.
Versegères
BRUSON 1080 M.
Tracouet 2200 m.
Vallon d'Arbi
LE CHÂBLE 821 M.
Hérémence
Croix de Coeur 2174 m.
Savoleyres 2354 m.
Prarion 1768 m.
THYON 2000 2100 M.
VERBIER 1500 M.
LES MASSES 1515 M.
LES COLLONS 1800 M.
Sembrancher
Pierre-Avoi 2473 m.
Martigny 10 km
VEYSONNAZ 1400 M.
NENDAZ 1400 M.
MAYENS-DE-L'OURS 1470 M.
Isérables
LA TZOUMAZ Mayens-de-Riddes 1500 M.
Vex
Aproz
Riddes
Sion

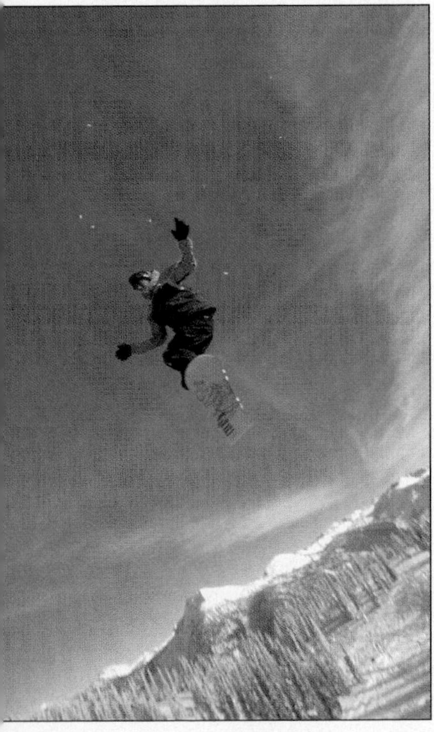

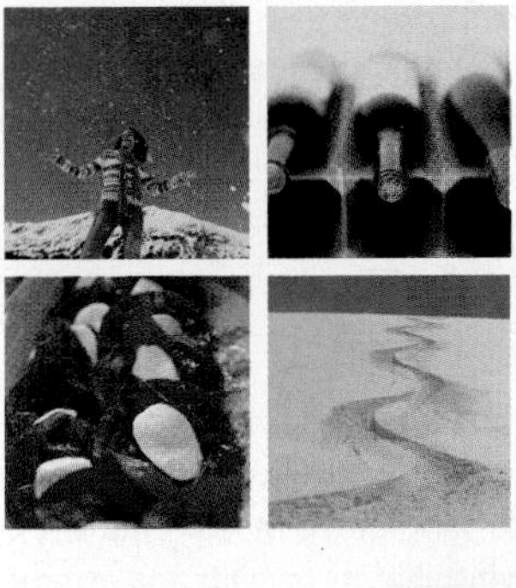

Novices make their first turns on a short nursery slope on the golf course and at Les Esserts. You can learn to ski in Verbier, but there are easier places in the Alps to do so. Verbier is a major centre for snowboarding. There is a giant terrain park at Les Chaux with separate snowcross and freestyle sectors, and a bar at the base area.

Learn

Verbier has a wide choice of ski schools, all with good reputations. **Powder Extreme, t** +41 (0)76 479 8761, specializes in off-piste ('excellent guiding and instruction'). British-run **Altitude, t** +41 (0)27 771 6006, is highly rated: 'The best lessons I have ever had' said one reporter. British-run **Warren Smith Ski Academy, t** +44 (0)1442 832 629, is rated 'well worth trying – Warren gave me some invaluable tips'. **ES European Snowsports, t** +41 (0)27 771 6222, offers courses for just six skiers including off-piste and women-only clinics. **La Maison du Sport, t** +41 (0)27 775 3363, is the official resort ski school. **Adrénaline, t** +41 (0)27 771 7459, **No Limits, t** +41 (0)27 771 5556, and **Swiss Snowboard School, t** +41 (0)27 775 3363, are the remaining competition. **Bureau des Guides** at La Maison du Sport and **La Fantastique, t** +41 (0)27 771 4141, are the mountain-guiding companies. **Eagles Hélicoptère, t** +41 (0)27 327 3060, and **Air Glaciers, t** +41 (0)27 329 1415, are the heli-skiing operations.

Children

Kid's Club, t +41 (0)27 775 3363, for skiers over four years, is run by La Maison du Sport at the Moulins nursery site, which has its own lift and restaurant. **Les Schtroumpfs, t** +41 (0)27 771 6585, also at Moulins, offers daycare for little ones aged three months to seven years.

Lunch

Cabane Mont Fort, t +41 (0)27 771 1384, is a popular mountain refuge off the La Chaux piste, and **Cabane du Tortin, t** +41 (0)27 288 1153, serves heart-warming food. **Chez Dany, t** +41 (0)27 771 2524, in the woods below the Ruinettes chair, is a resort institution. **Vieux-Verbier, t** +41 (0)27 771 1668, at Médran is cosy and well positioned. On Savoleyres, **Marlénaz, t** +41 (0)27 771 5441, is off-piste and has a good sun terrace. **Marmotte, t** +41 (0)27 771 6834, specializes in *Rösti*, and **Le Sonalon, t** +41 (0)27 771 7271, is popular. **Chez Simon, t** +41 (0)27 306 8055, is atmospheric and non-smoking. **Le Carrefour, t** +41 (0)27 771 7010, has a sunny terrace, **Namasté, t** +41 (0)27 771 5773, is an atmospheric old cabin on the piste at Savoleyres, and **Au Mayen, t** +41 (0)27 771 1894, serves local specialities.

Dine

Pierroz in Hotel Rosalp still has the finest international cuisine in town. The hotel's brasserie, **La Pinte, t** +41 (0)27 771 6323 for both, is informal and less expensive. **Caveau, t** +41 (0)27 771 2226, has raclette and fondues. The restaurant in **Hôtel Montpelier, t** +41 (0)27 771 6131, offers outstanding cuisine. **Appartement, t** +41 (0)27 771 6200, in Chalet d'Adrien specializes in French-international cuisine. **Chez Martin, t** +41 (0)27 771 2252, and **Al Capone, t** +41 (0)27 771 6774, serve pizzas. **Netsu, t** +41 (0)27 771 6272, is Japanese, **Verb'Asia, t** +41 (0)27 771 7581, is oriental, and **Chez Kamai, t** +41 (0)27 771 7628, is Indian.

Party

This is a party place, especially at weekends when wealthy players from London and Geneva hit town. **Le Farinet** in the Place Centrale is the most popular venue as the lifts close. Young skiers and snowboarders crush into the glass-sided terrace bar with live music. Thirty-somethings chill out inside over a bottle of wine in leather armchairs. **Offshore** with its pink VW Beetle centrepiece is a great place for après-ski drinks, and **Fer à Cheval** is busy by mid-afternoon. Resort staff flock to **Pub Mont Fort** for its cheap drinks. Later on, sophisticated **Crock No Name** provides the warm-up act for the night clubs of which the London- and Manhattan-priced **Farm Club** is still the leader. Moroccan-themed **Casbah** beneath Hotel Farinet, is an alternative. **Taratata** (known as Tara's) attracts a younger crowd. **Icebox** is the fourth choice. Clubs stay open until 4am.

Sleep

*******Le Chalet d'Adrien**, **t** +41 (0)27 771 6200, *www.chalet-adrien.com*, in Savoleyres, is small with individually decorated rooms, two restaurants and a spa.

******Hôtel Montpelier**, **t** +41 (0)27 771 6131, *www.hotelmontpelier.ch*, is inconvenient for the lifts but has attractive bedrooms and an indoor swimming pool.

******Hôtel Rosalp**, **t** +41 (0)27 771 6323, *www.rosalp.ch*, contains the resort's best restaurant and a spa that specializes in skin-ageing prevention.

******Hôtel Vanessa**, **t** +41 (0)27 775 2800, *www.hotelvanessa.ch*, is convenient, family-friendly, with good food.

*****Hôtel Bristol**, **t** +41 (0)27 771 6577, *www.bristol-verbier.ch*, is conveniently positioned and houses a disco on the first floor.

*****Le Mazot**, **t** +41 (0)27 775 2121, owned by former ski racer Serge Tacchini, is small and pleasant.

*****Hôtel Phénix**, **t** +41 (0)27 771 6844, *www.phenix-verbier.com*, is comfortable and central.

*****Hôtel Verbier**, **t** +41 (0)27 771 6688, *www.hotelverbier.ch*, in the village square, has a cosy sitting room.

****Hôtel Garbo**, **t** +41 (0)27 771 6272, *www.hotelgarbo.com*, has two restaurants – French and sushi – and is well positioned.

Chalet Kernow, **t** +44 (0)20 7385 8050, *skiverbier.com*, is a comfortable modern chalet sleeping 12, with delicious cuisine.

The Bunker, **t** +41 (0)27 771 6602, *www.thebunker.ch*, next to the sports centre, attracts a large number of young people to its good-value dormitory accommodation.

Villars

Profile

An underrated area for beginners, intermediates and families with easy airport access from Geneva. Its low altitude means snow-cover is unpredictable, but Les Diablerets glacier is open all year

* BEST FOR

Beginners, intermediates, families, airport access

ESSENTIALS

Altitude: 1300m (4,265ft)–2113m (6,932ft)

Further information: Villars: **t** +41 (0)24 495 3232, *www.villars.ch*, *www.tele-villars-gryon.ch*; Les Diablerets: **t** +41 (0)24 492 3358, *www.diablerets.ch*

Lifts in area: 36 (1 funicular, 3 cableways, 8 chairs, 24 drags) serving 100km of piste

Lift pass: Area (covers Villars, Les Diablerets glacier, Gryon, Leysin, Les Mosses) adult CHF261, child 9–15yrs CHF170, both for 6 days

Access: Geneva airport 1½hrs, railway station in resort

Resort

Villars is one of the original resorts in the Alps that first attracted British skiers, largely because it is one of the few places in Switzerland where foreigners can buy property in their own right without serious restriction.

Snow-cover at this low altitude is uncertain for much of the season, but the skiing is ideal for unadventurous intermediates and families who come here in large numbers to enjoy gentle slopes and magnificent scenery up above the Rhône Valley in the beautiful Vaudois Mountains.

The resort shares its ski area with Les Diablerets, a large village with mainly chalet accommodation and a 3209m glacier where limited skiing is always possible even in the driest of winters.

Mountain

Mountain access from Villars is by a cableway or by rack-and-pinion mountain railway that lead to Roc d'Orsay and the mid-mountain station of Bretaye at 1806m. A second gondola from the outlying hamlet of Barboleusaz provides an alternative means of mountain access.

From Bretaye a sequence of lifts and pistes leads across Les Chaux des Conches into the Diablerets sector, with a choice of runs down from 1949m Meilleret and 1727m Les Mazots to Vers L'Eglise and Les Diablerets itself. From here a gondola climbs the gentle pastureland to Isenau for some easy blue and slightly more challenging red runs. A bus takes you to Col du Pillon for the gondola up to the glacier which can also be reached by cable-car and chair from Reusch near Gstaad. The long run from the top takes you down the Combe d'Audon to Oldenalp at 1840m from where you can ride two chairs back up again in order to descend by cable-car to Col du Pillon and a bus back to Les Diablerets for the homeward journey to Villars. Terrain parks are at Bretaye and Les Chaux.

Learn

Villars Ski School, t +41 (0)24 495 4545, uses the graduated length method of teaching. **Riderschool, t** +41 (0)24 495 1600, is the dedicated boarder academy. **Gryon, t** +41 (0)24 498 2434, is warmly recommended. **Swiss Ski and Snowboard School, t** +41 (0)24 495 2210, is the traditional option. **Handicapt Sports & Loisirs, t** +41 (0)24 498 1028, is a sit-ski learning centre with a worldwide reputation. Off-piste guiding is available through **Villars Expérience, t** +41 (0)24 495 4138, and the ski schools.

In Les Diablerets, **Swiss Ski and Snowboard School, t** +41 (0)24 492 3358, is the place to learn.

Children

Snowli – the Swiss school's kindergarten – and **Villars Ski School** both teach children from three years at Bretaye. **La Trottinette, t** +41 (0)24 495 8888, down in the village, cares for non-skiers from two months to six years. In Les Diablerets, the **Swiss Ski and Snowboard School** has a kindergarten from four years. **Hotel Le Chamois, t** +41 (0)24 492 2653, has an in-house kindergarten, and **Diablodocus Park** is part of the ski and snowboard school, offering lessons and childcare. New last winter was a free lift pass for all children under nine years.

Lunch

Try **Hôtel du Lac de Bretaye, t** +41 (0)24 495 2192, and **Les Mazots** at Meilleret, **t** +41 (0)24 492 1023. **Le Col de Bretaye, t** +41 (0)24 495 2194, and **Les Chaux, t** +41

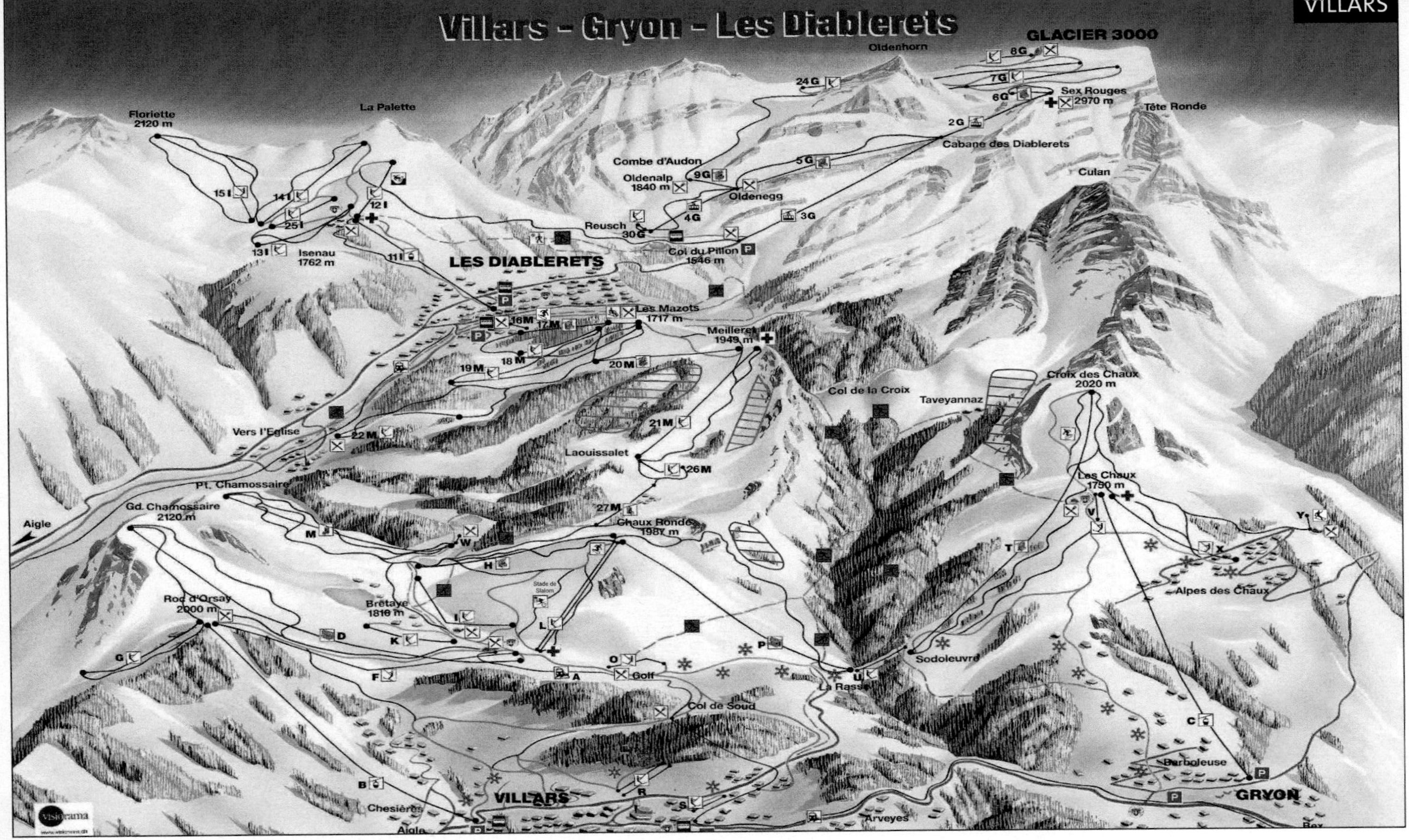
Villars - Gryon - Les Diablerets
GLACIER 3000
Oldenhorn
Sex Rouges
2970 m
Tête Ronde
Cabane des Diablerets
Culan
Floriette
2120 m
La Palette
Combe d'Audon
Oldenalp
1840 m
Oldenegg
Reusch
Col du Pillon
1546 m
Isenau
1762 m
LES DIABLERETS
Les Mazots
1717 m
Meilleret
1949 m
Col de la Croix
Taveyannaz
Croix des Chaux
2020 m
Vers l'Eglise
Laouissalet
Pt. Chamossaire
Gd. Chamossaire
2120 m
Aigle
Chaux Ronde
1987 m
Les Chaux
1750 m
Stade de Slalom
Bretaye
1810 m
Roc d'Orsay
2000 m
Alpes des Chaux
Sodoleuvre
Golf
La Rasse
Col de Soud
Barboleuse
Chesières
VILLARS
Arveyes
GRYON
Bex

(0)24 498 1187, are both recommended, and **Les Chevonnes, t** +41 (0)24 495 2131, is in a lovely lakeside setting at Bretaye.

Dine

Les Ecovets, t +41 (0)24 495 2378, specializes in regional dishes. **Le Vieux Villars, t** +41 (0)24 495 2525, is renowned for its fondue and raclette. **Le Soleil, t** +41 (0)24 495 4530, is a new gourmet restaurant. **Pasta & Basta, t** +41 (0)24 495 1818, in Chesières, **Le Sporting, t** +41 (0)24 495 1313, in Villars, and **L'Escale, t** +41 (0)24 498 1215, at Gryon below Les Chaux, are cheaper alternatives. In Les Diablerets, **Auberge de la Poste, t** +41 (0)24 492 3124, and **Café des Diablerets, t** +41 (0)24 492 0909, serve regional specialities.

Party

Après-ski includes live rock and pool at **Café Central** in Villars or **Harabee Café** in Barboleusaz, and drinking at **Charlie's Bar**, **L'Alchemiste**, **Murphy's Wine Bar**, the **Jazz** or **Blues Bars** in Villars or **Ragot d'Elfe** in Gryon. Dance the night away at **El Gringo** in Villars. Les Diablerets' nightlife is quiet and centres around a few bars and discos, including **La Diabletine** bar and internet café, **Atomix Bar**, **B'Bar** disco in Mon Abri, and **Pote Saloon** which is the other disco. **Les Vioz** is a good place for a *vin chaud* after the last run down.

Sleep

Villars:

★★★★★**Grand Hôtel du Parc, t** +41 (0)24 492 2828, *www.parcvillars.ch*, contains a choice of gastronomic and regional restaurants.

★★★★**Eurotel Victoria, t** +41 (0)24 492 3131, *www.forum.ch/eurotel-victoria-villars*, is located in the village centre and has spacious rooms.

★★★★**Hôtel du Golf, t** +41 (0)24 492 3838, *www.hotel-golf.ch*, is central, with attractive rooms and a wellness area.

★★★★**Hôtel La Renardière, t** +41 (0)24 495 2592, *www.larenardiere.ch*, has a home-from-home ambience and lovely wood-panelled bedrooms.

★★★**Hôtel Alpe Fleurie, t** +41 (0)24 492 3464 is a chalet-style hotel in the resort centre.

★★★**Hôtel Ecureuil, t** +41 (0)24 492 3737, *www.hotel-ecureuil.ch*, has been run by the same family for over 50 years and is child-friendly.

★**Hôtel Les Papillons, t** +41 (0)24 495 3484, between Villars and Gryon, is a small chalet-style B&B with attractive bedrooms.

Whitepod, t +41 (0)79 744 6219, *www.whitepod.com*, is a luxury village of geodesic domes with wood-burning stoves and real beds.

Les Diablerets:

★★★★**Eurotel-Victoria, t** +41 (0)24 492 3721, *www.eurotel-victoria.ch*, is the biggest hotel with large modern rooms and an indoor swimming pool ('very pleasant staff and good food').

★★★★**Hôtel des Diablerets, t** +41 (0)24 492 0909, *www.hoteldesdiablerets.ch*, is in the village centre.

★★★**Hôtel Le Chamois, t** +41 (0)24 492 265, *www.hotelchamois.ch*, is family-friendly with its own kindergarten.

Wengen

*** BEST FOR**

Big intermediate ski area, alpine charm, dramatic scenery

Profile

A car-free traditional resort with a large intermediate ski area linked to Grindelwald. Recommended for beginners and intermediates, as well as off-piste skiers, but not for families with small ski-age children

ESSENTIALS

Altitude: 1274m (4,180ft)–2320m (7,612ft)
Further information: t +41 (0)33 855 1414, *www.wengen-muerren.ch*, *www.wengen.com*
Lifts in area: 40 in Jungfrau Top Ski Region (5 funiculars, 5 cableways, 16 chairs, 14 drags) serving 221km of piste
Lift pass: Jungfrau (covers Grindelwald, Mürren, Wengen) adult CHF295, child 6–19yrs CHF148, both for 6 days
Access: Zurich airport 3hrs, Geneva airport 4hrs, railway station in resort

Resort

Wengen is one of the Edwardian cradles of modern skiing. Foreign – mainly British – visitors first arrived here in the late 19th century to gaze at the mighty peaks of the Eiger, Mönch and Jungfrau – and they came by train. The Jungfraubahn, the rack-and-pinion railway in the beautiful Bernese Oberland, was one of the engineering feats of the new Iron Age, climbing eventually through the granite heart of the Eiger to the 3454m Jungfraujoch, the highest railway station in Europe. It is now a UNESCO World Natural Heritage site that attracts tourists throughout the year from all over the world and notably Japan.

From 1911 the rail company took the commercial decision to keep the network open in winter and sports-minded visitors quickly discovered that it could be used as a ski-lift. Not all of these hardy tweed-clad pioneers approved of such easy uphill transport. They believed it offended the principle of 'no pain, no gain' and detracted from the achievement of skiing downhill. But in February 1925 the Downhill Only Club was formed in Wengen by British skiers to race against their Kandahar rivals encamped at Mürren on the other side of the Lauterbrunnen Valley. Both clubs are happily alive and active, and have as big a rivalry as ever in the 21st century.

Today the railway connecting the three resorts of Wengen, Grindelwald and Mürren still acts as the backbone of the shared Jungfrau ski region, along with a network of conventional ski-lifts.

Car-free Wengen sits on a sunny ledge nearly 500m above Lauterbrunnen and is reached only by rail in winter. Electric taxis and a few licensed motor vehicles provide the in-resort transport. The main street stretches back from the station to a modest collection of hotels, shops, restaurants, a giant skating rink and family-friendly nursery slopes. Hotels and private homes line the steep mountainside above.

In recent years, Wengen has lost some of its faded Edwardian ambience in favour of the high-tech demands of a modern ski resort. Nevertheless it remains a tranquil alpine backwater best suited to intermediate piste skiers and riders looking for distance over challenging gradient against one of the world's most spectacular mountain backdrops.

Sadly, the failure of the Swiss Ski School to offer afternoon group lessons makes it an inconvenient destination for families with small children.

WENGEN
Jungfraujoch
Top of Europe
3454 m 11333 ft
Schilthorn
Piz Gloria
2971 m 9748 ft
Eismeer
Eigerwand
Eigergletscher
2320 m 7612 ft
Birg
2676 m
Wildgerst
Gemsberg
berjoch
2501 m 8206 ft
Schilt
First
2168 m 7113 ft
Schreckfeld
Bort
Waldspitz
Faulhorn
2681 m 8796 ft
Bussalp
1800 m 5906 ft
Grindelwald
1034 m 3393 ft
Grund
Schwendi
Burglauenen
Lütschental
Gr. Scheidegg
Stepfi
Pfingstegg
Kl. Scheidegg
2061 m 6762 ft
Alpiglen
Wengernalpbahn
Brandegg
Holenstein
Männlichenbahn GGM
Lauberhorn
2473 m 8111 ft
"Lauberhorn Live" Rennstrecke
Tschuggen
Männlichen
2230 m 7317 ft
Männlichen-Gipfel
Männlichenbahn LWM
Wengernalp
1873 m 6145 ft
Allmend
Innerwengen
Slalom Strecke
Wengen
1274 m 4180 ft
Wengwald
Trümmelbach
Gimmelwald
1400 m 4593 ft
Mürren
1634 m 5361 ft
Stechelberg
922 m 3025 ft
Allmendhubel
1912 m 6273 ft
Maulerhubel
Winteregg
Stellifluh
Muttleren
Schwalmeren
Lauterbrunnen
796 m 2612 ft
Mürrenbahn
Grütschalp
1486 m 4379 ft
Isenfluh
Schynige Platte
Zweilütschinen
653 m 2142 ft
Breitlauenen
Saxeten
Gsteigwiler
Wilderswil
584 m 1916 ft
Matten
Heimwehfluh
Interlaken West
Interlaken
Interlaken Ost
Bönigen
Goldswil
Unterseen
Harder Kulm
Därligen
Leissigen
THUNERSEE
BRIENZERSEE
Iseltwald
Ringgenberg
Niederried
Waldegg
Vorsass
Beatenberg
1200 m 3940 ft
Meiringen - Grimsel - Sustenpass
Brünig - Luzern
Thun - Bern - Lötschberg - Brig - Milano

Mountain

'One of the most breathtaking places I have skied in' said one reporter. 'One of the most picturesque resorts in the world' said another, and a third called it 'The only place I have found where I can truly relax and enjoy my skiing'.

The commute up to the main skiing at Kleine Scheidegg is unquestionably more relaxing and scenic than the daily grind into Manhattan or the City of London. Swiss trains run to a precise timetable, with halts along the way. From Kleine Scheidegg you can drop back towards Wengen or take a run down the far side to Grindelwald. Trains also continue down to Grindelwald as well as up to the 2320m Eigergletscher. This is the highest point from which you can ski. The train then disappears behind the rock face and takes foot passengers on to the Jungfraujoch. Don't miss this excursion (the final section is not included in the lift pass), which stops at the famous windows in the North Face of the Eiger. From here mountain guides have launched dramatic rescue operations to save climbers stranded on the treacherous Eigerwand.

Alternative mountain access from Wengen is provided by a cable-car that rises to the 2230m Männlichen ridge separates the Lauterbrunnen and Grindelwald valleys. From here, a network of pistes and lifts brings you up to Kleine Scheidegg and the Eigergletscher. Long runs also continue down to the rail station at Grund near Grindelwald.

Each January, Wengen is the setting for the Lauberhorn, the longest – as well as one of the most celebrated and testing – downhill race in the World Cup Calendar. When not prepared for racing, the course that begins at the top of the Wixi chair provides a glorious 4.5km red descent back to Wengen. Advanced skiers and riders will find that even the handful of runs marked black on the piste map lack real challenge; however, the opportunities for lift-accessible off-piste are enormous. The dramatic White Hare, which begins from the foot of the Eigerwand and is reached from Eigergletscher, is a favourite.

Wengen has a terrain park with a variety of jumps and obstacles, served by the Wixi chair. Mürren is included in the lift pass and linked by train but not by piste. A day trip is viable, but distances are big and the trains are slow.

Learn

Swiss Ski School, t +41 (0)33 856 2022, gives three-hour morning group lessons from Sunday to Friday, as well as private lessons at any time. **Privat Ski and Snowboard School, t** +41 (0)33 855 5005, offers private tuition from young English-speaking instructors. **Swiss Snowsports School Kleine Scheidegg, t** +41 (0)33 855 1547, is based up the mountain.

Children

Swiss Ski and Snowboard School, t +41 (0)33 856 2022, runs morning-only group lessons, which makes life difficult for parents with small skiers who consequently never get the chance to explore far afield. Both the Swiss and **Privat Ski School, t** +41 (0)33 855 5005, offer private afternoon lessons. However, these constitute an expensive form of childcare and don't solve the problem of lunch-time babysitting. **Playhouse Wengen, t** +41 (0)33 855 1414, cares for non-skiers from 18 months to seven years. **Kinderhort Sunshine Männlichen, t** +41 (0)79 632 8178, accepts babies from four weeks at the top of Männlichen.

Lunch

Hotel Jungfrau, t +41 (0)33 855 1622, at Wengernalp has outstanding views from the terrace and the best food on the mountain. **Brandegg, t** +41 (0)33 853 1057, is famous for its apple fritters. **Kleine Scheidegg Bahnhof, t** +41 (0)33 828 7828, is a hotel and good restaurant as well as a station. **Mary's Café, t** +41 (0)33 855 2775, at the foot of the Lauberhorn race course, has wholesome and reasonably priced fare such as *Suppentopf* (beef and vegetable stew topped with cheese). Try also **Allmend, t** +41 (0)33 855 5800, for cheese fondue, **Eigergletscher, t** +41 (0)33 828 7888, and **Männlichen, t** +41 (0)33 853 1068.

Dine

With a few notable exceptions, restaurants in Wengen are almost all located in hotels. **Da Sina, t** +41 (0)33 855 3172, is a lively pizzeria. **Hirschenstübli, t** +41 (0)33 855 1544, in the Hotel Hirschen is renowned for its *fondue chinoise*. **Hotel Berghaus, t** +41 (0)33 855 2151, has a fish restaurant, and the **Bernerhof, t** +41 (0)33 855 2721, serves good fondue and raclette.

Party

At the end of the day, skiers and riders gather around the outdoor **Brunner Snowbar** on the home run. The last trains up the mountain are packed with families heading to Wengernalp for the 4km toboggan run back to the village. **Mary's Café** is ever popular. Later on the action moves to **Tanne Bar, Sina's Pub, Tiffany, The Underground** and **Chilis**.

Sleep

★★★★**Beausite Park Hotel, t** +41 (0)33 856 5161, *www.parkwengen.ch*, is in a peaceful location next to the Männlichen cableway above town. It has a leisure area with swimming pool.

★★★★**Hotel Regina, t** +41 (0)33 856 5858, *www.wengen.com/regina*, is a stately old hotel housing two good restaurants and rooms from a bygone age.

★★★★**Hotel Sunstar, t** +41 (0)33 856 5111, *www.sunstar.ch/wengen*, is one of the most conveniently placed hotels, containing family duplexes and a swimming pool. 'A model of Swiss efficiency' enthused one reporter.

★★★**Hotel Alpenruhe Kulm, t** +41 (0)33 856 2400, is set beside the woods with lovely views.

★★★**Hotel Brunner, t** +41 (0)33 855 2494, *www.wengen.com/hotel/brunner*, is ski-in/ski-out above the village, and family-friendly.

★★★**Hotel Eiger, t** +41 (0)33 855 1131, *www.eiger-wengen.ch*, is well positioned and a long-time British favourite.

★★★**Hotel Falken, t** +41 (0)33 856 5121, *www.hotelfalken.com*, is one of the resort's original Edwardian hotels and decorated with historic photographs. Rooms are quaintly old-fashioned.

★★**Hotel Bernerhof, t** +41 (0)33 855 2721, is said to be 'very friendly and the food is good'.

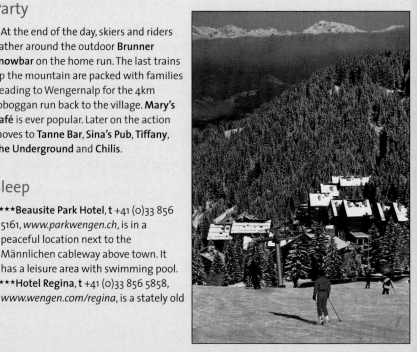

Zermatt

*BEST FOR

All levels of skier and rider, reliable snow-cover, mountain scenery, mountain restaurants

Profile

Ancient, historic climbing town with lashings of alpine charm, snow-sure skiing, luxury accommodation and the best mountain restaurants in the Alps. Suits all standards of skier and rider, as well as non-skiers

ESSENTIALS

Altitude: 1620m (5,314ft)–3899m (12,788ft)
Further information: t +41 (0)27 966 8100, *www.zermatt.ch*
Lifts in area: 57 in Zermatt, Cervinia and Valtournenche (2 funiculars, 19 cableways, 20 chairs, 16 drags) serving 313km of piste
Lift pass: Matterhorn Glacier Paradise (Zermatt, Cervinia and Valtournenche) adult CHF379, child 9–16yrs CHF190, both for 6 days
Access: Sion airport 1½hrs, Geneva airport 4hrs, railway station in resort

Resort

Zermatt is no stranger to change. Ever since Victorian mountaineer Edward Whymper controversially conquered the Matterhorn in 1865, with four of his companions falling to their deaths on the downward journey, Zermatt has regularly reinvented itself as a tourist destination. Most recently this has been in the form of a hi-tech ski resort by building a modern lift system to slowly replace the old network of sardine-can cable-cars and drag-lifts that had changed precious little during the previous 40 years. At the same time it has developed a range of smart hotels and sumptuous restaurants on the mountain that have few rivals anywhere else in the world.

The bustling little town, set at 1620m above the valley town of Visp, attracts well-heeled skiers and snowboarders who want to combine snowsports with excellent eating and nightlife. Faithful followers include Robbie Williams, the Duchess of York, Sir Bob Geldof, Ronan Keating, Tom Cruise, Diana Ross, Sir Paul McCartney, Nicole Kidman and Peter Gabriel, along with members of Pink Floyd and Dire Straits.

The town – actually it is no more than a large village, its size dictated by limited avalanche-safe building territory – dates back to the Middle Ages. Old blackened barns stand beside modern hotels and smart boutiques, and farmers still tend to their chickens and goats within 200m of the resort centre. Transport is by myriad high-speed electric taxis and an electric ski-bus system. These reduce noise and air pollution but can cause a dangerous traffic hazard to pedestrians.

Zermatt's ski area is linked via the Klein Matterhorn to Cervinia in Italy and the two resorts share a lift pass. Skiing continues here 365 days a year at 3900m on the border with Italy, with seven lifts and a vertical drop in summer of 1000m. The terrain park has a superpipe and a half-pipe open from the second week of July until the end of October.

Mountain

The skiing divides into three basic areas, two of them properly linked and the third tenuously so. Improvements to the lifts system have been dramatic in recent years since the various separate lift companies amalgamated.

Focus for experienced skiers and riders is on the Trockener Steg–Klein Matterhorn–Schwarzsee sector that is linked across

ZERMATT

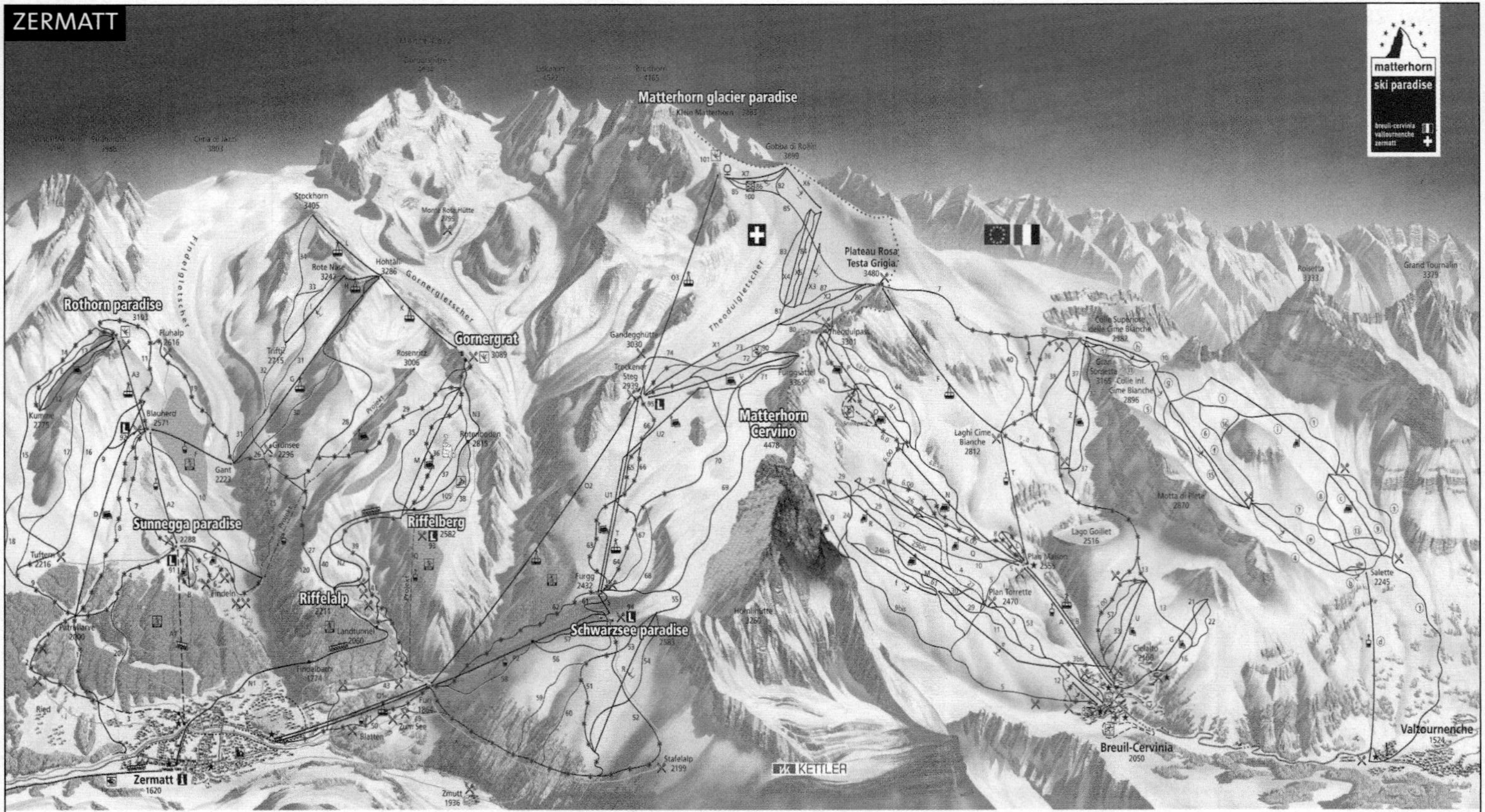

Bahnen
Transports
Transports

Piste leicht
Piste facile
Easy pistes

Piste mittel
Piste moyen
Medium pistes

Piste schwierig
Piste difficile
Difficult pistes

* * Piste beschneit
Piste enneigement artificiel
Piste with snowmaking

Abfahrtsroute
Itinéraires à ski
Downhill ski runs

Winterwanderweg
Sentiers de randonnée
Walking paths

Schlittelweg
Piste pour luges
Sledge track

Skibus
Ski-Bus
Ski bus

Landesgrenze
Frontière nationale
National boundary

Sommerski
Ski d'été
Summer skiing

Wild- und Waldschutzgebiet
Zone de protection de la forêt et de la faune
Forest and wildlife protected areas

★ Verkaufstelle Abonnemente
Vente d'abonnements
Ski-pass sale

Anfänger-Park
Domaine pour les débutants
Park for beginners

Igludorf
Le village d'igloos
Igloo-village

the Plateau Rosa to Cervinia in Italy. The Matterhorn Express gondola provides fast access to Furi and Schwarzsee. A cable-car from Furi takes you up to 2939m Trockener Steg, and another continues up to the Klein Matterhorn at 3820m. Plans are afoot to build a new eight-person gondola connecting Furi to Riffelberg in time for the start of this season. The area provides a wide range of scenic and occasionally demanding snow-sure intermediate skiing with magnificent views of the mighty Matterhorn. On sunny days, Zermatt-based skiers head over the top for the long intermediate run to Cervinia and an Italian lunch at half the price of Switzerland. Distances are huge and it is important to allow plenty of time for the return journey. Missing the last lift involves a six-hour taxi journey or, more sensibly, an overnight stay in a B&B.

The second area of Sunnegga is reached by an underground funicular from near the centre of town that takes you up to 2288m. A combination cableway, new last season – half gondola, half six-pack chair – brings you on up to Blauherd, replacing the slow old cable-car. The Sunnegga sector has some demanding pistes including the black roller coaster, Obere National FIS, as well as more benign red descents to the valley.

From 3103m Rothorn above Blauherd the area links via a long scenic piste and the Gant cable-car to the third sector of Gornergrat. This can also be accessed from the resort by a slow surface train that winds gently up the mountainside. Hohtälli above Gant and parallel Rote Nase-Stockhorn are the starting points for some of the best advanced pistes in the resort including the notorious Stockhorn descent to Triftji. However, these runs are often closed until mid-January because of insufficient snow.

The whole of Zermatt has enormous off-piste potential, with heli-skiing possible on the Monte Rosa and the Alphubeljoch. Snowboarding is a serious business with freeriding popular beneath Hohtälli. The winter terrain park is served by the Furggsattel lift above Trockener Steg.

Learn

Swiss Ski and Snowboarding School, **t** +41 (0)27 966 2466, used to run a tight and tired monopoly here that was broken some years ago by the younger and more go-ahead instructors of **Stoked The Ski and Snowboard School**, **t** +41 (0)27 967 7020. British-run **Summit Ski & Board School**, **t** +41 (0)27 967 0001, has since raised the game and now has 30 instructors and a cult following that includes the Duchess of York and Sir Bob Geldof and families. The other schools are **Almrausch Swiss Snow Sport School**, **t** +41 (0)27 967 0808, **European Snowsport**, **t** +41 (0)27 967 6787, **Independent Swiss Snowsport Instructors**, **t** +41 (0)27 967 7067, and **Prato Borni**, **t** +41 (0)27 967 5115. **Alpin Center**, **t** +41 (0)27 966 2460, provides guiding and **Air Zermatt**, **t** +41 (0)27 966 8686, heli-skiing.

Children

Summit, **t** +41 (0)27 967 0001, takes children in groups of six from six years, with New School courses for teenagers. Stoked's **Snowflakes Kids Club**, **t** +41 (0)27 967 4340, at the top of the Matterhorn Express at Schwarzsee cares for children from three years with lessons and play. **Snowli Snow Club**, **t** +41 (0)27 966 2466, run by the Swiss School is a kindergarten for four- to six-year-olds at Riffelberg. **Nico Kids Club**, **t** +41 (0)27 966 0777, in Hotel Nicoletta, accepts kids from two to eight years on weekdays. Childminding for children from two years is available at **Kinderclub Pumuckel**, **t** +41 (0)27 966 5000, in Hotel La Ginabelle, six days a week. **Kinderparadies**, **t** +41 (0)27 967 7252, cares for infants from three months and runs a babysitting service until 10pm. A list of recommended childminders is available from the tourist office.

Lunch

No resort in the world has a more enticing – and expensive – collection of welcoming mountain huts offering gourmet fare.

Chez Vrony, **t** +41 (0)27 967 2552, in Findeln is renowned for its *Rösti*, spicy fish soup, and spaghetti with prawns and wild mushrooms. The ancient hamlet of **Zum See**, **t** +41 (0)27 967 2045, houses a restaurant of the same name, serving delicious albeit pricey cuisine such as carpaccio of tuna with olive oil and lemon juice, Thai-style duck breast with basmati rice, and giant prawns with curry sauce and noodles. **Blatten**, **t** +41 (0)27 967 2096, below Furi, has 'fantastic *Rösti*'. Also at Furi is **Simi**, **t** +41 (0)27 967 2695, with a wood grill and serving Valais dishes at reasonable prices. **Alphittä**, **t** +41 (0)27 967 2114, at Riffelalp is wood-panelled and offers local specialities. **Fluhalp**, **t** +41 (0)27 967 2597, en route to Gant, offers fine food and the best views of the Matterhorn. **Stafelalp**, **t** +41 (0)27 967 3062, specializes in *Rösti* and sweet omelettes. **Pizzeria Cervino**, **t** +41 (0)27 967 1812, at Trockner Steg has 'no charm whatseoever, but the pizzas were excellent and cooked on a traditional wood-burning fire'. Wherever you go, even in low season, it is essential to book in advance.

Dine

Le Mazot, **t** +41 (0)27 966 0606, specializes in lamb cooked on an open grill. **Le Gitan**, **t** +41 (0)27 968 1940, has its own 'gypsy kebabs' and succulent giant prawns. The rustic **Schäferstube**, **t** +41 (0)27 966 7605, in Hotel Julen has lamb from its own flock.

Rua Thai, **t** +41 (0)27 966 6181, in Hotel Albana Real, has authentic Thai cuisine. **Casa Rustica**, **t** +41 (0)27 967 4858, has meat fondues and homely fare. **Mood's**, **t** +41 (0)27 967 8484, has a glass floor and gourmet nouvelle cuisine. **Myoko**, **t** +41 (0)27 966 8739, is an authentic sushi restaurant in the Seilerhaus.

Party

'Après-ski is OK but not wild' said one reporter. **Hennustall** is *the* piste-side bar on the way down from Furi. **Papperla** is always bursting at the seams at the end of the skiing day. **Elsie's Bar**, by the church, is a crowded but atmospheric place to go for champagne and oysters. The **Post Hotel** complex caters for everybody: upstairs is **Papa Caesar's** bar, downstairs is **Pink** with jazz, **Le Village** plays house music, and **Le Broken** is the traditional disco. The former owners of the Post have moved to Robbie Williams' favourite restaurant, **Mood's**, taking their loyal clientele with them. **Schneewittchen** is another popular meeting place. **Hotel Alex** nightclub attracts a 30-plus age group. Artist Heinz Julen's **Vernissage** is full of atmosphere with an art gallery, eclectic mix of ancient Valais furniture and light fittings made from recycled bicycle parts and bath plugs.

Sleep

★★★★★**Grand Hotel Zermatterhof**, **t** +41 (0)27 966 6600, *www.matterhorn-group.ch*, once a favourite of both Audrey Hepburn and Walt Disney, is a glamorous hotel with all its rooms recently refurbished with wood-panelling and murals.

★★★★★**Mont Cervin Palace**, **t** +41 (0)27 966 8888, *www.seiler-hotels.ch*, founded in

1851, has recently opened a three-storey Daniel Steiner Beauty Spa. It has some brand-new suites, and a wine cellar housing 10,000 bottles.

★★★★★**Riffelalp Resort 2222**, **t** +41 (0)27 966 0505, *www.zermatt.ch/riffelalp*, is a luxurious mini-resort at Gornergrat with an indoor pool with whirlpool and Europe's highest outdoor pool.

★★★★**Hotel Alex**, **t** +41 (0)27 966 7070, *www.hotelalexzermatt.com*, an alpine-Byzantine melange, has individually designed 'artistic' rooms, swimming pool and spa.

★★★★**Hotel Alpen Resort**, **t** +41 (0)27 966 3000, *www.alpenresort.com*, has family rooms and suites, as well as a spa, swimming pool, gym and an indoor tennis court.

★★★★**Hotel Ambassador**, **t** +41 (0)27 966 2611, *www.ambassador-zermatt.ch*, is comfortable, traditional, and rated 'excellent' by reporters.

★★★★**Hotel La Ginabelle**, **t** +41 (0)27 966 5000, *www.la.ginabelle.ch*, is family-friendly with a kids club.

★★★★**Seiler Hotel Monte Rosa**, **t** +41 (0)27 966 0333, *www.seiler-hotels.ch*, a favourite of Sir Winston Churchill and the base from which Edward Whymper, the Victorian mountaineer, set off to conquer the Matterhorn, is extremely central and guests can use the Mont Cervin spa.

★★★★**Seiler Hotel Nicoletta**, **t** +41 (0)27 966 0777, *www.seiler-hotels.ch*, offers guests the use of the Mont Cervin spa with swimming pool, and has its own kids club.

★★★★**Hotel Sonne**, **t** +41 (0)27 966 2066, *www.sonne.masch.com*, is family-run and chalet-style, with a wellness centre and a good restaurant.

★★★**Hotel Alpenroyal**, **t** +41 (0)27 966 6066, is warmly praised: 'An excellent location and the best food we have ever had in any hotel anywhere.'

★★★**Hotel Biner**, **t** +41 (0)27 966 5666, *www.hotel-biner-zermatt.ch*, near the railway station, has been recently renovated using all natural materials and offers five-star facilities including a spa with huge swimming pool.

★★★**Hotel Perren**, **t** +41 (0)27 966 5200, *www.hotel-perren.ch* has been welcoming guests since 1937 and has a relaxed and informal atmosphere.

Chalet Zaphir and Chalet Louise, **t** +44 (0)20 8682 5050, *www.scottdunn.com*, are luxury chalet-apartments sleeping 10 each, created by celebrated Swiss designer Heinz Julen.

Chalet Zen, **t** +44 (0)20 7384 3854, *www.descent.co.uk*, one of only a handful of stand-alone chalets available to rent in Zermatt, is decorated with antique furniture, rugs and paintings.

10

The Top Resorts: USA

Aspen, Colorado

*BEST SMALL SKI HOTEL 2007: Hotel Lenado

***BEST FOR**

Sophisto-cats, shoppers, all levels of skier and rider, ski gourmets

ESSENTIALS

Altitude: 7,945ft (2422m)–12,518ft (3815m)
Further information: **t** +1 970 925 1220, *www.aspensnowmass.com*
Lifts in area: 37 (1 cableway, 30 chairs, 6 drags) serving 4,893 acres of terrain
Lift pass: Area (covers all 4 mountains) adult \$198–360, child 7–17yrs \$180–225, both for 6 days
Access: Aspen airport 10mins, Denver airport 3½hrs, Eagle County/Vail airport 1½hrs

Profile

One of the top resorts in North America with skiing and snowboarding for all standards. The historic town has a wide choice of restaurants, shops and nightlife. Neighbouring Snowmass is the less expensive accommodation base

Resort

Aspen is too often dismissed by skiers who have never been there as a pretentious Hollywood-on-ice, a place for poseurs rather than *pisteurs*. In fact, nothing could be further from the truth. The reason why so many famous people make their home or take their holidays here is because they are fanatical skiers or riders who want some of the best facilities and challenging slopes that America has to offer. Stars with whom you may find yourself riding the gondola or a chair include Jack Nicholson, Michael Douglas, Melanie Griffiths and Antonio Banderas.

It is a wealthy town that was founded on money – back in the 1880s Aspen was briefly the silver-mining capital of the world. Its 14-year reign as a boom town ended in 1893 with the US adoption of the gold standard and by the early 1930s its population of 12,000 had plummeted to 350. But then came the discovery of 'white gold' and Aspen's rebirth as a ski town.

Its legacy from those early years is a collection of fine Victorian buildings including Hotel Jerome, the original inn. They have all been beautifully restored and more recent additions are constructed in sympathetic period style. Some 200 shops range from art galleries and designer boutiques like the new Prada store to sportswear outlets and beauty salons. No other resort in America has such a wonderful range of restaurants.

Property prices match Manhattan and London and the cost of living is higher than in any other major ski destination in North America. That said, Aspen is no more expensive than Courchevel 1850 or Val d'Isère. This is not a place for budget skiers and riders but, as in France, with a little careful research it is possible to enjoy a holiday here without spending a fortune.

The town centre at the foot of Aspen Mountain – also known as Ajax – is relatively compact. An efficient bus service connects outlying hotels as well as the three other ski areas of Buttermilk, Aspen Highlands and Snowmass. Snowmass (nine miles) and Highlands (three miles) are alternative places to base yourself if the town with its shops, restaurants and nightlife is not a priority.

Work has started on a new base village for Snowmass, which will make it a much more attractive option, with 246 hotel-style units, 349 condos, 10 town homes and two luxury hotels as well as shops and restaurants. The new base is now connected by an open cabriolet gondola to the existing Snowmass Mall.

You can fly direct to Aspen from Denver. The airport is only three miles from town. It's worth noting that the route is heavily booked during the winter and flights must be arranged well in advance.

Mountain

The skiing is divided into four separate areas linked by ski-bus. Furthest apart are Aspen Mountain and Snowmass (20 minutes). Each has its own character.

Buttermilk is a benign beginner and family area with lots of easy green runs served by the West Buttermilk Express and some marginally more taxing routes back to the base down the front face. The eastern side of the mountain is given over to runs marked black on the piste map, although they should present few difficulties to anyone who has just learned to ski parallel. An enormous terrain park is accessed by the Summit Express and runs from top to bottom.

Snowmass is the largest and most underrated sector which is suited to everyone from beginner to expert. It has a vertical drop of 3,904ft (1190m), one of the longest in North America. The upper mountain is mostly for advanced skiers with some truly steep terrain such as the Cirque headwall. Elk Camp and Big Burn have plenty of intermediate runs.

The new Sam's Knob Express lift opened last winter as part of $45 million of mountain improvements to complement the Base Village. It now takes skiers and riders to the top of 1,030ft Sam's Knob in nine-and-a-half minutes with a midway stop to access beginner runs. This season sees the opening of a new eight-person gondola from the base of Fanny Hill to Elk Camp, with a mid-station at the base of Funnel. Pipeline Park, served by the Burlingame chair, has three half-pipes and a warming yurt.

Aspen Highlands has some of the most radical terrain in America. Beginner and intermediate runs are found on the lower part of the mountain, but generally this is not a place for the faint-hearted. Highland Bowl, Steeple Chase and Olympic Bowl have awesome reputations. Last season it improved even further with the opening of a series of vertiginous runs served by the new Deep Temerity lift to the skier's left of Highland Bowl. This winter a further 25 acres of woodland trails have been cleared.

Aspen Mountain, immediately above the town and served by the venerable Silver Queen gondola, which this season receives a face-lift with a set of new six-person cabins. This is the domain of strong skiers. It is riddled with short, sharp and quite steep, double-black-diamond chutes, including the famous 'dump runs' such as Bear Paw, Short Snort and Zaugg Dump, which were created by miners' spoil. Walsh's is considered to be the most challenging.

Face of Bell leading down into Spar Gulch usually provides excellent tree-skiing. You don't have to be a double-diamond addict to ski on Aspen Mountain – you can ski top to bottom on blue runs – but the Little Nell approach to the gondola is quite steep and can be icy when covered in artificial snow. Aspen Mountain Powder Tours offers skiing and riding off the back of the mountain.

Learn

Ski and Snowboard School of Aspen/ Snowmass, t +1 970 925 1227, has branches on all four mountains. Courses include Too Cool For School teen skiing, **Aspen Adventures, t** +1 970 925 7625, and **Aspen Mountain Powder Tours, t** +1 970 920 0720.

LEVATION TOP:	11,212 ft/3,418 m
ERTICAL RISE:	3,267 ft/996 m
ERRAIN:	673 acres/273 hectares
ONGEST RUN:	3 miles/4.83 km
IFTS:	Silver Queen Gondola, 1 high-speed quad, 1 high-speed double, 2 quads, 3 doubles
IFT CAPACITY:	10,755 riders per hour
VERAGE ANNUAL SNOWFALL:	300 inches/762 cm
NOWMAKING CAPABILITIES:	210 acres/85 hectares (33% of area)
ASIEST TERRAIN:	None
IORE DIFFICULT TERRAIN:	48%
IOST DIFFICULT TERRAIN:	26%
XPERT TERRAIN:	26%
EASON DATES:	November 25, 2004 – April 10, 2005

mbols and color codes indicate the relative skiing difficulty r slopes and trails on Aspen Mountain only. For your own otection, do not start down a trail or slope until you know s degree of difficulty and never ski/ride a CLOSED trail.

Children

The ski school runs a full children's programme and kids aged 12 years and under must wear helmets. **Kids Room**, **t** +1 701 456 7888, provides childcare in town and a kindergarten, **t** +1 970 925 1227, is at each mountain base. At Snowmass, **Snow Cubs**, **t** +1 970 923 0563, caters for children aged from eight weeks with lessons from 18 months. **Big Burn Bears**, **t** + 1 970 923 0570, or the **Grizzlies**, **t** +1 970 923 0580, are clubs for older children. At Buttermilk, **Powder Pandas**, **t** +1 970 923 1227, cares for three- to six-year olds.

Lunch

Buttermilk has **Bumps**, **t** + 1 970 920 0991, at the base and the **Cliffhouse**, **t** +1 970 925 1220, at the top of the Summit Express.

At Snowmass, try **Gwyn's High Alpine**, **t** +1 970 923 3311, for grilled game and homemade desserts. **Sam's Knob**, **t** +1 970 925 1220, has good pasta and views of the Big Burn. **Ullrhof**, **t** +1 970 923 5143, is warmly recommended for its burgers, elk medallions, and Thai shrimp. **Up 4 Pizza**, **t** +1 970 925 1220, is quick and cheerful.

At Highlands, **Cloud Nine Alpine Bistro**, **t** +1 970 923 8715, is a small gourmet restaurant with magnificent views of the Maroon Bells. On Aspen Mountain, **Bonnie's**, **t** +1 970 925 1220, has wonderful white bean chilli and *Apfelstrudel*. **Ajax Tavern**, **t** +1 970 920 9333, by the Silver Queen gondola, has good food and is great for people-watching. **Benedict's**, **t** +1 970 920 6971, at the top of the gondola, is also recommended.

Dine

Most restaurants are expensive, but if you are prepared to eat at the bar you are served the same food in smaller portions at a greatly reduced price.

In Aspen, **Mezzaluna**, **t** +1 970 925 5882, serves pizza and other Italian cuisine. **Kenichi**, **t** + 1 970 920 2212, **Takah Sushi**, **t** +1 970 925 8588, and **Matsuhisa**, **t** +1 970 544 6628, all serve Japanese food. **Olives Aspen**, **t** + 1 970 920 7356, in the St Regis Resort, serves Mediterranean-inspired American food. **La Cocina**, **t** +1 970 925 9714, **Little Annie's**, **t** +1 970 925 1098, **Mother Lode**, **t** +1 970 925 7700, and **Wild Fig**, **t** +1 970 925 5160, are all warmly recommended. **Jimmy's**, **t** +1 970 925 6020, is said to be 'posh but not too posh'. In Snowmass, try **Mountain Dragon**, **t** +1 970 923 3576, and **Sage Bistro**, **t** +1 970 923 0923, at the Snowmass Club.

Party

The **Jerome Bar** or J-Bar is a popular resort rendezvous. The **Ajax Tavern** is always crowded at the end of the skiing day. **Elevation**, **Jimmy's**, the **Mogador** and **Club Chelsea** attract a sophisticated after-dinner crowd. **Shooters** is a country-and-western saloon with live bands. **Mezzaluna** serves inexpensive beers and pizza. The health-conscious head for **The Aspen Club and Spa** or the **Remede Spa** in the St Regis Resort. Those who have celebrity friends or are prepared to pay for temporary membership gather in the exclusive **Caribou Club**. **39 Degrees** is the Sky Hotel's all-day dining room/bar, serving Sushi Nachos and Asian Beef Summer Rolls. The signature cocktail is Botox Martini. It comes with two cherries – one wrinkled and one pristine.

Sleep

Aspen:

Luxury:

Hotel Jerome, **t** +1 970 920 1000, *www.hoteljerome.com*, is the original Victorian inn.

Hotel Lenado, **t** +1 970 925 6246, *www.hotellenado.com*, is a small, friendly B&B hotel full of rustic charm. Each of its 19 bedrooms has a carved four-poster bed. Some of them also have wood-burning stoves and whirlpool baths.

The Little Nell, **t** +1 970 920 4600, *www.thelittlenell.com,* is a five-star resort institution at the base of Aspen Mountain.

St Regis Resort Aspen, **t** +1 970 920 3300, *www.stregisaspen.com*, also at the base, has received a $35-million makeover and has a spa.

The Sky Hotel ,**t** +1 970 925 6760, *www.theskyhotel.com*, is a hip place to stay at the foot of Aspen Mountain, with an outdoor pool and hot tub. All suites have Jacuzzi baths and iPod 'music bars'.

Moderate/Budget:

Aspen Mountain Lodge, **t** +1 970 925 7650 *www.aspenmountainlodge.com*, has a pool and a hot tub.

Hotel Durant, **t** +1 970 925 8500, *www.durantaspen.com*, is two blocks from the centre and includes breakfast.

Innsbruck Inn, **t** +1 970 925 2980, is a favourite with the budget-conscious.

Limelite Lodge, **t** +1 970 925 3025, *www.limelite-lodge.com*, is centrally located and good value.

St Moritz Lodge, **t** +1 970 925 3220, *www.stmoritzlodge.com*, has triple-bed dormitories as well as regular rooms.

Snowmass:

Moderate/Budget:

Chamonix Inn, **t** +1 970 923 3232, *www.snowmass.ski.com*, has piste-side rental units with a pool.

Crestwood Inn, **t** +1 970 923 2450, *www.snowmass.ski.com*, are three-bedroom condos and town houses.

Silvertree Hotel, **t** +1 970 923 3520, *www.silvertreehotel.com*,is Snowmass' only full-service ski-in/ski-out hotel.

Snowmass Club, **t** +1 970 923 5600, *www.snowmassclub.com*, is a smart condo complex.

Snowmass Inn, **t** +1 970 923 4302, *www.snowmassinn.com*, is family owned and adjacent to the Village Mall.

Stonebridge Inn, **t** +1 970 923 2420, *www.stonebridgeinn.com*, has slope-side hotel rooms and suites.

Beaver Creek, Colorado

BEST FAMILY RESORT 2007

Profile

An up-market choice for families, with a good snow record and an excellent ski school. Not ideal for those on a budget

Resort

Beaver Creek is Vail's rich and beautiful sister who lives up a private road above the valley town of Avon, a 15-minute drive away along I-70. 'Couldn't believe the luxury' said one reporter. 'Why walk when you can stand on a motorized walkway?' Both resorts are owned by the same giant corporation, but each has its own character. Beaver Creek has a much more intimate atmosphere, lots of accommodation on the edge of the piste, and is more family oriented.

Unusually for North America, the resort is linked on mountain to two small hamlets – Arrowhead and Bachelor Gulch – that provide alternative bed-bases.

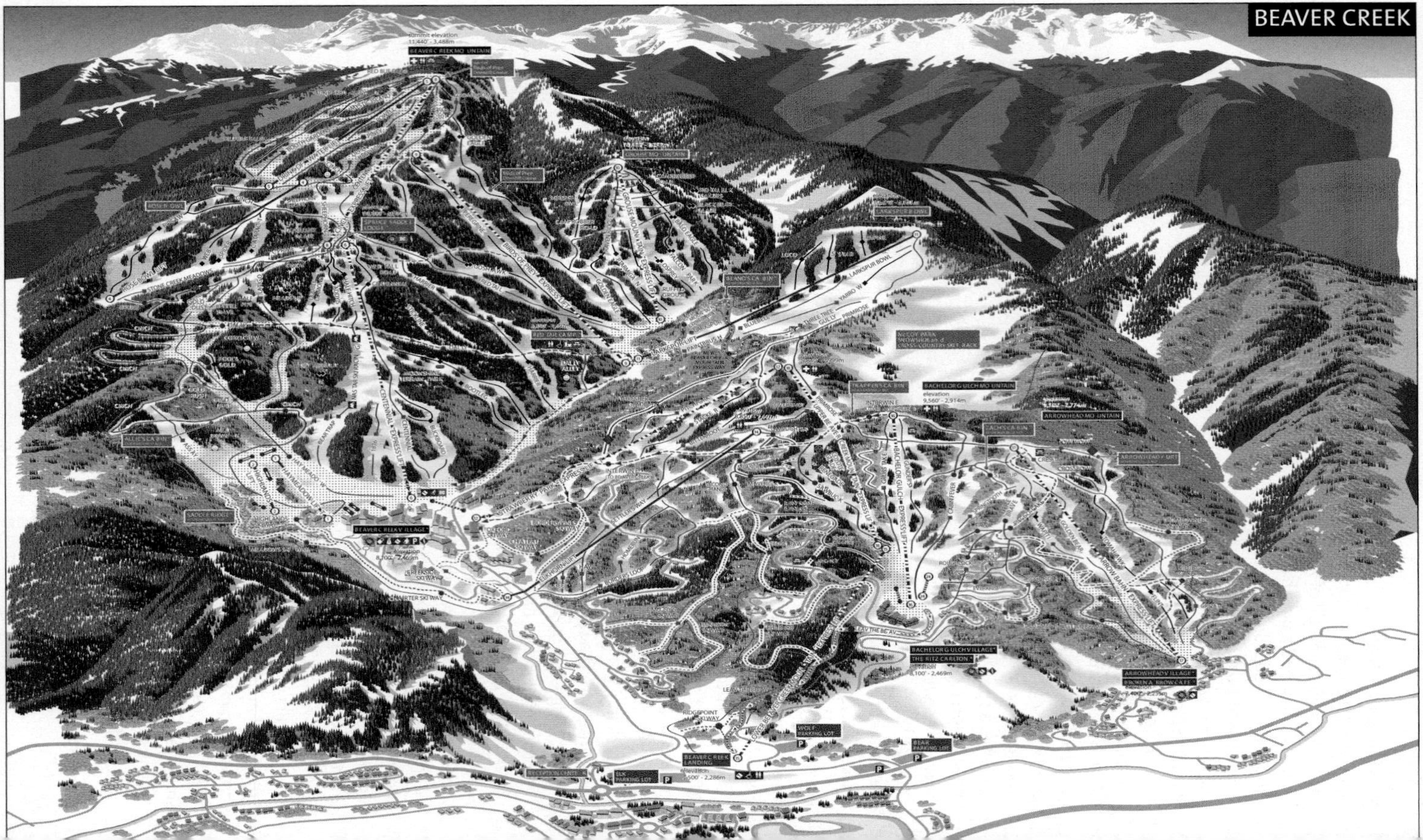
BEAVER CREEK
summit elevation
11,440' - 3,488m
BEAVER CREEK MOUNTAIN
GROUSE MOUNTAIN
GROUSE MOUNTAIN EXPRESS LIFT
BIRDS OF PREY EXPRESS LIFT
CENTENNIAL EXPRESS LIFT
CENTENNIAL
BLACKBOARD
LARKSPUR BOWL
LARKSPUR LIFT
THREE TREE GULLY
PRIMROSE
BACHELOR GULCH MOUNTAIN
elevation
9,560' - 2,914m
ARROWHEAD MOUNTAIN
BACHELOR GULCH EXPRESS LIFT
ARROW BAHN EXPRESS LIFT
GUNDER'S
CABINFEVER
TOMAHAWK
GOLDEN BEAR
WAPITI
STRAWBERRY PARK EXPRESS LIFT
HAYMEADOW LIFT
BEAVER CREEK VILLAGE
elevation
8,100' - 2,469m
CREEKSIDE SKIWAY
LEAVE THE BEAVER
BACHELOR GULCH VILLAGE
THE RITZ-CARLTON
elevation
8,100' - 2,469m
ARROWHEAD VILLAGE
BROKEN ARROW CAFE
RIDGEPOINT SKIWAY
WOLF PARKING LOT
BEAR PARKING LOT
BEAVER CREEK LANDING
elevation
7,500' - 2,286m
ELK PARKING LOT
RECEPTION CENTER

***BEST FOR**

Cosmopolitan sophistication, families, all levels of skier and rider

ESSENTIALS

Altitude: 8,100ft (2,470m)–11,440ft (3488m)
Further information: t +1 970 845 9090, *www.beavercreek.com*
Lifts in area: 14 (13 chairs, 1 drag) serving 1,805 acres of terrain
Lift pass: Colorado Ticket (covers Arapahoe Basin, Beaver Creek, Breckenridge, Keystone, Vail) adult $169–402, child 5–12yrs $186, both for 6 out of 9 days
Access: Denver airport 2½hrs, Eagle County/Vail airport 45mins

Focal point of the village is an open-air ice rink surrounded by designer boutiques, a plethora of art galleries where prices are only available on request, and sports shops that sell fur coats as well as ski gear. One outraged and thirsty reader protested that the cheapest bottle of wine in the resort's only off-licence was a bottle of 'undrinkable' Algerian *vin de table* priced at $14.99.

The resort's clientele is as sleekly groomed as its perfect corduroy pistes and this air of sophistication is reflected in a wide choice of luxury hotels and giant, well-appointed condos as well as fine dining establishments. Childcare facilities here are exceptionally good.

The lift ticket allows skiers and riders to go to Vail, Breckenridge, Keystone and Arapahoe Basin. A regular subsidized shuttle runs to and from Vail but you need a car to go further afield and sample the other Vail resorts – the bus service to these has been suspended through lack of interest.

Mountain

Despite its modest size, Beaver's ski area holds plenty of interest for all standards of skier and rider, but with the emphasis on intermediates.

The Centennial Express Chair – effortlessly reached from the heart of the village by a two-stage escalator – takes you up to the mid-mountain hub of Spruce Saddle with access to plenty of wide, undulating blue pistes back to the resort and off the shoulder down Stone Creek meadows into the Rose Bowl.

From Spruce Saddle, the Cinch Express chair takes you up to the top of the ski area for more intermediate terrain – or the much greater demands of the Birds of Prey downhill course, one of the toughest on the World Cup Circuit. When not prepared for racing, it tends to become severely mogulled between snowfalls and lives up to its double-diamond rating. Pick of the steep stuff is to be found on adjoining Grouse Mountain. Runs such as Royal Elk Glades, Bald Eagle, Falcon Park and Osprey served by the Grouse Mountain Express provide high-octane entertainment. The Rose Bowl lift also serves a range of black-diamond trails. After a major dump, powder opportunities here are exceptional. This season sees the addition of 180 acres of short, steep, gladed runs, known as the Stone Creek Chutes, with pitches of up to 44 degrees. For anyone staying here, a visit to Vail's Back Bowls and Blue Sky Basin is a must, but don't ignore the powder on your doorstep – this is where you will find the locals.

The easiest terrain is served by the Bachelor Gulch Express and the Arrow Bahn Express from Arrowhead, and novices and wobbly intermediates have a chance to explore the whole mountainside.

Beaver Creek has three terrain parks that attract as many twin-tipped skiers as they do snowboarders. Park 101, situated on Upper Sheephorn, is designed for park novices. Zoom is for accomplished riders, and has a half-pipe as well as the full range of obstacles.

Learn

Beaver Creek Ski and Snowboard School, **t** +1 970 845 5300, is part of the Vail school and has an excellent reputation both for the quality of instruction and the friendliness of the teachers ('best lesson I have ever had anywhere').

Children

The ski school runs the full range of classes and is again highly rated ('I really felt my children benefited hugely from the whole week of instruction – and they loved every minute of it'). **Small World Play School**, **t** +1 970 845 5325, provides all-day care for children from three years.

Lunch

Owing to the well-heeled nature of its clientele, Beaver Creek takes lunch more seriously than many American resorts – but unfortunately the public are unable to share the best part of it. At lunch time **Beano's Cabin**, **t** +1 970 949 9090, remains a private club. The same applies to **Zach's Cabin**, **t** +1 866 395 3185 (Pacific Rim cooking), and **Allie's Cabin**, **t** +1 970 845 5762, which has some fine wines. 'The few accessible outlets are heavily subscribed', said one reporter, 'and the best option is to return to the resort for lunch'. **Beaver Creek Tavern** offers gourmet burgers, and the **Broken Arrow Café** in Arrowhead has 'homemade soup and enormous club sandwiches'.

Dine

Splendido at the Chateau, **t** +1 970 845 8808, has Russian caviar and lobsters flown in from Maine. **SaddleRidge**, **t** +1 970 845 5762, houses a museum of Western memorabilia and serves game and seafood. **Allie's Cabin**, **t** +1 970 845 5762, and **Zach's Cabin**, **t** +1 866 395 3185, are open by night to all. **Beano's Cabin**, **t** +1 970 949 9090, reached by motorized sleigh, has memorable five-course meals. **Mirabelle**, **t** +1 970 949 7728, has contemporary Belgian and French cuisine. **traMonti**, **t** +1 970 949 5552, and **Toscanini**, **t** +1 970 845 5590, are both Italian. **Foxnut**, **t** +1 970 845 0700, has Asian fusion cuisine ('a pleasant change from the usual American fine dining').

Sato Sushi, **t** +1 970 926 7684, in the nearby town of Edwards, is off the beaten tourist track. It's popular with locals and has outstanding Japanese cuisine.

Party

Nightlife is distinctly muted in what is essentially a family resort. The **Coyote Café**, **Beaver Creek Chophouse** and **Dusty Boot Saloon** capture the main crowd, along with the **Beaver Creek Tavern** and **McCoy's** for live music. The **Black Family Ice Rink** is open until 10pm.

Sleep

★★★★★**The Charter**, **t** +1 970 949 6660, *www.thecharter.com*, at the base, has two restaurants, a spa and indoor pool.

★★★★★**Park Hyatt Resort & Spa**, **t** +1 970 949 1234, *beavercreek.hyatt.com*, has a renowned spa and two restaurants.

★★★★★**Ritz-Carlton**, **t** +1 970 748 6200, *www.ritzcarlton.com*, at the base of Bachelor Gulch, is like a small village in its own right and has a magnificent spa.

★★★★★**SaddleRidge**, **t** +1 970 845 5990, *www.beavercreekresortproperties.com*, consists of separate two-bedroom chalets furnished with Ralph Lauren fabrics and Western antiques.

★★★★**The Inn at Beaver Creek**, **t** +1 970 845 5990, *theinnatbc.coloradoreservationservice.com*, is slope-side and adjacent to the Strawberry Park Express lift.

★★★★**Elkhorn Lodge, t** +1 970 845 5990, is in a ski-in/ski-out position on the edge of the golf course ('extremely comfortable and spacious apartments with helpful concierge').

★★★★**Trapper's Cabin, t** +1 970 845 5900, *www.trapperscabincolorado.com*, is a rustic hideaway in the trees sleeping 10 people, reached on skis or by snowmobile.

Breckenridge, Colorado

Profile

Lively old mining town with a good nightlife. Large ski area with reliable snow conditions, but short runs. Snowboarding is popular. Time needed to acclimatize at this extremely high altitude

Resort

Breckenridge earned its inclusion in the map of the world in July 1887 when miners Tom Grove and Harry Lytton stumbled across a nugget of gold that weighed an astonishing 13lb 7oz. Tom's Baby, as it was christened, was the culmination of a 10-year mining boom that created the attractive Victorian town that is now one of Colorado's top ski destinations and still the most popular with overseas skiers.

The legacy of the boom years of the 19th century is a number of fine pastel-painted weatherboarded buildings along Main Street, the focal point of the resort with its wide range of shops and restaurants. Others have been created in a sympathetic style, while the late 20th-century ski-in/ski-out accommodation around the ski base is more utilitarian with few concessions to architectural frivolity. The skiing and riding is suitable for all standards but – the resort would beg to differ – is best for intermediates.

This season should see a transformation in resort transport. The long-awaited eight-person gondola from the main car parks off Main Street to Peak 7 and Peak 8 was under construction last summer and should be open in time for the start of the season.

Breckenridge shares a lift pass with Keystone, Vail, Beaver Creek and Arapahoe Basin, all of which are within easy reach. They are linked by a free bus service to Keystone and the local challenging ski area of A-Basin. Daily transport subsidized by the joint lift company connects Breckenridge with Vail and Beaver Creek, which are slightly further away. During a week or 10-day stay here you are strongly advised to explore further afield.

Visitors arriving at Denver from either coast or from overseas can easily reach Breckenridge in just 1½ hours, but it's easy to forget the enormous change in altitude. This, combined with low humidity, can cause dehydration and headaches that are exacerbated by exercise. Don't overdo it on your first day,

✱ BEST FOR

All levels of skier and rider, mogul-hoppers, snowboarders

ESSENTIALS

Altitude: 9,600ft (2927m)–12,998ft (3962m)

Further information: **t** +1 970 453 5000, *www.breckenridge.com*

Lifts in area: 28 (16 chairs, 4 drags, 8 carpets) serving 2,208 acres of terrain

Lift pass: Colorado Ticket (covers Arapahoe Basin, Beaver Creek, Breckenridge, Keystone, Vail) adult $169–402, child 5–12yrs $186, both for 6 out of 9 days

Access: Denver airport 1½hrs, Eagle County/Vail airport 1hr

drink plenty of water, and abstain from alcohol until your body has had a chance to acclimatize. One reader bought a can of oxygen from the supermarket ('keep sniffing it, it works'). Snow-cover in Breckenridge is usually the most abundant of all the Vail resorts.

Mountain

'Breckenfridge' is its apt nickname. The mercury can plunge at this high altitude and in mid-winter you need technical ski clothing to be comfortable. The skiing takes place on four side-by-side peaks in the Ten Mile Range alongside the town. Someone devoid of imagination originally named them Peaks 10, 9, 8 and 7 and no one else has so far found the courage to change them.

For the present, easiest access is by the Quicksilver Super 6 from the top of town that takes you up Peak 9 and into the system. All the peaks are well linked on mountain. In the future, skiers and riders will be able to access Peak 8 direct from Main Street and parking lots rather than by bus. Work has already started on the ambitious Skyway Skiway, which is due to be completed this season.

From the top of the Quicksilver, easy runs fan out to the Falcon SuperChair on Peak 10, the starting point for a network of predominantly advanced runs with some testing mogul-fields. It is also possible to ski to the Mercury and Beaver Run SuperChairs on Peak 9, which has some of the most inviting cruising in the resort, plus Gold King, a terrain park designed for learner freeriders. Peak 7 is built for cruising, with huge rollers on all seven new trails.

The opening of the SuperConnect lift has reduced queuing by integrating the ski area efficiently. It has eased access to Peak 8, otherwise reached by shuttle bus or the venerable Snowflake dog-leg chair from the edge of town.

The Vista Haus mid-station is the focal point for the chair-lifts that serve the network of blue and black trails on the lower slopes of Peak 8. The Independence SuperChair has extended Breckenridge's boundaries into a glade area cut from the forest on the lower slopes of Peak 7 that is suited to intermediates.

Breckenridge's expert terrain, created as a result of local demand for more 'European-style off-piste', covers the wide open upper slopes on Peaks 7, 8 and 9. The T-Bar takes snow-users into Peak 8's double-black-diamond zone, comprising Horseshoe, Contest, North and Cucumber Bowls, all of them ungroomed. Beyond that you're on your own, hiking over 12,000ft to the radical Peak-top runs. Whale's Tail and Peak 7 Bowl are 1,500ft vertical above the T-Bar, but the sterner test is Peak 8's Imperial Bowl, a 2,700ft vertical rise from the same starting point. This also accesses the Lake Chutes, which have slopes of up to 50 degrees.

Breckenridge was the first resort in Colorado to allow snowboarding and remains popular with riders who form 25 per cent of the winter clientele. The four dedicated areas include the Freeway Terrain Park and the Breckenridge Super-Pipe, which are equally attractive to twin-tippers.

Learn

Breckenridge Ski & Ride School, **t** +1 970 453 3272, has an excellent reputation with a wide range of courses, including some for teens and 50+.

Children

Breckenridge Children's Center, **t** +1 970 453 3258, offers slope-side crèches for kids from two months at Peak 8 and Peak 9. Both have pagers for parents to hire, provide lunches and offer a non-skiing, outdoor snow-play program. Advance

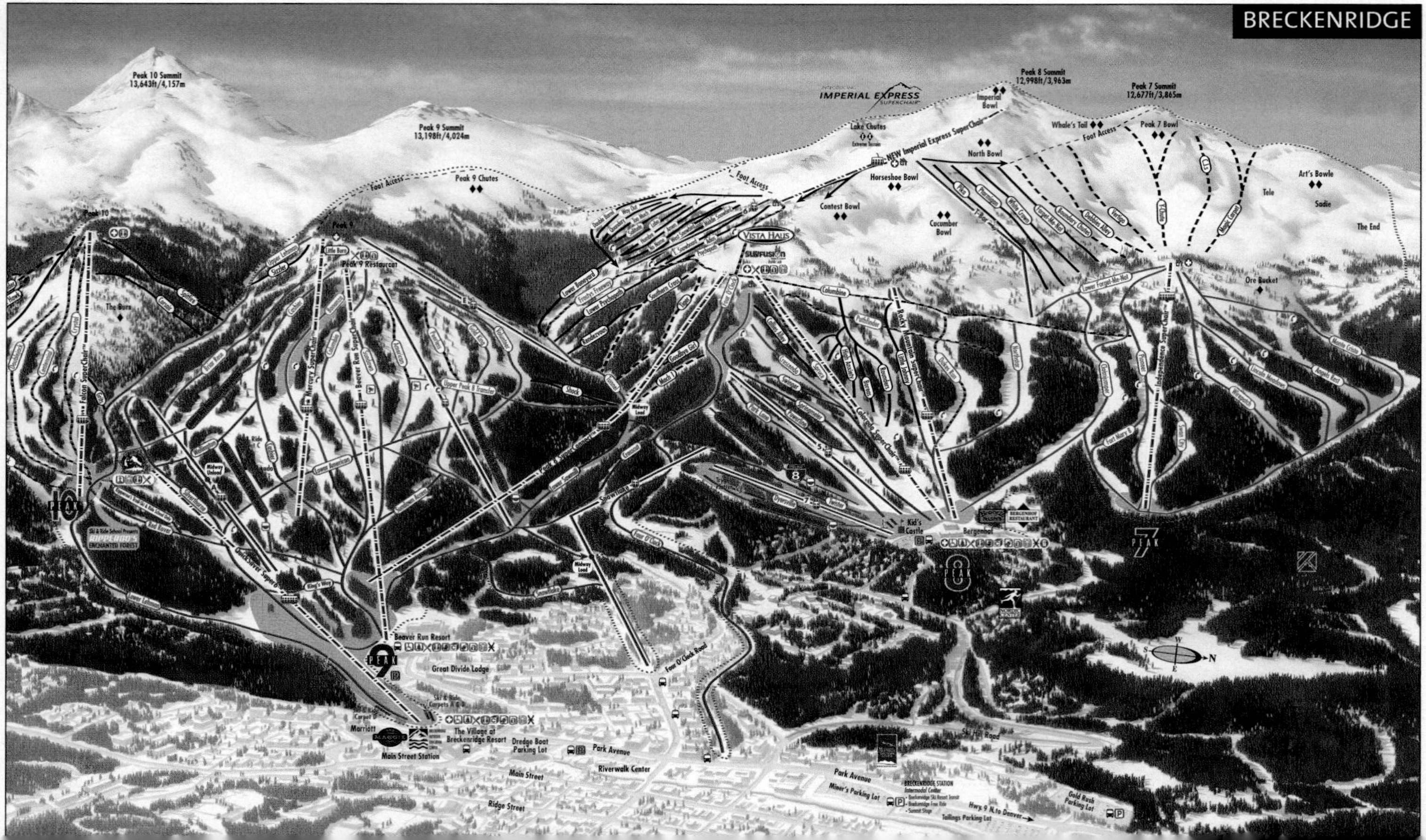
Peak 10 Summit
13,643ft/4,157m
Peak 9 Summit
13,198ft/4,024m
INTRODUCING IMPERIAL EXPRESS SUPERCHAIR
Peak 8 Summit
12,998ft/3,963m
Peak 7 Summit
12,677ft/3,865m
Imperial Bowl
Lake Chutes
Whale's Tail
Peak 7 Bowl
Foot Access
NEW Imperial Express SuperChair
North Bowl
Horseshoe Bowl
Art's Bowle
Tele
Sadie
The End
Peak 9 Chutes
Contest Bowl
Cucumber Bowl
Peak 10
Peak 9
Vista Haus
Peak 9 Restaurant
The Burn
Ore Bucket
Columbine
Rocky Mountain SuperChair
Independence SuperChair
Colorado SuperChair
Mercury SuperChair
Beaver Run SuperChair
Falcon SuperChair
Kid's Castle
Bergenhof
Beaver Run Resort
Great Divide Lodge
Four O'Clock Road
Marriott
Main Street Station
The Village at Breckenridge Resort
Dredge Boat Parking Lot
Park Avenue
Riverwalk Center
Main Street
Ridge Street
Park Avenue
Miner's Parking Lot
Ski Hill Road
Gold Rush Parking Lot
Hwy. 9 N. to Denver
Tailings Parking Lot
Breckenridge Station

reservations are essential during the busiest weeks.

Breckenridge Ski & Ride School accepts children from three years and is praised by reporters: 'I would definitely recommend Breckenridge to families with children who require warm coaxing into having lessons.'

Lunch

This is not a ski area for gourmets whose ideal skiing day involves a hard morning and lazy afternoon at a laden table. You can eat well in town, but good food on the mountain is harder to come by. Restaurants listed below without numbers belong to the resort, **t** +1 970 453 5000.

On Peak 9, **Le Bistro de Paris, t** +1 970 453 2572, is less burger-oriented, reasonably priced, and much the best bet. **Ten Mile Station**, at the top of the Quicksilver Chair, has a heated outdoor deck, a mining-themed food court, and a barbecue in fine weather. On Peak 8, **Border Burritos** at the Bergenhof has good-value salads and tacos, **The Vista Haus** food court at the top of the Colorado SuperChair has a great view of the Continental Divide, while the food is less spectacular.

Dine

Breckenridge has a choice of some 50 restaurants. In high season, booking is essential. **Hearthstone, t** +1 970 453 1148, is a converted Victorian brothel with loads of atmosphere and a creative Western menu. Try the granola-crusted elk chops. **South Ridge Seafood Grill, t** +1 970 547 0063, has oysters flown in daily from Chesapeake Bay. **The Blue River Bistro, t** +1 970 453 6974, and **Café Alpine, t** +1 970 453 8218, are fine-dining destinations. **Steak and Rib, t** +1 970 453 0063, is recommended.

Mi Casa, t +1 970 453 2071, is a good-value Mexican restaurant, and **Columbine Café, t** +1 970 547 4474 offers nutritious breakfasts. **The Red Orchid, t** +1 970 453 1881, specializes in Mandarin and Szechwan fare, **Mountain Flying Fish, t** +1 970 453 1502, and **Wasabi, t** +1 970 453 8311, are sushi restaurants, and **My Thai, t** +1 970 547 2887, is the fourth oriental offering. Italian eateries include **St. Bernard, t** +1 970 453 2572, **Fatty's, t** +1 970 453 9802, and **Giampetro, t** +1 970 453 3838. **Pierre's Riverwalk Café, t** +1 970 453 0989, blends American and French cuisine. If you don't want to go out, **Gourmet Cabby, t** +1 970 543 7788, will deliver food and drink from 30 restaurants to your condo.

Party

This is a lively town with young skiers and riders determined to party away the hours not spent on the mountain. **Mi Casa** serves mean jugs of Margaritas. Try also **Breckenridge Brewery**, **Sherpa & Yeti**, **Gold Pan Saloon** (the oldest bar in the US west of the Mississippi), **Downstairs at Eric's**, **Ullr's Sports Grille** and **Gracy O'Malleys**. **Julius Caesar** is a British-style pub.

Sleep

Breckenridge offers spacious rather than deluxe hotels, two large condominium resorts, several smaller apartment buildings and restored Victorian inns.

*****Beaver Run Resort, t** +1 970 453 6000, *www.beaverrun.com,*is a 500-room ski-in/ski-out condo complex praised for its 'excellent facilities'.

*****Breckenridge Mountain Lodge, t** +1 970 453 2333, *www.breckenridgemountainlodge.com,* provides budget accommodation at the end of Main Street, offering an 'Old West bed and breakfast experience'.

*****Great Divide Lodge, t** +1 970 453 4500, *www.greatdividelodge.com,* is near

Peak 9 base and is one of the only full-service hotels.

*****Lodge and Spa**, **t** +1 970 453 9300, *www.thelodgeatbreck.com*, is five minutes from town with a shuttle bus to the slopes.

*****The Mountain Thunder Lodge**, **t** +1 888 547 8092, *www.mtnthunderlodge.com*, contains comfortable studios, condos and suites below Peak 8.

The Canyons, Utah

* BEST MOUNTAIN RESTAURANT 2007
The Lookout Cabin

Profile

Purpose-built resort with convenient and extensive skiing for all standards. A good choice for foodies, including a superb mountain restaurant

Resort

The Canyons is one of three side-by-side ski areas an easy 40-minute drive from Salt Lake City. Leave the highway at Kimball Junction and you come first to The Canyons, followed by Park City Mountain Resort and then Deer Valley. Linking all three would involve the construction of just one lift. Rivalry has so far prevented this, but last season the three launched a joint adult and children's pass for foreign visitors that is only sold through tour operators, with a single rate throughout the season.

The Canyons is the relative newcomer. It has developed over a decade from a small, local ski area into what is now the fifth largest ski resort in the United States, with the facilities to attract international skiers and snowboarders. A further $400 million expansion over three years begins this season with a new lift opening up 200 acres of intermediate and expert terrain in the Dreamscape sector. The Utah Olympic Park, adjoining The Canyons, has a bobsleigh and luge track. It is also one of the few places in the world where beginners can try their hand at ski-jumping. Kimball Junction, just outside the resort, has a large collection of designer outlet stores with attractive prices.

Mountain

From the rather soulless purpose-built village, the Flight of the Canyons gondola rapidly conveys skiers and riders to the Red Lodge Pine mid-station. Lifts fan out from the top in all directions across the mainly tree-covered mountainside. The skiing suits all standards with lots of easy cruising runs as well as some more demanding terrain reached by the Super Condor Express and the Ninety Nine 90 Express at the 9,990ft summit of the ski area. Last season Dreamcatcher, a new

*BEST FOR

All levels of skier and rider, off-piste, mountain restaurant

ESSENTIALS

Altitude: 6,800ft (2073m)–9,990ft (3045m)

Further information: **t** +1 435 649 5400, *www.thecanyons.com*

Lifts in area: 15 (2 cableways, 12 chairs, 1 drag) serving 3,500 acres of terrain

Lift pass: Utah Three Resort Pass adult $408, child 7–12yrs $225, both for 6 out of 7 days

Access: Salt Lake City airport 40mins

THE CANYONS
MURDOCK PEAK
NINETY NINE 90
SWEET PEA
MAGIC CARPET
SUPER CONDOR EXPRESS
TOMBSTONE EXPRESS
THE ASPENS
THE PINES
TREE TIME
ESCAPADE WOODS
LOST WORLD
MYSTIC PINES
THE ABYSS
7 SISTERS CHUTES
SNOW MEADOW
NATURAL HALF PIPES
1 Canis Lupis
2 STH
3 Tube
4 Hurricane Alley
5 Tunnel of Fun
6 Pinball Alley
RED PINE LODGE AREA
TRAIL MAP LEGEND
Easiest
More Difficult
More Difficult
Most Difficult
Most Difficult
Surface Lift
Chairlift
Least difficult way down
Natural Halfpipes
Designated Kodak Photo Spots for the best photo opportunities at The Canyons
Ski Area Boundary
High-Speed Quad
Quad
Triple
Double
Gondola
Slow Skiing Zone
First Aid/Ski Patrol
Restroom
Restaurant
Day Care
Perfect Turn® Ski & Snowboard School at The Canyons
Access through gates only Gates subject to close
Freestyle Terrain Park Use extra Caution
This Orange Oval symbol designates Freestyle Terrain such as parks and pipes. SmartStyle represents Freestyle Terrain safety. Know it, Respect it, Use it!
Look before you leap. Scope around the jumps first, not over them. Know landings are clear and clear yourself out of the landing area.
Easy style it. Start small and work your way up. (Inverted aerials prohibited.)
Respect gets respect. From the liftline through the park.
Trail ratings are relative to other trails on our mountain only. They are in no way comparative to trails at other ski/snowboard areas.
RECCO
The Canyons neither encourages nor discourages backcountry skiing/riding. Backcountry terrain is not part of the ski resort. You are leaving the ski resort when you go through the backcountry access gates. This area is not controlled for avalanche safety, and people have died in avalanches in the backcountry. Skiers/snowboarders leaving The Canyons boundaries do so at their own risk. Backcountry skiers/riders should carry a beacon, shovel and probe. Never ski/ride alone. Read posted signs at backcountry access points before proceeding.
Call the Utah Avalanche Forecast Center at 1-435-658-5512 or 1-801-364-1581 for further information.
Reservations 1-888-CANYONS
General Information 1-435-649-5400
Snow Conditions 1-435-615-3456
www.thecanyons.com

quad-chair with a 1,600ft vertical drop, added 200 acres of intermediate and advanced gladed runs. The Canyons has two terrain parks for beginners and experts that are accessed by the Sun Peak lift.

Learn

The Canyons Ski & Snowboard School, **t** +1 435 615 3449, offers group and private tuition, and courses such as learn-to-ski packages, clinics with Olympic athletes, and telemark.

Children

The Canyons Ski & Snowboard School offers children's tuition, and **The Canyons Little Adventures Center**, **t** +1 435 615 8036, provides daycare for children from six weeks to four years.

Lunch

The Lookout Cabin, **t** +1 436 615 3406, at the top of the Golden Eagle and Short Cut chairs, is an unexpected gastronomic treat, a European-style mountain hut with a sophisticated menu and friendly service. Other mountain eateries, **t** +1 435 649 5400 for all, include **Red Pine Lodge**, at the top of the gondola, which has pizzas and deli sandwiches; **Sun Lodge**, at the base of the Sun Peak Express, which is less crowded and majors on grilled meat; and **Westgate Grill**, in the village, which has lots of atmosphere and an all-American menu.

Dine

The Cabin, **t** +1 435 615 8060, in The Canyons Grand Hotel, is one of the best mountain dining options in the region. Try the seafood mixed grill or the rack of venison. Join an evening excursion by snowcat to **The Viking Yurt**, **t** +1 435 615 9878, for a five-course Scandinavian dinner. There are several other good dining options to be found a short drive away in Park City.

Party

Late-night bars conform to the strictures of a private club licence in Utah, but temporary membership is easily obtained. **Doc's at the Gondola** is the main bar at The Canyons. In Park City, try **J.B. Mulligans Club and Pub**, **Wasatch Brew Pub Cantina** and **The Star Bar at Plan B** for live bands.

Sleep

All accommodation can be booked on **t** +1 800 472 6309, *www.the canyons.com*.

Luxury:

The Canyons Grand Hotel (formerly The Grand Summit Resort) is an impressive slope-side complex, with a spa and outdoor swimming pool.

The Miner's Club, **t** +1 435 615 8900, has elegant two- to four-bedroom condos. 'Very comfortable but isolated. You can ski to the door, but you need a courtesy car to reach the lifts.'

The Sundial Lodge has a rooftop hot tub and pool, daycare for kids, and all the rooms – from the studios to family-sized condos – are comfortably furnished.

Budget:

Holiday Inn Express Park City, **t** +1 435 658 1600, *www.hiexpress.com*, is a budget-priced option at Kimball Junction.

Copper Mountain, Colorado

*BEST FOR

Families, all levels of skier and rider, airport access

ESSENTIALS

Altitude: 9,712ft (2926m)–12,313ft (3767m)

Further information: **t** +1 970 968 2882, *www.coppercolorado.com*

Lifts in area: 21 (15 chairs, 6 drags) serving 2,450 acres of terrain

Lift pass: adult $220–348, child 6–13yrs $70–120, both for 6 days

Access: Denver airport 1½hrs

Profile

Recently redeveloped car-free resort with good facilities for families with young children. The skiing suits all standards and snowboarding is a particular strength. Currently still one of the best-kept secrets of Colorado

Resort

Since 1998, skiers driving north on Highway I-70, from one sleek Vail-owned resort to the other, cast barely a glance to their left at what, for over five years, was a construction site dominated by cranes. But now the steel gantries and booms have gone and Copper has emerged from its seemingly endless $400-million makeover since it was acquired by giant resort developer Intrawest. The new car-free base is set around four lodges and plazas with a good range of shops and restaurants.

Copper is no newcomer to skiing. It first opened as a ski area back in 1972. It has one of the best snow records in Colorado and the terrain suits all standards of skier and boarder, with plenty of powder opportunities.

Mountain

Copper is a serious snowboarding destination. Kidz terrain park, located near the top of the American Flyer lift, is for novices and has a mini-pipe. Night Riders Jib Park by the Burning Stones Plaza is floodlit on Friday and Saturday evenings. Catalyst is the main park with three distinct lines for different levels and a superpipe. New park zones under the American Flyer lift link up with Kidz and Catalyst to form a top-to-bottom park run.

The mountain summit is reached in eight minutes by the Super Bee chair-lift. The shape of the mountain naturally allows for one of the best-designed ski areas in the United States. The tree-lined trails become more difficult as you move towards the left of the piste map. Thus, advanced skiers and boarders tend to stick to the main face of Copper Peak and beginners will find little beyond their capabilities on the other side of the resort. In between, the terrain is mainly intermediate. Copper Bowl and Spaulding Bowl provide some of the best off-piste skiing in Colorado, with the latter full of natural jumps and lips for riders.

Learn

Ski & Ride School, **t** +1 866 841 2481, is at the Village and at Union Creek and offers a range of special courses including freestyle, Bumps Busters and Women's Wednesdays. **Over The Hill Gang**, **t** +1 970 968 3059, was founded here in 1976 for the over-45s and arranges guiding for different levels.

Children

Kids Jump Start, t +1 866 841 2481, at the Ski & Ride School offers lessons from three to 15 years. **Copper Freeride Camp, t** +1 866 385 0144, is a weekend course for ages 12 to 18 years. **Belly Button Babies, t** +1 970 968 2882, accepts children from six weeks to two years, and **Belly Button Bakery** provides indoor and outdoor play for children from two to four years.

Lunch

Try **Double Diamond, t** +1 970 968 2880, in the Foxpine Inn, for fried fish on Fridays. **The Blue Moose, t** +1 970 968 9666, by the American Eagle lift, serves New York-style pizzas and salads. **Creekside Pizza and Restaurant, t** +1 970 968 2033, is a local favourite offering 'hand-tossed' pizzas as well as pasta and barbecues. **Alpinista Mountain Bistro, t** +1 970 968 1144, is Copper's newest restaurant.

Dine

Alexander's, t +1 970 968 2165, on the Creek features contemporary cuisine and fine wines. The **Lazy Lizard Cantina, t** +1 970 968 0552, and **Salsa Mountain Cantina, t** +1 970 968 6300, are for Mexican cuisine. **Imperial Palace, t** +1 970 968 6688, in the Village Square Plaza serves low-cholesterol low-sodium Chinese dishes without any additives.

Party

Endo's Adrenaline Café sells huge sandwiches and is popular for après-ski. **Pravda** is a Russian vodka bar with the contemporary atmosphere of the Cold War Soviet era. **JJ's Rocky Mountain Tavern** in East Village has live entertainment and a 52ft bar. **McGillycuddy's** is a Celtic-style pub.

Sleep

Most accommodation is in apartments, with location the main choice to be made. Call **t** +1 888 219 2441 for all reservations. **The Village at Copper** is well placed for most of the dining and shopping. **East Village** is at the base of the intermediate to expert terrain, and **Union Creek** is at the base of the beginner terrain. Quality choices range from Platinum (with heated swimming pool, underground parking and fitness facilitites), through Gold (with hot tub) and Silver (spaciously designed) to Bronze (most affordable).

Crested Butte, Colorado

Profile

Attractive old town set a short drive away from the ski area base. Some excellent steep and deep off-piste and a well-regarded ski school. Its drawback is difficult international access

*BEST FOR

Steep 'n' deep, resort ambience, off the beaten track

ESSENTIALS

Altitude: 9,100ft (2774m) –12,162ft (3707m)
Further information: t +1 970 349 2303, *www.skicb.com*
Lifts in area: 13 (11 chairs, 2 drags) serving 1,073 acres of terrain
Lift pass: adult $372, youth 13–17yrs $282, child 7–12yrs $186, all for 6 days
Access: Gunnison airport 30mins, daily service from Denver airport to Gunnison

Resort

First thing you need to know about Crested Butte is how to pronounce it. A butte (as in 'beaut-iful') is a stand-alone mountain that provides the town with a reputation for challenging skiing that stretches far beyond Colorado. The small Victorian town is no newcomer to the ski scene. Miners from Scandinavia were competing in jumping and downhill races here at least a decade before alpine skiers attempted their first awkward turns in the Swiss Alps. The January 1887 edition of *Outing* magazine gave graphic details of a team skiing competition that had taken place in Crested Butte the previous year.

The resort is under new ownership and currently undergoing a major development plan. However, its remote location has meant that until now Crested Butte has remained something of a backwater. Visitors must first fly into Denver, catch a connecting flight to Gunnison and then a 30-minute transfer to the resort. For those coming from overseas it is not always possible to complete the journey in a single day. The ski area is located three miles from the town. Some 40 original buildings have been restored to their Victorian glory and others have been constructed in sympathetic style. Reporters warn of the need to acclimatize to the resort's high altitude.

Future plans involve a $57-million makeover that includes a new base area village called Mountaineer Square with 93 homes and the construction of a convention centre in the first phase.

Mountain

Crested Butte has some of the steepest lift-served terrain in North America and regularly hosts ski-extreme competitions. Most, but not all, of the mountain is suited to competent skiers and riders in search of new and challenging experiences. Main mountain access from the new Mountaineer Village is by the Red Lady Express and Silver Queen lifts. The first gives access to plenty of intermediate terrain, while the second takes you up into steep double-diamond territory.

The Prospect lift carries skiers from the Prospect housing development to the top of the Goldlink and Painter Boy lifts.

Last season saw an extensive land-scaping of the base area, and the replacement of the T-bars with a fixed-grip quad. This season the East River lift has been upgraded to a high-speed quad.

The resort is a favourite with snow-boarders. The Canaan terrain park, served by the Paradise lift, has a host of jumps and rails and a superpipe.

Learn

Crested Butte Ski and Snowboard School, t +1 970 349 2252, offers workshops on turning skills, all-terrain and ski-racing.

Children

Kids Ski and Snowboard World, t +1 970 349 2259, runs Baby Bears kindergarten for potty-trained toddlers, and Cuddly Bears from 13 months. Lessons are given from three years. The facilities in the Kids' Corral area have been updated.

Lunch

On the mountain, **Ice Bar and Restaurant, t** +1 970 349 2275, offers fine dining and exotic martinis. **Andiamo** in the Paradise Warming Hut, **t** +1 970 349 2274, has sound Italian cuisine and good service.

Dine

Crested Butte has more restaurants than you could possibly visit in a week. Recommended restaurants include **Buffalo Grille & Saloon**, **t** +1 970 349 9699, for buffalo and beef steaks. **The Secret Stash**, **t** +1 970 349 6245, is a 100-year-old miners' cabin with Japanese-style seating, serving Asian barbecue wings and gourmet pizzas. **Le Bosquet Restaurant**, **t** +1 970 349 5808, offers fine dining. **Lil's Land & Sea**, **t** +1 970 349 5457, serves fresh seafood, game and sushi. **Izzy's**, **t** +1 970 349 5630, specializes in stuffed Mediterranean crêpes. The **Firehouse Grill**, **t** +1 970 349 4666, in the Plaza building, is owned and operated by local firefighters and serves pizzas, pasta and steaks. **The Last Steep**, **t** +1 970 349 7007, is the resort's newest eatery, featuring affordable soups, salads and pasta.

Party

Hotspots include **Talk of the Town**, **Kochevar's** and the **Eldo**. The **Firehouse Grill** has pool tables. **Performing Arts** is the local theatre, with drama, music and comedies.

Sleep

****__The Grand Lodge__, **t** +1 970 349 8000, *www.sheratoncrestedbutte.com*, at the base area, is the finest full-service hotel in the resort and has an indoor swimming pool.

***__The Nordic Inn__, **t** +1 970 349 5542, *www.nordicinncb.com*, is a friendly family-run ski lodge.

Purple Mountain Lodge B&B and Spa, **t** +1 970 349 5888, *www.purplemountainlodge.com*, with five individually decorated rooms, offers massage and a hot tub.

Deer Valley, Utah

Profile

Glitzy up-market resort renowned for the immaculate grooming of its trails and guests alike, but with some surprisingly challenging skiing. Snowboarding is still not permitted

Resort

Deer Valley is the furthest from Salt Lake City of a trio of major resorts reached by a 40-minute drive to Kimball Junction. Its carefully nurtured reputation as the smartest – and most expensive – ski destination in America has done nothing to endear it to hard-core skiers who instinctively dismiss it as a place for middle-aged lower intermediates who are only happy if every wrinkle has been surgically removed from the slopes.

In fact, this is an unfair ageist misconception: the mountain at Deer Valley offers plenty of challenge for advanced skiers – but not for snow-boarders. You don't have to be old or rich

*BEST FOR

All levels of skier and rider, cosmopolitan ambience, trail grooming

ESSENTIALS

Altitude: 6,570ft (2003m) – 9,570ft (2917m)
Further information: **t** +1 435 649 1000, *www.deervalley.com*
Lifts in area: 21 (1 cableway, 20 chairs) serving 1,825 acres of terrain
Lift pass: Utah Three Resort Pass adult $408, child 7–12yrs $225, both for 6 out of 7 days
Access: Salt Lake City airport 40mins

DEER VALLEY
DEER VALLEY RESORT
25TH ANNIVERSARY
Heber City
Bald Mt. 9400 ft.
Flagstaff Mt. 9100 ft.
Empire Canyon 9570 ft.
Empire Canyon Lodge 8300 ft.
Silver Lake Lodge 8100 ft.
Bald Eagle Mt. 8400 ft.
Little Baldy Peak 7950 ft.
Snow Park Lodge 7200 ft.
Jordanelle Reservoir
Hwy 40
Deer Crest/ Mayflower Entrance
Jordanelle Ticket Office 6570 ft.
Royal Street
Access to Silver Lake Village
Wasatch Express
Sultan Express
Silver Strike Express
Northside Express
Ruby Express
Empire Express
Quincy Express
Silver Lake Express
Carpenter Express
Jordanelle Express Gondola
Closed Area
TNT Park
Attention:
It is a misdemeanor (Summit County Ordinance No. 91) to ski past rope lines, into closed areas or areas deemed unsafe by the Ski Patrol
LEGEND
Easier
Intermediate
Advanced Intermediate
Advanced
Expert
First Aid
Restrooms
Pay Phones
Historic Marker
Official Venue of the 2002 Winter Olympic Games:
Lifts
Ski Boundary
High Speed Lifts
Downloading Lifts
Designated Slow Ski Areas
Closed Areas
TNT Park
Food Service
Ski School
Race Course
Rossignol High Performance Test Center

as Croesus to ski here, although the latter helps. The resort remains a founding member of the tiny clutch of destinations around the world where snowboarding is still banned.

Deer Valley lies one mile to the south-east of Park City, up a winding mountain road lined with multi-million-dollar homes. It's so exclusive that the staff who unload the skis from your car and carry them to the snow won't accept tips. Any visit here should include days in Park City Mountain Resort (so close that skiers illegally go under the rope from one to the other) and The Canyons on the other side of the town of Park City.

Linking all three would involve the construction of just one lift. Rivalry has so far prevented this, but last season the three came a step closer by launching a joint adult and children's pass for foreign visitors that is only sold through tour operators, with a single rate throughout the season.

Mountain

Main mountain access from the car parks at Snow Park Lodge is by two parallel high-speed chairs that bring you up to Silver Lake Lodge mid-mountain hub. From here you can make your way up to lots of easy cruising terrain on Flagstaff Mountain and Empire Canyon. Both Sultan and Sterling chair-lifts have been upgraded to detachable-quads. The 9,400ft peak of Bald Mountain, reached by the Wasatch Express lift, is the starting point for some more challenging black-diamond terrain. The Daly Chutes and Daly Bowl, accessed from Empire Canyon, are steep powder tests.

Riders may be noticeable by their absence, but twin-tippers have their own Trick 'n' Turn rail park and a skiercross course on Empire Canyon.

Learn

The Deer Valley Ski School, t +1 435 649 1000, offers group and private lessons as well as Women on Wednesdays, and Men on Thursdays.

Children

Deer Valley Children's Center, t + 1 435 645 6648, cares for children from two months to 12 years. Deer Valley Ski School accepts children from four to 12 years, with clubs for different age groups and Teen Equipe lessons for 13- to 17-year-olds.

Lunch

For restaurants listed without numbers, call **t** +1 435 649 1000.

You can arrange a private lunch for two to 15 people at **Sunset Cabin, t** +1 435 645 6650, tucked away off Sunset run. At **Royal Street Café** at Silver Lake Lodge try the Vermont cheddar burger or the shrimp and lobster margarita appetizer served in a margarita glass. Try **Bald Mountain Pizza** at Silver Lake Lodge, **Empire Canyon Grill** as well as **Snow Park** for burgers and chilli.

Dine

Deer Valley has four evening restaurants: the **Seafood Buffet, t** +1 435 645 6632, at the Snow Park Lodge ('still good, but not as good as it used to be'). The **Mariposa, t** +1 435 645 6715, at Silver Lake Lodge, which offers fine dining, **Royal Street Café, t** +1 435 645 6724, at Silver Lake, and **Fireside Dining, t** +435 645 6632, in the Empire Canyon Lodge.

Party

The **Après Ski Lounge** at the Snow Park Lodge in Deer Valley is popular after skiing, but the best of the nightlife is on **Historic Main Street** in Park City, which has some 70 shops, bars and restaurants.

Sleep

Luxury:

The Lodges at Deer Valley, **t** +1 435 615 2600, is a condominium hotel built in Old West style with views across the Snow Park Ponds.

Goldener Hirsch Inn, **t** +1 435 649 7770, *www.goldenerhirschinn.com*, is an Austrian-style hotel with a fine restaurant.

Stein Eriksen Lodge, **t** +1 435 649 3700, at Silver Lake Village, has a Scandinavian feel and is named after the Norwegian legend who won gold at the 1954 Oslo Olympics and is 'father' of Deer Valley.

The Chateaux at Silver Lake, **t** +1 435 649 4040, is an elegant condo hotel with French country décor.

Heavenly, California/ Nevada

*BEST FOR

All levels of skier and rider, tree skiing, high rollers, scenery

ESSENTIALS

Altitude: 6,500ft (1982m)–10,067ft (3068m)
Further information: **t** +1 775 586 7000, *www.skiheavenly.com*
Lifts in area: 26 (2 cableways, 18 chairs, 6 drags) serving 4,800 acres of terrain
Lift pass: Interchangeable (covers Alpine Meadows, Heavenly, Kirkwood, Northstar-at-Tahoe, Sierra-at-Tahoe, Squaw Valley) adult $324, child 5–12yrs $120, both for 6 days
Access: Reno airport 1½hrs, Sacramento airport 2hrs, San Francisco airport 4hrs

Profile

Quirky resort straddling the California-Nevada border, with spectacular views of Lake Tahoe as well as the desert. Suits all standards, as well as party-goers and gamblers

Resort

The skiing and gambling town of South Lake Tahoe used to be famous for slow lifts and fast dealers, but all that has changed since Vail Resorts bought the adjoining 50-year-old ski resort of Heavenly five years ago. 'Vail West', as it has been dubbed, has since been the beneficiary of the lavish annual funding that is the hallmark of America's richest resort company.

The development of a village around the base of the gondola has created an identity that it previously lacked. Tacky is slowly giving way to trendy as the budget motels and T-shirt shops along the Californian end of the strip are torn down to give way to a burgeoning Marriott hotel and apartment complex as well as 40 shops and restaurants.

The Big Four casinos – Caesars, Harrah's, Harvey's and Horizon – that hug the Nevada side of the state line with California all offer the promise of instant riches. The monotonous clunk of one-arm bandits and the frenetic cries from the craps tables ring out 24 hours a day in the clock-less casinos.

Croupiers still shuffle decks faster than the eye can follow, but a modern gondola and $40 million of high-speed quads are gradually transforming mountain access.

In more serene California, quite literally on the other side of the road, gambling is

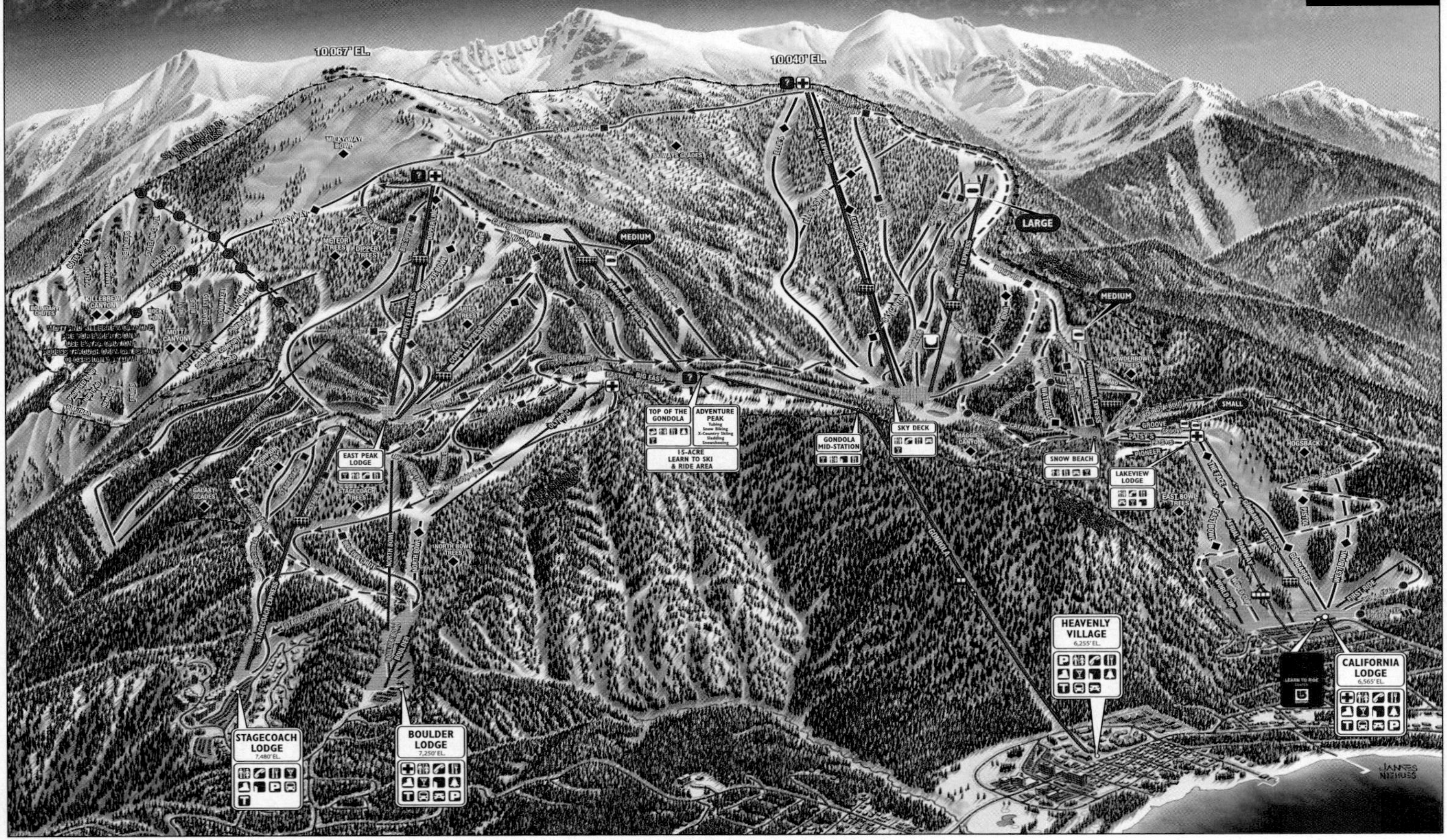

10,067' EL.
10,040' EL.
MILKYWAY BOWL
LARGE
MEDIUM
MEDIUM
SMALL
METEOR TREES
DIPPER TREES
KILLEBREW CANYON
MOTT CANYON
BOUNDARY CHUTES
GALAXY GLADES
NORTH BOWL TREES
POWDERBOWL TREES
HOGSBACK
EAST BOWL TREES
MAGGIE'S CANYON
BIG EASY
GONDOLA
EAST PEAK LODGE
TOP OF THE GONDOLA
ADVENTURE PEAK
Tubing
Snow Biking
X-Country Skiing
Sledding
Snowshoeing
15-ACRE LEARN TO SKI & RIDE AREA
GONDOLA MID-STATION
SKY DECK
SNOW BEACH
LAKEVIEW LODGE
HEAVENLY VILLAGE
6,255' EL.
CALIFORNIA LODGE
6,565' EL.
STAGECOACH LODGE
7,480' EL.
BOULDER LODGE
7,250' EL.

forbidden and the emphasis is on snow business rather than show business.

Heavenly is the largest of the 15 resorts that fringe the 72-mile shoreline of Lake Tahoe, the second largest and most beautiful mountain lake in the world behind Titicaca in Peru. Its position, straddling the frontier between two states, gives it an intriguing split personality. On the Californian side, the swirling azure waters – so deep that they never freeze over – are the ever-present backdrop. In Nevada, the slopes reach down towards the arid, painted desert.

The choice of where to stay is equally contrasting. California's part is more tranquil, with a peaceful waterfront and simple single-storey homes. Nevada's South Lake Tahoe has monstrous casino hotels where the ground floors are given over to 24hr slot machines. The third choice is more skier-oriented at the small and somewhat remote Nevada base areas.

Six resorts around the lake – Heavenly, Squaw Valley, Sierra-at-Tahoe, Kirkwood, Northstar and Alpine Meadows – share an interchangeable lift pass. Free shuttles operate from South Lake Tahoe to Sierra and Kirkwood. The Tahoe Queen paddle steamer provides a scenic way of reaching Squaw Valley on the North Shore. However, if you want to fully explore the region, it makes sense to hire a car.

Mountain

Unfortunately the gondola, built by the cash-strapped previous owners, stretches only three-quarters of the way up the mountain to a sunny balcony at just over 9,000ft. It provides great views of the lake and easy access to some of the best glade skiing in the whole of North America. Go left for Nevada, right for California, or stay put for tubing, tobogganing and cross-country skiing. The alternative is to start by chair or cable-car from California Lodge, or on the Nevada side from Stagecoach Lodge or Boulder Lodge.

The upper Californian side is generally fast, blue, cruising terrain, with the more difficult runs higher up. The notorious California Face, a vicious bump run, leads down to the California base area. Most of the trails are ideally suited to intermediates – long cruisers bordered by banks of pine trees and enhanced by the stunning view of the lake.

The Nevada Face consists mainly of blue trails, but this side of the mountain also houses the most advanced skiing and riding in Mott Canyon and Killebrew Canyon. Steep chutes are cut through the trees, with runs such as Snake Pit, Widowmaker and the difficult Boundary Chutes. If you happen across a visionary figure here with a Mohican haircut jumping off a 30ft cliff, that IS Glen Plake. The rebel extreme skier, who spent years dodging irritated ski patrollers, now works as an ambassador for the resort.

Links between the two sides involve a number of annoying flats that bring complaints from snowboarders. Heavenly has four terrain parks and a superpipe.

Learn

Resort-owned **Heavenly Ski School**, **t** +1 775 586 7000 x 6206, has the monopoly here. Quality of teaching is always a lottery. One reporter complained that his teacher was Argentinian and had only a rudimentary grasp of English.

Children

The **Daycare Center**, **t** +1 775 586 7000 x 6912, at the California Base Lodge takes non-skiers from six weeks. Private nannies are available from the **Nanny for a Day Program**. The ski school has a **Ski/Play Program** for kids from three years.

Lunch

On the California side, try **Café Blue** at the first stop on the gondola and **Adventure Peak Grill** at the top. **Lakeview Lodge** offers unrivalled views of Lake Tahoe and **Sky Deck** has a daily barbecue. On the Nevada side, **Slice of Heaven** at the Stagecoach base lodge is Italian, while **Black Diamond Cantina** at Boulder Lodge offers Mexican fare. For information on restaurants, **t** +1 775 586 7000.

Dine

Where once the ubiquitous burger ruled, you can now create your own Oriental stir-fry at **Fire + Ice**, **t** +1 530 542 6650, or dine on sushi and Hawaiian fusion cuisine at **Kalani's**, **t** +1 530 544 6100.

The best table in town is still **The Broiler Room**, **t** +1 775 588 3515, in Caesars, where gamblers can celebrate or console themselves on succulent steaks and fresh seafood flown in daily from the West Coast. In South Lake Tahoe, **The Summit**, **t** +1 775 588 6611, in Harrah's, is one of America's top 100 restaurants. **The Naked Fish**, **t** +1 530 541 3474, offers outstanding sushi and **The Chart House**, **t** +1 775 588 6276, is more expensive but has wonderful views. **The Red Hut**, **t** +1 775 588 7488, **Ernie's Coffee Shop**, **t** +1 530 541 2161, and **Heidi's Pancake House**, **t** +1 530 544 8113, all offer 'powder breakfasts'.

Party

Traditional après-ski is limited. You must head into South Lake Tahoe and try your hand at the green baize tables. As in Las Vegas, the by-product of casino culture is a wide range of cabaret acts and pop concerts featuring famous American and occasionally international artists.

Sleep

Luxury:

Tahoe Seasons Resort complex, **t** +1530 541 6700, *www.tahoeseasons.com*, is within walking distance of the lifts at the California base.

Moderate:

Caesars Tahoe, **t** +1 702 588 3515, *www.caesars.com*, has six restaurants including the Roman Feast Buffet, and houses Club Nero Nightclub, a lagoon-style swimming pool and a wedding chapel.

Harrah's Lake Tahoe, **t** +1 702 588 6611, *www.harrahs.com*, is a large casino-hotel at South Lake Tahoe.

Tahoe Lakeshore Lodge & Spa, **t** +1 530 541 2180, *www.tahoelakeshorelodge.com*, on the South Shore, has a view of the lake from every room, all of which are spacious and decorated with lodgepole pine furniture.

Embassy Suites Hotel, **t** +1 530 541 4418, is close to the gondola and has an indoor pool and a free cooked breakfast.

Harveys Resort & Casino, **t** +1 775 588 2411, *www.harrahs.com*, is located close to Heavenly's gondola base. It houses eight restaurants, 10 cocktail lounges, health club and the ubiquitous wedding chapel.

Best Western Station House Inn, **t** +1 530 542 1101, *www.stationhouseinn.com*, has a shuttle bus to the skiing, and features some 'spa rooms'.

Jackson Hole, Wyoming

Profile

Some of North America's most challenging trails and steepest backcountry terrain. Stay in the town of Jackson with its Wild West ambience, or for ski convenience at Teton Village. Wide range of moderate to extreme-luxury accommodation

Resort

Along with powder bums from all over the world, Jackson Hole manages to draw a glitteringly wealthy clientele worthy of Switzerland's St Moritz or France's Megève, and the reason for this lies in Jackson's long history of dude-ranching.

City Slickers have been answering the call of the wild in the Tetons ever since 1908 when rancher Louis Joy discovered that the urban rich would pay good money for chuck-waggon fare, lumpy mattresses and saddle sores. Little and much has changed since dude-ranching was overtaken by skiing.

The mighty Tetons remain unchallenged in their wild beauty.

Jackson Hole rancher Struthers Burt once wrote: 'You must search for the loveliness of America. It is not obvious, it is scattered. But when you find it, it touches you and binds you to it like a great secret oath taken in silence.' Presumably he was looking out of his window at the time.

The mountain range is captivating from the moment you step from the plane at Jackson Hole airport, where the runway is fringed by huge herds of grazing elk and the occasional enormous moose.

'It matched the vision I had of what beautiful is' said Harrison Ford, who forsook Hollywood for his 800-acre ranch here and has become part of the community. The occasional injured skier is astonished to find that his or her rescuer in a Bell 407 helicopter is Ford himself who has been known to spring into action when called out by the ski patrol.

A 15-minute car ride from the airport takes you to the quaint cowboy town of Jackson. The jet-lagged visitor usually assumes that the steep, groomed trails immediately above the town are his ski destination. Wrong. This mountain is the small and entirely separate resort of Snow King.

Jackson Hole Mountain Resort is located a further 20-minute drive away at Teton Village on the far side of the Snake River, an enticing trout stream that coils across the valley floor.

This leaves you with a dilemma as to where to base yourself. Both have hotels of equal stature. But the convenience of doorstep skiing has to be weighed against the shops, restaurants and nightlife of Jackson. If you can't make up your mind, you can stay in rural tranquillity between the two. Personally we now favour Teton Village since it has expanded into a real

* BEST FOR

Experts, romantics, luxury hotels

ESSENTIALS

Altitude: 6,311ft (1924m)–10,135ft (3135m)
Further information: **t** +1 307 733 2292, *www.jacksonhole.com*
Lifts in area: 11 (2 cableways, 9 chairs) serving 2,500 acres
Lift pass: adult $390, youth 15–21yrs $312, child 14yrs and under $195, all for 6 out of 8 days
Access: Jackson Hole airport 15mins from Jackson, 35mins from Teton Village

resort rather than just a base station. The police take a dim view of drink-driving and if you enjoy an evening out in Jackson it makes sense to travel by bus or taxi.

Some 8,000 elk and a host of celebrities, including Russell Crowe, Uma Thurman, Ralph Fiennes, Sandra Bullock and Jack Nicholson, agree that this is the best place in the Rockies to spend all or part of the winter. The winning combination of spectacular scenery, yesteryear cowboy values and what we consider to be some of the best skiing in North America make the long journey from Europe worthwhile.

To the chagrin of purist powderhounds, Teton Village has doubled in size in recent years. The establishment of such exotic hotels as the Amangani and the Four Seasons has brought a new breed of winter visitor who is not necessarily wedded to the mountainside from first to last lift. To the astonishment of local die-hards, some have even been seen out of ski clothes and carrying boutique shopping bags at lunch time rather than a pair of fat powder skis.

Focus in the quaint town of Jackson is on the main square with its archway made from hundreds of antlers naturally shed by elk in their winter reserve. Others have tried, but only Jackson – and Telluride on a smaller scale – has succeeded in welding the dusty gunslinging charisma of a Western frontier town to the hi-tech facilities of a modern ski resort.

Mountain

You don't have to be an expert to enjoy skiing or riding in Jackson Hole, but it sure helps. Much of the terrain is best described as 'difficult' to 'very difficult', although an increased amount of intermediate skiing can now be found on Apres Vous, the much more benign of the two adjoining mountains.

Focal point of the resort and lift system is – or, rather, was – the Aerial Tram, a venerable cable-car that took you slowly up to the 3185m summit of Rendezvous for Corbet's Couloir, a notorious heart-stopping gully reached by a 4m jump off a cornice. However, the Tram was involuntarily retired in summer 2006 with no permanent replacement in sight. After much heated discussion, a stopgap chair has now been built for this season from the top of the Sublette lift to the summit of Rendezvous. The gondola also has 18 more cabins to compensate for the uphill capacity lost from the Tram. The top of Rendezvous affords magnificent views and a choice of runs that initially look forbidding. The full range of bowls and chutes is radical in the extreme. However, in all but the most difficult snow conditions, confident intermediates will have no trouble in picking out manageable descents – provided they remember that, in Jackson, expert-only double-black-diamond trails take no prisoners. The Hobacks are a series of side-by-side and seemingly endless off-piste itineraries that will test the strongest legs.

The Bridger gondola provides access to the intermediate area between the two mountains as well as to some of the terrain that was served by the cable-car. A 20-minute hike up the Headwall opens up Casper Bowl. A further short walk takes you out of the resort area to Granite Bowl, a magnificent mile-long powder field followed by a wilderness traverse back to base, but it is avalanche-prone and so should not be attempted without a guide, transceivers and shovels. The same applies to Cody Peak and Rock Springs Bowls off Rendezvous Mountain.

The second mountain of Apres Vous is prime beginners' territory, with a beginner network of runs at the bottom served by the Teewinot quad, and more demanding, intermediate terrain at the top, which is served by the Apres Vous quad. A new triple-chair introduced this winter will ease intermediate traffic on

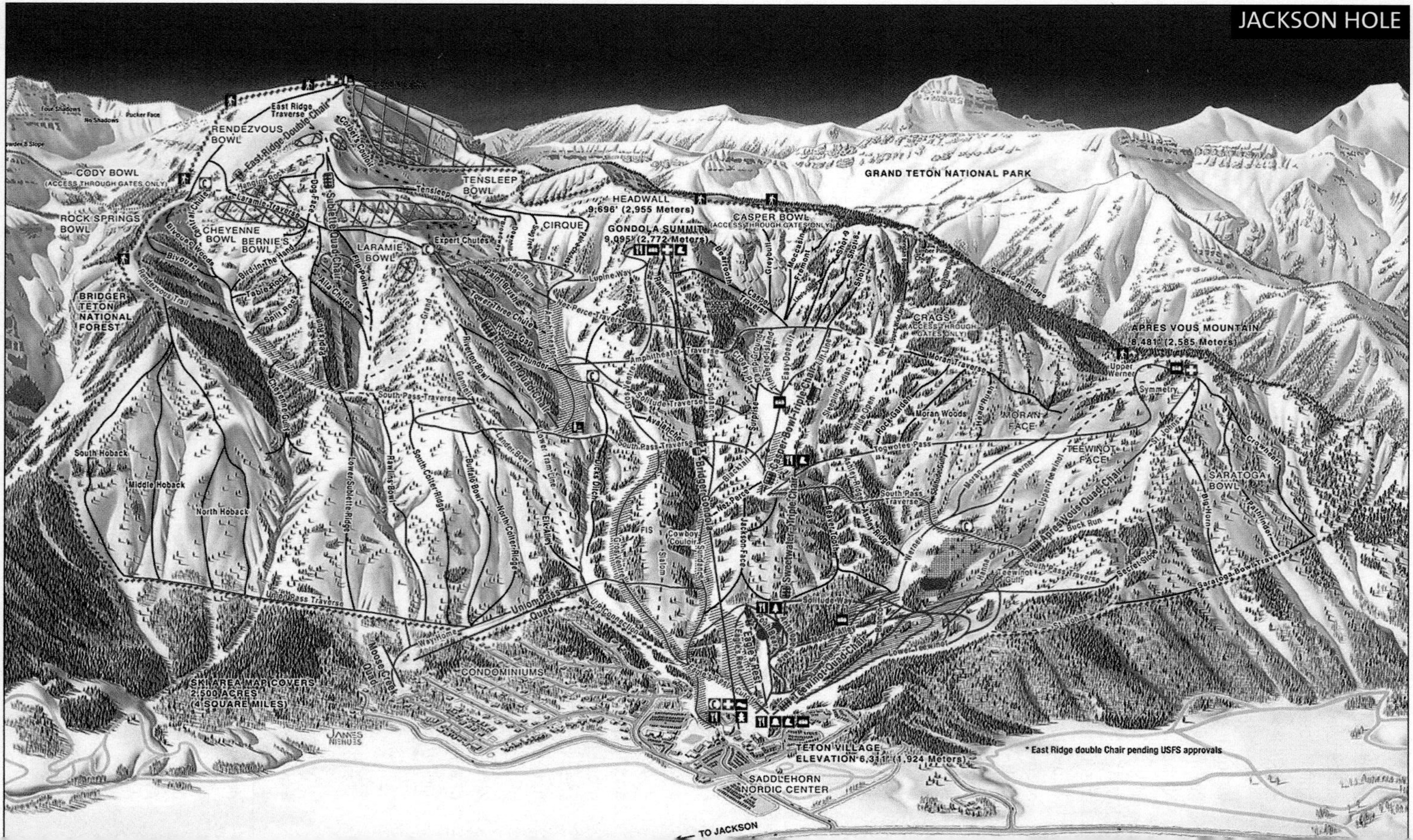
JACKSON HOLE
GRAND TETON NATIONAL PARK
RENDEZVOUS BOWL
CODY BOWL
(ACCESS THROUGH GATES ONLY)
ROCK SPRINGS BOWL
CHEYENNE BOWL
BERNIE'S BOWL
TENSLEEP BOWL
LARAMIE BOWL
CIRQUE
HEADWALL
9,696' (2,955 Meters)
GONDOLA SUMMIT
9,095' (2,772 Meters)
CASPER BOWL
(ACCESS THROUGH GATES ONLY)
CRAGS
(ACCESS THROUGH GATES ONLY)
APRES VOUS MOUNTAIN
8,481' (2,585 Meters)
MORAN FACE
TEEWINOT FACE
SARATOGA BOWL
BRIDGER TETON NATIONAL FOREST
East Ridge Traverse
East Ridge Double Chair
Sublette Quad Chair
Thunder Quad Chair
Bridger Gondola
Casper Bowl Triple Chair
Sweetwater Triple Chair
Apres Vous Quad Chair
Teewinot Quad Chair
Union Pass Quad
Moose Creek Quad
CONDOMINIUMS
SKI AREA MAP COVERS
2,500 ACRES
(4 SQUARE MILES)
TETON VILLAGE
ELEVATION 6,311' (1,924 Meters)
SADDLEHORN
NORDIC CENTER
TO JACKSON
* East Ridge double Chair pending USFS approvals

the Bridger gondola by providing a link to the Casper Bowl lift from the top of the Eagle's Rest chair. The adjacent freestyle terrain park and half-pipe is as popular with twin-tippers as it is with riders.

Learn

Jackson Hole Mountain Sports School, **t** +1 307 733 2292, has an outstanding reputation. Courses include Learn to Turn, Mountain Masters and Race Clinics. The demanding Steep and Deep Camp provides a safe introduction to Jackson's radical terrain. **Jackson Hole Alpine and Backcountry Guide Service**, **t** +1 307 739 2663, offers off-piste guiding. **High Mountain Heli-skiing**, **t** +1 307 733 3274, is another option.

Children

The slope-side **Kids' Ranch**, **t** +1 307 733 2292, has its own dedicated corral complete with a magic carpet lift and Fort Wyoming playground. It offers childcare from six months to three years, and ski programmes for three- to 14-year-olds. **Annie's Nannies**, **t** +1 307 733 8086, and **Babysitting by the Tetons**, **t** +1 307 730 0754, are the options available for non-skiers.

Keen teens can join **Team Extreme**, **t** +1 307 733 2292, a demanding four-day clinic for skiers and snowboarders aged from 12 to 17 years, which is aimed at children who have outgrown regular ski school.

Lunch

On-mountain lunches never used to be a strong feature, but the slope-side terrace of the **Four Seasons**, **t** +1 307 734 5040, is a welcome gourmet reward for a hard morning in the Hobacks. The new **Bridger Restaurant** is scheduled to open this winter at the top of the gondola. The other lunch-time venues worth considering are the **Mangy Moose**, **t** +1 307 733 4913, and upstairs at the **Alpenhof**, **t** +1 307 733 3242.

Dine

In Teton Village, the **Westbank Grill** in the Four Seasons has an international menu and cosy atmosphere. The **Mangy Moose**, **t** +1 307 733 4913, is a family favourite set in a vast barn. **GameFish**, **t** +1 307 732 6040, in the Snake River Lodge and Spa focuses on fish and smoked game, and **Masa Sushi**, **t** +1 307 732 2962, at Teton Pines golf course serves Japanese fare. **Calico**, **t** +1 307 733 2460, is a good-value Italian family restaurant on Teton Village Road. In Jackson, try **Nikai Sushi**, **t** +1 307 734 6490, and **Koshu's Wine Bar**, **t** +1 307 733 5283, which is popular with the locals. **Old Yellowstone Garage**, **t** +1 307 734 6161, is top-of-the-range Italian. Signature dishes at the **Snake River Grill**, **t** +1 307 733 0557, include smoked tuna carpaccio and pan-roasted Idaho trout. **Rendezvous Bistro**, **t** +1 307 739 1100, is run by the son of Snake River Grill's owner. Intimate **Wild Sage**, **t** +1 307 733 2000, at the Rusty Parrot is the first four-diamond restaurant in Wyoming.

Party

The slope-side **Peak** in the Four Seasons Resort attracts skiers at the end of the day, but Teton Village has little life after dark, with lights out almost everywhere by 11pm. **The Snake River Brewing Company** is popular with the locals. Those in search of serious drinking should head for the **Million Dollar Cowboy Bar** on Jackson's Town Square. This huge saloon has stools made from Western saddles, live music and pool tables, all of which is dominated by a stuffed grizzly bear. The local paper will tell you where to find live music each night – for example **The Stagecoach** in the nearby village of Wilson has music on Thursday evenings and the **Mangy Moose** in Teton Village on Saturdays. A word of warning: Jackson is strict about licensing laws, which forbid anyone under 21 to go to bars; over-21s must carry ID to show when asked.

Sleep

Luxury:

Amangani, t +1 307 734 7333, *www. amangani.com,* is a veritable palace set on a bluff halfway between Teton Village and Jackson town. Rooms are minimalist with ample use of black resin, animal hide and pale wood floors, as well as beautiful black slate bathrooms and wrap-around balconies.

Four Seasons Resort, t +1 307 734 5040, *www.fourseasons.com/jacksonhole,* has the best location of any hotel here. It is decorated with works of art by Miró and Giacometti and has slate floors and animal-hide upholstery. The substantial bedrooms and family-sized suites all have connecting marble bathrooms, and there is a kids' club and games room, state-of-the-art spa and fitness centre.

Moderate:

Rusty Parrot Lodge t +1 307 733 2000, *www.rustyparrot.com,* in Jackson, has a welcoming atmosphere with old terracotta floors, Persian rugs and an open fire in the lobby.

Spring Creek Resort, t +1 307 735 8833, *www.springcreekresort.com,* is next to the Amangani and contains traditional condos.

Snake River Lodge & Spa, t +1 307 732 6000, *snakeriverlodge.rockresorts.com,* is at the foot of the ski area and owned by Vail Resorts. It has a pleasant lobby and lounge area but dated rooms. The spa includes an attractive indoor-outdoor swimming pool among the rocks.

Teton Club, t +1 307 734 9777, *www. tetonclub.com,* is a very comfortable condo development in Teton Village with maid service and spa.

Teton Mountain Lodge, t +1 307 734 7111, *www.tetonlodge.com,* at Teton Village, is the newest lodge and is ideal for families. The condos contain cosy bedrooms and modern kitchens with huge fridges.

Teton Village Condos, t +1 307 733 3990, are spacious, well equipped, and a free bus ride from the slopes.

The Wort Hotel, t +1 307 733 2190, *www.worthotel.com,* a comfortable stagecoach inn close to the main square in Jackson, is the best situated in town.

Keystone, Colorado

Profile

As well as easy access from an international airport, the attractive purpose-built village has the largest night-skiing operation in North America

Resort

Keystone has been a Colorado community since the 1880s and is the only resort of that vintage that does not owe its existence to gold or silver strikes. For a while in those heady days, Old Keystone was the end of the line for the Denver, South Park (yes, of cartoon fame), and Pacific railroad. Not a lot happened here again until the 1960s when an enterprising group of developers persuaded the US Forest Service to let them build a ski resort. Its location, only

***BEST FOR**

Intermediates, night-skiing, airport access

ESSENTIALS

Altitude: 9,300ft (2835m)–12,200ft (3719m)
Further information: **t** +1 970 496 4386 or **t** +44 (0)1708 224 773, *www.keystone.snow.com*
Lifts in area: 15 (2 cableways, 11 chairs, 2 drags) serving 81 miles (130km) of piste
Lift pass: Colorado Ticket (covers Arapahoe Basin, Beaver Creek, Breckenridge, Keystone, Vail) adult $169–402, child 5–12yrs $186, both for 6 out of 9 days
Access: Denver airport 1¼hrs

75 miles on I-70 from Denver, made it attractive to local skiers. The establishment of what is now the largest floodlit night-skiing operation in North America appealed to city workers who could drive out after work as well as at weekends.

In the 1990s, Keystone underwent a complete makeover, with a new resort village constructed by Canadian ski property giant developer Intrawest. The result is a friendly family resort divided into the linked 'villages' of Lakeside and River Run. It has considerable atmosphere for somewhere that has been largely purpose-built. Keystone also has a substantial amount of intermediate skiing of its own and shares a lift pass with nearby Breckenridge and Arapahoe Basin as well as Vail and Beaver Creek, which are slightly further afield. The first two are linked by a free ski-bus and there is subsidized daily transport to the others. Skiers or riders spending a week or more here are strongly advised to explore the other Vail resorts as well as separate Copper Mountain.

Mountain

Skiing takes place on three interlinked mountains that lie one behind the other; each is progressively more challenging.

Main mountain access to Dercum, the closest peak to the resort, is by gondola or multiple-chair from River Run. Alternatively start from the other end of the strung-out resort with the Argentine chair from Mountain House. The easy and intermediate cruising runs on Dercum are floodlit for night-skiing. The gondola continues across to the summit of the second mountain, North Peak, which offers slightly more challenging terrain. Pistes and a quad-chair connect to the Outback at 12,220ft, which has steeps, trees and lots of bumps. From the top of the lift you can hike up the truly challenging South and North Bowls – but you need to be fit and acclimatized for a climb at this altitude.

Keystone's beginner and advanced terrain parks are located on the front side of Dercum Mountain in Pack Saddle Bowl.

Learn

Keystone Ski and Ride School, **t** +1 970 496 4170, offers group and private lessons.

Children

Keystone Children's Center and Snowplay Programs, **t** +1 970 496 4181, cares for babies from just two months at River Run and at the Mountain House base area.

Lunch

The Alpenglow Stube, **t** +1 800 354 4386, is the highest *haute cuisine* in North America. Signature dishes include ragout of blue crab, and duck foie gras with roast garlic hummus.

Dine

Ski Tip Lodge, **t** +1 877 625 1540, offers four-course menus. Almost as rustic is

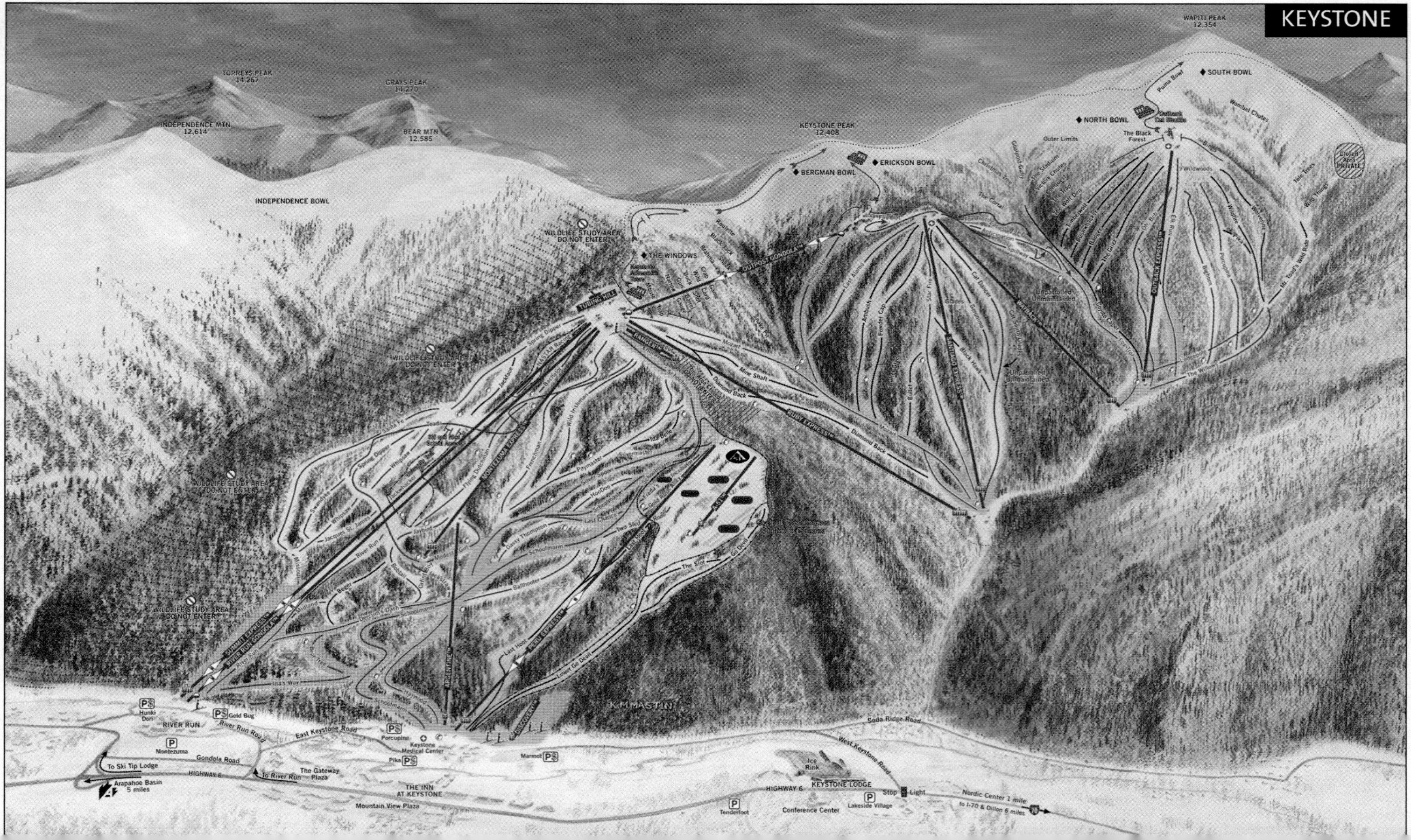
KEYSTONE
TORREYS PEAK 14,267
GRAYS PEAK 14,270
INDEPENDENCE MTN 12,614
BEAR MTN 12,585
KEYSTONE PEAK 12,408
WAPITI PEAK 12,354
INDEPENDENCE BOWL
BERGMAN BOWL
ERICKSON BOWL
NORTH BOWL
SOUTH BOWL
THE WINDOWS
WILDLIFE STUDY AREA DO NOT ENTER
OUTPOST GONDOLA
SANTIAGO EXPRESS
OUTBACK EXPRESS
RUBY EXPRESS
Diamond Back
Mine Shaft
Elk Run
The Black Forest
Outer Limits
Wombat Chutes
Puma Bowl
Mt. Toad's Wild Ride
Closed Area PRIVATE
K.M.MASTIN
River Run
RIVER RUN
Hunki Dori
Gold Bug
Montezuma
Gondola Road
River Run Road
East Keystone Road
Porcupine
Keystone Medical Center
Pika
Marmot
To Ski Tip Lodge
To River Run
The Gateway Plaza
HIGHWAY 6
Arapahoe Basin 5 miles
THE INN AT KEYSTONE
Mountain View Plaza
Tenderfoot
Conference Center
Lakeside Village
KEYSTONE LODGE
Ice Rink
West Keystone Road
Soda Ridge Road
Stop Light
Nordic Center 1 mile
to I-70 & Dillon 6 miles

the 1930s **Keystone Ranch**, **t** +1 970 496 4386, which serves 'Colorado Frontier and fine-dining, fusion cuisine'. **Champeaux**, **t** +1 970 496 2316, at Keystone Lodge in Lakeside Village, serves French country cuisine.

Party

Great Northern Tavern, **Kickapoo Tavern** and **Inxpot** provide snacks and après-ski entertainment, while **Snake River Saloon** has pool and live music. **Parrot Eyes** at River Run serves tacos, margaritas and draft beer.

Sleep

All accommodation can be booked through central reservations, **t** +1 970 496 4386.

Ski Tip Lodge, **t** +1 877 625 1540, *www.skitiplodge.com,* is an original and charming stagecoach inn. It offers B&B with a separate restaurant, and is a bus ride from the resort.

Keystone Ranch, **t** +1 877 204 7881, *www.keystoneranch.com,* is also a bus ride away from the skiing and offers good food.

Keystone Lodge, **t** +1 970 496 2316, has been recently renovated with smart guest rooms and loft suites.

Killington, Vermont

Profile

Chilly East Coast resort with phenomenal snowmaking capability and recommended ski school. Good accommodation, but resort lacks a village centre

*BEST FOR

Snow-making, long season, intermediates

ESSENTIALS

Altitude: 1,165ft (354m)–4,241ft (1293m)

Further information: **t** +1 802 422 1330, *www.killington.com*

Lifts in area: 31 (3 cableways, 22 chairs, 6 drags) serving 87 miles of trails

Lift pass: adult $234, youth 13–18yrs $204, child $174, all for 6 days

Access: Burlington airport 2hrs, Boston airport 3hrs

Resort

Killington is usually the first resort in the US to open each November and the last to close in May or June. The reason for this has nothing to do with nature's bounty, but with the most sophisticated snowmaking system on the planet. The resort claims 250 inches of natural snow each winter but this doesn't always fall to order. Instead, cannons mounted on 'giraffe' poles can blanket 1,182 acres with sufficient artificial cover to open terrain on all seven of its peaklets without a flake of the real thing.

Arriving by car on a crisp blue-sky day you may notice with gloom that the only clouds in the sky hang over your destination. But that's no cloud – just a prescribed mix of crystallized air-and-water falling from hundreds of snow cannons in the world's biggest broadside. Not only the pistes but the surrounding forest is laden with man-made snow that is manufactured in a dozen different qualities from adhesive base layers to fluffy finishes.

Killington's main shortcoming is that it lacks a heart – any one area that you can truly call the resort centre. Hotels, bars and restaurants sprawl along the five-mile approach road from the highway. However, plans for a new Killington Village have been revived, and work started in summer 2006 on a number of new homes. Reporters warn that it can be bitterly cold

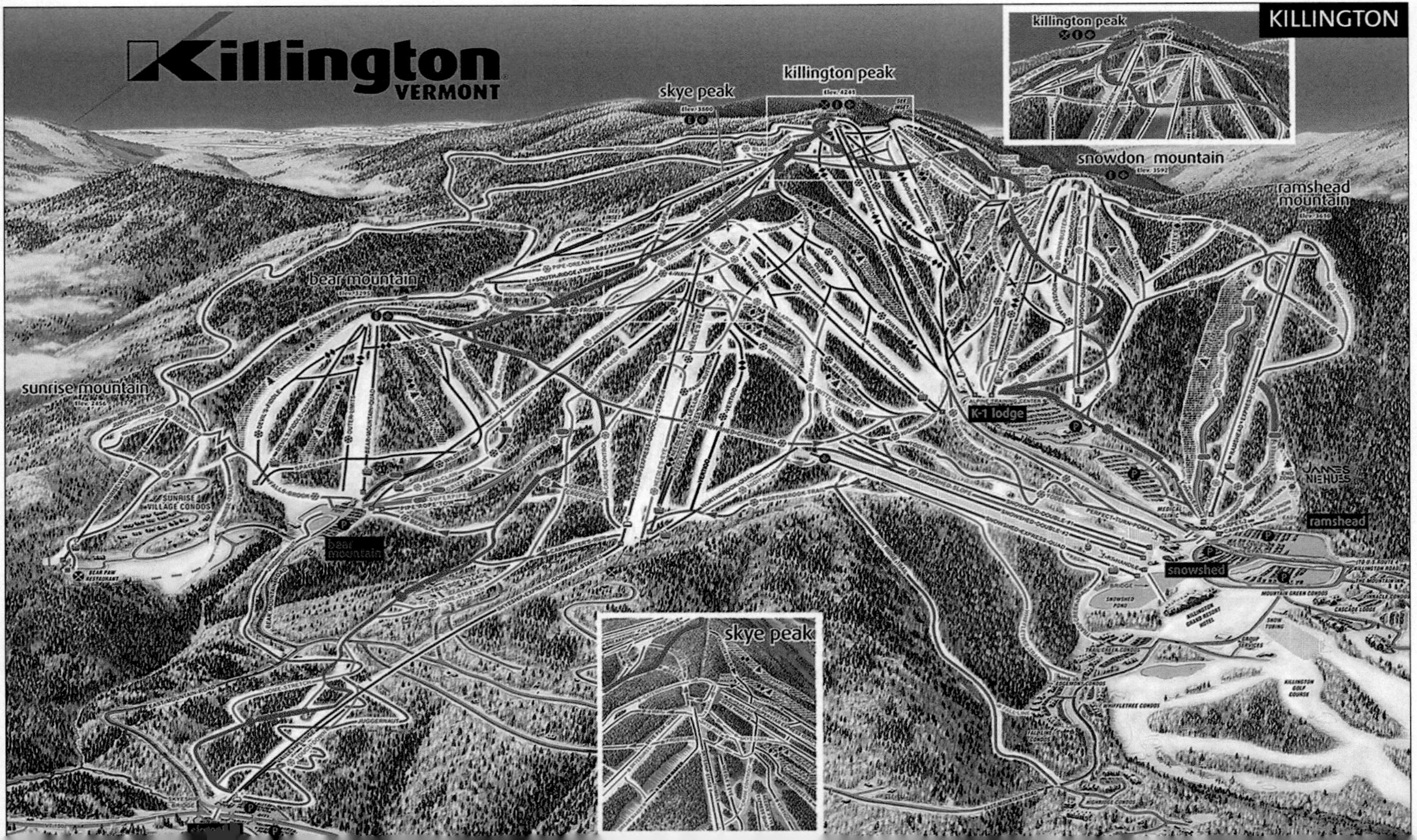
Killington
VERMONT
skye peak
killington peak
snowdon mountain
ramshead mountain
bear mountain
sunrise mountain
K-1 lodge
ramshead
snowshed
bear mountain
SUNRISE VILLAGE CONDOS
JAMES NIEHUES
skye peak
killington peak

here in mid-winter. The resort shares a lift pass with the neighbouring attractive little resort of Pico. Despite years of promises, a mountain link between the two has yet to be established.

Mountain

Killington claims to have skiing on seven mountains, but this is creative topography. The reality is one – 4,241ft Killington Peak, which has six shoulders. Together they form a naturally shaped ski area that extends for miles across a heavily wooded mountainside with a number of isolated condo-clad base areas. Snowshed, at the top of the road from the highway, is the main one with a clutch of high-speed chairs providing mountain access.

The much lower base of Skyship is served by a two-stage heated gondola that brings you up to Skye Peak 450ft below the top of the ski area. Killington suits all standards of skier and rider but the emphasis is on quantity rather variety – so many of the gladed runs have the same pitch that it is often hard to differentiate between them. The most demanding runs are to be found on the front face of Killington Peak, reached by the K1 Express gondola and on lower Bear Mountain. Killington is popular with snowboarders and has three terrain parks with a superpipe and a snowcross course.

Learn

The **Perfect Turn Ski School**, **t** +1 802 422 1234, uses the graduated length teaching method and has a good reputation for imparting the basics.

Children

Friendly Penguin Day Care, **t** +1 802 422 6222, is for kids aged six weeks to 23 months at the Ramshead Family Center and for up to six years at the Grand Hotel. Children as young as two years can join **First Tracks** for lessons, and **SnowZone** is ski or ride tuition for 13 to 18 years, **t** +1 800 923 9444 for all.

Lunch

Mountain Top Inn, **t** +1 802 483 6737, is traditional American. **Peak Restaurant**, **t** +1 802 422 6780, is a cafeteria on Killington Peak.

Dine

'Killington has a low-end feel to it. There are dozens of places to eat but the quality is generally moderate', reports one journalist. **Hemingway's**, **t** +1 802 422 3886, near the Skyship base serves good food but it is expensive. Other eateries include award-winning **Cascades**, **t** +1 802 422 3731, which has a casual atmosphere. **Casey's Caboose, t** +1 802 422 3539, serves traditional American. **Kong Chow**, **t** +1 802 775 5244, and **Sushi Yoshi**, **t** +1 802 422 4241, offer Asian dishes. **Santa Fe Steakhouse**, **t** +1 802 422 2124, is recommended. **The Wobbly Barn**, **t** +1 802 422 6171, has some of the best steaks and seafood in the area. **Peppers**, **t** +1 802 422 3177, in Killington Mall is reminiscent of a 1940s diner and is a good place for breakfast.

Party

Pickel Barrel on Killington Road is the hub of the evening action, with big-name bands playing every weekend. **Mogul's Pub** is also on Killington Road. **The Wobbly Barn** is where Killington's nightlife first began and still features world-class rock 'n' roll acts.

Sleep

Snowshed base is the best place to stay if you don't have a car.

Inn of the Six Mountains, **t** +1 800 228 4676, *www.sixmountains.com*, is close to the nightlife and a short drive from the base lodges. A courtesy taxi service is provided.

Killington Grand Resort Hotel, **t** +1 802 422 1330, *www.killington.com*, is a slope-side condominium-hotel.

Butternut on the Mountain, **t** +1 800 524 7654, *www.bestlodging.com*, is a no-smoking property with an indoor swimming pool and games room.

Vermont Inn, **t** +1 888 636 8107, *www.vermontinn.com*, is an 1840s farmhouse 10 miles out of town, offering individually decorated rooms, some with fireplaces or hot tubs.

Mammoth, California

Profile

Large but remote high-altitude ski area for all standards, with good sunshine and snow records. Particularly recommended for snowboarders

Resort

Skiing is no newcomer to the high Sierra Nevada mountain range that lies behind California's sunny coastline. As winter storms sweep in from the Pacific Ocean they attract some 400 inches of snow each winter, resulting in a season that lasts from November until June – or even July 4 in 2005. Back in the 1850s, some 30 years before skiing started in Switzerland, immigrant Scandinavian miners were using Lapp hunting skis as winter transport and weekend recreation.

Mammoth, named after the Mammoth Mining Company, which staked claim to the mountain after the discovery of gold here in 1878, has some of the best and most weather-reliable skiing in California. When it is not snowing, the sun shines for an average of 300 days each year. Mammoth it is, the largest single mountain ski and ride destination in North America.

The drawback is that it is a long way from anywhere. The local airstrip has been rebuilt but plans for services from Chicago and Dallas have so far failed to materialize.

Outside the main US holiday dates the resort is quiet mid-week, although young Los Angelinos drive up for the weekend in large numbers. Mammoth ski resort is just above the town of Mammoth Lakes and has been expanded at a cost of $830 million in recent years. The focal point is the three-year-old Village at Mammoth, which is the best place to begin and end your skiing day. The village is linked by gondola to the ski area.

A regular free shuttle bus runs to and from the ski-area bases at Main Lodge, Canyon Lodge and Juniper Springs and

* BEST FOR

All levels of skier, snow record, snowboarders

ESSENTIALS

Altitude: 7,953ft, (2424m)–11,053ft (3369m)
Further information: **t** +1 760 934 0745, *www.mammothmountain.com*
Lifts in area: 27 (3 cableways, 22 chairs, 2 drags) serving 3,500 acres of terrain
Lift pass: Area (Mammoth and June Mountain) adult $258, youth 13–18yrs $194, child 7–12yrs $129, all for 5 days
Access: Reno airport 3hrs, Los Angeles airport 5½hrs

MAMMOTH MOUNTAIN
CALIFORNIA
PANORAMA LOOKOUT
DAVE'S RUN
HUEVOS GRANDE
UPPER DRY CREEK
CLIMAX
UPPER ROAD RUNNER
HANGMAN'S HOLLOW
MJB'S
CORNICE BOWL
DROP OUT CHUTES
WIPE OUT CHUTES
BEYOND THE EDGE
DRAGON'S BACK
RICOCHET
WAZOO
DRAGON'S TAIL
GOLDHILL
SOLUTIDE
FACE OF FIVE
SLIVER
TRIANGLE
DRY CREEK
CHRISTMAS BOWL
CHINA BOWL
ROOSTER TAIL
EAST BOWL
CENTER BOWL
WEST BOWL
SADDLE BOWL
GREMLIN'S GULCH
ST. ANTON
SCOTTY'S
PARANOID FLATS
PHILIPPE'S
SANTIAGO BOWL
HEMLOCK RIDGE
HEMLOCK BOWL
OUTPOST 14
WHITE BARK BOWL
CHAIR 9
CHAIR 25
CHAIR 5
CHAIR 23
CHAIR 12
CHAIR 13
CHAIR 22
CHAIR 26
CHAIR 7
AVALANCHE CHUTES
ONE CHANCE
SPOOK
SLOT
QUICKSILVER
HAVEN'T THE FOGGIEST
BACK FOR MORE
SHAFT
GRIZZLY
VIVA
SUNSHINE
REPEAT 22
HOLIDAY
MANZANITA
LOWER GRIZZLY
SANCTUARY
WATERFALL
PANORAMA GONDOLA
FACE LIFT EXPRESS - 3
McCOY STATION
ST. MORITZ
WORLD CUP
WALL
GRAVY CHUTE
GLADES
POWDER BOWL
FASCINATION
FAR WEST
BROADWAY
BROADWAY EXPRESS
ROGER'S RIDGE
LOWER DRY CREEK
EASY RIDER
WALL STREET
LOST IN THE WOODS
STUMP ALLEY
DROP 18
STUMP ALLEY EXPRESS - 2
GOLD RUSH EXPRESS - 10
PATROLMEN'S
OVER EASY
MAMBO
EAGLE LODGE
EAGLE EXPRESS - 15
CANYON LODGE
CANYON EXPRESS - 16
SCHOOLYARD EXPRESS
CLOVER LEAF
BLUEJAY
DOWNHILL
ENCORE
ROLLER COASTER
CROSSWALK
VILLAGE GONDOLA
MOUNTAIN CENTER
THE MILL CAFE
MAIN LODGE
YODLER RESTAURANT & BAR
LOWER ROAD RUNNER

there is also a bus service to Mammoth Lakes. June Mountain, 20 miles away, is owned by Mammoth, shares the lift pass, and has easy intermediate runs in a spectacular setting.

Mountain

The Village Gondola takes you up to Canyon Lodge, giving access to some easy beginner and intermediate terrain as well as some testing double-diamonds such as Grizzly, Viva and Avalanche Chutes. However, the most challenging slopes are reached by the two-stage gondola from Main Lodge, which brings you up to Panorama Lookout at 11,053ft. From here and from Chair 23 you can traverse and drop into some phenomenal chutes and bowls such as Hangman's Hollow, Cornice Bowl and Beyond the Edge. The lower half of the mountain has plenty of cruising terrain and some good novice slopes but, overall, Mammoth is a mountain that will please good skiers and riders in search of testing gradients and fresh challenges.

Snowboarders are particularly at home in Mammoth and the Unbound terrain parks are considered among the best in North America with a superpipe and a super-duper pipe. JM2 at June Mountain has spines, pipes and rails.

Learn

Mammoth Ski and Snowboard School, **t** +1 760 934 0745, offers courses including teen skiing, Women Only and skiing for the disabled. **A J Kitt's Ski & Race Camp**, **t** +1 760 934 2571, organizes slalom and GS training. Off-piste guiding is through **Mammoth Mountaineering School**, **t** +1 760 924 9100.

Children

Small World Child Care, **t** +1 760 934 0646, looks after children from newborn to 12 years with ski or snowboard lessons for older ones.

Lunch

'Pretty poor' was how one reporter described the food available on the mountain. Choices include the **Mill Café**, **t** +1 760 934 2571, **Mountainside Grill**, **t** +1 760 934 0601, in the Mammoth Mountain Inn, and the **Yodler Restaurant and Pub**, **t** +1 760 934 2571 x 2234. In The Village at Mammoth try **Hennessey's**, **t** +1 760 934 8444, and **Lakanuki Café**, **t** +1 760 934 7447. **Parallax**, **t** +1 760 934 2571 x 3118, at McCoy Station serves Pacific Rim and Mediterranean cuisine.

Dine

Skadi, **t** +1 760 934 3902, and **Nevado's**, **t** +1 760 934 4466, offer gourmet fare. **Ocean Harvest**, **t** +1 760 934 8539, specializes in seafood. **Matsu**, **t** + 1 760 934 8277, offers an eclectic Far Eastern menu, including Thai and Chinese specialities. **Chart House**, **t** +1 760 934 4526, and **The Mogul**, **t** +1 760 934 3039, have fine steaks. **Alpenrose**, **t** +1 760 934 3077, offers cheese fondue. Other dining options in the Village include **Hennessey's**, **t** +1 760 934 8444, and **Pita Pit**, **t** +1 760 924 7482.

Party

Dublin's is a traditional-style Irish pub with the addition of 50 TVs lining the walls. If you want to dance the night away, go to **Fever**, the new nightspot inside Dublin's. **Lakanuki** is a hip mountain 'tiki bar' where you can try hula dancing in your ski boots while sipping tropical drinks. **Unbound** is a cool place to buy a new snowboard or hang out after a day in the terrain park. **Canyon Lodge** regularly has live bands. **The Clocktower** in Alpenhof Lodge and **Whiskey Creek** are popular meeting places in town.

Sleep

All accommodation can be reserved on **t** +1 760 934 0745.

Luxury/Moderate:

The Village at Mammoth, t +1 800 421 7005, *www.intrawestmammoth.com,* condos include Lincoln House, White Mountain Lodge and Grand Sierra Lodge.

Alpenhof Lodge, t +1 760 934 8558, *www.alpenhof-lodge.com,* is within easy access of the skiing and the town.

Mammoth Mountain Inn, t +1 760 934 2581, *www.mammothmountain.com,* is at the Main Lodge base.

Austria Hof Lodge, t +1 760 934 2764, *www.austriahof.com,* at the ski-area base, is good value, with some units containing fireplaces and hot tubs.

Canyon Lodge, Juniper Springs and **Sunstone Lodges, t** +1 760 924 1102, *www.mammothcondos.com,* offer slope-side self-catering.

Mammoth Lakes:

Shilo Inn Suites, t +1 760 934 4500, *www.shiloinns.com,*are conveniently located on Main Street.

June Mountain:

Double Eagle Resort & Spa, t +1 760 648 7004, *www.double-eagle-resort.com,* has a full-service spa, pool and health club.

Park City, Utah

Profile

Convenient resort for airport access, with a wide choice of nearby resorts. Good skiing for all levels and an excellent snow record. Recommended for gourmets

Resort

The Victorian mining town of Park City plays host to three of the most important ski resorts in Utah and is home of the finest and driest powder snow in the world. All three are located side-by-side on a five-mile stretch of mountainside an easy 40-minute drive from Salt Lake City. In the middle lies Park City Mountain Resort directly above the attractive old town of Park City.

Linking them would involve the construction of just one lift. Rivalry has so far prevented this, but the three have come a step closer by launching a joint adult and children's pass for foreign visitors that is only sold through tour operators, with a single rate throughout

*** BEST FOR**

All levels of skier and rider, powderhounds, ski gourmets

ESSENTIALS

Altitude: 6,900ft (2104m)–10,000ft (3049m)
Further information: **t** +1 435 649 8111, *www.parkcitymountain.com*
Lifts in area: 14 (14 chairs) serving 3,300 acres of terrain
Lift pass: Utah Three Resort Pass: adult $408, child 7–12yrs $225, both for 6 out of 7 days
Access: Salt Lake City airport 40mins

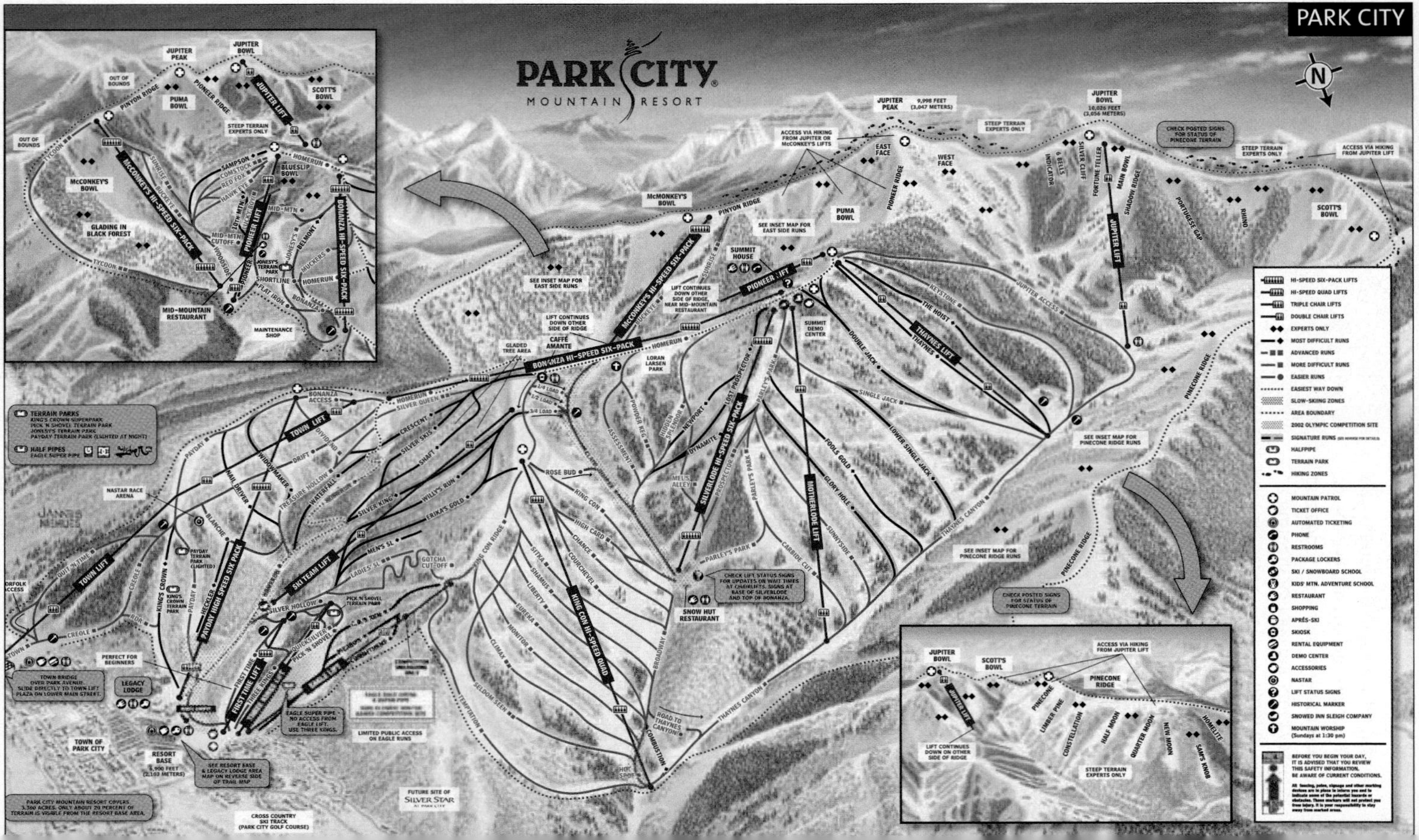
PARK CITY
MOUNTAIN RESORT
JUPITER PEAK 9,998 FEET (3,047 METERS)
JUPITER BOWL 10,026 FEET (3,056 METERS)
CHECK POSTED SIGNS FOR STATUS OF PINECONE TERRAIN
STEEP TERRAIN EXPERTS ONLY
ACCESS VIA HIKING FROM JUPITER LIFT
ACCESS VIA HIKING FROM JUPITER OR McCONKEY'S LIFTS
EAST FACE
WEST FACE
PIONEER RIDGE
PUMA BOWL
McMONKEY'S BOWL
PINYON RIDGE
6 BELLS
INDICATOR
SILVER CLIFF
FORTUNE TELLER
MAIN BOWL
SHADOW RIDGE
PORTUGESE GAP
RHINO
SCOTT'S BOWL
JUPITER LIFT
SEE INSET MAP FOR EAST SIDE RUNS
SUMMIT HOUSE
PIONEER LIFT
LIFT CONTINUES DOWN OTHER SIDE OF RIDGE, NEAR MID-MOUNTAIN RESTAURANT
McCONKEY'S HI-SPEED SIX-PACK
SUNRISE
BUCKEYE
LIFT CONTINUES DOWN OTHER SIDE OF RIDGE
CAFFÉ AMANTE
GLADED TREE AREA
BONANZA HI-SPEED SIX-PACK
HOMERUN
LORAN LARSEN PARK
SUMMIT DEMO CENTER
KEYSTONE
THE HOIST
THAYNES
THAYNES LIFT
JUPITER ACCESS
DOUBLE JACK
SINGLE JACK
LOWER SINGLE JACK
FOOLS GOLD
GLORY HOLE
SUNNYSIDE
MOTHERLODE LIFT
SEE INSET MAP FOR PINECONE RIDGE RUNS
PINECONE RIDGE
THAYNES CANYON
LOST PROSPECTOR
PARLEY'S PARK
SILVERLODE HI-SPEED SIX-PACK
NEWPORT
HIDDEN SPLENDOR
DYNAMITE
PROSPECTOR
MEL'S ALLEY
CARBIDE CUT
POWDER KEG
ASSESSMENT
CHECK LIFT STATUS SIGNS FOR UPDATES ON WAIT TIMES AT CHAIRLIFTS. SIGNS AT BASE OF SILVERLODE AND TOP OF BONANZA.
SNOW HUT RESTAURANT
ROSE BUD
KING CON
HIGH CARD
CHANCE
COURCHEVEL
SITKA
SHAMUS
LIBERTY
EUREKA
MONITOR
CLIMAX
SELDOM SEEN
TEMPTATION
KING CON RIDGE
KING CON HI-SPEED QUAD
BROADWAY
ROAD TO THAYNES CANYON
COMBUSTION
1/4 LOAD
1/2 LOAD
3/4 LOAD
BONANZA ACCESS
SILVER QUEEN
CRESCENT
SILVER SKIS
SHAFT
SILVER KING
WILLY'S RUN
ERIKA'S GOLD
MEN'S SL
LADIES' SL
GOTCHA CUT-OFF
SKI TEAM LIFT
SILVER HOLLOW
PICK 'N SHOVEL TERRAIN PARK
QUICKSILVER
PICK 'N SHOVEL
THREE KINGS
FIRST TIME
FIRST TIME LIFT
EAGLE SUPER PIPE - NO ACCESS FROM EAGLE LIFT. USE THREE KINGS.
LIMITED PUBLIC ACCESS ON EAGLE RUNS
FUTURE SITE OF SILVER STAR AT PARK CITY
CROSS COUNTRY SKI TRACK (PARK CITY GOLF COURSE)
TOWN LIFT
DIVIDEND
DRIFT
TREASURE HOLLOW
WATERFALL
WIDOWMAKER
NAIL DRIVER
PAYDAY
NASTAR RACE ARENA
BLANCHE
PAYDAY TERRAIN PARK (LIGHTED)
KING'S CROWN TERRAIN PARK
KING'S CROWN
HECKLER
PAYDAY HIGH SPEED SIX PACK
CREOLE
RDR
QUIT 'N TIME
NORFOLK ACCESS
PERFECT FOR BEGINNERS
LEGACY LODGE
TOWN BRIDGE OVER PARK AVENUE. SLIDE DIRECTLY TO TOWN LIFT PLAZA ON LOWER MAIN STREET.
TOWN OF PARK CITY
RESORT BASE 6,900 FEET (2,103 METERS)
SEE RESORT BASE & LEGACY LODGE AREA MAP ON REVERSE SIDE OF TRAIL MAP
PARK CITY MOUNTAIN RESORT COVERS 3,300 ACRES. ONLY ABOUT 29 PERCENT OF TERRAIN IS VISIBLE FROM THE RESORT BASE AREA.
TERRAIN PARKS
KING'S CROWN SUPERPARK
PICK 'N SHOVEL TERRAIN PARK
JONESY'S TERRAIN PARK
PAYDAY TERRAIN PARK (LIGHTED AT NIGHT)
HALF PIPES
EAGLE SUPER PIPE
OUT OF BOUNDS
TYCOON
McCONKEY'S BOWL
GLADING IN BLACK FOREST
SAMPSON
COMSTOCK
RED FOX
HAWK EYE
10th MTN
LUCKY BOY
MID-MTN
MID-MTN CUTOFF
WOODSIDE
BLUESLIP BOWL
JONESY'S
JONESY'S TERRAIN PARK
SHORTLINE
FLAT IRON
BELMONT
MUCKERS
BONANZA
MID-MOUNTAIN RESTAURANT
MAINTENANCE SHOP
PINECONE RIDGE
PINECONE
LIMBER PINE
CONSTELLATION
HALF MOON
QUARTER MOON
NEW MOON
HOMELITE
SAM'S KNOB
LIFT CONTINUES DOWN ON OTHER SIDE OF RIDGE
HI-SPEED SIX-PACK LIFTS
HI-SPEED QUAD LIFTS
TRIPLE CHAIR LIFTS
DOUBLE CHAIR LIFTS
EXPERTS ONLY
MOST DIFFICULT RUNS
ADVANCED RUNS
MORE DIFFICULT RUNS
EASIER RUNS
EASIEST WAY DOWN
SLOW-SKIING ZONES
AREA BOUNDARY
2002 OLYMPIC COMPETITION SITE
SIGNATURE RUNS
HALFPIPE
TERRAIN PARK
HIKING ZONES
MOUNTAIN PATROL
TICKET OFFICE
AUTOMATED TICKETING
PHONE
RESTROOMS
PACKAGE LOCKERS
SKI / SNOWBOARD SCHOOL
KIDS' MTN. ADVENTURE SCHOOL
RESTAURANT
SHOPPING
APRÈS-SKI
SKIOSK
RENTAL EQUIPMENT
DEMO CENTER
ACCESSORIES
NASTAR
LIFT STATUS SIGNS
HISTORICAL MARKER
SNOWED INN SLEIGH COMPANY
MOUNTAIN WORSHIP (Sundays at 1:30 pm)
BEFORE YOU BEGIN YOUR DAY, IT IS ADVISED THAT YOU REVIEW THIS SAFETY INFORMATION. BE AWARE OF CURRENT CONDITIONS.

the season. You can buy individual passes, but this ticket offers a considerable saving on window prices.

The heart of Park City is steep Main Street, lined with restored Victorian buildings and home to the Wasatch Brewery, the Egyptian Theater and a host of art galleries, boutiques, restaurants, bars and coffee shops. Mountain Resort at the foot of the pistes is a moderately well-designed complex on three levels, with shops, cafés and accommodation, set around a skating rink and a car park.

Mountain

Main mountain access is by two detachable six-person chairs that take 12 minutes to reach the Summit House Restaurant. Alternatively, you can get there by riding a triple-chair from the top end of town. It's a far automated cry from the early 1960s when the first skiers travelled up on an underground mine train before being brought to the surface on a hoist lift. The skiing is much more varied and challenging than is indicated by the lift map. The lower half of the mountain has plenty of easy intermediate terrain but much of it is given over to steepish gladed blacks. The top half, served by McConkey's Six-pack and the Jupiter lift, is a more serious proposition with an abundance of double-diamond chutes and bowls and still more off-piste opportunities for those prepared to hike along Pinecone Ridge.

Anyone spending a week or more here – Park City is a sensible accommodation base – is advised to not only explore Deer Valley and The Canyons but also Snowbird and Alta, which are a 45-minute drive away.

Learn

Park City Ski & Snowboard School, **t** +1 435 649 5496, has a justified reputation for some of the best cutting-edge technical instruction in the USA, as befits the town that is official home of the US ski team. Strong skiers and riders should try the **Mountain Experience** programme for exploring Jupiter Peak. Guided off-piste can be arranged through **Park City Powder Cats**, **t** +1 435 649 6596, **Ski Utah Interconnect Tour**, **t** +1 801 534 1907, and **Wasatch Powderbird Guides Heli-skiing**, **t** +1 801 742 2800.

Children

Park City Mountain Resort has no childcare facilities, but the town has no fewer than three non-ski kindergartens: **Annie's Nannies**, **t** +1 435 615 1935, **Creative Beginnings**, **t** +1 435 645 7315, and **Guardian Angel**, **t** +1 435 783 2662. The ski school provides lessons from three years.

Lunch

Legends has grills and fresh fish. **Summit House** near the top of the Bonanza lift has pizzas, grills and a large deck with views of Park City and beyond. **Mid-Mountain Lodge**, near the base of the Pioneer and McConkey lifts, is a modified version of an old miner's home with pasta, pizza and chilli. Further information on **t** +1 435 649 8111.

Dine

Chenez, **t** + 1 435 940 1909, is a French restaurant with an intimate ambience. **Zoom**, **t** +1 435 649 9108, owned by Robert Redford, is an old favourite, with Californian cuisine. **Adolph's**, **t** + 1 435 649 7177, is Swiss American with an emphasis on veal dishes. **Blind Dog**, **t** +1 435 655 0800, has 'outstanding' sushi. **Chimayo**, **t** +1 435 649 6222, serves Southwestern cuisine. **Café Terigo**, **t** +1 435 645 9555, is contemporary American ('great West

Coast mussels and Utah trout'). **Grappa Italian Restaurant**, **t** +1 435 645 0636, features traditional Tuscan dishes. **Claimjumper Steakhouse**, **t** +1 435 649 8051, is a carnivore's delight, and **Kampai Sushi**, **t** +1 435 649 0655 offers Japanese cuisine. **350 Main**, **t** +1 435 649 3140, has fresh seafood, while **The Riverhorse** on Main, **t** +1 435 649 3536, is hip American.

Party

This is the Mormon heartland but, contrary to popular belief, it is far from 'dry'. Draught beer in bars without a liquor licence is restricted to 3.2 per cent alcohol and according to one reader 'tastes like dishwater'. In a restaurant you may not be offered the wine list unless you ask for it. Liquor laws require pubs to be privately licensed, but temporary membership is easily obtained – the barman usually asks a local to 'sponsor' the stranger. Try **Legends at The Resort** in the Legacy Lodge at the base area. **No Name Saloon** displays the local Park City Rugby Club memorabilia on its walls. **J.B. Mulligans Club and Pub**, and **Wasatch Brew Pub Cantina** are popular along with **Spur Club**. The **Star Bar at Plan B** features live bands.

Sleep

Luxury:

Hotel Park City, **t** +1 435 200 2000, *www.hotelparkcity.com*, is an all-suite hotel in the style of a grand national park lodge of the early 1900s, and a leading Small Hotel of the World.

Silver King, **t** +1 435 649 5500, *www.silverkinghotel.com*, is a smart condo hotel one mile from Main Street.

Yarrow Resort Hotel, **t** +1 435 649 7000, *www.yarrowresort.com*, is a full-service hotel adjacent to the Holiday Village Mall.

Moderate:

Lodge at Mountain Village, **t** +1 435 649 8111, *www.parkcitymountain.com*, is a full-service hotel at the base area.

Marriott's Summit Watch, **t** +1 435 647 4100, *www.marriott.com*, is conveniently located at the lower end of Main Street.

Park City Marriott, **t** +1 435 649 2900, *www.parkcitymarriott.com*, is situated one mile from the downtown area.

Radisson Inn, **t** +1 435 649 5000, *www.radisson.com*, has spacious rooms and mountain views.

Budget:

Angel House Inn, **t** +1 435 647 0338, *www.angelhouseinn.com*, has nine rooms, each modelled on a different angel.

Best Western Landmark Inn, **t** +1 435 649 7300, *www.bwlandmarkinn.com*,is five miles out of town at Kimball Junction, but good value.

Holiday Inn Express Park City, **t** +1 435 658 1600, also at Kimball Juncton, is another budget-priced option.

Snowbird and Alta, Utah

Profile

Two contrastingly different, linked resorts for accomplished skiers and riders, with the best powder snow in the world. Snowboarding is not permitted in Alta

Resort

It is hard to find two more different resorts than Snowbird and adjoining Alta in Little Cottonwood Canyon, a 40-minute uphill drive from Salt Lake City. But, strangely, they admirably complement each other. Their alliance has created a formidable European-style ski circuit with two villages separated by some of the most exciting and radical terrain in North America. The canyon – Brigham Young and his 143 Mormon pioneers came this way in 1847 from Nebraska to found their city beside the great salt lake – is home to Champagne Powder. These talcum-like flakes are freeze-dried in their passage above the desert from the Pacific Ocean. They land here in the winter in copious quantities.

This annual phenomenon persuaded Texan oilman-turned-mountaineer Dick Bass to build Snowbird in the 1970s. Unfortunately, he chose the utilitarian concrete architecture of high-rise Tignes in France as a role model. Cliff Lodge with its 11-storey atrium dominates the resort. Snowbird Center, departure point for the Aerial Tram, a dated but renovated cable car, is the official heart of the village. The open space is surrounded by other nearby accommodation blocks and shops on three levels. Snowbird is no beauty, but very ski-convenient. Under its maximum-tog duvet of snow it is by no means unappealing.

Little Alta, higher up the canyon, is an altogether different proposition, a handful of lodges providing simple but exclusive accommodation favoured by 'old money' Americans and new money wannabes. Both hark back to halcyon Hemingway-esque days when handsome couples in cable-knit sweaters and white polo-necks sat around the fireplace at the end of day drinking mulled wine, while wooden skis were stretched and leather lace-up boots dried in the boiler room below. Skiing started in Alta in the 1930s and the first lodge was built in 1939.

The lifts all used to be fixed double-chairs that gave the formidable ski area an atmosphere reminiscent of St Anton in 1960. However, while retro-skiing has proved to be big business, ever-aloof Alta has been unable to ignore some of the refinements to the original invention of the wheel. Since its alliance with Snowbird after decades of bitter rivalry, a couple of detachable-quads – to the chagrin of Alta purists – have surreptitiously crept in to the system.

*BEST FOR

Powderhounds, ski convenience, airport access

ESSENTIALS

Altitude: 7,740ft (2359m)–11,000ft (3352m)
Further information: **Alta t** +1 801 359 1078, *www.altaskiarea.com*; **Snowbird t** +1 801 742 2222, *www.snowbird.com*
Lifts in area: 26 (1 cableway, 18 chairs, 7 drags) serving 4,700 acres of terrain
Lift pass: Snowbird: adult $198–288 for 6 days, child 12 years and under free with a paying adult
Alta/Snowbird: adult or child $348, for 6 days
Access: Salt Lake City airport 45mins

Mountain

The joint area is a world-class point of pilgrimage for anyone who is hooked on sliding down mountains and knows how to do it at a reasonably high level. The continued ban in Alta on snowboarding makes Little Cottonwood Canyon a more suitable destination for those who prefer two planks to one. The gradient of the double-diamonds and the off-piste in both resorts, backed by usually sensational snow-cover, has few rivals in North America. There is a reasonable amount of lower intermediate terrain in both resorts, as well as good novice slopes. Snowbird has a superpipe on the Big Emma run next to the Big Emma terrain park. The main terrain park is located by the Baby Thunder lift.

Main access from Snowbird is by cable-car straight up to 11,000ft Hidden Peak. Importantly, there are two easy routes down from the top. Better skiers and riders will head for Upper Cirque or Silver Fox, as well as High Baldy Traverse and the steep descents of Thunder Bowl. Mineral Basin, 500 acres of prime alpine terrain, provides the gateway to Alta. This is reached through a manned frontier gate to deter snowboarders.

The big innovation this season is the replacement of the old Peruvian lift with a high-speed quad. The new top-station is located below the steepest Chip's Run pitch. From here, a 600ft tunnel with a conveyor lift provides easy access for intermediates to Mineral Basin.

Main mountain access from Alta is by the Collins quad, gateway to an enormous range of intermediate and advanced runs back down the mountain and across to the Sugarloaf quad. A glance at the lift map shows a complete absence of double-black-diamond runs. Don't be deceived – it's just Alta's quirky way of doing things. They printed the first map decades before such gradings were invented and see no reason to change. Some of the most demanding terrain is reached from the Supreme triple-chair, and the most challenging routes are not on the lift map – you need to ask the locals. Also try the Ski Utah Interconnect, a guided day tour from Deer Valley to Snowbird via Solitude, Brighton and Alta.

Learn

Snowbird Mountain School, t +1 801 933 2170, has a sound reputation and the full range of ski and snowboard courses. **Alf Engen Ski School, t** +1 801 359 1078, is named after America's greatest skier of the 1930s, who taught skiing here in 1945–6. Guiding is with the **Ski Utah Interconnect Tour, t** +1 801 534 1907, or **Wasatch Powderbird Guides Heli-skiing, t** +1 801 742 2800. **Alta Snowcat Skiing, t** +1 801 799 2271, offers guided skiing – and even boarding – in Grizzly Gulch.

Children

Camp Snowbird, t +1 801 933 2256, at Cliff Lodge, looks after children from six weeks to 12 years. The **Mountain School, t** +1 801 933 2170, which is based at Camp Snowbird, gives lessons from three years.

Alta's Alf Engen Ski School, t +1 801 359 1078, provides children's lessons. **Alta Lodge Kids' Program, t** +1 801 742 3500, is aimed at its four- to 10-year-old residents and provides transport to and from ski school, as well as après-ski activities. **Alta Children's Center, t** +1 801 742 3042, offers daycare.

Lunch

The only eating place on the mountain at Snowbird is **Mid-Gad Restaurant, t** +1 801 933 2245. Serious lunchers must return to the base.

On the slopes at Alta, the new Watson Shelter, **t** +1 801 799 2296, at the Collins lift mid-station, offers grills and snacks. **Alf's Restaurant, t** +1 801 799 2295, serves lunch and snacks, while **Collins Grill, t** +1 801 799 2297, features French cuisine. **Albion Grill, t** +1 801 742 2500, is a cafeteria at Albion base area. **Alta Lodge, t** +1 801 742 3500, at Wildcat Base, serves breakfast, lunch and dinner. **Shallow Shaft, t** +1 801 742 2177, is one of the top restaurants in the USA.

Dine

Snowbird has a dozen restaurants; the **Aerie, t** +1 801 933 2160, at Cliff Lodge, serves continental cuisine, **The Keyhole, t** +1 801 933 2025, specializes in Southwestern food and the **Wildflower Restaurant, t** +1 801 933 2230, at Iron Blosam Lodge offers gourmet pizzas. **Lodge at Snowbird, t** +1 801 742 2222, has much the best cuisine in the resort. **El Chanate, t** +1 801 933 2218, is a new Mexican restaurant.

Shallow Shaft, t +1 801 742 2177, is much the best restaurant in Alta, but you need to book days in advance. At **Alta Lodge**, **t** +1 801 742 3500, wealthy guests from Boston and New York dine at communal tables. **Goldminer's Daughter**, **t** +1 801 742 2300, serves New Mexican fare at the mountain base.

Party

At Snowbird, **Aerie Lounge & Sushi Bar**, **Wildflower Lodge**, **Lodge Bistro Lounge** and **Keyhole Cantina** are the main meeting places. **The Tram Club** at Snowbird Center has billiards, video games, live music and 13 televisions. The **Aerie Lounge** has live jazz on Wednesdays and Saturdays.

In Alta, après-ski is limited to the slope-side hot tub or the screening of black-and-white ski films, followed by drinks taken around a roaring log fire. Guests at Alta Lodge swap tales in the **Sitzmark Club**.

Sleep

Snowbird, **t** +1 801 742 2222, for all reservations.

Cliff Lodge is the smartest address, with a major spa, a rooftop swimming pool and what claims to be the world's largest collection of Oriental rugs. The Cliff Club in the west wing has 54 three-room suites furnished in Mission style.

Lodge at Snowbird, by the cable-car, is the original lodge, completely renovated, with an outdoor pool and hot tub.

The Inn has simple studios, suites and an outdoor pool.

Iron Blosam Lodge is geared towards families, with its own spa and pool.

Alta:

Alta Lodge, **t** +1 801 742 3500, renovated in 1990, is a charming place that has been attracting visitors since 1939.

Alta Peruvian Lodge, **t** +1 801 742 3000, has a swimming pool.

Alta's Rustler Lodge, **t** +1 801 742 2200, has a heated outdoor pool.

Goldminer's Daughter Lodge, **t** +1 800 453 4573, is rustic and unassuming.

Alta Chalets, **t** +1 866 754 2426, are seven lovely ski-in/ski-out log homes and chalets, each with 4–8 bedrooms.

Squaw Valley, California

Profile

Scenic Lake Tahoe resort with good intermediate terrain and steep slopes. Also particularly good for snowboarding. For those with transport, the evening dining choices in the area are superb

Resort

Squaw Valley, despite a virtual absence of lifts at the time, managed, with a little help from Walt Disney, to convince the Olympic Committee that it should host the 1960 Winter Olympics, which were the first to be televized. Jean Vuarnet of France won gold in the downhill and went on to reinvent sunglasses. Squaw Valley has never looked back. The resort sits in natural splendour on the north shore of beautiful Lake Tahoe, home to 15 alpine resorts and eight cross-country centres with over 100 lifts in 17,520 acres of skiable terrain. Squaw has the best of it.

Its new Intrawest-built village provides the base area that it previously lacked, while no one has ever questioned the quality of the skiing. You need a car to

***BEST FOR**
Intermediate and advanced snowboarders

ESSENTIALS
Altitude: 6,200ft, (1890m) – 9,050ft (2758m)
Further information: **t** +1 530 583 6985, *www.squaw.com*
Lifts in area: 32 (3 cableways, 25 chairs, 4 drags) serving 4,000 acres of terrain
Lift pass: Interchangeable (covers Alpine Meadows, Heavenly, Kirkwood, Northstar-at-Tahoe, Sierra-at-Tahoe, Squaw Valley) adult $324, child 5–12yrs $120, both for 6 days
Access: Reno airport 1hr, San Francisco airport 4hrs

explore the other Lake Tahoe resorts included in the Interchangeable lift pass.

Tahoe City, a 10-minute drive away, is a small town providing an alternative bed-base with considerable atmosphere and some appealing restaurants.

Mountain

No less than seven lifts, including the Gold Coast Funitel gondola, give mountain access from the village, while the Squaw Valley Creek triple-chair provides an eighth way into the system. Val d'Isère in the French Alps is the only other ski destination with comparable diversity. The lifts lead up to six peaks: Granite Chief, Snow King, KT22, Squaw Peak, Emigrant and Broken Arrow. The area is divided into three sectors with the 32 lifts, rather than the runs, colour-graded. All the main lifts on KT22, Squaw Peak and Granite Chief are black-diamond, while those on Snow King and Emigrant are blue. Intermediates will find a huge amount of skiing – the highlight is a three-mile trail from the High Camp area to the mountain base. However, Squaw was birthplace of the American extreme skiing movement and offers a comprehensive menu of steep chutes. The most radical terrain is found off KT22, Headwall, Cornice II and Granite Chief chair-lifts.

Three terrain parks and three half-pipes, as well as exciting freeride terrain, make this a serious destination for snowboarders. All are accessed by the gondola or cable-car. Start in Belmont, move on to Central Park (floodlit at night), and then into the jumps and rails of Mainline Park.

Learn

Squaw Valley Ski and Snowboard School, **t** +1 530 581 7263, has a sound reputation. A new beginner double-chair built last winter make the learning process more enjoyable.

Children

Squaw Kids Children's Center, **t** +1 530 581 7166, takes children from three to 12 years. **Squaw Kids Ski & Snowboard School**, **t** +1 530 581 7263, gives lessons from four years.

Lunch

The resort has dozens of eateries and bars both on the mountain and in the base village. These include **Gold Coast**, **t** +1 530 583 6985, at the top of the Funitel in Squaw Valley, which features a barbecue, restaurants and bars on three levels. Newest addition is the **Crossroads Café**, which serves a wide selection of foods, including wraps, salads and sandwiches. **High Camp**, **t** +1 530 583 2555, has six different restaurants and bars, and the main dining room is open at night.

Dine

Dining in the area offers a huge choice of venues. Restaurants in the new Village include **Plump Jack Café**, **t** +1 530 583 5850, which is an 'American bistro' and **Fireside Pizza Co**, **t** +1 530 584 6150, offering gourmet pizzas 'with a sourdough crust and farm-fresh toppings'. **High Sierra Grill**, **t** +1 530 584 6100, has steaks and salads, and **Mamasake** sushi bar, **t** +1 530 584 0110, is a real treat. **Zenbu Tapas Lounge**, **t** +1 530 583 9900, upstairs in the Olympic House, has late-night 'Asian Tapas' and dancing. **Glissandi**, **t** +1 530 583 6300, in the Resort at Squaw Creek, is a high-priced Italian.

Ten minutes' drive away in Truckee are **Java Sushi**, **t** +1 530 582 1144, **China Garden Restaurant**, **t** +1 530 587 7625, and **Blue Agave Mexican Restaurant**, **t** +1 530 583 8113. **Cottonwood**, **t** +1 530 587 571, has seafood and live jazz.

In Tahoe City, **Wolfdale's**, **t** +1 530 583 5700, has 'Flavors of the West & Far East'. **Yama Sushi**, **t** +1 530 583 9262, is affordable and fun. **Bacchi's Inn t** +1 530 583 3324, is Italian, **Christy Hill**, **t** +1 530 583 8551, overlooking the lake, serves Californian cuisine with a French influence. **Sunnyside**, **t** +1 530 583 7200, serves seafood. **Izzy's Burger Spa**, **t** +1 530 583 4111, has great views and **Rosie's Café**, **t** +1 530 583 8504, is friendly.

Party

Bar One in the Olympic House features live music, pool and karaoke. Also in Olympic House, **Zenabu Tapas Lounge** is for late-night dining and dancing. Other post-slope options include **Le Chamois** at Village Green and **Red Dog Bar & Grill** at Far East Center. In the Village are **Plump Jack Café** which has live music twice a week, and **Auld Dubliner** pub, which was built in Ireland, dismantled, shipped over and reassembled. **High Camp** is open until 9pm with a Snowtubing Arena and Olympic Ice Pavilion in winter and Swimming Lagoon & Spa in the spring.

Sleep

★★★★**Resort at Squaw Creek**, **t** +1 530 583 6300, *www.squawcreek.com*, is a luxury ski-in/ski-out complex near the base with spa, swimming pool, ice rink and five in-house restaurants.

★★★★**Squaw Valley Lodge**, **t** +1 530 583 5500, *www.squawvalleylodge.com*, is ski-in/ski-out and contains condos with kitchens and hot tubs.

★★★★**The Village at Squaw Valley**, **t** +1 530 584, 1000 contains smart and well-equipped condos in the new base village. Shared facilities include a movie room, games room and billiards lounge.

PlumpJack Squaw Valley Inn, **t** +1 800 323 7666, dates back to 1959 and was upgraded in 1995 with attractively minimalist decoration and a renowned restaurant.

Olympic Village Inn, **t** +1 530 583 1576, served as the home to many of the 1960 Olympic athletes but was remodelled in 1982. It contains one-bedroom suites with kitchenettes and provides a shuttle bus to the ski base.

Tahoe City and Truckee provide alternative bed-bases for visiting other resorts in the area.

Steamboat, Colorado

Profile

A Wild West town set apart from the ski area base. The resort offers a good choice of restaurants. The ski area suits families and beginners, and is particularly good for snowboarders

Resort

The unlikely name of Steamboat Springs originated when three French fur trappers

***BEST FOR**

Resort ambience, families, snowboarders

ESSENTIALS

Altitude: 6,900ft (2103m)–10,568ft (3221m)
Further information: t +1 970 879 6111, *www.steamboat.com*
Lifts in area: 20 (1 cableway, 18 chairs, 1 drag) serving 2,939 acres of terrain
Lift pass: adult $330–402, youth 13–17yrs $246–318, child 6–12yrs $174–258, all for 6 days
Access: Eagle Airport 2hrs, Denver airport 3 hrs

exploring the River Yampa at the foot of Rabbit Ears Pass in 1865 thought they heard the chugging sound of a paddle steamer – only to find that it was actually the bubbling local mineral springs.

A lot of water has gone under the bridge since then and Steamboat has built a reputation as a Wild West ski town famous for its annual Cowboy Downhill when the skills of skiing and ranching come together. After negotiating a slalom course, competitors must first lasso a mountain host and then saddle a horse, before crossing the finishing line on skis. It produces a dramatic, and often hilarious, spectacle.

The history of skiing here goes back to 1914 when a bricklayer called Carl Howelsen organized a ski carnival and won every event. He possibly failed to mention that he had already won 14 trophies for ski jumping in his native Norway. Steamboat is an area that suits all standards of skier but is particularly suited to intermediates. Steamboat resort lies three miles from the town of Steamboat Springs and both offer a choice of hotels and condos.

Mountain

Main mountain access is by a gondola from the base area. This is a large resort with skiing on six linked peaks in the Routt National Forest: Mounts Werner, Sunshine, Storm, Thunderhead and Christie Peaks and Pioneer Ridge. It all adds up to 142 trails with a vertical drop of 3,688ft (1124m). Routt County's winter snowfall is traditionally measured by the number of fence wires it covers. *Three Wire Winter*, a quarterly journal produced by the local high school, is so called because in a typical winter, snow 30 inches deep will cover all three of the lower fence wires. In a seriously good winter, with snow depths of over 40 inches, the snow will cover the fourth.

This is home of some of Colorado's best powder and in a good winter the off-piste opportunities are exceptional. The modern lift system is backed up by extensive snowmaking. The resort is popular with riders and the 66ft Mavericks superpipe is the longest in North America.

Learn

Steamboat Ski and Snowboard School, **t** +1 970 871 5375, has a good reputation as befits a school that claims to have produced more Olympians than any other in the world. It incorporates the Billy Kid Performance Center, founded by the resort's most famous champion, which provides specialized coaching to get skiers off the 'intermediate plateau'. **Steamboat Powdercats**, **t** +1 970 871 4260, offers 10,000 acres of cat-skiing terrain only 20 minutes from the town on Buffalo Pass.

Children

The **Kids Vacation Center**, **t** +1 970 871 5375, accepts non-skiing children from six months and arranges ski lessons for older children.

Lunch

The most sophisticated lunch option is **Hazie's**, **t** +1 970 871 5150, at the top of the gondola, which serves New

MT. WERNER
10,568'
MORNINGSIDE PARK
(see inset)
STORM PEAK
10,372'
FRYING PAN
COWBOY COFFEE
SUNSHINE PEAK
10,384'
JUMP START
HOT CAKES
NO NAMES
EAST FACE
CHRISTMAS TREE BOWL
EAST
WEST
NORTH ST. PATS
CHUTE 3
CHUTE 2
CHUTE 1
OVER EASY
CROWTRACK
THE RIDGE
LAST CHANCE
FIRST CHANCE
BIG MEADOW
BUDDY'S RUN
TRAVERSE
STORM PEAK CATWALK
HIGHLINE
TOMAHAWK
TOMAHAWK CUT-OFF
KIT
CUB
QUICKDRAW
PUP
BUCKSHOT
RAMROD
FLINTLOCK
TRIANGLE 3
STORM PEAK NORTH
STORM PEAK SOUTH
KUUS' CRUISE
SUNDOWN LIFTLINE
SHADOWS
CLOSET
TWILIGHT
TWO O'CLOCK
ONE O'CLOCK
HIGH NOON
SUNSHINE
THREE O'CLOCK
FOOLS GOLD
CABIN FEVER
CINCH
NASH JUNCTION
FLYING Z
MEADOW LANE
FOUR POINTS HUT
9,716'
DAWN
DUSK
SUNSET
RAINBOW
CHISOLM TRAIL
ROYAL FLUSH
PERRY PARK
LONGHORN
DIAMOND HITCH
CYCLONE
TYPHOON
FETCHER GLADE
AMBUSH
MIDDLE RIB
PONY EXPRESS LIFTLINE
CHUCKWAGON
WJW
TORNADO
FOUR POINTS
NELSON'S RUN
TWISTER
HURRICANE
LIGHTS OUT
PRIEST CREEK
SUNDOWN EXPRESS
DUSTER
DAYBREAK
FAWN
SPIKE
SOUTH PEAK
ROWEX
WEST SIDE
BROADWAY
VELVET
SUNNYSIDE
MOONLIGHT
CHAPS
DROP OUT
VORTEX
STORM PEAK EXPRESS
TORNADO LANE
WHITE OUT
B.C. LIFTLINE
TOWER
ELKHEAD
OUTLAW
CANTER
LARIAT
PONY EXPRESS
RUDI'S RUN
FEATHER
BLIZZARD
LIGHTNING
WHY NOT
VAGABOND
OOPS
BURGESS CREEK
SURPRISE
SO WHAT
BETWIXT
THUNDERHEAD EXPRESS
CONCENTRATION
TED'S RIDGE
VERTIGO
HEAVENLY DAZE
VALLEY VIEW
RENDEZVOUS SADDLE
RAGNAR'S FINE DINING
9,325'
THUNDERHEAD
Hazie's FINE DINING
WESTERN BBQ
9,080'
MOTHER NATURE
EAGLES NEST
BC SKIWAY
NASTAR RACE AREA
MAVERICKS SUPERPIPE
BASHOR
TERRAIN PARK
VOO DOO
SEE ME
SEE YA
CHRISTIE III
CHRISTIE II
LOWER VALLEY VIEW
GONDOLA
VOGUE
GIGGLE GULCH
SWINGER
RIGHT-O-WAY
MAVERICKS
North America's Longest Superpipe
FREESTYLE TERRAIN PARK
BEAR RIVER BAR & GRILL
GONDOLA BASE
GONDOLA SQUARE
INFORMATION CENTER
BASE ELEVATION: 6,900'
VERTICAL DROP: 3,668'
SKI TIME SQUARE
STEAMBOAT GRAND

American cuisine. **Ragnar's**, **t** +1 970 871 5191, at Rendezvous Saddle, specializes in seafood, game, and beef. Try also **Gondola Pub & Grill**, **t** +1 970 879 4448, at Gondola Square.

Dine

At Steamboat Resort, **The Butcher Shop**, **t** +1 970 879 2484, has been feeding carnivores for 34 years. **The Cabin**, **t** +1 970 871 5550, features contemporary Colorado cuisine; try the Rocky Mountain Lamb Shanks. **La Montana**, **t** +1 970 879 5800, has Tex-Mex.

At Steamboat Springs, **Antares**, **t** +1 970 879 9939, **Giovanni's**, **t** +1 970 879 4141, and the **Steamboat Yacht Club**, **t** +1 970 879 4774, are all recommended. **Yama Chan's**, **t** +1 970 879 8862, is a great sushi restaurant. **The Cottonwood Grill**, **t** +1 970 879 2229, has tasty Pacific Rim cuisine.

Party

Skiers gather at the **Slopeside Grill** and **The Tugboat** in Times Square, as well as at **Mahogany Ridge** in downtown Steamboat Springs. Other popular bars include **Chaps** in the Grand Resort Hotel, **Bear River Bar & Grill**, **Dos Amigos** and **Levelz**.

Sleep

Steamboat base area

Luxury:

Bear Claw, **t** +1 970 879 6100, is a smart condo complex.

Sheraton Steamboat, **t** +1 970 879 2220, *www.sheraton.com/steamboat*, has Western décor.

Steamboat Grand Resort & Conference Center, **t** +1 970 871 5500, *www.steamboatgrand.com*, has a spa and fitness centre, a themed restaurant and 327 rooms.

Torian Plum, **t** +1 970 879 8811, offers comfortable furnished suites at the base area.

Budget:

Fairfield Inn, **t** +1 970 870 9000, has reasonably priced rooms close to the skiing.

Steamboat Springs

Moderate/Budget:

Alpiner Lodge, **t** +1 970 879 1430, is a low-cost Tyrolean-style lodge within walking distance of the shops and restaurants.

Hampton Inn & Suites, **t** +1 970 871 8900, *www.hamptonsteamboat.com*, is a new hotel located midway between the resort and downtown.

Harbor Hotel, **t** +1 970 879 1522, has simple rooms at budget prices.

Stowe, Vermont

Profile

Classic New England village surrounded by beautiful scenery, which suits all levels. Not all accommodation is convenient for the slopes and nightlife is quiet

Resort

Back in February 1914 when war clouds were gathering over Europe, a librarian from Dartmouth College called Nathaniel L. Goodrich made the first recorded descent on skis down Mount Mansfield. 'It was', he said, 'a lot of fun and very satisfying. But my stops – voluntary and otherwise – were very frequent'. What he achieved was rather greater than personal satisfaction. He had set in motion the

*** BEST FOR**

New England charm, all levels of skier and rider

ESSENTIALS

Altitude: 1,300ft (396m)–3,640ft (1109m)
Further information: **t** +1 802 253 3000, *www.stowe.com*
Lifts in area: 11 (1 cableway, 8 chairs, 2 drags) serving 63km of terrain
Lift pass: adult $269, child 6–12yrs $172, both for 6 days
Access: Montreal airport 2¼hrs, Boston airport 3¼hrs, Burlington 40mins

future prosperity of the charming 18th-century New England town of Stowe.

The trouble with Stowe is that the skiing takes place a full six miles from either Mount Mansfield or smaller and tamer Spruce Peak beside it. Hotels line the route, but wherever you stay is inconvenient for the skiing, the nightlife – or both. You need a car, but note that the police take a zero-tolerance stance on drink-driving. However, all that is set to change as Stowe Mountain Resort develops a new $400-million village at Spruce Peak that will act as a bed-base for both mountains. Work has already started, but the village will take 10 years to complete.

Stowe is the most patrician of all East Coast resorts with a pedigree going back to the 1920s and 1930s. It attracts wealthy Bostonians and New Yorkers, as well as 10 per cent of its skiers from Britain. The appeal lies in the quintessential Vermont town with its red-and-white weatherboarded houses set around a steepled white church on attractive Main Street, where most of the shops and restaurants, as well as some of the hotels, are located.

Mountain

Stowe probably needs to do more than build a couple of new lifts to access beginner and intermediate terrain – if the development at Spruce Peak is to become what is euphemistically billed as 'a dynamic alpine village with world-class amenities'. The Little Spruce Double, which has been carrying skiers up the mountain since 1963, has been replaced by a high-speed quad. From Spruce you can reach Smugglers' Notch ski area on the other side of the mountain, but the two do not share a lift pass and are not officially linked.

Anyone who has mastered the basics on Spruce will quickly want to progress to the 'real' skiing, which takes place a short shuttle-bus ride away on Mount Mansfield. Two fast lifts serve nearly all the trails. An eight-person gondola up to the Cliff House Restaurant offers a choice of mainly blue runs down, while the Cliff Trail links with the main part of Mansfield. On this sector a high-speed quad carries skiers to the self-service Octagon Café & Gallery, which commands superb views.

The main course on the mountain is the Front Four, a choice of fall-line double-diamond runs, which are steep and often glazed with ice. It is rightly said that if, in these testing conditions, you can stand up on, and ski gracefully down, Starr, Liftline, National and Goat, you can ski just about any pisted trail in the world.

Learn

Stowe Ski & Snowboard School, **t** +1 802 253 3000, offers group and private lessons.

Children

Cubs Daycare Center, t +1 802 253 3000, takes children from six weeks to six years.

Lunch

The **Cliff House Restaurant, t** +1 802 253 3000, at the Gondola Summit was recently renovated. **Fireside Tavern**, t +1 802 253 3656, at the slope-side Inn at the Mountain, serves grilled sandwiches and regional specials at lunch time.

Dine

Partridge Inn, **t** +1 802 253 8000, serves seafood in a typical New England ambience. Next door **Pie in the Sky**, **t** +1 802 253 5100, serves good-value wood-fired pizzas. **Blue Moon Café**, **t** +1 802 253 7006, features innovative cuisine based on seafood and game. **Olive's Bistro**, **t** +1 802 253 2033, has hand-painted murals and eclectic Mediterranean-Pacific cuisine. **Cactus Café**, **t** +1 802 253 7770, takes an imaginative approach to Mexican and American cuisine. **Red Basil**, **t** +1 802 253 4478, offers a mix of Thai dishes and sushi.

Party

José's Cantina at Midway Lodge and **The Den** at Mansfield Base Lodge are busy when the lifts close. In town, the **Shed Brewery** is the liveliest place. **Rusty Nail Bar & Grille** offers live weekend entertainment and pool tables. **The Matterhorn** has pool, darts and video games, as well as a sushi restaurant.

Sleep

Luxury:

Top Notch Resort & Spa, **t** +1 802 253 8585, *www.topnotch-resort.com*, has rooms decorated in sprigged English country-house style, and a spa that is rated one of the best in the country.

Trapp Family Lodge, **t** +1 802 253 8511, *www.trappfamily.com*, four miles out of town, is an opulent Tyrolean-style lodge containing the Mountain Kids Club and Activity Center providing activities for children. The Von Trapp Suite was once the private residence of Maria von Trapp.

Moderate:

Golden Eagle Resort, **t** +1 802 253 4811, *www.stoweagle.com*, along the road from Stowe, is friendly and offers accommodation for every budget, from comfortable rooms to large suites with fireplace and whirlpool bath.

Green Mountain Inn, **t** +1 802 253 7301, *www.greenmountaininn.com*, has been welcoming guests since 1833. It has an outdoor heated pool, two restaurants and a health club.

Honeywood Inn and Lodge, **t** +1 800 659 6289 or **t** +44 (0)800 085 7730, *www.honeywoodinn.com*, offers B&B accommodation at the Inn, with patchwork quilts, lacy pillows and curtains, and the Lodge has high ceilings and four-poster beds.

Inn at the Mountain, **t** +1 802 253 3656, *www.stowe.com/lodging/inn.php*, is the resort's only slope-side accommodation, offering 33 rooms and suites.

Stoweflake Mountain Resort & Spa, **t** +1 802 253 7355, *www.stoweflake.com*, houses two restaurants, a world-class spa and state-of-the-art fitness centre.

Sun Valley, Idaho

Profile

Charming resort based around an old Idaho mining town with a laid-back atmosphere. Good intermediate skiing, great restaurants and nightlife

Resort

America's oldest and most remote ski resort is completely confusing to the

***BEST FOR**
Intermediates, cosmopolitan ambience, resort charm

ESSENTIALS
Altitude: 5,750ft (1753m)–9,150ft (2789m)
Further information: **t** +1 208 622 4111, *www.sunvalley.com*
Lifts in area: 18 (18 chairs) serving 2,045 acres of skiable terrain
Lift pass: adult $240–390, child under 12yrs $136–210, both for 6 out of 7 days
Access: Sun Valley Airport 20mins

newcomer until you master the geography in this delightful corner of Idaho. Sun Valley was created in 1936 by Averell Harriman, chairman of the Union Pacific Railroad, as an all-American answer to the smart alpine resorts of St Moritz, Megève and St Anton, and as a way of 'roughing it in luxury'.

Sun Valley Lodge, made of poured concrete coloured to resemble wood, is the grand hotel in a rural village near the base that was constructed to house the big names of Hollywood. Ernest Hemingway wrote his earth-moving epic *For Whom The Bell Tolls* in room 206, which is kept as a museum. The room is surprisingly cramped by 21st-century ski resort standards. Sun Valley Inn is a later addition in similar style within the extensive manicured grounds. A small number of smart shops and restaurants compliment the carefully maintained original resort image.

It's all good historical fun, but the real skiing that you have come all this way to experience – and it is indeed a long way across the desert from anywhere to Sun Valley – lies not on little Dollar but on Bald Mountain a mile away to the west. This is directly above the quaint but vibrant Victorian mining town of Ketchum, much the most convenient place to stay. It would be a mistake, but you could easily spend an enjoyable week here without even visiting actual Sun Valley and little Dollar Mountain – and you still may find yourself riding a chair with Tom Hanks, Sheryl Crow, Jodie Foster, Hillary Swank, Clint Eastwood, Arnold Schwarzenegger, Demi Moore or Ashton Kutcher.

Mountain

In skiing terms, Sun Valley's biggest claim to fame is that it invented the chair-lift. In the heat of August in 1936, a system for shifting stems of bananas onto ships in Panama was installed. However, no allowance was made for the snowfall and subzero temperatures of the Rockies, and by the the start of the season it had completely ground to a halt. Lifts today are of more reliable design and Bald Mountain also has one of the world's most extensive automated snowmaking systems.

The skiing here suits all standards, but especially intermediates. Main mountain access is by quad-chair from River Run Plaza at one end of the town or from Warm Springs Day Lodge at the other. Both take you up to the Look Out restaurant where you can take a wide choice of routes back down or ride a triple chair to the 9,150ft summit for some challenging bowl skiing. The most demanding runs are in Easter Bowl. Snowboarding is popular, with a half-pipe on Lower Warm Springs and a new superpipe.

Learn

Sun Valley Ski and Snowboard School, **t** +1 208 622 2289, has a fine reputation and regularly has Austrian instructors.

Children

Sun Valley Playschool, **t** +1 208 622 2288, takes children aged six months to six years.

Lunch

For further information on restaurants listed without individual telephone number, call **t** +1 208 622 4111.

The **Roundhouse**, **t** +1 208 622 2371, at the top of the Exhibition and Cold Springs lift, offers a proper gourmet lunch in a warm atmosphere and is much the best place to eat. **Look Out** and **Seattle Ridge Lodge** are the above-average, self-service alternatives, along with **River Run Plaza** and **Warm Springs Day Lodge** at the bottom of Bald Mountain. At Sun Valley, **Gretchen's**, **t** +1 208 622 2144, has pasta and salads. **Trail Creek Cabin**, **t** +1 208 622 2135, one and a half miles east of Sun Valley and reached by sleigh or on cross-country skies, features prime rib, chops and an open log fire.

Dine

In Ketchum, **Michel's Christiania**, **t** +1 208 726 3388, is a French restaurant renowned for its *truite aux amandes* and *tournedos au Stilton*. **Chandler's**, **t** +1 208 726 1776, has Hawaiian *ahi* tuna, Alaskan halibut and local elk tenderloin. **Felix's**, **t** +1 208 726 1166, has Spanish Andalusian cuisine. The **Pioneer Saloon**, **t** +1 208 726 3139 – Clint Eastwood's favourite – is cheerful, much cheaper, and serves steaks. **Sushi on Second**, **t** +1 208 726 5181, is warmly recommended.

At Sun Valley, **Bald Mountain Pizza**, **t** +1 208 622 2143, has fine hand-tossed pizzas and a children' s games room, **The Ram**, **t** +1 208 622 2225, has local trout and lamb as well as fresh seafood. A relaxing and romantic way to end the day is by taking a sleigh ride to **Trail Creek Cabin**, t +1 208 622 2135, for dinner. It was popular with the Gable-Cooper-Gardner set and later became one of the watering holes of choice for Ernest Hemingway. Here you can eat prime rib, Idaho trout and barbecue ribs next to the log fire.

Party

Whiskey Jacques' on North Main in Ketchum has dancing and live music. The **Cellar Pub** is what is says it is. At Sun Valley, the **Boiler Room** has comedy shows, live bands and karaoke nights. **Duchin Lounge** is the piano bar in the Lodge.

Sleep

Luxury:

Sun Valley Lodge, **t** +1 208 622 4111, *www.sunvalley.com,*has a smart old-money atmosphere.

Sun Valley Inn, **t** +1 208 622 4111, *www.sunvalley.com*, is the slightly later addition that has been completely refurbished.

Les Saisons, **t** +1 208 727 1616, is warm and welcoming and contains condos with hickory wood floors, as well as a small spa and gym.

Thunder Spring, **t** +1 208 726 6060, *www.thunderspring.com*, contains impressive condos: bedrooms have wrought-iron bed frames, sitting rooms have polished wood floors and sofas with oversized velvet cushions and open-plan kitchens. There is a 25-m heated outdoor pool, and the 40,000sq-ft Zenergy centre houses a state-of-the-art gym, two indoor tennis courts and squash courts.

Knob Hill Inn, **t** +1 208 726 8010, *www.knobhillinn.com*, is a European-style Relais et Châteaux hotel.

Moderate:

Best Western Kentwood Lodge, **t** +1 208 726 4114, *www.bestwestern.com/kentwoodlodge*, is within easy reach of shops, nightlife and Bald Mountain.

Clarion Inn of Sun Valley, **t** +1 208 726 5900, *www.resortswest.net*, has spacious rooms and is centrally situated in Ketchum.

Taos, New Mexico

MOST CHILLED RESORT 2007

*** BEST FOR**

Exotic setting, steep 'n' deep, ski school

ESSENTIALS

Altitude: 9,207ft (2807m)–11,819ft (3603m)
Further information: t +1 505 776 2291, *www.skitaos.org*
Lifts in area: 11 (11 chairs) serving 1,294 acres of terrain
Lift pass: adult $324, youth 13–17yrs $264, child 7–12yrs $216, all for 6 days
Access: Santa Fe 1¼hrs, Albuquerque airport 2¼hrs

Profile

Quirky resort in desert surroundings with steep skiing and good ski-school tuition, but banned to snowboarders

Resort

Even by the diverse standards of America, with skiing scattered across a 2,500-mile continent, Taos – surrounded by the magical peaks of the Sangre de Cristo mountains – is a glorious one-off. Like D.H. Lawrence, Georgia O'Keeffe and Wild West frontiersman Kit Carson who all lived here, you don't have to ski to enjoy it, but you can have a lot more fun if you do. The original 1,000-year-old town with its adobe buildings and dominant Native American culture has been inspiring writers, artists and musicians for more than a century. The skiing – snowboarding is still not allowed here – takes place an 18-mile drive away up the road from the cactus and sage of the desert floor, into the alpine pines of the Carson National Forest. Like Jackson and Jackson Hole, you must choose between staying beside the ski hill or among the après-ski action. Our advice is to opt for the latter and base yourself in the town.

Taos Ski Valley (TSV) has a distinctly European atmosphere and, given that it sits on the same latitude as Rome, it usually has copious amounts of high-quality snow. It was this giant white basin that German-born Swiss Ernie Blake spotted from the window of his Cessna as he flew over the mountains in 1954. He took one look from the ground and moved there the following year to found the resort, which is still run by the family today.

The resort is a collection of lodges and condo buildings that line the banks of the Rio Hondo creek, linked by bridges and walkways near the base of what at first – and at second – glance looks like an extraordinarily steep mountain.

'Don't panic,' says the sign at the bottom of Al's run, the fall-line mogul field beneath the chair-lift, 'you are looking at 1/90th of Taos Ski Valley. We have easy skiing too.'

Mountain

The resort insists that Taos suits all standards of skier. But, while there is some good novice terrain and excellent ski instruction, this is a place for skiers who like their mountains steep and deep, or heavily mogulled between dumps. It seems strange that such a pinnacle in the desert can offer some of the toughest double-black-diamond skiing in North America. Oster and Stauffenberg, two of the most respected of these trails off the High Traverse are named after the German officers who plotted against Hitler – a statement of Ernie Blake's anti-Nazi stance during the Second World War. British skier Sir Arnold Lunn, founder of

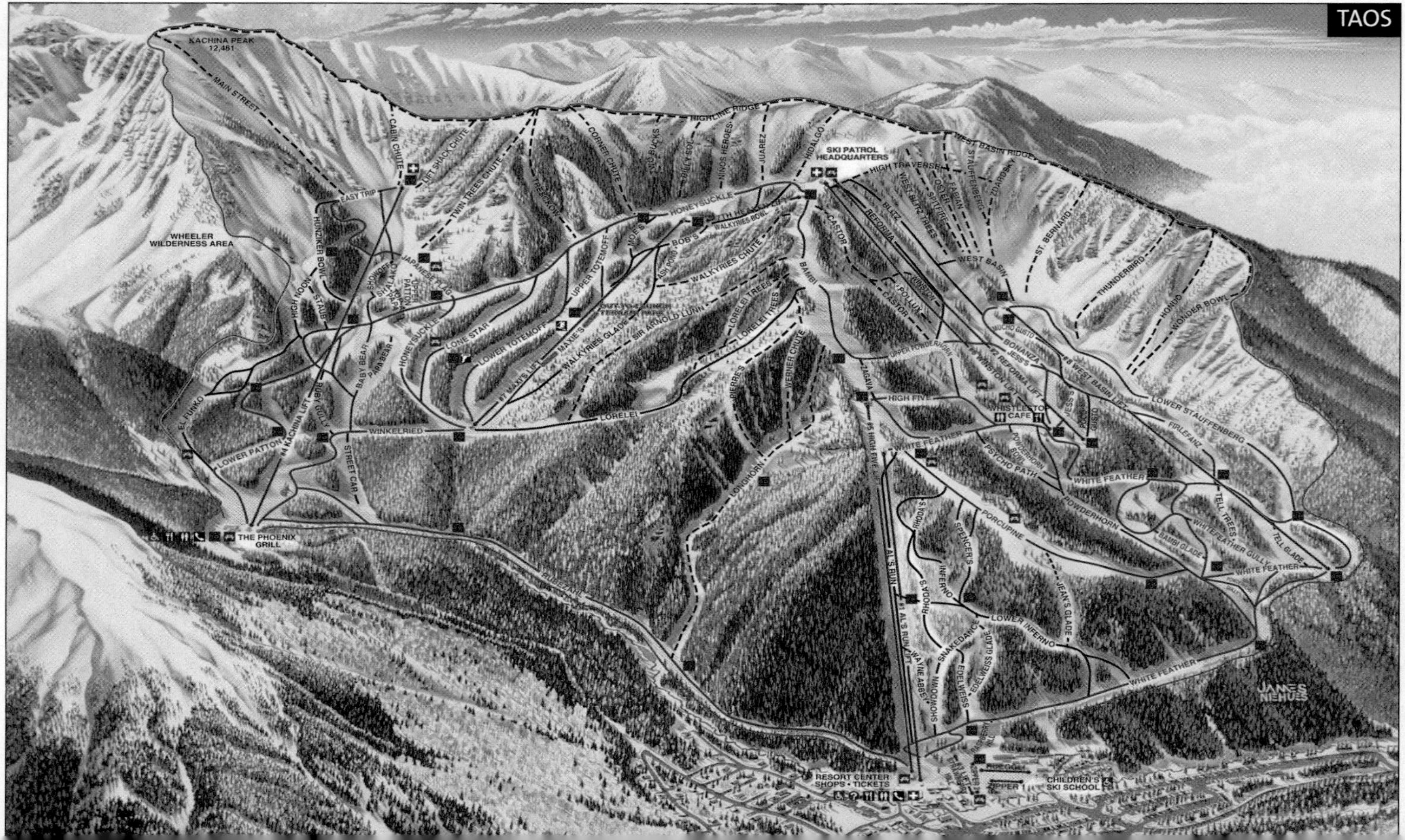
KACHINA PEAK
12,481
MAIN STREET
WHEELER
WILDERNESS AREA
CABIN CHUTE
LIFT SHACK CHUTE
EASY TRIP
HUNZIKER BOWL
HIGH NOON
STAUB
SHOWOFF
SHALAKO
JAPANESE FLAG
UPPER PATTON
PAPA
TWIN TREES CHUTE
TRESCKOW
CORNER CHUTE
TWO BUCKS
BILLY SOL
NINOS HEROES
JUAREZ
HIGHLINE RIDGE
HIDALGO
SKI PATROL
HEADQUARTERS
HIGH TRAVERSE
WEST BLITZ TREES
SPITFIRE
OSTER
FABIAN
STAUFFENBERG
ZDARSKY
WEST BASIN RIDGE
ST. BERNARD
THUNDERBIRD
HONDO
WONDER BOWL
HONEYSUCKLE
MOE'S
BOB'S
WALKYRIES BOWL
ASH POND
UPPER TOTEMOFF
LOWER TOTEMOFF
LONE STAR
MAXIE'S
WALKYRIES GLADE
WALKYRIES CHUTE
SIR ARNOLD LUNN
LORELEI TREES
BAMBI
CASTOR
POLLUX
KINSTON
REFORMA
BLITZ
WEST BASIN
MUCHO GUSTO
BONANZA
JESS'S
#2 REFORMA LIFT
#6 WINSTON LIFT
#8 WEST BASIN LIFT
LOWER STAUFFENBERG
FIRLEFANZ
UPPER POWDERHORN
ZAGAVA
HIGH FIVE
WHISTLESTOP
CAFE
POWDERHORN BOWL
PSYCHO PATH
GUSTO
WHITE FEATHER
TELL TREES
TELL GLADE
WHITEFEATHER GULLY
BAMBI GLADE
POWDERHORN
PORCUPINE
EL FUNKO
LOWER PATTON
#4 KACHINA LIFT
RUBY GULLY
BABY BEAR
PAPA BEAR
STREET CAR
WINKELRIED
#7 MAXIE'S LIFT
LORELEI
PIERRE'S
WERNER CHUTE
LONGHORN
#5 HIGH FIVE LIFT
AL'S RUN
#1 AL'S RUN LIFT
RHODA'S
SPENCER'S
INFERNO
JEAN'S GLADE
LOWER INFERNO
SNAKEDANCE
EDELWEISS
EDELWEISS GLADE
SHOWDOWN
WAYNE ABBEY
RUBEZAHL
THE PHOENIX
GRILL
RESORT CENTER
SHOPS • TICKETS
CHILDREN'S
SKI SCHOOL
JAMES
NIEHUES

slalom racing, is also remembered by his own trail. The terrain park for twin-tippers is located on Maxie's run under lift no. 7. It has a couple of big jumps, rails and a quarter-pipe.

Learn

Ernie Blake Ski School, **t** +1 505 776 2291 x 1355, provides tuition with a full range of courses and has an excellent reputation.

Children

Ernie Blake Ski School has a maximum class size of nine pupils. Little ones aged six weeks to three years are cared for by Bebekare and Kinderkare and skiers join Junior Elite. Kids' nights with entertainment and teen party nights are regularly organized.

Lunch

Rhoda's Restaurant, **t** +1 505 776 2291, slope-side in the Resort Centre, has an eclectic menu for hungry skiers. **The Phoenix Grill**, at the base of the quad-chair in Kachina Bowl, is the perfect spot for enjoying lunch and watching skiers go by. **The Whistlestop Café**, **t** +1 888 285 8920, at the base of no. 6 lift and close to the no. 2 quad, is the place to get a quick pizza or soup. **The Bavarian**, **t** +1 505 776 8020, is mid-mountain and – despite its name – looks like it is in Alpbach or Kitzbühel, with carved wooden furniture, staff in dirndl dresses and warmth provided by a tiled fireplace oven.

Dine

Rhoda's Restaurant, **t** +1 505 776 2291, features steaks, prime rib, salads, pasta, chicken and seafood at affordable prices. **De la Tierra**, **t** +1 505 758 3502, at El Monte Sagrado Living Resort & Spa serves regional and seasonal American dishes and has an impressive wine list. **Doc Martin's Restaurant**, **t** +1 505 758 1977, at the Historic Taos Inn at Taos, is an acclaimed fine-dining establishment. **Michael's Kitchen**, **t** +1 505 758 4178, in Taos, serves New York steaks and Tex-Mex. **Lambert's of Taos**, **t** +1 505 758 1009, serves contemporary American cuisine.

Party

The **Martini Tree Bar**, upstairs at Tenderfoot Katie's, is the hot place for après-ski action. The **Adobe Bar** at Historic Taos Inn serves 18 different tequilas and 14 margaritas, and features an adobe fireplace and jazz evenings. **Thunderbird Lodge** hosts live jazz.

Sleep

Luxury:

El Monte Sagrado, **t** +1 505 758 3502, *www.elmontesagrado. com,* in Taos town, offers 36 elegant suites and 'casitas' with décor inspired by Native American culture and local artists. The property has an exquisite spa and two restaurants.

Moderate:

St Bernard Hotel & Condos, **t** +1 505 776 2251, *www. stbernardtaos.com,* in TSV, is owned by Jean Mayer – technical director of the ski school. Rooms are normally fully booked for the season by early August. The hotel contains a kids' club and its bar has live music.

Snakedance Condos & Spa, **t** +1 505 776 2277, *www.snakedancecondos.com,* have evolved out of the old Inn at Snakedance and provide comfortable accommodation beside the main access lift.

Fechin Inn, **t** +1 505 751 1000, *www.fechin-inn.com,* has pleasant rooms and suites, together with a hot tub.

The Historic Taos Inn, **t** +1 505 758 2233, *www.taosinn.com*, is the old pub where Doc Martin dispensed medicine for 40 years. It has great authentic charm and a wicked menu of margaritas.

Hotel la Fonda de Taos, **t** +1 505 758 2211, *www.lafondataos.com*, atTaos Plaza, is the oldest hotel in town and houses the Forbidden Art collection by D.H. Lawrence that were banned as obscene in Britain.

Sagebrush Inn & Conference Center, **t** +1 505 758 2254, *www. sagebrushinn. com*, in Taos town, is an adobe building housing an impressive collection of Indian rugs and artefacts. The inn has been hosting visitors since the 1920s when the élite of New York and the East Coast would stop at Taos en route to Arizona.

Rio Hondo Condos, **t** +1 505 776 2347, *www.hondoproperties.com*, between Taos town and TSV, features 'casitas' – one-bedroomed guesthouses with bathroom, living room, two fireplaces and a hot tub.

Quail Inn Ridge Resort, **t** +1 505 776 2211, *www.quailridgeinn.com*, four miles from TSV, is in an adobe building and features a desert ambience, tennis courts and an outdoor swimming pool.

Telluride, Colorado

¥ BEST SKI RESORT 2007
¥ BEST LUXURY SKI HOTEL 2007:
The Peaks Resort & Golden Door Sp

Profile

Lovely old town with a wide choice of restaurants. Gondola to separate mountain village with further accommodation. Suits intermediate to advanced skiers and highly rated for snowboarding

Resort

The old mining town of Telluride, tucked away in a remote corner of the San Juan mountains, has a more colourful history and more present-day charm than any resort in North America. In 1889 Butch Cassidy and the Sundance Kid relieved the San Miguel Valley Bank of $24,000. Jack Dempsey washed dishes in a brothel here before finding his fists full of dollars elsewhere. In the 1890s Telluride built a power station and became the first town in the world to be lit by alternating electrical current. At the height of the gold rush 5,000 miners crowded into a town that supported one hotel and 100 brothels. Most probably it took its name either from tellurium, a non-metallic element in gold and silver ore or, less probably, from 'to hell you ride'.

The extra-wide streets, with their beautifully preserved Victorian buildings, including the New Sheridan Hotel and the original courthouse, were designed so that a carter could turn a full team of

***BEST FOR**

Strong skiers, luxury accommodation, snowboarders

ESSENTIALS

Altitude: 8,725ft (2660m)–12,247ft (3734m)
Further information: **t** +1 970 728 6900, *www.tellurideskiresort.com*
Lifts in area: 15 (2 cableways, 12 chairs, 1 drag) serving 1,700 acres of terrain
Lift pass: adult $388–438, child 6–12yrs $230–270, both for 6 out of 8 days
Access: Montrose airport 1¼hrs

oxen without difficulty. Modern traffic regulations limit speed to 15mph and cars give way to pedestrians. The old town is connected by gondola to the purpose-built Mountain Village Resort, four miles away by road. This provides a convenient – and increasingly extensive – bed-base.

In the late 1980s, Telluride caught the eye of Hollywood investors as it developed as a ski resort, attracting stars looking for an as yet uncommercialized Aspen. Tom Cruise has a home here, as does singer Alanis Morisette. Their presence helped to forge Telluride into one of the smartest destinations in America, with shops and restaurants of commensurate quality – and price.

The Mountain Village is reached from the old town by a gondola running 7am to midnight seven days a week. It was built in 1987, and linked in 1995 with a pedestrian centre surrounded by luxury condos and hotels, shops and restaurants. The most luxurious hotel here is The Peaks. At Mountain Village there is a further free gondola that links yet more properties. A new Four Seasons hotel and a St Regis are planned for The Mountain Village in the near future.

Mountain

The modest-sized ski area suits all standards with plenty of easy terrain, as well as some demanding steep chutes. The gondola rises steeply from the edge of the old town and doglegs down from the top station to Mountain Village. The backbone of the skiing is See Forever, a rolling blue run from Guiseppe's Restaurant at 11,890ft down to the village at 9,540ft. The whole area is made up of gladed runs with a good pitch for intermediate cruising. The sector immediately above the town is steeper with some tough fall-line options such as Kant-Mak-M, Spiral Stairs, and East and West Drain. Further challenging runs are served by the Gold Hill lift. The expansion into Prospect Bowl a few years ago greatly added to Telluride's appeal. A short hike from the top accesses La Rosa, Genevieve and Crystal – three of the steep double-black-diamonds in the resort.

Telluride Air Garden terrain park, served by the gondola from Mountain Village, has a new monster superpipe.

Learn

Telluride's Ski & Snowboard School, **t** +1 970 728 7507, offers adult group and private lessons as well as women's ski courses and adaptive skiing.

Children

The **Children's Nursery**, **t** +1 970 728 7531, is part of the Ski & Snowboard School and is for kids aged two months to three years. The ski school also offers lessons for skiers from three to 12 years, and a nightly activities programme for five to 12-year-olds. **Mountain Village Nursery**, **t** +1 970 728 7533, and **Annie's Nannies**, **t** +1 970 728 2991, are the alternatives for babysitting. The **Ski & Snowboard School** provides special teen programmes.

TELLURIDE
PALMYRA PEAK 13,320'
GUIDED HIKE-TO ACCESS ONLY
Book through Ski & Snowboard School
HIGH CAMP WARMING HUT
ELEVATION 11,815'
BALD MOUNTAIN 11,880'
ELEVATION 12,255'
TEMPTER HOUSE
GIUSEPPE'S RESTAURANT
ELEVATION 11,890'
TOPATEN NORDIC AND SNOWSHOE AREA
GORRONO RANCH RESTAURANT
STATION ST. SOPHIA 10,535'
ALLRED'S RESTAURANT
THRILL HILL
STATION VILLAGE PARKING 9,545'
TOWN OF MOUNTAIN VILLAGE 9,540'
TOWN OF TELLURIDE 8,750'
COONSKIN 8,725'
BIG BILLIE'S RESTAURANT
FREE GONDOLA
IN CASE OF EMERGENCY, CALL 911
The Telluride Ski Resort is located in the Uncompahgre National Forest and operates under special-use permit

Lunch

On-mountain dining is in a choice of five venues. **Allred's**, **t** +1 970 728 7474, a private club at lunch time, provides regional American dishes and fine wines. Try the Maine lobster bisque Asian and the spiced Muscovy duck. **Giuseppe's**, **t** +1 970 728 7503, has a cosy atmosphere and **Big Billie's**, **t** +1 970 728 7556, offers 'friendly family fare'. **Gorrono Ranch**, **t** +1 970 728 7566, is located on a late 19th-century Basque sheep herder's homestead. **That Pizza Place**, **t** +1 970 728 7499, is family-friendly and you can bake your own pizza.

Dine

Restaurants are one of Telluride's many great strengths. **Rustico**, **t** +1 970 728 4046, is Italian-owned and offers fresh-made pasta, wood-fired pizzas and one of the largest selections of Italian wines in Colorado. **Brown Dog**, **t** +1 970 728 8046, is the hippest pizza joint in town. **Honga's Lotus Petal**, **t** +1 970 728 5134, features an extensive selection of Asian cuisine. **BluePoint Grill**, **t** +1 970 728 8862, a block from the gondola base, is a hip seafood and steak house. **Harmon's**, **t** +1 970 728 3773, located in Telluride's historic train depot, serves modern American cuisine.

Up at Mountain Village is **Allred's**, **t** +1 970 728 7474, a private club by day but open to all at night. It provides regional American dishes and fine wines. Try the Maine lobster bisque Asian and the spiced Muscovy duck. **La Piazza**, **t** +1 970 728 0737, also in Mountain Village, is authentic northern Italian.

Party

Ski to the **Crunchy Porcupine** for cocktails. In town you can sip a martini and taste appetizers at the fashionable **Noir Bar** in the BluePoint restaurant, decorated with leather sofas, faux fur seats and a leopard-spotted carpet. **Fly Me to the Moon Saloon** has live music.

Sleep

Luxury:

Camel's Garden, **t** +1 888 772 2635, *www.camelsgarden.com*, is right next to the gondola station. It has 35 rooms and a spa.

Elk Mountain Resort, **t** +1 970 252 4900, *www.elkmountainresort.com*, is a member of The Small Luxury Hotels of the World, and features de luxe Lodge Rooms and three-bedroom cottages.

The Hotel Telluride, **t** +1 866 468 3501, *www.thehoteltelluride.com*, is a stylish boutique hotel housing an aromatherapy day spa. All bedrooms and suites contain feather beds with down duvets and embroidered sheets.

Inn at Lost Creek, **t** +1 970 728 5678, *www.innatlostcreek.com*, at Mountain Village, contains individually decorated rooms with de luxe kitchenettes.

Mountain Lodge, **t** +1 970 369 5000, *www.mountainlodgetelluride.com*, at Mountain Village, has comfortable condos, a pool and hot tub.

The Peaks Resort & Golden Door Spa, **t** +1 800 789 2220, *www.thepeaksresort.com*, at Mountain Village, is the ultimate in ski-in/ski-out hotels. It has a sumptuous five-storey spa with 44 treatment rooms including one for dog 'pawdicures'. The hotel contains some lovely suites and bedrooms, as well as a collection of three-bedroom cabins in its grounds. One of the hotel's pools has a water slide for kids. There is also a climbing wall, where Tom Cruise learnt the sport for *Mission Impossible 2*.

Moderate:

New Sheridan Hotel, **t** +1 800 200 1891, *www.newsheridan.com*, has been welcoming guests since 1891, four years after Telluride was founded. It is decorated in Victorian style and has a handsome mahogany bar. Its restaurant serves elk, ostrich and venison.

Ice House Lodge & Condos, t +1 800 544 3436, *www.icehouselodge.com*, is modern, central, smart and convenient for the gondola station. Adjoining the lodge are 16 luxury two- and three-bedroom condos.

Vail, Colorado

Profile

Pedestrianized village with smart hotels and restaurants. The extensive ski area has a reliable snow record, excellent ski school and substantial off-piste. A good choice for well-heeled families and skiers and riders of all levels

Resort

For most visitors, Vail is the one resort that is close to perfection. A large and easily accessible mountain offers beginner and intermediate trails immediately above the village that are nightly groomed into pristine condition. The back side is given over to hundreds of acres of lift-accessed, off-piste terrain that, after a fresh snow dump, becomes one of the world's greatest winter playgrounds.

The resort itself, built in Tyrolean style, promises a sophisticated winter wonderland borrowed from a Christmas card – and manages to deliver. Luxurious hotels are complemented by an outstanding array of restaurants and, by American standards, a busy nightlife.

The only people dissatisfied with this rose-tinted view of a snow-sure corner of Colorado are the 3 per cent of expert skiers and riders who find the gradient too tame in a destination that is more moneyed than mogulled. Chamonix or Jackson Hole it is not. This is skiing at its most comfortable, a state of affairs that would doubtless have been appreciated by eccentric Irish Baronet 'Lord' St George Gore when he passed through present-day Vail on a hunting trip in 1855 with no skis but with 112 horses and 50 dogs. While slaughtering 2,000 buffalo, 1,600 elk and 100 bears, he slept every night in a brass bed. The hedonistic trappings of his camp included a commode with a fur-lined seat, a library of rare books, and a silver dinner service.

Vail resort annually injects huge sums of cash into maintaining itself as the premier showcase of American skiing. In a move of which the likes of Tignes in France should take note, the centre of the ugly 1970s satellite of Lionshead has been demolished as part of a $380 million redevelopment programme. Last season skiers could only gawp at a giant hole in the ground where much of the accommodation had previously stood. The new building, The Arrabelle at Vail Square,

*BEST FOR

Large and varied ski area, excellent ski and snowboard tuition, non-skiers

ESSENTIALS

Altitude: 8,120ft (2475m)–11,570 ft (3526m)

Further information: t +1 970 476 9090, *www.vail.com*

Lifts in area: 34 (1 cableway, 24 chairs, 9 drags) serving 5,289 acres of terrain

Lift pass: Colorado Ticket (covers Arapahoe Basin, Beaver Creek, Breckenridge, Keystone, Vail) adult $169–402, child 5–12yrs $186, both for 6 out of 9 days

Access: Denver airport 2½hrs, Eagle County airport 40mins

houses 67 apartments along with shops, restaurants, and an ice rink. It is scheduled for completion by the start of the season.

Where you stay is important for reaching shops and restaurants, but not the slopes. The resort sprawls for seven miles along the busy I-70 freeway. The various lodging components are linked by an efficient bus service. Vail shares its lift pass with Beaver Creek 10 miles to the west, as well with Breckenridge, Keystone, and the small high-altitude ski area of Arapahoe Basin. A subsidized bus service runs between the resorts.

Mountain

Main mountain access is by the Vistabahn Express chair from Vail Village, but five other lifts at different points along the valley offer alternative routes. As a result, lift queues are rarely a problem. From the Mid-Vail hub, lifts and pistes fan out all along the front face of the mountain, offering an extraordinarily wide range of terrain. It is essentially an intermediate paradise spiced with some vicious bump runs such as Highline, Blue Ox and the infamous Roger's Run.

The Back Bowls, accessed from the top of the mountain, are ideally suited to beginner and inexperienced deep-snow skiers, who get a chance to find their feet in a controlled and lift-served environment with a mainly modest pitch. Nevertheless, it is rewarding for advanced skiers too, with plenty of good chutes, drop-offs and tree skiing.

Beyond the bowls lies Blue Sky Basin, Vail's most prized possession. This 645-acre area houses some truly stupendous off-piste served by the Skyline Express and Pete's Express lifts.

The Minturn Mile is an itinerary route that in the right snow conditions takes you down through some scenic and challenging terrain to the small town of Minturn; margaritas or pitchers of beer at the Saloon make a pleasant end to the outing.

Beginner areas are located at Golden Peak and at Eagle's Nest where there is also an activity centre – open in the evenings – with tubing, skating and snowmobiling. The Golden Peak terrain park features a 400ft superpipe with 18ft walls. There is also a smaller park on Bwana, which has jumps and rails.

Learn

Vail/Beaver Creek Ski and Snowboard School, **t** +1 970 476 3239, has a formidable reputation as an excellent, albeit expensive, learning academy. Courses include dedicated classes for teenagers, women's clinics, terrain park, and skiing for the disabled.

Children

Small World Play School, **t** +1 970 479 3285, at Golden Peak and at Lionshead is the non-ski kindergarten for children aged from eight weeks to six years. **Children's Ski and Snowboard School**, **t** +1 970 479 3280, at Golden Peak and **t** +1 970 479 4450, at Lionshead arranges classes for children from three to 12 years.

Lunch

Game Greek Restaurant, **t** +1 970 479 4275, offers American-French fusion cuisine. **Blue Moon**, **t** +1 970 479 4530, at Eagle's Nest has a relaxed atmosphere and specials such as Smoked duck *quesadilla* and Blackened catfish stuffed with a black bean-mango salsa. **Larkspur**, **t** +1 970 479 8050, in the Golden Peak base lodge has American cooking with a rustic French influence. **Cucina Rustica**, **t** +1 970 476 5011, at the Lodge at Vail has an excellent and reasonably-priced buffet. **Two Elk Lodge**, **t** +1 970 476 9090, on

VAIL

the ridge separating the Front Face from the China Bowl and Blue Sky Basin, is a huge self-service with Oriental dishes such as sushi and stir-fry with noodles or rice as well as the ubiquitous burger 'n' fries. **Bart & Yeti's**, **t** +1 970 474 2754, at Lionshead, is all-American. **Pepi's**, **t** +1 970 476 4671, has fine *moules marinière* and *Wienerschnitzel*. **Los Amigos**, **t** +1 970 476 5847, is a long-established Mexican restaurant.

Dine

Nozawa, **t** +1 970 476 9355, in the West Vail Lodge, has great sushi. **Terra Bistro**, **t** +1 970 476 6836, has an eclectic menu with Oriental-Italian fusion cuisine. **Montauk Seafood Grill**, **t** +1 970 476 2601, serves oysters flown in daily from both coasts, and Dungeness crab. **Russell's**, **t** +1 970 476 6700, offers fine steaks and seafood. **Campo de Fiori**, **t** +1 970 476 8994, specializes in pasta and risotto. **La Tour**, **t** +1 970 476 4403, is a celebrated French restaurant. Try the seared foie gras and the black truffle-scented pheasant breast. **Mezzaluna**, **t** +1 970 477 4410, has modern Italian-American cuisine. **Up The Creek**, **t** +1 970 476 8141, on the banks of Gore Creek, is renowned for its fresh fish, duck and pasta. **May Palace**, **t** +1 970 476 1657, is a good Chinese restaurant. The **Lancelot**, **t** +1 970 476 5828, specializes in prime rib. The **Wildflower**, **t** +1 970 476 5011, in the Lodge at Vail, is considered one of the top restaurants in Colorado. **Pazzo's Pizzeria**, **t** +1 970 476 9026, has sensibly priced pizzas and pasta.

Party

Chill out at the **Blue Moon** bar at Eagle's Nest after tubing, ski-biking, orienteering and a choice of other après-ski activities at **Adventure Ridge** at the top of the Eagle Bahn gondola. **Mickey's Piano Bar** at the Lodge is where to spot celebrities. **The Red Lion** in Bridge Street is the most popular après-ski bar with live music. The **Tap Room & Sanctuary** has dining and dancing. Numerically named **8150** is a fashionable nightclub. The **Ore House** offers happy-hour prices.

Sleep

Luxury:

The Lodge at Vail, **t** +1 970 476 5011, *www.lodgeatvail.com*, on the edge of the piste, is owned by the resort and remains one of the best addresses in the resort.

Sonnenalp Resort, **t** +1 970 476 5656, *www.sonnenalp.com*, is an elegant Bavarian-inspired hotel built in 1979 and still one of Vail's top places to stay.

Moderate:

Evergreen Lodge, **t** +1 970 476 7810, *www.evergreenvail.com*, located between Lionshead and Vail Village, heads the second rank.

Vail Marriott Mountain Resort & Spa, *www.marriott.com*, **t** +1 970 476 4444, at Lionshead, is a convenient and comfortable base.

Roost Lodge, **t** +1 970 476 5451, *www.roostlodge.com*, has recently been renovated and is a good-value place to stay in West Vail.

Vail Mountain Lodge and Spa, **t** +1 970 476 0700, *www.vailmountainlodge.com*, has been revamped and is highly recommended.

Antlers at Vail, **t** +1 970 476 2471, *www.antlersvail.com*, is a condo hotel on Gore Creek that recently underwent a $20-million refurbishment.

Winter Park, Colorado

***BEST FOR**

Families, airport convenience

ESSENTIALS

Altitude: 9,000ft (2743m)–12,050ft (3677m)

Further information: **t** +1 970 726 1564, *www.skiwinterpark.com*

Lifts in area: 21 (19 chairs, 2 drags) serving 2,770 acres of terrain

Lift pass: adult $220–348, child 6–13yrs $70–120, both for 6 days

Access: Denver Airport 90mins, ski train from Denver 2¼hrs

Profile

Unsophisticated family resort with plenty of advanced skiing, reasonably priced accommodation and a short airport transfer. Not recommended for night owls

Resort

Winter Park is the closest major ski destination to Denver and currently at the start of a mighty 15-year rebuild. The municipally owned ski area has now been leased to Canadian giant Intrawest over a 50-year period. Central to the expansion plan is the new Village at Winter Park Resort beside the base area, which will have 1,500 residential units and 24 shops and restaurants. The company is investing $70 million in the first phase, which includes the creation of a scenic lake from the Fraser River that runs through the base area. Work began in summer 2006 and completion of this initial project is scheduled for the start of the 2008–9 winter season.

All this augurs well for the future, but the problem for the present is that the town of Winter Park is an inconvenient two miles from the skiing. Plans to link the mountain to the town by gondola are included in the master plan but still seem to be a decade away. A regular bus service operates between the two but finishes at 10.30pm.

Mountain

Winter Park offers extensive terrain for all levels of skier and rider. The area naturally divides into two main sectors. Winter Park has beginner, intermediate and expert trails with main access by the Zephyr Express quad. More demanding Mary-Jane, named after a popular local prostitute of the 1920s, features hard bump skiing, some tree-level romps, as well as some expert double-diamond chutes from Vasquez Cirque. Main access is by a high-speed six-pack, which has replaced the Summit Express. Sorensen Park is a new five-acre learning area. Winter Park has three terrain parks and a 450ft superpipe. Neighbouring Berthoud Pass no longer operates as a ski area, but the off-piste runs from the top of the pass are superb. You will need a local guide and a strategically parked car.

Learn

Winter Park Resort Ski & Snowboard School, **t** +1 800 729 7907, runs a full range of courses.

Children

Kids Adventure Junction Center, **t** +1 970 726 1564, provides free pagers for parents and cares for non-skiing children from eight weeks to six years.

Lunch

Doc's Roadhouse, **t** +1 970 722 5450, at Zephyr Mountain Lodge, specializes in prime rib, **Club Car**, **t** +1 970 726 5514, at the Mary Jane Center and the **Dining Room** at the Lodge at Sunspot, **t** +1 970 726 1446, are the main mountain options.

Dine

Untamed Steakhouse, **t** +1 970 726 1111, has creative Colorado cuisine and live entertainment. **Carlos and Maria's**, **t** +1 970 726 9674, offers good Mexican food. **Deno's Mountain Bistro**, **t** +1 970 726 5332, serving steaks and seafood, is a resort institution. **Fontenot's Cajun Café**, **t** +1 970 726 4021, features Cajun dishes. **New Hong Kong**, **t** +1 970 726 9888, offers Szechwan, Mandarin, Cantonese and Thai specials.

Party

The **Derailer Bar** at West Portal Station is busy as the lifts close, but Winter Park is a family destination with limited après-ski entertainment. Try **Buckets Saloon**, **Smokin' Moe's**, **Moffat Station Restaurant and Brewery**, **Randi's Irish Saloon** and **Winter Park Pub**.

Sleep

Luxury:

For further information and reservations, call **t** +1 970 726 5587.

Zephyr Mountain Lodge provides rustic contemporary-style accommodation beside the lifts.

Moderate/Budget:

Beaver Creek Condos is a comfortably furnished complex a seven-minute shuttle ride from the slopes and five minutes from shops and restaurants.

Iron Horse Resort is the original condo complex with an outdoor pool.

Super 8 Motel, **t** +1 970 726 8088, close to the resort centre, features a 14-person indoor hot tub.

Winter Park Mountain Lodge has been extensively refurbished and is situated three minutes by shuttle bus from the base area.

A–Z of World Resorts

Abetone, Italy

t +39 0329 4207373, *www.abetone.org*
Altitude 1390m (4,560ft)–1900m (6,233ft)
Lifts 25
Tour operators Alpine Tours, Erna Low, SkiBound
Apennine resort within easy reach of Florence and Pisa.

Abondance, France

t +33 (0)4 50 73 02 90, *www.valdabondance.com*
Altitude 930m (3,050ft)–1800m (5,906ft)
Lifts 207 in Portes du Soleil
Tour operator Interhome
Small historic village 7km from La Chapelle d'Abondance. A regular bus service links the village with the Portes du Soleil area. Abondance has its own small ski area. Hotels include **La Rocaille, t** +33 (0)4 50 73 01 74, *www.larocaille.com*, **Hôtel Les Touristes, t** +33 (0)4 50 73 02 15, and **Le Ferraillon, t** +33 (0)4 50 73 07 75.

Adelboden and Lenk, Switzerland

Adelboden t +41 (0)33 673 8080, *www.adelboden.ch*
Lenk t +41 (0)33 733 3131, *www.lenk.ch*
Altitude 1068m (3,503ft)–2357m (7,733ft)
Lifts 56 in area
Tour operators Interhome, Kuoni, Swiss Travel Service.
The unspoilt village of Adelboden consists of chalets set on a sunny terrace below the Wildstrubel massif. Neighbouring Lenk is a spa village, and the two resorts share a 170km intermediate ski area with a good selection of mountain restaurants. 'By the end of February or early March there is always good snow, sunshine, few queues, and not many Brits', said one reporter. In Lenk, four-star **Sporthotel Wildstrubel, t** +42 (0)33 736 3111, *www.wildstrubel.ch*, is in a central position ('excellent food and leisure facilities, although decor is a little dated').

Alagna, Italy

See *Champoluc*, page 250
Tour operators Alpine Answers Select, Momentum, Original Travel, Ski 2, Ski Weekend

Alpbach, Austria

Page 37
Tour operators Crystal, Inghams, Interhome, Made to Measure

Alpe d'Huez, France

Page 143
Tour operators Airtours, Alpine Answers Select, Alpine Elements, Club Med, Crystal, Directski, Erna Low, First Choice, French Freedom, French Life, Frozenplanet, Inghams, Interhome, Lagrange, Made to Measure, Mark Warner, Momentum, Neilson, On The Piste, Panorama, Ski Activity, Ski Arrangements, SkiBound, Ski Expectations, Ski France, Ski Freshtracks, Ski Independence, Ski Miquel, Ski Supreme, Skiworld, Thomson, Tops, Wasteland

Alpendorf, Austria

See *Wagrain and the Salzburger Sportwelt*, page 86

Alpine Meadows, California, USA

t +1 530 583 4232, *www.skialpine.com*
Tour operator Ski the American Dream
Altitude 6,835ft (2083m)–8,637ft (2633m)
Lifts 14
Challenging small ski area next to Squaw Valley on Lake Tahoe with 2,400 acres of terrain suited to intermediate and advanced skiers and riders.

Alta, Utah, USA

See *Snowbird and Alta*, page 390
Tour operators Ski All America, Ski the American Dream, Ski Independence

Alta Pusteria, Italy

t +39 0474 913156, *www.three-peaks.info*
Altitude 1310m (4,298ft)–2000m (6,562ft)
Lifts 27
Seven small alpine ski areas within the Hochpustertal, which is a popular cross-country destination. Some 200km of trails begin around the scenic village of Sesto and charming Moso in the Val di Sesto, and around the thriving Tyrolean village of Dobbiaco and the ancient historic town of San Candido in the Val Pusteria. These head southwest to the quiet Val Fiscalina, with striking views of the Tre Cime di Lavaredo (the Three Peaks) en

route. A popular trail also leads south from Dobbiaco to Cortina d'Ampezzo. **Berghotel Tirol**, **t** +39 0474 710386, *www.berghotel.com*, is the hotel of choice in Sesto and **Hotel Villa Stefania**, **t** +39 0474 913588, *www.villastefania.com*, is a small hotel with a good restaurant in San Candido.

Altenmarkt, Austria

See *Wagrain and the Salzburger Sportwelt*, page 86
Tour operator Interhome

Alyeska, Alaska, USA

t +1 907 754 1111, *www.alyeskaresort.com*
Altitude 250ft (76m)–3,939ft (1200m)
Lifts 9
Tour operators Frontier Ski, Ski All America
Alaska's steep peaks offer excellent heli- and snowcat-skiing and fabulous scenery and have made this a cult destination for ski extremists. The cable-car conveniently starts inside the **Alyeska Prince Hotel**, **t** +1 907 754 1111, *www.princehotels.co.jp/alyeska-e*.

Andalo, Italy

t +39 0461 585570, *www.aptdolomitipaganella.com*
Altitude 1040m (3,412ft)–2125m (6,972ft)
Tour operators Equity/Rocket Ski, PGL, SkiBound
Lifts 18
Town dating back to the 12th century with pleasant intermediate skiing. This is the place where the World Cup started.

Andermatt, Switzerland

Page 299
Tour operators Momentum, Switzerland Travel Centre (Plus Travel)

Anzère, Switzerland

t +41 (0)27 399 2800, *www.anzere.ch*
Altitude 1500m (4,921ft)–2420m (7,940ft)
Lifts 11
Tour operator Interhome
Purpose-built neighbour of Crans-Montana and Aminona with 1970s apartment buildings and a loyal Swiss following.

Aonach Mor, Scotland

See *Nevis Range*, page 445
Tour operator Skisafe Travel

Aosta, Italy

See *Pila*, page 448
Tour operator Crystal

Apex, BC, Canada

t +1 250 292 8222, *www.apexresort.com*
Altitude 5,197ft (1575m)–7,197ft (2180m)
Lifts 4
Tour operators Frontier Ski, Ski Safari
Little-known village in the Okanagan Valley offering high-quality skiing without the crowds. The resort is 30 minutes' drive up a private road from the town of Penticton, and an hour from Kelowna airport. The varied runs include blues and easy black-diamonds on the front face, with the highest chair accessing some short and steep trails. Recommended hotels include **The Coast Inn Apex**, **t** +1 250 979 3939, **Saddleback Lodge**, **t** +1 250 292 8118, and the low-cost **Double Diamond Hostel**, **t** +1 250 292 8256.

Aprica, Italy

t +39 0342 746113, *www.apricaonline.com*
Altitude 1181m (3,875ft)–2361m (7,746ft)
Lifts 19
Tour operators Club Europe, PGL, SkiBound
Pleasant family resort 170km from Milan with 50km of piste.

Arabba, Italy

Page 238
Tour operators Inghams, Neilson, Original Travel, Ski Expectations

Arapahoe Basin, Colorado, USA

t +1 970 496 7077, *www.arapahoebasin.com*
Altitude 10,780ft (3283m)–13,050ft (3967m)
Lifts 5
Tour operators Ski Activity, Ski the American Dream, SkiBound
Arapahoe Basin (A-Basin) is a small high-altitude ski area with certain snow until May. Most of the trails suit beginners to intermediates, with the Pallavicini bump run one of the longest and steepest in North America. The nearest accommodation base is six miles away at Keystone. A-Basin shares a lift pass with Vail, Keystone, Breckenridge and Beaver Creek.

Arcalis, Andorra

See *Pal-Arinsal*, page 24

Les Arcs, France

Page 146

Tour operators Airtours, Alpine Answers Select, Alpine Elements, Club Med, Corporate Ski Company, Crystal, Directski, Equity/Rocket Ski, Erna Low, Esprit, First Choice, French Freedom, French Life, Frozenplanet, Inghams, Interhome, Lagrange, Made to Measure, Momentum, Neilson, On The Piste, PGL, Ski Activity, Ski Adventures, Ski Amis, Ski Arrangements, Ski France, Ski Freshtracks, Ski Independence, Skiworld, Thomson, Total Ski, Wasteland

Ardent, France

Altitude 1260m (4,134ft)–2466m (8,090ft)
Lifts 206 in Portes du Soleil area (14 cableways, 82 chairs, 110 drags)
Tour operators The Chalet Company, Family Ski Company

Charming little village linked into Les Lindarets near Avoriaz in the Portes du Soleil ski area by a 10-person gondola. **L'Escapade** is recommended for après-ski drinks.

Åre, Sweden

Page 286

Tour operators Neilson/Neilson School Groups

Argentière, France

Page 155

Tour operators AWWT, Board and Lodge, Collineige, Erna Low, French Life, Interhome, Lagrange, McNab, Mountain Retreats, Ski Freshtracks, Ski Hillwood, Ski Scott James, Ski Weekend, White Roc Weekends

Arinsal, Andorra

See *Pal-Arinsal*, page 24

Tour operators Airtours, Crystal, Directski, First Choice, Inghams, Neilson, Panorama, SkiBound, Ski Wild, Thomson

Arosa, Switzerland

t +41 (0)81 378 7020, *www.arosa.ch*
Altitude 1800m (5,904ft)–2653m (8,702ft)
Lifts 13
Tour operators Interhome, Kuoni, Made to Measure, Momentum, Powder Byrne, Swiss Travel Service, Switzerland Travel Centre (Plus Travel), White Roc Weekends

This pretty village offers the all-round winter-sports holiday with skiing for beginners to intermediates. Reporters rated the pistes as 'mainly wide, varied and really good fun to ski'. A new half-pipe opened the season before last. Recommended hotels include five-star **Arosa Kulm**, **t** +41 (0)81 378 8888, *www.arosakulm.ch*, and **Tschuggen Grand Hotel**, **t** +41 (0)81 378 9999, *www.tschuggen.ch*. **Hotel Cristallo**, **t** +41 (0)81 378 6868, *www.cristalloarosa.ch*, has bedrooms with four-posters, attractive **Hotel Arlenwald**, **t** +41 (0)81 377 1838, *www.arlenwaldhotel.ch*, has just eight rooms and is ski-in/ski-out. Stylish **Hotel Eden**, **t** +41 (0)81 377 0261, *www.edenarosa.ch*, has individually decorated bedrooms with a theatrical theme. **Hotel Alpensonne**, **t** +41 (0)81 377 1547, *www.hotelalpensonne.ch*, is another good choice.

Aspen and Snowmass, Colorado, USA

Page 346

Tour operators Alpine Answers Select, American Ski Classics, AWWT, Carrier, Crystal, CV Ski, Directski, Elegant Resorts, Erna Low, Lotus Supertravel, Made to Measure, Momentum, Rocky Mountain Adventures, Seasons in Style, Ski Activity, Ski All America, Ski the American Dream, Ski Expectations, Ski Freshtracks, Ski Independence, Ski Safari, Ski Solutions, Skiworld, Thomson, Trailfinders, United Vacations, Virgin

Auffach, Austria

See *Niederau*, page 59

Auris-en-Oisans, France

t +33 (0)4 76 80 13 52, *www.auris-en-oisans.com*
Altitude 1600m (5,249ft)–3330m (10,922ft)
Lifts 85 in linked area
Tour operator Lagrange

Purpose-built Auris is linked into the Alpe d'Huez ski area and is well placed for day trips to Les Deux Alpes, Serre Chevalier and La Grave.

Auron, France

t +33 (0)4 93 23 02 66, *www.auron.com*
Altitude 1165m (3,822ft)–2450m (8,038ft)
Lifts 12

Tour operators Club Pavilion/Concept, French Life, Lagrange
Traditional resort with a good atmosphere, linked to St-Etienne de Tinée and only 90km from Nice. The ski area provides good intermediate skiing on 130km of piste, with a recommended terrain park and ice-skating rink.

Aussois, France

t +33 (0)4 79 20 42 21, *www.aussois.com*
Altitude 1500m (4,921ft)–2750m (9,022ft)
Lifts 10
Tour operator Peak Retreats
Aussois is an easily accessible resort situated on a wide sunny plateau at the foot of the 3697m Dent Parrachée in the Maurienne Valley. The old village with its traditional stone-and-slate houses, shared in winter by man and beasts, is built around the central 'place' with its fountain and communal oven. The skiing is best suited to beginners and intermediates looking for easing cruising runs amid spectacular scenery. The village shares a joint lift pass with nearby La Norma and Valfréjus. It has 35km of cross-country trails.

Autrans, France

t +33 (0)4 76 95 30 70, *www.ot-autrans.fr*
Altitude 1050m (3,445ft)–1710m (5,610ft)
Lifts 12
Tour operator Lagrange
Small and attractive low-altitude ski area in the Vercors. **Auberge de la Croix Perrin**, **t** +33 (0)4 76 95 40 02, *www.aubergedelacroixperrin.com*, is a two-star hotel with eight bedrooms, set in the woods 5km from the village.

Aviemore, Scotland

See *Cairngorm Mountain (Aviemore)*, page 423
Tour operator Skisafe Travel

Avoriaz, France

Page 151
Tour operators Airtours, Chalet Snowboard, Club Med, Crystal, Directski, Erna Low, First Choice, French Freedom, French Life, Frozenplanet, Kuoni, Momentum, Neilson, On The Piste, Original Travel, Ski Arrangements, Ski Freshtracks, Ski Independence, Thomson, White Roc Weekends

Axalp, Switzerland

See *Meiringen-Hasliberg*, page 441

Axamer Lizum, Austria

t +43 (0)5125 9850, *www.innsbruck.info*
Altitude 874m (2,867ft)–2343m (7,687ft)
Lifts 10
Tour operators Crystal, Neilson School Groups, PGL, SkiBound, Thomson
The small modern resort offers the best skiing and snowboarding within easy reach of Innsbruck. Axamer is one of the top snowboarding destinations in Austria.

Bad Gastein and Bad Hofgastein, Austria

See *The Gasteinertal*, page 38
Tour operators Crystal, Directski, First Choice, Inghams, Interhome, Made to Measure, SkiBound, Ski Miquel, Ski Wild

Bad Kleinkirchheim and St Oswald, Austria

t +43 (0)4240 8212, *www.badkleinkirchheim.at*
Altitude 1080m (3,543ft)–2000m (6,560ft)
Lifts 26
Tour operators Alpine Tours, Crystal, PGL, SkiBound, Sloping Off, Solo's
Bad Kleinkirchheim (BKK) is the home resort of Austrian racing legend Franz Klammer. The 103km intermediate ski area is linked with the village of St Oswald. Accommodation includes five-star **Thermenhotel Ronacher**, **t** +43 (0)4240 282, which has a good spa.

Banff-Lake Louise, Alberta, Canada

Page 95
Tour operators Alpine Answers Select, American Ski Classics, AWWT, Crystal, CV Ski, First Choice, Frontier Ski, Inghams, Lotus Supertravel, Made to Measure, Momentum, Neilson/Neilson School Groups, Nonstopski, Rocky Mountain Adventures, Seasons in Style, Ski Activity, Ski All America, Ski the American Dream, Ski Arrangements, SkiBound, Ski Freshtracks, Ski Independence, Ski Safari, Skiworld, Solo's, Thomson, Trailfinders, United Vacations, Virgin

Bansko, Bulgaria

Page 133

Tour operators Balkan Holidays, Directski, Erna Low, First Choice, Inghams, Neilson/Neilson School Groups, Panorama, Thomson

Baqueira Beret, Spain

Page 293

Tour operator Ski Miquel

Bardonecchia, Italy

t +39 0122 99032, *www.bardonecchiaski.com*
Altitude 1290m (4,232ft)–2750m (9,022ft)
Lifts 24
Tour operators Corporate Ski Company, Crystal, Erna Low, Momentum, Neilson, Ski Arrangements, Ski High Days, Thomson

The busy market town is by the entrance to the Fréjus Tunnel and close to the resorts of Montgenèvre and Sestriere. It offers good value. 'The resort is very child-friendly and the pistes are well groomed. Many times I never saw another soul on the whole run down to the bottom' enthused a reporter. Three ski areas offer some challenging skiing with few crowds, and a choice of 11 mountain restaurants. The resort has recently added a new chair-lift and an eight-seater gondola.

Barèges and La Mongie, France

Barèges t +33 (0)5 62 92 16 00, *www.bareges.com*
La Mongie t +33 (0)5 62 91 94 15, *www.bagneresdebigorre-lamongie.com*
Altitude 1250m (4,100ft)–2350m (7,708ft)
Lifts 43 in linked area
Tour operators Borderline, Lagrange, Pyrenean Mountain Tours, Tangney Tours

Barèges and La Mongie make up the largest ski area in the Pyrenees, sharing pistes suited to all standards on both sides of the Col du Tourmalet. There is virtually no queuing due to a new fast six-seater chair. La Mongie is the better base for complete beginners, with 'lots of off-piste the locals don't seem to use'. The one-street spa village of Barèges has more atmosphere than its neighbour. Recommended hotels in Barèges include the two-star **Hôtel Igloo, t** +33 (0)5 62 92 68 10, *www.hotel-bareges.com*, which has been refurbished and has a good brasserie, and **Hôtel Alphée, t** +33 (0)5 62 92 68 39, offering cheap and tasty food. **Hôtel Europe, t** +33 (0)5 62 92 68 04, is also recommended. Accommodation in La Mongie includes three-star **Le Pourteilh, t** +33 (0)5 62 91 93 33, and **Résidence Le Montana, t** +33 (0)5 62 91 99 99.

Bariloche, Argentina

See *Gran Catedral (Bariloche)*, page 432

Beaver Creek, Colorado, USA

Page 351

Tour operators AWWT, Carrier, Crystal, CV Ski, Elegant Resorts, Made to Measure, Seasons in Style, Ski Activity, Ski All America, Ski the American Dream, Ski Independence, Ski Safari, Ski Wild, United Vacations

Le Bettex, France

See *St Gervais*, page 209

Big Mountain, USA

t +1 406 862 2900, *www.bigmtn.com*
Altitude 4,500ft (1372m)–7,000ft (2134m)
Lifts 13
Tour operators AWWT, Ski Independence

Large ski area at Whitefish, close to the Canadian border, with 3,000 acres of mainly bowl- and tree-skiing.

Big Sky, Montana, USA

t + 1 406 995 5000, *www.bigskyresort.com*
Altitude 6,800ft (2073m)–11,150ft (3398m)
Lifts 17
Tour operators AWWT, Momentum, Ski Activity, Ski the American Dream, Ski Independence, Ski Safari

Up-and-coming resort with uncrowded high-altitude skiing for all standards, situated 45 miles from Bozeman and 18 miles from Yellowstone National Park. The skiing takes place on three mountains with 150 marked runs in 3,600 acres of skiable terrain. The main action is on 11,150ft Lone Mountain reached by the Lone Peak Tram. Runs from the top include the steep Big Couloir, a vertiginous fall-line descent that requires considerable concentration. The Gullies and the exposed south face can be almost as challenging. The lower half of the mountain, together with the adjoining peaks of Andersite and Flat Iron provide plenty of intermediate gladed skiing. The 1,300ft terrain park is the longest in

Montana and has a half-pipe. Combined with neighbouring Yellowstone Club, to which it is linked, it would arguably be one of the biggest ski resorts in the USA. However, you have to be a multi-millionaire property owner to ski at strictly private Yellowstone. Big Sky has now buried the hatchet with adjoining little Moonlight Basin and the two now share a lift pass. **Big Sky Snowsports School**, **t** + 1 406 995 5743, has a sound reputation. Best hotel is **The Summit at Big Sky**. **Shoshone Condominium Hotel** has comfortable units with fireplaces. **Powder Ridge Cabins** are rustic-style with hand-hewn log finishes and three or four bedrooms (**t** + 1 406 995 5000 for all reservations).

Big White, BC, Canada

Page 99

Tour operators AWWT, Crystal, Frontier Ski, Made to Measure, Momentum, Ski Activity, Ski All America, Ski the American Dream, Ski Freshtracks, Ski Independence, Ski Safari

Bled, Slovenia

See *Bohinj*, page 136

Tour operators Crystal, Balkan Holidays, Directski, Thomson, Waymark

Blue Cow, Australia

See *Perisher-Blue*, page 448

Bohinj, Slovenia

Page 136

Tour operators Balkan Holidays, Crystal, Directski, Just Slovenia, Thomson

Bolzano, Italy

t +39 0473 279457, *www.ortlerskiarena.com*
Altitude 1459m (4,787 ft)–2070m (6,791ft)
Lifts 74 in Ortler Skiarena
Valley town that offers accessible nearby skiing at Meran 2000, Rittner Horn and a host of other resorts. Hotel choices include **Parkhotel Laurin**, **t** +39 0471 311000, *www.laurin.it*, **Hotel Kohlern**, **t** +39 0471 329978, and **Park-Hotel Holzner**, **t** +39 0471 345231, *www.parkhotel-holzner.com*, all with excellent restaurants.

Borca, Italy

See *Macugnaga*, page 440

Borgata, Italy

t +39 0122 755449, *www.montagnedoc.it*
Altitude 1840m (6,035ft)–2823m (9,262ft)
Lifts 93 in the Milky Way
Hamlet adjoining Sestriere in the Milky Way that acts as an alternative tranquil bed-base.

Bormio, Italy

Page 240

Tour operators Directski, Equity/Rocket Ski, Neilson School Groups, PGL, Ski Arrangements, Sloping Off

Borovets, Bulgaria

Page 137

Tour operators Airtours, Balkan Holidays, Crystal, Directski, First Choice, Frozenplanet, Inghams, Interhome, Neilson/Neilson School Groups, Panorama, Thomson

Les Bottières, France

See *Le Corbier*, page 427

Bourg-St-Maurice, France

See *Les Arcs*, page 146

Tour operators Erna Low, Neilson School Groups, Vanilla Ski

Breckenridge, Colorado, USA

Page 356

Tour operators Alpine Answers Select, Alpine Tracks, American Ski Classics, AWWT, Crystal, Erna Low, Inghams, Made to Measure, Neilson, Rocky Mountain Adventures, Ski Activity, Ski All America, Ski the American Dream, Ski Expectations, Ski Freshtracks, Ski Independence, Ski Safari, Ski Solutions, Ski Wild, Skiworld, Thomson, Trailfinders, United Vacations, Virgin

Briançon, France

See *Serre Chevalier*, page 212

Tour operator Lagrange

Brides-les-Bains, France

t +33 (0)4 79 55 20 64, *www.brides-les-bains.com*
Altitude 1400m (4,593ft)–2952m (9,685ft)
Lifts 198 in Trois Vallées
Tour operators Airtours, AWWT, Erna Low, First Choice, French Life, Lagrange, Peak Retreats, SkiBound, Ski Independence, Skiweekends

An alternative spa town choice for those wishing to ski the Trois Vallées ski area on a budget. 'Friendly and accessible' was how one reporter described it. It is linked by a gondola to Méribel. The town has 21 hotels including **Grand Hôtel des Thermes**, **t** + 33 (0)4 79 55 38 38.

Brienz, Switzerland

See *Meiringen–Hasliberg*, page 441

Brighton, Utah, USA

t +1 801 532 4731, *www.skibrighton.com*
Altitude 8,755ft (2668m)–10,750ft (3277m)
Lifts 8
Tour operator Ski the American Dream
Utah's oldest ski area was founded in 1936 and is located 45 minutes by road from Salt Lake City. Attractive resort best suited to intermediates. Brighton has some of the most extensive night-skiing in the country, with over 22 trails floodlit until 9pm six days per week. **The Brighton Lodge**, **t** +1 800 873 5512 x 236, *www.brightonresort.com*, is slope-side and friendly.

Brixen-im-Thale, Austria

t +43 (0)5334 8433, *www.brixenimthale.at*
Altitude 800m (2,624ft)–1829m (6,001ft)
Lifts 93 in SkiWelt
Traditional Tyrolean village near Kitzbühel, linked by gondola into the SkiWelt.

Bruson, Switzerland

t +41 (0)27 776 1682, *www.verbier.ch*
Altitude 1100m (3,543ft)–2445m (8,022ft)
Lifts 89 in Four Valleys
Small uncrowded resort near Verbier with some steep powder skiing. Bruson has a couple of hotels, and some apartments on the mountain. This is the next alpine village earmarked for development by Intrawest.

Cairngorm Mountain (Aviemore), Scotland

t +44 (0)1479 810 363, *www.cairngorm mountain.com*, *www.ski.visitscotland.com*
Altitude 550m (1,804ft)–1100m (3,608ft)
Lifts 17
Tour operator Ski Norwest
Aviemore is Britain's best-known ski resort – despite the fact that it is not a ski resort at all. The action takes place on Cairngorm Mountain, 10 miles to the east. Main mountain access is by funicular, and the skiing and riding are surprisingly challenging when conditions allow. In winter 2005/6 Cairngorm had some of the best cover in its history as a ski area. However, that is by no means always the case. The skiing at Cairngorm can be comparable to that of an alpine resort of similar size, but booking in advance is a risky business. Aviemore, the nearest town, is located about 120 miles north of Edinburgh and Glasgow on the A9. Recommended places to stay include the three-star **Cairngorm Hotel**, **t** +44 (0)1479 810 233, *www.cairngorm.com*, and the **Hilton Coylumbridge Hotel**, **t** +44 (0)1479 810 661, *www.hilton.co.uk/coylumbridge*.

Campitello, Italy

See *Canazei*, page 241
Tour operators Directski, Neilson

Campo Felice, Italy

t +39 06 943 00001, *www.campofelice.it*
Altitude 1410m (4,626ft)–2065m (6,775ft)
Lifts 14
Little resort with a good lift system and five restaurants, linked to village of Rocca di Cambio and within a one-hour drive of Rome.

Canazei, Italy

Page 241
Tour operators Directski, Equity/Rocket Ski, First Choice, Inghams, Interhome, Neilson, Thomson

Canillo, Andorra

See *Soldeu-El Tarter*, page 32

The Canyons, Utah, USA

Page 361
Tour operators AWWT, Ski All America, Ski the American Dream, Ski Independence, Ski Safari, Skiworld, United Vacations

Cardrona, New Zealand

See *Wanaka (Cardrona and Treble Cone)*, page 467

Les Carroz, France

t +33 (0)4 50 90 00 04, *www.lescarroz.com*
Altitude 1140m (3,740ft)–2480m (8,134ft)
Lifts 72 in Grand Massif

Tour operators Altitude Holidays, Erna Low, French Life, Lagrange, Peak Retreats, Ski Independence

One of the main resorts of the Grand Massif that is centred around Flaine. 'This is a gem,' enthuses one reporter, 'it oozes charm.' 'Genuinely friendly people', and 'a nice ordinary French village – you don't have to pay the earth for a cup of coffee', were the other favourable comments. **L'Igloo, t** + 33 (0)4 50 90 14 31, at the top of the Morillon chair is warmly praised as a lunch spot. The village is more architecturally appealing than Flaine and attracts families and weekend visitors. The cableway and chair are reached by efficient ski-bus from the village centre, and are within easy reach of hotels such as **Les Airelles, t** +33 (0)4 50 90 01 02, **Les Belles Pistes, t** +33 (0)4 50 90 00 17, and **Croix de Savoie, t** +33 (0)4 50 90 00 26. The old village has been renovated and apartment blocks including **MGM, t** +44 (0)20 7584 2841, have been added in keeping with the resort's style.

Castelrotto (Kastelruth), Italy

t +39 0471 706333, *www.castelrotto.com*
Altitude 1060m (3,478ft)–2180m (7,152ft)
Lifts 24 in Alpe di Siusi
Tour operator Inntravel

Village of the South Tyrol at the end of the Val Gardena near Ortisei with nearby access to Alpe di Siusi and Sella Ronda. Nearby Zanseralm is a resort dedicated to snowshoeing. **Hotel Cavallino d'Oro, t** +39 0471 706337, *www.cavallino.it*, is an ancient and pretty little hotel with quaint decoration. A ski-bus takes you to Alpe di Siusi under 30 minutes away.

Cauterets, France

t +33 (0)5 62 92 50 50, *www.cauterets.com*
Altitude 1000m (3,280ft)–2350m (7,710ft)
Lifts 15
Tour operators Lagrange, Leisure Direction

Small spa town 40km from Lourdes Tarbes airport, offering skiing mainly for beginners and intermediates. This takes place in the rather exposed Cirque du Lys bowl. A cable-car takes you up and brings you back again at the end of the day. One reporter complains of the 'very limited skiing' while another rates it 'ideal for novices'. Nearby Pont d'Espagne is a separate ski area with four lifts and 37km of cross-country trails. Recommended three-stars in Cauterets include **Hôtel Bordeaux, t** +33 (0)5 62 92 52 50, and **Hôtel-Résidence Aladin, t** +33 (0)5 62 92 60 00.

Cavalese, Italy

Page 244

Tour operators Alpine Tours, First Choice, SkiBound, Thomson

Celerina, Switzerland

t +41 (0)81 830 0011, *www.celerina.ch*
Altitude 1720m (5,643ft)–3057m (10,030ft)
Lifts 56 in area
Tour operator Made to Measure

Quiet alternative to St Moritz, with old frescoed houses and access on skis to the Corviglia ski area. **Cresta Kulm, t** +41 (0)81 836 8080, **Chesa Rosatsch, t** +41 (0)81 837 0101, and offbeat **Hotel Misani, t** +41 (0)81 833 3314, *www.hotelmisani.ch*, with its themed bedrooms, are the hotels of choice.

Cervinia, Italy

Page 246

Tour operators Alpine Answers Select, Club Med, Crystal, Elegant Resorts, First Choice, Inghams, Interhome, Momentum, Ski Arrangements, SkiBound, Ski Freshtracks, Ski Solutions, Thomson

Cesana-Sansicario, Italy

t +39 0122 89202, *www.montagnedoc.it*
Altitude 1350m (4,428ft)–2823m (9,262ft)
Lifts 92 in Milky Way

Cesana, setting for the Olympic Bobsleigh and Biathlon events, has been given something of a face-lift for the 2006 games. The attractive, albeit slightly shabby, 12th-century village is set on a busy road close to the Montgenèvre Pass. The chair-lifts accessing the skiing are a long walk from the village centre. Accommodation includes **Hotel Chaberton, t** +39 0122 89147, *www.hotelchaberton.com*. Halfway up the mountain lies the purpose-built village of Sansicario, made up mainly of apartment buildings and a shopping mall. The recommended place to stay here is **Hotel Rio Envers, t** +39 0122 811333.

Chamonix, France

Page 155

Tour operators Alpine Answers Select, Alpine Elements, Alpine Tracks, Alpine Weekends, AWWT, Barelli Ski, Bigfoot Travel, Board and Lodge, Classic Ski, Club Med, Club Pavilion/ Concept, Collineige, Concept Chalets, Corporate Ski Company, Crystal, Directski, Erna Low, Esprit, First Choice, Flexiski, French Freedom, French Life, Frozenplanet, High Mountain Holidays, Inghams, Interhome, Lagrange, Made to Measure, Momentum, Mountain Leap, Mountain Retreats, Neilson, Original Travel, Oxford Ski Company, Peak Retreats, Ski Activity, Ski Arrangements, Ski Expectations, Ski France, Ski Independence, Ski Solutions, Ski Weekend, Skiweekends, Snow Safari, Thomson, White Roc Weekends

Champagny-en-Vanoise, France

See *La Plagne*, page 200

Tour operators Barelli Ski, Erna Low, Lagrange, Made to Measure, Ski Independence

Champéry, Switzerland

t +41 (0)24 479 2020, *www.champery.ch*
Altitude 1053m (3,455ft)–2350m (7,708ft)
Lifts 206 in Portes du Soleil
Tour operators Alpine Answers Select, Alpine Tracks, Corporate Ski Company, Made to Measure, Momentum, Oak Hall, White Roc Weekends

Traditional village that is the main Swiss resort in the trans-frontier Portes du Soleil ski area. A large cable-car whisks you up to the mid-mountain station at Planachaux. Alternative access is by a new six-seater covered chair from Grand-Paradis up to Planachaux. In town, attractive wooden chalets, hotels, shops and restaurants line the main street, but the resort is finally beginning to modernize with a new ice hall featuring regular ice-hockey matches and a revamped sports centre. Recommended places to stay include comfortable **Hôtel Suisse, t** +41 (0)24 479 0707, **Hôtel National, t** +41 (0)24 479 1130, and **Hôtel Beau-Séjour, t** +41 (0)24 479 5858, *www.beausejour-champery.com*. **Auberge du Grand-Paradis, t** +41 (0)24 479 1167, *www.grandparadis.ch*, is well regarded, while **Hôtel la Rose des Alpes, t** +41 (0)24 479 2303, *www.rosedesalpes.com*, and **Pension La Mattaz, t** +41 (0)24 479 2002, are good value.

Champex-Lac, Switzerland

t +41 (0)27 783 2828, *www.champex.ch*
Altitude 1470m (4,823ft)–2188m (7,178ft)
Lifts 4

Charming small resort close to Verbier but not sharing its lift pass. The skiing is limited but never crowded, with some excellent tree-skiing. **Hôtel Belvédère, t** +41 (0)27 783 1114, *www.le-belvedere.ch*, is full of character.

Champoluc, Italy

Page 250

Tour operators Alpine Answers Select, Alpine Tracks, Crystal, Momentum, Ski Expectations, Ski 2

Champoussin, Switzerland

t +41 (0)24 476 8300, *www.portesdusoleil.com, www.royalalpageclub.com*
Altitude 1680m (5,512ft)–2350m (7,708ft)
Lifts 211 in Portes du Soleil
Tour operator Esprit

Champoussin in the Portes du Soleil is a mini-resort of modern, rustic-style buildings. Most are apartments, but the focal point is **Résidence Royal Alpage Club, t** +41 (0)2 447 68300, a hotel containing swimming pool, games room, disco and kindergarten.

Chamrousse, France

t +33 (0)4 76 89 92 65, *www.chamrousse.com*
Altitude 1700m (5,577ft)–2255m (7,398ft)
Lifts 26
Tour operators Erna Low, Lagrange

A rather unattractive but ski-convenient collection of buildings on the mountainside a 30-minute drive from Grenoble. The resort, scene of Jean-Claude Killy's clean sweep in the 1968 Grenoble Olympics, attracts a mainly French clientele and is popular with visitors from the city at weekends. **Hôtel Bellevue, t** +33 (0)4 76 89 97 73, is at the foot of the slopes. **Hôtel L'Hermitage, t** +33 (0)4 76 89 93 21, *www.hotel-hermitage.com*, is rated, along with the simpler **Hôtel Virage, t** +33 (0)4 76 89 90 63, and **Hôtel La Datcha, t** +33 (0)4 76 89 91 40.

La Chapelle d'Abondance, France

t +33 (0)450 73 51 41, *www.portesdusoleil.com/station/chapelle*
Altitude 1010m (3,313ft)–1700m (5,577ft)

Lifts 207 in Portes du Soleil
Tour operators Ski Addiction, Ski La Côte
This old straggling farming village is 6km from Châtel. On one side of the road two long chairs take you up to Crêt Béni, on the other side a gondola and chair take you to Châtel and Torgon. **Hôtel Les Cornettes, t** +33 (0)4 50 73 50 24, *www.lescornettes.com*, houses one of the area's best restaurants, and **Alti 1000, t** +33 (0)4 50 73 51 90, *www.valdabondance.com/alti-1000*, also has a swimming pool. The **Fer Rouge** pub is the local meeting place.

Château d'Oex, Switzerland

t +41 (0)26 924 25 25, *www.chateau-doex.ch*
Altitude 1050m (3,445ft)–2979m (9,744ft)
Lifts 62
Tour operator Alpine Tours
Small and attractive village sharing Gstaad's 250km ski area, and popular with hot-air-balloon enthusiasts. Accommodation includes **Gourmet-Hôtel Ermitage, t** +41 (0)26 924 6003, *www.gourmet-hotelermitage.ch*, and **Pension Le Vieux Chalet, t** +41 (0)26 924 6879, *www.hotels-suisse.ch/le-vieux-chalet/le-vieux-chalet.htm*, which is an old chalet with simple rooms and home cooking.

Châtel, France

t +33 (0)4 50 73 22 44, *www.chatel.com*
Altitude 1200m (3,936ft)–2350m (7,708ft)
Lifts 206 in Portes du Soleil
Tour operators First Choice, Freedom Holidays, Frozenplanet, Interhome, Lagrange, Momentum, Peak Retreats, Ski Addiction, Skialot, Ski Arrangements, Ski Independence, Ski Rosie, Snowfocus, Tops
The small farming village of Châtel is set in the vast Portes du Soleil ski area. Not a lot of planning has gone into the development of the village, which consists of buildings scattered up towards the Morgins Pass and Switzerland, and along the valley to the Linga lift with its access to Avoriaz. Reporters complain that lifts in the Super-Châtel sector are 'somewhat tired'. **Hôtel Fleur de Neige, t** +33 (0)4 50 73 20 10, *www.hotel-fleurdeneige.fr*, is a restaurant with rooms. **Hôtel Castellan, t** +33 (0)4 50 73 20 86, is renowned for its food, and **Hôtel Les Rhododendrons, t** +33 (0)4 50 73 24 04, is in the best position.

Le Chazelet, France

t +33 (0)4 76 79 95 73, *www.lagrave-lameije.com*
Altitude 1500m (4,921ft)–2100m (6,890ft)
Lifts 1
Close to the extreme skiing at La Grave, on the north face of the Meije, are the three more moderate areas of Le Chazelet, Villar d'Arène and the Col du Lautaret, which are ideal for beginners. If you are staying in La Grave (see page 177), this is the nearest place to find ski tuition for adults and children.

Clavière, Italy

t +39 0122 878856, *www.claviere.it*
Altitude 1760m (5,773ft)–2293m (7,523ft)
Lifts 92 in Milky Way
Tour operators Crystal, Equity/Rocket Ski, First Choice, SkiBound, Ski High Days
Set on the Franco-Italian border, the village is made up of a handful of hotels and shops. Clavière is linked into the giant Milky Way ski area, with access to the skiing above Montgenèvre and Cesana Torinese and easy home runs. Accommodation includes the **Grand Albergo Clavière, t** +39 0122 878787, **Passero Pellegrino, t** +39 0122 878914, **Hotel Pian del Sole, t** +39 0122 878085, and **Savoia, t** +39 0122 878803. Ski-in/ski-out **Sporthotel Sagnalonga, t** +39 0122 878856 is rated for its swimming pool. 'The hotel is in a perfect position and really cosy,' said one reporter, 'and the snowmobile ride up to the hotel at night was a great bonus for the kids.'

La Clusaz, France

Page 160
Tour operators Classic Ski, Crystal, Interhome, Lagrange, Made to Measure, Ski Activity, Ski Arrangements, SkiBound, Skitopia, Ski Weekend, Snowlife

Les Coches, France

See *La Plagne*, page 200
Tour operators Family Ski Company, Finlays, French Life, Lagrange, Mountain Sun, Ski Independence

Colfosco, Italy

See *Corvara*, page 257

El Colorado, Chile

See *Valle Nevado*, page 464

Compaccio (Compatsch), Italy

t +39 0471 704122, *www.schlern.info*
Altitude 1236m (4,055ft)–2949m (9,676ft)
Lifts 24 in Alpe di Siusi
Tour operators Equity/Rocket Ski, Inntravel
Small high-altitude hamlet above Ortisei with skiing in the Alpe di Siusi (Seiseralm) and a backdoor link into Sella Ronda ski area. Ski-in/ski-out **Hotel Urthaler, t** +39 0471 727919, *www.hotel-urthaler.com*, is a temple to all that is fresh and understated in hotel design of today.

Les Contamines-Montjoie, France

t +33 (0)4 50 47 01 58, *www.lescontamines.com*
Altitude 1164m (3,818ft)–2500m (8,202ft)
Lifts 24
Tour operators Classic Ski, Club Europe, Frozenplanet, Interhome, Lagrange, Ski Arrangements, Ski Weekend
The resort may be little known internationally, but it has a loyal following. Set a short distance from Megève, the long straggling village is based on one side of the river while the skiing is the opposite side. The lift access is a 1km walk from the town centre, although a frequent bus service provides welcome transport. It is immediately after a fresh snowfall when Les Contamines comes into its own, offering some delightful off-piste skiing. Three-stars **Hôtel La Chemenaz, t** +33 (0)4 50 47 02 44, *www.chemenaz.com*, is said to be friendly with good food, and **Chalet-Hôtel Camille Bonaventure, t** +33 (0)4 50 47 23 53, *www.camillebonaventure.com*, is new.

Copper Mountain, Colorado, USA

Page 364
Tour operators American Ski Classics, AWWT, Crystal, Equity/Rocket Ski, Erna Low, Neilson/Neilson School Groups, Ski Activity, Ski All America, Ski the American Dream, SkiBound, Ski Independence, Ski Safari, Thomson, United Vacations, Virgin

Le Corbier, France

t +33 (0)4 79 83 04 04, *www.le-corbier.com*, *www.sybelles.com*
Altitude 1550m (5,085ft)–2600m (8,530ft)
Lifts 76 in area
Tour operators Equity/Rocket Ski, Erna Low, Interhome, Lagrange, Ski Independence
Le Corbier is part of Les Sybelles, one of the largest ski areas in the Maurienne Valley, sharing 300km of terrain with the neighbouring resorts of Les Bottières, St Jean d'Arves, St Sorlin d'Arves and La Toussuire. The new Sybelles Express six-person chair-lift takes skiers up from the village centre to the top of Mont Corbier in eight minutes. The skiing is ideal for beginners and lower intermediates. Most of the accommodation in Le Corbier is in apartments. It also has a couple of two-stars: **Hôtel Mont Corbier, t** +33 (0)4 79 56 70 27, in the centre and **Le Grillon, t** +33 (0)4 79 56 72 59, 3km away towards Villarembert.

Coronet Peak, New Zealand

See *Queenstown (Coronet Peak and The Remarkables)*, page 451

Corrençon, France

See *Villard-de-Lans*, page 466

Cortina d'Ampezzo, Italy

Page 254
Tour operators Alpine Answers Select, Corporate Ski Company, Crystal, Elegant Resorts, Inghams, Made to Measure, Momentum, Original Travel, Ski Arrangements, Ski Equipe, Ski Expectations, Ski Freshtracks, Ski Solutions, Thomson, White Roc Weekends

Corvara, Italy

Page 257
Tour operators Momentum, Neilson, Pyrenean Mountain Tours

Courchevel, France

Page 161
Tour operators Airtours, Alpine Answers Select, Alpine Elements, Alp Leisure, Corporate Ski Company, Crystal, Descent International, Directski, Elegant Resorts, Erna Low, Esprit, Finlays, First Choice, Flexiski, French Freedom, French Life, Frozenplanet, Inghams, Jeffersons, Kaluma, Lagrange, Lotus Supertravel, Made to Measure, Mark Warner, Momentum, Mountain Leap, Neilson, Oxford Ski Company, PGL, Powder White, Scott Dunn Ski, Seasons in Style, Silver Ski, Le Ski, Ski Activity, Ski Amis, Ski Arrangements, Ski Deep, Ski Expectations,

Ski France, Ski Independence, Ski Link, Ski 'n' Action, Ski Olympic, Ski Power, Ski Solutions, Ski Val, Ski Weekend, Skiworld, Thomson, Total Ski, White Roc Weekends

Courmayeur, Italy

Page 258

Tour operators Alpine Answers Select, Alpine Weekends, Corporate Ski Company, Crystal, First Choice, Inghams, Interhome, Interski, Mark Warner, Momentum, Ski Arrangements, Ski Expectations, Ski Solutions, Ski Weekend, Thomson, White Roc Weekends

Crans-Montana, Switzerland

Page 300

Tour operators Corporate Ski Company, Crystal, Directski, Inghams, Interhome, Kuoni, Made to Measure, Momentum, Oxford Ski Company, PGL, Ski Freshtracks, Swiss Travel Service, Switzerland Travel Centre (Plus Travel)

Crested Butte, Colorado, USA

Page 365

Tour operators AWWT, Club Med, Ski Activity, Ski the American Dream, Ski Safari, United Vacations

Crest-Voland, France

See *Notre-Dame-de-Bellecombe*, page 446, and *Les Saisies*, page 454

Les Crosets, Switzerland

t +41 (0)24 477 2077, *www.lescrosets.com*
Altitude 1660m (5,445ft)–2350m (7,708ft)
Lifts 206 in Portes du Soleil
The hamlet of Les Crosets sits in the heart of the Portes du Soleil and is highly rated by riders. It has its own snowboard school and terrain park. This is not the most appealing of resorts and is best suited to serious skiers and boarders who favour early nights. **Hôtel Télécabine, t** + 41 (0)24 479 0300, *www.camillebonaventure.com*, is simple with good food.

Dachstein Glacier, Austria

See *Wagrain and the Salzburger Sportwelt*, page 86

La Daille, France

See *Val d'Isère*, page 221

Davos, Switzerland

Page 302

Tour operators Alpine Answers Select, Alpine Weekends, Corporate Ski Company, Flexiski, Frozenplanet, Headwater, Inghams, Interhome, Kaluma, Kuoni, Made to Measure, Momentum, PGL, Ski Expectations, Ski Freshtracks, Ski Gower, Swiss Travel Service, Switzerland Travel Centre (Plus Travel), White Roc Weekends

Deer Valley, Utah, USA

Page 367

Tour operators American Ski Classics, Momentum, Ski All America, Ski the American Dream, Ski Independence, Ski Safari

Les Deux Alpes, France

Page 169

Tour operators Airtours, Chalet Snowboard, Club Med, Crystal, Erna Low, First Choice, French Life, Frozenplanet, Inghams, Interhome, Lagrange, Made to Measure, Mark Warner, McNab, Momentum, Neilson, Panorama, Peak Retreats, Ski Activity, Ski Arrangements, SkiBound, Ski Independence, Ski Supreme, Skiworld, Thomson, Tops, Wasteland

Les Diablerets, Switzerland

See *Villars*, page 331

Tour operators Crystal, Equity/Rocket Ski, Interhome, Momentum, PGL, Ski Gower, Sloping Off, Solo's, Swiss Travel Service, Switzerland Travel Centre (Plus Travel), Thomson

Dienten, Austria

See *Maria Alm*, page 440

Dobbiaco, Italy

See *Alta Pusteria*, page 417

Tour operators Headwater, HF Holidays, Ramblers, Waymark

Durango, Colorado, USA

t +1 970 247 9000, *www.durangomountainresort.com*
Altitude 8,793ft (2680m)–10,822ft (3299m)
Lifts 10
Tour operator Ski Independence

Durango Mountain Resort in southern Colorado is a purpose-built, alpine-style resort with an old-town ambience. The skiing takes place on Purgatory Mountain. The resort makes an ideal two-centre trip combined with Telluride, which is just two and a half hours' drive away. Snowboarders and twin-tippers are well catered for with the Paradise Freestyle Arena and the Pitchfork Terrain Park. The Adaptive Sports Association is one of the best ski schools for disabled skiers in the USA. Hotels include **Purgatory Village Hotel**, **t** +1 970 385 2100, **The Inn at Durango Mountain**, **t** +1 970 247 9669, and **Sheraton Tamarron Resort**, **t** +1 970 259 2000. The **Twilight View Condos** are recommended.

Eichenhof, Austria

See *St Johann in Tirol*, page 75

Ellmau, Austria

t +43 (0)5358 2301, *www.ellmau.at*
Altitude 820m (2,690ft)–1829m (6,001ft)
Lifts 93 in SkiWelt
Tour operators Airtours, Crystal, Inghams, Interhome, Neilson/Neilson School Groups, Ski Astons, Ski Wild, Thomson
The largest resort of the SkiWelt offers good access into the lift system and a wide choice of accommodation. **Hotel Christoph**, **t** +43 (0)5358 3535, *www.hotel-christoph.com*, a five-minute walk from the main lift, has spacious rooms. **Hotel Hochfilzer**, **t** +43 (0)5358 2501, *www.hotel-hochfilzer.com*, and **Sporthotel Ellmau**, **t** +43 (0)5358 3755, *www.sporthotel-ellmau.com*, are both four-stars. The de luxe **Relais & Châteaux Der Bär**, **t** +43 (0)5358 2395, *www.hotelbaer.com*, has a spa.

Encamp, Andorra

See *Soldeu*, page 32

Engelberg, Switzerland

Page 306
Tour operators Alpine Answers Select, Corporate Ski Company, Crystal, Inntravel, Interhome, Kuoni, Made to Measure, Momentum, Oak Hall, Ski Gower, Swiss Travel Service, Switzerland Travel Centre (Plus Travel), Waymark, White Roc Weekends

Entrèves, Italy

See *Courmayeur*, page 258

Espace Diamant, France

See *Notre-Dame-de-Bellecombe*, page 446

Espace Killy, France

See *Val d'Isère*, page 221, and *Tignes*, page 217

Falls Creek and Mount Hotham, Australia

Falls Creek t +613 5758 3224, *www.fallscreek.com.au*
Mount Hotham t +613 5759 4444, *www.hotham.com.au*
Altitude 1450m (4,757ft)–1861m (6,105ft)
Lifts 13
These are the major resorts in Victoria, sharing a lift pass and linked by a six-minute helicopter ride. Falls Creek Alpine Resort is four hours' drive from Melbourne on the edge of the Bogong High Plains. A European-style, ski-in/ski-out village has accommodation among the gum trees. Australia's largest snowmaking system covers the main trails, and the resort has a good terrain park.

Mount Hotham is the highest alpine resort in Victoria, with most of the skiing taking place below the village. Dinner Plain, Mount Hotham's architect-designed sister village, provides good-value accommodation 10km from the mountain but linked by free ski-bus.

Le Fayet, France

See *St-Gervais*, page 209

Fernie, BC, Canada

Page 101
Tour operators Alpine Answers Select, American Ski Classics, AWWT, Crystal, Frontier Ski, Inghams, Made to Measure, Momentum, Neilson, Nonstopski, Ski Activity, Ski All America, Ski the American Dream, Ski Arrangements, Ski Freshtracks, Ski Independence, Ski Safari, Skiworld, Virgin

Fieberbrunn, Austria

t +43 (0)5354 56304, *www.pillerseetal.at*
Altitude 800m (2,625ft)–2020m (6,627ft)
Lifts 11
Tour operators Snowscape, Thomson, Tyrolean Adventures
Small and attractive ski area near St Johann in Tirol with a reputation for good snow and a network of long, easy tree-level runs. **Austria Trend Sporthotel Fontana**, **t** +43 (0)5354 56453,

www.austria-trend.at/fib, and **Hotel-Pension Lindauerhof**, **t** +43 (0)5354 56382, are convenient for the skiing, while **Schloss Rosenegg**, **t** +43 (0)5354 56201, is a 14th-century castle with bedrooms reached by spiral staircase, and dungeons and an armoury linked by an underground passageway.

Filzmoos, Austria

See *Wagrain and the Salzburger Sportwelt*, page 86

Tour operator Inghams

Finkenberg, Austria

See *Mayrhofen*, page 55

Tour operator Crystal

Fiss, Austria

t +43 (0)5476 62390, *www.serfaus-fiss-ladis.at*
Altitude 1427m (4,682ft)–2684m (8,806ft)
Lifts 53 in area
Tour operators Alpine Tours, Interhome
Small traditional village sharing a ski area with Ladis and larger Serfaus. The old village centre has been retained, with most of the houses built in the 16th and 17th centuries. The mainly stone houses have arched doorways and overhanging gabled roofs. The resort has 20 restaurants and cafés.

Flachau, Austria

See *Wagrain and the Salzburger Sportwelt*, page 86

Tour operators Interhome, Made to Measure

Flaine, France

Page 173

Tour operators Alpine Answers Select, Altitude Holidays, Classic Ski, Crystal, Erna Low, French Freedom, French Life, Inghams, Lagrange, Momentum, Neilson, On The Piste, PGL, Ski Arrangements, Ski Freshtracks, Ski Independence, Thomson

Flims, Switzerland

See *Laax*, page 315

Tour operators Alpine Answers Select, Corporate Ski Company, Frozenplanet, Interhome, Made to Measure, Momentum, Powder Byrne, Swiss Travel Service, Switzerland Travel Centre (Plus Travel), White Roc Weekends

Flumet, France

See *Notre-Dame-de-Bellecombe*, page 446, and *Les Saisies*, page 454

Folgarida, Italy

t +39 0463 901280, *www.valdisole.net*
Altitude 1300m (4,265ft)–2505m (8,219ft)
Lifts 47 in area
Tour operators Equity/Rocket Ski
Purpose-built resort linked to Marilleva, and to Madonna di Campiglio, which is 9km away. A total of 120km of linked skiing, popular with budget skiers and school groups.

Font-Romeu, France

t +33 (0)4 68 30 68 30, *www.font-romeu.fr*
Altitude 1700m (5,577ft)–2250m (7,382ft)
Lifts 26
Tour operators Lagrange, Solo's
Important resort in the Pyrenees, 90km from Perpignan. The skiing and purpose-built ski station are 4km from the old village and linked by gondola. The pistes are best suited to beginners, lower intermediates and families. Weekend queueing can be a problem. There are two dozen hotels and pensions, including three-star **Hôtel Carlit**, **t** +33 (0)4 68 30 80 30, *www.carlit-hotel.fr*, **Le Grand Tetras**, **t** +33 (0)4 68 30 01 20, *www.hotelgrandtetras.free.fr*, **La Montagne**, **t** +33 (0)4 68 30 36 44, and **Sun Valley**, **t** +33 (0)4 68 30 21 21, *www.hotelsunvalley.fr*.

La Foux d'Allos, France

See *Pra-Loup*, page 450

Tour operator Club Europe

Fulpmes, Austria

See *Neustift and the Stubaital*, page 58

Tour operator Crystal

Galtür, Austria

t +43 (0)5443 8521, *www.galtuer.com*
Altitude 1585m (5,200ft)–2300m (7,546ft)
Lifts 10
Tour operators Crystal, Directski, First Choice, Inghams, Made to Measure
Small resort with considerable atmosphere close to Ischgl. It suffered terribly in the February avalanches of 1999, but has since rebuilt its tourist trade with considerable success. Galtür's pistes are at Wirl, an outpost five minutes away by a free and frequent

shuttle bus. The skiing is gentle and well suited to beginners and families; the area is also a notable centre for ski-touring. The family-run **Fluchthorn Hotel, t** +43 (0)5443 8202, *www.fluchthorn-buentali.at*, offers a warm welcome in a central location. Four-star **Hotel Post, t** +43 (0)5443 84220, *www.hotel-post.at*, is convenient.

Gargellen, Austria

t +43 (0)5557 6303, *www.gargellen.at*
Altitude 1430m (4,692ft)–2300m (7,546ft)
Lifts 62 in area
Tour operator Made to Measure
The attractive chalet-style village in the Montafon area is close to the border with Switzerland and attacts a loyal international clientele. The ski area is shared with 10 other villages, with a total 222km of piste and 62 lifts, as well as extensive ski-touring on the Silvretta glaciers, and 100 km of cross-country ski runs. Hotels in Gargellen include the four-star **Madrisa, t** +43 (0)5557 6331, which was built as a country house at the beginning of the 20th century and opened as a hotel in the 1920s ('excellent, family-run, and very friendly. It is situated right by the beginner slope and you can ski back to the door'). **Hotel Heimspitze, t** +43 (0)5557 63190, *www.heimspitze.com*, is also rated. The resort has a modern eight-person gondola, and free ski-buses link Gargellen with the neighbouring resorts of Gaschurn and St Gallenkirch.

Garmisch-Partenkirchen, Germany

t +49 8821 1806,
www.garmisch-partenkirchen.de
Altitude 710m (2,330ft)–1330m (4,364ft)
Lifts 32 in Zugspitze
Tour operators Interhome, Moswin's Germany
The towns of Garmisch and Partenkirchen are surrounded by striking scenery and lie beneath the Zugspitze, Austria and Germany's highest mountain. Partenkirchen is an ancient Roman town dating back to 15 BC, while Garmisch has frescoed medieval houses. The towns were linked for Hitler's 1936 Winter Olympics. The ski area is made up of five mountains and offers 15km of the only glacier skiing in Germany. Although Garmisch has 18km of undemanding piste, the majority of runs are best suited to intermediate skiers and riders, with a terrain park featuring a superpipe. The mountain can be accessed from three starting places, including a cable-car and cog railway from Garmisch. The glacier can also be reached from the village of Ehrwald in Austria. Hotels include five-star **Reindl's, t** +49 8821 943870, and the four-star **Hotel Alpina, t** +49 8821 7830, *www.alpina-gap.de*.

Gaschurn, Austria

t +43 (0)5557 6303, *www.gargellen.at*
Altitude 1430m (4,692ft)–2300m (7,546ft)
Lifts 62 in area
Tour operator Made to Measure
The ski area is shared with 10 other villages of the Montafon area, with a total 222km of piste and 62 lifts, as well as extensive ski-touring. Free ski-buses link with the neighbouring resorts of Gargellen and St Gallenkirch.

The Gasteinertal, Austria

Page 38

Geilo, Norway

Page 287
Tour operators Alpine Tracks, Crystal, Headwater, Inntravel, Neilson/Neilson School Groups, Thomson

Les Gets, France

Page 194
Tour operators Descent International, Equity/Rocket Ski, First Choice, Gourmet Chalet Company, Lagrange, Made to Measure, Momentum, Oxford Ski Company, Peak Retreats, Reach4theAlps, Ski Activity, Ski Expectations, Ski Famille, Ski Hillwood, Ski Independence, Ski-n-doo, Total Ski, Wasteland, Wood Advent Farm

Glencoe and Glenshee, Scotland

Glencoe t +44 (0)1855 851 226,
www.ski-glencoe.co.uk
Glenshee t +44 (0)13397 41320,
www.ski-glenshee.co.uk
Altitude 304m (1,000ft) – 1109m (3,637ft)
Tour operator (Glenshee) Skisafe Travel
Glencoe is the original UK resort and has the longest black run in Scotland, while Glenshee has the largest lift system in Britain. However, both are victims of the changing European weather pattern and suffer from lack of snow

for much of the winter. When it does fall, both can offer good skiing, but it is impossible to book a holiday in advance and be certain of sufficient cover. Both have excellent ski schools. Near Glencoe, recommended accommodation is the **Macdonald Hotel, t** +44 (0)1855 831 539, *www.macdonaldhotel.co.uk*, and **Invercoe Highland Holiday Cottages, t** +44 (0)1855 811 210. For Glenshee, recommended hotels include **Callater Lodge Hotel, t** +44 (0)13397 41275, and **Braemar Lodge, t** +44 (0)13397 41627, at Braemar, **Dalmunzie House Hotel, t** +44 (0)1250 885 224, and the **Spittal Hotel, t** +44 (0)1250 885 215.

Going, Austria

t +43 (0)5358 2438, *www.going.at*
Altitude 800m (2,624ft)–1892m (6,207ft)
Lifts 93 in SkiWelt
Tour operators Interhome, Neilson, Solo's
Linked into the SkiWelt area, Going has some stunning views and a good nursery slope. One of the village highlights is five-star **Hotel Stanglwirt, t** +43 (0)5358 2000, *www.stanglwirt.com*, which has a Lipizzaner riding school.

Golden, BC, Canada

See *Kicking Horse*, page 109

Gosau, Austria

See *St Wolfgang*, page 454

Grächen, Switzerland

t +41 (0)27 955 6060, *www.graechen.ch*
Altitude 1615m (5,330ft)–2890m (9,537ft)
Lifts 13
Tour operator Interhome
Chalet-style village close to Saas-Fee and Zermatt. The ski area is accessed by a choice of two gondolas.

Gran Catedral (Bariloche), Argentina

t +54 2944 423776, *www.bariloche.com*
Altitude 1050m (3,445ft)–2050m (6,725ft)
Lifts 32
Tour operators Andes, Exsus, Lotus Supertravel
San Carlos de Bariloche, in Patagonia, is home to Gran Catedral – Argentina's oldest and most famous ski resort – better known as Bariloche. It is a large, attractive resort not far from the Chilean border. Sophisticated Bariloche is South America's biggest resort, boasting a modern lift system, 50 trails, a vertical drop of 1000m and the largest snowmaking system in South America. The area provides intermediate slopes with high-speed cruising and abundant off-piste. Hotels include the five-star **Panamericano, t** +54 2944 425847, *www.panamericanobariloche.com*, and four-star **Hotel Nevada, t** +54 2944 522778, *www.nevada.com.ar*, and **Hotel Edelweiss, t** +54 2944 445500, *www.edelweiss.com.ar.*

Le Grand Bornand, France

t +33 (0)4 50 02 78 00, *www.legrandbornand.com*
Altitude 950m (3,120ft)–2100m (6,890ft)
Lifts 39
Tour operators Interhome, Lagrange, Ski Arrangements
The charming village 10 minutes' drive from La Clusaz has extensive skiing comprising some 90km of piste, and offering something for all levels. The main ski station is at Le Chinaillon. The picturesque Col des Annes offers motorway cruising. From Lachat, at 2100m, the piste stretches out to the gentle slopes of Joyère. Snowboarders have some designated pistes and the new Aiguille Mountain terrain park provides a good playground. La Clusaz is an easy drive away. The three-star hotels are **Best Western Chalet Les Saytels, t** +33 (0)4 50 02 20 16, *www.bestwestern-chaletlessaytels.com*, and chalet-style **Les Cimes, t** +33 (0)4 50 27 00 38, *www.hotel-les-cimes.com*, with just 10 bedrooms.

Grand Targhee, Wyoming, USA

t +1 307 353 2300, *www.grandtarghee.com*
Altitude 8,000ft (2438m)–10,230ft (3118m)
Lifts 8
Tour operators AWWT, Ski Safari
This small purpose-built resort is just inside the Wyoming border and 47 miles from Jackson Hole. It boasts a wonderful snow record, which is why the main attraction is snowcat-skiing and -boarding. If you can't get a space on a snowcat, the resort's 2,000-acre ski area offers some challenge and plenty of powder. Prices are considerably lower than in Jackson Hole, and accommodation (**t** +1 800 827 4433 for booking office) includes **Teewinot Lodge, Targhee Lodge** and **Sioux Lodge Condominiums**.

Grandvalira, Andorra
See *Pas de la Casa*, page 29, and *Soldeu*, page 32

Grau Roig, Andorra
See *Pas de la Casa*, page 29

La Grave, France
Page 177
Tour operators Interhome, Lagrange, Momentum, Peak Retreats, Ski Arrangements

Gressoney, Italy
See *Champoluc*, page 250
Tour operators Alpine Answers Select, Crystal, Momentum, Ski Expectations

Grindelwald, Switzerland
Page 307
Tour operators Corporate Ski Company, Crystal, CV Ski, Elegant Resorts, Inghams, Interhome, Jeffersons, Kuoni, Made to Measure, Momentum, PGL, Powder Byrne, Seasons in Style, Ski Freshtracks, Solo's, Swiss Travel Service, Switzerland Travel Centre (Plus Travel), Thomson, White Roc Weekends

Grossarl, Austria
See *The Gasteinertal*, page 38
Small village with ski area linked to Dorfgastein.

Gstaad, Switzerland
Page 311
Tour operators Corporate Ski Company, Headwater, Made to Measure, Momentum, Seasons in Style, Ski Astons, Ski Expectations, White Roc Weekends

Guthega, Australia
See *Perisher-Blue*, page 448

Hafjell, Norway
See *Lillehammer*, page 439
Tour operator Crystal

Happo'one and Hakuba Valley, Japan
t +44 (0)20 7734 6870, *www.snowjapan.com*
Altitude 760m (2,493ft)–1830m (6,007ft)
Lifts 33

The pretty village of Happo'one is the biggest ski area in the Nagano Prefecture's resort-studded Hakuba Valley, and arguably the best ski resort in the country. The valley lies 200km from Tokyo, to which it is linked by the *shinkansen* (bullet train). The resort has some striking scenery, challenging terrain and longer-than-average runs. Accommodation includes **Hotel Omoshiro Hasshinchi, t** +81 0261 72 6663, at the resort base. The **Hotel Lady Diana & St George's, t** +81 0261 75 3525, is also rated.

Hasliberg, Switzerland
See *Meiringen-Hasliberg*, page 441

Haus-im-Ennstal, Austria
t +43 (0)3686 22340, *www.en.skiamade.com*
Altitude 750m (2,460ft)–2015m (6,611ft)
Lifts 64 in area
Tour operator Oak Hall
Haus is a peaceful little farming village linked into the Schladming ski area. **Hotel Gasthof Herrschaftstaverne, t** +43 (0)3686 2392, *www.herrschaftstaverne.at*, has a spa, traditional **Dorfhotel Kirchenwirt, t** +43 (0)3686 2228, *www.kirchenwirt.net*, is in the village centre. **Gasthof Reiter, t** +43 (0)3686 2225, *www.gasthofreiter.at*, is a delightful old chalet, and the **Panoramahotel Gürtl, t** +43 (0)3686 2383, *www.hotel-guertl.at*, is family-run.

Heavenly, California/Nevada, USA
Page 370
Tour operators American Ski Classics, AWWT, Directski, Equity/Rocket Ski, Erna Low, Neilson, Ski Activity, Ski All America, Ski the American Dream, SkiBound, Ski Freshtracks, Ski Independence, Ski Safari, Skiworld, Thomson, Trailfinders, United Vacations

Hemsedal, Norway
Page 289
Tour operators Alpine Tracks, Crystal, Neilson/Neilson School Groups, Thomson

Hintermoos and Hinterthal, Austria
See *Maria Alm*, page 440

Hintertux, Austria
See *Tux im Zillertal*, page 463

Hochsölden, Austria

See *Sölden*, page 82

Hopfgarten, Austria

t +43 (0)5335 2322, *www.hopfgarten.com*
Altitude 622m (2,040ft)–1829m (6,001ft)
Lifts 93 in SkiWelt
Tour operators Contiki, First Choice, PGL
The traditional village of Hopfgarten in the SkiWelt circuit is dominated by the twin yellow towers of its impressive church, yet despite its friendly atmosphere few British are attracted to the resort. The village is popular with Australians and New Zealanders. Accommodation includes **Aparthotel Hopfgarten**, **t** +43 (0)5335 3920, *www.hotel-hopfgarten.at*, and **Sporthotel Fuchs**, **t** +43 (0)5335 2420, *www.sporthotel-fuchs.at*.

Les Houches, France

Page 178
Tour operators Barelli Ski, Erna Low, French Life, Interhome, Lagrange, Peak Retreats, Ski Expectations, Ski Weekend, Snow Safari

Huez, France

t +33 (0)4 76 11 44 44, *www.alpedhuez.com*
Altitude 1120m (3,674ft)–3330m (10,922ft)
Lifts 85 in Alpe d'Huez area
Old village below Alpe d'Huez resort and connected by cable-car. **Hôtel L'Ancolie**, **t** +33 (0)4 76 11 13 13, is a renovated farmhouse with a recommended restaurant.

Humber Valley, Newfoundland, Canada

Page 105
Tour operators Barwell Leisure, Ski Safari

Hungerburg, Austria

See *Innsbruck*, opposite

Igls, Austria

t +43 (0)5125 9850, *www.innsbrucktourist.info*
Altitude 900m (2,953ft)–2247m (7,372ft)
Lifts 6
Tour operators Inghams, Made to Measure
The small village of Igls is set 5km from Innsbruck towards the Europabrücke and the Italian border. The skiing is limited, with the Olympic downhill run (of Franz Klammer fame) presenting the only real challenge. The village is made up of traditional hotels and coffee houses, some bracing winter walks, and the Olympic bob-run which is open to the public. **Sporthotel Igls**, **t** +43 (0)5123 77241, *www.sporthotel-igls.com*, has good food, the five-star **Schlosshotel**, **t** +43 (0)5123 77217, *www.schlosshotel-igls.com*, is highly recommended, and **Hotel Batzenhäusl**, **t** +43 (0)5123 8618, *www.batzenhaeusl.at*, is very comfortable.

Inneralpbach, Austria

See *Alpbach*, page 37

Innsbruck, Austria

t +43 (0)5125 9850, *www.innsbruck.info*
Altitude 580m (1,903ft)–2334m (6,250ft)
Lifts 60 in six ski areas
Tour operators Corporate Ski Company, Directski, Ramblers
Innsbruck is a minor ski resort in its own right, but its real significance is as a base for visiting the well-known resorts of the Tyrol and the Arlberg by bus or car. Hungerberg is the home ski area just outside the city, set on the steep south-facing slopes of the Hafelekar. The city's best hotel is the five-star **Europa-Tyrol**, **t** +43 (0)5125 9310, *www.europatyrol.com*. Four-stars include **Hotel-Restaurant Goldener Adler**, **t** +43 (0)5125 71111, **Hotel Penz**, **t** +43 (0)5125 75657, *www.the-penz.com*, and **Romantikhotel Schwarzer Adler**, **t** +43 (0)5125 87109. **Hotel Weisses Kreuz**, **t** +43 (0)5125 94790, *www.weisseskreuz.at*, is a 500-year-old hotel where Mozart stayed as a child.

Interlaken, Switzerland

t +41 (0)33 826 5300, *www.interlakentourism.ch*
Altitude 796m (2,612ft)–2971m (9,748ft)
Lifts 41 in Jungfrau Top Ski Region
Tour operators Kuoni, Ski Astons
Sophisticated and attractive Interlaken is positioned between two lakes at the foot of the dramatic Eiger, Mönch and Jungfrau mountains. The town provides a good base for mixed groups including non-skiers who would rather stay in a bustling town than in a ski resort. From the centre, it is a short train ride to Grindelwald, or to Lauterbrunnen where you can catch the cable-car to Mürren, or continue on the train to Wengen. The best place to stay is outwardly traditional **Grand**

Hotel Victoria-Jungfrau, **t** +33 (0)828 2828, *www.victoria-jungfrau.ch*, which has a state-of-the-art spa and strikingly minimalist rooms in a special spa wing.

Ischgl, Austria

Page 42

Tour operators Alpine Answers Select, Alpine Tracks, Crystal, First Choice, Frozenplanet, Inghams, Made to Measure, Momentum, Original Travel, Ski Solutions, Ski Wild

Isella, Italy

See *Macugnaga*, page 440

Isola 2000, France

t +33 (0)4 93 23 15 15, *www.isola2000.com*
Altitude 1800m (5,904ft)–2610m (8,561ft)
Lifts 22
Tour operators Club Pavilion/Concept, Crystal, Erna Low, French Life, Lagrange, Leisure Direction, PGL, Ski Arrangements

The purpose-built resort of Isola 2000 offers 120km of piste and was built by a British property company in the 1960s. Isola is the most southerly ski area in France but it is a particularly good place to find late-season snow. Created with families in mind, Isola has a decent collection of shops, bars, no-frills apartments and hotels, and a large, sunny nursery area. British skiers make up a large portion of the winter business, with many owning apartments in the resort. The ski area is limited, but varied enough for beginners, families with young children, and undemanding intermediates. A new gondola opened last season, greatly improving mountain access. The original building, the unattractive and soulless Front de Neige Centre, is right on the slopes. More aesthetically pleasing wood-clad additions behind it improve the resort's appeal. **La Marmotte**, **t** +33 (0)4 93 23 98 65, is warmly recommended for lunch. **Hôtel Le Chastillon**, **t** +33 (0)4 93 23 26 00 ('very dated, but clean and comfortable'), and **Hôtel Diva**, **t** + 33 (0)4 93 23 17 71, are the four-stars, while three-star **Hôtel de France**, **t** +33 (0)4 93 02 17 04 and **Hôtel Pas du Loup**, **t** +33 (0)4 93 23 27 00 are also recommended.

Itter, Austria

t +43 (0)5335 2670, *www.skiwelt.at*
Altitude 703m (2,306ft)–1829m (6,001ft)
Lifts 93 in SkiWelt

Itter is a small village with just 850 tourist beds, but a fast gondola nearby with no queues for the uphill journey, plus the longest run in the SkiWelt (8.5km), make it a quiet and good-value alternative to Söll. **Sporthotel Tirolerhof**, **t** +43 (0)5335 2690, *www.sporthotel-tirolerhof.com*, has a bowling alley.

Jackson Hole, Wyoming, USA

Page 374

Tour operators Alpine Answers Select, American Ski Classics, AWWT, Carrier, Crystal, Inghams, Lotus Supertravel, Momentum, Neilson, Seasons in Style, Ski Activity, Ski All America, Ski the American Dream, Ski Freshtracks, Ski Independence, Ski Safari, Skiworld, Trailfinders, United Vacations, Virgin

Jasper, Alberta, Canada

t +1 780 852 3816, *www.skimarmot.com*
Altitude 5,534ft (1686m)–8,534ft (2601m)
Lifts 8
Tour operators Crystal, Frontier Ski, Inghams, Made to Measure, Neilson/Neilson School Groups, Ski Activity, Ski All America, Ski the American Dream, SkiBound, Ski Independence, Ski Safari, Virgin

Arguably the most beautiful Canadian resort – and the most northerly – is set among the forests, glaciers, frozen lakes and waterfalls of Jasper National Park. The small but varied ski area is located at Marmot Basin, 20 minutes' drive out of town. The terrain is made up of open bowls, with steep chutes and glades cut through the trees. Eagle Ridge, Sugar Bowl and Birthday Bowl offer the most challenging skiing. **Château Jasper**, **t** +1 780 852 5644, *www.decorehotels.com/chateau*, is a comfortable place to stay.

June Mountain, California, USA

See *Mammoth*, page 384

Kandersteg, Switzerland

t +41 (0)33 675 8080, *www.kandersteg.ch*
Altitude 1200m (3,937ft)–1920m (6,299ft)
Lifts 7
Tour operators Headwater, HF Holidays, Inghams, Inntravel, Kuoni, Swiss Travel Service, Waymark

The charming village in the Bernese Oberland is popular with cross-country skiers and boasts 75km of loipe. But it also has some commendable alpine skiing for beginners. Hotels include the five-star **Royal Park**, **t** +41 (0)33 675 8888, *www.royalkandersteg.ch*, the four-stars **Waldhotel Doldenhorn**, **t** +41 (0)33 675 8181, *www.doldenhorn-ruedihus.ch*, with a wellness centre and sister hotel **Landgasthof Ruedihus**, **t** + 41 (0)33 675 8181, both full of atmosphere. Three-star **Victoria Ritter**, **t** +41 (0)33 675 8000, *www.hotel-victoria.ch*, is also recommended.

Kaprun, Austria

See *Zell am See and Kaprun*, page 90

Tour operators Airtours, Crystal, Directski, Esprit, First Choice, Interhome, Neilson/ Neilson School Groups, PGL, Ski Astons, Ski Wild, Thomson

Kelchsau, Austria

See *Söll and the SkiWelt*, page 83

Ketchum, Idaho, USA

See *Sun Valley*, page 400

Keystone, Colorado, USA

Page 378

Tour operators American Ski Classics, AWWT, Crystal, Erna Low, Frozenplanet, Ski Activity, Ski All America, Ski the American Dream, Ski Independence, Ski Safari, Thomson, United Vacations

Kicking Horse, BC, Canada

Page 109

Tour operators Alpine Answers Select, AWWT, Crystal, Frontier Ski, Made to Measure, Ski All America, Ski the American Dream, Ski Independence, Ski Safari

Killington, Vermont, USA

Page 381

Tour operators American Ski Classics, Crystal, Directski, Equity/Rocket Ski, Inghams, Neilson School Groups, Ski Activity, Ski All America, Ski the American Dream, Ski Arrangements, SkiBound, Ski Independence, Ski Safari, Solo's, Thomson, Trailfinders, United Vacations, Virgin

Kimberley, BC, Canada

t +1 250 427 4881, *www.skikimberley.com*
Altitude 4,035ft (1230m)–6,500ft (1981m)
Lifts 9
Tour operators Frontier Ski, Frozenplanet, Inghams, Ski Activity, Ski the American Dream, Ski Independence, Ski Safari

The log-cabin-style ski village is a five-minute drive from the Tyrolean-style town of Kimberley at the foot of the Purcell Mountains and ideal for a two-resort holiday combined with Fernie. The front face offers gentle slopes, while the backside area provides more challenge. There is night-skiing two nights a week on the longest floodlit trail in the country. In the rather spread-out ski village the choice of accommodation includes ski-in, ski-out **Polaris**, **t** +1 877 286 8828, and **Trickle Creek Residence Inn by Marriott**, **t** +1 877 282 1200.

Kirchberg, Austria

t +43 (0)5357 2309, *www.kirchberg.at*
Altitude 850m (2,788ft)–2000m (6,562ft)
Lifts 57
Tour operators Airtours, Directski, First Choice, Interhome, Neilson

Kirchberg shares the Hahnenkamm and the ski safari to Pass Thurn with nearby Kitzbühel and is now linked by a new eight-person cable-car to the 1956m Gampen above Westendorf in the SkiWelt. In theory this creates a single mammoth circuit of 150 lifts and over 400km of skiing, but you still have to take a bus from Westendorf to Brixen or Hopfgarten. A new wide piste has been created back down on the Kirchberg side. Kirchberg lacks the medieval charm of Kitzbühel but has considerable character. It has its own nursery area on the Gaisberg. **Tiroler Adler**, **t** +43 (0)5357 2327, *www.tiroler-adler.com*, is not particularly convenient but is one of the best hotels in town. **Hotel Alexander**, **t** +43 (0)5357 2222, *www.alexander.at*, and **Hotel Metzgerwirt**, **t** +43 (0)5357 2128, *www.metzgerwirt.at*, are recommended. **Restaurant Rosengarten** in **Hotel Taxacherhof**, **t** +43 (0)5357 2527, *www.taxacherhof.at*, is run by one of Austria's celebrated young chefs.

Kitzbühel, Austria

Page 46

Tour operators Airtours, Corporate Ski Company, Crystal, Directski, Elegant Resorts, First Choice, Inghams, Interhome, Made to Measure, Momentum, Neilson/Neilson School Groups, Original Travel, Panorama, PGL, Seasons in Style, Ski Activity, SkiBound, Ski Freshtracks, Ski Solutions, Ski Wild, Snowscape, Thomson, Tyrolean Adventures

Kleinarl, Austria

See *Wagrain and the Salzburger Sportwelt*, page 86

Klosters, Switzerland

Page 312

Tour operators Descent International, Flexiski, Inghams, Kuoni, Made to Measure, Mountain Leap, Oxford Ski Company, PGL, Powder Byrne, Seasons in Style, Ski Expectations, Ski Freshtracks, Ski Solutions, Swiss Travel Service, White Roc Weekends

Kranjska Gora, Slovenia

t +386 (0)4588 1768, *www.kranjska-gora.si*
Altitude 810m (2,667ft)–1630m (5,348ft)
Lifts 20
Tour operators Balkan Holidays, Crystal, Directski, Erna Low, First Choice, Inghams, Just Slovenia, Solo's, Thomson

This is Slovenia's best-known resort – but not necessarily its best. The village, set in a pretty flat-bottomed valley between craggy wooded mountains, has considerable charm and a level of sophistication that puts it on a par with any similar-sized Austrian or Italian resort. The 30km of skiing served by five chair-lifts and 15 drag-lifts lacks the variety and challenge of some of the other less famous resorts. However, Kranjska is an ideal base for beginners and early intermediates. The ski school, the Alpine Ski Club, has an excellent reputation, and the 5km toboggan run is not to be missed. Stay at the four-star **Hotel Kompas**, *www.hoteli-kompas.si*, or at the four-star **Hotel Lek**. The recommended alternatives are **Hotel Larix**, **Hotel Prisank**, **HIT Casino** and **Hotel Spik**. The **Razor apartments** are situated 200m from the lifts. Accommodation can be booked centrally **t** +386 (0)4588 1768, or through a tour operator.

Kronplatz, Italy

Page 263

Krvavec, Slovenia

t +386 (0)425 25 930, *www.rtc-krvavec.si*
Altitude 1450m (4,757ft)–1971m (6,466ft)
Lifts 12
Tour operator Just Slovenia

Ski area within a few minutes' drive of Ljubljana airport. The network of runs served by chair-lifts from the top of the modern access-gondola happily resembles a modest North American resort. In mid-winter you can even ski the whole way to the valley floor. The ski area has no village, but you can stay in the **A&S Hotel Krvavec**, **t** +386 (0)420 19 152, *www.hotel-as.com*. Some 90 per cent of the trails are covered by snow-cannon.

Kühtai, Austria

t +43 (0)5239 5222, *www.kuehtai.co.at*
Altitude 2020m (6,627ft)–2520m (8,268ft)
Lifts 12
Tour operators Crystal, Inghams

A pretty little Tyrolean village offering 40km of piste and a lack of queues. **Jagdschloss Kühtai**, **t** +43 (0)5239 5201, five minutes from the village centre, was once a hunting lodge and today is a hotel brimming with character. Four-star **Hotel Astoria**, **t** +43 (0)5239 5215, *www.hotelastoria.at*, is warmly praised.

Kvitfjell, Norway

See *Lillehammer*, page 439

Ladis, Austria

t +43 (0)5476 62390, *www.serfaus-fiss-ladis.at*
Altitude 1427m (4,682ft)–2684m (8,806ft)
Lifts 53 in area

Small village sharing a ski area with Fiss and much larger Serfaus.

Lake Louise, Alberta, Canada

See *Banff-Lake Louise*, page 95

Tour operators AWWT, Ski Safari

Lake Tahoe, California, USA

See *Heavenly*, page 370, and *Squaw Valley*, page 393

Lana, Italy

See *Monte San Vigilio*, page 442

Lauterbrunnen, Switzerland

t +41 (0)37 856 8568, *www.wengen-muerren.ch*
Altitude 796m (2,612ft)–2971m (9,748ft)
Lifts 41 in Jungfrau Top Ski Region
Tour operators Oak Hall, Re-lax Holidays, Ski Miquel

Lauterbrunnen is the railway junction town near Interlaken that provides a cheap alternative to the better-known resorts of Mürren and Wengen. Hotels offer a convenient, if rather characterless, base from which to explore the skiing in this corner of the Bernese Oberland. Mürren, reached by a steep rack-and-pinion railway, is the easier to get to. Try three-star **Hotel Schützen, t** +41 (0)33 855 2032, *www.hotelschuetzen.com*, and **Hotel Silberhorn, t** +41 (0)33 856 2210, *www.silberhorn.com*.

Lech, Austria

Page 50

Tour operators Alpine Answers Select, Alpine Tracks, Crystal, CV Ski, Elegant Resorts, Erna Low, Flexiski, Inghams, Kaluma, Made to Measure, Momentum, Original Travel, Seasons in Style, Ski Activity, Ski Expectations, Ski Solutions, Total Ski, White Roc Weekends

The Lecht, Scotland

t +44 (0)1975 651 440, *www.lecht.co.uk*
Altitude 643m (2,109ft)–793m (2,600ft)
Lifts 14

Scotland's smallest ski area has a network of short lifts on both sides of the A939 Cock Bridge–Tomintoul road. It lies 56 miles west of Aberdeen and about 45 miles from Glenshee and Cairngorm. The area is best suited to beginners and intermediates living within reasonable driving distance. The longest run is 900m. The nearest accommodation is the **Allargue Arms, t** +44 (0)1975 651 410, *www.allarguearmshotel.co.uk*, three miles away at Corgarff.

Las Leñas, Argentina

t +54 262 747 1100 (in Buenos Aires 1 313 1300), *www.laslenas.com*
Altitude 2240m (7,349ft)–3431m (11,257ft)
Lifts 11
Tour operators AWWT, Exsus, Scott Dunn Latin America

Las Leñas can be the most challenging resort in South America. But it depends entirely upon the weather and the operation or closure of a single lift. If there is sufficient stable snow and little enough wind to open the avalanche-prone Marte chair then strong skiers and riders are in for the finest feast in the southern hemisphere. The lift provides the only mechanized access to some extraordinary off-piste with plunging powder bowls and vertiginous couloirs. The area is exposed to avalanche danger and dotted with cliffs. It's the kind of place where you never follow lone tracks to see where they go and a local guide is essential. On the other hand, if the Marte chair is closed, Las Leñas reverts to being a fun but bland Andean resort – a treeless wilderness that is not necessarily worth the 90-minute flight from Buenos Aires to Malargue and the one-hour bus transfer. You can also fly to San Rafael, a three-hour drive from the resort. All accommodation is in hotels and lodges within a short walk or ski of the lift. The five-star **Hotel Piscis, t** +54 262 747 1100, is the most luxurious, featuring what claims to be the highest ski-resort casino in the world. The **Aries, t** +54 262 742 7120, has its own cinema.

Lenk, Switzerland

See *Adelboden and Lenk*, page 417

Lenzerheide and Valbella, Switzerland

t +41 (0)81 385 1120, *www.lenzerheide.ch*
Altitude 1500m (4,920ft)–2865m (9,397ft)
Lifts 34 in area
Tour operator Made to Measure

These linked resorts at either end of the beautiful Heidsee have considerable charm and lots of mainly intermediate skiing. They used to attract a high number of British families but have declined in popularity for no discernible reason. The lift system has been steadily updated. None of the terrain is particularly difficult, and it makes a pleasant holiday centre where most of the clientele are Swiss. It is best suited to families and intermediate skiers and riders. Recommended hotels include the four-star **Sunstar, t** +41 (0)81 384 0121, and **Romantik Guarda Val, t** +41 (0)81 385 8585, *www.guardaval.ch*. Valbella has less charm. Both the four-star **Posthotel Valbella, t** +41 (0)81 384 1212, *www.posthotelvalbella.ch*, and the **Valbella Inn**, **t** +41 (0)81 384 3636, *www.valbellainn.ch*, are recommended.

Leogang, Austria

t +43 (0)6583 8234, *www.leogang-saalfelden.at*
Altitude 800m (2,625ft)–2096m (6,877ft)
Lifts 55 in area
Tour operators Inntravel, Tyrolean Adventures
The village is a collection of 10 farming hamlets with a modern gondola taking you to Berghaus Asitz at 1758m, where a quad-chair and six-seater chair link into the Saalbach-Hinterglemm area. Four-star **Hotel Salzburgerhof**, **t** +43 (0)6583 7310, *www.salzburgerhof.co.at*, is convenient.

Levi, Finland

Page 290
Tour operators Inghams

Leysin, Switzerland

t +41 (0)24 494 2244, *www.leysin.ch*
Altitude 1330m (4,363ft)– 2200m (7,218ft)
Lifts 15
Tour operators Interhome, Sloping Off, Switzerland Travel Centre (Plus Travel)
The village above the town of Aigle has historically been associated with finishing schools, health clinics and cut-price student holidays. Today it is also one of the top resorts in Switzerland for snowboarders, with the advantage of the 50km area having virtually no drag-lifts. 'Uncrowded – once or twice in January we were the only people on the piste,' said one reporter. **Garderie Arc en Ciel**, **t** +41 (0)24 494 1200, cares for children from newborn to seven years. Best-situated accommodation is the four-star **Hotel Classic-Terrasse**, **t** +41 (0)24 493 0606, with spacious rooms, and the simpler **Bel-Air**, **t** +41 (0)24 494 1339. **The Hiking Sheep**, **t** +41 (0)24 494 3535, is a renovated Art Deco building run as a hostel with good dormitories.

Lillehammer, Norway

t +47 612 89800, *www.lillehammerturist.no*, *www.hafjell.com*
Altitude 200m (656ft)–1050m (3,444ft)
Lifts 11
Tour operators Crystal, Directski, Original Travel, Waymark
Lillehammer is cosy little town with a single main street of weatherboard houses that was a surprising (given that it has such limited skiing) but successful choice for the 1994 Winter Olympics. The closest skiing is 15 minutes away at Hafjell. Kvitfjell, 50km from Lillehammer, has only 18km of pistes but provides more demanding terrain. **Radisson SAS Lillehammer**, **t** +47 612 86000, *www.lillehammerhotel.no*, **Rica Victoria**, **t** +47 612 50049, and **First Hotel Breiseth**, **t** +47 612 47777, *www.breiseth.com*, are all recommended.

Livigno, Italy

Page 264
Tour operators Airtours, Directski, Equity/Rocket Ski, Inghams, Interhome, Neilson, Panorama, Ski Arrangements

Long-Zhu Erlongshan, China

t +86 451 791 3640
Altitude 266m (872ft)–1371m (4,500ft)
Lifts 4
This is the second most important resort in the Heilongjiang province after larger Yabuli. It is situated at Bin Xian, 56km from Harbin. The ski area is currently being developed by the Beijing Long-Zhu Leisure Group, which is pumping millions of dollars into mountain facilities.

Loveland, Colorado, USA

t +1 303 571 5580, *www.skiloveland.com*
Altitude 10,600ft (3231m)–13,010ft (3965m)
Lifts 11
This small, high ski resort competes annually with Killington to be the first US resort to open at the end of October or in early November. It is set on the Continental Divide 53 miles west of Denver and 12 miles east of Silverthorne. The resort is a local favourite due to its reliable snow-cover and low prices. The most convenient accommodation is **Silver Mine Lodge**, **t** +1 877 733 2656, in Silver Plume 10 miles from Loveland, at **Georgetown Mountain Inn**, **t** +1 303 569 3201, at Georgetown 12 miles away, or at **Peck House**, **t** +1 303 569 9870, in Empire 14 miles away.

Luosto, Finland

t +358 16 624 367, *www.luosto.fi*
Altitude 203m (665ft)–531m (1,750ft)
Lifts 4
Tour operator Canterbury Travel

Geographically in the centre of Lapland, Luosto is easily accessible from Rovaniemi airport. The resort has seven pistes that are best suited to families. Pyhä is 20km away and offers a further 10 pistes and four lifts. Luosto offers 74km of cross-country trails, 25km of which are floodlit. Other activities in the area include snowmobile or reindeer safaris through the forest, snowshoe hiking, and dinner in a kota (Sámi teepee). Don't miss a visit to Lampivaara amethyst mine, and watch the Northern Lights through the glass-roofed Pohjan Kruunu kota. Stay in the village of log cottages or in the new **Hotel Luostontunturi**, *www.luostotunturi.com*, that houses an 'amethyst spa'.

Macugnaga, Italy

t +39 0324 65119, *www.macugnaga-online.it*
Altitude 1327m (4,353ft)–2984m (9,790ft)
Lifts 12
Tour operators Neilson/Neilson School Groups
This resort is made up of five villages: Borca, Isella, Pecetto, Pestarena and Staffa. They are set at the foot of the Monte Rosa, close to the Swiss border and two hours' from Turin. The skiing is mainly of intermediate level. Due to the resort's proximity to the border, many of the buildings are Swiss in style. The dozen hotels include **Hotel Dufour, t** +39 0324 65529, in Staffa's main square, and **Hotel Zumstein, t** +39 0324 65490, *www.zumstein.macugnaga.it*. **Hotel Girasole, t** +39 0324 65052, has 'large rooms, good service and food – but no frills'.

Madesimo, Italy

t +39 0343 53015, *www.madesimo.com*
Altitude 1530m (5,018ft)–2984m (9,790ft)
Lifts 19
Tour operators Frozenplanet, Inghams
This attractive old village with narrow streets and a scattering of converted farmhouses has a considerable international following among families who want a quiet resort offering plenty of snow-sure intermediate skiing. It lies close to the Swiss border, a two-hour drive from Bergamo and it is possible to take a day trip from here to St Moritz. The skiing in the Valle Spluga ski area is mostly intermediate and takes place on the usually uncrowded slopes of the Pizzo Groppera, with long trails leading into neighbouring Valle di Lei. The area boasts mostly red runs and some challenging black, including the famous Canelone run. Hotels include four-star **Emet, t** +39 0343 53395, family-run **Andossi, t** +39 0343 57000, *www.hotelandossi.com*, **Hotel Harlequin, t** +39 0343 53005, which is well located, and **Hotel Cascata e Crystal, t** +39 0343 53108, with a swimming pool and mini-club.

Madonna di Campiglio, Italy

Page 265
Tour operators Crystal, Directski, Equity/Rocket Ski, First Choice, Inghams, Interhome, Ski Arrangements, Ski Expectations, Ski Freshtracks, Solo's

Mammoth, California, USA

Page 384
Tour operators American Ski Classics, AWWT, Crystal, Made to Measure, Ski Activity, Ski All America, Ski the American Dream, Ski Independence, Ski Safari, United Vacations, Virgin

Marble Mountain, Newfoundland, Canada

See *Humber Valley*, page 105

Maria Alm, Austria

t +43 (0)6584 7816, *www.mariaalm.at*
Altitude 800m (2,625ft)–2000m (6,562ft)
Lifts 39
Tour operators Club Europe, Ski Astons
This unspoilt village close to Zell am See is dominated by a church boasting the highest spire in Salzburgerland and has won awards as the region's most beautiful village. Lots of intermediate skiing linked to Saalfelden, Hinterthal, Hintermoos, Dienten, and Mühlbach. It is included in the giant Ski Amadé lift pass.

Mariborsko Pohorje, Slovenia

t +386 (0)260 36 554, *www.pohorje.org*
Altitude 325m (1,066ft)–1347m (4,419ft)
Lifts 20
Maribor is Slovenia's second largest city and the modest slopes above it are home each January to the Golden Fox Trophy, one of the most important events in the Women's World Cup calendar. The 80km of trails are backed up by snow-cannon, and low temperatures usually ensure top to bottom skiing. Stay at the base in the luxurious five-star

Hotel Habakuk, t +386 (0)230 08 100, *www.termemb.si*, or the more modest three-star **Hotel Tisa**, t +386 (0)260 36 100.

Marilleva, Italy

t +39 0463 901280, *www.valdisole.net*
Altitude 1300m (4,265)–2505m (8,219ft)
Lifts 47 in area
Tour operators Interhome, PGL
Purpose-built resort linked to Folgarida and to Madonna di Campiglio which is 9km away. A total of 120km of linked skiing, popular with budget skiers and school groups.

Marmot Basin, Alberta, Canada

See *Jasper*, page 435

La Massana, Andorra

See *Pal-Arinsal*, page 24
Tour operator First Choice

Le Massif, Québec, Canada

t +1 418 632 5876, *www.lemassif.com*
Altitude 118ft (36m)–2,644ft (806m)
Lifts 5
Tour operators Frontier Ski, Ski All America, Ski the American Dream, SkiBound, Ski Safari
Le Massif is under new ownership and the mountain is currently undergoing a Can$5 million makeover to turn it into a four-seasons resort. As a ski centre it has the unusual attribute of being upside down. You park your car at the top of the mountain and ski all the way down to take the first lift. The resort and mountain are perched on the bank of the mighty St Lawrence, a 45-minute drive from Québec City and have one of the most enchanting views of any ski destination in the world. So steep is the angle of descent down the principal run that you feel that at any moment you are liable to tumble off the mountain and on to the majestic ice floes of the river far below. The resort suits all standards of skier and is used as a training centre by the Canadian national team.

Mayrhofen, Austria

Page 55
Tour operators Crystal, Equity/Rocket Ski, First Choice, HF Holidays, Inghams, Neilson/Neilson School Groups, Ski Activity, Ski Astons, Ski Freshtracks, Ski Wild, Snowcoach, Thomson

Megève, France

Page 179
Tour operators Alpine Answers Select, Classic Ski, Corporate Ski Company, Erna Low, French Life, Frozenplanet, Interhome, Lagrange, Leisure Direction, Made to Measure, Momentum, Mountain Leap, Original Travel, Peak Retreats, Simon Butler Skiing, Ski Arrangements, Ski Barrett-Boyce, Ski Expectations, Ski Independence, Ski Solutions, Stanford Skiing, White Roc Weekends

Meiringen-Hasliberg, Switzerland

t +41 (0)33 972 5050, *www.alpenregion.ch*
Altitude 1061m (3,481ft)–2433m (7,982ft)
Lifts 22
Tour operators Kuoni, PGL
Meiringen-Hasliberg is the key component of four linked villages that form the Alpen Region in the Bernese Oberland, between Lucerne and Interlaken. Brienz, Axalp, Hasliberg and Meiringen offer modest intermediate ski areas set against an awesome alpine backdrop. Meiringen is known to all Sherlock Holmes fans for the Reichenbach Falls, where Sir Arthur Conan Doyle's character fell to his untimely death during his final struggle with arch villain Moriarty. The Alpen Region is great for riding, with natural obstacles that form Switzerland's first 'natural snowboard park'. In Meiringen, **Alpin Sherpa, t** +41 (0)33 972 5252, *www.alpinsherpa.ch*, **Parkhotel du Sauvage**, **t** +41 (0)33 971 4141, *www.sauvage.ch*, and three-star **Sporthotel Sherlock Holmes, t** +41 (0)33 972 9889, *www.sherlock.ch*, are recommended. In Hasliberg try **Hotel Bären**, **t** +41 (0)33 971 6022, *www.hotel-restaurant-baeren.ch*, and the **Bellevue, t** +41 (0)33 971 2341. In Brienz, recommended places to stay include **Hotel Brienz, t** +41 (0)33 951 3551, and **Grandhotel Giessbach, t** +41 (0)33 952 2525.

Les Menuires, France

Page 184
Tour operators Club Med, Directski, Erna Low, Family Ski Company, First Choice, French Freedom, French Life, Interhome, Neilson, PGL, Silver Ski, Ski Arrangements, SkiBound, Ski Independence, Ski Olympic, Ski Supreme, Skitopia, Wasteland

Meran 2000, Italy

t +39 0473 279457, *www.hafling.com*
Altitude 1650m (5,413ft)–2300m (7,546ft)
Lifts 7 in resort, 74 in Ortler Skiarena
The South Tyrol village, close to Bolzano, is 30 minutes' drive from the ski area with its 36km of piste served by two cableways and six other lifts. The resort is part of the Ortler Skiarena, with 13 unconnected resorts on one lift pass. Some 260km of piste is served by eight cableways and 66 chairs and drags. Hotels in Meran 2000 are headed by **La Pergola Residence, t** +39 0473 201435, *www.pergola-residence.it*, on a hillside outside the village. It opened in 2005 and was designed by Matteo Thun, whose signature style is clear lines and wide-open spaces, using wood, stone, glass and traditional wickerwork. Guests tell the kitchen what they want to eat using organic products straight from the farm. Other hotels include **Romantik Hotel Staffler, t** +39 0472 771136, **Grand Hotel Palace, t** +39 0473 271000, *www.palace.it*, **Hotel Sissi, t** +39 0473 231062, *www.hotel-adria.com*, and **Castel Fragsburg, t** +39 0473 244071, *www.fragsburg.com*.

Méribel, France

Page 187
Tour operators Airtours, Alpine Action, Alpine Answers Select, Alpine Elements, Alp Leisure, AWWT, Belvedere Chalets, Bonne Neige, Club Med, Cooltip, Corporate Ski Company, Crystal, Descent International, Directski, Elegant Resorts, Erna Low, First Choice, Flexiski, Four Winds Meriski, French Freedom, French Life, Inghams, Interhome, Kaluma, Lagrange, Lotus Supertravel, Made to Measure, Mark Warner, Momentum, Mountain Leap, Neilson, Oxford Ski Company, PGL, Purple Ski, Scott Dunn Ski, Seasons in Style, Silver Ski, Ski Activity, Ski Amis, Ski Basics, Ski Beat, Ski Blanc, Ski Collection, Ski Cuisine, Ski Expectations, Ski France, Ski Freshtracks, Ski Independence, Ski Olympic, Ski Solutions, Ski Weekend, Skiworld, Snowcoach, Snowline, Thomson, Total Ski, VIP, Wasteland, White Roc Weekends

Mieders, Austria

See *Neustift and the Stubaital*, page 58

The Milky Way, Italy

See *Clavière*, page 426; *Montgenèvre*, page 193; *Sauze d'Oulx*, page 274; *Sestriere*, page 280

Mittersill, Austria

See *Kitzbühel*, page 46

Moena, Italy

See *Canazei*, page 241

La Mongie, France

See *Barèges and La Mongie*, page 421
Tour operators Lagrange, Tangney Tours

Montafon, Austria

See *Gargellen*, page 431, *Gaschurn*, page 431, *St Gallenkirch*, page 453, *Schruns*, page 456, and *Tschagguns*, page 463
Tour operator Made to Measure
The Montafon Valley lies in the south of the Vorarlberg, in Austria's southwestern corner. Its 11 villages lie at altitudes between 600m (1,968ft) and 1430m (4,690ft) and they are surrounded by three mountain chains including peaks as high as the Piz Buin at 3312m (10,896ft).

Montalbert, France

See *La Plagne*, page 200
Tour operators French Life, Interhome, Lagrange

Montchavin, France

See *La Plagne*, page 200

Monte San Vigilio, Italy

t +39 0473 561770, *www.lana.net*
Altitude 1500m (4,921ft)–1800m (5,906ft)
Lifts 3
From the town of Lana, a cable-car with real leather seats – a 1970s replacement of the original cabin built in 1912 – takes you up to a lone building in the small ski area of Monte San Vigilio. The building is **Hotel Vigilius, t** +39 0473 556600, *www.vigilius.it*, which is a true mountain hideaway oozing understated elegance. The Asian-European-fusion spa has an infinity swimming pool. Skiing is on the gentle Vigiljoch with a choice of three lifts outside the door or a ride down the cable-car and on to the more extensive resorts of Val d'Ultimo (20mins' drive) or Val Senales (1¼hrs).

Montgenèvre, France

Page 193

Tour operators Airtours, Club Europe, Crystal, Equity/Rocket Ski, French Life, Lagrange, Leisure Direction, Neilson, SkiBound, Ski Etoile

Montriond, France

t +33 (0)4 50 79 12 81, *www.portesdusoleil.com*
Altitude 950m (3,116ft)–2350m (7,708ft)
Lifts 211 in Portes du Soleil
Montriond is a suburb of Morzine, with no real centre and a collection of simple, good-value hotels. A bus links the village to the gondola that accesses the Portes du Soleil ski area. The British Alpine Ski and Snowboarding School has a branch in the resort.

Mont-Sainte-Anne, Québec, Canada

t +1 418 827 4561, *www.mont-sainte-anne.com*
Altitude 575ft (175m)– 2,625ft (800m)
Lifts 15
Tour operators Frontier Ski, Ski All America, Ski the American Dream, SkiBound, Ski Safari
This is one the best ski areas in eastern Canada, situated only a half-hour drive from Québec City, with lots of intermediate slopes of a respectable gradient that are interspersed with much more challenging double-black-diamonds. As all destinations in Québec, the mercury can plummet unbelievably low in mid-winter and occasionally the resort considers it is just too dangerously cold to open the lifts. But Canadians wrap up well in technical clothing and take low temperatures in their stride. On weekdays, city dwellers pop out to catch a few runs after work. Some 15 trails are floodlit for night-skiing in what is the biggest illuminated vertical drop (2,000ft) in Canada. **Château Mont-Sainte-Anne**, **t** +1 418 827 5211 is at the base area, and the **Chalets Mont-Sainte-Anne**, **t** +1 418 827 5776 condominium complex is nearby.

Morgins, Switzerland

t +41 (0)24 477 2361, *www.morgins.ch*
Altitude 1350m (4,428ft)–2000m (7,710ft)
Lifts 211 in Portes du Soleil
Tour operators Ski Morgins, Ski Rosie
Morgins is a laid-back resort a short distance from Châtel on the Swiss–French side of the Portes du Soleil circuit. Most of the accommodation is in chalets and apartments. The two-stars are **Hôtel La Reine des Alpes**, **t** +41 (0)24 477 1143, and **Hôtel Beau-Site**, **t** +41 (0)24 477 1138.

Morillon, France

t +33 (0)4 50 90 15 76, *www.ot-morillon.fr*
Altitude 700m (2,296ft)–2480m (8,134ft)
Lifts 78 in Grand Massif
Tour operators Altitude Holidays, Erna Low, French Life, Lagrange, Peak Retreats
The old village of Morillon in the beautiful Giffre Valley has a 16th-century church and is linked by road or gondola to the purpose-built satellite of Morillon 1100 ('in a fantastic position'). Together they have some 10,000 visitor beds and make a popular second-home resort for the French. Morillon has seven of its own lifts and is linked into the Grand Massif ski area, of which Flaine is the best-known resort. Two-star **Hotel Le Morillon**, **t** +33 (0)4 50 90 10 32, *www.hotellemorillon.com*, has a recommended restaurant.

Morzine, France

Page 194

Tour operators Alpine Answers Select, Alpine Escapes, Alpine Tracks, Alpine Weekends, AWWT, Chalet Chocolat, The Chalet Company, Chalet Snowboard, Challenge Activ, Corporate Ski Company, Crystal, Esprit, First Choice, French Life, Frozenplanet, Inghams, Lagrange, Made to Measure, Momentum, Mountain Highs, Neilson School Groups, Peak retreats, PGL, Reach4theAlps, Ski Activity, Ski Arrangements, SkiBound, Ski Chamois, Ski Expectations, Ski Independence, Snowline, Thomson, Trail Alpine, White Roc Weekends

Moso, Italy

See *Alta Pusteria*, page 417

Mount Buller, Australia

t +61 35777 6077, *www.mtbuller.com.au*
Altitude 1390m (4,559ft)–1804m (5,917ft)
Lifts 22
Mount Buller is the major area for Melbourne-based skiers, located a three-and-a-half-hour (250km) drive northeast from the city. It has the largest lift capacity in the country. There are some long cruising runs, as well as some

genuine black-diamond runs. The scenery is impressive, with panoramic views across the gum forests. Boutique hotel **The Breathtaker**, **t** +61 35777 6377, *www.breathtaker.com.au*, is Australia's first mountain spa hotel. The **Schuss Lodge**, **t** +61 35777 6007, *www.schuss.asn.au/Buller.html*, is a small hotel with great views.

Mount Hotham, Australia

See *Falls Creek and Mount Hotham*, page 429

Mount Hutt, New Zealand

t +64 (0)3 302 8811, *www.mthutt.co.nz*
Altitude 1585m (5,200ft)–2075m (6,808ft)
Lifts 9

New Zealand's best-known resort is a 35-minute drive from Methven and 90 minutes from Christchurch airport. It has wonderful views across the Canterbury Plains and is normally the first resort to open in Australasia each winter. Although the weather is unpredictable, the skiing can be excellent and Mount Hutt has some of the most extensive snowmaking in this part of the world. The village of Methven has a good choice of accommodation.

Mount Ruapehu, New Zealand

t +64 (0)7 892 3738, *www.mtruapehu.com*
Altitude 1605m (5,266ft)–2322m (7,616ft) bottom
Lifts Turoa 9, Whakapapa 14

Mount Ruapehu is in the midst of North Island's Tongariro National Park and is the country's biggest and busiest ski area. Over the next two years the lift company plans to invest NZ$30million in upgrading the lift system and installing snowmaking equipment. The area comprises Whakapapa on the northwestern side of the volcano, and Turoa, on the southwestern slopes. Mount Ruapehu is renowned for its unpredictable weather – on a good day the skiing can be excellent but during a wet and windy white-out the visibility can be so poor that the resort is barely skiable. In bad weather the mountain can shut down for days on end. Happy Valley is New Zealand's largest beginner area, tucked away from the main slopes at Whakapapa. It normally opens in mid-June before the rest of the area. Turoa shares a pass and has Australasia's biggest vertical drop of 720m. Unfortunately there is no easy way to get from resort to resort on snow. Turoa is always the last resort in the country to close in early November, and offers fabulous spring skiing.

Whakapapa village, 6km from the mountain, boasts the smart and pricey **Grand Château**, **t** +64 (0)7 892 3809, *www.chateau.co.nz*, while the cheaper **Skotel**, **t** +64 (0)7 892 3719, *www.skotel.com*, is nearby. **Adventure Lodge & Motel**, **t** +64 (0)7 892 2991, *www.adventurenationalpark.co.nz*, with a spa, and **Howard's Lodge**, **t** +64 (0)7 892 2827, *www.howardslodge.co.nz*, are at National Park Village 22km away, but convenient for both ski fields.

Lively Ohakune provides a wide choice of accommodation including **Powderhorn Château**, **t** +64 (0)7 385 8888.

Mühlbach, Austria

See *Maria Alm*, page 440

Mürren, Switzerland

Page 317

Tour operators Inghams, Kuoni, Made to Measure, Momentum, Ski Freshtracks, Ski Solutions, Swiss Travel Service, Switzerland Travel Centre (Plus Travel)

Naeba, Japan

t +44 (0)20 7734 6870, *www.snowjapan.co.uk*
Altitude 900m (2,953ft)–1800m (5,905ft)
Lifts 28

This is one of the busiest ski areas in the Niigata Prefecture in the northern Japanese Alps, with 24-hour skiing. It is presided over by the **Naeba Prince**, **t** +81 25 789 2211, *www.princehotelsjapan.com* – the world's largest ski hotel containing a shopping mall, spa, amusement centre and over 40 restaurants. At weekends, when packed bullet trains and buses disgorge their human cargo, an absurd number of skiers floods the slopes – the record stands at 40,000 in one weekend – so at least at 4am there is some chance of finding a place to turn.

Nakiska, BC, Canada

t +403 256 8473, *www.skinakiska.com*

Altitude 5,003ft (1524m)–7,415ft (2215m)
Lifts 4
Tour operator Ski the American Dream
Small ski area just 83km from Calgary and a venue for the 1988 Olympics.

Nasserein, Austria

See *St Anton*, page 69
Tour operator Albus Travel

Nassfeld, Austria

t +43 (0)4285 8241, *www.skiarena.at*, *www.hermagor.com*
Altitude 600m (1,969ft)–1500m (4,921ft)
Lifts 40
Tour operators Crystal, PGL, Ski Wild, Thomson
The Carinthian resort offers mainly intermediate skiing and claims to have the longest cable-car in the Alps – the Millennium-Express is 6000m and takes 17 minutes to climb from the valley. However, the resort is increasing in popularity, which means crowds during peak season. The 11 four-stars include **Alpen Adria**, **t** +43 (0)4282 2666, *www.alpenadriahotel.at*, **Berghotel Presslauer**, **t** +43 (0)4285 209, *www.berghotel-presslauer.at*, and **Hotel Berghof**, **t** +43 (0)4285 8271, *www.berghof-nassfeld.at*. **Cube**, *www.cube-hotels.com*, is a new concept in hotels that combines function with cutting-edge design. The building doesn't have rooms: it has minimalist 'cube boxes'. Each box has its own 'showroom' used to dry clothing and store sports equipment. Cube doesn't have any stairs: it has 'gateways'. The whole building is constructed in glass and concrete, with the maximum use of light.

Nelson, BC, Canada

See *Whitewater*, page 468

Nendaz, Switzerland

t +41 (0)27 289 5589, *www.nendaz.ch*
Altitude 1365m (4,478ft)–3330m (10,925ft)
Lifts 89 in Four Valleys
Tour operators Frozenplanet, Interhome, OTP
Nendaz is a cheaper alternative bed-base to Verbier, although access into the Four Valleys skiing from here is complicated. A free ski-bus operates between Nendaz and Siviez and a new fast chair takes you up from Siviez towards Veysonnaz. **Neige Aventure Ski School**, **t** +41 (0)27 288 3131, received rave reviews ('best I've come across for young children in 35 years of skiing').

Neuberg, Austria

See *Wagrain and the Salzburger Sportwelt*, page 86

Neustift, Austria

Page 58
Tour operators Alpine Tours, Esprit, Made to Measure, Ski Astons

Nevis Range, Scotland

t +44 (0)1397 705 825 snow info/**t** +44 (0)1397 703 781 tourist info, *www.nevisrange.co.uk*, *www.ski.visitscotland.com*
Altitude 655m (2,148ft)–1221m (4,006ft)
Lifts 12
Tour operators Skisafe Travel
This is Scotland's premier ski resort, a compact but challenging ski area that is reached by a modern six-seater gondola. It is situated near Ben Nevis – Britain's highest peak – seven miles north of the ancient town of Fort William which provides accommodation. You can also find B&Bs in the pretty nearby hamlet of Torlundy. In good snow conditions Nevis (sometimes known as Aonach Mor) can offer just as good skiing as its alpine counterparts of similar size. The Braveheart chair accesses the back bowls of the Coire Dubh, which provide outstanding off-piste opportunities after a fresh snowfall. Last season it had generally good conditions, but like all Scottish resorts Nevis Range suffers from lack of regular cover in these troubled times of global warming. Nineteenth-century **Inverlochy Castle**, **t** +44 (0)1397 702 177, *www.inverlochycastlehotel.com*, is a convenient and luxurious place to stay.

Niederau, Austria

Page 59
Tour operators Airtours, Directski, First Choice, Inghams, Interhome, Neilson/Neilson School Groups, Panorama, PGL, Thomson

La Norma, France

t +33 (0)4 79 20 31 46, *www.la-norma.com*
Altitude 1350m (4,429ft)–2750m (9,022ft)
Lifts 18
Tour operators Erna Low, Interhome, Lagrange, Leisure Direction, Peak Retreats

The car-free family ski resort in the Maurienne Valley has wooden ski-in, ski-out buildings that blend into the scenery. **Hôtel-Restaurant, l'Auberge Pastorale, t** +33 (0)4 79 05 02 63, *www.auberge-pastorale.com*, is 5km away at Le Bourget, and offers traditional cuisine. Most of the other accommodation is in apartments, including **Les Chalets et Balcons de la Vanoise, t** +33 (0)4 79 20 22 18, and **Les Balcons d'Anaïs, t** +33 (0)4 79 20 22 31, *www.goelia.com*.

Northstar-at-Tahoe, California, USA

See *Heavenly*, page 370

t +1 530 562 1010, *www.northstarattahoe.com*
Altitude 6,330ft (1929m)–8,610ft (2624m)
Lifts 17
Tour operators Ski the American Dream, SkiBound, United Vacations

Notre-Dame-de-Bellecombe, France

t +33 (0)4 79 31 61 40, *www.notredamedebellecombe.com*
Altitude 1150m (3,773ft)–2070m (6,791ft)
Lifts 72 in area
Tour operators Peak Retreats, SkiBound
Pretty village in the rural Val d'Arly between Megève and Albertville with a distinctive bulb-shaped bell tower that dates back to the 11th century. Ski area is linked to Flumet and Praz-sur-Arly. It is also connected to Les Saisies and Crest-Voland as part of the Espace Diamant area.

Nozawa Onsen, Japan

t +44 (0)20 7734 6870, *www.snowjapan.co.uk*
Altitude 560m (1,837ft)–1650m (5,414ft)
Lifts 29
The neighbour to better-known Shiga Kogen is an attractive spa village with old-world charm. The busy, narrow streets are marred by traffic and imbued with the aroma of sulphur from the 13 public hot-spring bathhouses. The slopes are reached by a steep uphill walk, followed by two long escalators. The ski terrain is varied with some steep pitches. Accommodation is mainly in *ryokans* (inns) and small hotels, with **Kameya Ryokan, t** +82 269 852124 recommended.

Oberau, Austria

See *Niederau*, page 59

Tour operators Directski, Inghams, Neilson

Obergurgl-Hochgurgl, Austria

Page 61

Tour operators Airtours, Corporate Ski Company, Crystal, Esprit, First Choice, Inghams, Made to Measure, Momentum, Neilson, Panorama, Ski Activity, Ski Expectations, Ski Freshtracks, Ski Solutions, Thomson

Oberlech, Austria

See *Lech*, page 50

Oberndorf, Austria

See *St Johann in Tirol*, page 75

Tour operator Tyrolean Adventures

Obertauern, Austria

Page 64

Tour operators Alpine Answers Select, Club Europe, Directski, Inghams, SkiBound, Snowscape, Thomson

Oppdal, Norway

t +47 724 00470, *www.oppdal.com*
Altitude 545m (1,788ft)–1300m (4,265ft)
Lifts 16
One of Norway's most northerly and largest downhill resorts, 120km south of Trondheim, Oppdal has three ski areas: Stölen, Hovden and Vangslia, some good off-piste skiing, and 60km of cross-country trails. **Quality Hotel Oppdal, t** +47 724 00700, is in the village centre, **Nor Alpin Hotel, t** +47 724 21611, is recommended, and **Vangslia Fjelltun, t** +47 724 00801, contains piste-side log-built apartments.

Orcières-Merlette, France

t +33 (0)4 92 55 89 89, *www.orcieres.com*
Altitude 1850m (6,070ft)–2725m (8,944ft)
Lifts 30
Tour operators French Life, Interhome, Lagrange
Remote purpose-built resort and – from an architectural perspective – visually challenging resort with an almost exclusively French clientele in the Southern French Alps 45 minutes from Gap. Merlette is set just above Orcières.

Ordino, Andorra
See *Pal-Arinsal* page 24

Les Orres, France
t +33 (0)4 92 44 01 61, *www.lesorres.com*
Altitude 1550m (5,085ft)–2720m (8,924ft)
Lifts 23
Tour operators Equity/Rocket Ski, Lagrange, Sloping Off
Pleasant resort in the southern French Alps with 88km of skiing in heavily wooded terrain. The resort has five two-star hotels, including **La Portette, t** +33 (0)4 92 44 00 02, *www.laportette.com*, next to a drag-lift at the foot of the slopes.

Ortisei, Italy
Page 268
Tour operators Inghams, Interhome

Oz-en-Oisans, France
t +33 (0)4 76 80 78 01, *www.oz-en-oisans.com*
Altitude 1350m (4,429ft)–3330m (10,922ft)
Lifts 84 in area
Tour operators Erna Low, Lagrange, Ski Activity, Ski Independence, Skiworld, Wasteland
The purpose-built village of Oz Station is set above the old village of Oz-en-Oisans and provides a backdoor into the Alpe d'Huez lift system. The small **Hotel Le Hors Piste, t** +33 (0)4 76 79 40 25, *www.lehorspiste.com*, is the only hotel.

Pal, Andorra
Page 24
Tour operator Directski

Pamporovo, Bulgaria
t +359 (0)2987 9778, *www.bulgariatravel.org*
Altitude 1450m (4,757ft)–1925m (6,316ft)
Lifts 8
Tour operators Balkan Holidays, Crystal, Directski, First Choice, Inghams, Panorama, Solo's, Thomson
The small resort is located 85km from the attractive old town of Plovdiv. Most of the accommodation is in the handful of hotels straggling between the centre and the lift station. At the top of the mountain of Snezhanka is the Bulgarian telecom tower. Pamporovo boasts an average of 272 sunny days each year, although it does not always snow on the other days. Lift queues are rare, except for a 15-minute spell in the morning when all the ski school classes set off together. Ski school instructors are said to speak 'great English'. It is advisable to book hotels through one of the many tour operators to the resort. Reporters criticize hotel food. **Hotel Orlovets** was newly built in 2005, with a swimming pool and spa facilities. **Hotel Pamporovo** is a recommended four-star in the resort centre. **Hotel Finlandia** is of a good standard but lacking in atmosphere. **Hotel Murgavets** has a spa with fitness room, whirlpool, massage and beauty treatments. **Hotel Snezhanka** is said to be 'very cosy' with good food. **Hotel Perelik** is basic but clean – avoid rooms above the disco that closes at 3am. The hotel also houses Pamporovo's main shopping centre. The après-ski is lively.

Panorama, BC, Canada
Page 112
Tour operators Inghams, Oak Hall, Ski Activity, Ski All America, Ski the American Dream, Ski Independence

Paradiski, France
See *Les Arcs*, page 146; *Peisey-Vallandry*, page 448; *La Plagne*, page 200

Park City, Utah, USA
Page 387
Tour operators Alpine Answers Select, American Ski Classics, AWWT, Crystal, Equity/Rocket Ski, Momentum, Ski Activity, Ski All America, Ski the American Dream, Ski Independence, Ski Safari, Skiworld, Thomson, United Vacations

La Parva, Chile
See *Valle Nevado*, page 464
Tour operators Andes, Scott Dunn Latin America

Pas de la Casa, Andorra
Page 29
Tour operators Airtours, Crystal, Directski, First Choice, Inghams, Lagrange, Neilson, Panorama, Thomson

Passo Tonale, Italy

Page 270

Tour operators Airtours, Alpine Tours, Club Europe, Crystal, Directski, Equity/Rocket Ski, First Choice, Inghams, Neilson/Neilson School Groups, PGL, SkiBound, Sloping Off, Thomson

Pecetto, Italy

See *Macugnaga*, page 440

Peisey-Vallandry, France

t +33 (0)4 79 07 94 28, *www.peisey-vallandry.com*
Altitude 1350m (4,428ft)–3226m (10,581ft)
Lifts 144 in Paradiski
Tour operators Alpine Elements, Club Med, Erna Low, Esprit, French Life, Lagrange, Ski Hiver, Ski Independence, Ski Olympic, Snow Monkey Chalets

Vallandry and the other low-lying villages of Peisey and Nancroix in Paradiski used to be regarded as a tree-level bolt hole in bad weather. The only other winter visitors were a few French families who stayed here to avoid the commercial realities of the true *stations de ski*. All that changed with the opening of the £12 million Vanoise Express, a double-decker cable-car linking Les Arcs to La Plagne. These two major resorts now form the single ski area of Paradiski with 420km of piste. The delightful village of Vallandry, with its wide and well-groomed pistes, is situated just below the cable-car station. From this quiet little base, your biggest decision each day is whether to ski the slopes of Les Arcs or to take the link and explore La Plagne. What Vallandry offers that larger resorts cannot is a true village ambience, for the village still boasts more cows than people. The village has 80 chalets, some low-rise apartments, and a couple of hotels. **L'Orée des Cimes**, **t** +44 (0)870 750 6820, is an MGM development, and a four-star **Club Med** village opened last season.

Perisher-Blue, Australia

t +61 26459 4419, *www.perisherblue.com.au*
Altitude 1605m (5,264ft)–2034m (6,672ft)
Lifts 47

Perisher in New South Wales is part of the largest ski area in Australia and is linked to Blue Cow, Guthega and Smiggins. You get there by driving up the Kosciuszko Road, or better by train – the Skitube takes you through 10km of tunnels on a 20-minute journey to Perisher and Blue Cow from Bullocks Flat. Snowcats take you from the Perisher terminal to your lodge. The country's first eight-person chair was installed here. Blue Cow has a high proportion of advanced terrain, and more than half the trails are intermediate. Excelerator is the longest run in the Perisher-Blue area. Guthega has some short challenging runs and its half-pipe is rated the best in Australia. The whole area has recently been the subject of a Aus$750,000 makeover. **Perisher Valley Hotel**, **t** +61 26459 4455, is said to offer the best accommodation. **Perisher Manor**, **t** +61 26457 5291, *www.perishermanor.com.au*, is ski-in/ski-out, and smoking is banned at **The Lodge**, **t** +61 26457 5341, *www.thelodgesmiggins.com.au*, at Smiggins.

Pestarena, Italy

See *Macugnaga*, page 440

Pila, Italy

t +39 0165 521148, *www.pila.it*
Altitude 1750m (5,741ft)–2750m (9,022ft)
Lifts 12
Tour operators Crystal, Interski, Momentum, Thomson

Pila is a compact but surprisingly challenging ski area with pistes of mainly intermediate level, but with lots of accessible off-piste. The gentle blue run, Grimond, is enjoyable for beginners, while The Wall is a long run that provides a challenge for experts. An impressive gondola links with the regional capital of Aosta in 18 minutes, making it feasible to commute. The old Roman town, although blighted by commercial development, has a delightful pedestrianized centre. Accommodation in Pila includes ski-in/ski-out **Hotel Etoile de Neige**, **t** +39 0165 521541, *www.etoiledeneige.it* ('relaxing atmosphere and good food'), **Hotel Pila 2000**, **t** +39 0165 521148 ('modern and efficient, with friendly staff and fantastic food'), and **Hotel Printemps**, **t** +39 0165 521246, while in Aosta you can stay at **Hotel Europe**, **t** +39 0165 236363, in the centre.

Pitztal, Austria

t +43 (0)5414 86999/5413 8288 (Pitztaler Glacier), *www.tiscover.at/pitztal*
Altitude 2880m (9,446ft)–3440m (11,283ft)
Lifts 11
The Pitztal region in the Tyrol is made up of four villages, with St Leonhard the main accommodation base close to the Pitztaler Glacier and Rifflsee ski area. The skiing at Rifflsee is for all standards. The glacier skiing is accessed by funicular and the highest gondola in Austria. The area has a wide range of hotels, including the four-star ski-in/ski-out **Alpinhotel**, **t** +43 (0)5413 86361, at the glacier base station.

La Plagne, France

Page 200
Tour operators Airtours, Alpine Answers Select, Club Med, Crystal, Equity/Rocket Ski, Esprit, First Choice, French Life, French Freedom, Frozenplanet, Inghams, Interhome, Lagrange, Made to Measure, Mark Warner, Momentum, Neilson, On The Piste, Ski Activity, Ski Amis, Ski Arrangements, Ski Beat, SkiBound, Ski Expectations, Ski France, Ski Freshtracks, Ski Independence, Ski Olympic, Ski Supreme, Skiworld, Thomson

Plan-Peisey, France

See *Les Arcs*, page 146

Poiana Brasov, Romania

Page 139
Tour operators Airtours, Balkan Holidays, Frozenplanet, Inghams, Neilson/Neilson School Groups, Solo's

Pont d'Espagne, France

See *Cauterets*, page 424

Ponte di Legno, Italy

See *Passo Tonale*, page 270

Pontresina, Switzerland

t +41 (0)81 838 8300, *www.pontresina.com*
Altitude 1800m (5,904ft)–2978m (9,770ft)
Lifts 56 in St Moritz area
Tour operator Made to Measure
Pontresina is midway between the Diavolezza and Corviglia ski areas of St Moritz. **Grand Hotel Kronenhof**, **t** +41 (0)81 842 0111, *www.kronenhof.com*, is a five-star, **Saratz Hotel**, **t** +41 (0)81 839 4000, *www.saratz.ch*, is a four-star that mixes traditional with modern design. **Kochendorfer's Albris**, **t** +41 (0)81 838 8040, is a relatively inexpensive three-star. **Hotel Steinbock**, **t** +41 (0)81 842 6371, is comfortable.

Portes du Soleil, France/Switzerland

See *Avoriaz*, page 151; *Champéry*, page 425; *Châtel*, page 426; *Morgins*, page 443; *Morzine*, page 194

Portillo, Chile

t +56 2 263 0606, *www.skiportillo.com*
Altitude 2512m (8,241ft)–3348m (10,984ft)
Lifts 15
Tour operators Andes, AWWT, Crystal, Exsus Travel, Lotus Supertravel, Momentum, Scott Dunn Latin America, Ski Safari
Chile's oldest ski area is the best-known resort but not necessarily the best resort in South America. It affable American-born owner runs the hotel and mountain with impeccable efficiency. Portillo lies 160km north of Santiago on the frontier with Argentina. The brilliant yellow **Hotel Portillo** sits in a deep cleft in the Andes on the shore of the beautiful Laguna de Inca surrounded by towering peaks including 6960m Aconcagua, the highest mountain in the southern hemisphere. The sophisticated hotel attracts both the United States and Austrian national teams who spend part of each off-season training here. Their hi-tech presence is in sharp contrast to the bygone era that lingers in the lakeside dining room, harking back to winters when Harris tweed plus-fours rather than latex catsuits were worn at breakfast. The walls are covered in antique leather, and waiters wear bow ties and formal red jackets. The number of guests in the whole resort is limited to just 450. The food is outstanding, service is exemplary, but most of the rooms are rather small. Free daycare and après-ski activities are provided for children aged three to six years, with lessons available from three years. **Tio Bob's** is the only mountain restaurant with a daily selection of grilled meats and salads. The main dining room in the hotel specializes in Chilean seafood. The skiing is suited to all standards, with plenty of

intermediate terrain as well as some dramatically steeper slopes. The two infamous *va et vient* lifts – multiple drag-lifts without pylons designed by Poma to access steep avalanche-prone slopes – tow you up the mountain at a knee-juddering 22kph. 'The only drawback is that the slopes are limited in variety and size, and you can cover the whole lot in a day,' said a reporter.

Pradollano, Spain

See *Sierra Nevada*, page 457

Pragelato, Italy

t +39 0122 740011, *www.pragelatoresort.com*
Altitude 2035m (6,675ft)–2823m (9,262ft)
Lifts 88 in Milky Way
This old village 10km by road down the valley from Sestriere has been given a face-lift as the ski jumping venue and an accommodation base for the Olympics. A new cable-car is to connect it to Sestriere and accommodation is in the new **Pragelato Resort**, **t** +39 0122 740011, *www.pragelatoresort.com*, which has 205 chalet-style units with a spa. **Antica Osteria**, **t** + 39 0122 785300, a converted cowshed with a vaulted ceiling, is the best restaurant in the region.

Pralognan-la-Vanoise, France

t +33 (0)4 79 08 79 08, *www.pralognan.com*
Altitude 1400m (4,593ft)–2350m (7,710ft)
Lifts 12
Tour operators Erna Low, Lagrange, Ski Independence
Attractive family resort with good cross-country skiing and modest alpine skiing between Courchevel and La Plagne. **La Vanoise**, **t** +33 (0)4 79 08 70 34, *www.hoteldelavanoise.fr*, is the resort's only three-star hotel, situated in the village centre and a few steps from the nearest lift. The village also has three two-star hotels. Dog-sledding is a new sport offered in the resort.

Pra-Loup, France

t +33 (0)4 92 84 10 04, *www.praloup.com*
Altitude 1600m (5,249ft)–2500m (8,202ft)
Lifts 53 with La Foux d'Allos
Tour operators Equity/Rocket Ski, French Life, Lagrange, Leisure Direction
Pra-Loup shares a ski area with neighbouring La Foux d'Allos. The skiing takes place on two main mountains, accessed by cable-car from the top of the village of 1600. Pra-Loup has a wide choice of beginner and intermediate runs, including a variety of open-bowl skiing, good tree-level runs and extensive off-piste. Weekend queueing can, however, be a problem. The resort is divided into the two villages of 1500 and 1600, which are linked by chair and made up of a collection of 1960s hotels and apartments. Try **Hôtel Club Les Bergers**, **t** +33 (0)4 92 84 14 54, *www.hotel-soleil-pra-loup.cote.azur.fr*, or **Hôtel Le Prieuré**, **t** +33 (0)4 92 84 11 43.

Puy-St-Vincent, France

t +33 (0)4 92 23 35 80, *www.puystvincent.com*
Altitude 1400m (4,593ft)–2750m (9,022ft)
Lifts 16
Tour operators Erna Low, Interhome, Lagrange, Snowbizz Vacances
Puy-St-Vincent (PSV) is an established resort that was extremely popular with British families in the 1970s. It is located 20km from Briançon on the edge of the Ecrins National Park. Its microclimate usually ensures secure late-season snow-cover, along with 300 days of sunshine per year. As one reporter put it: 'Excellent for families, much quieter than other more famous resorts even at peak times.'
PSV 1400 is an unspoilt mountain village connected by a new six-pack to PSV 1600. Newer *résidences*, a few chalets and shops and restaurants have been built on the edge of the piste, and the higher village is the better bet if you want doorstep skiing. The 67km of piste in the small but challenging area has enough variety to suit all standards, although most runs are classified as blue or red. From PSV 1600, two chair-lifts give easy access to the main skiing, and queues are rare outside school holidays. The resort has a small terrain park that is floodlit at night, and a cross-country track. The best of the apartments here are in the **Mona Lisa** building. Three-star **Hôtel Saint Roche**, **t** +33 (0)4 92 23 32 79, is down at 1400.

Pyhä, Finland

See *Luosto*, page 439

Québec City, Canada

t +1 418 649 2608, *www.quebecregion.com*
Altitude Stoneham: 695ft (420m)–2,075ft (632m)/Mont-Sainte-Anne: 575ft (175m)–2,625ft (800m)
Lifts Stoneham 8, Mont-Sainte-Anne 15
Tour operators Carrier, Crystal, Neilson School Groups, Virgin, Waymark

Romantic, beautifully preserved – and reasonably priced – Québec acts as a bed-base from which to explore the nearby ski areas, each of which is worth a day or two's exploration. A regular shuttle bus operates between the city, Stoneham (20-minute drive) and Mont-Sainte-Anne (30 minutes away). Le Massif (30 minutes) offers dramatic piste views of the frozen St Lawrence River. The city was built in 1608 and its cobbled streets added in the 18th century. The city has a wide choice of restaurants, shops and art galleries, and is home to a thriving club scene. The **Fairmont Château Frontenac, t** +1 418 692 3861, *www.fairmont.com/frontenac*, is a prominent hotel at the heart of the city overlooking the St Lawrence River.

Queenstown (Coronet Peak and The Remarkables), New Zealand

Coronet Peak t +64 (0)3 442 4634
The Remarkables t +64 (0)3 442 4617, *www.queenstown-nz.co.nz*
Altitude 1200m (3,937ft)–1957m (6,421ft)
Lifts 10

Six resorts come under the marketing umbrella of the Southern Lakelands, based around Queenstown and Wanaka. Queenstown is a lively and picturesque lakeside town situated in the south-west of the South Island. It is flanked by two separate resorts. The traditional but modernized resort is Coronet Peak, with six lifts providing a variety of good all-round skiing. The nursery slope now claims the longest magic carpet lift (146m) in the world. The resort has recently installed a new six-seater chair. *The Remarkables* was constructed more recently. The resort is visually exciting, but has fewer options than Coronet Peak. From Queenstown, The Remarkables range seems impossibly steep, but the ski area is in gentle bowls. A new snowmaking system has been installed for the 2006–7 season in the Sugar Bowl area. The **Remarkables Lodge, t** +64 (0)3 442 2720, is highly rated and closest to the resort.

Radstadt, Austria

See *Wagrain and the Salzburger Sportwelt*, page 86

Ramsau, Austria

Tour operators HF Holidays, Inntravel

Small village near Schladming that is strong on cross-country skiing.

Rauris, Austria

t +43 (0)6544 20022, *www.rauris.net*
Altitude 950m (3,114ft)–2200m (7,253ft)
Lifts 10
Tour operator Crystal

Old gold mining village with beginner and family skiing in the Hohe Tauern mountains between the Gasteinertal and Zell am See.

Reberty, France

See *Les Menuires*, page 184

Red Resort, BC, Canada

Page 115
Tour operators AWWT, Frontier Ski, Nonstopski, Ski Independence, Ski Safari

Reith, Austria

See *Alpbach*, page 37

The Remarkables

See *Queenstown* (*Coronet Peak and The Remarkables*) opposite

Riksgränsen, Sweden

t +46 (0)980 400 800, *www.riksgransen.nu*
Altitude 500m (1,640ft)–909m (2,982ft)
Lifts 5
Tour operator Original Travel

The resort in Swedish Lapland is 300km into the Arctic Circle yet just 1½ hours from Stockholm. This far north the sun doesn't set during midsummer (mid-May to mid-June), so you can ski, snowboard or heli-ski even in the early hours of the morning. **Hotel Riksgränsen, t** +46 980 400 800, is the accommodation of choice with a spa and swimming pool.

Risoul, France

Page 205

Tour operators Crystal, First Choice, Interhome, Lagrange, Leisure Direction, Neilson School Groups, On The Piste, Ski Arrangements, SkiBound, Ski Independence, Wasteland

Rittnerhorn (Corno Renon), Italy

t +39 0471 352993, *www.ortlerskiarena.com*
Altitude 1530m (5,020ft) – 2070m (6,791ft)
Lifts 74 in Ortler Skiarena
To the north of Bolzano is a small village that is especially good for families, with 8km of piste, one gondola and three drag-lifts. The resort is part of the Ortler Skiarena, with 13 unconnected resorts covered by one lift pass. A total 260km of piste is served by eight cableways and 66 chair- and drag-lifts.

Rocca di Cambio, Italy

See *Campo Felice*, page 423

Rohrmoos, Austria

t +43 (0)3687 61147, *www.rohrmoos.at*
Altitude 870m (2,854ft)–1850m (6,070ft)
Lifts 46 in Schladming area
The spread-out satellite of Schladming has ski-in/ski-out accommodation and is unchallenging. Try **Hotel Austria**, **t** +43 (0)3687 61444, **Hotel Seiterhof**, **t** +43 (0)3687 61194, *www.seiterhof.com*, or **Hotel Waldfrieden**, **t** +43 (0)3687 61487, *www.waldfrieden.at*, all of which are good value. Smarter **Hotel Schwaigerhof**, **t** +43 (0)3687 61422, *www.schwaigerhof.at*, is on the edge of the piste and has a swimming pool. **Hotel Schütterhof**, **t** +43 (0)3687 61205, is recommended.

La Rosière, France

Page 207

Tour operators Crystal, Erna Low, Esprit, Interhome, Leisure Direction, Ski Amis, Ski Arrangements, Ski Beat, Ski Independence, Ski Olympic, Thomson

Ruapehu, New Zealand

See *Mount Ruapehu*, page 444

Saalbach-Hinterglemm, Austria

Page 65

Tour operators Airtours, Alpine Answers Select, Board and Lodge, Club Europe, Crystal, Directski, Equity/Rocket Ski, Erna Low, First Choice, Inghams, Interhome, Neilson, Panorama, PGL, Ski Activity, Ski Astons, SkiBound, Thomson

Saalfelden, Austria

See *Maria Alm*, page 440

Saas-Fee, Switzerland

Page 320

Tour operators Alpine Answers Select, Crystal, Erna Low, Esprit, Inghams, Interhome, Kuoni, Made to Measure, Momentum, Oak Hall, OTP, PGL, Ski Freshtracks, Ski Independence, Ski Solutions, Swiss Travel Service, Switzerland Travel Centre (Plus Travel), Thomson, Total Ski

St Anton, Austria

Page 69

Tour operators Airtours, Albus Travel, Alpine Answers Select, Corporate Ski Company, Crystal, Directski, Elegant Resorts, Erna Low, Esprit, First Choice, Flexiski, Frozenplanet, Kaluma, Inghams, Interhome, Lotus Supertravel, Made to Measure, Mark Warner, Momentum, Neilson, Original Travel, Scott Dunn, Seasons in Style, Simply Ski, Ski Activity, Ski Equipe, Ski Expectations, Ski Solutions, Ski St Anton, Ski Total, Ski Val, Ski Wild, Skiworld, Snowscape, Solo's, Thomson, White Roc Weekends

St Christoph, Austria

t +43 (0)5446 22690, *www.stantonamarlberg.com*
Altitude 1800m (5,906ft)–2811m (9,222ft)
Lifts 82 on Arlberg Ski Pass
Tour operators Elegant Resorts, Flexiski, Jeffersons, Kaluma, Made to Measure, Momentum, Powder Byrne, Scott Dunn Ski, Seasons in Style
St Christoph is a delightful village directly linked into St Anton ski area. It consists of a small collection of restaurants and hotels, of which the luxury **Arlberg-Hospiz**, **t** +43 (0)5446 2611, *www.hospiz.com*, is the most famous and comfortable. St Christoph has five other hotels as well as the **Bundes Ski Academy**, where future ski and snowboard instructors are trained. The resort is a peacful alternative to bustling St Anton.

St-Christophe-en-Oisans, France

Small village linked off-piste with La Grave.
See page 177

Sainte-Foy, France

Page 208
Tour operators Alpine Answers Select, Alpine Elements, Alpine Weekends, Erna Low, Frozenplanet, Leisure Direction, Peak Leisure, Première Neige, Ski Arrangements, Ski Independence

St-François-Longchamp, France

See *Valmorel*, page 228
Tour operators Erna Low, French Life, Interhome, Lagrange, Peak Retreats, Ski Independence

St Gallenkirch, Austria

t +43 (0)5557 66000, *www.stgallenkirch.at*
Altitude 1430m (4,692ft)–2300m (7,546ft)
Lifts 62 in area
Tour operator Made to Measure
Part of the extensive Montafon area with its 11 villages and a total 222km of piste and 62 lifts.

St-Gervais, France

Page 209
Tour operators Erna Low, French Life, Interhome, Lagrange, Leisure Direction, Peak Retreats, PGL, Snowcoach

St-Jean-d'Arves, France

See *Le Corbier*, page 427
Tour operators Crystal, First Choice, French Life, Peak Retreats, Ski France, Thomson

St-Jean-d'Aulps, France

Independent village in Portes du Soleil ski area.

St Johann im Pongau, Austria

See *Wagrain and the Salzburger Sportwelt*, page 86

St Johann in Tirol, Austria

Page 75
Tour operators Crystal, Directski, Ski Wild, Snowscape, Thomson

St-Lary, France

t +33 (0)5 62 39 50 81, *www.saintlary.com*
Altitude 830m (2,723ft)–2515m (8,251ft)
Lifts 32
Tour operators French Life, HF Holidays, Lagrange, Leisure Direction
This village, located 80km from Lourdes, is typically Pyrenean with stone-built houses and one narrow main street. The skiing is suitable for beginners to intermediates, and it takes four minutes to walk from the village centre to the cable-car to St-Lary Pla d'Adet, a small modern ski station with some accommodation. This is linked by road and by lift to an alternative base at St-Lary La Cabane. The fourth base area of St-Lary Espiaube is also reached by road, or on skis from Soum de Matte. The ski area is mainly treeless and lacks variety. It extends into the neighbouring Auron Valley and up the snow-sure glacier on Mont Pichaleye. **Hôtel Mercure Coralia**, **t** +33 (0)5 62 99 50 00, **Hôtel La Terrasse Fleurie**, **t** +33 (0)5 62 40 76 00, *www.la-terrasse-fleurie.com*, and **Les Arches**, **t** +33 (0)5 62 49 10 10, *www.hotel-les-arches.com*, are all recommended, while **Hôtel Christiania**, **t** +33 (0)5 62 98 40 62, *www.christiania-pyrenees.com*, is a more recent addition. At Espiaube, **Hôtel La Sapinière**, **t** +33 (0)5 62 98 44 04, provides reasonable accommodation.

St-Martin-de-Belleville, France

Page 211
Tour operators Les Chalets de St Martin, Erna Low, First Choice, Kaluma, Leisure Direction, Ski Independence, Skitopia, Thomson

St Michael, Austria

t +43 (0)6477 8913, *www.stmichael-lungau.at*
Altitude 1100m (3,609ft)–2411m (7,910ft)
Lifts 38
Tour operators Alpine Tours, Club Europe, Equity/Rocket Ski
Pretty, traditional village and intermediate ski area near Obertauern on the border of Salzburgerland and Carinthia.

St Moritz, Switzerland

Page 322
Tour operators Alpine Answers Select, Club Med, Corporate Ski Company, Descent International, Elegant Resorts, Flexiski, Inghams, Interhome, Jeffersons, Kuoni, Made to Measure, Momentum, Oak Hall, Original

Travel, Oxford Ski Company, Powder Byrne, Scott Dunn Ski, Seasons in Style, Ski Gower, Ski Solutions, Swiss Travel Service, Switzerland Travel Centre (Plus Travel)

Saint-Nicolas-de-Véroce, France

See *St-Gervais*, page 209

St-Sorlin-d'Arves, France

t +33 (0)4 79 59 71 77, *www.saintsorlindarves.com*, *www.sybelles.com*
Altitude 1550m (5,085ft)–2620m (8,595ft)
Lifts 75
Tour operators Crystal, First Choice, French Life, Lagrange, Leisure Direction, Peak Resorts, Peak Retreats, SkiBound, Ski France, Ski Independence, Thomson, Wasteland

Quaint mountain village of carefully preserved Savoyard farmhouses and long-established shops built around an early 17th-century Baroque church in the Maurienne Valley. The village is part of the 310km Les Sybelles ski area linked to St-Jean, Le Corbier and La Toussuire. It holds the coveted 'Les P'tits Montagnards' label for good children's facilities. The skiing is best suited to intermediates and has two terrain parks and 16km of cross-country trails. Hotels in the village include two-stars **La Balme, t** +33 (0)4 79 59 71 71, *www.hotel-balme.com*, and **Hôtel Beausoleil, t** +33 (0)4 79 59 71 42, *www.hotel-beausoleil.com*. The village has more than a dozen restaurants and the local ski area boasts three mountain eateries.

St Wolfgang, Austria

t +43 (0)6138 8003, *www.stwolfgang.at*
Altitude 550m (1,800ft)–1600m (4,763ft)
Lifts 8
Tour operators Crystal, Directski, First Choice, Inghams, Thomson

The 16th-century village ('so quiet, it's unreal – absolutely no nightlife') at the centre of Austria's lake district acts as a pleasant base for those wishing to ski the modest Postalm plateau, a magnificent 35-minute drive. Additional skiing is available at Gosau, an hour away. St Wolfgang's nursery slope is just outside the village. Four-star **Hotel Cortisen, t** +43 (0)6138 2376, *www.cortisen.at*, is warmly praised by readers.

Les Saisies, France

t +33 (0)4 79 38 90 30, *www.lessaisies.com*
Altitude 1650m (5,413ft)–1941m (6,368ft)
Lifts 29; 84 in Espace Diamant
Tour operators Classic Ski, Erna Low, French Life, Lagrange, Leisure Direction, Peak Retreats, Ski Independence

Les Saisies sits in a delightfully scenic position on the ridge dominating the Arly and Beaufortain valleys in a beautiful area of woodland and alpine pastures 30km from Albertville that is sometimes called the French Tyrol. It is primarily a cross-country resort with 140km of loipe, but it also has 64km of piste, of which more than half are on easy tree-lined slopes. 'A great resort for families,' said one reporter, but 'not many English-speaking instructors' complained another. Accommodation is headed by three-star **Hôtel Le Calgary, t** +33 (0)4 79 38 98 38, in the village centre, with a health club, swimming pool and gourmet restaurants. Les Saisies first attracted international fame when it was chosen as the venue for cross-country skiing for the 1992 Winter Olympics. But it also has extensive alpine pistes. Les Saisies is now in the new Espace Diamant, a ski area of 84 lifts covering 175km of pistes that connect the neighbouring resorts of Crest-Voland, Notre-Dame-de-Bellecombe, and Flumet. Les Saisies also provides a backdoor entrance to Les Contamines.

Sälen, Sweden

t +46 (0)28 018700, *www.skistar.com*
Altitude 366m (1,201ft)–620m (2,034ft)
Lifts 77

The town of Sälen, 53km from the better-known resort of Trysil, has a range of ski areas close by. These are Lindvallen, which is linked to smaller Högfjället, and two more linked resorts of Tandådalen and Hundfjället. Yet more small resorts include Kläppen and Stöten. Most of the pistes are of intermediate standard, although there are over 30 black runs in the area. The Trollskogen – or Enchanted Forest – at Hundfjället is a children's forest trail featuring 400 trolls in theatrical stage sets complete with sound effects. Lindvallen has the first ski-in/ski-out McDonald's. **Högfjälls Hotel, t** +46 (0)28 087000, *www.salen-hotell.se* is a comfortable piste-side hotel in the area, with facilities that include a spa and a sushi restaurant.

Salzburger Sportwelt, Austria

See *Wagrain*, page 86

Samnaun, Switzerland

t +41 (0)81 868 5858, *www.samnaun.ch*
Altitude 1840m (6,035ft)–2864m (9,394ft)
Lifts 44 in Ischgl-Samnaun area
Samnaun lives off its duty-free status and its linked ski area with Ischgl in Austria. The resort has a loyal Swiss following. Hotels include **Chasa Montana, t** +41 (0)81 861 9000, *www.hotelchasamontana.ch*, **Hotel Post, t** +41 (0)81 861 9200, and **Hotel Silvretta, t** +41 (0)81 86 1 95 00, *www.hotel-silvretta.ch*.

Samoëns, France

t +33 (0)4 50 34 40 28, *www.samoens.com*
Altitude 700m (2,296ft)–2480m (8,134ft)
Lifts 78 in Grand Massif
Tour operators Altitude Holidays, French Life, Interhome, Lagrange, Peak Retreats, Ski Independence
The resort is linked into the Grand Massif ski area, of which Flaine is the major resort. It is easily accessible, just 45 minutes' drive from Geneva and an easy drive from Calais. 'There is a real warmth about the village,' enthused a reporter. However, it is fairly quiet in the evenings. Traditional bars and restaurants abound in this 'authentic French village'. The long-awaited Red Devil Gondola now whisks you up from Samoëns 720 to the ski area at 1600m in eight minutes. Hotels include three-star **Neige et Roc, t** +33 (0)4 50 34 40 72, *www.neigeetroc.com*, and **Hôtel Les Drugères, t** +33 (0)4 50 34 43 84, which has good food. The B&Bs **Chez Bobeau, t** +33 (0)4 50 34 98 95, and **Les Gîtes de Plampraz, t** +33 (0)4 50 34 95 98, are recommended. For something a little different, try **Le Château du Bérouze, t** +33 (0)4 50 34 95 72, *www.chateauduberouze.com*, a charming old manor house run by a New Zealand couple.

San Candido, Italy

See *Alta Pusteria*, page 417
Tour operator Waymark

San Cassiano, Italy

Page 271
Tour operators Momentum, Mountain Sun, Powder Byrne, Ski 2

San Martino (Reinswald), Italy

t +39 0471 623091, *www.sarntal.com*, *www.reinswald.com*
Altitude 1570m (5,151ft)–2460m (8,071ft)
Lifts 5 in resort, 74 in Ortler Skiarena
The South Tyrol village, in the Val Sarentino, has a modern gondola and three drag-lifts serving some 12km of piste. The resort is part of the Ortler Skiarena, with 13 small resorts covered by one lift pass. A total 260km of piste is served by eight cableways and 66 chair- and drag-lifts. For skiing at San Martino you can stay 15 minutes' drive away at the charming **Hotel Bad Schörgau, t** +39 0471 623048, *www.bad-schoergau.com*.

San Martino di Castrozza, Italy

t +39 0439 768867, *www.sanmartino.com*
Altitude 1450m (4,757ft)–2385m (7,825ft)
Lifts 17
San Martino is on the eastern edge of the Trentino Dolomites, surrounded by wild forest with soaring mountain peaks above. In 1700, the violin-maker Stradivari used to go into the same woods to select the spruce for his violins. Skiing started at San Martino di Castrozza in the early 1930s, and it has developed into three separate areas (two of which are linked). The resort lacks high-season queues and snowboarders, and has the charm of a low-profile ski station, although the majority of lifts are old-fashioned and slow. Accommodation includes four-star **Hotel Savoia, t** +39 0439 68094, and three-star **Hotel-Residence Colfosco, t** +39 0439 68224.

Santa Caterina, Italy

t +39 0342 935598, *www.valtellinaonline.com*
Altitude 1738m (5,702ft)–2725m (8,940ft)
Lifts 8
Tour operators Airtours, Neilson School Groups
The quiet village, 30 minutes by bus from Bormio, is ideal for families and beginners. It is set up a mountain road that is a dead-end in winter when the Gavia Pass is closed. Local skiing is on the northeast-facing slopes of the

Sobretta. The higher slopes are fairly steep and there are some intermediate trails through the trees. Comfortable **San Matteo Hotel**, **t** +39 0342 925121, *www.hotelsmatteo.com*, has good food.

Sauze d'Oulx, Italy

Page 274

Tour operators Airtours, Club Pavilion/Concept, Crystal, Directski, First Choice, Inghams, Momentum, Neilson, Panorama, Ski Arrangements, Ski Freshtracks, Ski High Days, Thomson

Savognin, Switzerland

t +41 (0)81 659 1616, *www.savognin.ch*
Altitude 1200m (3,937ft)–2715m (8,907ft)
Lifts 17

Attractive village close to St Moritz and Davos. It has recently added a cutting-edge new **Cube Hotel**, *www.cube-hotels.com* (see Nassfeld)

Scheffau, Austria

t +43 (0)5358 7373, *www.scheffau.com*
Altitude 752m (2,467ft)–1829m (6,001ft)
Lifts 93 in SkiWelt
Tour operators Crystal, Esprit, Neilson/Neilson School Groups, PGL, Ski Astons, Ski Wild, Thomson

Hotel residents in Scheffau are given priority in the queue for the sometimes-crowded eight-person gondola, which links into the giant SkiWelt circuit. A new six-pack replaces the old Weissachlift this season. **Hotel Alpin Scheffau**, **t** +43 (0)5358 85560, *www.hotelalpinscheffau.at*, has comfortable rooms and a swimming pool. The resort is a quieter alternative to popular Söll. Après-ski is muted apart from the Red Bull tent beside the gondola, which is crowded for a couple of hours when the lifts close.

Schladming, Austria

Page 76

Tour operators Alpine Answers Select, Crystal, Equity/Rocket Ski, Interhome, Neilson School Groups, Oak Hall, PGL, SkiBound, Sloping Off

Schlick 2000, Austria

See *Neustift and the Stubaital*, page 58

Schönberg, Austria

See *Neustift and the Stubaital*, page 58

Schruns, Austria

t +43 (0)5556 721660, *www.schruns-tschagguns.at*
Altitude 700m (2,296ft)–1300m (4,265ft)
Lifts 11
Tour operators j2ski.com, Made to Measure

Schruns in the Montafon area is one of the smaller resorts in the country, with 40km of fairly low-lying piste. The skiing is ideal for beginners and the resort is easily accessible from Friedrichshafen airport, which is an hour away, and Innsbruck which is 90 minutes. Ten other villages of the Montafon area are nearby, giving access to a total 222km of piste and 62 lifts.

Schwendau, Austria

Small village close to Mayrhofen (see page 55).

Seefeld, Austria

Page 79

Tour operators Crystal, Directski, Headwater, Inghams, Interhome, Thomson, Waymark

Sella Ronda, Italy

See *Arabba*, page 238; *Canazei*, page 241; *Corvara*, page 257; *San Cassiano*, page 271; *Selva Gardena*, page 277

Selva Gardena, Italy

Page 277

Tour operators Alpine Answers Select, Crystal, Esprit, First Choice, Inghams, Momentum, Neilson, Ski Arrangements, Ski Expectations, Thomson, Total Ski

Serfaus, Austria

t +43 (0)5476 62390, *www.serfaus-fiss-ladis.at*
Altitude 1427m (4,682ft)–2684m (8,806ft)
Lifts 53 in area
Tour operators Alpine Tours, Made to Measure

Smart Serfaus attracts a mainly Austrian, German and Dutch clientele to its beginner and intermediate slopes and its luxury hotels. The village is car-free and has an unusual underground railway, which runs on air cushions rather like a hovercraft. This transports snow-users from the far end of the village to the ski-lifts and contributes to the resort's serene atmosphere. The 175km ski area, linked to the villages of Fiss and Ladis, boasts a terrain park, permanent racing slopes, and an impressive 25 mountain restaurants. The slopes are floodlit for night-skiing and there is a new tubing park and mini snowmobile course at the Komperdell lift in Serfaus. Serfaus specializes in health treatments, with five spa hotels including the **Löwe und Bär**, **t** +43 (0)5476 6058, *www.loewebaer.com*, **Wellnesshotel Cervosa**, **t** +43 (0)5476 62110, *www.cervosa.com*, and **Wellnesshotel Schalber**, **t** +43 (0)5476 6770, *www.schalber.at*. **Gourmet-Hotel Maximilian**, **t** +43 (0)5476 6520, *www.maximilian.at*, is, as its name suggests, renowned for its food. The four-stars at Fiss include **Hotel Bergblick**, **t** +43 (0)5476 6364, *www.bergblick.com*, **Verwöhnhotel Chesa-Monte**, **t** +43 (0)5476 6406, *www.chesa-monte.at*, and **Hotel Gebhard**, **t** +43 (0)5476 6617, *www.hotel-gebhard.at*, while in Ladis they include **Hotel Sonnleit'n**, **t** +43 (0)5472 2660, *www.sonnleiten.co.at*, and **Hotel Goies**, **t** +43 (0)5472 6133, *www.hotel-goies.at*, which houses the Vitality Schlössl spa.

Serrada-Folgaria, Italy

t +39 0464 720538, *www.folgariaski.com*
Altitude 1169m (3,835ft)–2060m (6,758ft)
Lifts 42
Tour operators Equity/Rocket Ski, Neilson School Groups, PGL, SkiBound, Sloping Off

Good-value, mainly beginner and easy intermediate ski area in the Dolomites that is popular with school groups. Folgaria is made up of seven hamlets of which Serrada has the low-cost accommodation. **Golf Hotel**, **t** +39 0464 723114, *www.golfhotelfolgaria.it*, in the Costa area, has a choice of hotel rooms or apartments. The resort also has more than 20 three-star hotels and résidences.

Serre Chevalier, France

Page 212
Tour operators Alpine Elements, Club Med, Crystal, Equity/Rocket Ski, Erna Low, First Choice, French Life, Frozenplanet, Hannibals, Inghams, Interhome, Lagrange, Momentum, Neilson/Neilson School Groups, Ski Activity, Ski Arrangements, SkiBound, Ski Expectations, Ski Independence, Ski Miquel, Skitopia, Sloping Off, Thomson

Sestriere, Italy

Page 280
Tour operators Alpine Answers Select, Crystal, Equity/Rocket Ski, First Choice, Inghams, Interhome, Momentum, Neilson, Ski Arrangements, Thomson

Shiga Kogen, Japan

t +44 (0)20 7734 6870, *www.snowjapan.co.uk*
Altitude 1228m (4,028ft)–2305m (7,562ft)
Lifts 71

This is Nagano's largest ski area, and was the venue for the majority of ski events at the 1998 Winter Olympics. It is a mixture of 21 different ski bases, served by 71 lifts, dotted over six interlinked mountains. None of the sectors is big or particularly difficult; in alpine terms, the whole area would make up just three or four linked resorts of reasonable size. A competent skier or rider could cover all the terrain in a couple of days. Accommodation includes **Villa Alpen**, **t** +81 269 34 2731, which has its own ski school and equipment rental shop in the Sun Valley resort, and **Hotel La Neige Higashikan**, **t** +81 261 72 7111, at Shiga Kogen.

Sierra-at-Tahoe, California, USA

t +1 530 659 7453, *www.sierrattahoe.com*
Altitude 6,640ft (2024m)–8,852ft (2698m)
Lifts 9
Tour operator Ski the American Dream

Lake Tahoe resort set in 2,000 acres with plenty of sunny intermediate skiing and no fewer than six terrain parks with two half-pipes for skiers and riders.

Sierra Nevada, Spain

t +34 95 824 91 00, *www.sierranevadaski.com*
Altitude 2100m (6,888ft)–3470m (11,385ft)
Lifts 19
Tour operator Thomson

The Andalucian resort of Sierra Nevada is 32km from Granada, and offers mainland Europe's most southerly skiing. The presence of a ski resort here seems at complete odds with the nearby resorts of Marbella and Malaga, under two hours away. The purpose-built and somewhat charmless village of Pradollano is where most skiers stay. The ski area is vulnerable to bad weather, the mountain range is often exposed to high winds, and skiing is as likely to be interrupted by too much snow as too little. But when conditions are good the skiing can be excellent, and is best suited to beginners and intermediates. On a clear day you can see from the top across to North Africa. During fiesta time the resort can be crowded due to its proximity to Granada and the Costa del Sol. Accommodation includes **Hotel Sol Melia Sol y Nieve**, **t** +34 95 848 03 00, and the four-star **Sol Melia Sierra Nevada**, **t** +34 95 848 04 00 (both *www.solmelia.com*), which are convenient and pleasant. Four-star **Hotel Maribel**, **t** +34 95 824 91 11, is highly rated.

Silver Star, BC, Canada

Page 117

Tour operators Alpine Answers Select, AWWT, Crystal, Frontier Ski, Ski Activity, Ski All America, Ski the American Dream, Ski Independence, Ski Safari

Sinaia, Romania

t +40 1 614 5160 or +44 (0)20 7224 3692, *www.romaniantourism.com*
Altitude 855m (2,805ft)–2219m (7,280ft)
Lifts 10

Sinaia is a spa town where the Romanian royal family used to spend their summers after King Karol I built beautiful Peles Castle in the 1870s. Its once-smart hotels and casinos have an air of faded grandeur. The skiing is basic, but the setting is delightful. The long and easy runs down the front of the mountain are poorly marked and therefore challenging in uncertain visibility. The main area is on exposed slopes behind the mountain. Four-star hotels include **New Montana**, **t** +40 (0)244 312751, *www.newmontana.ro*, **Hotel Anda**, **t** +40 (0)244 306020, *www.hotel.anda.tourneo.ro*, and the recently renovated **Palace Hotel**, **t** +40 (0)244 312051, *www.sinaia.biz*. Three-star **Hotel Sinaia**, **t** +40 (0)244 311551, *www.sinaia.hotel.tourneo.ro*, is also rated.

Siviez, Switzerland

t +41 (0)27 289 5589, *www.nendaz.ch*
Altitude 1730m (5,676ft)–3330m (10,925ft)
Lifts 89 in Four Valleys
Tour operator Interhome

Sunny Siviez is a budget option for those wanting to ski the Four Valleys. A high-speed chair links to the Gentianes–Mont-Fort cable-cars of Verbier. Accommodation is in one hotel, a soulless apartment block and a youth hostel.

Sixt Fer à Cheval, France

t +33 (0)4 50 34 49 36, *www.sixtferacheval.com*
Altitude 1600m (5,248ft)–2480m (8,134ft)
Lifts 73 in Le Grand Massif
Tour operators Lagrange, Peak Retreats

The small 9th-century village of Sixt in the Grand Massif ski area is linked via the Piste des Cascades, a 14km blue trail, to the resort of Flaine.

SkiWelt, Austria

See *Söll and the SkiWelt*, Page 83

Smiggins, Australia

See *Perisher-Blue*, page 448

Smugglers' Notch, Vermont, USA

t +1 800 451 8752, *www.smuggs.com*
Altitude 1,030ft (314m)–3,640ft (1109m)
Lifts 8
Tour operators Neilson School Groups, Virgin

The resort has carved a niche for itself in the family market, but you would not choose to come to 'Smuggs' if you did not have small children. The key is convenience, with the lifts and accommodation within a 1,000ft radius, and apartments designed with families in mind. Smuggs is a small, unadorned village consisting mainly of condos. Morse is the beginners' mountain, conveniently situated in the village centre. Another novice area, Morse Highlands, is set halfway up the mountain. More adept skiers move on from Morse to the other two mountains, which are reached by bus or on skis. Madonna Mountain offers some pleasant trails, and Sterling has long intermediate runs. **Snow Sport University**, **t** +1 802 644 1293, is the highly respected ski and snowboard school. But children are what Smuggs is all about, and they are cared for at **Treasures Child Care Center**, **t** +1 800 451 8752, which features underfloor heating and giant fish tanks.

Snowbird and Alta, Utah, USA

Page 390

Tour operators Alpine Answers Select, American Ski Classics, AWWT, Momentum, Ski All America, Ski the American Dream, Ski Independence, Ski Safari, United Vacations

Snow King, Wyoming, USA

t +1 307 733 5200, *www.snowking.com*
Altitude 6,237ft (1901m)–7,808ft (2380m)
Lifts 4
This small ski area is confusingly in Jackson town but quite separate from Jackson Hole resort. The quiet ski area offers ample scope for a day's (or night's) skiing. The closest accommodation is the **Snow King Resort Hotel and Condominiums**, **t** +1 307 733 5200, at the base.

Snowmass, USA

See *Aspen and Snowmass*, page 419

Solda (Sulden), Italy

t +39 0473 737060, *www.sulden.com*
Altitude 1905m (6,185ft)–2625m (8,612ft)
Lifts 11
The South Tyrol village with its 11 lifts and 40km of piste offers some extensive skiing and is also home to the magnificent four-star **Hotel Post**, **t** +39 0473 613024, *www.hotelpost.it*, with an indoor pool and spa. The resort is part of the Ortler Skiarena, with 13 separate resorts sharing one lift pass. A total 260km of piste is served by eight cableways and 66 chair- and drag-lifts.

Sölden, Austria

Page 82
Tour operators Airtours, Frozenplanet, Panorama, Neilson, Thomson

Soldeu, Andorra

Page 32
Tour operators Airtours, Club Pavilion/Concept, Crystal, Directski, First Choice, Inghams, Lagrange, Neilson, Panorama, Ski Freshtracks, Ski Wild, Thomson

Solitude Mountain Resort, Utah, USA

t +1 801 534 1400, *www.skisolitude.com*
Altitude 7,988ft (2435m)–10,035ft (3059m)
Lifts 8
Tour operators Ski the American Dream, Ski Independence
Solitude is located 45 minutes' drive from Salt Lake City in the heart of Big Cottonwood Canyon in Utah's Wasatch National Forest. The underrated, ski-in, ski-out resort is family owned and full of charm. Some 50 per cent of the trails are rated intermediate. All accommodation (**t** +1 801 536 5707 for reservations) is of a good standard, with comfortable ski-in, ski-out apartments in **Creekside Lodge** and **Powderhorn Lodge**, as well as at the four-star **Inn at Solitude**, which houses the St Bernard's restaurant and a spa. **The Crossings** town houses are well equipped. **Silver Fork Lodge**, **t** +1 801 533 9977, in the Wasatch National Forest overlooks **Solitude**.

Söll, Austria

See *Söll and the SkiWelt*, page 83
Tour operators Airtours, Crystal, Directski, First Choice, Inghams, Neilson/Neilson School Groups, Panorama, PGL, Ski Activity, Ski Astons, Ski Freshtracks, Ski Hillwood, Ski Wild, Thomson

Squaw Valley, California, USA

Page 393
Tour operators American Ski Classics, AWWT, Ski All America, Ski the American Dream, Ski Expectations, Ski Independence, Ski Safari, United Vacations

Staffa, Italy

See *Macugnaga*, page 440

Steamboat, Colorado, USA

Page 395
Tour operators American Ski Classics, Crystal, Erna Low, Lotus Supertravel, Made to Measure, Ski Activity, Ski All America, Ski the American Dream, Ski Independence, Ski Safari, Skiworld, Thomson, United Vacations, Virgin

Stoneham, Quebec, Canada

t +1 418 848 2415, *www.ski-stoneham.com*
Altitude 695ft (420m)–2,075ft (632m)
Lifts 8
Tour operators Frontier Ski, Ski All America, Ski the American Dream, SkiBound, Ski Safari
Stoneham is known for having the most extensive night-skiing in Canada. Its 17 illuminated trails are open daily from 3pm to 10pm, making it popular with local skiers from Québec City – only a 20-minute drive away – on weekday evenings. With 32 trails spread over four mountains, Stoneham is one of the three largest ski areas in the province. It

boasts three terrain parks, including a superpipe with 17ft walls, and a 1km-long boardercross course. **Stoneham Hotel**, **t** +1 418 848 2411, is the only lodging at the base.

Stowe, Vermont, USA

Page 398

Tour operators American Ski Classics, Crystal, Erna Low, Neilson School Groups, Ski All America, Ski the American Dream, Ski Arrangements, SkiBound, Ski Independence, Ski Safari, Trailfinders, United Vacations, Virgin

Stubaital, Austria

See *Neustift and the Stubaital*, page 58

Stuben, Austria

t +43 (0)5582 399, *www.stuben.com*
Altitude 1407m (4,616ft) –2811m (9,222ft)
Lifts 86 on Arlberg Ski Pass

The village is called after the warm parlour – or *Stube* – of a solitary house on the Arlberg Pass where pilgrims used to shelter in the eighteenth century. Only 32 houses have been added since, and Stuben has just 104 residents and 650 guest beds. Four-star **Hotel Post**, **t** +43 (0)5582 7616, *www.hotelpost.com*, was where mailcoach drivers changed horses for the steep journey up the pass. With its small collection of five hotels and restaurants, Stuben is an ideal base for exploring St Anton and the Arlberg.

Sundance, Utah, USA

t +1 801 225 4107, *www.sundanceresort.com*
Altitude 6,100ft (1859m)–8,250ft (2515m)
Lifts 4
Tour operators Ski All America, Ski the American Dream, Ski Independence, Ski Safari

This traditional little Utah resort, created by film star Robert Redford, has old boardwalks and an atmosphere of a bygone era. It is a 55-minute drive from Salt Lake City and lift queues are rare. Sundance offers a variety of terrain ranging from wide, open trails to bowl skiing and is recommended for families. Accommodation is in the elegant-rustic **Sundance Cottages**, **t** +1 801 225 4107.

Sunday River, Maine, USA

t +1 207 824 3000, *www.sundayriver.com*
Altitude 800ft (244m)–3,140ft (957m)
Lifts 18
Tour operators American Ski Classics, Crystal, Ski the American Dream, SkiBound, Ski Independence, Ski Safari, Virgin

Sunday River, six miles north of Bethel in Maine, is one of the largest East Coast resorts. The picturesque state suffers at times from sparse natural snow, but given low temperatures this is of little consequence thanks to the snow-cannons that can cover up to 92 per cent of the total terrain. 'A good selection of runs,' said a reporter. 'The resort offers blacks and double-blacks with steep inclines.' The quality of the skiing compares favourably with that of a medium-sized alpine resort. Fortunately, Sunday River is far enough from New York not to suffer from the overcrowding to which other Vermont resorts are prone. Sunday River is flanked at one end by the **Grand Summit Hotel**, **t** +1 207 824 3500, and at the other by the **Jordan Grand Resort**, **t** +1 207 824 5000. In between lies the base area beneath a ridge of eight peaks offering a variety of terrain. 'Après-ski is non-existent with the village of Bethel a ghost town at night with the exception of a few pokey bars' complained a reporter.

Sun Peaks, BC, Canada

Page 119

Tour operators Alpine Answers Select, AWWT, Crystal, Frontier Ski, Made to Measure, Ski Activity, Ski All America, Ski the American Dream, Ski Freshtracks, Ski Independence, Ski Safari

Sun Valley, Idaho

Page 400

Tour operators AWWT, Ski Activity, Ski All America, Ski Independence, Ski Safari

Les Sybelles, France

See *Le Corbier*, page 427; *St-Jean-d'Arves*, page 453; *St-Sorlin-d'Arves*, page 454, and *La Toussuire*, page 462

La Tania, France

Page 216

Tour operators Airtours, Alpine Action, Alpine Answers Select, Crystal, Directski, Erna Low, First Choice, French Freedom, French Life, Frozenplanet, Lagrange, Momentum, Neilson, Silver Ski, Le Ski, Ski Activity, Ski Amis, Ski Arrangements, Ski Beat, Ski Deep, Ski France, Ski Freshtracks, Ski Independence, Ski Power, Skiweekends, Snowline, Thomson

Taos, New Mexico, USA

Page 403

Tour operators AWWT, Ski Activity, Ski the American Dream, Ski Independence, Ski Safari

El Tarter, Andorra

See *Soldeu-El Tarter*, page 32

Tour operators Airtours, Directski, First Choice, Panorama

Telfes, Austria

See *Neustift and the Stubaital*, page 58

Telluride, Colorado, USA

Page 406

Tour operators American Ski Classics, AWWT, Crystal, Lotus Supertravel, Ski All America, Ski the American Dream, Ski Independence, Ski Safari, United Vacations

Termas de Chillán, Chile

t +562 233 1313, *www.andesweb.com*

Altitude 1800m (5,900ft)– 2500m (8,200ft)

Lifts 9

Tour operators Andes, Elegant Resorts, Exsus Travel, Momentum, Scott Dunn Latin America, Ski Safari

South America's most exotic resort is set against a backdrop of smoking volcanoes and bubbling sulphur springs, 480km south of Santiago and 80km east of Chillán. The resort boasts some of the country's longest runs, with some 28 groomed trails spread across varied terrain. The excellent off-piste includes the 14km Shangri-La run, and Pirigallo – one of the resort's most celebrated itineraries, which comes complete with fumaroles belching sulphur fumes. The **Gran Hotel**, **t** +562 233 1313, has expensive ski-in/ski-out accommodation and a steaming indoor/outdoor swimming pool fed by pipes from the volcano. Reporters recommend renting a cabin in the village, which at US$20 per day is cheaper than any of the hotels.

Thierbach, Austria

See *Niederau*, page 59

Thredbo, Australia

t +61 (0)26459 4100, *www.thredbo.com.au*

Altitude 1365m (4,478ft)– 2037m (6,683ft)

Lifts 12

Thredbo, in the Kosciuszko National Park of New South Wales, is Australia's leading resort. It was founded in the early 1950s by Austrian and Czech immigrants who helped build the Snowy Mountain hydroelectric scheme. Aussies make either a six-hour drive from Sydney or the two-and-a-half-hour journey by road from Canberra, but you can also fly to Cooma, 80km away. The lifts serve some of the best intermediate terrain in the country and this is consequently Australia's nearest equivalent to a European ski resort – with the addition of gum trees. Four quads among the dozen lifts whisk skiers and boarders above the treeline. From here you progress to the summit on T-bars, which are better suited to the altitude's windier conditions. Because the snow record is unpredictable, the resort has invested heavily in snowmaking, and boasts the largest system in the southern hemisphere. Hotels include **The Alpenhorn**, **t** +61 (0)2 6457 6223, *www.alphorn.com.au*, **Black Bear Inn**, **t** +61 (0)2 6457 6216, *www.blackbearinn.com.au*, **Candlelight Lodge**, **t** +61 (0)2 6457 6049, *www.candlelightlodge.com.au*, **High Country Mountain Resort**, **t** +61 (0)2 6456 2511, and **Thredbo Alpine Hotel**, **t** +61 (0)2 6459 4100, which has a new-look pub called **The Pub**. Nearby **Crackenback Farm**, **t** +61 (0)2 6456 2198, *www.crackenback.com.au*, is a four-star country guesthouse. **Eagle's Nest**, at the top of the Kosciuszko Express, is the highest mountain restaurant in Australia and sometimes opens for sunset dinners. Reporters rated the resort 'astonishingly expensive for what it offers'.

La Thuile, Italy

Page 283

Tour operators Alpine Answers Select, Crystal, Inghams, Interski, Momentum, Neilson, Ski Arrangements, Thomson

Thyon-Les Collons, Switzerland

t +41 (0)27 281 2727, *www.thyon-region.ch*

Altitude 1500m (4,920ft)–3330m (10,925ft)

Lifts 89 in Four Valleys

The unexpected piste-side community is situated at the top of the Mayen-de-l'Ours gondola. It is little more than a collection of apartment blocks and a hotel linked into the Four Valleys ski area, of which Verbier is the major resort.

Tignes, France

Page 217

Tour operators Alpine Answers Select, Alpine Elements, Chalet Iguana, Club Med, Corporate Ski Company, Crystal, Directski, Erna Low, Esprit, First Choice, French Life, Frozenplanet, Inghams, Interhome, Lagrange, Made to Measure, Mark Warner, Momentum, Mountain Sun, Neilson, On The Piste, Ski Activity, Ski Amis, Ski Arrangements, SkiBound, Ski Expectations, Ski France, Ski Freshtracks, Ski Independence, Ski Olympic, Ski Solutions, Ski Supreme, Skitopia, Ski Val, Skiworld, Snowstar, Thomson, Total Ski, Wasteland, White Roc Weekends

Torgon, Switzerland

t +41 (0)24 481 3131, *www.torgon.ch*

Altitude 1100m (3,608ft)–2350m (7,708ft)

Lifts 207 in Portes du Soleil

Tour operator Interhome

Torgon is one of the least-visited resorts of the Portes du Soleil, a small purpose-built Swiss outpost of 1960s A-frame buildings on a sunny balcony above the Rhône and close to Lac Léman. It is reached on skis either from Châtel or from La Chapelle d'Abondance. Accommodation is in modest apartments. The resort is best suited to families looking for a quiet offbeat holiday spot with no other distractions apart from skiing.

La Toussuire, France

t +33 (0)4 79 83 06 06, *www.la-toussuire.com, www.sybelles.com*

Altitude 1800m (5,905ft)–2620m (8,596ft)

Lifts 75

Tour operators Erna Low, French Life, Interhome, Lagrange

Village in the 310km Les Sybelles ski area in the Maurienne Valley, linked to St-Jean, Le Corbier and St-Sorlin. The two three-star hotels are **Les Airelles**, **t** +33 (0)4 79 56 75 88, *www.hotel-les-airelles.com*, and **Les Soldanelles**, **t** +33 (0)4 79 56 75 29, *www.hotelsoldanelles.com*.

Trafoi, Italy

t +39 0473 613015, *www.inmontagna.net/trafoi.htm*

Altitude 1570m (5,151ft)–2550m (8,366ft)

Lifts 74 in area

Little Trafoi in the South Tyrol has only four lifts and 15km of piste but plenty of other skiing within a short drive of the village and included in the same lift pass. The resort is part of the Ortler Skiarena, with 13 unconnected resorts covered by one lift pass. There is a total 260km of piste in the area. Three-star **Hotel Madatsch**, **t** +39 0473 611767, at Trafoi is a comfortable spot in which to base yourself.

Treble Cone, New Zealand

See *Wanaka* (*Cardrona and Treble Cone*), page 467

Tremblant, Québec, Canada

Page 121

Tour operators Crystal, CV Ski, Elegant Resorts, Equity/Rocket Ski, Erna Low, Frontier Ski, Inghams, Lotus Supertravel, Neilson/Neilson School Groups, Ski All America, Ski the American Dream, SkiBound, Ski Independence, Ski Safari, Ski Wild, Thomson, Trailfinders, United Vacations, Virgin

Trois Vallées, France

See *Brides-les-Bains*, page 422; *Courchevel*, page 161; *Les Menuires*, page 184; *Méribel*, page 187; *St-Martin-de-Belleville*, page 211; *La Tania*, page 216; *Val Thorens*, page 230

Trysil, Norway

t +47 624 51000, *www.trysil.com*
Altitude 600m (1,969ft)–1132m (3,714ft)
Lifts 25
Tour operators Alpine Tracks, Neilson School Groups

Norway's largest ski area is ideal for families. 'An awesome resort', said reporters. 'Waiting times at lifts were very small.' Trysil is situated a two-and-a-half-hour drive from Oslo and has some of the most reliable snow-cover in Norway. The village is not picturesque compared to alpine resorts and does not offer much après-ski. Its pistes spread across the wooded slopes of Trysilfjellet and run 75 is rated for adventurous skiers and boarders. Instruction is highly rated and teachers are said to speak good English. The excellent accommodation is in hotels, apartments, and the many new *hyttes* (cabins). **Trysilfjell Aparthotel**, **t** +47 624 52350, is on the slopes. **Norlandia Trysil Hotel**, **t** +47 624 50833, *www.norlandia.no/trysil*, and **Trysil-Knut**, **t** +47 624 48000, are based in the old village of Trysil, 2km away from the slopes. Reporters recommend avoiding staying in the Fageråsen area as the slopes there are 'quite flat'.

Tschagguns, Austria

t +43 (0)5556 721660, *www.schruns-tschagguns.at*
Altitude 1430m (4,692ft)–2300m (7,546ft)
Lifts 62 in area
Tour operator Made to Measure

Tschagguns is part of the vast Montafon region with its 11 villages and a total 222km of piste and 62 lifts, as well as extensive ski-touring on the Silvretta glaciers and 100km of cross-country trails.

Turoa, New Zealand

See *Mount Ruapehu*, page 444

Tux im Zillertal, Austria

t +43 (0)5287 8506, *www.tux.at*
Altitude 1500m (4,920ft)–3250m (10,663ft)
Lifts 21 on Hintertux Glacier

Tux im Zillertal is made up of five villages in the Tuxer valley, the main one of which is Hintertux. It boasts the steepest glacier skiing in Austria and is usually open 365 days a year (20km of the piste is open all summer). It also offers the most advanced skiing and snowboarding on the otherwise low-altitude Zillertal Superskipass. The glacier is prone to overcrowding in winter when conditions are poor elsewhere, but hotel guests receive priority in the lift queue. Nowhere on the glacier is the skiing particularly challenging, with most runs groomed and free of bumps. However, the pistes are considered to be the best year-round downhill training ground in Europe, and national teams spend much of their summer here. The handful of modern, four-star hotels in Hintertux includes **Hotel Bergfried**, **t** +43 (0)5287 87239, *www.bergfried.at*, which has a swimming pool surrounded by rock walls.

Vail, Colorado, USA

Page 410

Tour operators American Ski Classics, Alpine Answers Select, Alpine Tracks, AWWT, Carrier, Crystal, CV Ski, Elegant Resorts, Erna Low, Inghams, Lotus Supertravel, Made to Measure, Momentum, Neilson, Rocky Mountain Adventures, Seasons in Style, Ski Activity, Ski All America, Ski the American Dream, Ski Expectations, Ski Freshtracks, Ski Independence, Ski Safari, Ski Solutions, Ski Wild, Skiworld, Thomson, Trailfinders, United Vacations, Virgin

Valbella, Switzerland

See *Lenzerheide and Valbella*, page 438

Val Cenis, France

t +33 (0)4 79 05 23 66, *www.valcenis.com*
Altitude 1400m (4,593ft)–2800m (9,186ft)
Lifts 22
Tour operators AWWT, Erna Low, Lagrange, MGS Ski, Peak Retreats, Snowcoach

The old unspoilt villages of Lanslebourg and Lanslevillard in the Haute Maurienne join together to form the resort of Val Cenis. The villages have a traditional community ambience. The skiing is for all standards, particularly beginners to intermediates. The eight two-star hotels include **La Vieille Poste**, **t** +33 (0)4 79 05 93 47, *www.lavieilleposte.com* ('too much good food'), and **Le Val Cenis**, **t** +33 (0)4 79 05 80 31. **CIS Centre International de Sejour**, **t** +33 (0)4 79 05 92 30, is warmly recommended by reporters.

Val di Fassa, Italy

See *Canazei*, page 241

Val di Fiemme, Italy

See *Cavalese*, page 244

Tour operators Neilson School Groups, Ramblers, Waymark

Val d'Isère, France

Page 221

Tour operators Airtours, Alpine Answers Select, Alpine Weekends, Club Med, Corporate Ski Company, Crystal, CV Ski, Descent International, Directski, Elegant Resorts, Erna Low, Esprit, Flexiski, Finlays, First Choice, French Freedom, French Life, Frozenplanet, Inghams, Interhome, Lagrange, Le Ski, Lotus Supertravel, Made to Measure, Mark Warner, Momentum, Mountain Leap, Neilson, On The Piste, Oxford Ski Company, Scott Dunn Ski, Silver Ski, Ski Activity, Ski Amis, Ski Arrangements, Ski Beat, SkiBound, Ski Expectations, Ski France, Ski Freshtracks, Ski Independence, Ski Olympic, Ski Solutions, Ski Supreme, Ski Val, Ski Weekend, Skiworld, Snowline, Thomson, Total Ski, Val d'Isère à la Carte, VIP, Wasteland, White Roc Weekends, YSE

Val d'Ultimo, Italy

See *Monte San Vigilio*, page 442

Val Fiscalina, Italy

See *Alta Pusteria*, page 417

Valfréjus, France

t +33 (0)4 79 05 33 83, *www.valfrejus.com*
Altitude 1550m (5,085ft)–2737m (8,980ft)
Lifts 12
Tour operators Erna Low, Lagrange, Peak Retreats

The modern resort of Valfréjus is built around the old wood-and-stone hamlet of Charmaix above the town of Modane. The skiing is mainly above the treeline on steep and sometimes mogulled slopes. **Hôtel Club MMV Le Valfréjus**, **t** +33 (0)4 92 12 62 12, is a Savoyard-style three-star in the centre of the village, while **Le Grand Vallon**, **t** +33 (0)4 79 05 08 07, is a two-star with good views.

Valle Nevado, Chile

t +56 2 206 0027, *www.vallenevado.com*
Altitude 2860m (9,383ft)–3670m (12,040ft)
Lifts 11
Tour operators Andes, Crystal, Exsus Travel, Lotus Supertravel, Momentum, Scott Dunn Latin America, Ski Safari

Valle Nevado was constructed by the French in the 1980s and is situated just 64km from Santiago, making it the closest resort to a capital city. The resort is linked by lift to the resorts of La Parva and El Colorado to create a small-sized version of an alpine ski circuit. A variety of slopes offer mainly intermediate skiing, and experienced skiers and riders can also take advantage of some of the world's best-value heli-skiing which goes up to a breathtaking 5000m. Reporters rated the pistes 'pretty well maintained'. The most comfortable accommodation is in **Hotel Valle Nevado**. The slightly cheaper options are **La Puerta del Sol** and **Tres Puntas** (bookings advisable through tour operators). **La Parva** is an enclave of smart holiday homes for wealthy city dwellers, while **El Colorado** is a purpose-built base for the adjoining old village of Farellones. Due to the extremely high altitude, visitors arriving from sea level may feel some discomfort for the first few days and are advised to drink plenty of water and refrain from drinking alcohol.

Vallnord, Andorra

See *Pal-Arinsal*, page 24

Valloire, France

t +33 (0)4 79 59 03 96, *www.valloire.net*
Altitude 1430m (4,690ft)–2600m (8,528ft)
Lifts 33
Tour operators Crystal, Erna Low, Ski France, French Life, Lagrange, Peak Retreats, SkiBound, Ski Independence, Thomson

The large and attractive village of Valloire is set in an isolated bowl above the Maurienne Valley. It is still very much a traditional French farming community without a lot of nightlife. The skiing, linked to Valmeinier, is divided between three areas on adjacent mountains accessed by two gondolas a few minutes' walk from the village centre. The ski area is mainly intermediate with some long runs. 'If you want to learn, go somewhere else,' warned a snowboarder; 'the pistes are better suited to skiing than boarding, as even the green runs are very narrow.' Accommodation includes three-stars **Les Oursons**, **t** +33 (0)4 79 59 01 37, *www.hotel-les-oursons.com*, with a swimming pool, **Grand Hôtel de Valloire et du Galibier**, **t** +33 (0)4 79 59 00 95, *www.grand-hotel-valloire.com*, opposite the lifts, **Hôtel Rapin**, **t** +33 (0)4 79 59 06 02, *www.hotel-rapin.com*, which contains gastronomic restaurant **Le Matafan**, and a wide range of chalets and apartments.

Valmeinier, France

t +33 (0)4 79 59 53 69, *www.valmeinier.com*
Altitude 1430m (4,690ft)–2600m (8,528ft)
Lifts 33
Tour operators Crystal, Erna Low, French Freedom, French Life, Lagrange, Neilson School Groups, On The Piste, Ski Independence, Snowcoach, Thomson

The skiing is linked to that of Valloire in the Maurienne Valley (see above). 'Not really suitable for complete beginners, and the attitude of the ESF is cavalier to say the least', complained a reporter. Accommodation choices include **Auberge Le Grand Fourchon**, **t** +33 (0)4 79 59 21 01, *www.fourchon.com*, **Hôtel L'Aigle**, **t** +33 (0)4 79 59 24 31, with an outdoor hot tub, and **Hôtel Club Les Carrettes**, **t** +33 (0)4 79 59 25 45, which provides full-board, a mini-club and evening entertainment.

Valmorel, France

Page 228
Tour operators Crystal, Erna Low, French Life, Neilson/Neilson School Groups, Ski Amis, Ski Independence, Ski Supreme, Thomson

Val Senales (Schnalstal), Italy

t +39 0473 662171, *www.schnalstal.com*
Altitude 2005m (6,578ft)–3250m (10,663ft)
Lifts 12

The principal destination in the Ortler Skiarena, with 13 unconnected resorts all covered by one lift pass. A total 260km of prepared piste is served by eight cableways and 66 chair- and drag-lifts. This is the main village of the scenic Vinschgau and base for one of Europe's largest year-round ski areas with guaranteed snow, six lifts in summer at the top of the Ghiacciai cable-car and another five in winter. **Berghotel Grawand**, **t** +39 0473 662118, *www.grawand.com*, located at 3212m on the glacier, is a simple two-star hotel that houses the only on-mountain eatery and a small museum dedicated to Ötzi, the Neolithic man found preserved in the ice above the ski area in 1991. Other hotels include three-star **Hotel Schwarzer Adler**, **t** +39 0473 669652, which has been in the same family for four generations.

Val Thorens, France

Page 230
Tour operators Airtours, Alpine Elements, Club Med, Crystal, Directski, Erna Low, First Choice, French Freedom, French Life, Frozenplanet, Inghams, Interhome, Lagrange, Made to Measure, Momentum, Neilson, Ski Activity, Ski Amis, Ski Arrangements, Ski Expectations, Ski France, Ski Freshtracks, Ski Independence, Ski Solutions, Ski Supreme, Skiworld, Thomson, Total Ski, Wasteland

Valtournenche, Italy

t +39 0166 92055, *www.cervinia.it*
Altitude 1524m (5,000ft)–3883m (12,740ft)
Lifts 59 with Zermatt

The old village is 9km by road from Cervinia, but linked into the same ski area. Valtournenche provides good-value accommodation in a genuine village ambience unspoilt by tourism. **Albergo Grandes Murailles**, **t** +39 0166 932956, *www.hotelgmurailles.com*, is a small hotel with lots of atmosphere.

Vars 1850, France

t +33 (0)4 92 46 51 31, *www.vars-ski.com*
Altitude 1850m (6,068ft)–2750m (9,020ft)
Lifts 57 with Risoul
Tour operators Erna Low, Interhome, Lagrange, Neilson School Groups, Tops, Wasteland

Vars 1850 is larger, less attractive and not as welcoming to the non-French as neighbouring Risoul 1850. The old village is linked by drag-lift to the modern station, but you have to walk across town to reach the Vars gondola and chair to Risoul 1850. Beginners can learn in the village where there are two drags and some gentle green runs. Intermediates have a good choice of runs above and below the treeline, and some wide-open bowl skiing.

Accommodation is in apartment buildings such as **Résidence l'Albane** and **l'Ecrin des Neiges**.

Vaujany, France

Page 233

Tour operators Erna Low, Lagrange, Peak Retreats, Ski Independence, Ski Peak

Vent, Austria

t +43 (0)5254 8193, *www.vent.at*
Altitude 1900m (6,234ft)–2680m (8,793ft)
Lifts 4

The small village has just 900 beds but offers some good off-piste skiing. The seven hotels include **Familyhotel Vent**, **t** +43 (0)5254 8102, which houses a kindergarten. A free ski-bus links with Sölden and Obergurgl.

Verbier, Switzerland

Page 326

Tour operators Alpine Answers Select, Corporate Ski Company, Crystal, Descent International, Erna Low, First Choice, Flexiski, Inghams, Interhome, Kaluma, Lotus Supertravel, Made to Measure, Momentum, Mountain Leap, Oxford Ski Company, Peak Ski, The Powder Co, Powder White, Simply Ski, Ski Activity, Ski Activity, Ski Expectations, Ski Freshtracks, Ski Independence, Ski Solutions, Ski Verbier, Ski Weekend, Ski with Julia, Skiworld, Swiss Travel Service, Thomson, Total Ski, White Roc Weekends

Veysonnaz, Switzerland

t +41 (0)27 207 1053, *www.veysonnaz.ch*
Altitude 1400m (4,593ft)–3330m (10,925ft)
Lifts 89 in Four Valleys

This resort, used as a training base by the Swiss national team, is reached by a winding 13km mountain road from Sion. It is part of the 412km Four Valleys circuit and provides a useful backdoor into the steeps of Mont Fort. A new eight-person gondola brings you up to the mid-station and Veysonnaz's own considerable ski area can also be accessed from a second base area 3km away by road at Mayen-de-l'Ours. A bus connects the two. **Hôtel Magrappé**, **t** +41 (0)27 207 1817, is comfortable and friendly.

Villard-de-Lans, France

t +33 (0)4 76 95 10 38, *www.ot-villard-de-lans.fr*
Altitude 1160m (3,806ft)–2170m (7,119ft)
Lifts 29
Tour operators AWWT, Interhome, Lagrange

This rural French community attracts weekend skiers from nearby Grenoble rather than an international clientele. The pistes, best suited to beginners and low intermediates, are at Côte 2000 – a rather unappealing *station de ski* situated a 2km bus ride from the resort. Together with the resort of Corrençon, Villard-de-Lans is also a popular venue for cross-country skiing. Recommended hotels include three-star **Le Christiania**, **t** +33 (0)4 76 95 12 51, **Le Dauphin**, **t** +33 (0)4 76 95 95 25, and two-star **Les Bruyères**, **t** +33 (0)4 76 95 11 83.

Villard-Reculas, France

t +33 (0)4 76 80 45 69, *www.villard-reculas.com*
Altitude 1500m (4,921ft)–3330m (10,922ft)
Lifts 84 in area
Tour operator La Source

This isolated farming hamlet is perched on the mountainside below Alpe d'Huez and above the valley town of Bourg-en-Oisans. A quad chair-lift links it to the top of Signal de L'Homme and the rest of the large Alpe d'Huez circuit,which includes Vaujany, Auris and Oz-en-Oisans. **Bonsoir Clara**, **t** +33 (0)4 76 80 37 20, is warmly recommended for dinner. Accommodation is at **Hôtel Beaux Monts**, **t** +33 (0)4 76 80 43 14, and in a few converted barns.

Villaroger, France

Tour operator Optimum Ski

Villars, Switzerland

Page 331

Tour operators Club Med, Corporate Ski Company, Crystal, Erna Low, Inghams, Interhome, Kuoni, Made to Measure, Momentum, Original Travel, OTP, PGL, Ski Independence, Ski Solutions, Ski Weekend, Swiss Travel Service, Switzerland Travel Centre (Plus Travel), Thomson

Vorderlansersbach, Austria

Small village up the valley from Mayrhofen.

Voss, Norway

t +47 565 20800, *www.visitvoss.no*
Altitude 91m (300ft)–945m (3,100ft)
Lifts 9
Tour operators Alpine Tracks, Crystal, Inghams, Neilson School Groups

Despite its low altitude, Voss provides a reasonable ski area for beginners and lower intermediates, but it can become busy at weekends. 'Extremely quiet slopes and very well groomed', enthused a reporter; 'The mountain is deserted during the week,' said another. But 'On the minus side, very poor mountain restaurants – cheeseburgers pall a little after six days and there is no beer on the mountain'. For more experienced skiers and boaders, the resort has three black runs and some off-piste. Cross-country skiers will not be disappointed with 60km of prepared loipe close to the centre, with more on offer in the valleys around the area. **Hotel Fleischer, t** +47 565 20500, *www.fleischers.no*, is traditional.

Wagrain, Austria

Page 86

Waidring, Austria

t +43 (0)5353 5242, *www.tiscover.com/waidring*
Altitude 780m (2,558ft)–1860m (6,102ft)
Lifts 8
Tour operators Thomson, Tyrolean Adventures

This unspoilt village is less under 20km away from St Johann in Tyrol and is situated in the same snow pocket as Fieberbrunn. The peaceful resort is known for its family skiing, with convenient nursery slopes in the village centre. The main skiing is at Steinplatte, 4km from the village and ideal for beginners and intermediates. **Hotel Waidringerhof, t** +43 (0)5353 5228, *www.waidringerhof.at*, has a swimming pool, and the central **Hotel Tiroler Adler, t** +43 (0)5353 5311, *www.tiroler-adler.at*, is also rated.

Wanaka (Cardrona and Treble Cone), New Zealand

Cardrona t +64 (0)3 443 8651
Treble Cone t +64 (0)3 443 7443
www.cardrona.com, www.lakewanaka.co.nz, www.treblecone.co.nz
Altitude Cardrona 1670m (5,479ft)–2060m (6,759ft), Treble Cone 1200m (3,936ft)–1860m (6,102ft)
Lifts 9 in Cardona and Treble Cone

Wanaka is an alternative bed-base to Queenstown from which to explore the main South Island skiing. From here, the ski areas of Cardrona and Treble Cone, as well as the Waiorau Nordic Ski Area and the Wanaka Snow Park (New Zealand's first whole-mountain terrain park) are all within a 30-minute drive. The road between Queenstown and Wanaka is sealed, but reporters warn it is 'a test of nerves', making the other Southern Lakelands resorts of Coronet Peak and The Remarkables even more accessible. Cardrona's ski field is well suited to beginners and intermediates with several wide and gentle slopes. It is known for its dry snow and reliable season, which runs from late June until early October. The area boasts the country's largest terrain park and four half-pipes. Wanaka is also the gateway to Treble Cone, with 'scenery that has to be seen to be believed'. One of the country's top resorts, it boasts New Zealand's first six-seater chair. Advanced skiers – and snowboarders in particular – are well catered for but the area is quite limited for beginners. The area's best off-piste is found by hiking 20 minutes to the summit. There is good heli-skiing nearby in the Harris Mountains.

Wengen, Switzerland

Page 335

Tour operators Club Med, Crystal, Inghams, Interhome, Kuoni, Made to Measure, Momentum, Oak Hall, Re-lax Holidays, Ski Expectations, Ski Freshtracks, Ski Solutions, Swiss Travel Service, Switzerland Travel Centre (Plus Travel), Thomson

Westendorf, Austria

Page 89

Tour operators Inghams, Interhome, Thomson

Whakapapa, New Zealand

See *Mount Ruapehu*, page 444

Whistler, BC, Canada

Page 124

Tour operators Alpine Answers Select, American Ski Classics, AWWT, Carrier, Cold Comforts, Crystal, CV Ski, Elegant Resorts, Equity/Rocket Ski, Erna Low, First Choice,

Frontier Ski, Frozenplanet, Inghams, Kaluma, Lotus Supertravel, Made to Measure, Momentum, Neilson, Rocky Mountain Adventures, Seasons in Style, Ski Activity, Ski All America, Ski the American Dream, Ski Arrangements, SkiBound, Ski Expectations, Ski Freshtracks, Ski Independence, Ski Miquel, Ski Safari,
Ski Solutions, Ski Wild, Skiworld, Solo's, Thomson, Total Ski, Trailfinders, United Vacations, Virgin

Whitewater, BC, Canada

t +1 250 354 4944, *www.skiwhitewater.com, www.nelsonbc.ca*

Altitude 5,400ft (1646m)–6,700ft (2042m)

Lifts 3

Tour Operators Frontier Ski, Ski Safari

Whitewater is a pleasant little ski area close to the atmospheric Victorian town of Nelson. Its two lifts give direct access to challenging trails through the trees as well as some great – but avalanche-prone – off-piste. Some 20 per cent of the terrain is made up of easy runs, while the remainder is divided equally between intermediate and advanced skiing. But the real attraction is Nelson. The lakeside town, close to the Montana border, was the point of arrival in Canada for hundreds of hippies fleeing the draft during the Vietnam War. Some of them travelled no further.

Inn the Garden, t +1 250 352 3226, is a recommended B&B.

Wildschönau, Austria

See *Niederau*, page 59

Winter Park, Colorado, USA

Page 414

Tour operators American Ski Classics, AWWT, Crystal, Equity/Rocket Ski, Erna Low, Lotus Supertravel, Neilson/Neilson School Groups, Ski Activity, Ski All America, Ski the American Dream, SkiBound, Ski Independence, Skiworld, Thomson, United Vacations, Virgin

Wirl, Austria

See *Galtür*, page 430

Yabuli, China

t +86 451 345 5088, *www.yabuliskiresort.com*

Altitude 1374m (4,508ft)–1944m (6,378ft)

Lifts 9

Yabuli is China's most important resort. It was initially developed at a cost of $210m, and was the venue for the 1996 Asian Winter Games. Situated 194km north-west of the city of Harbin, the resort is open 120 days a year and is attempting to double its present ski terrain. However, development is being held back by an apparent lack of agreement between the government and the 10 Chinese investors. The longest run is 5km and there is a vertical drop of 600m. Yabuli is also the location for a separate ski area used until now for competitions and by army skiers. There is a plan to link the two areas to create China's most extensive ski area. The hotel of choice is four-star **Windmill Villa, t** +86 451 345 5168, close to the slopes.

Yellowstone Club, Montana, USA

t +1 406 995 4900, *www.theyellowstoneclub.com*

Altitude 7160ft (2182m)–9,860ft (3005m)

Lifts 13

The world's only private ski resort covers an area of 6,000 acres of perfectly manicured piste – that's an area bigger than Breckenridge – but you'll never see more than 30 people on the slopes on a busy day. Of the total 12 lifts, 11 are high-speed covered chairs, the pistes are so smooth that you never see a pebble or a mogul. The ski area is supplemented by neighbouring Big Sky, with its 11 lifts and 150 runs that can be skied by YC members but not vice versa. To join you have to be proposed by another member. Then you have to buy property here, with prices starting at $795,000. Three lodges – Rainbow, Warren Miller and Timberline – house restaurants, bars, and a ski shop. Some 20 lovely little log cabins are available to members' friends and to prospective buyers.

Zakopane, Poland

t +48 18 2020400, *www.zakopane.pl*

Altitude 838m (2,749ft)–2301m (7,549ft)

Lifts 16

Tour operators Interhome, Poltours

Skiing has been popular in Zakopane for over a hundred years. The earliest international ski competition took place here in 1910. The resort offers plenty of scope, from beginner runs to the more difficult. The best skiing can usually be found in the Kasprowy Wierch area.

Zao, Japan

t +44 (0)20 7734 6870, *www.zao-spa.or.jp*, *www.snowjapan.com*
Altitude 780m (2,599ft)–1736m (5,696ft)
Lifts 42
Zao, in the Yamagata Prefecture, retains its spa-town charm in spite of being one of the biggest resorts in Japan. It is located two and a half hours from Tokyo by *shinkansen* (bullet train), and its slopes are reached by ancient cable-car. They are famous throughout the country because of a huge forest of 'snow-ghosts' – fir trees that become encrusted with hoarfrost and snow to form a vast collection of monster shapes. Some 90 per cent of this large ski area is suited to beginners and intermediates, and the resort has little to entice advanced skiers. Accommodation is mainly in traditional *ryokan* inns, which include the recommended **Zao Onsen Eko**, **t** +23 6949533.

Zauchensee, Austria

See *Wagrain and the Salzburger Sportwelt*, page 86
Tour operators Ski Hillwood, Sloping Off

Zell am See, Austria

See *Zell am See and Kaprun*, page 90
Tour operators Airtours, Club Europe, Crystal, Directski, Erna Low, First Choice, Inghams, Interhome, Neilson/Neilson School Groups, PGL, Ski Activity, Ski Astons, SkiBound, Ski Freshtracks, Ski Wild, Snowscape, Thomson

Zell am Ziller, Austria

t +43 (0)5282 22810, *www.zell.at*
Altitude 1250m (4,101ft)–2505m (8,219ft)
Lifts 55 in area
Tour operators Equity/Rocket Ski, Neilson School Groups, PGL, Ski Astons, Sloping Off
Zell am Ziller is the second most substantial valley resort in the Zillertal area after Mayrhofen. The two areas, Kreuzjoch or Gerlosstein, are set away from the town. Kreuzjoch is reached by swift, eight-person gondola, and Gerlosstein has twin cable-cars. There is an influx of visitors from Germany each weekend. Four-star **Sport und Wellnesshotel Theresa**, **t** +43 (0)5282 22860, *www.theresa.at*, and three-star **Hotel Englhof**, **t** +43 (0)5282 3134, are rated.

Zermatt, Switzerland

Page 339
Tour operators Alpine Answers Select, Corporate Ski Company, Crystal, CV Ski, Descent International, Elegant Resorts, Erna Low, Frozenplanet, Inghams, Interhome, Kuoni, Lotus Supertravel, Made to Measure, Momentum, Oak Hall, OTP, Powder Byrne, Scott Dunn Ski, Seasons in Style, Ski Expectations, Ski Freshtracks, Ski Independence, Ski Solutions, Swiss Travel Service, Switzerland Travel Centre (Plus Travel), Thomson, Total Ski, VIP, White Roc Weekends, Zermatt Holidays

Zillertal 3000, Austria

See *Mayrhofen*, page 55

Zug, Austria

See *Lech and Zürs*, page 50

Zürs, Austria

See *Lech and Zürs*, page 50
Tour operators Alpine Answers Select, Corporate Ski Company, Crystal, Elegant Resorts, Inghams, Kaluma, Made to Measure, Momentum, Powder Byrne, Seasons in Style

Directory

Tour Operators

The 200 ski and board operators listed below offer inclusive ski and board holiday packages, but you should be aware that not all of them are fully bonded. Before parting with any money it makes sense to discover what would happen in the event of a company going bust before you travel or while you are abroad. One extra safeguard, which may entitle you to a refund in such an event, is to pay by credit card direct to the company rather than to a travel agent.

Airtours Ski & Snowboard: Holiday House, Sandbrook Park, Sandbrook Way, Rochdale OL11 1SA
t +44 (0)870 241 8964, *www.airtours.co.uk, www.mytravel.com*
Mass-market UK subsidiary of Mytravel, with hotel, chalet and apartment holidays in Andorra, Austria, Bulgaria, Canada, France, Italy and Romania

Albus Travel: Hill Farm Barn, Angel Hill, Earl Stonham, Stowmarket IP14 5DP
t +44 (0)1449 711 952, *www.albustravel.com*
Winter and summer holidays with flights to choice of two catered chalets and an apartment in St Anton (*see* page 72)

Alpine Action: Marine Suite, The Old Town Hall, Southwick BN42 4AX
t +44 (0)1273 597 940, *www.alpineaction.co.uk*
Small family-run operator with chalets in Méribel and La Tania

Alpine Answers Select: The Business Village, 3–9 Broomhill Road, London SW18 4JQ
t +44 (0)20 8871 4656, *www.alpineanswers.co.uk*
Well-established tailor-made arm of specialist ski travel agency

Alpine Elements: 1 Risborough Street, London SE1 0HF
t +44 (0)8700 111 360, *www.alpineelements.co.uk*
Luxury and standard catered ski and snowboard chalet holidays in France

Alpine Tours: The Ardmour Group, Berkshire College, Burchetts Green SL6 6QR
t +44 (0)1628 826 699,

www.alpinetours.co.uk
Long-established schools and groups operator to Austria, Italy, Switzerland and Spain

Alpine Tracks: 40 High Street, Menai Bridge, Anglesey LL59 5EF
t +44 (0)1248 717 440, *www.alpinetracks.com*
Chalet and hotel holidays in Champoluc, Ischgl, Lech, Morzine, Breckenridge and Vail. Also ski-touring, off-piste and mountain awareness courses (*see* page 52)

Alpine Weekends: 95 Dora Road, London SW19 7JT
t +44 (0)20 8944 9762, *www.alpineweekends.com*
Bespoke breaks in France, Italy and Switzerland, with off-piste, heli-skiing and ski-touring

Alp Leisure: La Nouvaz, 73120 Courchevel, France
t +33 (0)4 79 00 59 42, *ww.alpleisure.com*
Tailor-made luxury holidays to privately owned chalets in Méribel and Courchevel 1850. Selected chalets available all year round

Altitude Holidays: Suite 787, 2 Old Brompton Road, London SW7 3DQ
t +44 (0)870 870 7669, *www.altitudeholidays.com*
Chalets and apartments, catered and self-catered in Flaine, Les Carroz, Samoëns and Morillon

American Ski Classics: Mortlake Business Centre, 20 Mortlake High Street, London SW14 8JN
t +44 (0)20 8607 9988, *www.americanskiclassics.com*
Hotels and apartments in over 20 resorts in North America

Andes: 37A St Andrews Street, Castle Douglas DG7 1EN
t +44 (0)1556 503 929, *www.andes.org.uk*
South American skiing and climbing specialist, with holidays and ski-tours to Chile and Argentina

AWWT: 1 Lonsdale Gardens, Tunbridge Wells TN1 1NU
t +44 (0)1892 511 894, *www.awwt.co.uk*
Tailor-made holidays to North America

Balkan Holidays: Sofia House, 19 Conduit Street, London W1S 2BH
t +44 (0)845 130 1114, *www.balkanholidays.co.uk*
Mass-market operator to Bulgaria, Romania, Slovenia, Serbia and Turkey

Balkan Tours: 61 Ann Street, Belfast BT1 4EE
t +44 (0)28 9024 6795, *www.balkan.co.uk*
Long-established holiday specialist to Bulgaria and Romania, with direct flights from Belfast and Dublin

Barelli Ski: 19 Sefton Park Road, St Andrew's, Bristol BS7 9AN
t +44 (0)870 220 1500, *www.barelliski.co.uk*
Accommodation-only holidays to 20 chalets in Chamonix, Les Houches and Champagny-en-Vanoise

Barwell Leisure: The Coach House, Elm Road, Chessington, KT9 1AW
t +44 (0)20 8786 3071, *www.barwell.co.uk*
Specialist to Humber Valley Resort in Newfoundland (*see* page 107)

Belvedere Chalets: Peach House, Gangbridge Lane, St Mary Bourne SP11 6EW
t +44 (0)1264 738 257, *www.belvedereproperties.net*
Small specialist operator with five superb catered chalets in Méribel

Bigfoot Travel: Winchcombe House, 123–126 Bartholomew Street, Newbury RG14 5BN
t +44 (0)870 300 5874, *www.bigfoot-travel.co.uk*
Hotels, chalets and apartments in the Chamonix Valley

Board and Lodge: 18 Belsize Grove, London NW3 4UN
t +44 (0)20 7419 0722, *www.boardnlodge.com*
Snowboarding holidays in Argentière, Chamonix, Saalbach and Slovenia

Bonne Neige Ski Holidays: PO Box 42, Crewe CW2 7FH
t +44 (0)1270 256 966, *www.bonne-neige-ski.com*
Small independent tour operator, with two luxury catered chalets and family-run hotel in Méribel
(see page 190

Borderline: 16 Place St Clément, 65120 Luz, France
t + 33 (0)5 62 92 68 95, *www.borderlinehols.com*
Well-established operator with own hotel and self-catering properties in Barèges in the French Pyrenees

Canterbury Travel: 42 High Street, Northwood HA6 1BL
t +44 (0)1923 822 388, *www.laplandmagic.com*
Lapland specialist with holidays to Luosto in Finland

Carrier: 1 Lakeside, Cheadle SK8 3GW
t +44 (0)1625 547 040, *www.carrier.co.uk*
Luxury tailor-made holidays in Aspen, Beaver Creek, Jackson Hole, Vail, Québec and Whistler

Chalet Chocolat: Glebe Cottage, Philleigh, Truro TR2 5NB
t +44 (0)1872 580 814, *www.chalet-chocolat.co.uk*
Luxury catered chalet in Morzine

The Chalet Company: 1 Cluanie Orchard, Melford Road, Cavendish CO10 8AA
t +44 (0)871 717 4208 or **t** +33 (0)450 79 68 40, *www.thechaletco.com*
Smart catered chalets in Morzine and Ardent in the Portes du Soleil

Chalet Snowboard: Dell House, Bodham NR25 6NG
t +44 (0)870 800 4020, *www.chaletsnowboard.co.uk*
Specialist snowboard holidays and freestyle camps based in company's own chalets in Morzine and Avoriaz. Summer camps in Les Deux Alpes

Les Chalets de St Martin: Chalet Roussette, 73440 St-Martin-de-Belleville, France
t +33 (0)4 79 08 91 77, *www.leschalets.co.uk*
Catered chalet in St-Martin-de-Belleville

Challenge Activ: Chalet Flori, L'Ele, Montriond 74110, France
t +44 (0)871 717 4113, *www.challenge-activ.com*
Activity holiday specialist with catered chalet in Morzine

Classic Ski: Ober Road, Brockenhurst SO42 7ST
t +44 (0)1590 623 400, *www.classicski.co.uk*
Established operator with holidays in the French Alps including tuition for singles and couples over 50yrs, weekday flights and flexible-length stays

Club Europe: Fairway House, 53 Dartmouth Road, London SE23 3HN
t +44 (0)800 496 4996, *www.club-europe.co.uk*
Schools operator with ski programmes in Austria, France and Italy

Club Med: 1st Floor, Gemini House, 10–18 Putney Hill, London SW15 6AA
t +44 (0)845 367 6767, *www.clubmed.co.uk*
Club villages in France, Switzerland, Italy, Japan and the USA. Flights, transfers, full-board accommodation, ski pass, tuition, après-ski entertainment and insurance all included in the price, as well as childcare in many resorts

Club Pavilion/Concept Holidays: 56 Lansdowne Place, Hove BN3 1FG
t +44 (0)870 241 0427, *www.conceptholidays.co.uk*
Specialists in low-cost ski and weekend breaks

Cold Comforts: 22 Chilbolton Avenue, Winchester SO22 5HD
t +44 (0)800 404 9297,

www.cold-comforts.com
Tailor-made holidays to Whistler, with ski-guiding, flexible-length holidays, and Sun Peaks add-ons (*see* page 128)

Collineige: 30–32 High Street, Frimley GU16 7JD
t +44 (0)1276 24262, *www.collineige.com*
Large portfolio of catered and uncatered chalets in Chamonix and Argentière. Guiding/instruction on request. Chalets available winter and summer (*see* page 157)

Concept Chalets: 3 Cholswell Court, Shippon, Abingdon OX13 6HX
t +44 (0)1865 390 807, *www.conceptchalets.com*
Luxury catered chalets with spa in Chamonix

Contiki: Wells House, 15 Elmfield Road, Bromley BR1 1LS
t +44 (0)20 8290 6422, *www.contiki.com*
Holidays for 18–35s in Hopfgarten, Austria, by coach or air

Cooltip Mountain Holidays: Ashcourt, Main Street, Long Riston, Hull HU11 5JF
t +44 (0)1964 563 563, *www.cooltip.com*
Small operator with catered chalet-apartments in Méribel

The Corporate Ski Company: Olympic House, 196 The Broadway, Wimbledon SW19 1RY
t +44 (0)20 8542 8555, *www.thecorporateskicompany.co.uk*
Corporate ski trips to major resorts in the Alps

Crystal Holidays: King's Place, 12–42 Wood Street, Kingston-upon-Thames KT1 1SH
t +44 (0)870 160 6040, *www.crystalski.co.uk*
Mass-market operator with UK's largest choice of resorts and properties throughout Europe, North and South America

CV Ski: Thames Wharf Studios, Rainville Road, London W6 9HA
t +44 (0)870 062 3425, *www.cvski.co.uk*
Luxury hotel holidays in Austria, Canada, France, Italy, Switzerland and the USA

Descent International: Riverbank House, Putney Bridge Approach, London SW6 3JD
t +44 (0)20 7384 3854, *www.descent.co.uk*
Luxury operator positioned at the extreme upper end of the chalet market, with properties in Courchevel, Les Gets, Méribel, Val d'Isère, Klosters, Verbier and Zermatt (*see* page 191)

Directski.com: Block 10–4, Blanchardstown Corporate Park, Dublin 15, Ireland
t +44 (0)800 587 0945, *www.directski.com*
Major Dublin-based online operator with holidays to Andorra, Austria, Bulgaria, Canada, France, Italy, Norway, Slovenia and the USA (*see* pages 28, 346)

Elegant Resorts: The Old Palace, Chester CH1 1RB
t +44 (0)1244 897 333, *www.elegantresorts.co.uk*
Worldwide 4- and 5-star de luxe hotel and chalet tour operator with an established reputation in skiing (*see* page 52)

Elemental Adventure: Kitts Farm, Churt GU10 2PH
t +44 (0)870 738 7838, *www.eaheli.com*
Heli-skiing in Alaska, Argentina, Canada, Greenland, Himalayas, Russia, Sweden and Turkey

Equity Ski: Dukes Lane House, 47 Middle Street, Brighton BN1 1AL
t +44 (0)1273 299 299, *www.equityski.co.uk*
All-inclusive ski holidays to 34 resorts in Austria, France, Italy, Switzerland and North America

Erna Low: 9 Reece Mews, London SW7 3HE
t +44 (0)870 750 6820/**t** +44 (0)20 7584 7820 (brochure line), *www.ernalow.co.uk*
The oldest independent ski tour operator, with wide selection of apartments in Austria, Bulgaria, France,

Italy, Slovenia and Switzerland, as well as hotels. Also ski programme to selected resorts in North America and spa holidays to a wide range of resorts (*see* inside front cover, pages 147, 203)

Esprit Ski: 185 Fleet Road, Fleet GU51 3BL
t +44 (0)1252 618 300,
www.esprit-holidays.co.uk
Family specialist to 17 resorts in Austria, France, Italy and Switzerland, with dedicated nurseries, ski classes and activity clubs (*see* pages 19, 72, 147, 165, 197)

Exsus Travel: 23 Heddon Street, London W1B 4BQ
t +44 (0)20 7292 5050, *www.exsus.com*
Specialist tailor-made operator to South America, with luxury accommodation

Family Ski Company: Bank Chambers, Walwyn Road, Colwall, Malvern WR13 6QG
t +44 (0)1684 540 333,
www.familyski.co.uk
Family ski specialist with dedicated child facilities. Catered chalets in Portes du Soleil, Paradiski and the Trois Vallées. Provides helpers at the ski schools' *jardins de neige* working with Family Ski Company
(see page 19

Finlays: 2 Abbotsford Court Business Centre, Kelso TD5 7BQ
t +44 (0)1573 226 611, *www.finlayski.com*
Long-established small Scottish chalet company with a dedicated following in Courchevel, Val d'Isère and Paradiski (*see* page 142)

First Choice Ski: First Choice House, London Road, Crawley RH10 2GX
t +44 (0)870 754 3477,
www.firstchoice.co.uk/ski
Mainstream winter sports operator with a collection of chalets, hotels and apartments in Europe and North America

Flexiski: Olivier House, 18 Marine Parade, Brighton BN2 1TL
t +44 (0)870 909 0754, *www.flexiski.com*
Luxury arm of First Choice Ski (see above), with holidays of variable length to chalets and hotels in Austria, France and Switzerland. Also runs a corporate breaks programme (*see* page 164)

Four Winds Meriski: 1st Floor, Carpenters Buildings, Carpenters Lane, Cirencester GL7 1EE
t +44 (0)1285 648 518,
www.fourwindsresorts.com
Luxury family chalet operator in Méribel (*see* page 190)

Freedom Holidays: PO Box 46, Petworth GU28 9ZX
t +44 (0)1798 861 881,
www.freedomholidays.co.uk
Tailor-made weekends and weeks in apartments, chalets and hotels in Châtel in the Portes du Soleil

French Freedom Holidays: 44 Newdown Road, Southpark, Scunthorpe DN17 2TX
t +44 (0)1724 290 660,
www.skifrance4less.co.uk
Self-drive and fly-drive holidays to the French Alps

French Life Ski: Spring Mill, Earby, Barnoldswick, Lancs BB94 0AA
t +44 (0)870 197 6963,
www.frenchlifeski.co.uk
Budget ski holidays for the independent traveller, mainly focused on self-drive to the French Alps. Also short breaks

Frontier Ski: 6 Sydenham Avenue, London SE26 6UH
t +44 (0)20 8776 8709,
www.frontier-ski.co.uk
Canadian specialist with a dedicated following (*see* page 128)

Frozenplanet.co.uk:
t +44 (0)7947 331 606,
www.frozenplanet.co.uk
Online operator offering ski and snowboard holidays worldwide

Gourmet Chalet Company: 15 Scalebor Square, Burley-in-Wharfedale, Ilkley LS29 7SP
t +44 (0)871 218 0480,
www.gourmet-chalet.com
Luxury catered chalet in Les Gets with transfers

Hannibals: Farriers, Little Olantigh Road, Wye, Ashford TN25 5DQ
t +44 (0)1233 813 105, *www.hannibals.co.uk*
Established specialist operator with hotels, chalets and self-catering apartments in Serre Chevalier

Headwater Holidays: The Old School House, Chester Road, Northwich CW8 1LE
t +44 (0)1606 720 033, *www.headwater.com*
Cross-country ski programme in France, Italy, Austria, Switzerland and Scandinavia, winter discovery weeks in North America

HF Holidays: Imperial House, Edgware Road, London NW9 5AL
t +44 (0)20 8905 9558, *www.hfholidays.co.uk*
Group holidays with instruction in cross-country skiing and snowshoeing in Austria, France and Switzerland

High Mountain Holidays: 39 Bartholomew Close, Ducklington OX29 7UJ
t +44 (0)1993 775 540, *www.highmountain.co.uk*
Chamonix specialist with apartments, hotels and eight chalets. Weekends and short stays, off-piste courses

Huski Chalet Holidays: 14 Warren Road, Nork, Banstead, Surrey SM7 1LA
t +44 (0)8000 97176, *www.huski.com*
Long-established Chamonix chalet operator, also offering hotels, apartments and weekend skiing

Independent Luxury Chalets: 62 Lydon Grove, London, SW18 4LN
t +44(0)20 8875 5656
www.independtluxurytravel.co.uk
Luxury Chalet in St. Jean d'Aulps near Morzine

Inghams: 10–18 Putney Hill, London SW15 6AX
t +44 (0)20 8780 4433, *www.inghams.co.uk*
Major tour operator with chalets and hotel holidays in 90 resorts in 12 countries. Top end of the mass market but also has separate luxury programme

Inntravel: Nr Castle Howard, York YO60 7JU
t +44 (0)1653 617 906, *www.inntravel.co.uk*
Cross-country, snowshoeing and alpine skiing in Austria, Finland, France, Italy, Scandinavia, Switzerland and USA

Interhome: 383 Richmond Road, Twickenham TW1 2EF
t +44 (0)20 8891 1294, *www.interhome.co.uk*
Swiss company (part of Hotelplan/Inghams group) with a large database of self-catering ski-drive chalets and apartments throughout the Alps (*see* page 7)

Interski: Acorn Park, Commercial Gate, Mansfield NG18 1EX
t +44 (0)1623 456 333, *www.interski.co.uk*
Long-established schools operator to

DIRECTORY Tour Operators

Courmayeur and the Aosta Valley. Also has own BASI ski school and equipment rental

James Orr Heliski: 12 Rose & Crown Walk, Saffron Walden CB10 1JH
t +44 (0)1799 516 964, *www.heliski.co.uk*
Established agent for heli-skiing holidays in Canada

Jeffersons Private Jet Holidays: Mill House, Millers Way, London W6 7NA
t +44 (0)870 850 8181,
www.jeffersons.com
Short breaks by private jet/helicopter to selected resorts with own airstrip (Courchevel, Grindelwald, Lech, St Christoph am Arlberg, St Moritz). Limousine transfers and luxury accommodation

Just Slovenia: The Barns, Woodlands End, Mells, Frome BA11 3QD
t +44 (0)1373 814 230,
www.justslovenia.co.uk
Specialist tour operator offering tailor-made holidays to Slovenia

Kaluma Travel: 1st Floor Offices, 263 Putney Bridge Road, London SW15 2PU
t +44 (0)870 442 8044,
www.kalumatravel.co.uk
Luxury ski holiday specialist in France, Austria and Switzerland. Also flexible-length trips and weekend breaks. Corporate programme also available (*see* page 165)

Kuoni Travel: Kuoni House, Deepdene Avenue, Dorking RH5 4AZ
t +44 (0)1306 747 000, *www.kuoni.co.uk*
Long-established mainstream hotel operator to Switzerland

Lagrange: 168 Shepherds Bush Road, London W6 7PB
t +44 (0)20 7371 6111,
www.lagrange-holidays.co.uk
British branch of giant French operator with a wide range of self-catering accommodation in 100 resorts in the Alps and the Pyrenees (*see* page 157)

Leisure Direction: Image House, Station Road, London N17 9LR
t +44 (0)20 8324 4042,
www.leisuredirection.co.uk
Established ski-drive operator to 36 French resorts

Lotus Supertravel: Sandpiper House, 39 Queen Elizabeth Street, London SE1 2BT
t +44 (0)20 7962 9933,
www.supertravel.co.uk
High-quality chalets and tailor-made holidays to Europe, North America and Chile

Made To Measure Holidays: 1 South Street, Chichester PO19 1EH
t +44 (0)1243 533 333,
www.mtmhols.co.uk
Long-established operator specializing in tailor-made and flexible holidays to a wide range of resorts in Europe and North America (*see* page 6)

Mark Warner: 10 Old Court Place, London W8 4PL
t +44 (0)870 770 4226,
www.markwarner.co.uk
Family holiday specialist with over

30 years' experience, offering chalet-hotel holidays with childcare and adult-only holidays in eight major French resorts, as well as Courmayeur and St Anton (*see* inside back cover)

McNab Mountain Sports: Harbour House, Crinan, Lochgilphead PA31 8SW
t +44 (0)1546 830 243, **t** +33 (0)4 50 54 22 84, *www.mcnab.snowboarding.com*
Off-piste snowboarding courses and technical clinics based at catered chalet in Argentière. Also summer freestyle/freeride snowboard camps in Les Deux Alpes

MGS Ski: 109 Castle Street, Saffron Walden CB10 1BQ
t +44 (0)1799 525 984, *www.mgsski.com*
Small, well-established family operator offering apartments in Val Cenis in France

Momentum Ski: 162 Munster Road, London SW6 6AT
t +44 (0)20 7371 9111, *www.momentumski.com*
Tailor-made operator specializing in weeks and weekends to the Alps and North America, together with a corporate programme. Italy and Switzerland are a particular strength (*see* page 261)

Moswin's Germany: The Birds Building, Fleckney Road, Kibworth LE8 0HJ
t +44 (0)870 062 5040, *www.moswin.com*
Holidays in Garmisch-Partenkirchen in Germany and cross-country skiing in Berchtesgaden

Mountain Heaven: 1 Cholmondeley Road, West Kirby, Wirral CH48 7HB
t +44 (0)151 625 1921, *www.mountainheaven.co.uk*
Self-catering apartments in La Plagne/Montalbert

Mountain Highs: Chalet Marcassin, Le Clos de Renève, 74430 Seytroux, France
t +44 (0)121 550 9321 or **t** +33 (0)4 50 79 29 54, *www.mountainhighs.co.uk*
Three catered chalets in Morzine, with optional ferry crossings, transfers and childcare

Mountain Leap: 25 Eccleston Square, London SW1V 1NS
t +44 (0)20 7931 0621, *www.mountainleap.com*
Tailor-made holidays to Chamonix, Courchevel, Megève, Méribel, Val d'Isère, Klosters and Verbier. Also large groups and corporate hospitality events

Mountain Retreats: Guilton Ash, Tile Barn, Woolton Hill, Newbury RG20 9UX
t+44 (0)1635 253 946, *www.mountainretreats.co.uk*
Small company offering luxury catered ski-in/ski-out accommodation in Chamonix Valley

Mountain Sun: Fillis Cottage, The Street, Kingston near Lewes BN7 3NT
t +44 (0)7941 196 517, *www.mountainsunltd.com*
Three catered chalets in Paradiski, Tignes and San Cassiano

Mountain Tracks: The Business Village, 3 Broomhill Road, London SW18 4JQ
t +44 (0)20 8877 5773, *www.mountaintracks.co.uk*
Off-piste trips, ski-touring, heli-skiing and avalanche awareness courses worldwide

Native Travels: 26 Andover Green, Bovington BH20 6LN
t +44 (0)192 946 3774 *www.naturetreks.co.uk*
Beginner ski courses, off-piste and dog-sledding in Scandinavia

Neilson: Locksview, Brighton Marina, Brighton BN2 5HA
t +44 (0)870 333 3347, *www.neilson.co.uk*
Major tour operator with hotels, apartments and chalets in Andorra, Austria, Bulgaria, France, Italy, Norway, Romania and Sweden and North America. The company is part of Thomas Cook (*see* page 126)

Neilson School Groups: Locksview, Brighton Marina, Brighton BN2 5HA
t +44 (0)870 333 3620,

www.neilsonschools.com
Schools and adult groups operator

Nonstopski: Shakespeare House, 168 Lavender Hill, London SW11 5TF
t +44 (0)870 241 8070, *www.nonstopski.com*
Learn-to-be-a-ski-instructor courses in Banff, Fernie and Red Mountain in Canada

Oak Hall Skiing and Snowboarding: Oak Hall, Otford TN15 6XF
t +44 (0)1732 763 131, *www.oakhall.co.uk*
Christian holidays for 20s and 30s to Austria and Switzerland

On The Piste: 28 Great King Street, Macclesfield SK11 6PL
t +44 (0)1625 503 111, *www.onthepiste.com*
French Alps specialist offering tailor-made travel for school groups, students and adults by coach or air

Optimum Ski: Chalet Tarentaise, Le Pré, 73640 Villaroger, France
t +44 (0)8702 406 198, *www.optimumski.com*
BASI trainer-run ski courses in Villaroger near Les Arcs with accommodation in large chalet

Original Travel Company: Crombie Mews, 11a Abercrombie Street, London SW11 2JB
t +44 (0)20 7978 7333, *www.originaltravel.co.uk*
Up-market short-break specialist offering heli-skiing, ski-touring and off-piste in Austria, Canada, France, Italy, Switzerland, Sweden and the USA

OTP (On The Piste Holidays): 2 Oldfield Court, Cranes Park Crescent, Surbiton KT5 8AW
t +44 (0)871 871 8034, *www.otp.co.uk*
Holidays to Nendaz, Saas-Fee, Villars and Zermatt

The Oxford Ski Company: Field Cottage, Hazelton, Rodmarton, Cirencester GL7 6PG
t +44 (0)870 787 1785, *www.oxfordski.com*
Tailor-made luxury holidays for private and corporate clients in luxury private chalets in France and Switzerland

Panorama Holidays: Panorama House, Vale Road, Portslade BN41 1HP
t +44 (0)870 750 5060, **t** +44 (0)870 241 5026 (24hr brochure line), *www.panoramaski.co.uk*
Budget-priced chalets, hotels and apartments in Andorra, Austria, Bulgaria, France, Italy and Slovenia. Part of the Mytravel group

Peak Leisure: The Old Post Office, Steventon, Basingstoke RG25 3BA
t +44 (0)870 760 5610, *www.peak-leisure.co.uk*
Independent catered chalet in Ste-Foy, flexible-length stays with transfers

Peak Retreats: 2.4 Central Point, Kirpal Road, Portsmouth, PO3 6FH
t +44 (0)870 770 0408, *www.peakretreats.co.uk*
French Alps specialist for self-catering chalets, apartments and family-run hotels in offbeat resorts (*see* page 197)

Peak Ski: White Lilacs House, Water Lane, Bovingdon HP3 0NA
t +44 (0)1442 832 629, *www.peakski.co.uk*
Independent operator offering catered chalets in Verbier

PGL Ski: Alton Court, Penyard Lane, Ross-on-Wye HR9 5GL
t +44 (0)870 162 6622, *www.pgl.co.uk*
Major schools operator to Austria, France, Italy, Switzerland and USA

Poltours: 20 The Avenue, London W13 8PH
t + 44 (0)208 810 5625, *www.poltours.co.uk*
Tailor-made ski holidays to Zakopane in Poland

Powder Byrne: 250 Upper Richmond Road, London SW15 6TG
t +44 (0)20 8246 5300, *www.powderbyrne.com*
Luxury family ski holidays to Austria, Italy, France and Switzerland, with exclusive children's clubs and crèches (*see* page 341)

The Powder Co: Case Postale 1454, Verbier 1936, Switzerland **t** +44 (0)778 813 622, **t** +41 (0)79427 9778, *www.thepowderco.com* Luxury chalets in Verbier

Powder Skiing in North America: 61 Doneraile Street, London SW6 6EW **t** +44 (0)20 7736 8191, *www.canadianmountainholidays.com* Agent for CMH Heli-ski in Canada, with international flights

Powder White: 213 Earlsfield Road, London SW18 3DE **t** +44 (0)20 8355 8836, *www.powderwhite.co.uk* Luxury chalets in Courchevel, Verbier, and Val d'Isère with flexible catering arrangements (*see* page 329)

Première Neige: 19 East London Street, Edinburgh EH7 4ZD **t** +44 (0)709 2000 300 or **t** +33 (0)4 79 06 30 55, *www.premiere-neige.com* Catered chalets and apartments in Sainte-Foy. Guided ski safaris to other resorts in the region

Purple Ski: Holmbury House, Skittle Green, Bledlow HP27 9PJ **t** +44 (0)1885 488 799, *www.purpleski.com* Small luxury chalet operator in Méribel

Pyrenean Mountain Tours: 2 Rectory Cottages, Wolverton, Tadley RG26 5RS **t** +44 (0)1635 297 209, *www.pyrenees.co.uk* Small operator with ski, ski-touring and snowshoeing holidays to hotels and self-catering apartments in Barèges in the French Pyrenees and Corvara in the Dolomites

Ramblers Holidays: PO Box 43, Welwyn Garden City AL8 6PQ **t** +44 (0)1707 331 133, *www.ramblersholidays.co.uk* Walking holidays specialist with group cross-country holiday programme to Achenkirch and Innsbruck in Austria, Dobbiaco and Val di Fiemme in Italy

Reach4theAlps: Chalet Sol Ré, Essert La Pierre, 74430 St Jean d'Aulps, France **t** +44 (0)1382 731 719, *www.reach4thealps.com* Independent chalet company offering a high standard of catered accommodation with chalets in Morzine and Les Gets

Re-lax Holidays: 2 Shirley Road, Enfield EN2 6SB **t** +44 (0)20 8360 1185, *www.re-laxholidays.co.uk* Holidays to hotels in Lauterbrunnen and Wengen, with flights or self-drive

Rocket Ski: Dukes Lane House, 47 Middle Street, Brighton BN1 1AL **t** +44 (0)1273 262 626, *www.rocketski.com* Online booking service for components of holidays to Austria, France and Italy

Rocky Mountain Adventures: 6 Denstone Close, Woolton, Liverpool L25 8SJ **t** +44 (0)870 366 5442, *www.rockymountain.co.uk* Full-season chalet holidays in Aspen, Breckenridge, Vail, Banff and Whistler

Scott Dunn Latin America: Fovant Mews, 12 Noyna Road, London SW17 7PH **t** +44 (0)20 8682 5030, *www.scottdunn.com* Holidays to major resorts in Argentina and Chile

Scott Dunn Ski: Fovant Mews, 12 Noyna Road, London SW17 7PH **t** +44 (0)20 8682 5050, *www.scottdunn.com* Up-market operator with a portfolio of luxury catered chalets in Courchevel 1850, Méribel, St Anton, Val d'Isère and Zermatt. Also runs its own childcare operation (*see* pages 71, 223)

Seasons in Style: Lakeside, St David's Park, Nr Chester CH5 3YE **t** +44 (0)1244 302 000, *www.seasonsinstyle.co.uk* Five-star worldwide hotel operator with a ski programme to Austria, France, Switzerland, USA and Canada

Silver Ski: Conifers House, Grove Green Lane, Maidstone ME14 5JW
t +44 (0)1622 735 544, *www.silverski.co.uk*
No-nonsense catered chalets in Paradiski, Trois Vallées and Val d'Isère

Simon Butler Skiing: Portsmouth Road, Ripley GU23 6EY
t +44 (0)870 873 0001, *www.simonbutlerskiing.co.uk*
Holidays to chalet-hotels in Megève, including instruction

Le Ski: 25 Holly Terrace, Huddersfield HD1 6JW
t +44 (0)870 754 4444, *www.leski.com*
Long-established family-run company with chalets in Courchevel 1650, Val d'Isère and La Tania. Offers childcare, free ski guiding and owns a complex of six chalets in Val d'Isère (*see* page 163)

Ski 2:The Old Forge, High Street, Twyford SO21 1RF
t +44 (0)1962 713 330, *www.ski-2.com*
Champoluc and San Cassiano specialist, with its own crèche, offering total flexibility of travel dates and length of stay. Also runs own ski, freeride and snowboard school (*see* page 273)

Ski Activity: Lawmuir House, Methven PH1 3SZ
t +44 (0)1738 840 888, *www.skiactivity.com*
Chalets, hotels and apartments in 11 resorts in France, as well as in Verbier and 25 resorts in North America

Ski Addiction: The Cottage, Fontridge Lane, Etchingham, East Sussex TN19 7DD
t +44 (0)1580 819 354, *www.skiaddiction.co.uk*
Holidays in Châtel and La Chapelle d'Abondance in the Portes du Soleil. Short breaks, and instruction

Ski Adventures: 14a Graham Road, Malvern WR14 2HN
t +44 (0)1684 560 707, *www.skiadventures.co.uk*
Piste-side catered chalet accommodation in Les Arcs 1600

Ski All America: 117 St Margarets Road, Twickenham TW1 2LH
t +44 (0)870 167 6676, *www.skiallamerica.com*
Chalets, hotels and apartments in a large portfolio of resorts in North and South America

Skialot: 119 Apple Grove, Enfield EN1 3DB
t + 44 (0)845 004 3622, *www.skialot.com*
Catered chalet in Châtel, with draught beer on tap from chalet's own microbrewery

Ski the American Dream: 31 Beaufort Court, Admirals Way, Waterside, South Quay, London E14 9XL
t +44 (0)870 350 7547, *www.skidream.com*
The UK's original independent ski holiday specialist operator to North America, now under new ownership (*see* page 346)

Ski Amis: 122–126 High Road, London NW6 4HY
t +44 (0)20 7692 0850, *www.skiamis.com*
Well-established company offering catered and self-catered apartments and chalets in the French Alps

Ski Arrangements: The Reading Rooms, Sandy Lane, Crich, Matlock DE4 5DE
t +44 (0)8700 110 565, *www.skiarrangements.com*
Flexible-length ski holidays to France, Italy and Canada, staying in apartments, chalets and hotels

Ski Astons: Clerkenleap, Broomhall, Worcester WR5 3HR
t +44 (0)1905 829 200, *www.skiastons.co.uk*
Schools specialist with all-inclusive holidays to resorts in Austria and Switzerland

Ski Barrett-Boyce: 3 Mayfields, Brighton Road, Lower Kingswood KT20 6QZ
t +44 (0)1737 831 184, *www.skibb.com*
Family-run company offering chalet holidays in Megève, with instruction and childcare

Ski Basics: 95 West Avenue, Oldfield Park, Bath BA2 3QB
t +44 (0)1225 444 143, *www.skibasics.co.uk*
Méribel specialist with eight chalets, offering ski courses with Inspired to Ski

Ski Beat: Metro House, Northgate, Chichester PO19 1BE
t +44 (0)1243 780 405, *www.skibeat.co.uk*
Long-established operator with chalets in Méribel, Paradiski, La Tania, La Rosière and Val d'Isère. Crèches in La Plagne, Les Arcs and La Tania (*see* page 203)

Ski Blanc: 89 Palmerston Road, Buckhurst Hill, Essex IG9 5NH
t +44 (0)20 8502 9082, *www.skiblanc.co.uk*
Small operator with a range of catered chalets in Méribel-Les-Allues

Ski Bon: 6 St Paul's Terrace, Northampton NN2 6ET
t +44 (0)1604 247 723, *www.skibon.com*
Holidays to two catered chalets in Méribel, with self-drive, sleeper-coach travel or airport transfers

SkiBound: Olivier House, 18 Marine Parade, Brighton BN2 1TL
t +44 (0)870 900 3242, *www.skibound.co.uk*
Market leader for school trips to Austria, France, Italy and North America. Part of the First Choice group

Ski Chamois: 18 Lawn Road, Doncaster DN1 2JF
t +44 (0)1302 369 006, *www.skichamois.co.uk*
Small chalet-hotel operator in Morzine, with own childcare programme

Ski La Côte: 33 Dale Road, Welton, Brough HU15 1PE
t +44 (0)1482 668 357, *www.ski-la-cote.karoo.net*
Catered chalet in La Chapelle d'Abondance, with airport transfers and instruction, but not flights

Ski Cuisine: 49 Burgess Road, Southend-on-Sea SS1 3AX
t +44 (0)1702 589 543, *www.skicuisine.co.uk*
Small company with six gourmet-catered chalets in Méribel

Ski Deep: 5 The Orchard, St Johns Hill Road, Woking GU21 7RF
t +44 (0)1483 722 706, *www.skideep.com*
Catered chalets in Courchevel and La Tania, with instruction

Ski Equipe: Victoria House, 19/21 Ack Lane East, Bramhall, Cheshire SK7 2PR
t +44 (0)870 444 5533, *www.ski-equipe.co.uk*
Small operator with chalets and hotels in Cortina d'Ampezzo and St Anton

Ski Etoile: Glebelands, Clun, Shropshire SY7 8JH
t +44 (0)1588 640 442, *www.skietoile.co.uk*
Flexible holidays to Montgenèvre with hotels, chalets and apartments

Ski Expectations: Jasmine Cottage, Manor Lane, Great Chesterford CB10 1PJ
t +44 (0)1799 531 888, *www.skiexpectations.com*
Small tailor-made hotel and catered-chalet operator to major resorts in Europe, Canada and North America

Ski Famille: Unit 10, Chesterton Mill, French's Road, Cambridge CB4 3NP
t +44 (0)845 644 3764, *www.skifamille.co.uk*
Specialist family-run chalet operator for families in Les Gets, with free childcare programme (*see* page 19)

Ski France: Unit 14, Croydon House Business Centre, 1 Peall Road, Croydon CR0 3EX
t +44 (0)870 251 0006, *www.skifrance.co.uk*
Travel by rail, air or self-drive to France, with chalets, hotels and apartments

Ski Freshtracks: The White House, 57–63 Church Road, Wimbledon, London SW19 5SB
t +44 (0)845 458 0784, *www.skifreshtracks.co.uk*

Ski Club of Great Britain's programme where you can ski or snowboard with a group of similar ability for weeks, weekends or on specialist courses. Carefully selected leaders, instructors and guides (*see* page 4)

Ski Gower: 2 High Street, Studley B80 7HJ
t +44 (0)1527 851 411
Tailor-made holidays in Switzerland for schools and groups

Ski High Days: Fire Clay House, Netham Road, Bristol BS5 9PJ
t +44 (0)117 955 1814, *www.skihighdays.com*
Group tour operator with an increasingly large presence in Sauze d'Oulx, Clavière and Bardonecchia in Italy (*see* page 277)

Ski Hillwood: Lavender Lodge, Dunny Lane, Chipperfield WD4 9DD
t +44 (0)1923 290 700, *www.hillwood-holidays.co.uk*
Long-established specialist family operator with childcare programme to Söll and Zauchensee in Austria, Les Gets and Argentière in France

Ski Hiver: 29 Place House Close, Fareham PO15 5BH
t +44 (0)1329 847 788, *www.skihiver.co.uk*
Catered chalets with childcare in Peisey-Nancroix and Plan-Peisey in Paradiski

Ski Independence: 5 Thistle Street, Edinburgh EH2 1DF
t +44 (0)845 310 3030, *www.ski-i.com*
Largest independent operator to USA and Canada, with hotels, chalets and apartments in 40 resorts. Also extensive programme to 30 French and 4 Swiss resorts, with option to fly or drive for week or weekend stays (*see* page 127)

Ski Link: 25 Hopfield Avenue, Byfleet, West Byfleet, Surrey KT14 7PE
t +44 (0)871 218 0174, *www.ski-link.co.uk*
Online operator with catered chalets and hotels in Courchevel

Ski Miquel: 73 High Street, Uppermill, Oldham OL3 6AP
t +44 (0)1457 821 200, *www.miquelhols.co.uk*
Long-established chalet, hotel and apartment operator to Alpe d'Huez, Bad Gastein, Baqueira-Beret, Lauterbrunnen, Serre Chevalier and Whistler (*see* page 128)

Ski Morgins:The Barn House, 1 Bury Court Barns, Wigmore HR6 9US
t +44 (0)1568 770 681, *www.skimorgins.com*
Small specialist operator to Morgins in Switzerland

Ski 'n' Action: Maison Beaufort, rue des Beauforts, Le Praz, Courchevel 73120, France
t +44 (0)1707 251 696, *www.ski-n-action.com*
Catered chalet in Le Praz Courchevel 1300

Ski-n-doo: Les Clos, 74260 Les Gets, France
t +44 (0)871 900 8126, *www.ski-n-doo.com*
Upmarket catered chalets in Les Gets

Ski Norwest: 8 Foxholes Cottages, Foxholes Road, Horwich, Bolton BL6 6AL
t +44 (0)1204 668 468, *www.skinorwest.com*
Weekend and midweek ski and snowboarding breaks to Aviemore

Ski Olympic: PO Box 396, Doncaster DN5 7YS
t +44 (0)1302 328 820, *www.skiolympic.com*
Chalets and hotels in seven French resorts, including own chalet-hotel at Vallandry in Paradiski

Ski Peak: Barts End, Crossways Road, Grayshott GU26 6HD
t +44 (0)1428 608 070, *www.skipeak.com*
Small, dedicated operator with its own chalets and apartments and its own hotel in Vaujany in the Alpe d'Huez ski area. Provides a British nanny for the resort crèche. Chalets available all year round (*see* page 236)

Ski Power: The Gables, Coopers Hill Road, Nutfield RH1 5PD
t +44 (0)1737 823 232, *www.skipower.co.uk*

Catered chalets in La Tania and Courchevel 1650

Ski Rosie: L'Alpage 8B, route du Petit Châtel, 74390 Châtel, France
t +33 (0)4 50 81 31 00, *www.skirosie.com*
Long-established operator with one catered chalet in Morgins, apartments and hotels in Châtel

Ski Safari: 1 Amber House, St Johns Road, Hove BN3 2EZ
t +44 (0)1273 224 060, *www.skisafari.com*
North America expert with high-quality hotels and apartments. Self-drive adventures a speciality. Also holidays in Chile

Skisafe Travel: Unit 4, Braehead Estate, Old Govan Road, Renfrew PA4 8XJ
t +44 (0)141 885 1423, *www.osatravel.co.uk*
Family-run operation in Aviemore, Nevis Range and Glenshee

Ski St Anton: Avon House, Albany Park Estate, Frimley Road, Camberley GU16 7PL
t +44 (0)1276 61072, *www.skistanton.net*
One-resort specialist with hotels, luxury catered chalets and flexible-length holidays

Ski Scott James: Byre Cottage, Sessay, Thirsk YO7 3BE
t +44 (0)1845 501 139, *www.skiscottjames.co.uk*
Catered chalets in Argentière, with off-piste courses

Ski Solutions à la Carte: 84 Pembroke Road, London W8 6NX
t +44 (0)20 7471 7777, *www.skisolutions.com*
Tailor-made arm of specialist ski travel agency, with hotels and apartments in all major resorts in the Alps and North America. Staff have intimate knowledge of the resorts and properties (*see* page 52)

Ski Supreme: 24 Howard Court, Nerston Estate, East Kilbride G74 4QZ
t +44 (0)1355 260 547, *www.skisupreme.co.uk*
Self-drive and accommodation-only holidays in France

Skitopia: 40 Lemon Street, Truro TR1 2NS
t +44 (0)1872 272 767, *www.skitopia.com*, *www.skitopia.biz*
Hotel and chalet holidays to the French Alps and Italy for schools and adults

Ski Val: The Ski Barn, Middlemoor, Tavistock PL19 9DY
t +44 (0)870 746 3030, *www.skival.co.uk*
Catered chalets and chalet-hotels in Courchevel, Tignes, Val d'Isère and St Anton

Ski Verbier: Thames Wharf Studios, Rainville Road, London W6 9HA
t +44 (0)20 7385 8050, *www.skiverbier.com*
Well-established up-market operator in Verbier, with 16 catered chalets and its own four-star hotel. Chalets available all year round. Private nannies, and separate corporate programme (*see* page 329

Ski Weekend: Darts Farm Village, Topsham, Exeter EX3 0QH
t +44 (0)870 060 0615, *www.skiweekend.com*
Weekends and short breaks combined with high-mountain guiding and specialist courses, to Chamonix Valley and destinations in Switzerland and Italy. Corporate programme also available

Skiweekends: 4 Post Office Walk, Fore Street, Hertford SG14 1DL
t +44 (0)870 442 3400, *www.skiweekends.com*
Budget weekend and short break specialist. Coach and air packages to Brides-les-Bains, La Tania and Chamonix

Ski Wild: Corner Cottage, Woodlands Lane, Stoke d'Abernon, Surrey KT11 3QA
t +44 (0)870 746 9668, *www.skiwild.co.uk*
Tailor-made holidays in Andorra, Austria, France and North America

Ski with Julia: East Lodge Farm, Stanton, Broadway WR12 7NH

t +44 (0)1386 584 478, *www.skijulia.co.uk*
Three catered chalets in Verbier

Skiworld: Skiworld House, 3 Vencourt Place, London W6 9NU
t +44 (0)870 241 6723 (Europe), t +44 (0)870 787 9720 (North America), *www.skiworld.ltd.uk*
Largest independent ski-tour operator, with major chalet programme in the Alps and North America

Sloping Off: 47 Middle Street, Brighton BN1 1AL
t +44 (0)1273 886 888, *www.sloping-off.co.uk*
Schools and groups operator to resorts in Austria, France, Italy and Switzerland

Snowbizz Vacances: 69 High Street, Maxey PE6 9EE
t +44 (0)1778 341 455, *www.snowbizz.co.uk*
Small, long-established operator to Puy-St-Vincent in France, including extensive childcare and own ski-school programme with race-training for children 10–16yrs

Snowcoach: 146–148 London Road, St Albans AL1 1PQ
t +44 (0)1727 866 177, *www.snowcoach.co.uk*
Specialist ski and snowboard operator offering high-quality accommodation and good-value holidays to France and Austria

Snowfocus: Chalet La Sonnaille, 74390 Châtel, France
t +44 (0)1392 479 555, *www.snowfocus.com*
Two catered chalets for weeks and weekend breaks in Châtel

Snowlife: Chanson de la Mer, rue de la Falaise, Trinity, Jersey JE3 5BD
t +44 (0)1534 863 630, *www.snowlife.co.uk*
Catered chalet with childcare in La Clusaz

Snowline: Collingbourne House, 140–142 Wandsworth High Street, London SW18 4JJ
t +44 (0)870 112 3118, *www.snowline.co.uk*
Well-established chalet operator with wide range of 28 catered properties in Morzine, Méribel, La Tania and Val d'Isère. Childcare service with private nannies in Trois Vallées, plus crèche in Val d'Isère (*see* pages 197, 227)

Snow Monkey Chalets: Maison Rose, 73210 Peisey-Nancroix, France
t +44 (0)20 7387 0095, *www.snowmonkeychalets.co.uk*
Comfortable catered chalets in Paradiski

Snow Safari: Chalet Savoy, 1351 route des Chavants, 74310 Les Houches, France
t +33 (0)4 50 54 56 63, *www.chaletsavoy.com*
Small chalet specialist to Chamonix Valley with mountain guiding and instruction.

Snowscape: Restdale House, 32–33 Foregate Street, Worcester WR1 1EE
t +44 (0)1905 357 760, *www.snowscape.co.uk*
Weekly and flexible holidays to Austria for groups and individuals

Snowstar: 38 Nicola Close, South Croydon CR2 6NB
t +44 (0)870 068 6611, *www.snowstarholidays.com*
Catered chalet holidays in Tignes

Solo's Holidays: 54–58 High Street, Edgware HA8 7EJ
t +44 (0)8700 720 700, *www.solosholidays.co.uk*
Holidays for singles in 14 resorts in Austria, France, Italy, Switzerland, Romania, Bulgaria, Slovenia, Canada and USA

La Source: 14 The Grove, Brookmans Park, Hatfield AL9 7RN
t +44 (0)1707 655 988, *www.lasource.org.uk*
Luxury catered chalet in Villard-Reculas near Alpe d'Huez

Stanford Skiing: 479 Unthank Road, Norwich NR4 7QN
t +44 (0)1603 477 471,

www.stanfordskiing.co.uk
Long-established specialist operator with chalets and hotels in Megève (see page 181)

Swiss Travel Service: Bridge House, 55–59 High Road, Broxbourne EN10 7DT
t +44 (0)870 191 7145, *www.swisstravel.co.uk*
Major hotel operator to 19 resorts in Switzerland. Travel by scheduled flight with rail transfers, or by rail or car from UK

Switzerland Travel Centre (Plus Travel): 30 Bedford Street, London, WC2E 9ED
t +44 (0)20 7420 4900, *www.stc.co.uk*
Specialist hotel operator to 16 Swiss resorts

Tangney Tours: 3 Station Court, Borough Green TN15 8AF
t +44 (0)1732 886 666, *www.tangney-tours.com*
Pilgrim charter operator to Lourdes, with a small ski programme in nearby Barèges in the French Pyrenees

Thomson Ski & Snowboarding: King's Place, 12–42 Wood Street, Kingston-upon-Thames KT1 1JY
t +44 (0)870 606 1470, *www.thomson-ski.co.uk*
Major tour operator to over 80 resorts in 11 countries, with group discounts and childcare facilities

Tops Ski Chalets and Club Hotels: Lees House, 21 Dyke Road, Brighton BN1 3GD
t +44 (0)1273 774 666, *www.topstravel.co.uk*
Chalets and club hotels in Alpe d'Huez, Châtel, Les Deux Alpes and Vars

Total Ski: 185 Fleet Road, Fleet GU51 3BL
t +44 (0)870 163 3633, *www.skitotal.com*
Large portfolio of catered chalets in 14 resorts in Austria, France, Italy, Switzerland and Canada (*see* pages 72, 147, 165, 197, 227)

Trail Alpine: Cordelia House, James Park, Dyserth, Rhyl LL48 6AG
t +44 (0)870 750 6560,

www.trailalpine.co.uk
Small operator with a chalet in Morzine

Trailfinders: 194 Kensington High Street, London W8 7RG
t +44 (0)845 050 5900, *www.trailfinders.com*
Largest independent travel company in UK, with tailor-made programmes to resorts including Banff-Lake Louise, Whistler, Breckenridge, Heavenly and Killington

Tyrolean Adventures: 15 Willow Close, Weston-super-Mare BS22 7XF
t +44 (0)7779 764 858, *www.tyroleanadventures.com*
Small operator offering holidays by coach, inclusive of ski pass and ski hire, based at a hotel in Hochfilzen near Kitzbühel. Discounts for those choosing to fly or using their own transport

United Vacations/Ski Freedom: PO Box 377, Bromley BR1 1LY
t +44 (0)870 606 1006,

www.unitedvacations.co.uk
Tour operator arm of United Airlines, offering a tailor-made service to 25 resorts across USA and Canada

Val d'Isère à la Carte: La Hure, rue de la Motte, St Martins, Guernsey GY4 6ER
t +44 (0)1481 236 800, *www.skivaldisere.co.uk*
Tailor-made holidays and booking service for all components of holidays to Val d'Isère, but not flights (*see* page 227)

Vanilla Ski: Avoca Cottage, Woodside Road, Chiddingfold GU8 4RJ
t +44 (0)1932 860 696, *www.vanillaski.com*
Catered chalet near Bourg-St-Maurice, with day trips organized to nearby resorts

VIP: Collingbourne House, 140–142 Wandsworth High Street, London SW18 4JJ
t +44 (0)8701 123 119, *www.vip-chalets.com*
Well-established luxury chalet operator with a large portfolio of properties in Val d'Isère, Méribel and Zermatt, with childcare service and private nannies. Crèche in Val d'Isère (*see* page 227)

Virgin Snow: The Galleria, Station Road, Crawley RH10 1WW
t +44 (0)870 990 4212, *www.virgin.com/holidays*
The tour-operator arm of Virgin Atlantic. Offers hotel and fly-drive holidays to 22 resorts across North America

Wasteland Ski Company: 9 Disraeli Road, London SW15 2DR
t +44 (0)870 844 4644, *www.wastelandski.com*
The largest student operator with dedicated events team. Works with over 100 university snowsports clubs in UK. Also good-value chalets for non-students

Waymark Holidays: 44 Windsor Road, Slough SL1 2EJ
t +44 (0)1753 516 477, *www.waymarkholidays.com*
Long-established cross-country ski operator to hotels in Austria, France, Italy, Switzerland, Norway, Finland, Slovenia, USA and Canada

White Roc Weekends: 69 Westbourne Grove, London W2 4UJ
t +44 (0)20 7792 1188, *www.whiteroc.co.uk*
Weekend and longer tailor-made holidays for individual and corporate clients to Austria, France, Italy, Spain and Switzerland, with a choice of 25 resorts and an emphasis on characterful, good-quality hotels (*see* page 7)

Wood Advent Farm: Roadwater, Exmoor National Park, TA24 0RR
t +44 (0)1984 640 920, *www.skilesgets.com*
Catered chalet in Les Gets

YSE: Church House, Abbey Close, Sherborne, Dorset DT9 3LQ
t +44 (0)845 1221 414, *www.yseski.co.uk*

Large Val d'Isère specialist with a wide range of chalets, from comfortable to luxurious, with travel by charter flights (*see* page 227)

Zermatt Holidays: PO Box 378, 3920 Zermatt, Switzerland
t +41 (0)27 966 0101, *www.zermattholidays.com*
Resort specialist with chalets and apartments, including long-term rentals

Ski Travel Agents

Alpine Answers
t +44 (0)20 8871 4656, *www.alpineanswers.co.uk*
Also a tour operator

Chalet World (London)
t +44 (0)20 7373 2096, *www.chaletworld.co.uk*
Agency for tour operator chalets

Chalet World Ski
t +44 (0)1743 231 199, *www.chaletworldski.co.uk*
Chalet agents to major alpine resorts

Erna Low
t +44 (0)20 7584 2841, *www.ernalow.co.uk*
Agent for Paradiski, Intrawest Europe and MGM apartments. Also a tour operator (*see* inside front cover, page 203)

The First Resort
t +44 (0)8700 556 300, *www.thefirstresort.com*
Online holiday booking, cheap flights and information for snow-users

Ifyouski
www.ifyouski.com
Online agency

Iglu
t +44 (0)20 8542 6658, *www.iglu.com*
Online travel and accommodation

Independent Ski Links
t +44 (0)1964 533 905, *www.ski-links.com*
Agency offering holidays to the Alps and North America

Momentum Ski
t +44 (0)20 7371 9111, *www.momentumski.com*
London-based agency, also a tour operator (*see* page 261)

Mountain Beds
t +44 (0)20 7924 2650, *www.mountainbeds.co.uk*
Apartment bookings for Verbier

Mountain Rooms & Chalets
t +44 (0)700 2000 456, *www.mountainrooms.com*
Chalets and apartments for rent in Val d'Isère

Packyourskis
t +44 (0)1892 673 406, *www.packyourskis.com*
Online agents for ski destinations and flights

Ski Deals
t +44 (0)8000 273 158, *www.skideals.com*
Online holiday agency

Ski McNeill
t +44 (0)28 9066 6699, *www.skimcneill.com*
Small independent ski travel agency

Ski Solutions
t +44 (0)20 7471 7700, *www.skisolutions.com*
The original ski travel agency, also a tour operator (*see* page 52)

Ski & Surf
t +44 (0)20 8958 2418, *www.skisurf.com*
Independent ski travel agency

Ski Tracer
t +44 (0)8704 205 882, *www.skitracer.com*
Ski specialist agency arm of Skiworld

Ski Travel Centre
t +44 (0)141 649 9696, *www.skitravelcentre.co.uk*
Scotland's biggest ski travel agency

Snow Finders
t +44 (0)1858 466 888, *www.snowfinders.com*
Independent ski travel agency

Snowhounds
t +44 (0)1243 788 487, *www.snowhounds.co.uk*
Ski specialist agency arm of Ski Beat

Snow-Line
t +44 (0)8700 507 025, *www.snow-line.co.uk*
Large and long-established ski travel agency (*see* page 165)

World Ski & Travel
t +44 (0)870 043 4122, *www.worldski.co.uk*
Specialist ski travel agency

Travelling by Air

Airlines

Adria Airways
t +386 (0)136 91000, *www.adria-airways.com*

Air 2000/First Choice
t +44 (0)870 900 3213, *www.firstchoice.co.uk*

Air Canada
t +44 (0)870 220 1111, *www.aircanada.ca*

Air France
t +44 (0)870 142 4343, *www.airfrance.co.uk*

Alitalia
t +44 (0)870 544 8259, *www.alitalia.co.uk*

American Airlines
t +44 (0)20 7365 0777, *www.aa.com*

Austrian Airlines
t +44 (0)20 7766 0300, *www.aua.com*

bmibaby
t +44 (0)870 264 2229, *www.bmibaby.com*

British Airways
t +44 (0)870 850 9850, *www.ba.com*

Continental Airlines
t +44 (0)1293 776 464, *www.continental.com*

Darwin Airline
t +41 800 177 177, *www.darwinairline.com*

Delta Airlines
t +44 (0)800 414 767, *www.delta.com*

easyJet
t +44 (0)905 821 0905, *www.easyjet.com*

Excel Airways
t +44 (0)870 169 0169, *www.xl.com*

Flybe
t +44 (0)871 700 0535, *www.flybe.com*

Jet 2
t +44 (0)870 737 8282, *www.jet2.com*

JMC/Thomas Cook
t +44 (0)870 750 5711, *www.thomascook.com*

Lufthansa
t +44 (0)845 773 7747, *www.lufthansa.com*

Monarch Airlines
t +44 (0)1582 400 000, *www.flymonarch.com*

Mytravel/Airtours
t +44 (0)870 241 5333, *www.mytravel.com*

Northwest Airlines
t +44 (0)870 507 4074, *www.nwa.com*

Ryanair
t +44 (0)871 246 0000, *www.ryanair.com*

Swiss International Airlines
t +44 (0)845 601 0956, *www.swiss.com*

Thomsonfly
t +44 (0)800 107 1517, *www.thomsonfly.com*

United Airlines
t +44 (0)845 844 4777, *www.unitedairlines.co.uk*

Virgin Atlantic Airways
t +44 (0)1293 747 747, *www.virgin-atlantic.com*

Wizzair
t +48 22 351 9499, *www.wizzair.com*

Zoom
t +44 (0)870 240 0055, *www.flyzoom.com*

Travel extras

Airport Parking Shop
www.airport-parking-shop.co.uk
Online comparison of car parks and meet-and-greet prices at UK airports

and ferry ports. Choice of 14 car parks at Heathrow

First Luggage
t +44 (0)845 270 0670, *www.firstluggage.com*
Take the hassle out of travelling by having your skis and suitcases collected from your home and delivered to any European ski resort (*see* page 6)

Holiday Extras
t +44 (0)870 844 4186, *www.holidayextras.co.uk*
A selection of hotels (with/without parking), car parks and lounges at airports across the UK, as well as chauffeur transfers, car hire to and from the airport, foreign exchange and travel insurance

Ski Hoppa
t +44 (0)871 855 0350, *www.skihoppa.com*
Airport shuttle bus in Andorra, Austria and France

Ski Taxis
t +44 (0)870 444 1880, *www.skitaxis.com*
Taking the hassle out of airport transfers

Travel Supermarket
www.travelsupermarket.com
Price comparisons for flights and car hire

Travelling by Car

Breakdown insurance

AA Five Star Services
t +44 (0)800 444 500, *www.theaa.com*

Autohome
t +44 (0)800 371 280, *www.autohome.co.uk*

Britannia Rescue
t +44 (0)800 591 563, *www.britanniarescue.com*

Direct Line Rescue
t +44 (0)845 246 8702, *www.directline.com*

Europ Assistance
t +44 (0)1444 44 22 11, *www.europ-assistance.co.uk*

Green Flag National Breakdown
t +44 (0)141 349 0516, *www.greenflag.com*

Mondial Assistance
t +44 (0)20 8681 2525, *www.mondial-assistance.co.uk*

RAC Travel Services
t +44 (0)800 55 00 55, *www.rac.co.uk*

Channel crossings

Brittany Ferries
t +44 (0)870 366 5333, *www.brittanyferries.com*
Portsmouth–Caen

Eurotunnel
t +44 (0)870 535 3535, *www.eurotunnel.com*
Folkestone–Calais (*see* page 3)

Norfolkline
t +44 (0)870 870 1020, *www.norfolkline.com*
Dover–Dunkerque (*see* page 5)

P&O Ferries
t +44 (0)870 598 0333, *www.poferries.com*
Various routes

Seafrance
t +44 (0)870 571 1711, *www.seafrance.com*
Dover–Calais

Stena Line
t +44 (0)870 570 7070, *www.stenaline.com*
Harwich–Hook of Holland

Ski roof-boxes

Karrite Europe
t +44 (0)1440 760 000, *www.karrite.co.uk*

The Roof Box Company
t +44 (0)1539 621 884, *www.roofbox.co.uk*

Thule
t +44 (0)1275 340 404, *www.thule.co.uk*

Snow chains

AA
t +44 (0)870 550 0600, *www.theaa.com*

Brindley Chains
t +44 (0)1925 825 555, *www.brindley-chains.co.uk*
Polar Automotive
t +44 (0)1892 519 933, *www.snowchains.com*
RAC
t +44 (0)800 55 00 55, *www.rac.co.uk*
Rud Chains
t +44 (0)1227 276 611, *www.rud.co.uk*
Snowchains
t +44 (0)1732 884 408, *www.snowchains.co.uk*

Travelling by Rail

Eurostar
t +44 (0)8705 186 186, *www.eurostar.com*

A weekly overnight service leaves London Waterloo on Friday evening, arriving in the Tarentaise valley the following morning. The return train departs on Saturday evening. An additional daytime service departs on Saturday morning, in each direction

Rail Europe
t +44 (0)870 124 4646, *www.raileurope.co.uk* or *www.sncf.com*

Agents for tour operators' chartered Snowtrain, which leaves Calais on Friday night, arriving in the French Alps on Saturday morning, and departs on Saturday evening, arriving in Calais Sunday morning

Also agents for SNCF couchette service departing Paris Gare du Nord for the Alps on Friday evening, arriving Saturday morning, and leaving the Alps on Saturday evening, arriving Sunday morning. Services connect with Eurostar to London Waterloo but involve a change of train, though not of station

Also agents for SNCF daily and couchette Intercity services to the French Alps from Paris Gare de Lyon

National Tourist Offices

Andorran Delegation
t +44 (0)20 8874 4806, *www.andorra.ad*
Argentinian Embassy
t +44 (0)20 7318 1300, *www.argentina/embassy/uk.org*
Australia
t +44 (0)9068 633235 (brochure line), *www.australia.com*
Austria
t +44 (0)845 101 1818, *www.austria.info*
Bulgaria
t +44 (0)20 7584 9400, *www.bulgariaski.com*
Canada
t +44 (0)9068 715000 (brochure line), *www.travelcanada.ca*
Chile
t +44 (0)20 7580 1023, *www.visitchile.org*
Czech Republic
t +44 (0)9063 640641 (brochure line), *www.visitczechia.cz*
Finland
t +44 (0)20 7365 2512, *www.visitfinland.com*
France
t +44 (0)9068 244123 (brochure line), *www.franceguide.com*, *www.skifrance.fr*
Italy
t +44 (0)20 7408 1254, *www.enit.it*
Japan
t +44 (0)20 7734 9638, *www.seejapan.co.uk*
New Zealand
t +44 (0)9050 606060, *www.newzealand.com*
Norway
t +44 (0)9063 022003 (brochure line), *www.visitnorway.com*
Poland
t +44 (0)8700 675 010 (brochure line), *www.poland.dial.pipex.com*
Romania
t +44 (0)20 7224 3692, *www.romaniatourism.com*

Scotland
t +44 (0)845 22 55 121 (brochure line), *www.visitscotland.com*
Slovenia
t +44 (0)870 225 5305, *www.slovenia.info*
Spain
t +44 (0)20 7486 8077, *www.tourspain.co.uk*, *www.spain.info*
Sweden
t +44 (0)20 7108 6168, *www.visit-sweden.com*
Switzerland
t +44 (0)20 7420 4900, *www.myswitzerland.com*
USA
Switchboard t +44 (0)20 7499 9000
Visa Information Line t +44 (0)9068 200 290 (24hr), *www.unitedstatesvisas.gov*
California
www.visitcalifornia.com
Colorado
www.visitcolorado.com
Maine
www.visitmaine.com
Nevada
t +44 (0)870 523 8832 (brochure line), *www.visitnevada.com*
New England
www.skinewengland.com
New Hampshire
www.visitnh.gov
Rocky Mountain International
t +44 (0)9063 640 655, *www.rmi-realamerica.com*

Ski-related Organizations

Association of British Tour Operators to France (ABTOF)
t +44 (0)1989 769 140, *www.holidayfrance.org.uk*
Association of British Travel Agents (ABTA)
t +44 (0)20 7637 2444, *www.abta.com*
Association of Independent Tour Operators (AITO)
t +44 (0)20 8744 9280,
t +44 (0)870 751 8080 (brochure line), *www.aito.co.uk*
The Back Up Trust
t +44 (0)20 8875 1805, *www.backuptrust.org.uk*
Charity for disabled skiers
British Alpine Racing Academy
t +44 (0)1634 685 909, *www.alpine-racing.co.uk*
Summer and winter race training for adults and children in Europe, New Zealand and North America
British Association of Ski Patrollers
t +44 (0)1855 811 443, *www.basp.org.uk*
Safety officers at Scottish resorts and UK artificial slopes
British Association of Snowsport Instructors (BASI)
t +44 (0)1479 861 717, *www.basi.org.uk*
British Bobskeleton Association
t +44 (0)1225 323 696 *www.british-bobsleigh.com*
British Bobsleigh Association
t +44 (0)1225 386 802, *www.british-bobsleigh.com*
British Mountain Guides
t +44 (0)1834 871 694, *www.bmg.org.uk*
British Ski Academy
t +44 (0)20 8399 1181, t +33 (0)4 50 54 40 59, *www.britskiacad.org.uk*
British Ski Club for the Disabled
t +44 (0)1747 828 515, *www.bscd.org.uk*
Disability Snowsport
t +44 (0)1479 861 272, *www.disabilitysnowsport.org.uk*
Freestyle Snowsports
www.freestylesnowsports.co.uk
International School of Mountaineering
t +44 (0)1766 890 441, *www.alpin-ism.com*
Ski Club of Great Britain
t +44 (0)20 8410 2000, *www.skiclub.co.uk*
The leading club for British skiers
Snowsport England
t +44 (0)121 501 2314, *www.snowsportengland.org.uk*

Snowsport GB
t +44 (0)131 445 7676, *www.snowsportgb.com*
Snowsport Industries of Great Britain
t +44 (0)131 557 3012, *www.snowlife.org.uk*
Snowsport Scotland
t +44 (0)131 445 4151, *www.snowsportscotland.org*
Snowsport Wales
t +44 (0)29 2056 1904, *www.snowsportwales.net*
World Ski & Snowboard Club
t +44 (0)870 043 4122, *www.worldski.co.uk*

Artificial Snow Slopes

Reall-ski, Canterbury, Kent
t +44 (0)1227 833 944, *www.reall-ski.co.uk*
Ski simulator centre
Tamworth SnowDome, Staffordshire
t +44 (0)8705 000 011, *www.snowdome.co.uk*
Xscape, Braehead, Glasgow
t +44 (0)871 222 5672, *www.xscape.co.uk*
Xscape, Castleford, West Yorkshire
t +44 (0)871 222 5671, *www.xscape.co.uk*
Xscape, Milton Keynes
t +44 (0)871 222 5670, *www.xscape.co.uk*

Dry Slopes

A full list of the 70 slopes is available from the Ski Club of Great Britain

Bearsden Ski Club, Glasgow
t +44 (0)141 943 1500, *www.skibearsden.co.uk*
Gloucester Ski and Snowboard Centre
t +44 (0)8702 400 375, *www.gloucesterski.co.uk*
Hemel Ski Centre, Hemel Hempstead
t +44 (0)1442 241 321, *www.hemel-ski.co.uk*
Llandudno Ski and Snowboard Centre
t +44 (0)1492 874 707, *www.llandudnoskislope.co.uk*
Midlothian Ski Centre, Edinburgh
t +44 (0)131 445 4433, *www.midlothian.gov.uk*
Rossendale Ski Centre, Lancashire
t +44 (0)1706 226 457, *www.ski-rossendale.co.uk*
Sheffield Ski Village
t +44 (0)114 276 9459, *www.sheffieldskivillage.co.uk*
Wycombe Summit, High Wycombe
t +44 (0)1494 474 711, *www.wycombesummit.com*

Real Snow Slopes

Opening times dependent on snow conditions

Allenheads, Northumberland
t +44 (0)1670 715 719, *www.ski-allenheads.co.uk*
Carlisle Ski Club, Alston, Cumbria
t +44 (0)1228 561 634, *www.thepriceofcheese.com*
Weardale Ski Club, Shield, Northumberland
t +44 (0)191 534 6251, *www.skiweardale.co.uk*

Ski Recruitment Agencies

Free Radicals
www.freeradicals.co.uk
Jobs in the Alps
www.jobs-in-the-alps.com
Natives
t +44 (0)870 046 3377, *www.natives.co.uk*
(*see* page 142)
Ski Connection
www.skiconnection.co.uk
Voovs.com Ltd
t +44 (0)1707 396 511, *www.voovs.com*

Gap-year Skiing

Base Camp Group
t +44 (0)20 7243 6222, *www.basecampgroup.com*
Ski and snowboard instructor courses in Méribel, Val d'Isère, Kicking Horse and Whistler. Also ski season jobs, powder and freestyle camps

Bunac/Gap Canada
t +44 (0)20 7251 3472, *www.bunac.org*
Student work opportunities in Australia, New Zealand and North America

Nonstopski
t +44 (0)870 241 8070, *www.nonstopski.com*
Intensive instruction in Fernie, Red Mountain and Banff, with the aim of qualifying as a Level 1 Canadian ski or board instructor

Peak Leaders
t +44 (0)1337 860 079, *www.peakleaders.co.uk*
Gap-year instructor courses

Powdertrip
t +44 (0)8454 900 480, *www.powder-trip.com*
Instructor courses in Kicking Horse and ski clinics in Fernie

Ski Le Gap
t +44 (0)800 328 0345, *www.skilegap.com*
Instructors' programme in Tremblant for UK gap-year students

Snowskool
t +44 (0)871 223 0060, *www.snowskool.co.uk*
Ski and snowboard instructor courses in Banff and Big White

Ski Property Companies

Erna Low
t +44 (0)20 7590 1624, *www.ernalowproperty.co.uk*
Purchase of ski chalets and apartments throughout Europe and North America (*see* inside front cover, page 203)

Investors in Property
t +44 (0)20 8905 5511, *www.investorsinproperty.com*
Sale of ski chalets and apartments in the Swiss, French and Austrian resorts (*see* page 298)

Clothing and Equipment Retailers

For a full list, see *www.snowlife.org.uk*

47 Degrees
t +44 (0)20 7384 1747, *www.47degrees.com*

Blacks
t +44 (0)800 214 890, *www.blacks.co.uk*

Boardwise
t +44 (0)8707 504 421, *www.boardwise.com*

Cotswold Outdoor
t +44 (0)870 442 7755 *www.cotswoldoutdoor.com*

Ellis Brigham
t +44 (0)161 833 0746, *www.ellis-brigham.com*

Lockwoods
t +44 (0)1926 339 388, *www.lockwoodsoutdoor.co.uk*

Sheactive
t +44 (0)20 7836 0440, *www.sheactive.co.uk*

Snow + Rock
t +44 (0)845 100 1011, *www.snowandrock.com*

Ski Clothing Rental

Captains Cabin
t +44 (0)1732 464 463, *www.theski-shop.co.uk*

edge2edge
t +44 (0)870 241 1316, *ww.edge2edge.co.uk*

Ski Force
t +44 (0)1543 411 249, *www.ski-force.co.uk*

Ski Togs Hire
t +44 (0)20 8993 9883, *www.skitogshire.co.uk*

Ski West
t +44 (0)1453 819 247, *www.ski-west.co.uk*

Weather and Snow

www.avalanches.org
Collective avalanche warning site for Europe

www.lawine.at
Avalanche warnings for Austria

www.meteo.fr
French weather forecasts

www.skiclub.co.uk
Snow reports and six-day weather forecasts on more than 250 resorts across Europe and North America

www.slf.ch
Avalanche warnings for Switzerland

www.snow-forecast.com
Worldwide snow data

Ski Travel Insurance

American Express
t +44 (0)800 028 7573, *www.americanexpress.co.uk*

BIBA
t +44 (0)870 950 1790, *www.biba.org.uk*

Columbus Direct
t +44 (0)845 330 8518, *www.columbusdirect.com*

Direct Travel Insurance
t +44 (0)845 605 2700, *www.direct-travel.co.uk*

Endsleigh Insurance Services
t +44 (0)800 028 3571, *www.endsleigh.co.uk*

Europ Assistance
t +44 (0)1444 444 692, *www.europ-assistance.co.uk*

Fogg Travel Insurance
t +44 (0)1623 631 331, *www.fogginsure.co.uk*

Insure & Go
t +44 (0)870 901 3674, *www.insureandgo.com*

James Hampden
t +44 (0)870 220 0634, *www.primary1.co.uk*

Liverpool Victoria
t +44 (0)1202 292 333, *www.liverpool-victoria.co.uk*

Medicover
t +44 (0)870 735 3600, *www.medi-cover.co.uk*

Mondial Assistance
t +44 (0)20 8681 2525, *www.mondial-assistance.co.uk*

MPI
t +44 (0)1428 664 265, *www.mpibrokers.com*

MRL Insurance Direct
t +44 (0)870 876 7677, *www.mrlinsurance.co.uk*

Options
t +44 (0)870 876 7878, *www.optionsinsurance.co.uk*

Primary Insurance
t +44 (0)870 220 0634, *www.primaryinsurance.co.uk*

Ski Club of Great Britain
t +44 (0)8700 759 759, *www.skiclub.co.uk*

Snowcard Insurance Services
t +44 (0)1327 262 805, *www.snowcard.co.uk* (*see* page 273)

Sportscover Direct
t +44 (0)845 120 6400, t +44 (0)117 922 6222, *www.sportscover.co.uk*

Travel & General Group
t +44 (0)845 345 2487, *www.tagdirect.co.uk*

WorldSki
t +44 (0)870 428 8706, *www.worldski.co.uk*

Worldwide Insure
t +44 (0)870 112 8100, *www.worldwideinsure.com*